VISUAL DEVELOPER magazine

Building NT 4 Web Servers

Building NT 4 Web Servers

Jeff Bankston

an International Thomson Publishing company I(T)P®

Albany, NY • Belmont, CA • Bonn • Boston • Cincinnati • Detroit • Johannesburg • London
Madrid • Melbourne • Mexico City • New York • Paris • Singapore • Tokyo • Toronto • Washington

Publisher	Keith Weiskamp
Project Editor	Denise Constantine
Production Coordinator	Nomi Schalit
Cover Artist	Gary Smith/Performance Design
Cover Design	Anthony Stock
Interior Design	Nicole Colón
Compositor	Rob Mauhar
Copyeditor	Mary Millhollon
Proofreader	Meredith Brittain
Indexer	Kirsten King
CD-ROM Development	Robert Clarfield

Visual Developer Building NT 4 Web Servers
ISBN: 1-57610-165-7

The Coriolis Group, Inc.
An International Thomson Publishing Company
14455 N. Hayden Road, Suite 220
Scottsdale, Arizona 85260

602/483-0192
FAX 602/483-0193
http://www.coriolis.com

Printed in the United States of America
10 9 8 7 6 5 4 3 2 1

Acknowledgments

Second edition books are largely published in response to user demand for good information and timely solutions to today's problems of computers. This revision is no less important than the initial release, and is improved upon in several areas. More information about intranets has been added and more programmatical examples of how to implement an NT Web Server is used to reinforce the thought. Throughout this book, changes have been made with the release of Microsoft's NT Server v4.0 and the new Internet Information Server v3.0. The many problems and issues that had to be resolved were accomplished by my in-house staff, and are due tremendous thanks.

No book is possible without the guidance and direction of the publisher, Keith Weiskamp and project editor, Denise Constantine. My agent, Valda Hilley, President of Convergent Press Literary Group, has led me with uncanny insights and a serene posture. To a large degree, parts of this book were written by my associate authors Rob Thayer, Robert Ellis, and Marshall Copeland. Their contributions have made it a better book.

Last but not least, my darling wife has put up with all of us—publisher, editors, myself, and the many long nights required to do this update. I couldn't have done it without Anja Marie's patience and support.

AUTHOR BIOS

Jeff Bankston is the VP of Operations for BCI Associates, Inc., a Systems Integrator and Network Design company, based in Panama City, Fl. He is the senior designer for the company designing medium and large scale network infrastructures along with specifying complete electronics solutions. He is also the author of *Web Browsing with The Microsoft Network* and *Building and Maintaining an NT Web Server*.

Robert H. Ellis is an experienced system administrator. He has many years experience of supporting numerous multi-user and network operating systems. He is the author of several technical articles and a contributor to numerous computer and technical books.

Rob Thayer runs Thayer Technologies, a consulting firm that provides programming services for medium-to-large-sized businesses such as Motorola, Sperry, and MCI.

CONTENTS

INTRODUCTION

Jeff Bankston

The second edition of *Building And Maintaining An NT Web Server* is renamed *Visual Developer Building NT 4 Web Servers* to more appropriately fit the changing face of the Internet. This book focuses on Web sites and the technologies that have matured within the past year. These technologies, including CGI and ActiveX, have beaten new paths to users' keyboards. Using new technologies, users are finding more of what they want to see on the Web, without sacrificing the ease of Web browsing that most users have come to enjoy.

But, what happens when Web users find themselves building a Web server? Just as in the first edition, this book is written for users turned Web administrators, as well as for folks needing to create or enhance their personal or corporate Web presence. This book is *not* a comprehensive instructional guide on using NT 4. The text assumes that you have experience with NT 4 and that you are adept at navigating NT 4's architecture.

More and more businesses are finding themselves on the Internet, competing with businesses down the block and around the world. This second edition involves the business usage of intranets and the Internet, showing you how to exploit the new functionalities of NT 4, including proxy servers and Active Server Pages. *Visual Developer Building NT 4 Web Servers* is designed to show you how to get your business onto the Internet, serving the public community, your private business' user base, or a combination of both. It also shows you how to run your applications on your Web server locally, as a logged in user, or remotely, if you happen to be traveling. Various forms of server communications are explored and exploited to increase your Web server's potency, while keeping costs under control. This book also introduces some of the best tools that you can use to build a solid foundation for the future of your Web server.

Creating a network server isn't too difficult. Not surprisingly, the key lies in preparation. Your Web server requires some careful consideration and a whole lot of planning. This book provides a structured planning guide to help you reach the Web, making your business known to the world. Of course, you must be prepared to spend time, money, and a few sleepless nights putting it all together, but, with this book in hand, you won't be working in the dark. Read on. You'll see what you need to do, when to do it, and what not to do as you create a presence on the Web.

This book is structured into five key parts, which reflect the major topics of Web server creation and management:

- *Part 1*—Discusses the finer details of building a physical server. This section discusses how to manage the rigors of the Web and plan for the number of users you expect to see.
- *Part 2*—Shows you how to install NT 4 from scratch and perform the basic configuration of Internet Information Server version 3. Both of these applications can help ensure the successful development of your Web server.
- *Part 3*—Explores Common Gateway Interface (CGI) and Visual Basic. This section discusses how to expand your Web server's power and flexibility. A generous helping of Active Server Pages and ActiveX technologies are thrown in here, and you'll learn how to use programmatical methods to conduct your business activities while accessing the Web server from the Internet.
- *Part 4*—Takes a look at two new Web servers not included in the first edition of this book—Oracle's Web Server and Netscape's FastTrack.
- *Part 5*—Goes into some depth of disaster recovery. In addition, this section addresses some critical maintenance issues for Web servers and physical servers.

To compliment the topics mentioned in the preceding list, a CD-ROM accompanies this book. The CD-ROM contains demo and evaluation software for use on your Web site.

This book concentrates on the tasks you'll encounter when you create your very own Web server. The tasks are numerous and varied. So, be prepared to be flexible in your past thinking of how to run a site. Not every network server is capable of running a Web server, and not every Web server is up to the task of serving both Internet and intranet users.

Finally, this book will help provide you with a firm grasp on how to plan, propose, create, and present your Web server. You'll learn how to best approach the decision makers with your Web server plan, and you'll learn how to gather the necessary figures to help estimate how much it will cost to get your business online. You'll see some of the new Web technologies in action and what they can do for your Web site. You'll know what to expect in terms of server administration, emergency and normal maintenance, and system upgrades. Above all, after this book shows you what is entailed in creating and maintaining a Web server, so you'll appreciate the talent and effort necessary to run a successful server.

If you need technical support or have questions about the book, please send email to me at bciassoc@panama.gulf.net or to the Coriolis Group at robertc@coriolis.com.

Part 1

Planning An NT Web Server

1

Overview Of Web Technologies

Jeff Bankston

Welcome to the first chapter of *Building NT 4 Web Servers*. This chapter focuses on the main types of Internet technologies and presents a foundation for later chapters on how to effectively employ NT Server as a Web server. The bulk of this chapter provides an overview of Web technologies and how the technologies can affect what you intend to do with your Web server. In addition, you'll learn a few of the finer points of Web servers. Subsequent chapters delve deeper into the issues for each topic presented in this chapter.

There are as many possible operating environments for NT Server as there are needs to be filled, but the Web is one environment that has absolutely exploded over the past few years. This was foreseen by some, neglected by others, and secretly supported by few. Not until NT Server took the reins and charged ahead as a Web solutions platform did the Internet blow open the doors of opportunity. Ease of administration, clean integration into the Internet, and breadth of tools are some of the reasons why NT is so easy to install and support.

I say "blow open the doors" because, for years, the Web seemed to be the private territory of Unix systems with all of Unix's cryptic background. Couple this with the somewhat primitive text-based way that Web users actually navigated the Web, and change was due. Not only was it due, but it *had* to happen if the Internet were to evolve.

Let me make one comparison clear in every respect. When I talk about the *Web*, this reference is to the many public Internet servers, connections, interconnections, and backroom links to private servers all over the world. The Web is, in every sense of the word, the conglomeration of servers that makes up the *Internet*. However, many people refer to the Web as simply the mass of HTTP links from Web server to Web server. This simplified view of the Web is what has radically changed in recent months. The Web now uses simple list servers, massive parallel processors handling monstrous databases, and everything in between.

The Web's capabilities span FTPing from Web pages to clients, subscribing to news services, using forms to request product information, and on and on. There are many services that now consume the Web in all its glory. To effectively conduct all these services, networks must use a common language. The language used to conduct Web conversations is called *TCP/IP*, or *Transmission Control Protocol/Internet Protocol*. The two protocol types, TCP and IP, collectively make up the connections we call the *Internet*. Utilizing TCP/IP to get messages across the wires are several other forms of *protocols*, including:

- *HTTP*—Hypertext Transfer Protocol. Used by Web servers to display and process HTML (Hypertext Markup Language) Web pages.
- *FTP*—File Transfer Protocol. Used to move files from place to place.
- *MIME*—Multipart Internet Mail Engine. A method of differentiating file types by associating a file format type to a particular type of message.
- *Gopher*—A way to browse directory structures and look at files. The forerunner to FTP, Gopher is sometimes viewed as antiquated, but Gopher is actually faster than HTTP or FTP.

This chapter focuses on identifying the following primary functions of the Web:

- Email systems
- Gopher
- File transfers
- Security and the Web

- Proxy servers
- Routing issues and the Web
- Electronic commerce
- Electronic classrooms

Let's take these eight principal functions of the Internet and see how they're used to create the beast we know and love as the World Wide Web.

Email Systems

From the beginning of the Internet, back in the days when it was known as ARPAnet, electronic mail has been one of the backbone services of the Net. When the Internet was evolving, totally funded, controlled, and used by the U.S. Department of Defense, email and file transfers were the overriding uses of the network. (We'll address file transfers and FTP in the next section.) Clearly, email is nothing new—it has simply grown.

Email is nothing more than the formatting, moving, and deciphering of text using the Internet as the medium for transmission. It consumes an estimated 60 percent of all traffic moving across the Internet. The text you're reading now is exactly the type of information that flows across the Internet in email applications. It's as plain as plain can be.

Data transmissions on the Internet are not secured and are susceptible to interception and decoding by less than optimal people. While changes are in the making to secure selective transmissions, the vast majority of the Internet is open to surreptitious usage.

The most common use of email is to send messages, but email can also be used to transmit files. When an email message is used to transfer files, the files are attached and converted from a binary format to the textual equivalent. Why? Because the Internet only handles textual transmissions for email. The process involved is called *UUEncoding/UUDecoding*, and this is the process that converts a binary file into text.

When an email message makes it to the distant end mail server, the server detects that the mail just received has an attachment. Upon further examination, the mail server sees what format of UUEncoding was used to create the binary file attachment. Some of the more common coding schemes are Base64, XXE extended format, and BINHEX (used by Macintosh computers and some others). The mail server then attempts to automatically decode the file and return it back to the binary entity it once was. If this conversion is not possible, automatically speaking, then the contents of the encoded file are placed inside of the original email itself. Following is an example of information received in an email message indicating the presence of an attached file, and Figure 1.1 shows Netscape's email client:

Name: afcesa.pab
Type: unspecified type (application/octet-stream)
Encoding: base64

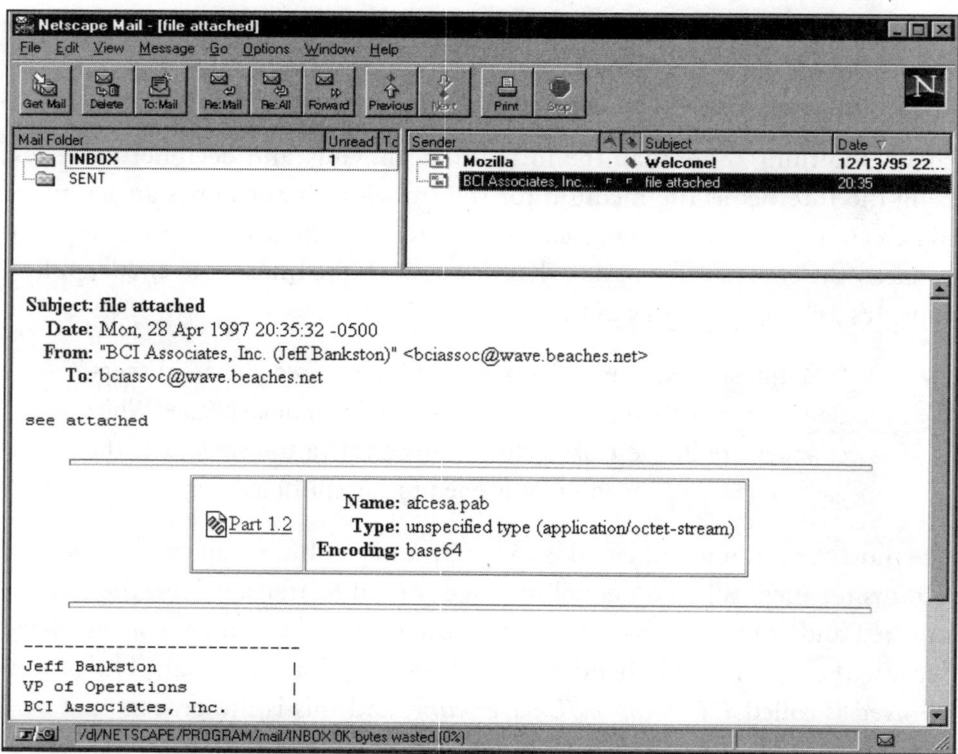

Figure 1.1
Netscape's email client.

You can view the source of email transmissions in most email clients. Many email clients, such as Eudora, display the email source information in the body of each message. Other clients display source information when you choose the proper menu option. For example, you can view the source of an email in Microsoft Internet Explorer by selecting File|Properties|Details. What appears next is the contents of an email when the source of the email is viewed in Netscape:

```
Received: from sysmgrjb (p1s29.beaches.net [206.240.81.62])
        by wave.beaches.net (8.8.5/8.8.5) with SMTP id UAA01910
        for <bciassoc@mail.beaches.net>; Mon, 28 Apr 1997 20:32:48 -0500
(CDT)
X-UIDL: 862277583.000
Message-Id: <2.2.32.19970429013532.0091a3bc@mail.beaches.net>
X-Sender: bciassoc@mail.beaches.net
X-Mailer: Windows Eudora Pro Version 2.2 (32)
Mime-Version: 1.0
Content-Type:multipart/mixed; boundary="=====================_862295732==_"
Date: Mon, 28 Apr 1997 20:35:32 -0500
To: bciassoc@wave.beaches.net
From: "BCI Associates, Inc. (Jeff Bankston)" <bciassoc@wave.beaches.net>
Subject: file attached
X-Attachments: C:\EXCHANGE\afcesa.pab;
Status: U
X-Mozilla-Status: 0001

--=====================_862295732==_
Content-Type: text/plain; charset="us-ascii"
see attached
--=====================_862295732==_
Content-Type: application/octet-stream; name="afcesa.pab"
Content-Transfer-Encoding: base64
Content-Disposition: attachment; filename="afcesa.pab"
```


```
IUJETl9orb9CQQ4AFgABAQAAAAAAAAANAAAACEAAAAHAAAAAAQAAAAEAAAABAAAAAQAAAAEAAA
ABAAAAAQAAAAEAAAABAAAAAQAAAAEAAAABAAAAAQAAAAEAAAABAAAAAQAAAAEAAAABAAAAAQAAA
AEAAAABAAAAAQAAAAEAAAABAAAAAQAAAAEAAAABAAAAAQAAAAEAAAABAAAAAQAAAAEAAAAAAAA
IAAAABEAACAIwAAAAwAACAAAAAAVgAAHgAAAABQAAABAAAA4AAAAAAAAAAAAAAAAAAAAAAAAAA
AAAAAAAAAAAAAAAAAAAAAAAAAAAAAAAAAAAAAAAAAAAAAAAAAAAAAAAAAAAAAAAAAAAAAAAAAAAA
AAAAAAAAAAAAAAAAAAAAAAAAAAAAAAAAAAAAAAAAAAAAAAAAAAAAAAAAAAAAAAAAAAAAB/////
```


This is the essence of electronic mail—just another way to say hello or get information from one person to another. The next Internet function presented is something of a different type of animal on the Web.

Gopher

Following a close second to email and email attachments is the straightforward movement of files across the Internet. Currently, file transfers using FTP (discussed in the next section) comprise some 20 percent of all Internet traffic. But in the not-so-distant past, another function, Gopher, provided the file transfer needs during the developmental phase of FTP.

Gopher is a tool used to handle file and directory searches. Gopher, as stated earlier, is the forerunner to Web services and does not use any of the fancy HTML codes or commands. Using a Gopher server is very easy, and it involves nothing more than pointing Gopher's root level directory to the lowest level directory that you want to view or share with viewers.

But what about when you want to get files or see what's up on a Gopher server? How do you know where to start looking for files? In time, you'll create your own list of favorite Gopher sites. In the meantime, there are still tons of Gopher navigational aids out there that can help serve your informational needs. Veronica and Jughead servers are two popular aids in Gopher navigation.

Veronica Servers

Veronica servers perform searches of available Gopher servers in a listed area of the Web or within a known search group of Gopher servers. Figure 1.2 shows the results of a Veronica search using Hgopher client.

Jughead Servers

To further assist sifting through the massive amounts of Gopher data, Jughead servers can be established. Jughead servers confine Gopher data searches to search parameters defined by a system administrator. The parameters can be a specific group of Gopher servers, one section of one Gopher server, or any combination. Basically, Jughead scales down searchable data to a smaller, more manageable data set.

While Gopher presents some opportune situations for Web server development, creating Veronica and Jughead server searches are beyond the scope of this book. There are several things that have to be done to create these two servers, and they require special coordination. If you decide to implement a Gopher server and feel the need to work with Veronica or Jughead, contact the folks at the University of Minnesota.

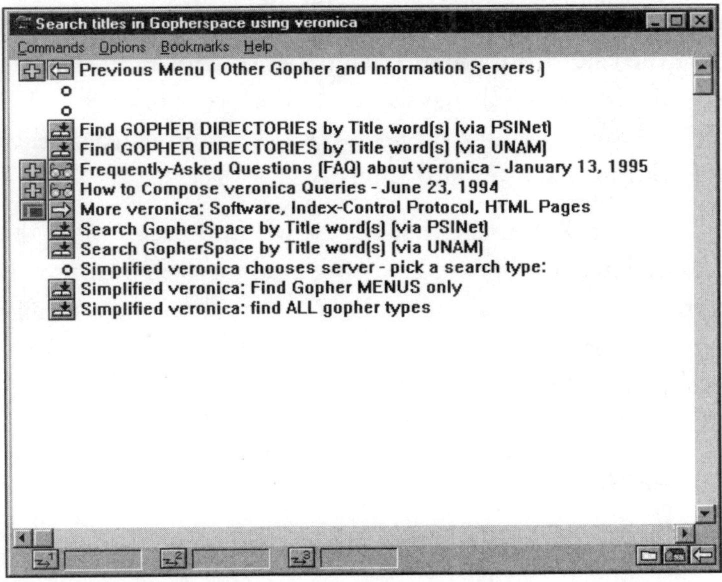

Figure 1.2
Veronica server search using Hgopher client.

FTP

As mentioned earlier, file transfer activities using the File Transfer Protocol (FTP) comprise some 20 percent of all Internet traffic. File transferring and email messaging are the dominant functions on the Web. In fact, many sites will easily have FTP servers of very large proportions as opposed to Web servers with HTML pages. One reason for this is that FTP servers can, and are, routinely used as network servers but share out the same files for FTP.

Let's say that the root directory structure for your FTP site was D:\PROJECTS\. Let's further say that the entire directory structure beneath this location was:

D:\PROJECTS\SYSTEMS

D:\PROJECTS\INCOMING

D:\PROJECTS\PUBLIC

D:\PROJECTS\PRIVATE

D:\PROJECTS\PRIVATE\CONFIDENTIAL

In the normal course of business, your NT Server provides file access to these areas for all of the users from the internal network. However, the external users coming across the Internet only have access to the areas of D:\PROJECTS where NTFS security allows them to go. This is how a common area on the server can be used for both internal users and Internet FTP access.

This is one aspect of Web usage that has grown into much more than anyone expected. Internal network servers are being used for Web purposes, both internal and external to businesses. Internal and external servers are called *intranet* and *Internet* Web servers, respectively. In later chapters, these entities will be further defined and explained. For now, suffice it to say that if you want to move files across the Net, using FTP is the preferred way to go.

> ***Note:** Email is used to a very large degree to send someone a short message, but email clients often convolute mail servers when monstrous files are attached to email messages. While possible, emailing large attachments defeats the entire purpose of having multiple protocols for the Net. If you intend to transfer large files, you should use FTP.*

Security And The Web

Security is always an issue for Internet users, but it's even more so for Internet server administrators. Most Web servers are open to the public, but usually they are only partially available for usage. This regulation of Web servers presents the most challenging part of Web manipulation to date. How much do you make available to the world? How much, and how far, do you tuck under the covers for the internal users of a business? This is a topic that generates heat, strife, and much discussion in many Internet server administrator circles. Naturally, most enterprises want to help those seeking enlightenment on the Web, but not at too high of a price or risk.

You'll have to address a number of issues to ensure your server is a safe place to surf. Following are some of the key issues to consider for the security of a network server and, in particular, a Web server:

- User security on the NT Server
- IP address security in the router

- Share-level security on the NT Server
- Proxy server security
- Web Server security at the application level

NT Server is a platform that allows you to secure a server to prevent most surreptitious entries. It does have one limitation that still baffles many administrators. When a share is created inside NT Server (and this is discussed in Chapter 5), the name of the share is made public. Not the contents of the share, but the *name.* Even if proper security is set on the NT Server, the name is still known. Within Unix servers, any and all parts of a server can be made to be totally hidden and secured, which is the preferred method of security.

Chapter 19 will delve into significantly deeper issues of security on NT Server. For now, it's good to keep in mind that the Internet is completely nonsecure, as far as the public is concerned. One form of security can be established at the router for some form of firewall. This isn't an ironclad security option, but it's a very good start. There are many forms of security available, including proxy servers. In the next section, we'll take a look at proxy servers. Later, in Chapter 8, we'll implement Microsoft's Proxy Server so you can see how you can tighten up your site's privacy through the use of a proxy server.

Proxy Servers

Proxy servers provide a really neat function on the Web. This is largely considered to be the poor Web site's secure environment option when a full firewall system can't be afforded. A firewall looks at an incoming TCP request, determines if the request is valid for the site based on a number of parameters, and either allows the request to pass onto the Web server or rejects the request. Proxy servers do something similar except that a proxy server bases the request on an IP address or group of IP classes.

Let's say you have a group of users in your internal network, and they're not subject to the network's proxy server software. The users can access the Web server directly. If they need to go to the public Internet, they can use the proxy server to create the connection to the Internet based on an IP address. Think of it as an IP filter allowing selective IP requests to flow in and out of your server. Figure 1.3 displays how proxy servers can be implemented on each server, or on just one.

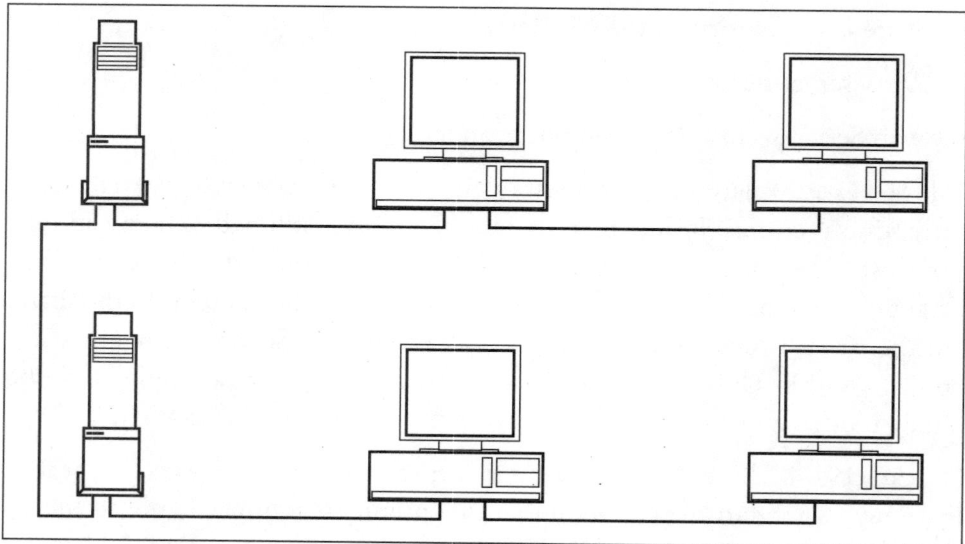

Figure 1.3
Two networks, two proxy servers.

Notice in Figure 1.3 that each server has two network interface cards installed in each machine. Proxy software installed in these servers filters requests from one network to another. Now, let's say that someone on the public Internet attempts to come into your Web server. The proxy server intercepts the request, evaluates the request, and determines if the request is a valid connection to your Web server. It either accepts or rejects the request at that point. The Web server never sees an invalid request.

Routing Issues And The Web

Routing is one of the touchier Internet topics, and routing issues have yet to be resolved to the satisfaction of most Internet administrators. The router is a lot like a traffic cop in the middle of an intersection where a red light doesn't work. You enter the intersection with your turn signal on (hopefully) to show your intentions. The policeman then indicates yes or no with hand signals. If the intersection has one road barricaded, you can't go down that road, no matter what. You know which way you want to go, but the policeman gives the final approval.

Routers, Routers, Everywhere

Basically, a router receives a packet of data, looks to see where the packet needs to go, and sends the packet to the proper connection, if possible. If the transmission is not possible, the packet is returned to the sender, in much the same way that you'd be denied access to a blocked-off street. The router acts like a traffic cop in another way—it doesn't modify a data packet that comes into the router any more than the traffic cop modifies your vehicle. The traffic cop simply allows you to pass or reroutes you, depending on the situation. It's either yes or no.

The downside to using a router is the cost of such a device. If you're routing the same protocol, as in TCP/IP to TCP/IP networks, then less versatile routers are required at a cost of perhaps $1,000 or less. If you've got to route and filter packets of data for say IPX, TCP/IP, and Macintosh systems, then a much more powerful and capable router is required. Such a device could easily top $10,000 from one of the best vendors.

Similar to Internet routing is the use of a simple server link sometimes referred to as *internal routing*. Internal routing occurs when, instead of having one network interface card (NIC) in a server, a server has two NICs installed which are then cabled together. This situation forms a physical separation between networks, yet allows for a logical connection when the proper software is used. Such is a common practice between Novell Netware IPX networks and Microsoft Windows NT Server NETBeui networks. The two are incompatible network protocols and can't see one another without internal routing. The same results can be achieved by simply connecting both servers to a router.

So, what's the big deal with internal versus external routers? The external device is much faster because its only job in life is to receive data packets and forward them to the appropriate network. Figure 1.4 illustrates this point. Keep in mind that the router has to be told which physical port on the router handles the data for which destination, and many routers have as many as eight ports to handle. If the data being moved stays on the same physical network, then it never has to be routed, and performance is never an issue.

The server performing internal routing has plenty of other jobs to handle, as well, and the internal routing function simply adds to the workload.

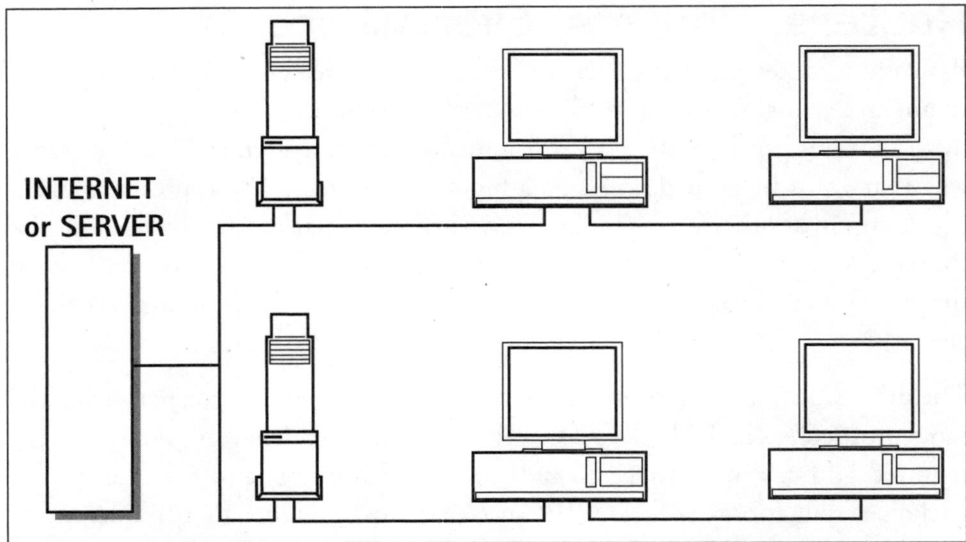

Figure 1.4
Basic router processing.

The Internet Routing Scheme

Now that you've seen how networks and routers work, let's look at how this pertains to Microsoft Windows NT Server and the Web. The Internet is made up of literally thousands of networks interconnected by a massive number of routers of all types and designs. Because these network systems are so diverse, the common thread among them is the protocol—the language computers use to communicate. English is the predominant language of the United States. In France, it's French. And, in Japan, it's Japanese. All across the world, countries and even divisions within countries have their own dialects. If you had to connect computers together and bridge the language barrier among the world's possible languages, then you would be faced with a highly formidable task, indeed. It would be really nice if there were a way everyone could easily understand one another, but that option got fouled up a few thousand years ago.

In the computer world, a very similar dialectical situation exists. Novell servers speak IPX as their native tongue. Microsoft's dialect is NETBeui and NetBIOS. Banyan VINES has its own version of communicating called VINES-IP. None of these languages knows anything about the other, so to connect each of these systems together calls for a common language, or protocol. TCP/IP is it. *Transmission*

Control Protocol/Internet Protocol is the name, seamless connectivity is the game. If you install TCP/IP in each of the servers mentioned, then all of the servers can talk to each other regardless of the underlying server languages. What this does is form a common bond from Hong Kong to Vienna to Los Angeles (ad infinitum). Remember the lost common language a few thousand years ago? Well, we can't get that back, but TCP/IP creates a universal language for computers. Even as I write this manuscript, I'm connected to my Internet provider and checking mail, grabbing a file from an Internet site in Germany, and browsing the Web at Microsoft's campus.

Figure 1.5 clearly shows how the Internet is put together. From my computer, I can check on several things at one time, as I said earlier. Emailing, file transferring, and Web browsing are commonly processed simultaneously. TCP/IP allows this by using sockets. *Sockets* are connections between the application software and operating system. Having the ability to create and manage multiple sockets is one feature TCP/IP uses that makes your world on the Web so much fun. Multiple sockets are very important, as you'll see in later chapters. Later, we're going to build a Web server capable of supporting multiple users and performing multiple functions. When you see these things happening, you'll understand

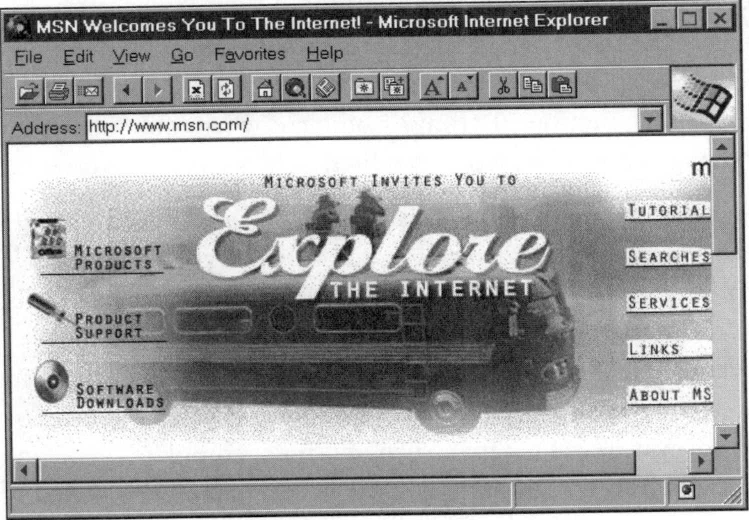

Figure 1.5
A walk on the Internet.

it can occur because of sockets. And when simultaneous processing doesn't occur, knowing about sockets will seem even more important!

Electronic Commerce

There are quite a few ways to make money on the Web, and many businesses are doing it. Let's take a few minutes to look at some of the ways to exploit the opportunities that abound on the Web. One of the ways to keep your CFO a happy camper is to show how the Web server can be manipulated to further the cause of the bottom line. All across the Internet, there are many ways to find information, yet few ways to use it to good order and purpose. This section will introduce you to a few ideas on how to use available information to leverage your business's Web server into a more profitable venture. In a manner of speaking, you'll bring together several aspects of the Web to your server and entice customers to use you as a sole point of contact. The next sections are an introduction to the same-titled sections in Chapter 3 where each topic will be explored in some detail. For now, let's just take a peek at the ideas that you'll cover in more detail at that time.

Marketing Surveys

Have you ever been sent one of those goofy marketing surveys that asks you to verify all sorts of personal information, including your income, number of kids, and social security number? I always wondered what could come out of a decent marketing survey if someone conducted the survey with clear vision.

Well, there's one way to do just that and have the information stored away in a database for good usage later. In Chapter 3, we'll explore all sorts of ways to handle marketing data, but for now, let's presume that a form is filled in and the data is tucked away for later usage. When could you use such a survey to good benefit? Well, Netscape and Microsoft both use forms when users want to download their Web server software. (See Figure 1.6.) This is a good ploy—if you want their software, even a demo, then you must complete the form in its entirety! No gaps and no substitutions—the form must be completed.

After a form is filled in, the resultant data is sent to the back-end tools. The back-end tools process each request and assign return mail messages that let users know the status of their requests. I've never known one of Microsoft's or

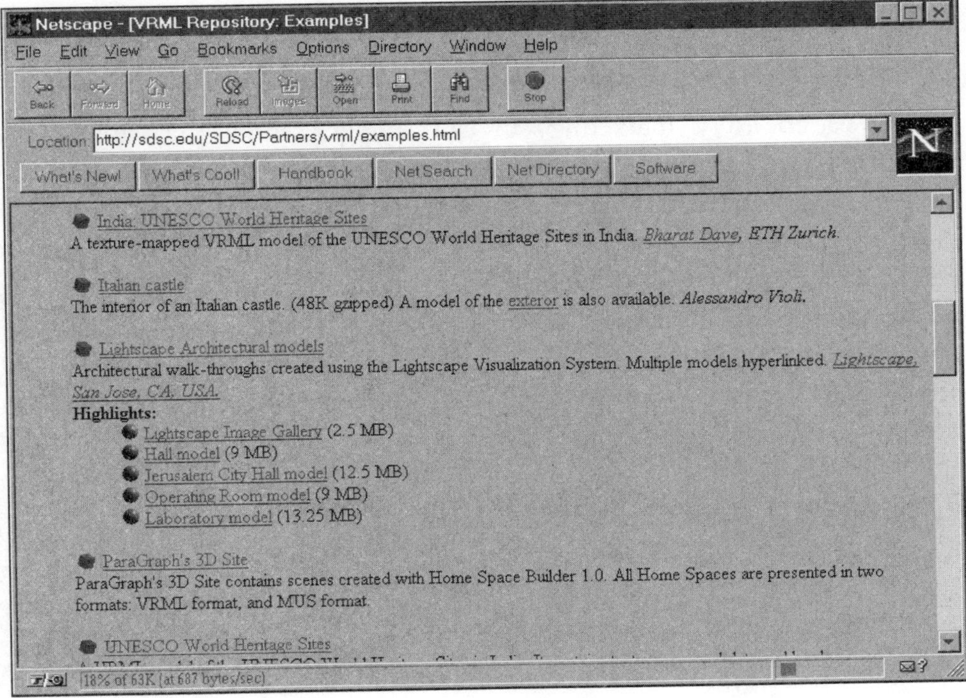

Figure 1.6
Downloading the Microsoft Internet Information Server.

Netscape's forms to be turned down, but I do know that each time a form is submitted, information—marketing information—is gathered for the company's own purposes. And I assure you, the information is used for something, or they wouldn't have gone through the trouble to create and maintain the forms in the first place.

Following is a list of some ways you can use your Web server to gather information of, what I call, a useful nature:

- Determine the types of operating systems your software users have.
- Gather data on problem calls to your computer repair shop.
- Register the software your users buy.
- Classify suggestions or complaints about the service of the Web server.
- Ask vendors to participate in an information-only request for proposal study.

- Update product FAQs remotely.
- Query users concerning what they want in a new or enhanced product.

So you see, not every "marketing" survey is simply a pain in the behind. Take your individual wants, needs, and company desires forward into the following sections, and imagine how and where you could use such a form to solve a particular need or fill a gap in your server software. Remember, these surveys generate files and use disk space, so customers offering forms using your server should be charged for the usage of the disk. Also, if a set of surveys reaches a set demand or the results hit a specific volume, then you can generate email to call attention to this fact. You can also bill for the volume of email generated. You don't always have to bill to store data, but it's a potential you'll have to evaluate.

Creating New Servers

If you can build a new Web server or rebuild an existing one, you have the potential for a decent contract as an Internet consultant. Obviously, this is a biggie. Chapter 2 goes over Web server requirements from both the hardware and software standpoint, and it discusses how to develop a Web server game plan. So, what tasks are involved in developing a Web server? Here's a quick summary of some of the tasks addressed in Chapter 2:

- Perform a site survey to determine the actual needs of the server.
- Talk to your customers and as many of your customers' users as possible, to determine the overall purpose of the site.
- Propose a Web server platform and finalize it.
- Install and configure the prototype server.
- Review your final configuration.
- Perform acceptance testing.

Potentially, most of these tasks can turn into billable tasks. At one time or another, I've worked with people on site surveys, writing proposals and bid requests, system reviews, quality acceptance testing, and final acceptance testing. Why wouldn't the same person do all of these tasks for a Web server? Think of it this way: If you have five sets of eyes and ideas on a subject, you are more likely to find most of the flaws in any good game plan for a server.

Logistics Issues

Where there are servers and connectivity, there is the potential for disaster and mayhem. These two brothers seem to run hand in hand with Murphy and his law, so modern computing infrastructures are bound to fail at some point. This is the basic and most important premise of support issues. There are a tons of support topics, but here's a list of issues that will cause the greatest consternation among CEOs:

- When a Web server goes down, the business starts losing money immediately.
- When a Web server goes down, critical customers lose connectivity to other sites. Not a direct loss of money to you, but your customers are now without *their* money-making functions.
- If a natural disaster strikes, a Web server could be unrecoverable.
- If a man-made disaster strikes, the Web server could be unrecoverable.

Each of these items is catastrophic to a business, either in the basic premise that the data has been destroyed or the access to the data has been removed. I added the last two to differentiate between flash fires over the weekend at the office and hurricane warnings, which allow you to grab the server and evacuate the state. In all of the listed circumstances, the opportunity to supply services to the customer is very possible, and especially probable, if the customer is very interested in the long-term survival of the site.

Not only that, but critical data on a server should be, as any wise Webmaster should know, backed up consistently over the weeks of having a server built and put online. This means purchasing a good tape drive, software, and a whole slew of tapes if these items weren't purchased in the initial server build. Power-protection devices, utility software, and other issues such as this encumber the customer with a host of logistics questions. Chapter 4 covers these issues in detail.

Billing Issues

Of course, all of this has to be paid for somehow. Not the server, I mean, but the services that your customers use and allow their own customers to use. If you use the Web server to do double duty as a partial Internet Service Provider, then your customers may need someone to track the online time used by those connected to the Web server. You can also have billing set in place for selling FTP disk space, Web pages, and the like. All of these are opportunities that you can provide on your Web server to help your customers or, if the need exists, for your customers to support and sell excess server space to their customers. It's a lot like leasing a building and then subleasing each of the suites to more customers.

Server Maintenance

All servers, at one time or another, need some kind of support, whether it's minor maintenance, training a new user, training a Webmaster how to use the server, installing new hardware, or even providing routine support. There are plenty of businesses out there that love to have the Web server earning them money, but they don't have the time, inclination, or the personnel to perform normal maintenance. Take, for example, one customer I recently supported in a 200-user network. The company hired me when they had plenty of their own computer people available to do the job, but they believed that they could save money by having their employees perform different, and hopefully more productive, jobs. So, they hired outside technical support to do the same job their own employees used to do. Outsourcing service and support of networking systems is quickly becoming common practice.

Included in server-maintenance theory is the ability of a customer to have someone (presumably you or your business) create, test, maintain, and support their Web server or Web businesses while they simply use the results of the Web server's performance. There are tons of server actions performed by outside maintenance sources, and much of them are done remotely across the Internet. All you have to do is prepare the server for remote access by you or your assistant.

Sales Projects

Every vendor of a product seeks ways to promote and even sell the product on the Internet. Just like the billboard on the road, or the evening TV show, Web pages are a superb form of advertising your products.

It's significantly easier to create an advertisement, and much faster, by using your Web page as one. When your widgets change characteristics overnight, your Web page can change as fast to meet the need.

Beta Test Projects

Beta testing is one part of the Web that is so underused that it's not even funny. One of the things I've done on my own server is to involve several external users and people I can trust to both use the Web server and beat it up, at the same time. This is by design and necessity to find the flaws in the design of my server. In Chapter 3, we'll discuss how you can set up your Web server as a beta test site. Keep in mind that such a site is likely to need the resources of a full-blown powerful server.

Beta testing is a process of using new software in an effort to find bugs or shortcomings in the software, so expect to have problems. You should plan on having extra tape backups of the software and of the entire server itself in case of disaster.

Internet Service Providers

The Internet Service Provider (ISP) business is booming around the globe. We'll discuss what it takes to be an Internet Service Provider in Chapter 3. The long and short of it is that a very competitive market is evolving. Chapter 3 will go into more details, but the average ISP will need at least 107 customers of the $19.95 variety for a 50-line ISP to break even. This takes into account the initial costs of modems, the monthly line charges (on average, that is), and two employees to run the show.

All too often, small ISPs that establish roots in small communities where there is no other competition find themselves at risk of losing business when large providers like UUNet come to town. Our small town of Panama City, Florida, recently began experiencing this just as soon as UUNet and a mid-range provider established new service. The previous providers were of the $19.95 all you can eat variety, but these larger providers run an average of $25.00 for 100 hours, and $1.50 an hour for each hour beyond the 100.

Why is this significant? Sure, cost is always important, but these two larger providers have full-time tech support, significantly better expansion capabilities, and more hardware resources to provide for all of my connectivity needs. For a business looking for a long-term business relationship, these larger providers are the way to go. Chapter 3 will expound upon these principles.

Training And The Web Server

In this section, let's focus on your Webmaster. What are the qualifications of this person? Smart and quick to learn, but how experienced is this person? How will he or she respond to a crisis under the pressure of dozens of users calling to find out why they're not able to connect? What kind of a public relations expert did you hire? If you think these considerations are a joke, then you're in for quite a shock! Quite a shock indeed.

The best thing you can do when hiring a Webmaster is to use peer evaluation. When you interview potential Webmasters, collaborate with an associate you trust and who has a significant level of expertise with the Internet and Microsoft Windows NT. This process isn't something to sneeze at. Then, after you hire a Webmaster, keep in mind that there are Microsoft Certified Training Centers all across the country. It is well worth the investment to have your Webmaster learn a few things about Microsoft Windows NT Server and networking in general. A generous sprinkling of systems administration background wouldn't hurt, either.

Running A List Server

A list server is nothing more than a mechanism to send the same message to multiple recipients yet only use one email address. Let's say that there are six persons in the outside sales team that need to get information about hot topics and new sales tactics, and they need this information hourly. Would you like to create an email message each hour to six people and type in six addresses?

That wouldn't be terribly painful, just not an exciting venture. Now, how about that same informational update to over a hundred employees? That would indeed be painful. List servers come onto the scene by providing automatic mailing lists for just such a purpose. Unfortunately, there are few list servers for NT Server. Chapter 3 will talk more about list servers.

Electronic Classrooms

Now here's one really new and interesting aspect of Web usage that is sure to grow at a tremendous rate. Imagine taking computer classes over your modem! This is happening as we speak. Well, perhaps not college accredited courses, but how would you like to learn how to design, build, and maintain NT Web Servers via modem in a neat virtual classroom?

One example of this is the Ziff-Davis University classes taught from the Cambridge, Massachusetts office of Ziff-Davis. There's a monster Web server or two hosting the software running on a Sun Sparc Server, and it's somewhat like a news or list server, only better. The software is custom written to take advantage of the many benefits of the Web yet maintain security. That's about all I can say about it for now except that it's in operation and fully functional at **www.zdu.com**. Figure 1.7 shows the ZDNet University Web site.

There are rumors flying around the Web that there are several more of these types of learning centers coming into the scene, but to date, only ZDU has the breadth and depth to offer these types of courses. If this idea catches on, I fully expect to see more services offered as the online community grows.

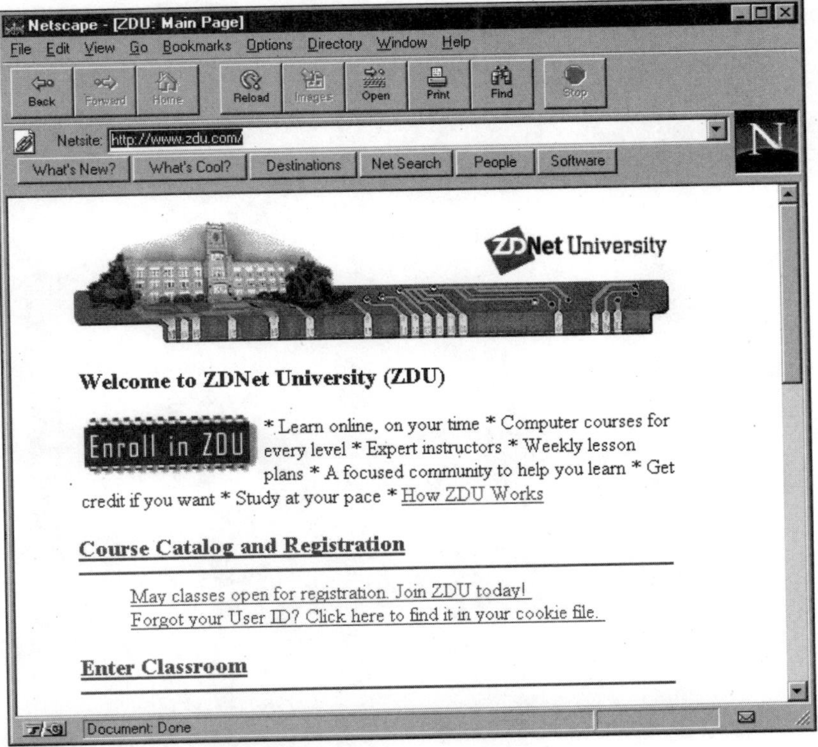

Figure 1.7
Ziff-Davis University.

Summary

Chapter 1 presents many of the opportunities that Web servers offer to enterprising customers and businesses. Not all of these concepts will be implemented in this book, but this chapter offers ideas of how, what, and why these functions are brought to bear on a paying customer base. As you read onward, keep in mind that for everything you employ on the Web, there are several different flavors of each that portend to bring newer and more exciting ways to expand your site into the future. All it takes is time and money....

2

Developing Your Web Server Game Plan

Jeff Bankston

This chapter will play a significant role in your Web site. You'll be better able to determine why you or your business wants a Web site, what to expect in the way of things to do and obstacles to overcome on the way, and more. You'll get a secondhand look at a real-life Web site that was built from the ground up—mine! I'll make a few comparisons, at various points, to other Web sites I've been involved in, ranging from other NT Servers to Sun Microsystems-based Unix servers. Each offers a unique perspective on what you'll do, or need, for your site.

Specifically, this chapter addresses:

- Designing your site from scratch from a desired need or goal
- Planning the hardware construction of your site
- Acquiring your domain name and address
- Acquiring the physical communications link
- Designing and planning the actual software installations

Systems Integration—The Process Of Planning

Systems and network integration is one of two primary functions of my business, and one that I've enjoyed tremendously over the years. I've been pleased with the success I've had, the customers I've helped, and the business relationships I've forged. Perhaps the one thing that has brought me the most pleasure has been the reward of having a customer thank me for keeping them from jumping off into an abyss of wasted money and development time in their projects. I want to keep you from jumping into the abyss, too, so together we'll be developing the Web Server Master Plan. This plan will keep you on the straight and narrow as you embark on your Web adventure. The plan is included on the accompanying CD-ROM as plan.doc. The document starts off as plan01.doc and increments upward to the final document, plan05.doc. By breaking the plan into segments, you will be able to see what tasks you need to tackle and in what order.

Most of my customers are small businesses with goals and aspirations exceeding those of their big cousins in corporate America, but they don't have the cash to handle the project. Even those that do have the cash—or investment partners—to handle Web site projects, don't have a firm grip on what they're getting into until it's too late. It's not until the server is built, the software is installed, and a few customers are online that they realize what they *should have* done.

Sure, you can make improvements during off-peak hours or by scheduling downtime and notifying the customers. (In fact, scheduled maintenance is very worthwhile and should be performed once a week at a minimum. We'll get to this concern later on.) But why recover from continual problems when you can get it right the first time? The solution is really quite simple, and I already mentioned it—planning. Developing a workable plan is the primary purpose of this chapter. When you set out to tackle the Web, you'll need to consider many different things, starting with why you want this site.

Why Set Up A Web Site?

Somewhere along the line, someone mentioned that Joe Blow from Company ABC found a really neat piece of software that helped his business in some way. So, being the savvy businessperson that you are, you inquire about the source of this information. "The Web," he replies. "Can't be," you scoff. "That large conglomeration of computers and gobbledygook?" You eventually find out that not only did Joe find the software on the Web, but it was even *easy*! "Wow!" you think to yourself. "I wish we could do that for our customers."

Well, you can, and it's one of the most frequently chosen reasons for having a Web site. Customer support of your product is chewing your right financial arm off at the elbow, and the CFO knows it. What if you could give your customers complete access to your tech support databases and reference materials? And automate it for remote access? Now, that's a superb reason for a Web site. And these same customers have computer-literate technical folks on staff to wade through everything you offer.

Now, imagine your business has 500 PC users split up into several groups. There's an Engineering department, an Accounting department, a Logistics department, and, of course, the HeadShed. Each department has unique needs and support issues, so why burden them all with the same server? Or the same server topics? Again, here comes Microsoft Windows NT Server to the rescue. NT's disk sharing and resource utilization makes for a fine separation of unwanted groups of topics or users.

In the planning stages of this book, I considered several different ways I could write it. My publisher and I had many discussions determining the goals we wanted to meet. You, too, will have to determine your goals—whether they be technical support for your customers or meeting the needs of your company internally—if you want your Web site to be a success, not to mention pain free (well, almost). So, let's get right to it.

Determining Goals For The Site

We're going to use my own Web site as a target environment for this chapter. We've discussed some pretty ambitious goals. Before we can set any plans into motion with any degree of success, it's important to know what we want to accomplish. The following four goals represent the core of our support issues:

- Private Web access for our Internet-based customers
- NT Server Remote Access Service for our WFWG, Win95, and WinNT Workstation customers
- Intranet services for employees

- Direct server-to-server connections for our major customers to our NT Web and LAN servers

Sure, this seems like a not-too-demanding list of things to accomplish, but you'd be amazed at the hoops we'll jump through, prerequisite tasks we need to complete, and the little issues that can easily derail or compromise installation. For instance, will the customers be accessing data using the CGI scripts on the server? Will any users be doing programming for you? If so, they'll need special access, including rights and permissions. Did you get the proper licensing for network access? Like I said, the little things. Now that we have these four primary objectives defined, we can begin to plan for the future. Using this approach, we might even be able to purchase the equipment now that we'll need to successfully meet these goals.

Of course, the four goals are our primary concern, but the bigger picture holds more for us. Next, I'll let you know what our other goals are and how we want to implement them.

Alternative Goals For The Site

Even the best leaders have to work out kinks in their great plans for conquering the world. But the rewards are well worth the effort. Our situation is no different and also holds the prospect of financial and personal rewards if implemented correctly. Unfortunately, we have a limited time scale—two to four years. However, considering the turnover rate of today's technology, even one year can be construed as excessive. For instance, I purchased a 2 gigabyte SCSI-2 drive last year in July for $990, and today the price is down to $600. Motherboards and other component parts of my server have similarly come down in price at the rate of 40 percent or more. Overall, a server that cost $3,500 in July of 1996 now can be purchased for under $2,000. That's a mighty big drop, and you can consider it all lost money if your server isn't earning you a solid return. The moral: Make sure you are earning a solid return!

You should have alternatives ready to put into play or even as a supplement to your existing strategy. In my business, we're planning to offer a few more services to preferred customers. Here's a list of the ones we'll be implementing:

- Public Internet Service Provider (ISP) connections to the Web server over a dialup modem.

- In the rural areas of my county, all phone calls are either local long distance or toll calls at the rate of 25 to 50 cents per call. Using NT Server's Remote Access features, we're offering direct connections to our networks. The 1-800 number offers a value-added incentive to do business with us.
- Public bulletin board access for home-based businesses and personal users needing technical support for their computers. These customers represent a huge growing market across the nation, as more people begin working at home.
- We're offering private intranet services for our business partners using NT Server as the baseline platform.

As you can see, there's plenty to do in a short span of planning. Obviously, you'll have to evaluate the merit of any project you do with the return on the investment. And remember, in the business world, time also equals money. If the task will be one of low cost in terms of up-front funding but high cost in terms of time to get it going, it may not be as viable as it appears. One more factor, and a very important one at that, is to check out the market presence around you to see if any other companies have implemented similar services. You'd be foolish to set up a Web site where a major ISP with a healthy customer base has already set down roots—unless you've found a top-secret way to entice their customer base to your site.

Most ISPs do not offer private Web access to transfer files and other related confidential information. This is one way in which your Web site could garner membership—by offering secured access customer-to-customer or customer-to-your-business.

Customer Interaction

Now that you've defined the goals and aspirations for your Web site, it's time to begin drafting the initial planning document that you'll use during this process. Wait a minute, this is only a Web site, you say. Just build or buy a new machine and start loading the software, right? Well, I wouldn't. The people that'll be using your site may or may not have special needs. They may have Macintosh computers and need to access your Microsoft Windows NT Server. Not exactly what I'd call a compatible set of kids playing in the sandbox. Also, they may not even have modems! Are you going to leave them in the dark to decide how to get connected? I'd surely hope not if you want to keep these people as paying customers.

You should definitely involve your customer base in this very critical stage of planning. While you're developing your master document, talk to them. Perhaps a telephone conference with them and several of your people will get the creative juices flowing and uncover idiosyncrasies, such as a customer having insufficient phone lines to handle the needs. Alternatively, you could create a small survey and mail it to each customer asking what they'd like to see, how they intend to connect to the Web server or the BBS, if they have special needs, and so forth. These are the small behind-the-scenes issues that can (and usually do) cripple the best of plans. Here are some key issues for you to consider:

- How is this site being offered to the customer? Extra charge to existing contracts? Gratis for preferred customers?
- How many of the customers' employees are you going to grant this access to?
- Are there hourly usage limits?
- Will there be restrictions to accessing the Web site—time of day or day of week?
- How will you assist customers in getting connected? When it breaks?
- What existing hardware and software does the customer have now to access your site? Any upgrades required?

This is but a sampling of the issues you'll have to consider when you speak with each customer. Oh, with each one? Doesn't this apply to most of them? Not really. It could, but it's only a starting point for the work you've now got in front of you. I hope you didn't think this was going to be a walk in the park. It'll take some significant planning, but the rewards are worth it in a well-designed Web site.

Your First Rough Draft

Our first set of plans is the rough draft, which is located on the CD-ROM in a file called plan01.doc. As you can see, it's nothing more that a condensed version of the last few pages. We'll be adding more detail to the plan as we consider all of the alternatives to this site. As with any good plan, our document will undergo a lot of revisions before the site is firmly established. One AutoCAD drawing I saw during a recent design stage went through 140 changes. We won't go quite that far, but it's important that you understand that your plan is a living document.

This rough draft should give you some idea of what you're likely to want in your Web site, even if it's nothing more than a skeletal picture of the site. Don't let this bother you. If your site goes through a dozen changes or drafts, then I'd say that's about normal. As I've stated before, it's far better to make mistakes now and correct them now than to wait until the site is operational. There's nothing worse than a handful of irate customers to ruin your Web site dreams, not to mention the business.

Initial Design Review

When you've created a baseline game plan, and have reviewed and/or edited it for the tenth time, it's time to get the entire gang together and conduct an internal formal business review of how you intend to implement the initial goals of the Web site. At this stage, you (hopefully) have not yet purchased anything, nor have you issued a request for quotes to any computer resellers. This is the best time to make changes or clear up any misgivings that may exist about the Web site. It's terribly important that everything is laid out on the design table at this time. Make no bones about it—mistakes from here on out can be costly and delay the implementation of the site. Additionally, mistakes can be quite costly down the road when the site needs to be updated because the plan was too shortsighted.

So, just how does this initial design review help us? It states the obvious needs for the site—you plan the purchases, set the tempo for the site, involve the customers so they know what to expect, and show your CFO what to expect in next month's accounts-payable bin. Aside from that, the review also uncovers some of life's little unexpected matters, such as how much training is needed and for whom. The review shows you how much you knew about building sites, how much you didn't know, and an idea of what to expect in the future. You learn all of these educational things before spending a penny and committing to the site. This is the ideal time to delay creation or modify the intent of the site.

Whether you know it or not, an initial design review, if you take notes and do an outline, provides you with a baseline document usable for writing a site's guidance and manuals; remember, someone has to operate the site. This task entails daily administration, security issues, customer contacts, and related matters. You'll probably want to devote a single person to the site's overall needs, and this person is usually called a *Webmaster*. You may have someone that can do double duty in two or more positions, but many businesses create a new position dedicated to that job. For the first six months of the site, I'd highly advise the business to devote a knowledgeable networking person to this task.

Okay, let's say you've had your series of meetings and decided on a core set of needs the business would like to support for the customer base. The site is still to be a private venture for the first year. In order of importance, here are the most strategic goals to be addressed in this first version of the site:

- Provide required server access for customers.
- Provide employee services, such as traveling sales representatives checking on leads and orders.
- Give the Webmaster and MIS full access for remote control and administration.

To provide the solutions for this target environment, your customers need to be polled to determine their requirements and special needs. Once this review has been completed, you will have identified the following system-level issues that have to be addressed with the site (the following list contains sample figures from my own site-building work). These concerns are common to all of your customers:

- A need exists to have at least 50MB of disk storage for your 15 most preferred customers.
- Your site will need 700MB of temporary storage for file transfers, program operations, and such.
- Disk space growth is estimated at 20 percent per year per customer for the next five years.
- The business has five customers whose data is critical to the point that a loss of one hour of downtime can cost as much as $5,000. Data protection and recovery are of the utmost importance.
- Only 10 people will have no possible need for Internet access, but rather need simple file transfer from the Web site's server locations. This group represents those people who have no earthly idea what the Internet is, how to operate it, and have no time to learn it.

In-Progress Design Review

Now that we've made some concrete decisions regarding system-level issues, it's time to get down to the final decisions. We know the goals of the site, the minimum requirements of the site, and the customers' requirements. The designers of the site have a firm grasp of the requirements, and these people may indeed be the same team that builds the server. In fact, that's the most desirable position possible but not always doable. At this stage, if your designers and builders are not the same team, it's time to hand off the project to the builders. Your game plan should now look something like plan02.doc. And it's this stage of the plan—the part that has all those final decisions in writing—that needs to go to the builders of the site. Let's take a look at the nuts and bolts of the plan at this point.

Choice Of Servers

I'll state a couple of blanket opinions about the Web server hardware as suggestions because you already know that Microsoft Windows NT Server can handle the task with great aplomb. Get the best affordable server hardware possible, and buy brand-name equipment from the start. There's Dell, AST Research, Gateway 2000, IBM, Compaq, and a host of other vendors that will meet your every need in server hardware. All will suffice and provide years of reliable service. However, the age-old adage is still true—you pay extra for a good name, but you also get what you pay for. I've built quite a few computers from scratch, ranging from simple desktop machines all the way up to multiprocessor network behemoths. In time, I learned how to pick and choose the parts needed, by vendors, to have a very reliable system. By the same token, if you build your machine this way, you can expect to be totally responsible for all hardware and warranty support for the server.

On the other hand, if you buy a pre-built server, most will come with some level of on-site support or provide warranty support by phone with the vendor. Be cautious about on-site support! On-site, to the majority of vendors, means that they've contracted with a computer shop near you to take care of your needs if the server requires it. I'm not knocking these local providers of support, but most of them have no clue about your situation and specific needs. You'll have to spend time on the phone with the vendor to diagnose the problem, and then the vendor will tell the local support shop what they need to bring to you to fix the problem. If it doesn't work, then they'll have to try again. Usually, the vendor sends the parts to the local shop, which then brings them to you. If more parts are needed, then your site sits down a bit longer until the vendor gets the additional parts to the local shop.

In situations where Web servers are in critical positions, this situation is totally unacceptable. Sites with servers this important must be staffed by networking technicians that can handle any job that comes around. For this reason, you may opt to purchase the server without site support and handle that issue on your own. Even if your package does come with on-site support, just ignore it unless doing so would void the warranty. Yet another option is to purchase additional hardware as spare units ready for use should the main equipment go out.

All About Spare Hardware

If you purchase spare hardware, the most important thing you can do is to proof test it just as soon as you can to validate its readiness for the job. If this is to be a critical hard drive that contains the operating system, then you should prepare the drive and reload the operating system to the point that it's configured as close to normal site operations as possible. This includes creating the core user accounts, permissions, security, and so on. Once you've tested and prepared the unit, then store it in a safe location *that several people know about.* Yes, that's right! I went to a customer's site once where the server hard drive was having measurable difficulty processing data. The customer had a spare drive handy because the inventory said they did. The person holding the inventory knew that the network administrator kept the drive in the logistics room, which looked like my eight-year-old son's room. After two hours of searching, the decision was made to call the on-vacation administrator who could not be reached. Unfortunately, this person wouldn't be back for two more days—just about the amount of time required for me to order a new drive and have it installed.

As it turned out, all of the network spare hardware was placed in an unlocked cabinet behind the kitchen in the office. Readily accessible, but no one knew where it was, so the site spent the next two days down. I'm glad I wasn't there when the administrator came back!

Core Server Requirements

Okay, enough war stories about misguided intentions. It's time to get down to the nitty-gritty of Web server design. As I mentioned before, Web servers have different requirements than normal network servers. This is true of our server, as well. We'll tailor the Web server to our customers' needs with an emphasis on future business plans. Later in this chapter, we'll go over the actual hardware and software requirements of the site, and issues surrounding their use. If you're in a smaller organization, you'll be able to build your server from scratch using clone parts and hardware. If you're in a large organization, you probably have a logistics department that has buying power with numerous vendors. In that case, you'll probably buy brand-name servers already built to a large degree. In a later section, we'll talk about the actual server requirements. Also, data links will be explained, and you'll see how I went through the data communications jungle with my providers.

Final Process Review

When you've made it this far, you can pat yourself on the back because you've survived the most important parts of making your Web site a reality. But you're not done yet. After building the physical server, installing the software, and proof testing the basics, you need to consult with your customers (and employees) again to see if their requirements have changed. This is still the best time to make changes to the server and site configuration without altering the bottom line too much and risking the wrath of the CFO.

This stage is called a *final process review* of the site, and you conduct the review as you would conduct the initial design review. The difference, however, is that you've purchased all of the required hardware and software. The pieces of the puzzle have been put together, you're finishing most of the construction process, and you can consider the site 95 percent completed. It's not yet online and ready for business, but you're close to it.

What, then, are the relative merits of this review? Well, for one thing, you've had the chance to use the server and see how the hardware performs. You can, in fact, build the Web site and make it operational as a test bed for the MIS group to pound upon and see how it reacts. If you don't have an MIS group, let some of your computer hacker buddies beat on it. You'd be surprised at what you'll uncover in the way of anomalies when you first proof test it. You'll also learn what amount of disk space is consumed when the core software is installed and brought to life. Just remember that this is perhaps the last time you'll be able to make the changes necessary to give your customers a bandage-free site that flows and works smoothly. Bandage-free because once the server is brought online, you want your only downtime to occur when you're performing basic tasks and installing patches to bugs.

Unfortunately, mistakes happen. Every time you make adjustments or quick fixes, you're opening your site up for potential trouble. I once saw the most simple and fundamental of site inspections go bad and cause a minicomputer to be down for 48 hours when all they wanted to do was oil the bearings of a cooling fan. True story! To get to the fan, a shelf had to be removed. To remove the shelf, a 10-pin connector had to be moved out of the way to get to a screw on the shelf. When that connector was moved, its safety hooks broke from old age and removed primary signal connections to eight disk drives on the critical run of disk drives for the processor—and down came the system. All for the love of oiling a bearing on a $2 fan. The repair of the connector cost $650 in labor and time lost ordering a new connector.

The moral to this story is to get it as close to perfect as possible before taking the site public, or private, as it is in this case. It's really never too late to fix what needs to be fixed, but it's always too late when you fix what isn't broken.

What's left to do? Something called *site acceptance*, which is sometimes tied into site testing and qualifications. It's a lot like Boeing Aircraft Corporation building a new jet and selling it to Delta Airlines. You can bet that Boeing has a solid reputation as a premier builder of planes, but Delta is still going to test the plane before giving Boeing a single penny. So, Delta test pilots will fly it, land it, and wring it out for all it's worth. If they give the thumbs up, then the plane is accepted for commercial service.

Site Acceptance

But, we're not flying airplanes here! Web sites aren't nearly as critical as airplanes, where lives are at stake, you say. I'd agree with that from the humanistic standpoint, but could you accept your company's data being stolen and destroyed by intruders? Or could you accept one of your best customers getting faulty data from the Web site and making a bad decision because of it?

I didn't think so, and I definitely would not want to be in the board room while a customer was yelling at the CEO who then flares up at the CFO because she approved the purchases for the site. I think I'd rather have a site tested to the highest level possible. Don't go to extremes, but make sure the site is protected from intruders with a good firewall. Make sure the allowed users have the proper permissions to get them into the server areas necessary to do their jobs. Make sure the essentials and important stuff are covered. You'll have to sit down with your customers and tell them what they'll see, what's expected of them, and what you'll work with them to achieve. When all else fails, have a good set of server backups handy.

So, the equivalent to having your site signed off and accepted as a formal site would be to have every customer begin a 30-day testing period. This test period should be as in-depth and intense as possible. Transfer as much data as possible, use as many of those forms and CGI scripts as possible, and beat the server as hard as possible. While your customers are doing this, check the NT Server error and monitor logs to see what's going on and how the physical server is performing. You'll also want to pay special attention to the communications link and observe the statistics of the link. How's that critical portion of the site performing?

When this acceptance testing period is over, you should gather all the data together for analysis. Look for weak spots in the performance of the server, and review the performance log files of Microsoft Windows NT Server's diagnostics. This information is critical in deciding if you're ready to put the Web site online officially or if you need to make final changes. At this point, your planning document should resemble plan03.doc.

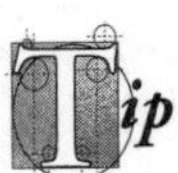

This is a great time to show the CFO that her money was well spent because you've built a primo server.

Planning For Private And Public Web Sites

A Web server is a Web server, true or false? It is, unless you're using the same server for both private (intranet) and public (Internet) usage. What's the difference between these two server types, you ask? An *intranet* Web server, shown in Figure 2.1, is one that is attached to the business network as a whole. An *Internet* server, shown in Figure 2.2, is a completely standalone server that is not attached to the network and is accessible to the general public. This perspective of using a Web server can be confusing and is worth a few words. Intranet Web servers are those in which the server itself allows network users to access the Internet by routing TCP/IP traffic from the network across the wire. Internet Web servers are those in which the users accessing the Web site do so from across the Internet itself. This server typically is a Microsoft Windows NT Server sitting all by itself and not connected to anything else but the Internet. You're probably scratching your head wondering, "Do I have separate physical servers for each? Is it worth that kind of an investment? Why would I want separate servers?" These are some great questions that deserve detailed answers.

The Differences Between Intranet And Internet Web Servers

You can see from Figures 2.1 and 2.2 that the physical differences are apparent, but what about the logical ones? The users allowed to log on are the most prevalent issue. When they log onto the Internet Web server, this server is the only place they can go. Users do their work, get the files they want, and leave. Not much else to do, not much else they could do anyhow. They still have full access across the server just like any other Web site for which they have rights. The

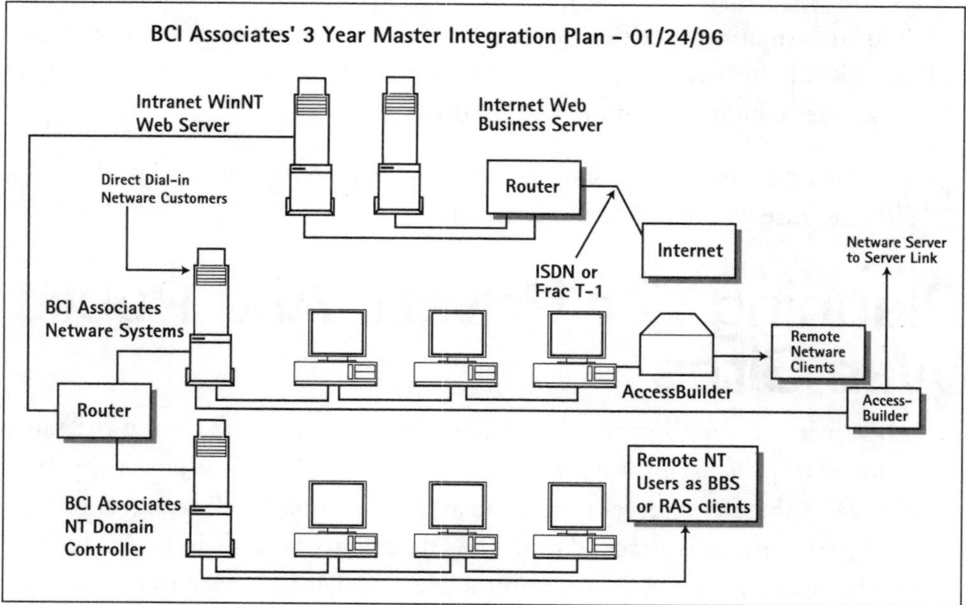

Figure 2.1
Internet and intranet Web servers, on the same network.

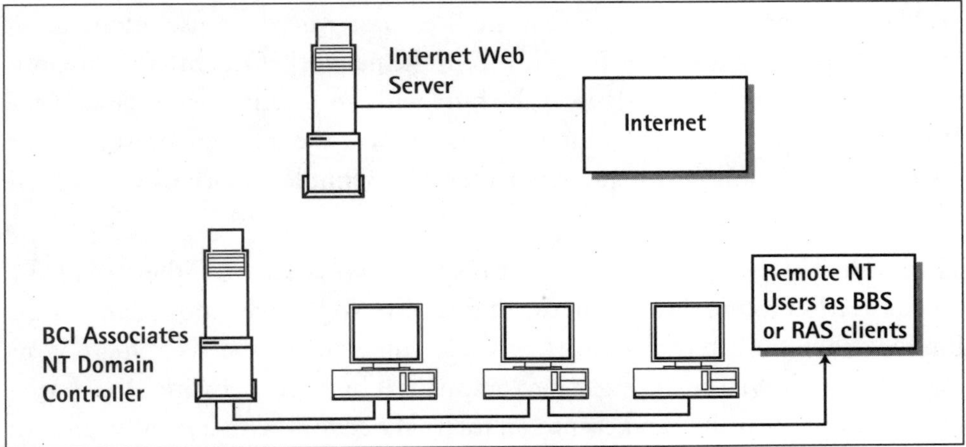

Figure 2.2
Standalone Internet Web server, not connected to the network.

Internet Web server can only be administered from the console instead of through remote links by the Webmaster. The Internet Web server also requires more local hardware to accomplish some tasks, such as backing up the server.

As I mentioned previously, intranet Web servers provide the ability for network users to access the Internet from their network workstations. If necessary, users can access Internet sites or their own Web server. They need special routing hardware, which is usually installed at the server, to get their network request out to the Internet. These workstations have to run TCP/IP software, in addition to any other Internet client software, for their network I/O cards to be able to connect to the Internet. The system administrator of the network has global access to the Web server and any other resources on the network. This makes updates not only easier but accessible from any place where the Webmaster can log in.

Examining The Dangers Of The Two Server Types

What possible dangers does the Internet Web site have to deal with? There's no possible intrusion into the business network. If the server crashes, no other part of the business is affected. So, what is affected? The term *danger* isn't exactly accurate. The potential problems are generally operational, such as when the administrator who has to access the core functions of the server when something goes wrong is on vacation and no one else is trained to handle server problems. There's also a chance that the Webmaster needs to use resources on the Web server that are accessible only from the network. Other than situations like this, there's not much that can be hurt with an Internet Web server. One other possible drawback of an Internet server is that the machine must have the horsepower to handle any request, whether it be a simple FTP transfer or a CGI SQL Server request.

The intranet Web server, by contrast, has a lot to worry about. If there's a physical connection to the business network from the Web server connecting to the Internet, then the internal network is just as vulnerable as the Web site. A virus that gets into a Web site can get into an internal business network. A user that can get into a Web site can get into an internal network with a goodly amount of hacking. It doesn't seem like a pretty picture, and it might not be at times, so let's get into the reasons why each has good points.

Another point of interest for the intranet Web server is that most planning goes into internal servicing of the users. Did any planning go into the Internet usage? What would happen if you decided to take this intranet Web server public? You would find out that all of the design went into internal security, safety, and disaster issues. Oops!

Perhaps the best thing designers of a system can do is plan for the best and the worst in each platform. Then, implement the Web server for the desired position with an ever-clear point to the other position. This is one way the most versatile sites stay ready for the future.

The Benefits Of The Two Server Types

Internet Web servers are, all other things being equal, faster than their intranet site siblings. No other kind of traffic has to be routed or processed from users or other sources, as shown in Figure 2.3. Other resources include back-end SQL Servers that process CGI requests for data and related queries. If the Web site has to be taken down for maintenance, no other part of the business infrastructure is affected.

The intranet Web site has a lot going for it in the plus column. Included here is the Webmaster's ability to access and administer any other part of the network from the Web server to which he has rights. The intranet Web server, having connectivity to the other business resources, offers redundancy for Web server

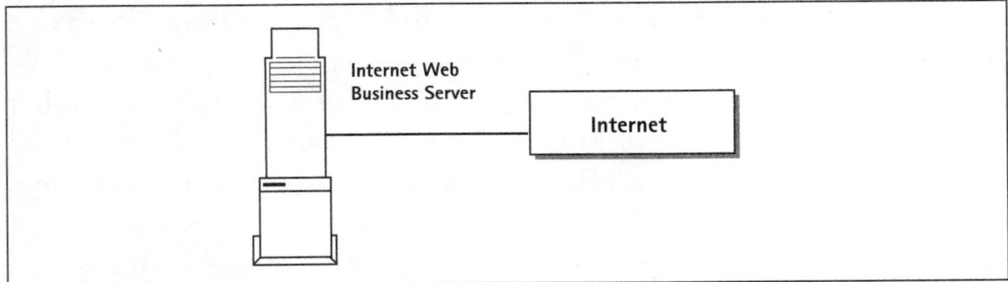

Figure 2.3
Truly standalone Web server.

resources, such as the file repositories. This redundancy comes in many forms and offers several advantages. For example, if your network runs Windows NT Workstation and uses NTFS partitions, you can use TCP/IP in the workstations and perform nearly any Web task to the network workstation that can be performed to the Web server itself. Figure 2.4 illustrates intranet Web site processing.

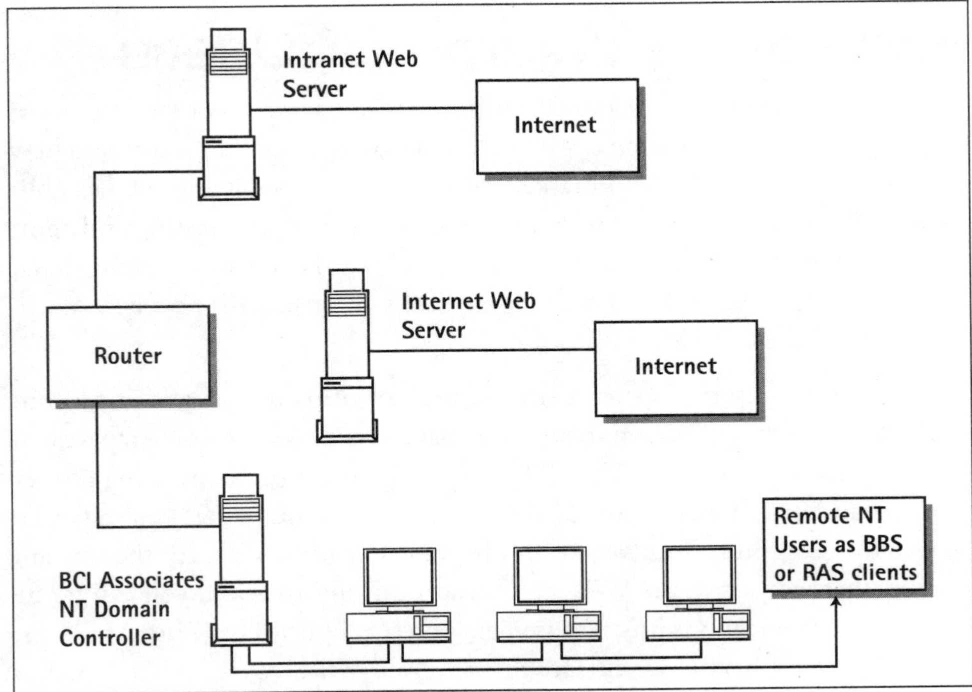

Figure 2.4
Intranet and Internet Web servers prepared for connection.

An intranet Web server provides a key aspect to critical processing of Web sites because it gives you instant redundancy and protection. Microsoft Windows NT Server offers directory replication for security of data, true enough, but having accessible alternatives is nice. Consider this: Your site comes to life and flourishes for two years. Your plans are largely successful, and the site brings much joy to the CFO. The Web site only needs a few configuration changes and a new software package to make everyone content with the Web site.

This changes dramatically when word gets out that your Web site offers wonderful services and you suddenly have three new prospective clients. Each company has its own requirements, and all three appear to be really hot tickets. You don't want to lose them at any cost. How do you leverage the intranet Web site to your advantage? The solution is simple. Use one of the Windows NT workstations on the network as a temporary Web site running any one of the Web server software packages I'll discuss in Part 2 of this book. By the way, Windows 95 can operate as a Web site given the appropriate hardware.

Estimating Volume Of Users

Figuring out how many users will visit your site has to be one of the most frustrating aspects of creating a Web site. You can guess all you want as to how popular your site will be, and market the site until you're blue in the face, but what it all boils down to is how you present the site with interesting and compelling information. You've got to make the site worth someone's online dollar and make it sparkle so they'll come back. If the site performs poorly, you can count on a decline in visitors.

You need to recoup the cost of a site—unless, of course, money is of no concern. Money is a huge concern to me, and I have to have some form of repayment to recoup the cost of a site. The CFO isn't likely to continue investing money into a dead horse, I assure you. If this is a private business site, you've got an edge in the user count. You should already know to within 5 percent the amount of users that will access the Web server. With this information, you can figure out the communications link requirements pretty closely. The volume of users, and the bandwidth requirements for the same, are critical to building the proper Web server.

> ***Note:*** *For the remainder of this chapter, all discussions will focus on a private intranet Web server. While there are distinct issues that differentiate a private from a public Web server, most of the discussion applies to both.*

So, let's state the figures that will drive us to the decisions that lie ahead. Let's assume that we've got five customers employing five people who will access the Web server by way of the Internet. Because direct Internet users do not have specific bandwidth requirements like modem users do, direct Internet users can retrieve and manipulate data on the Web server as fast as the Web server can process it. For our purposes, let's say that each direct Internet user equals a modem user at 28.8Kbps speed.

Our clients also employ four direct modem users that will dial into the Web server for Web server access using modems of 28.8Kbps speed rating. These users will be the traveling folks that can never tell where they'll be in relation to a local Internet point of presence. You'll have 1-800 numbers for these users because you value their business. Table 2.1 summarizes the connection speeds and type of access that we know will occur.

I've thrown in the third connection of a server-to-server link because there's a chance that one of these customers may need to have his or her Microsoft Windows NT Server directly integrated into your environment. Later on, when we discuss links, I'll introduce you to something called *ISDN*, which is rapidly becoming the next communications wave to overtake computing. ISDN has been around for quite some time, but it has only recently become viable in terms of its widespread presence and lowered cost. ISDN, which is illustrated in Figure 2.5, is a fantastic solution for linking servers together over dialup routers for local solutions. From this perspective, the important point to note is the

Table 2.1

Summation of Web server connection requirements.

Volume of Users	Type of Access	Speed of Connection	Cumulative Bandwidth
4	Modem	28.8Kbps	115.2KB
5	Internet	28.8Kbps	144.0KB
1	Server to Server	10Mbps	10Mbps

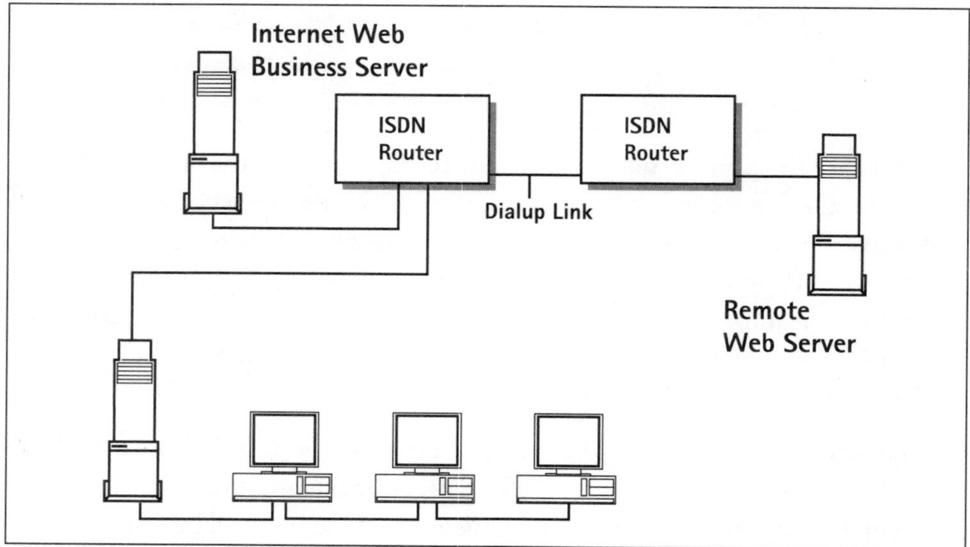

Figure 2.5
Low-capacity Web server using ISDN.

Internet connection speeds. ISDN's maximum rate is 128Kbps, and our link requires up to 144Kbps if all four users connect to the Web server at the same time. This implies that ISDN isn't right for us capacity-wise, but you'll soon see this is not necessarily true.

Look at Figure 2.5 carefully because there are hidden costs with this circuit. Although ISDN has the capacity to run at 128Kbps link speed, it's a digital service that requires numerous checks to be performed before it can be brought into play. ISDN also must be available within your local area, to some extent. Don't let a measly 128Kbps connection between servers give you the impression this is insufficient. Nothing could be further from the truth unless you've got servers constantly passing tons of data. For the vast majority of sites, ISDN is a decent alternative. If this concept sounds confusing, don't worry. We'll discuss ISDN in depth shortly.

There's a new technology coming of age called *cable modems* that promises to bring speeds of up to 5Mbps using standard copper wiring to the home and business that would blow ISDN out of the water! More realistically, if the technology survives, the average data rates that could be expected are more probable to be 1.5Mbps or so. Still, it's a far cry from standard modems.

Types Of Connections For Corporate Users

Let's take a few minutes to discuss the types of connections we may need. There are as many ways to get connected as there are directions for the wind to blow, but the four most prevalent are:

- Microsoft Windows NT Server's Remote Access Server
- Internet access to your Web server
- Bulletin board dialup service using a modem
- Server-to-server connections

NT Server's Remote Access Server (RAS)

If you've ever logged into a network, then you know you have to supply a user name and a password to gain access to the resources of the network, such as a printer or files on the network server. These are the most basic and fundamental workings of a network infrastructure. As a member of the network users group, you have specific access rights, belong to membership groups for centralized control, and a host of other things. These things you do at the office from your desk or other suitable accommodations.

However, when you're away on vacation or traveling for the company, you're no longer a user on the network, right? Sure, but that is only applicable as far as a modem will take you. When you need to get back to the office, and you're running software compatible with Microsoft Windows NT Server's RAS functions, you can use a modem to connect back to the main network server, as shown in Figure 2.6. This compatible software comes in the form of Windows 95, Windows for Workgroups, and Windows NT Workstation. When you use this type of connection, you'll log into the network just like you do from your desktop. The only difference is that the speed of the modem controls the performance of your work.

This is a very easy way to continue working while you're away and check up on things at the office. (Perhaps your spouse would rather you *couldn't* connect to the office when you're supposed to be enjoying a relaxing trip to Mexico!) When you connect to the server, you appear to the server just like you do when connected locally. You can check mail, run applications, move files, and anything else you might want to do, including print. Once again, the only difference is

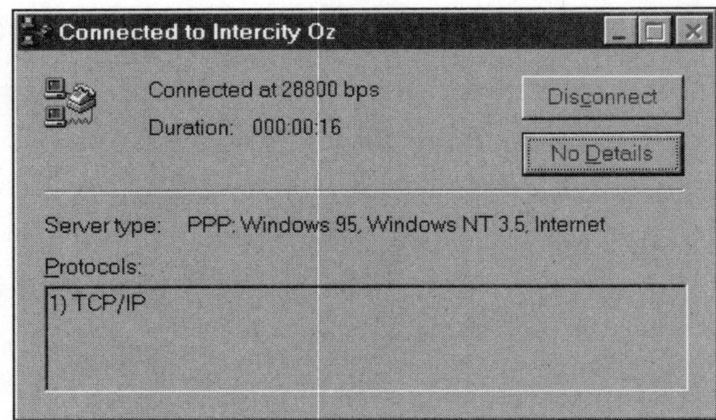

Figure 2.6
Dialup networking and TCP/IP.

the speed at which things happen. This is where a fast modem or even an ISDN dialup adapter is nice to have.

Direct Internet Access From The Web

The next form of connectivity that we'll need to employ is direct Internet connections. We've stated that we'll have up to five concurrent users on our site at any given time. If we make a blanket statement that we consider each connection will be at 28.8Kbps, then we'll need 144Kbps of throughput. This seems inappropriate for ISDN's maximum of 128Kbps, but is it? Let's dissect this situation and see why it should work just fine.

When users connect to your Web server directly across the Internet, they may be doing so from a workstation on a network, from a PC using a modem from their Internet Service Provider, or from a Sun workstation that doubles as a server at some university. You just don't know which one, and any of those could, in fact, be powered to download files at 56Kbps transfer rates. Just two of those users maxes out the ISDN connection alone! Unless you've got continued service requirements like this, what actually happens is that as much as 75 percent free bandwidth is available as data flows across the line.

When a user connects to your Web server, the initial log-on procedure is but a momentary blip in the performance of the link. When files are transferred or a Web page is accessed, the data is moved relatively quickly, and the link is again idle. These bursts of traffic are what most sites experience during the course of normal operations. As such, an ISDN-equipped site could support as many as

18 users with compression turned on and resulting in an equivalent transfer rate of about 9.6Kbps. So, let's keep this in mind as we progress forward. A 9.6Kbps link may not seem like much when it comes to Internet access, but remember that the most we're anticipating during this startup period is five concurrent users. In a section to come shortly, you'll see why I'm suggesting ISDN as a startup, and we'll consider dedicated links at that time.

Bulletin Board Access For Modem Users

In a worst-case scenario, you may have some users that have no reason, purpose, experience, or wherewithal to use the Internet. All they need to do is read/send mail and move files. If these people had one of the prerequisites mentioned earlier for NT Server's Remote Access Server, then they could simply use dialup RAS connections. However, quite a few of them (in fact, most) have standard laptops running standard DOS and Windows software. None of these laptops are equipped to run Windows NT Workstation or Windows 95. They could, however, be running Windows for Workgroups with the Remote Access Server add-in programs.

This would solve the problem of access, and it would enable them to have direct access to the Web server. These users would appear as normal users on the network, as far as the NT server is concerned. However, as a practical matter, we can't count on that. What we can count on is that if these people have DOS or Windows communications software, then they can get connected to our bulletin board. From the BBS, they could perform an operation called a *door*. This operation works like a door in your house. Open the door, and you leave the BBS and go into another room, such as another BBS. In this case, the door leads to the Web server and full Internet access.

Server-To-Server Connections

Another interesting aspect of this process is the technique of connecting a customer's network server to our server and then routing TCP/IP traffic from them to us and out to the Internet. This is normal life for many sites and isn't anything special in the world of networking. It's new for customers that have never experienced life on the Internet nor considered alternative ways of connectivity. All that happens here is that, in a Microsoft Windows NT Server domain model, the customer's network server is a member of the NT domain. When the customer's server connects to our regular NT network, which our

Web server is part of, we route the customer's TCP/IP traffic across our Web server out to the Internet.

Server-to-server connections are just another form of indirect Internet access. This type of situation lends itself to ISDN connectivity and remote access server products to form the core link. Cable modems and newer modem technology like x2 modems (56Kbps) are enabling more usage of server-to-server linkages.

If it looks like the traffic is getting to be too much, you can always increase the link capacity. The point is to provide whatever services your customers need. Keep them happy, and it'll all come together.

Monitoring Connected Users For Future Estimates

When you get the site operational, use the tools provided with the Web server software for monitoring the activity of the server. The tools will show you how much of the site is in use and by whom. Microsoft Windows NT Server itself has server diagnostic tools and monitoring tools, shown operating in Figure 2.7, that show how many users are connected, to where, and for how long. You can see how much of the server's resources are being used, how much of these resources are free for the system, and an average loading factor on the physical server. Over time, all of these statistics will be necessary to determine future upgrades and to find problem areas of the Web server's capabilities.

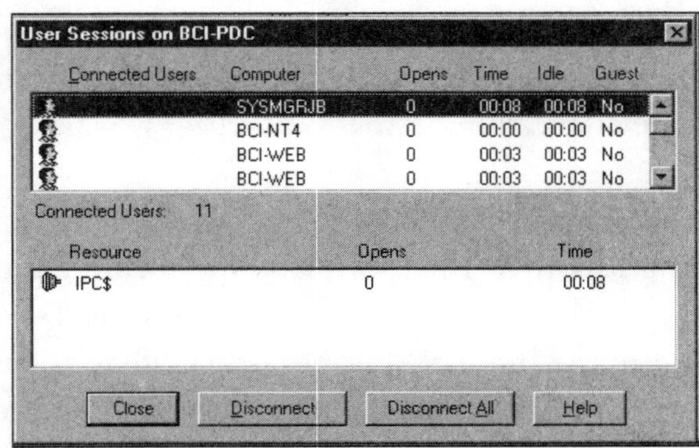

Figure 2.7
Routing monitoring by IP address for usage.

You can define monitoring parameters, which allow you to review average CPU time, interrupts per second, and other related information. Simply save all information for later analysis. As a matter of policy, you should gather these log statistics once a week and review them as well. In the case of my own servers, my Web server doubles as a Microsoft Windows NT Server Backup Domain Control (BDC). Periodically, this BDC resynchronizes with the network's Primary Domain Controller (PDC). When this occurs, the BDC's user databases are updated with any changes to the PDC, including new users, changed rights and permissions, and so forth.

Internet Link Capacity

We've already discussed ISDN as a solution for connecting 20 or fewer users, and where permanent connections are not required. That's fine, but what are the alternatives? There are numerous alternatives to ISDN for more demanding needs, so let's examine these. Table 2.2 illustrates some of the connectivity options available in today's market. Understand that even though these options exist now, they may not be available in your immediate area.

This table was built from data I gathered by calling several vendors, including AT&T, SprintLink, and others involved in the communications business while I was building my site. As you can see, it can get quite pricey very quickly. The CFO would have a canary if you put the bill on her desk for a T3 link. So, what I did was use a 28.8Kbps modem link to proof test the basics of the Web server

TABLE 2.2

RELATIVE MERITS OF DIFFERENT COMMUNICATIONS LINKS.

Available	Type of Connection	Speed of Link	Startup Cost	Monthly Cost
Immediate	Modem access	Up to 28.8Kbps	None	Up to $30
30–60 days	Dialup ISDN	Up to 128Kbps	Up to three months free	Varies, but can be as little as $400
30–90 days	Dedicated *FT1	56Kbps to 768Kbps	$3,500 (56Kbps) $12,000 (768Kbps)	$1,650 for 56Kbps $4,800 for 768Kbps (graduated)
30–90 days	Dedicated T1	1.544Mbps	$15,000	$6,000
90–120 days	Dedicated T3	45.1Mbps	$135,000	$75,000
90–120 days	Frame Relay	56Kbps on demand	$3,000	$1,200

*FT1 means fractional T1 speeds which range from 56Kbps up through 768Kbps.

until I was sure that all was well and that the site was going into full-scale operation. This is a real money-saving trick. All you're really doing at this stage is building the Web pages, getting the basics built, making sure it works, and showing the CFO you have an idea of what you're doing.

So, what do these speeds have in common with your needs? Most of them are flexible enough to suit your needs, except for the modem link. But even modems have witnessed a boost in technology that upped their throughput to 33.6Kbps and over 57.6Kbps with compression turned on for a single link. This advance puts the pressure on single-line ISDN, which is 64Kbps normal and over 135Kbps with compression turned on. Using the plain ISDN connect last week, I got 13.6Kbps effective transfer rates on files, which equates to roughly 136Kbps link speed. Not bad at all! But, when the data really gets moving, these modem and ISDN links begin to suffer from a decided lack of horsepower. It's now time to explore the real world of dedicated connectivity.

Upgrading The Link To Meet The Need

As you probably know, modem lines are capable of what modems do, and nothing more. Frequently, we see even less productivity with noisy lines and moisture in the lines, and ISDN tops out at 128Kbps with multiplexed channels. When this happens, you'll need more room to grow. This is where the downside to ISDN hits squarely in the pocketbook. Whatever investment in ISDN you've made to date is usually down the tubes. It has been fun, but that's about the extent of it.

The new faster links require different hardware on both ends. Because ISDN is a digitally mastered modem, it's sometimes considered to be a "smart" modem. As such, the local telephone company or source is also running similar ISDN equipment, so it's not likely to be able to support your upgrades on the same equipment. All the way around, new equipment and costs are jumping right out at you. Table 2.3 shows the costs that I incurred with my local Bell South office when setting up my 128Kbps multiplexed dialup ISDN in comparison to a similar 128Kbps FT1 dedicated link with SprintLink.

> ***Note:*** *If you decide to go with ISDN, be careful that you know what the rates are. In some locales, ISDN has gone up on a monthly charge plus a per-minute fee of one cent per minute. Bell South recently did this, so a full-time ISDN connection now exceeds $800 a month! 128K Fractional T1 is now cheaper than ISDN, and it's a permanent connection.*

TABLE 2.3

ACTUAL CONNECTIVITY COSTS.

Function	Startup Cost	Monthly Fee	Lease Required
128Kbps ISDN basic	$210	$93 flat rate	None (Bell South)
ISDN Internet Acct	None	$395 flat rate	None (UUNet Tech)
ISDN Router	$1,100	N/A	One-time cost
128Kbps FT1 dedicated	$2,800	$1,200	1 year (Sprint, all functions)
FT1 Router	N/A	$275	1 year

You can see that my monthly ISDN cost is $488 for 128Kbps, no matter how much or how little I use it. I have to purchase an ISDN router for this link, and my provider configures it for me. All I have to do is connect it up, and away I go. If the link drops out, the ISDN router will automatically try to reconnect all the time. The only issue here is that if the link goes down, and the router can't connect (usually a physical problem on the wire), then the site is down until this can be repaired. Bell South treats this as a standard phone line outage, which is exactly what it is. The *D* in *ISDN* stands for *digital*, which means that the data traveling across the line is digitized data moving along a standard telephone link.

This repair process can take up to a week at times, but they try to get to it within 48 hours during the normal workweek. If the link goes down on Friday morning, then I can pretty much count on my site being down over the weekend. By contrast, if the SprintLink goes down on a dedicated circuit, Sprint reroutes the link to another spare circuit. If the outage is between my site and the closest point of presence, then Sprint gets to work on it right away without delay. They realize that the reason you've got the dedicated link is for business purposes, so they waste no time at all in circuit restoration.

This is the reason dedicated links exist. If you want to compare raw costs per link, you'd see that the dedicated link is more expensive at a 3:1 ratio. So, why all the fuss over these links? My suggestion is to use a 28.8Kbps modem to get the Web server talking to your provider. This is quick and painless. So far, no obligations. Next, if your immediate user count is 20 or fewer, try using dialup ISDN to proof the rest of the site. If that proves less than optimal, you can always jump to the dedicated FT1, which should solve all but your most demanding needs.

If you intend to build your site as an Internet Service Provider, don't waste your time and money on a 56Kbps link of any type! I've had to bail out three customers that thought 56Kbps was sufficient but could not possibly serve the public with more than five users connected. The lowest speed you should consider for a customer desiring to be an ISP is a 384K FT1. You can always bump up the speed to full T1, if necessary.

What Happens When You're Way Off?

Ah, yes. Someone didn't heed the preceding warning block and has gotten into a jam and a half. In the situation described previously, I found that I was able to upgrade the link, with SprintLink and AT&T, from 56Kbps all the way up to full T1 using most if not all of the existing equipment that these customers had in service for 56Kbps. Not too much of a hassle, but that's not even the half of it. The major factor was that the Web server itself was built on a 486DX4-100 processor and 32MB of memory for 10 users on the 56Kbps link. Even though the link was upgraded to T1, the Web server wasn't up to the task of handling 30 concurrent users!

Faulty planning all the way around and misguided intentions left this wanna-be Internet Service Provider hanging in the breeze and counting change to foot the bill. I watched the server's console and noticed that the time clock wasn't updating at all. Yes, a locked up server and on a T1 connection. If you calculate the average cost to the provider per second, the dialup ISDN at 128Kbps is 67 cents per hour while the full T1 is around $2 per hour. You do the math and tell me if the CFO would be ticked off if the server was down over the weekend and no one noticed.

In the next section, we'll go over the actual Web server hardware and software requirements for building a respectable Web server that won't embarrass you, your CFO, or the customers. By now, your plan should look something like plan04.doc. Keep in mind that your server requirements may change, but this should help you consider the many aspects of creating a Web site.

Web Server System Requirements

We've talked a lot about the planning stages and some requirements to building a good site. Planning is always key to a successful site, so it's time to start naming names and taking notes about hardware. As a matter of standard practice, I generally don't back one hardware vendor over another unless my years of systems design clearly point out a winner that's head and shoulders above others. There are just certain things in life that mean more to me, and one's a reliable vendor of hardware and software.

System Hardware

In considering our goals for the customers, we've concluded that we may have as many as 25 concurrent users online at any one time. In the future, it's feasible that our Web server will have as many as 100 users at one time. In light of this consideration, I feel justified in saying that for proper performance, you should start the server at a Pentium-120 or higher with at least 64MB of memory. By the time NT itself gets running and the Web server software starts going, the server will have used 26MB RAM. Once the ancillary software starts and a few users get logged on, you'll easily be using 32MB of memory.

Because you're running a Web server with business data, RAID 5 disk subsystem components are essential to a successful site. The two most common forms of RAID are type 1 and type 5. Type 1 is nothing more than a mirroring of a drive. Type 5 is used in database operations where security of the data is paramount. Figure 2.8 illustrates the RAID disk subsystems. The idea here is that a set of SCSI disk drives are teamed with a SCSI controller to form one logical drive out of several physical drives. The end result is data safety, because in RAID systems no one physical drive holds all the data. It's spread out among the cluster of drives in such a way that if one physical drive quits running, you can replace the bad drive and let the operating system rebuild the data.

Many Web servers are afterthoughts for company marketing and are not deemed essential to the bottom line, so these do not run RAID. However, if you intend to process a lot of requests, you should consider RAID because these systems are generally faster in response than singular disk drives. The expense can't be

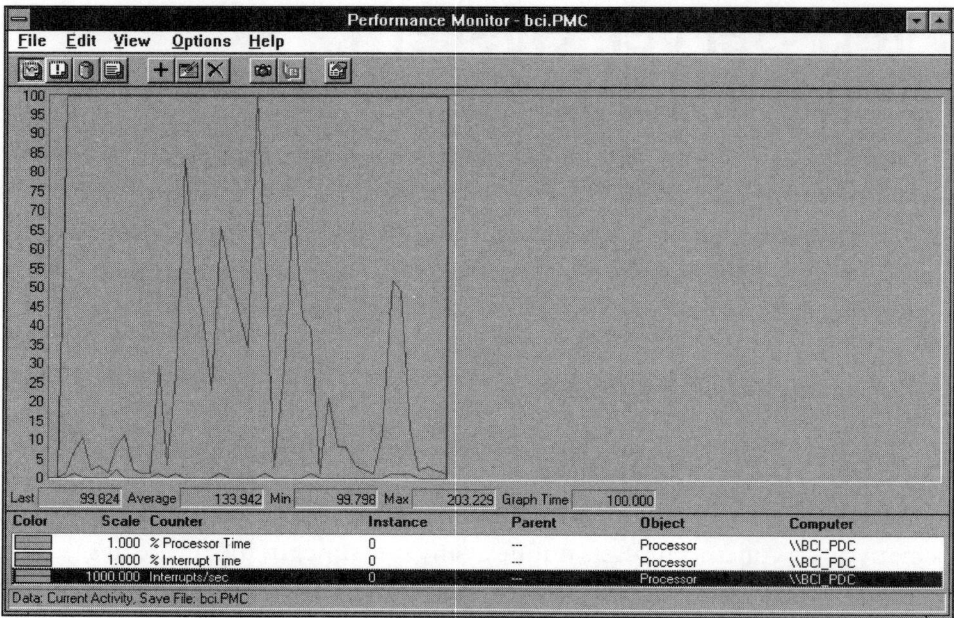

Figure 2.8
Server monitoring.

ignored, either. RAID subsystems require a special controller card. There are plenty on the market now that are up to the task, including Mylex, Adaptec, BusLogic, Seagate, and more. I've personally used the Mylex DAC-960 RAID controller and have had very good success with it. One glaring problem exists with RAID—if a drive quits, the controller or operating system *has to notify you!*

Yes, I had a drive die once and found that my Banyan VINES operating system continued to operate—although sluggishly due to the dead drive. The only way I knew the drive had quit was by the amount of user problems with their data. The RAID was restoring the data on the fly as users needed the data, and this imposed a significant overhead on the server in addition to normal operations for 200 users. Using the system logs, I identified the failed drive, replaced it, and let RAID rebuild the data.

If you choose RAID, make sure the controller works with NT, but also make sure it has provisions to notify NT of a failure and/or otherwise handle the event.

With the advent of SCSI-3 disk drives and the increased performance they can bring, I recommend you use them. Because you'll need three drives as a minimum for the RAID 5 factor, choose drives of sufficient capacity to last you. For example, if you choose 2GB units, then 3 drives result in an effective storage of 4GB, because 33 percent of the cumulative drives is used for RAID overhead. The same 3-drive set of 4GB units gives you an effective storage of around 9GB, which should suffice for most starting Web sites. One last comment on RAID: Although not really documented anywhere, I've found that instead of using 3 drives of 2GB, 5 drives of 2GB are your best bet for a faster-performing system. If one drive in the three-drive set dies, the data is stored on only two drives. A system rebuild or continuing operations will be very sluggish. In a five-drive setup, a downed drive leaves four units still operational. I have found this to be a more reliable situation. The proverbial "more is merrier" rings true in this case.

Okay, that's it for the core of the server—processor, memory, and disk drives—so, let's hit the ancillary equipment. Because the server doesn't have much interaction at the console, the video subsystem is negligible. I use plain 16-bit SVGA cards to keep the cost down. No use putting a Ferrari engine in a VW, because the frame would fall apart at Mach 2. Same thing with the keyboard. I use a standard 84-key keyboard. For the mouse, I'm partial to the Microsoft Serial mouse for the touch and feel because most operations under Microsoft Windows NT Server are mouse driven. Certainly, you are free to pick your favorite rodent. For serial ports, two are fine, but make sure they're using the 16550 UART-designed models.

My Web server is aided by the use of a four-port serial card from Equinox Corp. in Sunrise, Florida. I know. I said I seldom bespeak a single vendor's name. Well, I renege here because this SST-4 four-port serial card from Equinox works like a dream with NT and my BBS software, Wildcat for NT Server. When I find something that works this well, I've just gotta say it! One of the best attributes about this card is if you have two serial ports on the Web server to start, this card starts its ports off as serial port three. If a Web server has four ports on it, the SST-4 starts off as port five. Effortless operations, to be sure. Equinox can be reached at 800-275-3500 ext. 247 or across the Internet at **info@equinox.com**. Equinox has many other cards supplying up to 256 ports on a Microsoft Windows NT Server. I will provide more information about this card in Chapter 12, when we get into generalized Web site administration.

Next, you certainly want to protect your data with good backups. Don't waste your time fiddling around with tape drives of less than 500MB, and don't waste your time with a Travan drive. DAT is considerably faster than Travan drives. Get one of the speedy Digital Audio Tapes (DAT) version 3, which can give you up to 8GB on a single tape. As the site grows, you'll surely need the capacity. One more thing is that if you implement the idea of having another workstation on the network serve as an FTP site, then that'll need to be backed up, as well. With a good DAT drive, you can backup across the network with ease. New software is flooding the market. Third-party vendors have really come through to solve your most demanding backup needs with Microsoft Windows NT Server. Again, while I don't normally bespeak of a preferred vendor of software, I found that Cheyenne's ARCServe for NT does an excellent job with NT. Excellent enough that I'm willing to say that.

Let's see, what's left? Oh yes, case and power supply. Make very sure that the case is large enough to support your projected expansion, and make sure there are cooling fans installed in it! Heat is the number one killer of computer systems, followed closely by power disturbances. You can be most assured that power protection is paramount to the server's extended life span. To calculate the required capacity needs, add up all of the amperage draw of the components that you want to protect. Multiply the amperage by 120 to give you the wattage. The surge load of the protected equipment can be as high as three times the maximum operating amperage draw—an important technicality to keep you from blowing up the Uninterrupted Power Supply (UPS) and frying everything in sight. Now that you know the power consumption of the devices, pick a UPS from your favorite vendor. Take its rating, which is in volt-amperes, and multiply that by .707 to get the true wattage rating that the UPS can handle.

Never, never, never put a laser printer on a UPS unless that UPS is rated at over 5,000 watts of protection! The average desktop laser printer runs at a nominal 8 amperes of continuous power with an initial surge load that can exceed 30 amperes for less than a second. Even though the wall power breaker may handle this load, a UPS is much more sensitive to these power transitions and will attempt to supply the correct power to the printer, mistaking the initial surge as a loss of power. This error has often resulted in fried laser printers, fried UPSs, or both. And that's not to mention the possibility of an electrical fire.

Let's do an example and then discuss the types of power protection. Before getting into the example, I'd like to emphasize the difference between the terms *volt-amperes* and *wattage*. The two are drastically different in their meaning and application, but the industry has seen fit to use the ratings in what I've seen to be contradictory places. When you go to the computer store and see a UPS on the shelf, it'll have a numerical rating on the outside of the box. This is the *volt-ampere* rating which indicates a relative value of the UPS's input voltage and power. The true effective capacity of the device is the *wattage* rating. Take the volt-ampere rating on the box and multiply it by .707 to get the wattage rating. My server has a 300 watt power supply for all of the internal components of the server. While none of them are drawing full power, the most that is being drawn is 300 watts, which is the maximum rating of the power supply. My monitor pulls 6 amperes on startup and 2 amperes continuous running. So, the monitor uses 2 amperes multiplied by 120 volts equals 240 watts of power. The combined needs of the monitor and computer total 540 watts of power. So to get the best UPS for my system, I'll need a UPS of 771 volt-amperes or higher to properly sustain the system during normal runtime.

Two other power-protection devices—*online UPS* and *sine wave UPS*—differ from the standard UPS in that not only do they provide backup power to the computer, but they also provide a higher degree of filtering and protection from power transients, such as brownouts and line sags. Think about when the refrigerator or furnace comes on in the house. Many homes experience a brief dimming of lights. This is called a *sag* and occurs when the line voltage momentarily drops below 100 volts. While the power is low, your wonderful power company senses the decrease of power and the transformer outside your house dutifully boosts up power to compensate. By the time that occurs, the furnace has caught up and now the excess voltage reaches as high as 150 volts. This is called a *surge*. Sags and surges, pictured in Figure 2.9, of less than 20 volts are not normally noticed in computers, but larger swings can cause computers to reboot. A more devastating form of power problem is called a *spike*. Spikes, which are illustrated in Figure 2.10, do some real damage when they hit the electronic world, because standard power supplies aren't built to handle the

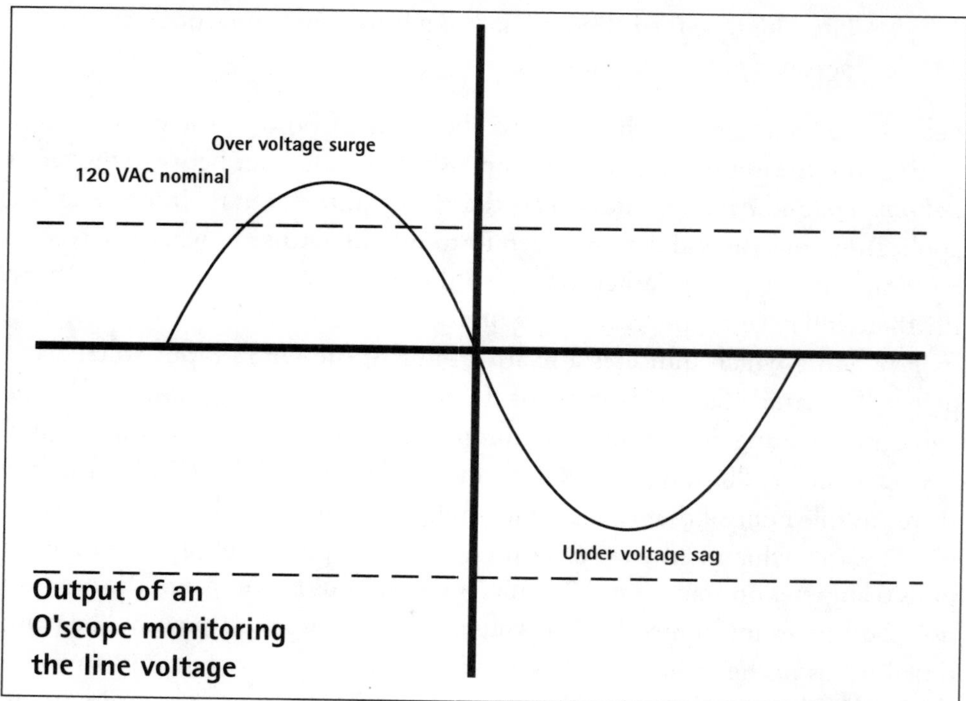

Figure 2.9
Power sag and surge.

momentary power spike of up to 10,000 volts that can sometimes occur in less than one-tenth of a second.

To counter these types of power anomalies, protection devices, such as the online filter, exist to stabilize the line at 120 volts nominal. When these unruly power waves hit the beaches of your Web server, nothing will occur except normal operations.

System Software

Next, let's peruse some of the software that is required to get your Web server operational. Of course, there's Microsoft Windows NT Server itself. This takes about an hour to install, and about two hours to configure, get the network protocols working, add a few users, set basic security and permissions, and otherwise get the server running. Plan on a day to do this, just to be safe. Then, there's the Web server software. This isn't too terribly difficult to do for any of

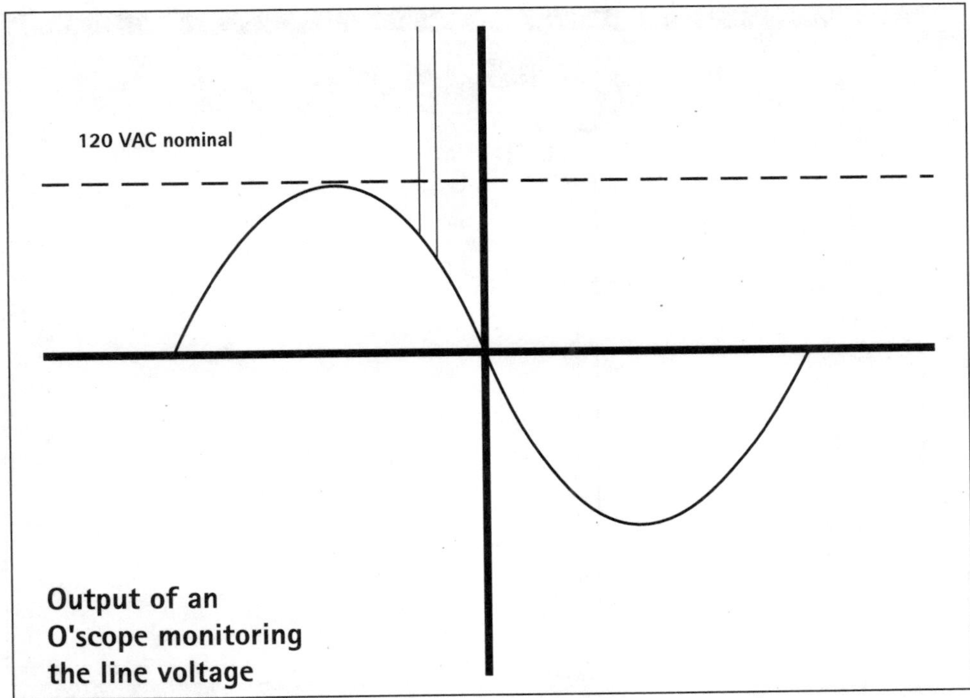

Figure 2.10
Power spike.

the packages that we'll look at, but just the same, it takes time to accomplish. Next, there's the FTP configuration. FTP takes only a few minutes to install and set up, but it's a disaster to fix if you don't define your directories properly. Try to choose a proper layout based upon your needs and the types of software to be stored. Figure 2.11 shows a simplified tree structure of my FTP site.

Finally, you'll need to install all of the ancillary tools, such as Visual Basic for the CGI work. If you're using Microsoft SQL Server as the backend engine, this is a tremendous load on the server. Count on using over 150MB of disk space and a full day to configure it, at least. Table 2.4 summarizes the configuration requirements for the server software. The table only summarizes the major tools you'll be needing. You're bound to run across some smaller tools that you're sure to want to install.

Basically, you can have the server installed and operational with the minimum taskings in a day and a half, or two full working days if you're taking your time.

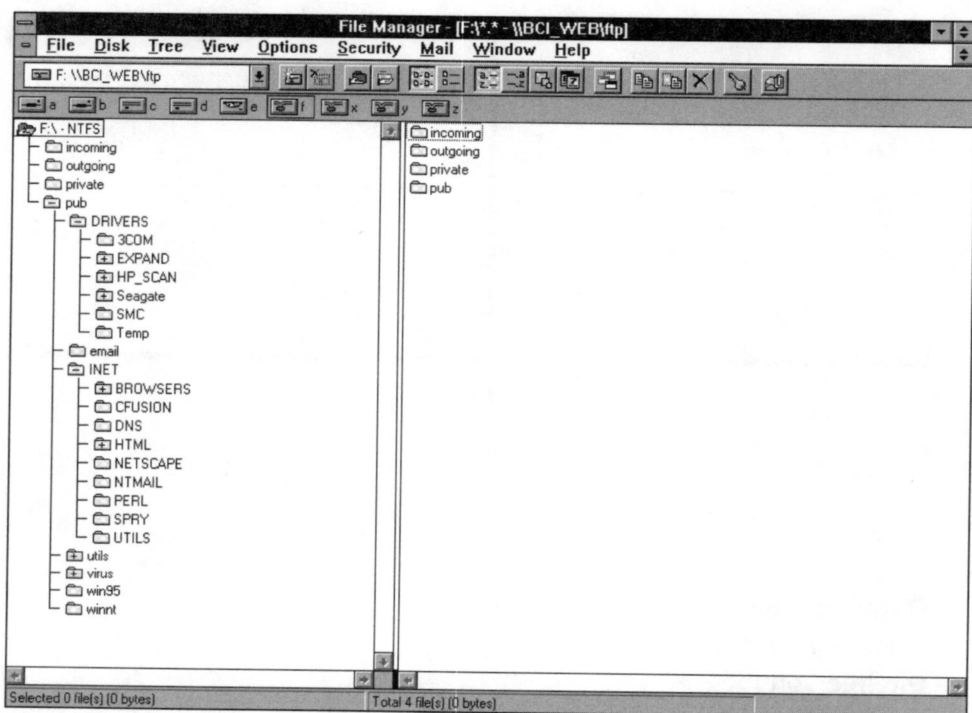

Figure 2.11
FTP site directory structure.

Table 2.4

Relative configuration requirements of server software.

Software	Space Size	Time to Install/Configure	Required to Use
NT Server	100MB	8 hours	Yes
Web Server	~50MB	4 hours	Yes
FTP Service	10MB	1 hour	Yes
FTP Space	>500MB	1 hour	Yes
Email	25MB	3 hours	No
Gopher Server	10MB	1 hour	No
Remote Access	5MB	½ hour	No
Bulletin Board	10MB	3 hours	No

The FTP space requirement of 500MB is a starting point for your needs, and, as I mentioned earlier, you should set aside as much disk space as you can imagine is required. Starting out with 1GB is not unreasonable.

The Webmaster

The Webmaster is the single most important position in the company after the Web server comes online, as far as the server is concerned. This person is the server's primary caregiver. When the Web server acts up, the Webmaster fixes it. When it needs help for a user, the Webmaster takes care of the account issues. When the disk fills up and crashes the server, the Webmaster is the one that the CFO chews on when someone says that all it takes is money to fix it. Any way you look at it, the Webmaster is the focal point of the daily operations for the Web server.

As such, the Webmaster is worthy of some training on Microsoft Windows NT Server and how to accomplish the many daily tasks required to maintain accounts and user needs. Once NT is set up, it's very reliable and easy to deal with. However, in the changing world of the Internet and the World Wide Web, the Webmaster may find it a busy day at the office every day. The Webmaster should have a solid TCP/IP background and know the terms and troubleshooting techniques of the average network infrastructure. The Webmaster should be well versed in data recovery and server restorations in the unlikely event of a crash of the worst magnitude.

All in all, the Webmaster is the "top dog" of the Web for your company. Ideally, the Webmaster will have at least one assistant who knows the hows, whys, and wherefores of the Web server and the Webmaster's procedures for maintaining the same. A little written policy goes a long way towards solving the needs of users.

When you plan on the mailboxes for the Webmaster, plan on three to start: INFO, SALES, and WEBMASTER. These are the three most commonly referred to and used mailboxes. Even if you don't use SALES, the name can be changed and used for something else. However, I've found that three is the bare minimum that a Webmaster should have.

Future Plans For The Site

All the while that a site is being built or otherwise being planned, always strive to be looking forward to the needs of the site. In this day and age, even if the site doesn't pan out in a year's time, the components of the server can be used elsewhere. For instance, a 2GB drive can be used to expand the storage on a workstation that is highly graphic in nature. Or, you may have a programmer on staff that has lots of experience and is branching off into Windows programming. This person could use a powerful PC, and the Microsoft Windows NT Server operating system could be removed and reloaded with something else. The server has lots of memory, disk space, and other goodies that would make it a fine programming platform.

These are the things that could be useful later on or make future Web server upgrades easier to do. One of the worst possible things that a new Web site can do is focus on one technology and one vendor to solve all of the site's needs. This just isn't practical, and it's downright wasteful of company resources. True, SCSI can take care of storage needs quite easily, but I saw a test site that used IDE drives go into production using one IDE drive as the sole storage medium. IDE works great and is inexpensive, but it leaves very little room for expansion when it occurs. To add more storage, you'll have to down the site and add a drive or a new SCSI controller and drive. All of this takes time, which keeps your customers offline.

Where You're Located—The IP Address

How do people know where to find you on the Internet? Why through your address, of course. Just as your friends locate your home by its street address, users locate your Web site through your *Internet Protocol* (IP) address. An IP address is a 32-bit (or 8-byte) numerical designation of the placement of a computer within the global network that we call the Internet. If you don't have an address, no one can find you.

You need to make your presence known publicly by officially registering yourself. The *Domain Name Service (DNS)* locates everyone who is officially registered on the Internet. More on this topic later.

The IP Address Of Where You Live

IP addresses are composed of 32 bits of format in an octet base. This means that IP addresses will never exceed the number nine. My server's address is 206.139.150.10 and has an *alias* of **www.bciassoc.com** for the time being. By the time this book goes to print, I'll have a more permanent situation in which the IP address will change and the Web site will be **www.bciassoc.com**. An alias? What's that? Well, the human-readable form of a name is easier to remember than the numerical one, so the DNS registers my name of **www.bciassoc.com** and equates it to 206.139.150.10. This means that when you enter **www.bciassoc.com** in your Web browser, DNS looks the alphabetical name up in the directory listing and translates it into the numerical one. Why does it do this?

To get from one location on the Internet to another, a device called a *router* is used to move the data in the appropriate ways to get from point A to point B. Routers know nothing of alpha names, only numerical addresses. What's more, routers have the numerical designations in a listing called a *router table,* which tells the router how to send data from place to place.

From Figure 2.12, you can see that the steps to get from place to place are as follows:

1. Server examines the destination address typed in.
2. If numerical, bypass DNS (Step 3) and go to Step 4.
3. If alpha, use DNS to obtain numerical address.
4. Send desired IP address to your closest router. Router then finds closest connection point to hand off the same request and get to the next router. Process continues until destination IP address is reached or fails.
5. Destination IP address device either responds with an authoritative return or errors out.
6. Destination IP address device then processes request to provide data.

While these steps present a simplified version of the process, you can still see why your request can sometimes take forever. The request has to make the route from location to location. If one path fails, the request, in a sense, backs up and tries another path. This process is called *finding the path* and can be

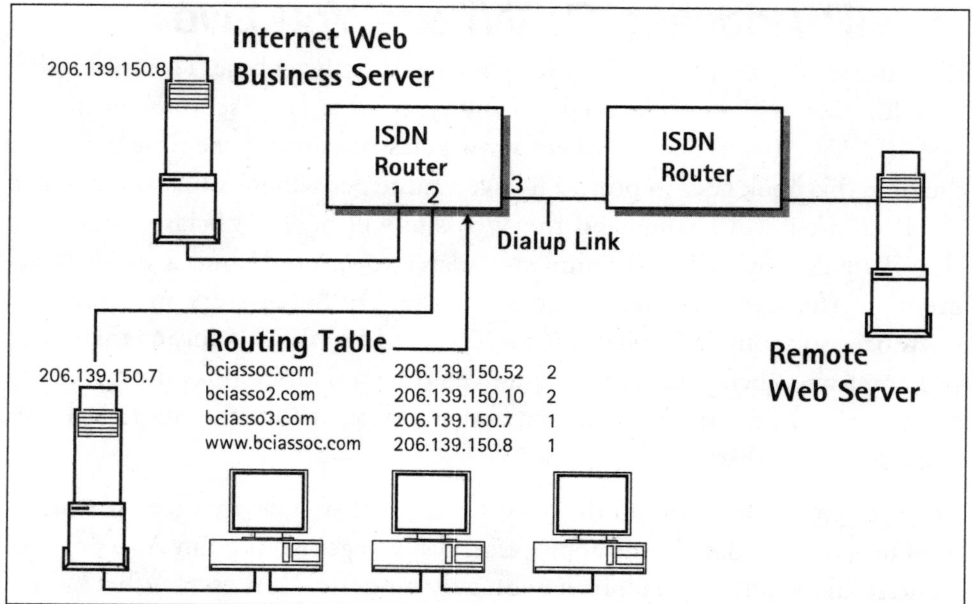

Figure 2.12
Routing table.

followed by a really neat Microsoft Windows NT Server utility called *TraceRoute*. Examine Listing 2.1, and you'll see how TraceRoute can be used to see where the data has to go and what it has to go through to get around. As a sample, I did a trace from my modem connection to my Internet Service Provider to Microsoft Corporation's Web server, **www.microsoft.com**.

Listing 2.1 Actual TraceRoute to Microsoft's Web server.

```
Tracing route to www.microsoft.com [198.105.232.4]

over a maximum of 30 hops:
  1   161 ms   150 ms   146 ms  gulf98.interoz.com [204.49.131.98]

  2   158 ms   146 ms   148 ms  router.interoz.com [204.49.131.1]

  3   171 ms   145 ms   167 ms  ciscol-gulfnetpc.mariana.cntfl.com
                                [204.49.129.5]

  4     *        *        *     Request timed out.

  5     *        *        *     Request timed out.
```

```
 6   197 ms   174 ms   171 ms  204.49.62.2
 7   180 ms   172 ms   195 ms  cisco_5.cntfl.com [204.49.7.2]
 8   187 ms   200 ms   188 ms  cisco-sl.cntfl.com [199.44.9.65]
 9   216 ms   211 ms   212 ms  borderl-serial3-5.Atlanta.mci.net
                               [204.70.16.65]
10   214 ms   201 ms   356 ms  core-fddi-0.Atlanta.mci.net [204.70.2.49]
11   219 ms   190 ms   206 ms  core2-aip-4.Atlanta.mci.net [204.70.1.70]
12   327 ms   219 ms   228 ms  corel-hssi-2.Dallas.mci.net
                               [204.70.1.114]
13   237 ms   259 ms   276 ms  core-hssi-3.KansasCity.mci.net
                               [204.70.1.118]
14   295 ms   232 ms   262 ms  core2-hssi-2.Denver.mci.net
                               [204.70.1.157]
15   325 ms   283 ms   296 ms  core-hssi-4.Seattle.mci.net [204.70.1.90]
16   295 ms   311 ms   273 ms  borderl-fddi-0.Seattle.mci.net
                               [204.70.2.146]
17   321 ms   302 ms   324 ms  nwnet.Seattle.mci.net [204.70.52.6]
18   333 ms   309 ms   333 ms  seabrl-gw.nwnet.net [192.147.179.5]
19   367 ms   267 ms   288 ms  microsoft-t3-gw.nwnet.net [198.104.192.9]
20   313 ms   280 ms   297 ms  131.107.249.3
21   339 ms   274 ms   311 ms  www.microsoft.com [198.105.232.4]

Trace complete.
```

The first thing you should notice is that the **Trace** function did a DNS resolution as the very first item. Why press onward if the alpha address is not a valid site? When the alpha address *resolves*, as it's called, it means that the Microsoft site was properly registered with the people that handle the DNS services—AT&T. Also, notice that two of the sites timed out and had to be retraced along an alternate route. The principal services that the Internet operates by are:

- *Directory And Database Services*—Provided by AT&T Corp., these services provide all of the information for finding people, places, and sites on the Internet. Think of them as the "White Pages" of the Internet.
- *Network Registration Services*—Provided by Network Solutions, Inc., this service creates and registers the domain and IP addresses of customers. To obtain new domain registrations, Network Solutions normally deals directly with Internet Service Providers or with users, such as myself, that have a domain but connect to an Internet Service Provider.

Now, look back at the trace and notice how many of the first IP addresses use the number 204 during the trace. This number represents the class of addresses. There are three distinct classes of IP addresses governed by the size of the networks involved. Class A addresses are for the largest networks, while class C represents the smallest networks. Table 2.5 illustrates this concept. The term *hosts* represents the number of PCs connected to the particular network. For instance, my current provider uses a class C address of 206.139.150.xxx which allows for addresses of 206.139.150.0 through 206.139.150.254. If this provider ever exceeded 255 concurrent users, then they'd have to get another block of IP addresses for another network.

Significance Of Class Membership

Each computer and each network has a significance on the Internet and is classified by its hierarchical position, or pecking order, on the Internet as a whole. When the number of host computers supported by an ISP is large (as with an enterprise-wide network with 50,000 computers), then the ISP takes on a class A address. The number of servers is few, but the number of supported users is quite large. By contrast, most of the ISPs being sold to us little users by modem are class C addresses. During testing, the address for my Web server is

TABLE 2.5

IP CLASS ADDRESSES.

Class	Number of Networks	Number of Hosts
A 1–126	126	16,777,214
B 128–191	16,384	65,534
C 192–223	1,097,151	254

206.139.150.10. The leading 206 indicates a class C designation. Class C is by far the most common network you'll see from a provider. Class A is generally reserved for development and internal use by InterNIC.

When you apply for and obtain a class address—we'll use the class C block that I obtained for my server—you receive the address from the available pool of your provider. The provider gets them assigned from InterNIC's master pool of IP addresses. Along with the address, I had to select a domain name for my server. Selecting a domain name is not mandatory, but it's advisable, so you can have an alpha name for your site. If you go to **www.internic.net** and choose the registration services, there's a query that you can use to see if a particular domain name already exists, as shown in Figure 2.13. I applied for my name, *bciassoc.com*, but I checked with InterNIC first to see if it was available. When the domain name application process is completed, InterNIC sends confirmation of the domain name. As of May 1997, the registration cost was $100 for a two-year period.

The next step is to associate the two addresses (the numerical and alphabetical) in the DNS listing from your provider. You can maintain your own DNS if you

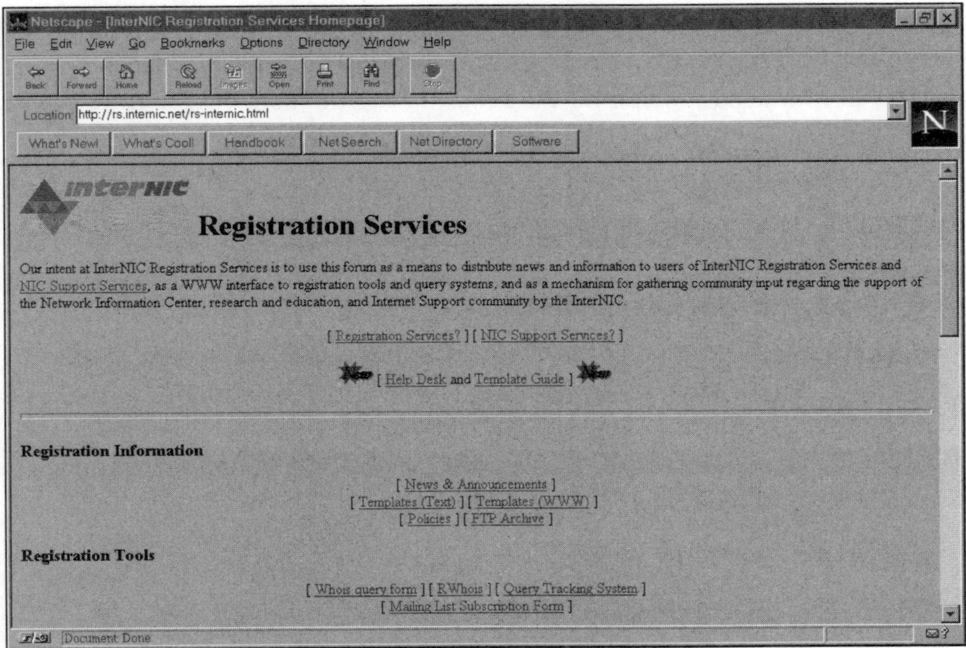

Figure 2.13
InterNIC registration services.

like or pay a nominal fee to have your provider do it. The DNS basically tells other computers that **www.bciassoc.com** refers to 206.139.150.10. Table 2.6 shows a sample DNS resolution file.

The DNS is nothing more than a simple text file that allows any computer to determine the IP address for any server. Once the data makes it to the server, the internal router on the network takes over and sends the requests to the appropriate location. This DNS process is also the source of many headaches. Have you ever gotten the ill-fated message that an alias cannot be resolved? This error occurs because the destination can't be found, the destination isn't properly (or at all) registered with the NIC, or the server is truly offline.

Your Relationship With Your Vendor

So, now you've obtained a domain and block of IP addresses for your Web server, and you're officially online. One thing you should remember is that you don't own the block of IP addresses. You're paying for them by virtue of the monthly service fees you pay to the ISP for the account. The domain is yours to keep as long as you keep it active. If for some reason you leave the ISP, then the registered block of IP addresses returns to the free IP pool of the ISP. Getting the connection back with someone else requires you to go through the same process all over again, including the DNS for the domain. By the time you've made it here, your Web Plan should look similar to plan05.doc.

The Connection—Getting Online With A Domain

Way back in the beginning of the chapter, I mentioned that we'll need to form a *domain* for our Web server to get online. This is still true, and now's the time

TABLE 2.6

SAMPLE DNS RESOLUTION FILE.

Name	IP Address
BCIASSOC.COM	204.49.131.245
BCIASSOC2.COM	204.49.131.245
TEST.SERV.COM	204.49.131.245

to do that. I also mentioned that you should get to the Network Solutions site. Let's go through this process in detail now and make the final process bear fruit.

What Is A Domain?

If you've got Microsoft Windows NT Server experience, then you may have knowledge of the domain model. If you do, just bear with me as I explain the difference between a Microsoft Windows NT Server domain and an Internet domain model. One of the most useful things you can do is get a copy of the Microsoft Windows NT Server Resource Kit. The kit contains a program called the Domain Model Planning Guide that you can use to create your most basic game plan for Microsoft Windows NT Server. This guide will also prove to be helpful for planning your Web server.

Basically, a domain is a territory. Consider this analogy: The lion of Africa has an invisible area of land that he patrols and claims ownership to by virtue of his own way of knowing the perimeter of land. You can't define the territory as concretely as a lion does, but you can observe him over time and get a rough idea of the area that he commands. A business has a territory that's within its control, as well. For the most part, a business can define a range in terms of buildings or specific desktops. This is not always practical to do, so creating a domain from an abstract thought makes planning and control easier to manage.

Your Place In The World—Creating Your Domain

Let's take a look at the Internet domain. You can choose an Internet domain name based on a number of factors, including the name of the business, a favorite product of the business, or some closely relevant idea of the business. Because the Internet places few restrictions on domain names, you could choose a name that has no relevance to your business, but I wouldn't hold your breath waiting for visits if you go this route.

The Domain Registration Process

My business' name is BCI Associates, so I chose bciassoc.com as an abbreviation of the business name. With a name picked out, and several backup names in case yours is already taken, head off to InterNIC and do a check for the

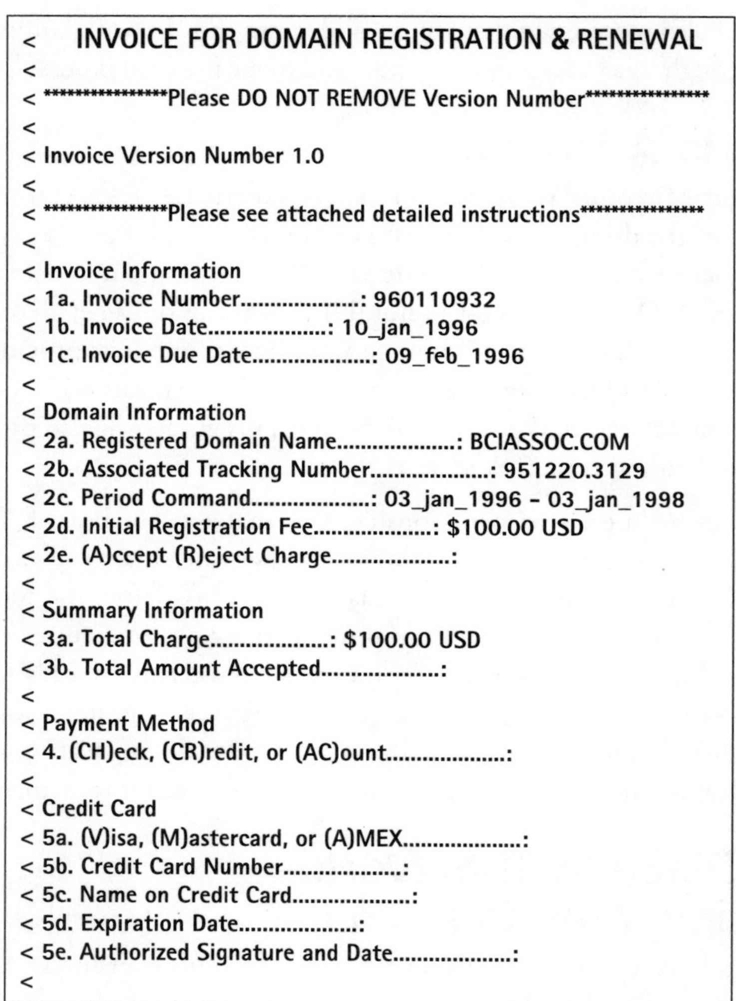

```
<   INVOICE FOR DOMAIN REGISTRATION & RENEWAL
<
< ****************Please DO NOT REMOVE Version Number****************
<
< Invoice Version Number 1.0
<
< ****************Please see attached detailed instructions****************
<
< Invoice Information
< 1a. Invoice Number....................: 960110932
< 1b. Invoice Date....................: 10_jan_1996
< 1c. Invoice Due Date....................: 09_feb_1996
<
< Domain Information
< 2a. Registered Domain Name....................: BCIASSOC.COM
< 2b. Associated Tracking Number....................: 951220.3129
< 2c. Period Command....................: 03_jan_1996 - 03_jan_1998
< 2d. Initial Registration Fee....................: $100.00 USD
< 2e. (A)ccept (R)eject Charge....................:
<
< Summary Information
< 3a. Total Charge....................: $100.00 USD
< 3b. Total Amount Accepted....................:
<
< Payment Method
< 4. (CH)eck, (CR)redit, or (AC)ount....................:
<
< Credit Card
< 5a. (V)isa, (M)astercard, or (A)MEX....................:
< 5b. Credit Card Number....................:
< 5c. Name on Credit Card....................:
< 5d. Expiration Date....................:
< 5e. Authorized Signature and Date....................:
<
```

Figure 2.14
InterNIC domain registration.

domain name. Figure 2.14 shows the NIC registration documents. If you're getting your server connection from an existing ISP, then chances are, they'll submit the papers for you and report back with the domain name and a block of registered IP addresses. If not, then you can submit the domain name electronically to InterNIC, as I did. You'll receive confirmation by email, or by fax if you choose, of the name selection or a message indicating that you need to try again. You'll also receive an electronic bill for the registration with instructions on how to pay it. That's all there is to it.

Types Of Domain Connections

Types of domain connections? What kind of a section is this, you ask? Well, I just wanted to point out a few differences in how a server is connected to the Internet and why it affects the connection. If you use a modem to make the link, the server still uses an IP address to get connected but is obviously limited to the speed of the modem. You should keep this in mind when it comes time to work with time-sensitive connections and test your Web server. Even though I said you can use a modem to proof test the Web server, and that still stands true, keep in mind that if the phone line gets ratty, then data is easily corrupted and some operational parts of the server can get lost in the shuffle. If you used RAS to make the connection, run the RAS monitor, and watch for the little red light to come on the monitor indicating corrupted data transmissions. If this happens once every minute, then there's the real possibility that the modem line is completely unreliable. Also, in a modem connection, no users on the internal network can get out to the Internet.

Making the connection with the dialup ISDN terminal adapter is the next best solution. This solves, for all practical purposes, the dirty line problems. However, like the modem, no internal network routing can be performed.

As a third option, using a dialup ISDN device such as the Ascend series of routers provides both reliable digital circuits and internal network routing functions. This little gem gets your users onto the Internet from your internal business networks. The drawback? More than 15 or 20 users will choke up this link.

The best way to get your domain online is the dedicated link, which keeps you online all the time and at faster rates. You pay for this extra speed, but you can get higher processing rates on the same port with a few minor changes at the ISP.

Getting An Online Connection

Getting the actual connection can be a real trial in patience, but one way to get started is to use a known list of sites, such as the one found at **www.yahoo.com/Business/Corporations/Internet_Access_Providers/Indices**, which I found by using the Yahoo! search engine. This is a very good list of the major and some not-so-major ISPs around the nation. Keep in mind that there are perhaps 10 times this number of sites. Don't discount the spare room in a large closet, either. Servers and modems can fit almost anywhere!

Other than modems, the local exchange carrier controls the ISDN to your server if you choose that route. Such major vendors as AT&T long-distance services aren't yet allowed to compete in the market, but that appears to be changing, thanks to Congress. Dedicated and switched Internet links can be had from SprintLink, MCI, and AT&T.

All About Email

As common as the modem is these days, the email process is used so often that I've heard that whole businesses would collapse if email was to end. That's a bit of an exaggeration, but you get the idea. Electronic mail has quickly replaced the telephone and the post office as the most often used form of communication in a business environment.

What Is Electronic Mail?

Email is the electronic form of the paper letter, nothing more. Email is also the single largest component of a Web server that promises to kill a new server. Why is that, you ask? I was recently a victim of an email flurry on a system where some nitwit sent the email to "*@*@*", which is a global address on our email system. What actually transpired was that over 20,000 users got the email message, and over half of them didn't have the sense to realize what the message was and replied to it. Now, in addition to that return email, the original is attached to the reply so now 10,000 new messages are floating around that are twice the size of the first message. In a very short time, about 200 servers started croaking under the load of the email running loose in the wide area network.

So, what is email? An ever-convenient method to converse with someone, a group of people, or the world. If you're not careful about this, you'll bring the world to its electronic knees. Yes, it can be done (and is on occasion). And that's not the only dastardly deed of which email is guilty. Let's find out what other evils lurk in email.

Attachments And The Dark Side

Email with an attached file is a neat way to move files from one place to another. So, you've been introduced to the evil email product, but did you think to consider what would occur if an errantly attached file was sent to the same global users? It would crash that system in a hurry. Furthermore, in some email systems, if an email is sent to a group of 25 users, and all have the same attachment, and one of those 25 users can't receive the email, guess what happens? Yes, *all 25* get the same email sent to them all over again! Even if those first 24 got the message, the last one caused the retransmission to the failed delivery point. However, the email system has no way of knowing that the list of recipients is more than just one user. If one fails, all of the recipients get the message again. When you pick an email system, make sure it doesn't do this to you!

Multiple Recipients

If you've got a list of users that you need to send the same letter, you can compose each individual message offline—to save connection fees—then go online and transmit them all at once, but that means creating a bunch of individual messages. A better solution is to use a mailing list. Mailing lists save on time and money by creating one message and sending it to everyone on the list. This is the essence of what is known on the Internet as a *list server*, or *listserv* for short. You can subscribe to a listserv to get on a common mailing list for messages, updates from a vendor, and such. Your Web server may or may not provide a listserv for your customers for you to update them on coming events, upgrades, special product notifications, and so on.

However, list servers are for disseminating fixed information (usually) and discussion groups. The information isn't normally for dynamic usage like a Web page would be using Perl or VB.

Return Receipts, And What They Don't Mean

When you send out an email message, you can do much like the post office does and request a return receipt for both delivery and for when it gets read. That's a nice idea and has the best of intentions, but it's worthless in many situations. Here's why. Think back to the router example of the intranet network. When an email leaves the source, weaving its way through the Internet, it passes through many gateways on its way to its final destination. A return receipt is generated by the first point capable of responding. This may or may not be the final destination. So, you can see how the return receipt misleads the source into thinking that the mail made it when in fact it may not have.

The second most useless part of an email receipt is that is doesn't indicate whether or not the recipient has actually *read* the email. If the recipient stores the email in a folder but never actually reads the message, the "message read" receipt never gets sent back to the sender. We know that the email made it past the first server because the return receipt was generated. Perhaps it's stuck in the processing software on the user's server, and the user is totally unaware that mail has been lost. Unfortunately, this happens all too often. Be careful when you select your email package.

Utilities At Your Disposal

As you administer your new site, you'll find some indispensable resources that are crucial in keeping the server operational and working smoothly. Downtime or poor operation could cost you potential customers, so you'd better be ready.

Basic System Tools

Some of the most basic tools are free, and you've got a pile of them. A couple of them I'll talk about shortly, but first, here are the tools included with the Microsoft Windows NT Server installation:

- *Server Diagnostics*—Allows you to track the progress of each part of the server, ranging from memory utilization to CPU time slices to ancillary devices in use.
- *System, Security, And Applications Log Files*—Generated by NT Server itself, log files provide an ongoing analysis of recorded events such as failed logons, successful directory accesses, time on the system, and more.
- *Server Performance Monitoring*—Let's you examine and chart the performance of the server.
- *User Statistics*—Used to see how the users are utilizing the server.

Recovery Tools

The recovery tools provided with NT amount to a precious disk that maintains a copy of the boot record, system files, user and system critical files, and a means to boot the server when it dies. It can restore the core part of the system that would otherwise prevent it from booting up. You can make a new emergency disk by running the RDISK program in the SYSTEM32 directory. Follow the instructions, and it updates your emergency disk easily. In addition to that, you might want to make a backup of the disk registries and critical areas by running the Disk Administrator and saving the configuration, as shown in Figure 2.15. A worthwhile gesture, I assure you. Wait until you've been caught in a failure, and you'll *never* forget to do it again!

Basic Supported Backup Tools

The NT-supported backup program is a no frills, few thrills program designed to work with the most common backup tape drive in the industry. Any common Travan or DAT drive should work fine. The program performs routine backups in an orderly manner and professes to use compression when it's running. Depending on how much data you've got that changes, QIC tapes are next to useless in a full-scale server implementation. Your best bet is to use one of the commercial-strength solutions from any one of the available products supporting up to 8GB on one tape.

Watching The Attached Users (Admin Tools)

One of the neat administrative tools that comes with Microsoft Windows NT Server allows you to monitor the users connected to the server, where they are in the system, what they're doing, and many other things. If you open the Administrative Tools group, then run the Server Manager program, shown in Figure 2.16,

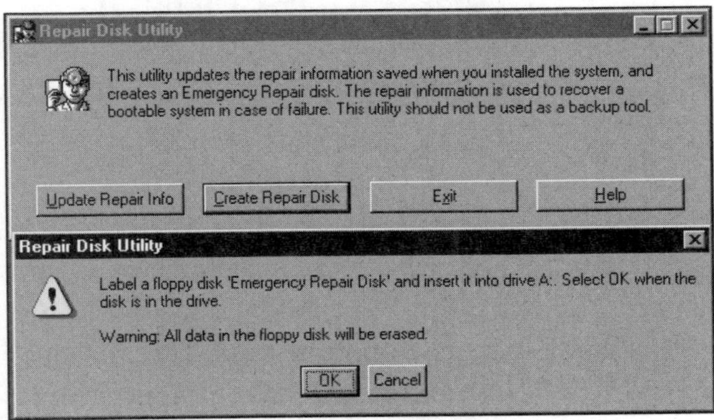

Figure 2.15
Emergency disk.

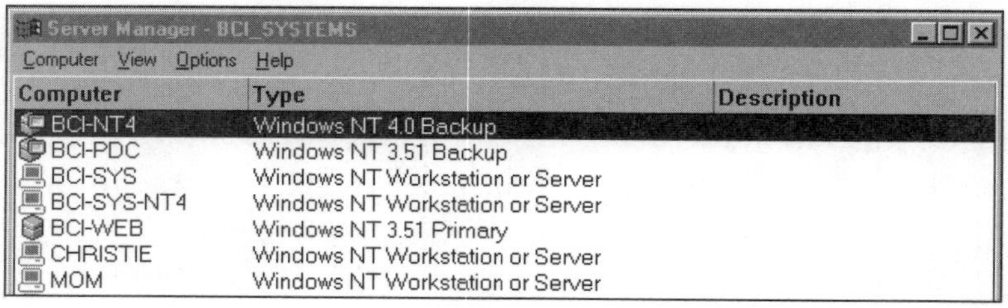

Server Manager - BCI_SYSTEMS

Computer View Options Help

Computer	Type	Description
BCI-NT4	Windows NT 4.0 Backup	
BCI-PDC	Windows NT 3.51 Backup	
BCI-SYS	Windows NT Workstation or Server	
BCI-SYS-NT4	Windows NT Workstation or Server	
BCI-WEB	Windows NT 3.51 Primary	
CHRISTIE	Windows NT Workstation or Server	
MOM	Windows NT Workstation or Server	

Figure 2.16
Server Manager.

you'll see a concise listing of users connected to the Web server and to any other computer in the network. This is a normal function of the Microsoft Windows NT Server, but I thought it interesting enough to tell you about it.

NT Resource Kit

As I mentioned earlier, this double CD-ROM set with accompanied documentation is perhaps the single most important set of documents next to the Microsoft Windows NT Server docs, themselves. The RK includes a host of utilities and functions, such as the Domain Planner, Net Watcher, a UUEncoder and Decoder, support for multiple desktops, an image editor, and more. The RK is shown in Figure 2.17. I paid $395 for the full set in March 1997, and it is probably still close to that now. If you're serious about maintaining your Web site in top working order, this is definitely required reading.

Microsoft TechNet Subscription

The last item I want to go over with you is called the TechNet subscription. TechNet is a whopping double CD-ROM set issued monthly, and every month's arrival offers to install and update your existing installation of the TechNet database indices. This guide is chock-full of technical tips, new driver updates, the Microsoft Knowledge base, and tools and tips to maintain nearly any Microsoft product. While it's true that we're installing and maintaining mostly third-party software onto Microsoft Windows NT Server, the plain and simple fact is that TechNet contains installation notes and fixes for many other applications as they relate to NT or other Microsoft products. Are you trying to configure Microsoft SQL Server for your Web server's databases? Check TechNet to see if there's a technical note or tip on how to do what you want. TechNet's main screen is shown in Figure 2.18.

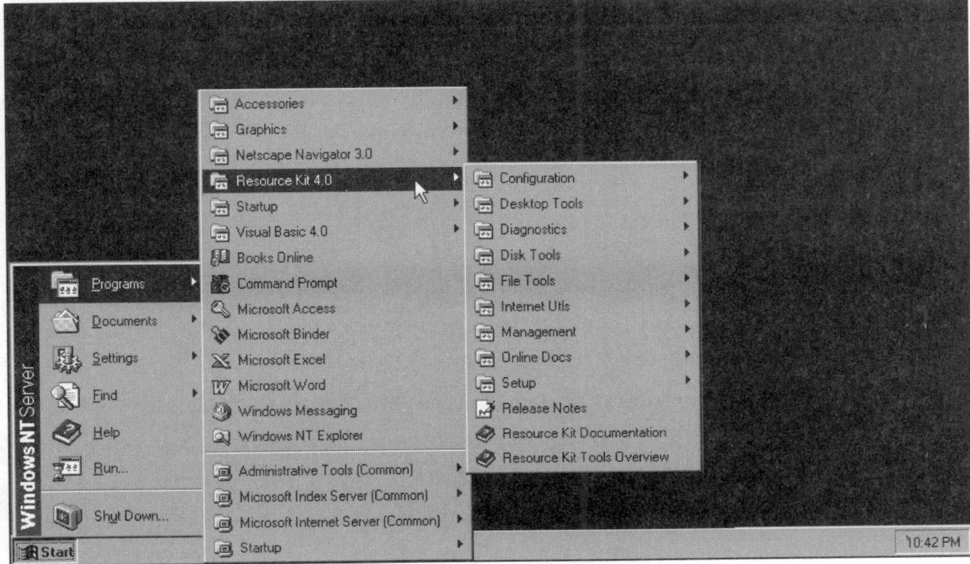

Figure 2.17
NT Server v4.0 Resource Kit.

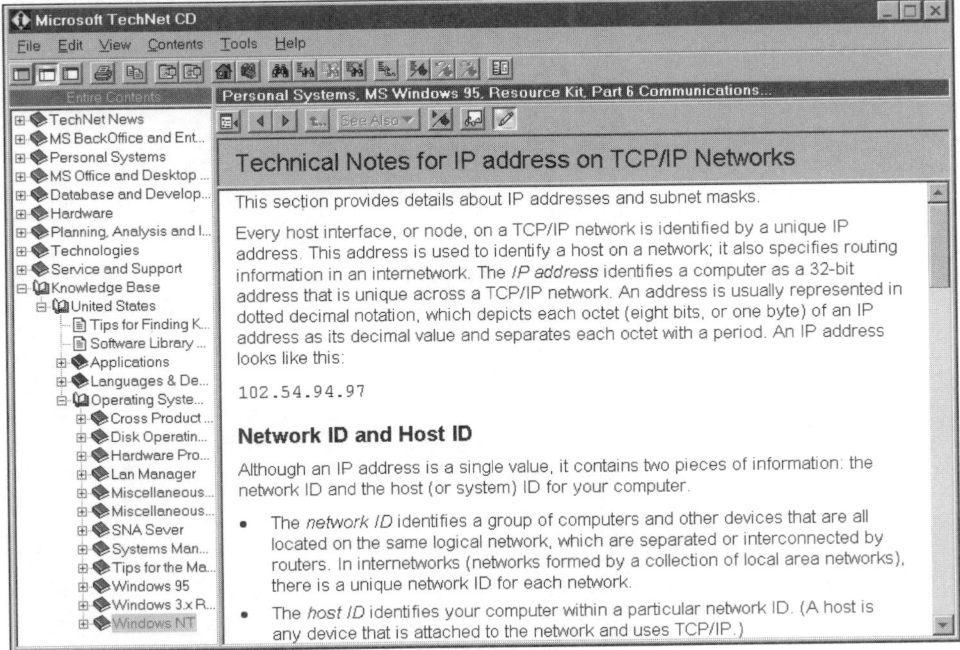

Figure 2.18
Microsoft's TechNet.

While these are the predominant tools that make the Web server easy to administer, we'll be talking about other tools in Chapter 12. Appendix B also provides an in-depth look into the resources mentioned in this chapter, with specific emphasis on working with the server when problems arise.

Summary

This has been a complex, but fun-filled chapter! We covered many topics, including defining the Web site as a whole, why we're doing it, what we'll use to build the site, our basic working parameters, and a host of related matters. We've defined the nominal and best-case hardware for the server and why some of the choices were made. I also addressed such important issues as communications links, including the ups and downs of the choices available. I hope this discussion has prepared you to accept or reject some of the theories you've had about your own site and alerted you to some of the things to be watching out for during construction. You definitely need to keep the CFO hard hat on during all phases of server building, but let the CEO and customers know what fun and newfound productivity they'll receive as a result of all their hard work and patience!

3

Web Services From A Business Perspective

Jeff Bankston

Now that you have a solid understanding of Windows NT Server and how to create a strategy for implementing a successful Web server, I would like to show you how, in addition to your other business needs, your Web server can function as a money-making machine. I know, you've already decided that the Web site would be private—to keep it to your customers—but once you've seen the unparalleled opportunities that the Web offers, you're likely to change your mind.

Specifically, in this chapter, we'll explore:

- Selling Web pages on the server
- Selling or leasing disk space on your server
- Consultant roles you can perform on the Web, for a fee
- Operating your site as a beta test site center
- Advertising on the Web

- Running a news service
- Operating an Internet list server for your customers
- Implementing front-end tools for your business data

There's plenty more, and I'd love to share them with you, but the book would then be large enough to boost a small child at the dinner table.

Selling Web Pages

Perhaps one of the most pervasive topics on the World Wide Web is the subject of selling Web pages stored on a Web server. You've got the server, so why not use it to its fullest extent. We'll get into the details in a moment, but before I get in too deep, I want to define a few terms. A *Web page* is an HTML document that displays on a Web browser. A *home page* is simply the topmost Web page of a particular Web site. *HTML*, or *Hypertext Markup Language*, is the language used to create a Web page—the graphics and links you see are part of the HTML code. HTML has seen several incarnations and enhancements, of which v3.2 is the latest. It supports an improved set of commands, including better audio, video, and representative markups to help make the most of your Web sites. Finally, a *link* is a portion of the HTML code that is used to launch users through cyberspace to another location containing related information.

To further clarify these concepts, let's hop to the Microsoft home page, shown in Figure 3.1, at **www.microsoft.com**, and make note of some key ideas there. I'll assume you're using Netscape's Navigator for this little expedition. However, if you're using Microsoft's Internet Explorer, you will find it to be quite similar in operation to Netscape.

This is the very first Web page that is accessible when you access the Microsoft Corporation via the Internet. This is its home on the Internet, hence the term *home page*. All of the links are underlined and displayed in blue. This display is Netscape's default, and you can change the default anytime you want. Continuing our tour, move your mouse to the Microsoft Internet Explorer link. Notice the arrow turns into a hand with a finger pointing to the link. This symbol shows you the text is, in fact, a link to another site or another place on this site. In this case, the link is to another Microsoft location—perhaps even on this same server. At the bottom of Microsoft's home page, the link **www.cdt.org/speech.html** takes you to another site altogether.

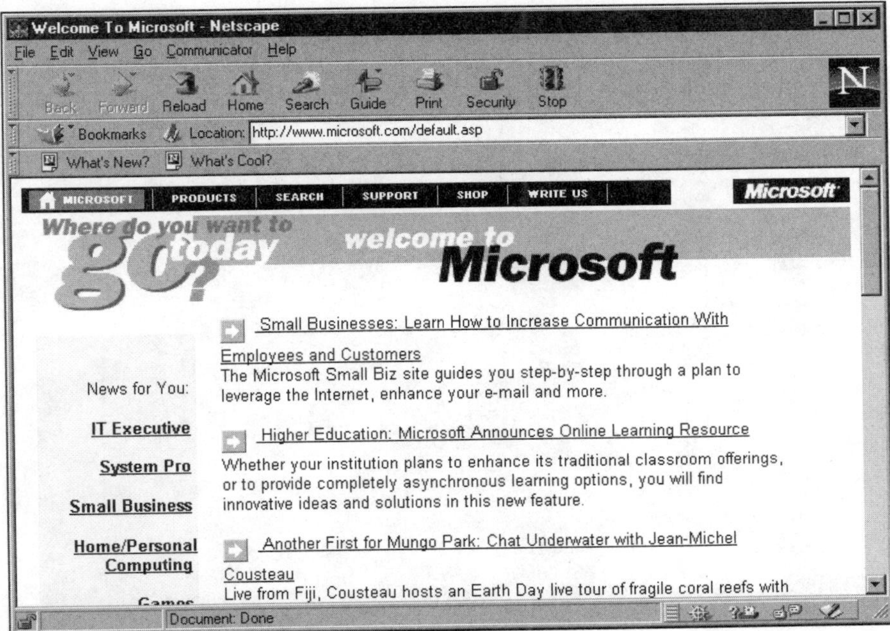

Figure 3.1
Microsoft's home page.

Now, let's hop over to The Coriolis Group's site, **www.coriolis.com** as shown in Figure 3.2.

Notice the bottom portion of the figure is subdivided into frames of information. Frames, which are simply a way to organize a Web site, are one of the latest rages of the Web to hit the streets. A *frame* is nothing more than HTML code that focuses Web page content so common items are contained within a frame, much like glass windows are sectioned off in frames. Each frame is independent from the others, yet sometimes related in content.

As your site prospers, you should consider adding frames to your home page, as a way to advertise your customers. If your Web server is as capable as the one we created in Chapter 2, then it will weather the additional hits without any problem. You'll make extra money for little or no work, and your customers will have just one more reason to praise your existence!

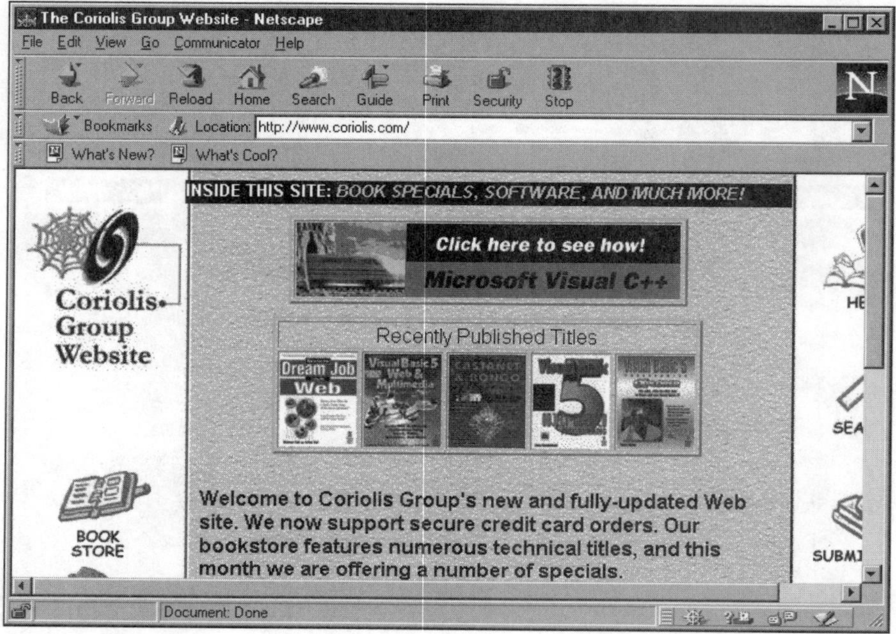

Figure 3.2
The Coriolis Group's home page.

There's one small drawback: maintenance. What does all of this have to do with maintenance, you ask? Consider this: You change and control your site as you deem necessary for the customers, and for good business, as well. Those other sites? Well, they're doing the same, which means that if you have links that cross to other sites, then at one time or another, you'll wind up with useless links that don't go anywhere. When links break down, someone has to fix them and pay for it! So, without further ado, let's proceed onward to the topics of maintenance and money.

Maintenance

The maintenance of a Web page involves several aspects of programmatical venturing. HTML is a fairly easy language to learn and master. As I mentioned earlier, there are lots of interesting things that you can do with HTML—display neat graphics, link to other sites, link to your own information, and much more. If your company won an award for excellence in its field, you might want to add a graphic of the award and list your accomplishment on your site. Or, maybe a client who keeps a page on your server tells you about a really cool site on widget technology that he wants added to his page. So, off you go to add a link to this site. Sounds like a piece of cake, right? Well, it is, as long as you're careful.

You make your first changes on the test files, save them, and test them. Looks fine until you put them in place. The first person that accesses the page gets sent off to Siberia! Not exactly what you wanted. Puzzled, you start debugging the problem. Are you responsible? Sure, you maintain these pages! The customer pays you for this, so, dutifully, you go off and find out, two days later, that the site you're referencing has moved and not bothered to let anyone know. You programmed everything perfectly, but it wasn't your fault. And it certainly wasn't the customer's fault. Now, what do you do?

This is but one of the many problems of Web page maintenance that will confront and confound you. What is your level of responsibility towards the customer and Web page maintenance? Generally, the amount of responsibility is determined in your negotiations with the customer at the onset of your service. You have several options: You can post the Web page into the server when the customer creates or modifies the page; you can give the customer access to the page storage location and let him create, modify, and process the page; or you can handle the modifications yourself. These factors affect the ways you can make money on the site processing Web pages.

The Cost Of Money

Ah, yes. It all boils down to money. Doesn't everything? If you decide to sell Web page space, then be prepared for several new issues to arise, such as a crashing end to the privatization of your Web server. Once you go public, you'll have to contend with a whole new set of administrative issues. See Chapter 2 for information regarding those issues. Aside from these concerns, you need to decide how much you want to charge for your Web pages and what criteria you want to use to determine the cost and rates for ongoing Web page support.

This can be a bothersome issue for customers who don't understand what a Web page can do on the Internet, so on goes your PR hat. First, you must explain what a Web page can do for them, such as:

- Offer standard advertising of products and services on an ongoing basis, unlike a newspaper that charges for a finite period of time.

- Offer prompt and timely updates to information on the Web pages in response to changing market conditions or new customer products offered on the market.
- Offer other Web connections to relevant products, technical support, and product updates via the Web page links.
- Empower customers with the ability to provide customer support to their own end users.

After you've shown them how beneficial a Web page can be, you need to discuss maintenance issues, such as:

- Frequent changes require time-consuming effort on your part, and effort does not come cheaply.
- Maintenance costs can be large if pages are maintained on a per-change basis.
- Complex Web page modifications can cause echoed problems, if one change causes another page's links to be broken. For instance, if a customer's home page has links to 15 other pages on his site, and those 15 pages each have 10 distinct links, one change to a link in a strategic location can cause half of those links to break.
- Subservient actions on a Web page can cause the need for lots of disk storage on a Web server, costing more for disk space than the Web pages themselves.

As with other business ventures, to build up a reputable and profitable Web business, you need to invest capital. In other words, you need to spend money to make money. Consider this analogy: You own a small business making and selling widgets from your home. The first year, your office consisted of a workbench in the garage. You had one employee—yourself—and you used existing tools and space. As widgets became more popular, you sold more and needed help to build and ship them. Your garage became increasingly crowded with no room to grow. So, to make more money and sell more widgets, you had to hire more people and build an attachment to the garage. A Web-based business is no different. If you profit from the Web pages and your buyers demand more, then you should create more pages or enhance existing pages to further reflect your mission.

Now that you know what's involved—and there is a lot of stuff to digest here—I bet you're wondering what kind of figures you can expect to see. Most sites charge $25 per page per month to store their customers' pages. Pages are generally limited to 3,000 bytes. This price includes only posting and storage fees. If the customer wants changes, many sites charge around $35 per month per page, and they average about four changes per month. If this is a really hot site that requires many changes each month to keep up with the changing market conditions, then charging up to $100 per page per month is not unreasonable. However, when a customer's changes get this numerous and frequent, they generally hire their own Internet expert or negotiate special rates with you to maintain their pages.

You have to be very careful when you agree to do page maintenance because the volume of changes can soon find you making changes on a full-time basis. When you get to that point, it's time to assess your position on the issue. Do you hire a Web page maintainer or train the customer to do more on his or her own, losing the user's monthly payments? I hope you don't choose the latter. After all, you're doing this for the money. My advice is to have your eye on an HTML expert, preferably waiting in the wings, if possible.

You also need to consider if the maintenance agreement with the customer includes keeping the last few revisions around for historical reasons. If this is the case, then your disk storage requirements rise sharply. Suppose 10 customers have five Web pages, each page averaging 3K in size. If the last three revisions had to be held for historical reasons, then you're storing four sets of pages for each customer. That's 600K of disk storage per customer. While that's not a huge number, consider these same 10 customers create two more pages for each of the existing pages. This addition jumps the storage to around 1MB for basic Web services. I've seen sites that have 200 customers in this situation, which means 120MB of disk space is used just for Web page contents—and that's only counting text content. Most pages use graphics of some kind to enhance the display, so add 30MB for each of these 10 customers. Add another 30MB for sound files or other enhancements. We're talking a whole lot of storage here. These issues should play a role in your decision of whether to pursue the business of selling Web pages. Either way, you'll, at the very least, be dealing with your own Web pages, so let's talk a little bit about the languages—HTML and VRML—that you'll be using for your own needs.

An Introduction To HTML

Web pages are written in HTML—a text formatting language that tells a browser how to interpret and display pages like the ones you saw in Figures 3.1 and 3.2. HTML is simple to learn and use, and there are several programs and utilities available that allow you to create HTML pages with ease. Check out the Word for Windows utility add-in, which is free, or the shareware program HTML Assistant. Both are neat and simple to use, and produce code like that shown in the code fragment in Listing 3.1. The resulting Web page is shown in Figure 3.3.

Listing 3.1 Sample Web page HTML code.

```
<TITLE>Panama City, Fla.'s Premier Web Site</TITLE>
<H1>Welcome to BCI Associates</H1>
<H2>A Systems Integration Firm</H2>
<P><P>
<H3>We're pleased you've chosen to visit our site, and welcome your
  comments.</H3>
```

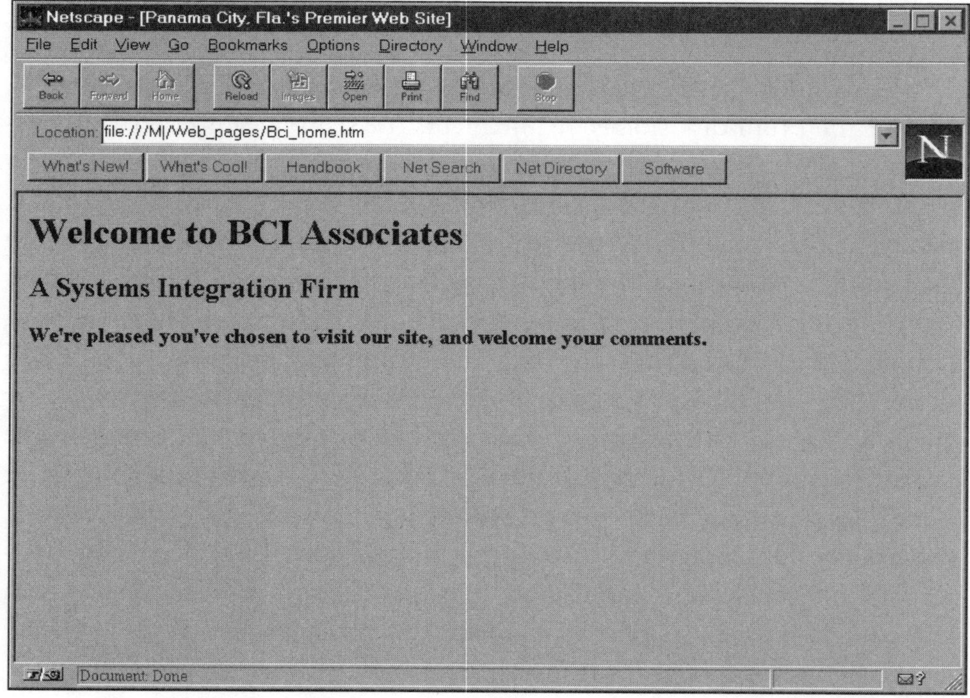

Figure 3.3
Sample Web page.

Notice that this doesn't have all of the <HEAD> or <TITLE> tags in it. This is merely intended to show you what HTML code looks like, and the resulting Web page. I'm not going to get into an HTML discussion because there are already dozens of books out there to tell you how to write and debug HTML pages. What I'm going to do is emphasize a few items of interest that can help you make your Web pages more exciting. The code in Listing 3.1 is in plain old HTML from the earliest days. Since then, numerous changes and enhancements have been made to the language. HTML 3.2 is the current version. To understand some of these concepts, let's look at the HTML source from the Netscape site, which uses the frames feature we discussed earlier. Listing 3.2 shows the HTML used by Netscape to create frames. To learn more about the different elements of HTML, try the Internet site **www.sandia.gov/sci_compute/elements.html**.

Listing 3.2 Netscape's frame source listing.

```
<FRAMESET ROWS="*,93">
   <FRAME
      NAME="content"
      SRC="/ndx.html"
      MARGINHEIGHT=5
      MARGINWIDTH=10
      SCROLLING = "auto"
      NORESIZE>
<FRAMESET COLS="150,160,160,*">
   <FRAME
      NAME="frame1"
      SRC="/navigate/f1.html"
      MARGINHEIGHT=3
      MARGINWIDTH=0
      SCROLLING = "no"
      NORESIZE>
   <FRAME
      NAME="frame2"
      SRC="/navigate/f2.html"
      MARGINHEIGHT=4
      MARGINWIDTH=0
      SCROLLING = "no"
      NORESIZE>
   <FRAME
      NAME="frame3"
      SRC="/navigate/f3.html"
      MARGINHEIGHT=4
```

```
        MARGINWIDTH=0
        SCROLLING = "no"
        NORESIZE>
    <FRAME
        NAME="frame4"
        SRC="/navigate/f4.html"
        MARGINHEIGHT=4
        MARGINWIDTH=0
        SCROLLING = "no"
        NORESIZE>
</FRAMESET>
</FRAMESET>
```

Netscape's home page is an excellent example of how to spruce up a site to provide customers with a site that's worth their online charges. You don't have to have the latest version of HTML to do this, but it helps. The downside to creating such a site lies in the HTML learning curve—using the latest versions of HTML can and usually does take up more of the Webmaster's valuable time. When you decide to go fancy, a dedicated Web page creator almost becomes mandatory.

Another neat thing you can do with Web pages is to create a search engine for databases. This is done by using a form to enter data as a request to find something and then submitting the form to a back-end processor, such as SQL Server or Oracle database engines. Let's look at the ever-famous Yahoo! search Web page, where hundreds of thousands of people visit each month to find information on the Web. Listing 3.3 shows a portion of the HTML code for the page, while Figure 3.4 shows the actual page.

Listing 3.3 The Yahoo! search engine.

```
<FORM METHOD=GET action="http://search.yahoo.com/bin/search">
<INPUT SIZE=30 NAME=p>   <INPUT TYPE=submit VALUE=Search>
    <A HREF="/search.html">Options</A>
```

The extracted source, which is partway down the listing, shows the search function. The user types in the requested search parameters or data to find, or selects the Options link to specify the conditions of the search. This step is useful to help narrow the search to the pertinent information so users don't get 10,000 sites returned in the results.

And that's the brief rundown on HTML. If you'd like further information, I suggest you pick up a copy of *The New Netscape & HTML EXplorer* by Urban A. LeJeune

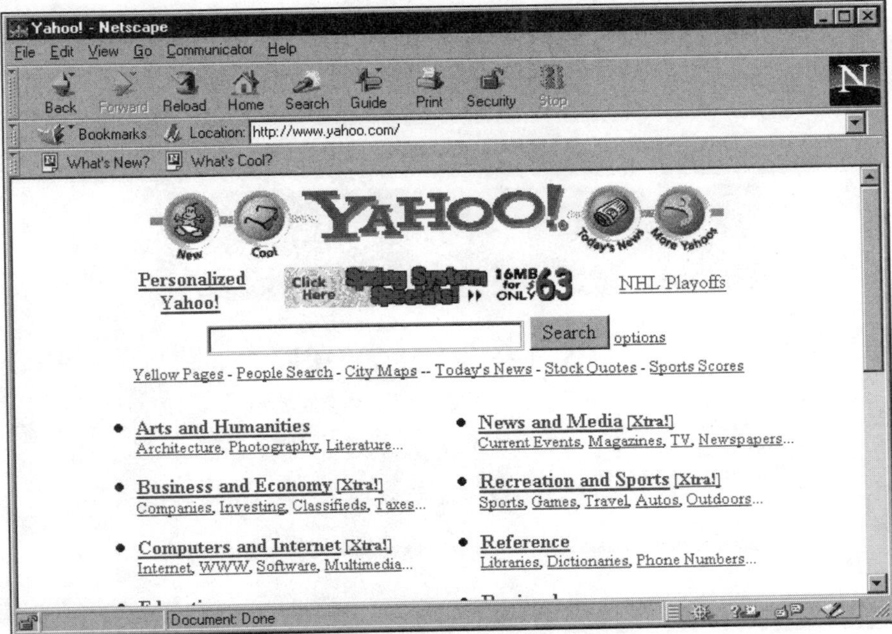

Figure 3.4
Yahoo! Web site.

(The Coriolis Group Books, 1996, ISBN 1-883577-91-8). This superb reference goes into many aspects of HTML, CGI, forms, and scripting, to provide you with a detailed background of using the language. Next, we'll talk about a newcomer to the Web—VRML.

An Introduction To VRML

Virtual Reality Modeling Language, or VRML, sprang onto the Web about two years ago and provides an interesting extension to the Web page by using a 3D technique. This newcomer is astounding and demanding at the same time. To use VRML, add the VRML add-in component to your HTML-capable browser, and head off to the Netscape home site for a preview. When I was last there, they had a VRML graphic on screen as part of their home page. You might also want to check out the VRML Forum, shown in Figure 3.5, at **http://vag.vrml.org/www-vrml**. If you don't have a VRML add-in for Netscape Navigator, go to **http://home.netscape.com:80**, and check out the new add-in products.

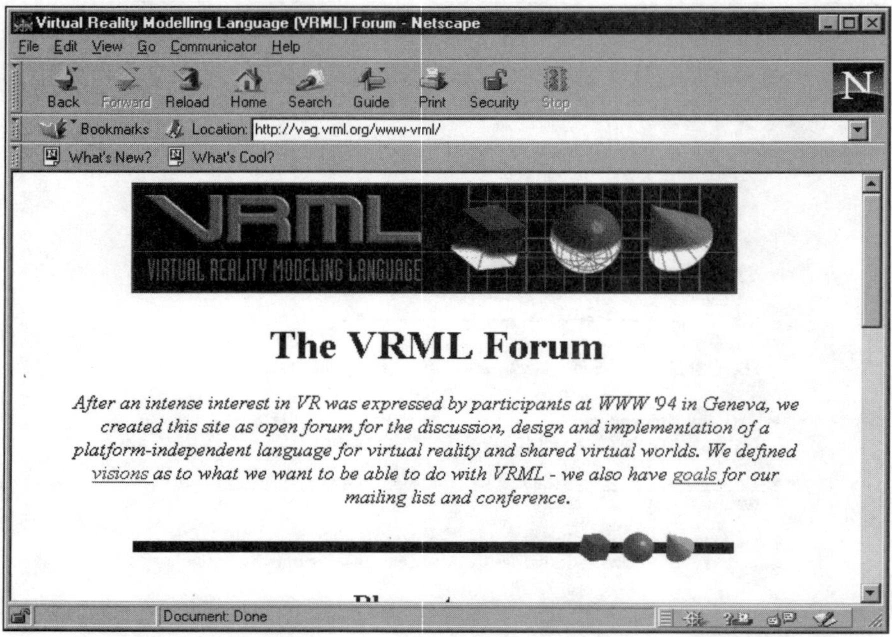

Figure 3.5
The VRML Forum.

VRML adds a three-dimensional view of Web sites and graphics called *VRML worlds*. It's a lot like having a whole new perspective on sites. It requires a new level of programming and support, but VRML adds plenty of spice to a Web page. If you decide to implement VRML, you might consider having a shareware or one of the freeware VRML add-ins available to your customers to use. One often-used tactic is to offer the viewer on your Web page and let the person know that your Web page requires a VRML viewer. The VRML Forum has a listing of many available VRML viewers.

Adding Sound And Video To Web Pages

Two of the most appealing aspects of Web pages are the addition of sound and video files. Sound comes in several forms, including WAV sound files and AVI video files, which include full sound capabilities in addition to video capabilities. WAV sound files are usually small in size and are used for such sounds as the alarms and radio files found in your Windows installation. Less than 50K in size, these files transfer from the Web to your system relatively quickly and easily. The catch is that either your operating system has to support these files or you'll have to get an add-in product that plays the files for you.

Netscape allows you to add this support by using *helper applications.* Simply download the product you need and install it on your system. Then, add the helper application to Netscape's list of supported applications. Windows 95 supports audio WAVs and video MPEGs with built-in viewers. When either of these two types of files are downloaded as a result of surfing a Web page, Windows 95 starts the correct helper application automatically.

Both popular audio file types, WAV and AVI files, can be a great advantage to your Web page, but don't get overzealous. Video files are often very large, sometimes exceeding 5MB in size. Just wait until a user hits one of these links and spends the next 30 minutes downloading the video file only to find out she went to the wrong link. She can cancel the file transfer, right? Yes, she can, but she may not know she is at the wrong place until it's too late!

The moral of the story is that sound and video can enhance your site and presentations, but you should caution the Web surfer that these files exist and you should post their relative sizes right next to the link. For an example of this technique, stop in at **http://sdsc.edu/SDSC/Partners/vrml/examples.html**, which is shown in Figure 3.6. This is a VRML site, but the lesson still applies.

Selling FTP Space

Ah, yes—more money issues. Your business has spent thousands of dollars building a Web site, and your CFO would like to see some of this capital come back to the company. Can't blame the CFO, for sure, because this is what the Web site is supposed to be doing by being properly planned for at the onset. To accommodate your customers' storage needs without incurring additional costs for unplanned disk upgrades (based on your discussions with them and the 10MB that's generally offered gratis), you decide to purchase a 4GB drive at the onset of the project.

However, after your site becomes operational, some of the customers have decided that there is no need for disk space at all, regardless of the cost (or lack of cost). You're stuck with lots of extra real estate. What to do, what to do. My

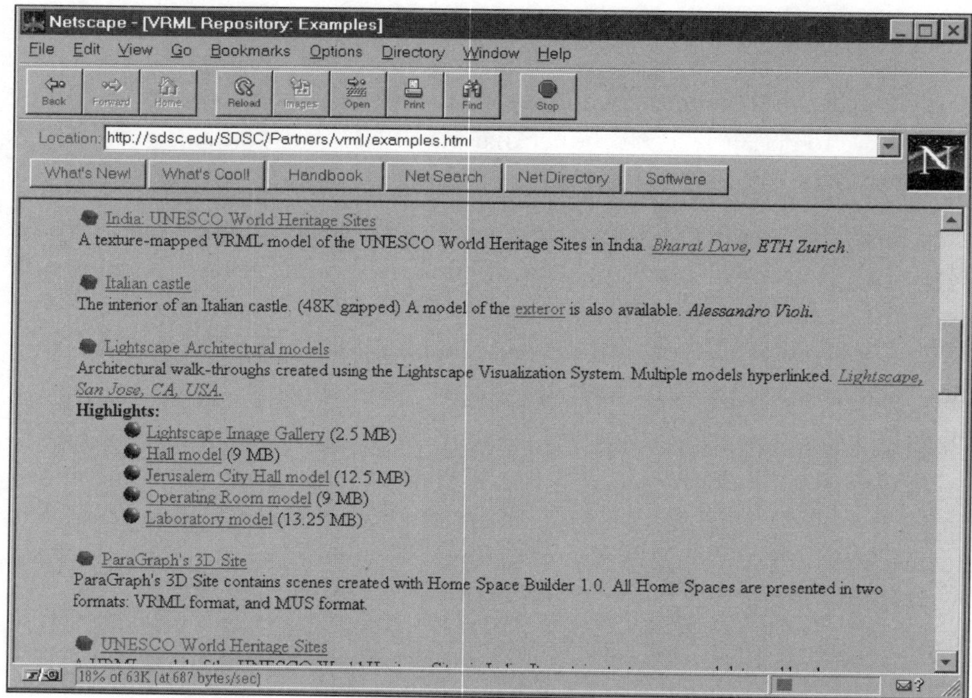

Figure 3.6
Examples of VRML.

suggestion: Sell the space as rented "office space" to complement the Web pages you've sold earlier. Now, your customers that have Web pages can store the files that complement the Web pages right on the same server!

As an example, let's examine the HTML code from McAfee's Web page offer to download its anti-virus software from its Web site (see Listing 3.4). Pay special attention to its usage of HTML to get to an FTP site.

Listing 3.4 References to site links.

```
<HEAD><TITLE> Download updated McAfee files</TITLE></HEAD>
<BODY BGCOLOR="ffffff">

<P>
<P><CENTER> <IMG SRC="/gif/downban.gif" align="Middle" alt=""></P>

<P>
Fully functional, 30 day evaluation copies of all McAfee software
packages are available from these McAfee Associates FTP servers.
```

```
<UL><UL>
   <EM>Note:</EM>  You can select the <U><I>00-index.txt</I></U>
   files in any directory for some clues as to which directories
   contain which packages. For example, for anti-virus products
   you'd look in the <B>/pub/anti-virus/</B> directory. </UL></UL>
</P>

<P><HR><H2>
<A HREF="ftp://mcafee.com/pub">
Download Evaluation Copies of McAfee Products</A><BR><BR>

<A HREF="ftp://mcafee.com/pub/3rdparty">
Download Third Party Products</A> </H2></P>
```

Figure 3.7 shows the actual site. Notice the FTP link at **www.mcafee.com/down/download.html**. Nothing more than HTML code, no trickery. This is how you can implement FTP within your Web pages without actually having an FTP server running. The FTP protocol itself is one of the MIME subsets and can be called from just about any Internet protocol.

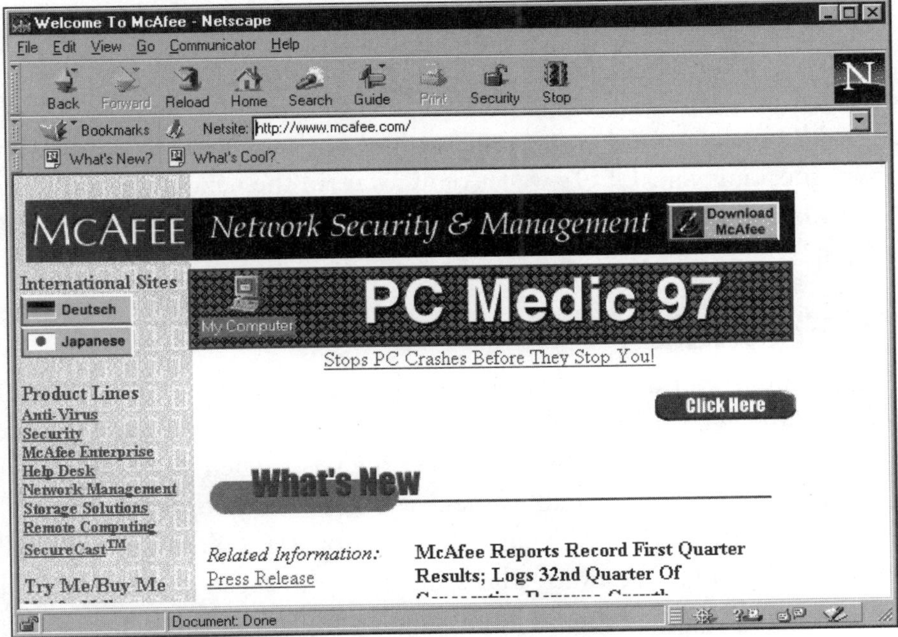

Figure 3.7
Downloading file updates via FTP in a Web page.

Pretty neat stuff! So, keeping with the tone of providing the customer with a viable business solution, the use of Web links can achieve all sorts of productive tasks. If your customer so desires, you can maintain complete libraries of files for their users by simply posting the file to the FTP site and changing the Web link. This technique is especially helpful for novice users—they can simply enter the URL to go right to a file location.

Enough said about the necessities—what about money? This depends on a number of factors, but essentially you'll have to negotiate rates with each customer. One site I know of provides 10MB free with each account, whether they use it or not. Exceeding that allocated amount results in fees ranging from block increases of 1MB at a time to a per-kilobyte charge. Generally, fees are $1 per MB per month per account, above the initial supplied amount. For a user of 125MB with a 10MB initial allocation, the fee would be $115 per month. Because it would take two years for this user to spend the amount of storage fees that would equal the cost of a decent-size drive to support this locally on the user's own PC, this provides both a needed and economical service. Of course, if you have 20 users with the same disk requirements, then you'll soon wind up with a disk farm to satisfy their needs, as shown in Figure 3.8.

How's that for supporting the user's storage needs? Using a monster disk array along with optical storage is a unique method of giving users dynamic storage without breaking your CFO's wallet right away. In the next few sections, we'll go over some related needs of an FTP storehouse, aside from the obvious fees to pay for it.

File Formats

In the computer world, there are as many file formats as there are wrong turns to take on the Web. However, you'll generally run across the more common types of files. It's nice to be aware of these file types when you start servicing your customers, because not all of them will know how to handle these files. Hey, there's another use for Web pages! Informational specifications called *FAQs*, or Frequently Asked Questions. These are short info sheets that provide pertinent information about common topics. For example, you could have an entire FAQ series on how to process files. Table 3.1 lists a few of the more common files, something about them, and how to process them.

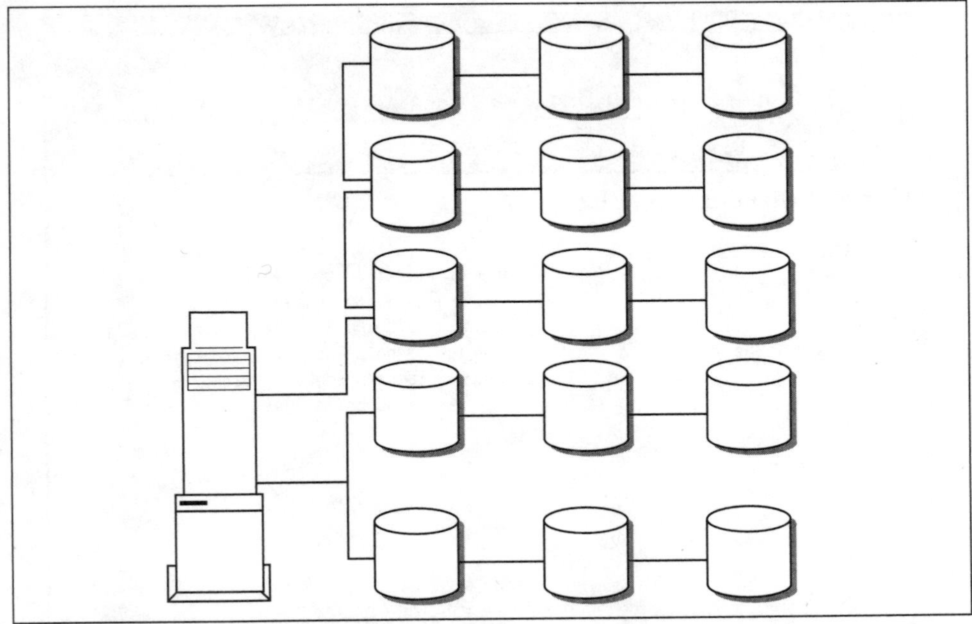

Figure 3.8
What you don't want in a server farm.

These are but a few of the files you'll find scattered across the Internet, but they're the ones you're most likely to run across and have to process. To help your clients out, you might consider purchasing the required files and posting them on your server so your clients can use these archives. These programs don't take up much space and are relatively inexpensive. One more thing you

TABLE 3.1

SEVERAL FILE FORMATS FOUND ON THE WEB.

File Type	Extension	Native Environment	Processor
DOS archive	ZIP	PKWare's PKZIP	PKUNZIP.EXE v2.04g
DOS Archive	EXE	PKWare's Self Extractor	ZIP2EXE.EXE
DOS Archive	LZH	Lharc, by Yoshi	LHA.COM
DOS Archive	ARC	DOS archives	ARCE.COM
Unix Workstation	Z	native Unix	Unix System
Unix Workstation	TAR	native Unix	TAR archiver on Unix

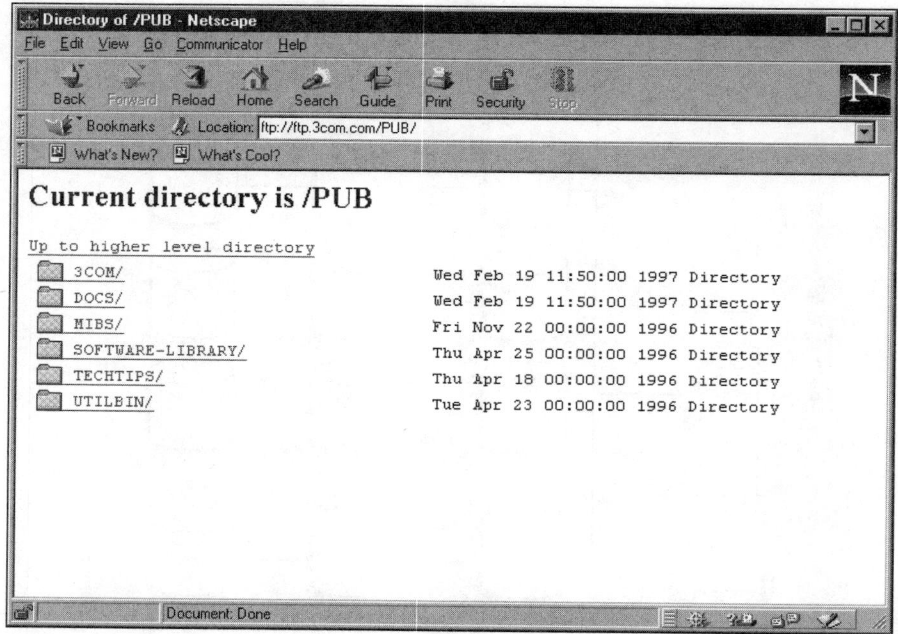

Figure 3.9
3Com's FTP viewed from a browser.

might want to consider placing on your site is a program to process long file names. Figure 3.9 shows the 3Com FTP site root directory. Although several of the file names listed in the directory are standard DOS-style file names—up to eight characters plus a three-character extension—you can see a few that have longer names. If you look deeper into 3Com's directory tree, you'll see that some of the directory names are also longer than eight characters.

All of these longer names get truncated in displays and files of regular DOS formats, such as DOS and Windows 3.x. Windows 95, Windows NT Workstation, Windows NT Server, and OS/2 all support long file names, but if you *download* one of these long file name files, DOS users will see the name truncated. For example, the file name TEST_SYSTEM_FILE.EXE would be shortened to TEST_S~1.EXE. The *1* stands for the first iteration of the named file. Figure 3.10 shows an example of truncated files.

The situation becomes sticky when you download a file with a long file name, extract the short file name version, and then run the program. You may get an

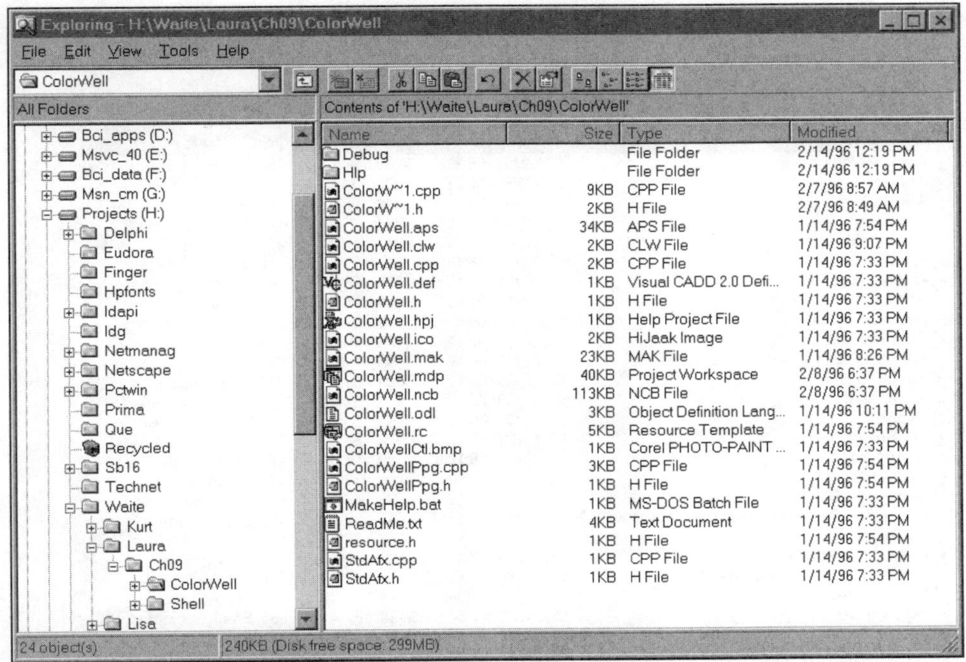

Figure 3.10
Long file names truncated.

error message indicating that the program cannot find some of the files required to run the program. Sure it can't find them, the names have been truncated! Files with the ~ symbol (called a *tilde*) are unusable as far as the programs that use these files are concerned, although DOS, Windows, and Unix can work with them just fine. You'll have to rename them to the correct names to use them. But how do you do that?

Using a program like WinZIP v6, open the archive to see the long file names preserved. From there, simply re-enter the correct file name. Figure 3.11 shows an archiver that preserves long file names.

Self-extracting files are the most commonly used because they require nothing on the part of the user except the ability to type in the name of the file. This also has the benefit of sharing files with unknown systems or destinations because, if they can run a DOS program, the self-extractor can be used to get to the files. I prefer to use self-extracting files whenever possible.

WinZip - CHAPTER9.ZIP

File Actions Options Help

New Open Add Extract View CheckOut

Name	Date	Time	Size	Ratio	Packed	Path
AppBarWnd.cpp	02/02/96	08:23	7,983	64%	2,858	Shell\AppBar\
AppBar.aps	02/02/96	08:21	33,936	74%	8,881	Shell\AppBar\
AppBar.clw	02/02/96	08:21	1,340	59%	543	Shell\AppBar\
AppBar.rc	02/02/96	08:21	5,344	73%	1,463	Shell\AppBar\
resource.h	02/02/96	08:21	1,012	63%	372	Shell\AppBar\
appbar menu.tif	02/02/96	08:16	201,548	99%	2,432	Shell\images\
AppBar.cpp	02/02/96	08:10	1,318	58%	560	Shell\AppBar\
AppBarWnd.h	02/02/96	00:43	1,453	55%	654	Shell\AppBar\
Subfolder.mdp	02/02/96	00:31	37,888	94%	2,285	Shell\Subfolder\
Subfolder.ncb	02/02/96	00:31	107,520	90%	10,713	Shell\Subfolder\
AppBarData.h	02/02/96	00:19	1,207	54%	558	Shell\AppBar\
AboutDlg.cpp	02/02/96	00:12	1,009	59%	411	Shell\AppBar\
AboutDlg.h	02/02/96	00:12	809	52%	388	Shell\AppBar\
AppBar.h	02/02/96	00:10	755	53%	354	Shell\AppBar\
AppBar.ico	02/02/96	00:10	1,078	68%	341	Shell\AppBar\res\
AppBar.rc2	02/02/96	00:10	398	57%	170	Shell\AppBar\res\
StdAfx.cpp	02/02/96	00:10	204	34%	134	Shell\AppBar\
StdAfx.h	02/02/96	00:10	502	44%	283	Shell\AppBar\
subfolder - change to the DLL version of MFC.tif	02/01/96	21:57	601,443	99%	7,463	Shell\images\
Subfolder.dll	02/01/96	19:11	57,856	77%	13,350	Shell\Subfolder\Debug\
early version of Subfolders.tif	02/01/96	17:43	15,197	66%	5,115	Shell\images\
create new class CProperties.tif	02/01/96	17:42	19,621	29%	13,880	Shell\images\
Subfolder.mak	02/01/96	17:34	11,674	83%	1,946	Shell\Subfolder\
Subfolder.aps	02/01/96	17:33	42,180	77%	9,658	Shell\Subfolder\
Subfolder.clw	02/01/96	17:33	1,213	60%	485	Shell\Subfolder\
Subfolder.rc	02/01/96	17:33	4,642	71%	1,362	Shell\Subfolder\
SubfolderPage.cpp	02/01/96	17:21	6,643	64%	2,424	Shell\Subfolder\

Selected 0 files, 0 bytes | Total 136 files, 2,161KB

Figure 3.11
Preserving long file names in an archive.

Storage Requirements

Alas, one of the main functions of a Web site now comes into focus. Every Web server has to have sufficient disk space to run normally, and you should give yourself enough for emergencies, as well. Counting the operating system and basic Web server software, along with the basic utilities, you'll use in excess of 400MB of disk space just to get started. For a new site, I suggest that you have 500 percent of disk space free above the disk space used. For instance, if you've occupied 400MB after the installation of NT Server and all of your Web server software, then you should have an additional 2,000MB free for the inevitable expansion that will occur in the coming months as the other issues of Web servers come to light. This may seem excessive at first, but trust me. Been there, done that, felt that. And it hurts when you get caught by the ears!

I've seen this aspect of Web server development bite many planners squarely in the wahoo. But it doesn't have to be this way. One way to ease the sting is to use

SCSI controllers and devices. By using SCSI controllers, you can operate as normal and then add storage like you usually do to SCSI controllers—one device at a time. It's nothing to shut down the Web server and pull the cover to add a new drive. Fire it back up, format the drive, and boom—you're back online! You repeat the process each time you near capacity with the current drives. This approach presumes you're using standard drive architectures and not RAID. If you're using RAID, this is another story entirely. To increase RAID storage, you'll have to do a complete backup of all of the data on the RAID, add the new drive, reformat the entire RAID system, and then restore the data. This is true of nearly all RAID systems because RAID treats all of the physical drives as a logical unit of one drive. So, misplan your RAID storage, and you could be in for an exciting night at the office.

Perhaps one of the most underused storage mediums in the industry is optical solutions. You see plenty of CD-ROM drives and jukeboxes for CDs, but how many rewritable drives are in the business office? One estimate recently placed the corporate environment as the next big push for computer resellers with rewritable optical solutions. These solutions include everything from small zip drives, such as the Bernoulli 100MB floptical unit, all the way up to the big 8-inch, 12-gigabyte platters. At one time, I contemplated the purchase of a 5 1/2-inch, 1.2GB rewritable drive for my storage needs. The drive and controller cost $1,700, and the media cost $49 per blank disk. Not exactly what you'd consider economical, so these kind of drives languished in the market. The next optical drive to make its debut was a little 3 1/2 inch magneto optical drive like the Fujitsu DynaMo unit. This little gem holds about 217MB of data after being formatted. It's the same size as a standard 3 1/2 -inch floppy, but twice as thick. The price of the drive, which is SCSI-1 compliant, was $700 when I bought mine, and the media was $19 apiece. Now, the drive is priced at barely $500, but the media price hasn't dropped much.

When you are determining your storage requirements, the primary piece of information you'll need to know is: How much storage are you using on a weekly basis, and what percentage of that number is actual Web server storage? Obviously, if you've had to add a physical disk, you know the impact on the Web server. Now, if you use a very large rewritable optical drive, you can amass up to 2.4GB of storage using two of the 5 1/2-inch SCSI rewritable drives. When the media fills up, just replace it with a fresh disk. An instant 1.2GB per drive ready to go!

However, a time may come when you need access to the data on an existing disk but the disk will have to be changed out. If you're traveling 2,000 miles away, that's kind of hard to do, because the physical disk will have to be switched. One solution to this problem is to go with jukebox optical disks the size of CD-ROMs that are used in a device that closely resembles the jukebox full of 45 records in the old ice cream shop. It's an expensive device, but with it, you can store up to a terabyte of data that is immediately accessible to users. Jukeboxes are especially useful because a 50-platter device can use up to 50 CD disks that will switch automatically under software control, so you won't have to physically switch the disks.

So, you can see that optical storage is a very viable alternative to many storage solutions. This type of storage provides you not only with adequate storage requirements for the present, but for the near and far future of your Web site. Figure 3.12 illustrates the architecture I built for my Web server initially for testing, and then for the final Web server. I used it to test the "proof of concept" model of the site and security of data.

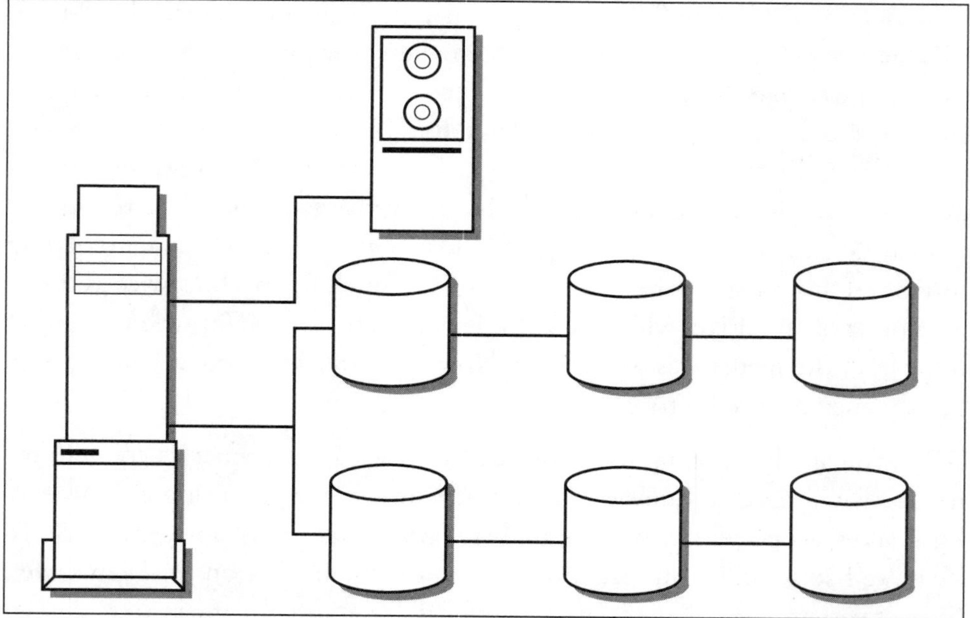

Figure 3.12
Storage prototyping.

Employing A Hierarchical Tree Structure For Your Web Server

A hierarchical tree structure? What does this have to do with anything, you ask? Well, in a nutshell, your users will find it easier to navigate a responsible tree structure than to wander around your site trying to figure out what's what. Let's begin by examining the directory structure of my Web server, as viewed from Explorer. This view is shown in Figure 3.13. Figure 3.14 shows the same directory tree as seen from an FTP logon from the Internet.

See the difference? While you can see the full tree from File Manager, the FTP view is considerably different. Why in the world would you use a subdirectory of *games* under the *drivers* directory? You wouldn't, so creating such would cause much distress for one of your regular visitors trying to get the latest update to a game you wrote. This is a quiet and seldom seriously thought out process that deserves some attention. In planning your FTP usage, keep in mind the Web

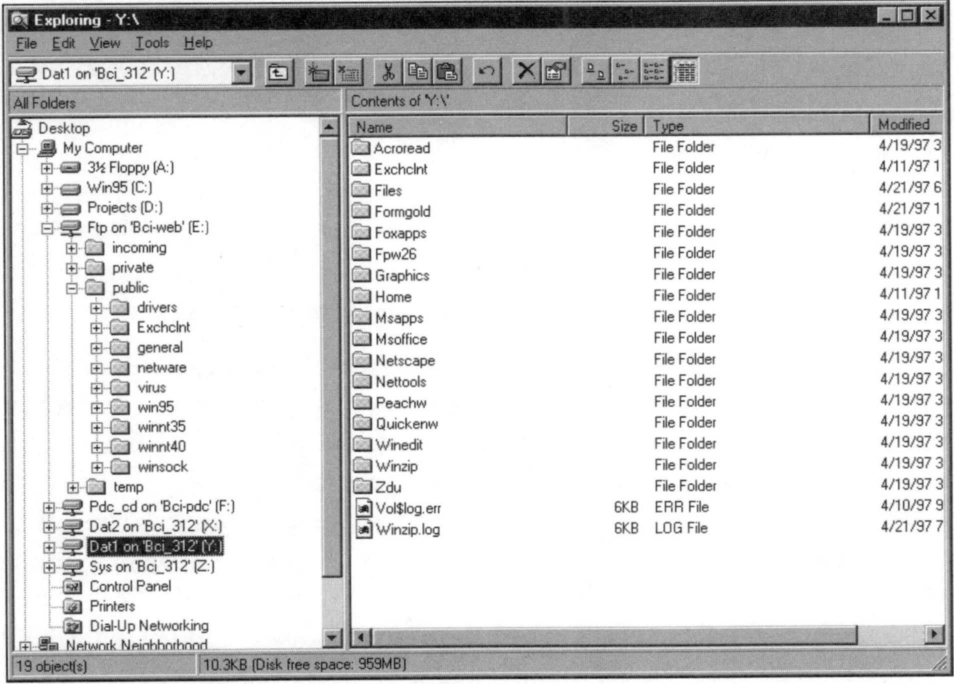

Figure 3.13
Explorer view of FTP site.

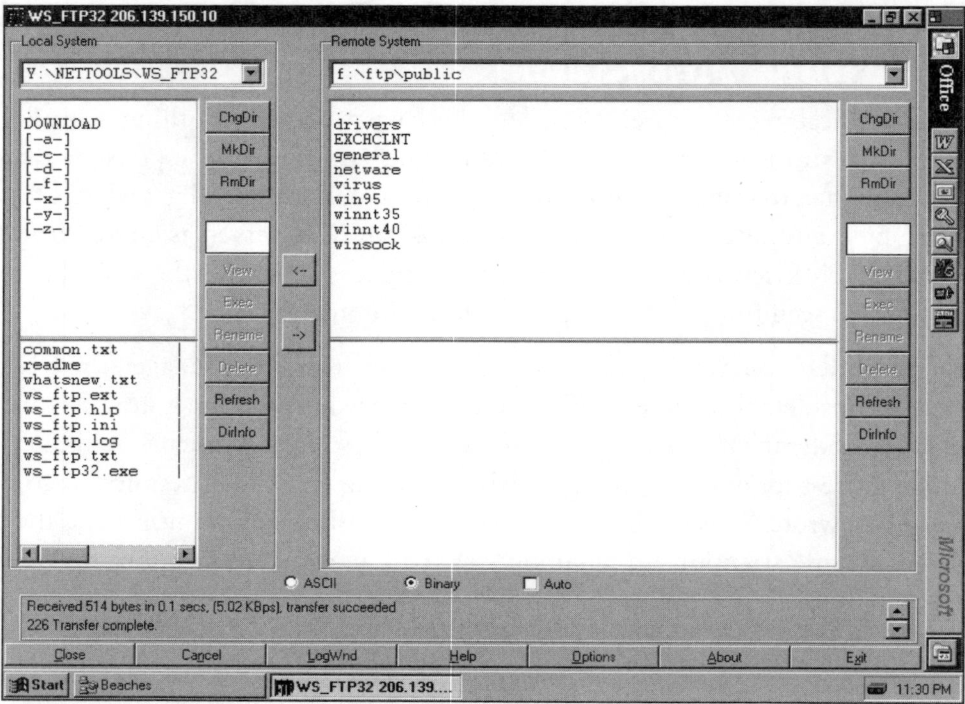

Figure 3.14
The same view from FTP software.

server as a whole. How are you serving your customers and the business in general? Are there program or data files that the business's most important customers need to access on an ongoing basis? Are these files top secret?

If they are, I guess you'd better protect them. (We'll talk about security in a moment.) How about those games updates? Give them away to any customer as a freebie, and you'll need to grant public access. Microsoft Windows NT Server makes this kind of sharing of data as easy as pie, but there's a little trick to remember. When you grant the proper permissions to users, don't forget to share the directory! Set the same permissions to the same groups you do in the Security settings of Explorer. Once this is done, sit back, and enjoy the secured environment of file access. Figure 3.15 shows the groups I've added to the FTP access. These are the basics of my site, and new users need only be added to a group when new groups are created on the Web server.

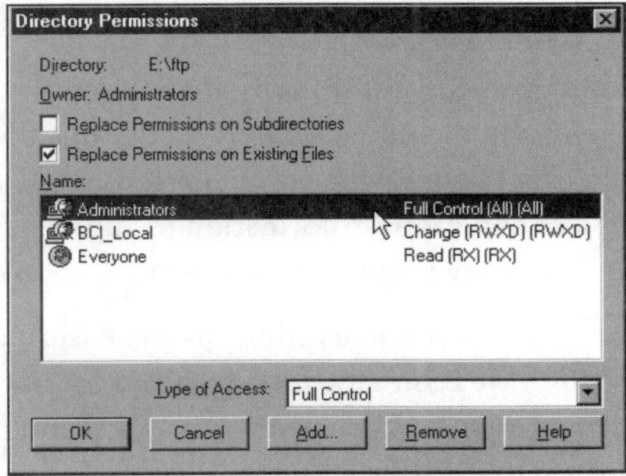

Figure 3.15
Security permissions.

Client Access

Perhaps the single most important part of the Web server is security. Security is crucial to the proper growth and livelihood of your new toy. Give the wrong access, and your best customer's most vital business plans could end up in the wrong hands. It's a lot like jumping off into a pit of punji sticks. You know it's going to hurt, and you shouldn't do it, so be careful, and *don't* do it! Because your customers connect to the Web server in different ways, you have to institute proper security and procedures for all connection avenues.

Network clients have a different set of concerns than BBS users, as do Remote Access Server (RAS) users, and you'll have to address them at the proper time. If you have supersensitive issues, then you should consider using a firewall for limited Internet access.

Web Server Consultant Services

One of the ways you can keep your CFO happy is to show how the Web server can be manipulated to further the cause of the bottom line. All across the Internet, there are ways to find information, but organization of that information is in a sorry state. This section introduces you to a few ideas on how to use that information to leverage your business's Web server for a more profitable venture. In a manner of speaking, you'll bring together several aspects of the Web for your server and entice customers to use you as a sole point of contact.

Marketing Surveys

Have you ever been sent one of those goofy marketing surveys that just chill your bones? They generally include questions requesting all sorts of information that you would never ever give out to anyone, let alone a stupid form. They ask you to verify all sorts of personal information including your income, number of kids, and social security number. I never send mine back.

Well, there's one way to set up a marketing survey, ensuring 100 percent response, and store the information away in a database for use at a later time. If you want what is offered at a site, even just a software demo package, then you must complete a survey form in its entirety. No gaps and no substitutions, it must be completed. Both Netscape and Microsoft use this technique for users wanting to download their Web server software. Their surveys take the form of an application, although I've never known anyone to be turned down. Figure 3.16 shows the survey you get when you download the Microsoft Internet Information Server v3 trial version.

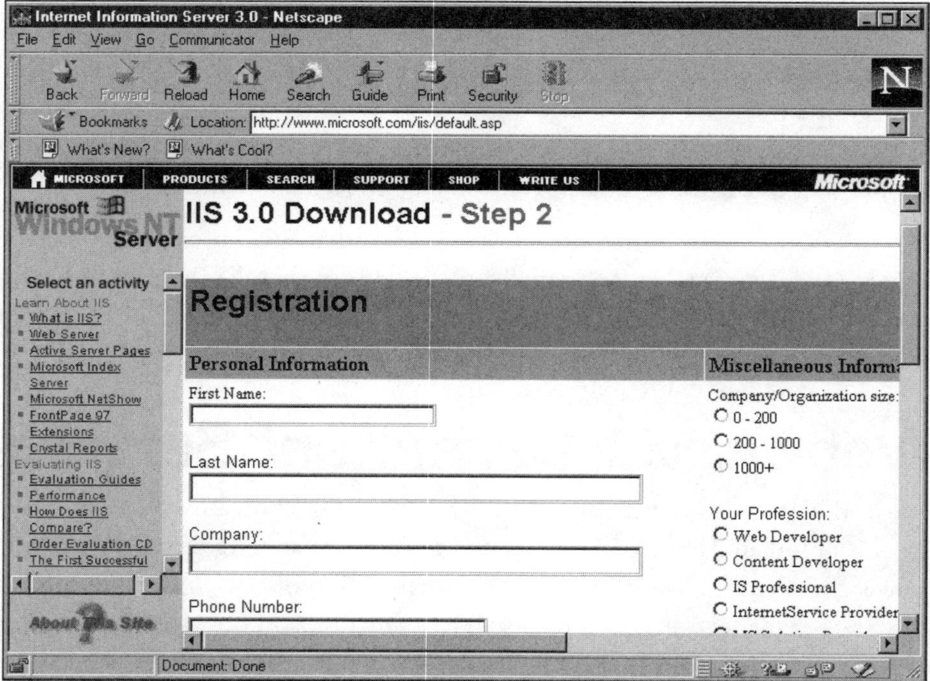

Figure 3.16
Form to fill out for download registration.

After you fill in the form, the data is sent to the Microsoft server back-end tools that process the request, and they send you a return mail message that lets you know the status of your request. Although I do not know what these companies use their information for, I assure you, it's used for something or else they would not have gone to the trouble to create and maintain the form.

Your Web server can be of great help on your (or your customer's) data gathering venture. Here are some suggestions for information you can request and ways to use your server to gather data:

- Find the type of operating system your software users have.
- Gather data on problem calls to your computer repair shop.
- Register any of your software that a user has bought.
- Send in a suggestion or complaint on the service of the Web server.
- Perform an information-only request for proposals from vendors.
- Send in product FAQ updates remotely.
- Ask users what they want in a new or enhanced product.

So you see, not every marketing survey is a real pain in the behind. Take your individual wants, needs, and company desires forward to the following sections and imagine how and where you could use such a form to solve a particular need or fill the gap in something the server software can't do. Remember that these surveys generate files and use disk space, so if a customer of yours is requesting surveys, the disk space they use goes up. Also, if a set of surveys reaches a set demand or the results hit a specific volume, then you can generate email to someone to pay special attention to this fact. You can also be billing for the volume of email generated. You don't always have to bill for this data, but it's a potential you'll have.

Creating New Servers

If you can build a new Web server or rebuild an existing one, you have a very lucrative potential to become a consultant. We're not talking about just any old physical server. This is a full-fledged machine capable of supporting tremendous amounts of activity, data storage, and services for a Web site. In Chapter 2, we discussed Web server requirements from both a hardware and software standpoint. Let's quickly review these points:

- Perform a site survey to determine the actual needs of the server.
- Talk to the customer and many of the customer's users to determine the overall purpose of the site.
- Propose a Web server platform, and finalize it.
- Install and configure the prototype server.
- Conduct a final configuration review.
- Perform acceptance testing.

Most of these tasks could turn into billable services if you were an Internet consultant.

Logistics Issues

Where there are servers and connectivity, there's the potential for disaster and mayhem. These two brothers seem to run hand in hand with Murphy and his law, so modern computing infrastructures are bound to fail at some point. This is the basic and most important premise of support issues. Here's a list of the most important issues that will cause great consternation to the CEO:

- If the Web server goes down, the business starts losing money immediately.
- If the Web server goes down, critical customers lose connectivity to other sites. Not a direct loss of money to you, but your customers are now without *their* money-making functions.
- If natural disaster strikes, the Web server would be unable to be recovered.
- If man-made disaster strikes, the Web server would be unable to be recovered.

Each of these items is catastrophic to the business, either in the basic premise that the data has been destroyed or the access to the data has been removed. I added the last two to differentiate between unavoidable disasters, such as flash fires at the office over the weekend, and avoidable disasters, like hurricanes, that generally come with a warning. In all of those circumstances, the opportunity to avoid disaster and continue supplying services to the customer is very possible.

Critical data on the server should be backed up consistently over the weeks that the server is being built and then put online. This means purchasing a good tape drive, software, and a whole slew of tapes if these items weren't purchased in the initial server build. Power-protection devices, utility software, and other issues such as this encumber the customer with a host of logistics questions that you can answer.

Billing Issues

Of course, all of this has to be paid for somehow. Not the server, but the services that the customer uses and allows their own customers to use. If you use the Web server to do double duty as a partial Internet Service Provider, then the customer may need someone to track the online time used by those connected to the Web server. You can also have billing set in place for selling FTP disk space, Web pages, and the like. All of these things allow you to use your Web server to help your customers, or if the need exists, for your customers to support and sell excess server space to their customers. It's a lot like leasing a building and then subleasing each of the suites.

Server Maintenance

All servers at one time or another need some kind of support, whether it's minor maintenance, training the new user, training the Webmaster on how to use the server, installing new hardware, or even providing routine support. There are plenty of businesses out there that would love to have the Web server earning its keep but haven't the time, inclination, or the personnel to perform normal maintenance.

A perfect example of this is a past client of mine. I supported this client's 200-user network. The customer had plenty of his own computer people available to do the job, but he believed that he could save money by having his employees work a different and hopefully more productive job. The change was to hire outside technical support to do the same job that his own employees used to do. It's becoming more common these days to *outsource* service and support of networking systems.

Along the same vein, you can always find companies that need someone to create, test, maintain, and support their Web servers or Web businesses while they simply use the results of the Web server's performance. Most server actions can be and are performed by outside maintenance sources, and many of these tasks are done remotely across the Internet. All you have to do is prepare the server for remote access by you or your assistant.

Sales Projects

By now, you've gotten the idea that Web servers are a massive advertising machine, if nothing else. This is how and why most sites realize significant gains in their products or are accepted by the public. Well, not completely, but with the explosive growth of the Internet, the Web holds the best promise for small companies to look just like large ones. This is perhaps one of the best benefits of the Web. On the Web, a two-employee company seems just as large as IBM or Compaq. If you can create and maintain an enticing Web page, then you're likely to have a lot of visitors because of that fact alone. Web surfers like to see what all of the hubbub is about, even if they're not buying. And window-shopping has led to a substantial amount of sales.

Your most important sales event or product can be advertised on your home page as a current event. In fact, most Web sites actively involved in these kinds of sales have a "Coming Events" section. You'll also find lots of "New and Improved" or "News Flash" sections. If you head off to Novell's home site at **www.novell.com**, you'll see a "What's New" item at the left center of Novell's home page, as shown in Figure 3.17.

Look for these kinds of updates to clue you into the latest and greatest. Software vendors like Netscape often change their home page daily to keep up with the changing times. Be prepared to do the same for your customers if you expect them to get the most out of the Web server.

Beta Test Projects

This is one part of the Web that is so underused it's not even funny. If you've ever been involved with the beta testing of new or improved products, you undoubtedly know that CompuServe has many forums for these vendors to host private testing forums for their products. Although this technique is still popular, many vendors have moved to private BBSs to do some of their testing. Few, if any, that I know of use the Web for such activities, although Microsoft

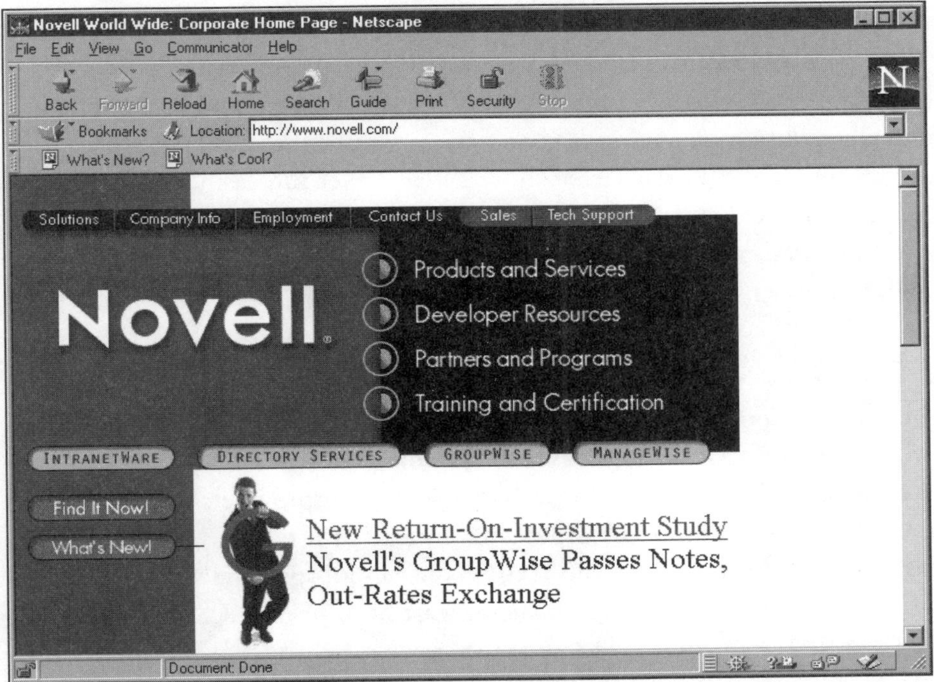

Figure 3.17
Novell's home page.

Windows NT Server is fully capable of supporting private ownership and private operations.

So, how would one set up a Web server as a beta test site? Well, for one thing, design it to support as many users as you see posting bug reports, downloading file updates, and generally accessing the Web server at the same time. I was once refused admittance to a beta forum on CompuServe in which the maximum number of users was 250, so I was at least number 251 trying to get online.

To support that many concurrent users on a Web server, you'd have to have at least a T1 link, a dual Pentium 166MHz server, and about 256MB of RAM. This would be a massive server with a price tag to match, about $25,000. Who would such a server benefit? Actually, the business producing product ABC that manipulates the widgets discussed earlier needs to have some software debugged and prepared for the masses. A beta test Web server is perfect for this situation and should be explored.

Here's how it would work: You use Web pages to let users know of updates, an FTP server to download updates or post bug reports, a list server to carry on conversations about the beta project, an email server to send comments in or generally talk to others in private, and private home directories to store miscellaneous software. So, you can see how a Web server can easily double as a beta test site, just like CompuServe forums do. Next, let's review the possibilities of using this very same configured server not as a beta test site but as an Internet Service Provider.

Internet Service Providers

The Internet Service Provider (ISP) business is booming all across the country, and it's expanding in Europe, as well. Let me give you a brief tour of what it takes to be an ISP. I've been actively working with providers in my local area and have done vast amounts of research into what it takes to provide Internet services. Do you remember the Web server we built in Chapter 2? Well, take that Web server and make sure it has at least 8GB of disk space and is configured as a RAID 5 system. Also, start the server off with 64MB of memory and be prepared to boost it up to 128MB if necessary.

To provide decent access to the Internet, you'll need to use a T1 line, which costs $7,000 to install and about $3,200 a month in access fees for a full-time dedicated connection, depending on your physical location in your country and your communications provider. So to become an ISP, you're already looking at an initial investment of about $15,000 for hardware, software, and communications, with recurring costs of $3,200 a month for the link. Let's not forget modems for the T1 link. Decent 28.8Kbps modems can be had for about $200 (less for external modems), and you'll need a pile of them. If your site grows much beyond 50 modems, then having a rack-mounted modem bank is a much neater solution.

How many is a pile? Well, to recoup just the monthly line charges of $3,200, and this doesn't count the administration costs of the site, you'll have to have 128 paying customers at $25 a month. In these days of Internet providers on every corner, most ISPs are charging between $20 and $35 a month for unlimited access. Another popular pricing scheme charges $19.95 for 20 hours a month and $1.25 for each additional hour.

ISPs often make money back by selling Web page services, as we discussed earlier, but that takes disk space and possibly the addition of another worker at the site. You can also sponsor special events in your hometown using your Web server, so there's use for an ISP. Even if you have people that don't use Windows 95 or Windows NT Workstation, some of them surely use Windows 3.1 and can get the Windows for Workgroups add-in. Native Windows operating systems connect to NT Server very easily and reduce connectivity problems significantly. If these users don't have any of the Windows-based software, then using a TCP/IP protocol software, such as Trumpet Winsock, is a superb solution. Because Microsoft Windows NT Server uses a point-to-point protocol (PPP) schema to make remote connections, then Trumpet and other packages such as Netmanage's Chameleon TCP/IP software works well. As you can see, there are alternatives out there to solve the connectivity needs of the most finicky user.

The one issue that escapes some ISPs is that new Internet users have no software at all to start out! If they join up, how are you going to get them connected to your server? When you sign on new users, mail them an installation kit, and then assist them over the phone to get connected. One 3 1/2-inch floppy, one package of shareware, and you've got another happy Internet user. Once connected to the Internet, they can get as much software as they want or that you can store on your own Web server.

Training And The Web Server

For this section, let's talk about your Webmaster. What are the qualifications of this person? How will she respond to a crisis? How well will she handle the pressure of dozens of users calling to find out why they're not able to connect? If you think this is a joke or could never happen to you, then you're in for quite a shock! Quite a shock indeed, and a heck of a rude awakening.

I suggest that you have someone with a significant level of expertise with the Internet and Microsoft Windows NT Server perform a peer evaluation of the proposed Webmaster. You should also consider sending your Webmaster to a Microsoft Certified Training Center to provide advanced training with the Microsoft Windows NT Server and networking in general. Add to this a generous sprinkling of systems administration knowledge, and you've got one competent Webmaster.

Advertising On The Web

As your Web site expands, you may want to take it public and earn more, as I mentioned earlier in this chapter. Advertising is the most obvious and most lucrative approach, but how do you get up to speed? In this section, we'll explore advertising and identify how your business can leverage various functions of a Web server to make money and provide a competitive advantage.

Running A List Server

List servers perform automated mailing and messaging functions, and are nothing more than an automated BBS in which a message you post gets automatically sent back to a defined number of users. Let's take a look at a listserv we'll call *ABC.* This listserv has members one through five. If user one posts a new message to the listserv, then member two can reply to it. However, the reply not only goes to member one, who created the message, but also to members three through five. In the meantime, member four also replies to member one. Member four's reply gets sent to all list users, as well. As you can see, this is a great way to disseminate information but can result in massive amounts of data being transmitted across the server. Remember the suggestion I had for a rather large hard drive for the server? Thought I was joking, eh?

Later in this book, we'll examine the list server in depth. We'll be use NTList from SoftDisk Corporation as our Microsoft Windows NT Server list server. NTList is included on the accompanying CD-ROM. It's fully functional, but you have to apply for a key to use the product at **www.ntsoftdisk.com**. Having said that, I'd like to let you preview the steps that will be necessary to form a list server:

1. Install the list server software.
2. Define new lists.
3. Add users to the list.
4. Specify distribution.
5. Monitor disk space and performance.

Not much to it, but there are a few things to watch for, and disk space is one. If you're planning on running many lists, then running them on a separate physical or logical disk from the FTP, Web, and operating systems is a good idea. Periodic purging of old list members and message traffic is also a good idea.

Another excellent use for a listserv, and this is one that is used all the time, is for users to subscribe to a list and receive messages for updated products, materials, services, and notices of problems. I subscribe to several in which I receive the Microsoft Windows NT Server BackOffice mail for happenings and updates to BackOffice. I also receive updates from several book publishers, so I know when new books hit the marketplace. The NTList product I used for this book sends me update notices, bug fixes, and enhancement notices.

Business Resources

Every business—including your Web site—needs to have backing of one type or another. When I was looking for support for my business in some expansion projects, AT&T Capital Services (**www.att.com**) was one that I turned to for help. There's similar support available all across the Web in the form of research shops, search engines like Lycos and Yahoo!, but also the Microsoft Knowledge Base articles. The next section will talk about Gopher and how that can help you, but for now, let's keep the discussion to what you can do for your customers.

An exciting prospect of customer support is self-help, in which customers use your resources to help themselves. If the problem is something a customer can't resolve, then you come to the rescue—and that means money in your pocket. One way to help your customers help themselves is to use a networked CD-ROM tower. This device allows seven drives to function as a single entity by using software that maps all the drives to one drive letter. You could then purchase a network license for products such as Microsoft's TechNet technical solutions resource and put it on the network for your customers.

While you may think that paying $2,000 for a networked CD and another $5,000 for the CD-ROM tower is a bit pricey, consider the alternatives. Last summer, one of my clients' servers crashed and died a horrible death. Upon finding that the problem was a bad hard drive controller, they were fully capable of replacing it and bringing the server back online knowing that they'd have to update the NOS drivers for the new controller. However, restarting the server yielded numerous system crashes that were unresolvable and seemingly pointed to another, more serious problem.

In reality, the problem was that the new controller's native operating mode was to support drives faster than those that existed in the server at that time. So, he was hung out to dry, right? Wrong. Using one of these CDs for technical support, he found the solution was to jumper the new controller to operate at a mode of data transfer that was compatible with the existing drives. But isn't that what the manuals are for, you ask? Well, the manuals for the controller cover installing the controller and installing the NOS drivers, and that's about it. A few minor troubleshooting tips and hints, but nothing of the magnitude he saw. What about tech support? Tech support can be wonderful, but consider this: Your drive crashes at 2 A.M. on a Saturday morning of a three-day weekend. A critical business decision has to be made bright and early Tuesday morning, and you can't get through. Somebody's toes are in the wringer over this one if it doesn't get fixed.

This situation really happened to a very good customer, and now he is an even better customer! Why? We had a CD-ROM of technical support handy on our server; he dialed into our 1-800 link and found the solution. It was a single-user version of the network edition, but it did the job nicely, thank you. Oh, and Murphy truly rules the roost in the computer room after midnight. 'Nuff said.

Using Gopher

If you've ever used the Web as a single user rambling through the Internet, then you've probably used a Gopher server to help you find information. Gopher got its name from the mascot of the University of Minnesota, where the gopher is a native animal of the area and the Gopher server started. Gophers make their way around by burrowing through the small areas to find virtually anything! The Internet Web server packages we'll use in future chapters will exploit Gopher servers in much the same way. Unless you're using the Microsoft Internet Information Server, which has a gopher server built right into the software package, you'll have to purchase a gopher server. One excellent place to find NT products is at the Beverly Hills Web site, shown in Figure 3.18 and located at **www.bhs.com**.

This site is dedicated to serving the needs of the Microsoft Windows NT Server community, and it is one of my top picks for products and general information about Microsoft Windows NT Server. They perform some really serious checks across the Web for new and exciting products, and they also sponsor many topics, such as finding NT support, services, and NT user groups.

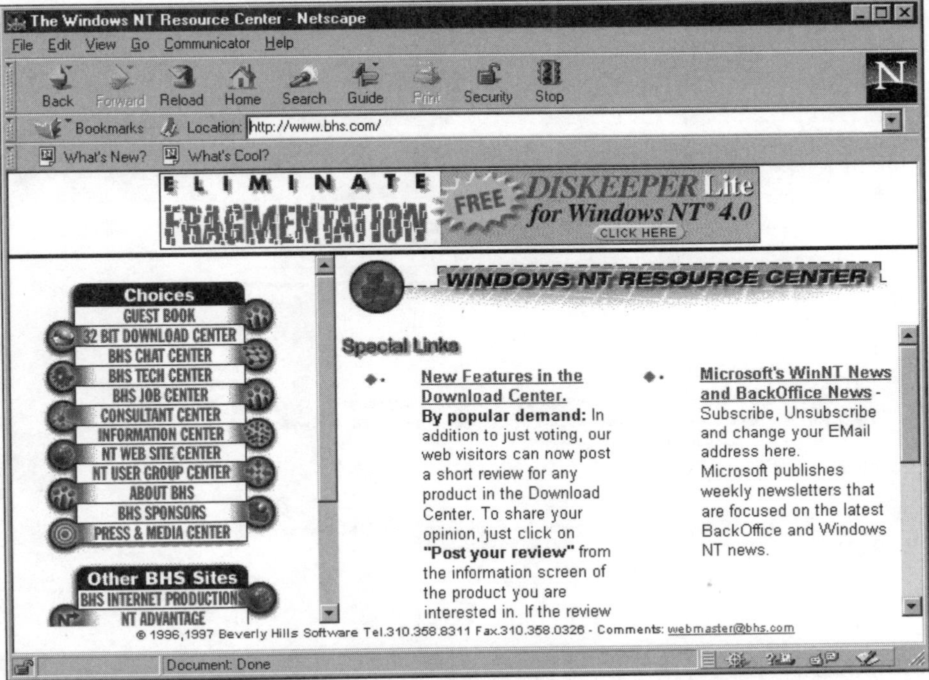

Figure 3.18
Beverly Hills Software.

Internet Shopping Malls For Advertising

Shopping on the Web for the general public has grown significantly over the last two years. It has become such a lucrative business that many Web sites have included links to stores offering related items or just fun stuff, as a courtesy to their clientele. Sometimes, you can find good deals on a vacation plan or cruise, and other times, you'll run across a Web site like the one shown in Figure 3.19.

The PC Cyber Shop (**http://web2.pc-today.com/browse.html**) is chock-full of computer deals. When you've browsed the Web as long as most of us have, you eventually compile a Web link base of dozens of juicy places to go and find things, do things, or just keep you informed. There's so much out there that many larger companies, and some small ones, too, devote one person a day to cruising the Web locating sites with similar content to their site (a real dream job). Adding these links to your Web server for your customer base is a good business move and excellent advertising on the Web.

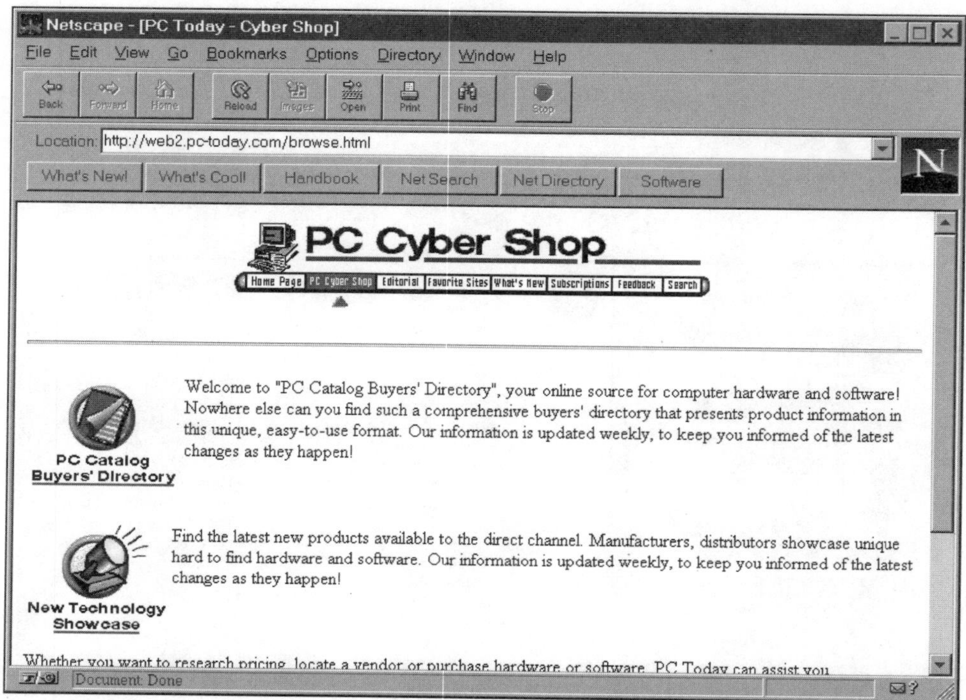

Figure 3.19
Internet shopping.

Think about the prospect of having a link on your Web page that has a button icon right next to it telling the reader about a new tool your business now has ready or a really sweet deal for new clients. All they have to do is click on the button one inch from the links, and voila! Instant advertising for you on their way to other sites on the Web.

Etiquette On The Web

One of the last things I want to discuss about advertising is when and where to do it, and when and where not to do it. You see, there's an unspoken set of rules by which you must abide if you wish to prosper on the Web. If you send email or advertising to an unwanted party or parties, then count on getting some unruly responses, called *flames*, about your requests and/or your heritage. People pay for email accounts and other useful items on the Web, and to receive someone's unwanted literature about products and paraphernalia is a sure bet to get you smacked.

If you receive a large volume of flames regarding an unsolicited message, your server may slow down tremendously. This happened recently at an East Coast company that violated the unwritten rule of the Web, and these folks got slammed with enough email that their ISP crashed their twin Web servers. Needless to say, this company got kicked off the ISP as soon as it found out what happened.

The moral to the story of advertising is that if you want to pitch your goods and services, do it on your own server, so people come to you. Don't send unsolicited email to anyone if you don't want to have their unhappy responses swamping your server. If you want to advertise outside of your server's realm, go to one of the many shopping malls that exist all across the Web, and buy office space on their servers. If you don't know where to look, go to **http://guide-p.infoseek.com/Titles?qt=shopping+mall** and look at the list that comes up. Figure 3.20 shows the search results.

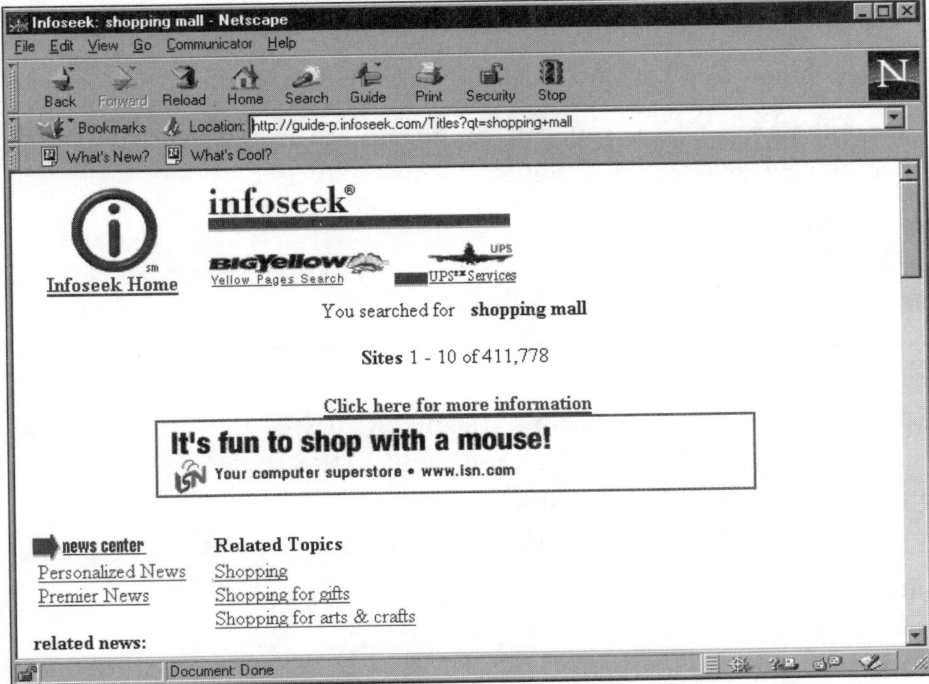

Figure 3.20
Infoseek searching the Web.

News Services

Running a news service is much like operating a business. You've got customers with different needs, different expectations of what news is, and how to use it to their benefit. When you consider adding a news service to your offerings, you need to determine the volume of news so that you can decide whether to use a completely different physical server or just install the software on the same server as the Web server itself. If you don't have a news service from your ISP, you might be interested in trying one of these free services:

- **news.sisna.com**
- **mediasoft.net**
- **ulke.himolde.no**
- **news.cis.nctu.edu.tw**
- **ccnews.ke.sanet.sk**
- **news.ak.net**

If one of these won't work, you may have to resort to using a paid service to feed you a full news system. Try one of the following services:

a2i communications
1211 Park Avenue #202
San Jose, CA 95126
Data: (408) 293-9010 (v.32bis, v.32), (408) 293-9020 (PEP)
(log in as "guest")
Telnet: a2i.rahul.net [192.160.13.1] (log in as "guest")
FTP: ftp.rahul.net [192.160.13.1], get /pub/BLURB
Email: info@rahul.net (a daemon will auto-reply)
(UUCP, news feeds, mail feeds, MX forwarding, name service)

Anterior Technology
P.O. Box 1206
Menlo Park, CA 94026-1206
Voice: (415) 328-5615
Fax: (415) 322-1753
Email: info@fernwood.mpk.ca.us
(UUCP, connectivity, name service, MX forwarding, news feeds)

CERFnet
P.O. Box 85608
San Diego, CA 92186-9784
Voice: (800) 876-CERF
Email: help@cerf.net
(connectivity, name service, MX forwarding, news feeds)

Colorado SuperNet, Inc.
Attn: David C. Menges
Colorado School of Mines
1500 Illinois
Golden, CO 80401
Voice: (303) 273-3471
Email: dcm@csn.org
(UUCP, news feeds)

connect.com.au (Australia)
Attn: Hugh Irvine (hugh@connect.com.au)
Ben Golding (bgg@connect.com.au)
Voice: 61 3 528 2239
(UUCP, connectivity, name service, MX forwarding, news feed, PPP, SLIP)

Demon Internet Systems
Email: internet@demon.co.uk
(Internet access, SLIP, PPP, name service)

DPC Systems
537 Cloverleaf Drive
Monrovia, CA 91016 (Los Angeles County)
Voice: (818) 305-5733
Fax: (818) 305-5735
Data: (818) 305-8444
Email: connect@dpcsys.com
(UUCP, name service, MX forwarding, news feeds)

ExNet Systems Ltd
37 Honley Road
Catford
London, SE6 2HY, UK

Voice: 44 81 244 0077
Fax: 44 81 244 0078
Email: exnet@exnet.com or exnet@exnet.co.uk
(UUCP, mail and news feeds)

Gordian
20361 Irvine Avenue
Santa Ana Heights, CA 92707 (Orange County)
Voice: (714) 850-0205
Fax: (714) 850-0533
Email: uucp-request@gordian.com
(UUCP, name service, MX forwarding, news feeds (for SoCal sites only))

Hatch Communications
8635 Falmouth Avenue, Suite 105
Playa del Rey, CA 90293
Voice: (310) 305-8758
Email: info@hatch.socal.com
(UUCP Usenet news and email, SLIP connections for FTP and Telnet)

HoloNet
Information Access Technologies, Inc.
46 Shattuck Square, Suite 11
Berkeley, CA 94704-1152
Voice: (510) 704-0160
Fax: (510) 704-8019
Modem: (510) 704-1058
Telnet: holonet.net
Email: info@holonet.net (automated reply)
Support: support@holonet.net
(UUCP/Usenet feeds, local to 850+ cities nationwide)

infocom
Public Access Unix
White Bridge House
Old Bath Road
Charvil, Berkshire
United Kingdom
RG10 9QJ

Voice: 44 [0] 734 344000
Fax: 44 [0] 734 320988
Data: 44 [0] 734 340055 (you can register online interactively)
Email: info@infocom.co.uk (send a message with ALL in the subject)
(UUCP, Usenet Feeds and Internet Email to Unix, DOS, ATARI, AMIGA, MAC)

Internet Initiative Japan, Inc.
Hoshigaoka Bldg.
2-11-2, Nagata-Cho
Chiyoda-ku, Tokyo 100 Japan
Voice: 81 3 3580 3781
Fax: 81 3 3580 3782
Email: info@iij.ad.jp
(UUCP, news feeds, mail feeds, MX forwarding, name service, anonymous FTP and UUCP services, domain registration)

Iowa Network Services
312 8th Street, Suite 730
Des Moines, IA 50309
Voice: (800) 546-6587
Fax: (515) 830-0345
FTP: ftp.netins.net
WWW: http://www.netins.net/
Gopher: gopher.netins.net
Email: info@netins.net
(UUCP, news feeds, mail feeds, MX forwarding, name service, domain registration, SLIP)

JvNCnet
B6 von Neumann Hall
Princeton University
Princeton, NJ 08543
Voice: (800) 35-TIGER
Email: market@jvnc.net
(connectivity, name service, MX forwarding, news feeds)

MSEN, Inc.
628 Brooks Street
Ann Arbor, MI 48103

Voice: (313) 998-4562
FTP: ftp.msen.com [148.59.1.2], see /pub/vendor/msen/*
Email: info@msen.com
(UUCP, connectivity, name service, MX forwarding, news feeds)

MV Communications, Inc.
P.O. Box 4963
Manchester, NH 03108-4963
Voice: (603) 429-2223
Data: (603) 429-1735 (log in as "info" or "rates")
Email: info@mv.mv.com
(UUCP, name service, MX forwarding, news feeds)

NEARnet (New England Academic and Research Network)
10 Moulton Street
Cambridge, MA 02138
Voice: (617) 873-8730
Fax: (617) 873-5620
Email: nearnet-join@nic.near.net
(connectivity, name service, MX forwarding, news feeds (for NEARnet sites))

Netcom—Online Communication Services
4000 Moorpark Avenue, Suite 209
San Jose, CA 95117
Voice: (408) 554-UNIX
Data: (408) 241-9760 (login "guest," no password)
Telnet: netcom.netcom.com [192.100.81.100] (login "guest")
Email: info@netcom.com
(UUCP, connectivity, name service, MX forwarding, news feeds, other services)

NET GmbH—Network Expert Team
Figarostr. 3
70597 Stuttgart, Germany
Voice: 49 711 97689-21
Data: 49 711 97689-22 (login "guest," no password)
Fax: 49 711 97689-33
Email: info@N-E-T.de

(Internet access, SLIP/PPP, ISDN, UUCP, connectivity, name service, MX forwarding, news feeds, mail feeds, domain registration, other services)

Northwest Nexus Inc.
P.O. Box 40597
Bellevue, WA 98015-4597
Voice: (206) 455-3505
Data: (206) 382-6245 (log in as "new")
Fax: (206) 455-4672
Email: info@nwnexus.wa.com
(Internet access, SLIP/PPP (dialup, dedicated, 56K, FT-1), UUCP, news feeds, mail feeds, MX forwarding, name service, NIC registration, Nutshell books)

The PC User Group
P.O. Box 360
Harrow
London
Voice: 44 81 863 1191
Fax: 44 81 963 6095
Email: hostmaster@ibmpcug.co.uk or hostmaster@ibmpcug.uucp
(UUCP, mail and news feeds)

Performance Systems International, Inc.
11800 Sunrise Valley Drive, Suite 1100
Reston, VA 22091
Voice: (703) 620-6651 or (800) 827-7482
Computerized info: all-info@psi.com
Human-based info: info@psi.com
(UUCP, connectivity, name service, MX forwarding, news feeds)

Portal Communications Company
20863 Stevens Creek Boulevard, Suite 200
Cupertino, CA 95014
Voice: (408) 973-9111
Fax: (408) 725-1580
Data: (408) 973-8091 (V.32/PEP) Call for local node near you. Nodes provided by Sprintnet or Tymnet have additional charges.

Telnet: portal.com
Email: CS@portal.com
(UUCP, news feeds, mail feeds, MX forwarding, mailing lists, file archives, domain registration, FTP, SLIP/PPP, commercial menu-based online service, shell, Telnet, irc, Gopher, interface software available for Amiga, PC, and Sun)

SURAnet
8400 Baltimore Boulevard
College Park, MD 20742
Voice: (301) 982-3214
Fax: (301) 982-4605
Email: news-admin@sura.net
(connectivity, name service (for SURAnet sites), news feeds (for SURAnet sites))

TDK Consulting Services
119 University Ave. East
Waterloo, Ontario
Canada N2J 2W9
Voice: (519) 888-0766
Fax: (519) 747-0881
Email: info@tdkcs.waterloo.on.ca
(UUCP, news/mail feeds)

Telerama
Luce McQuillin Corporation
P.O. Box 60024
Pittsburgh, PA 15211
Voice: (412) 481-3505
Fax: (412) 481-8568
28.8 K: (412) 481-2392
Email: info@telerama.lm.com
(UUCP))

UUNET Canada, Inc.
1 Yonge St., Suite 1400
Toronto, Ontario

Canada M5E 1J9
Voice: (416) 368-6621
Fax: (416) 369-0515
Email: info@uunet.ca or uunet-ca@uunet.uu.net
(UUCP, connectivity, name service, MX forwarding, news feeds)

UUNET Technologies Inc.
3110 Fairview Park Drive, Suite 570
Falls Church, VA 22042
Voice: (703) 204-8000
Fax: (703) 204-8001
Email: info@uunet.uu.net
AlterNet (network connectivity) info: alternet-info@uunet.uu.net
(UUCP, connectivity, name service, MX forwarding, news feeds)

UUNORTH, Inc.
Box 445, Station E
Toronto, Ontario
Canada M6H 4E3
Voice: (416) 537-4930 or (416) 225-UNIX
Fax: (416) 537-4890

Xenon Systems
Attn: Julian Macassey
742 1/2 North Hayworth Avenue
Hollywood, CA 90046-7142
Voice: (213) 654-4495
Email: postmaster@bongo.tele.com
(UUCP, news feeds, mail feeds)

XMission
P.O. Box 510063
Salt Lake City, UT 84151-0063
Data: (801) 539-0900 (log in as "guest")
Telnet: xmission.com [198.60.22.2] (log in as "guest")
FTP: xmission.com [198.60.22.2], get/pricing
Email: support@xmission.com
(UUCP, news feeds, mail feeds, MX forwarding, name service, SLIP/PPP)

XS4ALL
Postbus 22864
1100 DJ Amsterdam, Holland
Voice: 31 20 6200294
Data: 31 20 6222174 (V.34 28k8)
31 20 6265060 (ZyXEL 19k2)
Fax: 31 20 6222753
Email: account@xs4all.nl
(Internet access, SLIP/PPP, ISDN, UUCP, name service, MX forwarding, news feeds, WWW home pages)

News Servers

News servers operate on many different protocols, but the most commonly used is called *NNTP*, or *Network News Transport Protocol.* The predominant news server, however, is ruled by Unix machines using the *UUCP*, or *Unix-to-Unix Copy Protocol.* These servers run under one of two operating modes: SUCK feed, which means that your news server receives only the news that you ask for, and forced-feed systems, which means you get the entire newsgroup system. This latter method means that, at any one time, you could be receiving as much as 4GB of news articles and updates daily.

And, at that kind of volume, a lowly ISDN or FT1 link is next to useless. For that reason, most ISPs generally use an established news server or tag onto another server for the feed. This approach usually incurs some charges for your site, but it's worth it in the long run if you're shorthanded in the maintenance and support department. The following information was extracted from the Usenet news FAQ, which is stored in its entirety on the CD-ROM included with this book as file newsfaq.txt.

If you just want to read Usenet yourself, then putting your machine onto Usenet is probably not what you want to do. The process of doing so can be time-consuming, and regular maintenance is also required. Furthermore, the resources consumed by a full Usenet setup on a machine are significant. You need to consider the following:

- *Disk space for the programs*—A few MB for the binaries, another couple of MB for any sources you keep online.

- *Disk space for the articles*—Currently (as of August, 1995) around 450MB a day, although it's possible to minimize the amount of disk space consumed by articles by carefully selecting which newsgroups and/or hierarchies you wish to receive.
- *Communications bandwidth*—For practicality, you should have either a 14.4Kbps/28.8Kbps modem link or 56Kbps or faster NNTP link. It's no longer possible to run a full feed over 28.8Kbps modems or 56Kbps TCP/IP NNTP links.
- *Fees*—If you're paying someone to provide you with a news feed.

A serious Usenet server system, carrying all of the standard eight Usenet hierarchies, a large hunk of alt.*, and various regionals is typically going to need a Sparc 2 or better, with 32MB or more of RAM, and at least 3GB of disk space. One particularly good high-end, but inexpensive, configuration is INN 1.4unoff2 on an HP 9000/712 system, with 96MB of RAM and 5GB of disk space.

A home system can usually fit into a much smaller machine, such as a Sun 3 or 386-class PC compatible, plus 25MB to 50MB of disk for news. Until recently, one supporter's home machine was an AT&T 3b1 (about the performance of an IBM PC/AT) with 60MB of disk. The setup worked just fine for a small news feed and a fair amount of email.

If you plan on running a Microsoft Windows NT Server as a news feed, plan on running equivalent news servers.

If you decide to create your own news server, pay close attention to Chapters 5 through 8, where we'll install, configure, and test run four Web servers. At the same time, we'll integrate a news server in those environments so you can see how it's done.

Newsgroups

News services are structured according to the intended topics. There were nearly 20,000 newsgroups the last time I checked, and more are being created weekly. However, fewer than a dozen core newsgroups form the classifications of the rest of the entire news service. Here's a rundown on the major groups:

- *alt*—Alternative news, which involves everything from cooking to submarine screen door maintenance.
- *comp*—Anything related to computers.
- *biz*—Business matters.
- *rec*—Recreational issues.
- *news*—Learn about newsgroups.

The CD-ROM included with this book contains a file called newsgrps.txt, which lists all the current newsgroups. From this reference, you can search—offline—for any prospective newsgroups you may want to join.

Naughty News

Ah, yes. The wild and wooly Internet offers many things to many people, including some of the not-so-charming aspects of the Web. Your business should tag the marketplace you intend to use to please your customers and steer clear of the less-than-desirable remaining groups. You can subscribe your server to the most applicable groups and filter out the undesirables in much the same way a client does.

After you've used enough newsgroups to last you a lifetime, you'll realize that the existing newsgroups are about as complicated and useless to some people as screen doors on a submarine. At this point, Webmasters often decide to create a newsgroup to solve a particular need instead of finding groups that only partially meet the needs of their customers.

A word of warning is worthwhile. The Congress of the United States is working on legislation that would have ISPs regulated for content in an effort to stem the tide of smut on the Net. While this really smacks in the face of legislating morality, is it really? Is it a burden on the standards of free speech? If ISPs don't start doing something about the content on the Internet on a world-wide basis, we all may find ourselves in a position of facing such legislation on a global basis. The best thing ISPs can do (in the gospel according to Jeff) is to begin policing ourselves for a better Internet before someone does it for us.

End of speech.

Front-End Tools To Access Your Business's Data

I want to give you a preview of how your business can leverage the Web with many different methods. This last section goes over some of the ways that HTML, CGI, and scripting can manipulate data and return favorable and useful results to your users.

HTML

Hypertext is a neat way to create and build Web pages along with handling the usual support issues. I pointed out earlier that HTML is nothing more than a textual markup language that is interpreted by Web server software and executes certain commands. It has a defined set of commands, just like what is considered to be regular programming languages such as C or C++. Unlike those compiled languages, though, HTML has to be parsed into distinct commands. If these commands are not readable, then it fails. There are dozens of HTML authoring tools available to you, many of them are free, and just as many of them are quite expensive.

When we install the Web servers and create basic Web server home pages, we'll be using HTML Assistant Professional v2. We'll create dual HTML versions of Web pages because not everyone uses a Web browser client that works with HTML v3.2.

CGI And Visual Basic

Users interface with HTML to enter data presented in a form made easy for the user to understand. Once data is entered, it's ushered back to software running on the Microsoft Windows NT Server. The software packages that process the data are called *backend servers*, and include packages such as Microsoft SQL Server, Oracle, and Sybase. These backend servers cannot interpret HTML, so a middle processing system is required. Enter the Common Gateway Interface, or CGI. CGI comes to the rescue along with some programming language to tie these two—CGI and the backend—together. Because these CGI functions are likely to change weekly, it's nice to use an easy and effective programming language. We'll be using Microsoft's Visual Basic for this task, and the source code is supplied on the CD-ROM for your altering pleasure.

Scripting

Scripts are another form of utilizing data entered into an HTML form. In this case, the data is used to automate sets of actions to get a desired result. For example, you can use scripts to register a user onto a list or a product listing database. Scripts are basically a kind of batch file for the Web.

Summary

In this chapter, we've learned about many things dealing with business on the Web. There's so much to cover that you could easily write an entire book about business on the Web from a purely business perspective. The topics we covered included:

- Selling Web pages
- Offering FTP space on a server
- Giving Internet Service Provider-style services
- Learning about Web server requirements
- Learning how to entice your customers with new business arrangements on the Web
- Learning about advertising on the Web

I hope you found this information enlightening. There are a lot of business opportunities on the Web just waiting to be discovered. After completing this chapter, you should feel up to the challenge!

4 Practical Hardware Solutions

Jeff Bankston

Chapter 4 is our first big step into actually building our Web server. The previous three chapters provide an excellent introduction into the hows, whys, and wherefores of business Web servers. Now, it's time to explore the inner workings of your Web server. We'll begin our exploration by examining the hardware designs of different servers. I'll present three options for server configurations, providing information on specific vendors' types of systems and designs that will help you keep that pestering CFO happy for a time. More specifically, we'll cover the following:

- Styles of Web servers you can build
- Memory requirements for the server as a whole
- RAID subsystems
- Internet connectivity options
- Web server applications and disk usage
- Server backup operations

- Ways to avoid the temperature demon
- Power-protection devices

When you finish with this chapter, you'll be armed to the teeth with genuine practical data to make the installation of the Web server software a cinch. All of this information comes from years of experience, research, hours of lost sleep, and months of reading in my technical library. It thrills me to no end to be able to bring this to you, so let's proceed! If you want to shake up your current distributor, take a look at the Web page at **www.pc-today.com/browse.html**, and check out the vast array of computer components advertised there.

Selecting And Setting Up Your NT Server Hardware

In this section, I will specifically address the core issues behind, or rather within, a Web server—that is, the hardware ideally geared to the Web server. As I mentioned before, I won't be covering the installation of a Microsoft Windows NT Server; I assume that you already fully understand that process. My goal is to illuminate the reasons why a normal network server may or may not serve your purposes as a Web server, depending on the volume of traffic you'll have and what you can expect to invest to ensure you're building a productive Web server. The next three sections profile the minimum, average, and optimum physical server hardware needed to perform as a prototype, low-volume usage, and a very serious Web server, respectively. Each section is broken down further for consideration of the processor, memory, disk systems, and other I/O devices, such as serial ports.

Minimum Server Hardware

I consider this server setup to be a testbed environment to get your server baselined. If nothing else, you can use this model to get your thoughts together and decide upon a course of action without getting into too many money, time, and configuration issues. For this discussion, I'm using a standard desktop PC (by the end of 1996 standards). This server model is likewise suitable for low-volume user groups of fewer than 50 users.

Processor

As processors go, the 90MHz processor is largely considered to be the minimum to use. As for vendor, I use Intel, but I've also used AMD successfully. Other specialists have reported using Cyrix and others with no problems. The 90MHz processor is capable of performing at the rate of 3.7 MIPs, or millions of instructions per second. At one time, this was considered to be a real barnburner of a CPU, but it has since been overshadowed by stronger performers.

The other aspect of Pentium processors is the use of the internal 8K cache located inside the processor. A *cache* is a temporary holding area for data while the CPU processes the data. You can think of a cache as a small hand-held shopping bag—like one of those little hand-carried plastic baskets you use when you only need to pick up a few items. This is where you keep your goodies before you get to the checkout stand. If you think you've forgotten something, you simply refer to the carrier to see if it's there. If not, you go back to the aisle and get one of whatever you need.

A cache is used in much the same way, as shown in Figure 4.1. The CPU retrieves data from the disk drive for its usage, but it also keeps a copy of the most recently ordered 4K worth of information in the cache. If the CPU needs more information to work on, it refers to the cache. If the cache has it, then the CPU gets it from there. If not, the CPU retrieves it from the disk in a second disk access. Because the cache is closer to the CPU electronically, and the cache is faster than the disk system, this process has a net effect of speeding up overall system operation to a degree. To further clarify, I'm talking about the *internal* or level 1 (L1) cache (within the physical processor itself), not the level 2 cache installed on the motherboard.

However, not all caching operations are good. As in much of life, too much of a good thing isn't always good for you...or your CPU. Just like parking lots, the larger a cache is, the more time it takes to find the desired information—or car, in the case of the parking lot. The CPU will then spend much of its time waddling around looking for information that may or may not be present. To put this into perspective, the cache system in these slower 90MHz CPUs runs at an average of 35 nanoseconds access time. This means that to get to the data inside the cache, it takes an average of 35 nanoseconds to set up the physical cache chips to be accessed plus 250 nanoseconds to set the rise time and circuit access

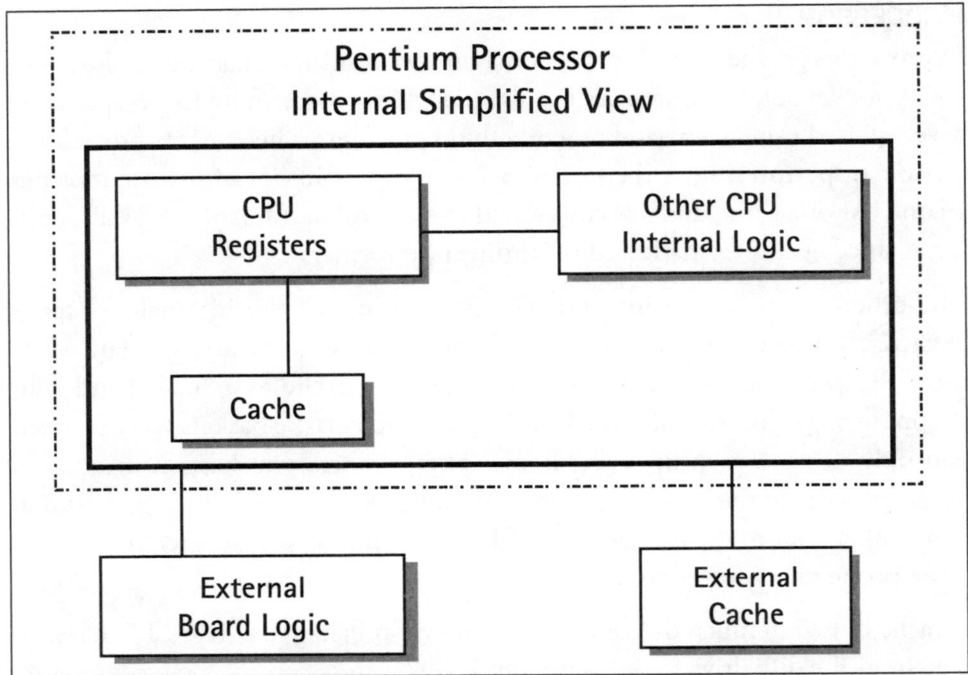

Figure 4.1
Pentium processor simplified internal diagram.

time. Additional overhead for the cache can amount to as much as 25 more nanoseconds. These figures are general times meant to keep the intricate details out of this discussion, but you get the idea. Now, we're up to 310 nanoseconds of processing time, or roughly one third of a microsecond.

So, what's a nanosecond? It's one thousandth of a millionth of a second, or one billionth of a second. That's humming right along as far as you and I are concerned, but it's relatively slow as far as the processor is concerned. The CPU itself can handle 3.7 million instructions per second. If you do a little quick math, then you'll see that if one cache operation were to support one CPU instruction, then only six cache access cycles would be available per CPU instruction cycle. This isn't a very hospitable working relationship between the two, so something has got to give. Normally, such a CPU/cache system would support in excess of a 20:1 ratio. When we get into our discussion on faster systems, I'll show you how this problematic situation is cured, resulting in much improved system throughput.

MEMORY

Our minimum server must start out with at least 32MB of memory, no matter how you configure it. Because of their initial configuration and the popularity of the 30-pin memory modules, these Pentium and earlier 486 processor systems have a widespread installation base. Unfortunately, the popularity of the 30-pin memory presents a unique problem for the industry. Most, if not all, of these 486 processors and earlier Pentiums are installed in motherboards that exclusively use these 30-pin memory modules and only use 8 memory slots. This means that the Microsoft Windows NT Server installation had better work on 32MB of memory, or you've got a problem. Memory is not upgradable in most of these systems unless you use one of the add-in 16-bit memory cards, such as the AST RAMPage. These are fine devices, but on the ISA bus, they're murder on performance. In many situations, these add-in memory cards exceed the cost of a motherboard upgrade.

The problem? On a normal installation of Microsoft Windows NT Server, up to 24MB of this main memory is in use to get the server off the ground. Use the RAS component, and another 4MB of RAM is in use. So, you can see from this that these minimum servers are good for prototyping and a few users, perhaps up to 10 concurrent users either from your network or dialing in remotely. One solution to this is to use some of the new memory conversion modules on the market. These conversion modules take 4 of the 30-pin modules and effectively make them a single 16MB module. Another approach is to purchase an adapter that uses the newer 72-pin memory and mates it to the 30-pin memory slot of the motherboard. The kicker is that the motherboard's memory controller has to have a legal memory configuration available to support this new memory capacity. A *legal memory configuration* is one where the memory module you install must match the motherboard's allowable usage.

On 486 and above systems, you must install 4 of these 30-pin modules at a time to have a proper installation. Because these are 32-bit computers, the memory must also match. The 30-pin modules are 8 data bits wide, so 4 of them must be used at a time. These four modules together are called a *bank* of memory. Table 4.1 illustrates part of the legal configuration of my 486 testbed's system. All amounts are in megabytes.

It's important to notice the placement of the memory modules to accommodate these values. There's no place for 24MBs of memory, nor can 4Mx9 modules

TABLE 4.1

AN EXAMPLE OF A LEGAL MEMORY CONFIGURATION.

Amount	Type	Bank 0	Bank 1
4	1Mx9	1Mx9	
8	1Mx9	1Mx9	1Mx9
16	4Mx9	4Mx9	
20	mixed	4Mx9	1Mx9
32	4Mx9	4Mx9	4Mx9

be placed in Bank 1 by themselves, as they can be in Bank 0. You must carefully consider these restrictions if you want to have a successful server. What do you do when it's time to increase memory? Blame the CFO for not funding a better server? Not likely. This table shows one reason why these systems are best relegated to test servers or desktop PCs for a user.

Disk Systems

Disk drives have evolved over the years into something that none of us ever thought was possible. Certainly, this is one of the most important parts of the server that exists, and it's also the most neglected. While it's nothing to swap out a disk drive or add in new storage, this isn't the case with Microsoft Windows NT Server when it comes to Web servers. Although this process was a cinch in Windows 3.1—all you had to do was complete a full backup across the drive, install the new drive, and restore the old software—NT's intricacies change the situation radically.

Many of the existing computers today still have 300 to 500MB hard drives installed, which is fine for desktop or prototype Web servers installing the bare minimum software. When you get into production servers, however, do yourself a favor, and stay away from drives with less than 1GB of space—even if it means using the 486DX we've talked about here with its 500MB drive and adding a second drive of 1GB, as shown in Figure 4.2. Such a scenario may exist for a 486DX2-66 that used to reside on a desktop running a 340MB IDE drive. As common as these are, very inexpensive drives of nearly 2GB capacity exist now for EIDE and SCSI. It's simply a matter of adding a second drive or perhaps a second controller, if you choose to go the SCSI route.

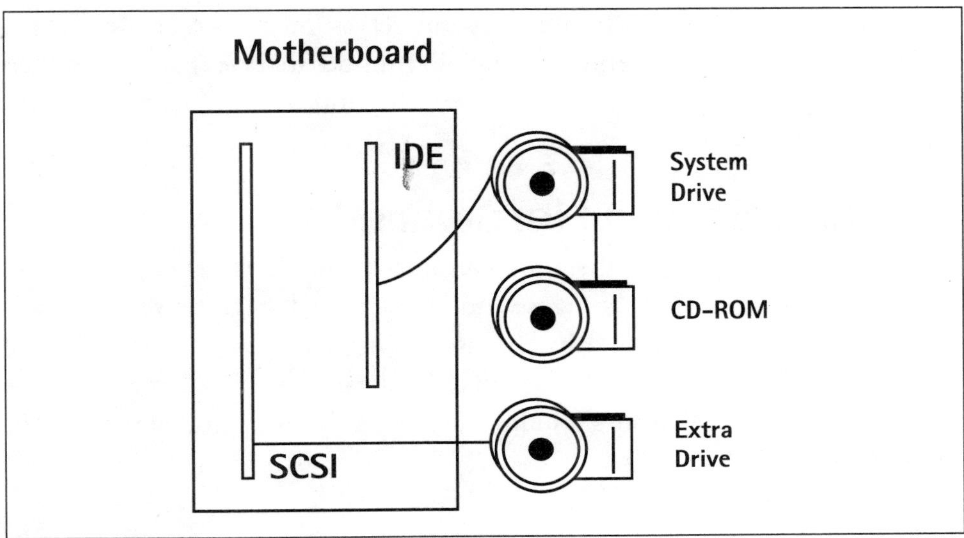

Figure 4.2
Simplified diagram of a disk subsystem.

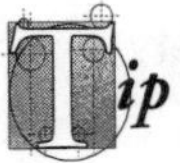

Give yourself the capacity required of even a bare Web server. As soon as you figure out what you'll be using the Web site for, you can then migrate the extra drive out of this minimum configured server into a more powerful one by removing the drive and controller as a pair, if the controller is usable in the new system.

I/O Devices

Always the topic of conversation but never remembered until after the fact, the I/O devices may or may not be important to your server. With this minimum server, you'll surely have the basics of I/O installed: two serial ports and one parallel port. A game port may or may not be installed; it's obviously not required, and it won't hurt anything by being there. This basic I/O card is necessary for the mouse to run on the serial port because most of these older systems used a serial mouse. The second serial port is useful as a modem port for an external modem, so you can remotely log in and take care of your assigned duties.

I'll get into specifics in the next section, but these older I/O cards do not have the capacity to sustain high-speed modem data transmissions. As such, they're relegated to the role of maintenance connections and general data usage. I wouldn't count on them at all for serious communications. One of the minimum devices used is a 14.4Kbps modem to proof test the server links to other sites. While 14.4Kbps seems aggravatingly slow for data, consider that this bare-bones Web server is being used to propagate ideas into reality and, as such, needs no serious money thrown at it.

Average Server Hardware

This is where we begin to bring our server into the modern day of computing. Not all the way, mind you, but close enough that you'll begin to see how Web server performance is affected by the use of better hardware to support the software. We'll also begin exploring some hardware not considered to be the normal usage in the Microsoft Windows NT Server world, but that will benefit us for the Web server.

Processor

The processor now graduates into something a bit more powerful. As I mentioned before, the absolute minimum processor from the previous section was a 66MHz 486DX model, but today the 486 goes all the way up to 120MHz speed demons. Sure, the Pentiums rule the roost around the PC these days, but does this mean the high-end 486s should be forgotten? Intel has killed off the 60, 66, and 75MHz Pentiums so far with rumors that the 90 and 100MHz processors aren't far behind, given the advances in processor design. As of March 1997, the 200MHz Pentium Pro is out on the streets and tearing up the competition with the high-end processors. The prices match, I assure you, but that's the price you pay for performance!

A Pentium 166 handles the system at about 8 times the horsepower of a 486DX4-100 because of its sheer speed and enhanced design. One of my customers uses a Pentium 90 single processor network server to handle 150+ users on a daily basis, running Unix on the server, and averaging a 60 percent server utilization. This leaves 40 percent of the processor's abilities available for those extra-demanding times.

To put it in another perspective, my testbed 486DX2-66 running 32MB of memory recently averaged 85 percent utilization when I was downloading files from one network station directly to the server, had a second machine downloading files via a modem and then moving the files across the network, and had a third user accessing the Web server doing his thing. Memory utilization was at 95 percent to match the processor's load factor. This means that a fourth user was likely to cause all sorts of problems if a demanding task was requested of the Web server. It all points to considering the Pentium 133 as the average Web server's processor of choice. Because Intel is killing off the 486 line and the earlier releases of Pentiums up to 100MHz, the Pentium 120 is likely to become the minimum processor available for your average Web server. This isn't necessarily a bad thing. The next section, about memory, ties into the processor to show how they complement one another.

Memory

This is where building a Web server gets interesting. To start things off on a good foot, you'll want to put at least 32MB of memory in this system, leaving room for growth. It doesn't matter what the makeup of the memory is at this time, but 32 is a good figure to start with and get you going. An average Web site means including FTP and Telnet capabilities and perhaps one Web server software package to support users browsing the Web. Don't include Microsoft Windows NT Server's remote access into this equation, as 32MB will just about be used up for this server. You can have as much FTP storage as you want, just watch the extra applications you may want to run.

Memory Types

I said that memory type and design influences the performance of a system, and now I'll explain how and why. The form itself—30-pin or 72-pin memory modules—doesn't matter. What does matter is the speed of the module now that you're getting into a more serious Web server. I'll explain briefly. The speed rating of the module is rated in nanoseconds and represents the average time required for the processor to retrieve the data in the module itself. If the processor has to do too much waiting to get data out of memory, then the processor waits for one clock cycle while the memory bus controller catches up.

It's a lot like sitting at a red light with three cars in front of you, and the first car in line has a very timid driver. This person won't press onward when the light turns green for fear of a last-minute driver buzzing the intersection, and the light is one of those 45-second wonders. You'll eventually get through, but it takes time. If the processor (you) has to wait for someone else to get going (the timid driver), the only recourse is to wait until this situation is resolved.

One way to resolve this is by using something called *page mode interleaving* of the memory system. This means that while one part of memory is waiting to have data placed into it, the other part of memory is being used by the processor. When the first part of memory gets its data, the other part will be done servicing the processor. Now, the processor switches to the second part of memory that was being filled while the first part was being used, and the processor doesn't miss a beat...usually. Figure 4.3 illustrates page mode interleaving. While this is a really simplistic view of memory management, this is the basic structure of how the processor uses memory for different tasks. The processor is perhaps 6 to 10 times faster than the memory subsystem, and page mode is one way to speed things up.

So, how do you know if your memory uses page mode? You don't. Check the motherboard's manual or the computer's manual if you were shipped a whole box complete, and see what kind and type of memory it takes. I say this because on some systems, in order to use page mode, you have to install two of whatever type of memory you choose to install. If it's 16MB modules, then two are required.

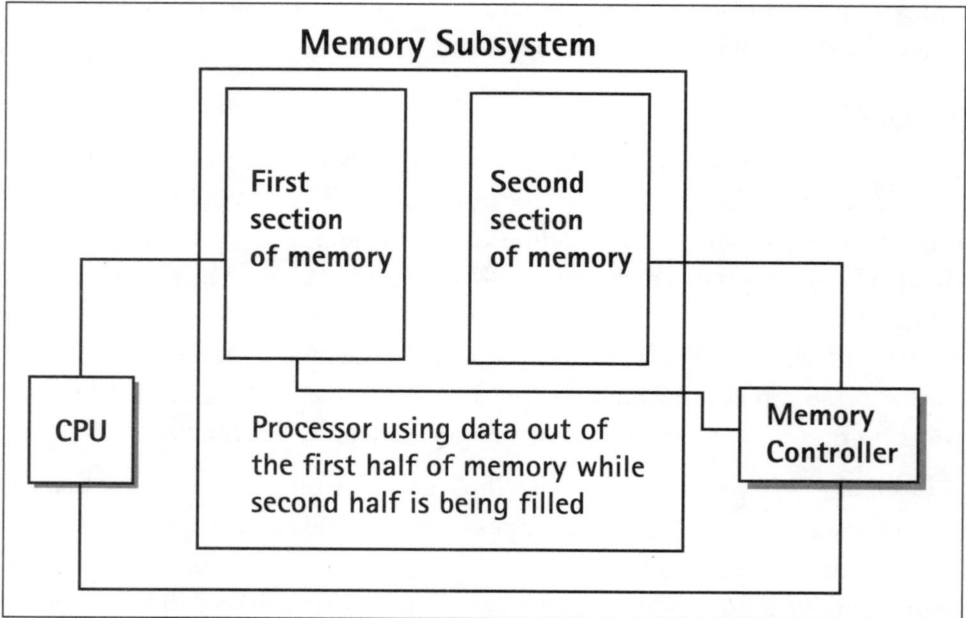

Figure 4.3
Memory subsystem.

Guess what? Back to the CFO for more money! That should go over like a lead brick in a balloon shop, but rest assured that most motherboards shipped today use this kind of memory architecture built into the motherboard itself. It's just something to be aware of.

The use of faster memory in a page mode interleaved motherboard can improve system performance by as much as 40 percent. If you can find them, use the 40-nanosecond variety for best performance. While more expensive, they're worth it in the long run.

Memory Architectures And Capacity

I already said that 32MB is the minimum acceptable for a mid-range Web server. This gets you running and operational. As you plot and plan this system, you'll find an increasing number of motherboards that accept a mix of the older 30-pin SIMMs and the newer 72-pin variety. Fear not, you can mix them and save the old investment. The caveat is threefold.

- If you mix the two types, be sure they're of the same rated speed.
- Be careful about the adapter board you buy for the 30-pin modules—cheap adapters result in dangerous performance and possible system crashes.
- Be sure the memory used on the adapter and the 72-pin modules are either both parity or non-parity. Neither can be of a mixed type.

Failure to observe these three caveats in one form or another has often resulted in the loss of data, many hours of operational time, and money trying to find the cause of the system crashes.

I'm not telling you not to use the older 30-pin modules, but be wise when you do. I said before that I don't often specify one vendor over others, but I will this time. The Minden Group makes an adapter for using 4 of the 30-pin SIMMs in one 72-pin socket, and this adapter has worked beautifully in my servers. The adapter is very simple to use, and I've found it at various computer stores for as little as $35 retail.

So, what's this parity business? You gurus hang tight for a minute. For you nonbelievers, here's the scoop. The old 30-pin modules are nearly all parity types. Parity means that the computer uses an extra data bit to form a type of error-correction code in case the data gets corrupted. Nearly all PCs use odd parity. If you looked at the ASCII representation of the letter *A*, its binary equivalent is 01000001, or a hexidecimal 41. If you look at the number of bits that are set, you'll see an even number of them, two to be specific. This letter has even parity, so the parity bit is 1, or said to be *set*.

Parity is used to correct for data loss, and it's common in the older systems, which are less reliable than current-day systems. Newer motherboards are no longer supporting parity memory because of the significantly increased reliability of all computer components. There's a more powerful form of error control called *ECC*, or *Error Correcting and Control*, in which the motherboard's memory controller can detect two-bit errors and correct one of them. ECC has been around for many years and is popular in minicomputers. The catch? 32MB of standard memory is about $250, whereas 32MB of ECC memory is typically 3 times that, if not more.

This means that if you use one of the adapters for 30-pin memory, make sure the adapter supports these parity memory modules (like the 30 pinners) in a parity or non-parity motherboard. My most recent motherboard purchases were non-parity boards, and they're working wonderfully in my Web servers. I'm also using the Minden adapters for some of the older 30-pin memory. The key here is that if the motherboard uses parity memory (the ninth data bit), then you must use parity memory. If the motherboard uses non-parity memory, you can use either parity or non-parity. As of May 1997, 16MB non-parity memory was $40 to $65 cheaper per 72-pin module, so the per-server savings are obvious.

Cache Subsystem

One more way to expedite your server's performance is by the use of a level 2 (L2) cache system. As I mentioned earlier, the level 1 (L1) cache, shown in Figure 4.4, is built into the internals of the 486, 586, and Pentium processors and acts as a small amount of very fast memory in which a copy of the most recently used data is stored. An L2 cache, shown in Figure 4.5, is exterior to the processor and installed onto the motherboard itself. For a discussion on cache systems, see the "Processor" section under the heading *Minimum Server Hardware* in this chapter.

The L1 cache is 8K in the 486 series and 16K in the Pentiums. While this seems to be too small to do any good, Intel Corporation has tested and published that this cache delivers a rate of 90 to 95 percent hit rates. A *hit* in cache terms means

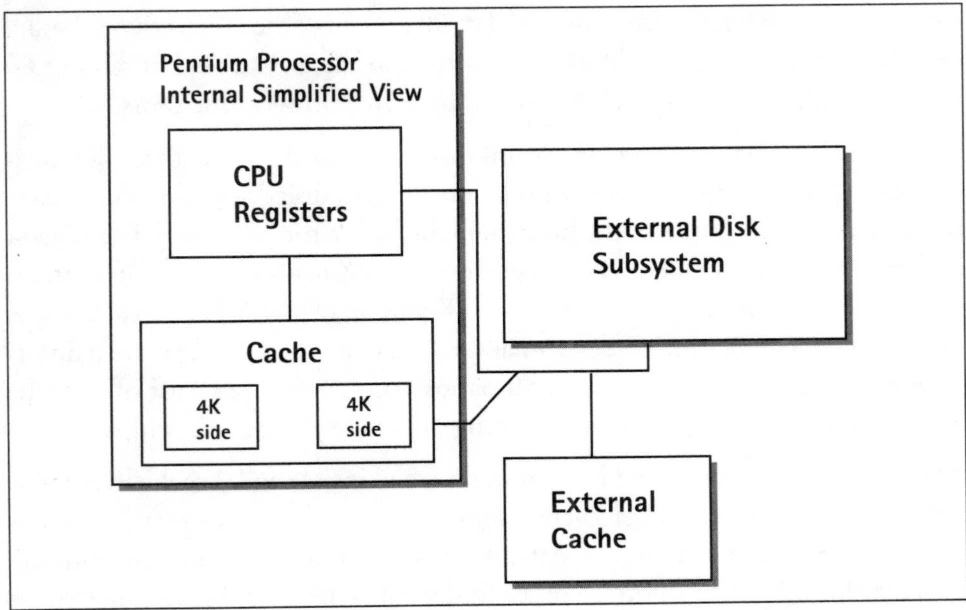

Figure 4.4
Level 1 cache system.

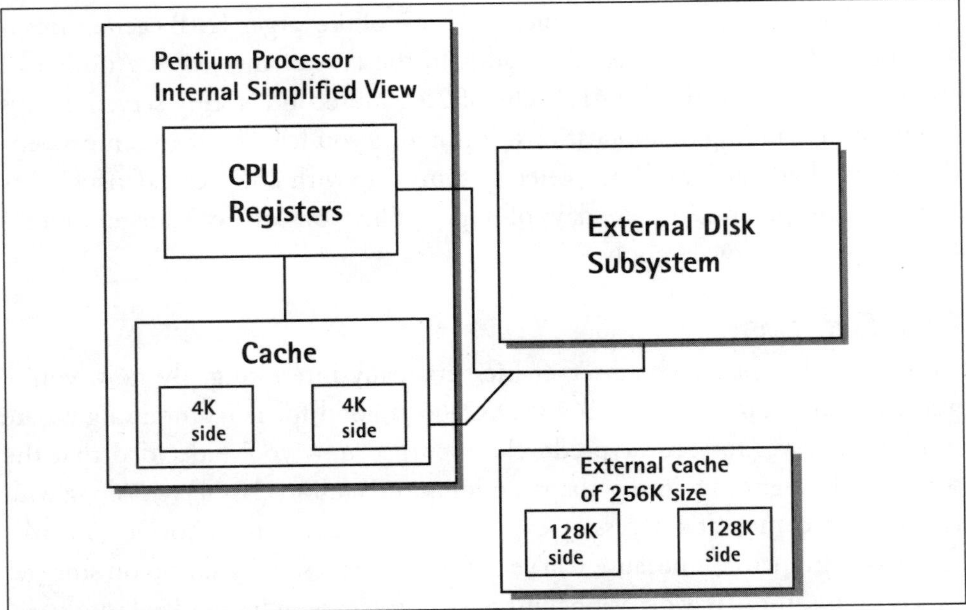

Figure 4.5
Level 2 cache system.

that the processor has found the desired data 90 percent of the time in the cache and only 10 percent of the time has had to go back to the disk drive. Hit rates of 80 percent or higher are acceptable and common in Pentium processors.

One of the keys to the performance gains that this cache delivers is that not only is the cache still closer to the processor than the physical disk drives, but it's still electronic data storage, just like the built-in cache inside the processor. The biggest difference between L1 and L2 cache is the size: L1 is 8K in 486s and 16K in Pentium class, while onboard L2 cache is at least 32K and up to 1MB. The L2 cache varies in speed, but a decent cache uses 15-nanosecond chips. The performance difference between 15-nanosecond and 50-nanosecond chips is a factor of 5, and a cost variance of perhaps twice, depending on where you buy the chips.

There's one thing you should keep in mind when installing L2 cache. Keep it to 256K or even 128K. Larger cache chips frequently result in marginal gains because the increased volume of data in the cache means that the processor has to wade through more information to find what it needs. Now, you may think that because the processor is such a barnburner, this isn't a problem. In fact, it really isn't that big of an issue in terms of a Web server, but if you decide that you want to use your current network server to double as the Web server, then every bit matters. Of course, the increased cost of the larger 1MB cache chips is a marginal factor but, nonetheless, adds to the cost of the server. Another of Intel's tests reported that a 64K cache of 20 nanoseconds rating served all but the most demanding of applications. If it makes you feel any better, most vendors of motherboards and completed systems ship with 256K cache installed as standard equipment. In these days of huge applications, the old adage "more is better" does not always apply.

Disk Systems

This is another place where server life gets really interesting. By now, you've guessed that about all a 16MB 486DX2-66 is good for is maintaining a bare minimum server for prototype development, so now you've decided that the server needs to grow up into perhaps a minimum Pentium class server. Along with that growth comes, at a necessary expense, the storage system. You've gone to a larger system, perhaps because you've got more users, so why skimp on storage? Likely as not, those few occasional users and prototyping has evolved into a real need for a full server. Alas, the need finally catches up with the expense.

For the minimum Web server requirements, I stated that an enhanced IDE drive is suitable for storage. This is still true enough for a mid-range server but be aware that four EIDE devices is the most you can put in one system and maintain decent performance. Okay, let me restate that. Under normal circumstances, only two EIDE controllers can be used in the system at one time and maintain decent performance, or even run at all. That may not seem like much, but I said EIDE *devices*, which means a tape drive, CD-ROM drive, or other such device. Both CD-ROMs and tape drives have become very cost-effective solutions these days for storage mediums, and they are commonly seen. One variety of CD-ROM plugs directly into the sound card, which is one IDE controller. The system drive obviously needs a controller and one drive. Strike another. This leaves you down to a possible one controller to be added and possibly two hard disks.

That's a lot of *maybes* and *could bes*. To ease yourself out of a lot of pain and anguish later on, this mid-range Web server could exist using the primary disk controller running one of those really fast EIDE drives, such as the Western Digital 1.65GB EIDE Caviar drive or a Seagate 1.28GB Medalist Fast ATA-2 drive. For the system files of Microsoft Windows NT Server, either of those is fine. You're not likely to add much more software that could fill the drive right away, so this should suffice to get you going. Both drives have access times as fast as any SCSI-2 drive, so don't let the thought of a fast IDE-style drive keep you from using it as a system drive.

In addition to the system drive, one configuration I prefer for myself and my clients is the use of a secondary SCSI-2 or SCSI-3 controller, in which the tape backup unit and the disk hosting the Web software are stored. If you use a RAID 5 controller, then you can use some of the now-inexpensive SCSI drives of the 2GB range to form the RAID. I priced these 2GB drives recently as low as $650 retail! Not bad at all. But, you say you're not interested in RAID just yet? Fine, use a secondary SCSI-2 controller to keep the cost down and use single drives. Just remember to backup often, at least daily. If you use multiple drives on this SCSI controller, you can use a single drive for the Web server software and another separate drive as the FTP device.

Figure 4.6 is a recap of the disk configuration I favor for the mid-range Web server, which walks an even line between the prototype server and the forthcoming best-case Web server. This particular configuration offers a safety net,

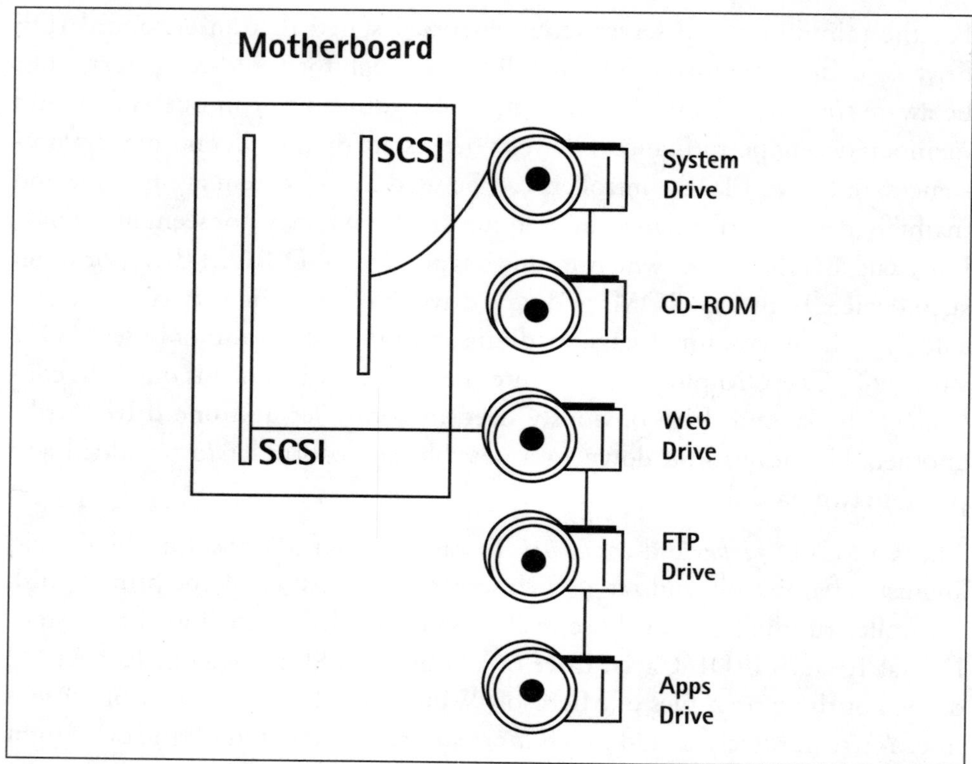

Figure 4.6
Split-level disk subsystem.

in that any one device can fail and not take out the other services. Sure, NT itself has been known to self-destruct like any other NOS, but it wouldn't take out the Web software. Why destroy all the configurations?

I/O Devices

The I/O devices won't differ a whole lot from the prototyping system we defined earlier, except that now you're likely to be using serial ports that are 16550 style. These are enhanced serial I/O units that buffer data at higher speeds above 9,600Kbps, and prevent loss of data if the main processor can't get to the data quick enough. In addition, you might consider using four serial ports to provide a little extra access to the server beyond the normal Internet connections. One possibility is to set up a BBS for local customers that don't have an Internet provider handy. Simply have them dialup into your Wildcat NT BBS, as we discussed in the last chapter, and then gateway out to the Internet. Not only is this doable, but it's very practical. We'll get into more detail on the subject later in this book.

Optimum Server Hardware

Now the time has come to talk about some serious money. This is the Web server that separates the kid's game PC from the one that would make the most devout programmer drool. This is also the one system that will serve all but the most demanding of environments. This is surely the last server of any sort that you'll have to buy any time soon. Wake up and pay attention, because when you put this one in front of the CFO, he or she will definitely have a cow!

Processor

It's time to belly up to the bar and be serious. It has been well established that the Pentium class processors are the king of the hill for Intel-based systems. Recently (late fall 1996), the 200MHz Pentium Pro came onto the market with the splash and marketing flair that Intel does so well. This is a killer processor that dwarfs anything the best 486 is capable of, and it makes the earlier sub-100MHz Pentiums eat its dust. To build the best Web server so you won't have to go out and upgrade in 6 months, specify a motherboard or pre-built computer that supports the 200MHz and also supports multiple processors, either by inserting the processor into another chip socket or adding another card. Microsoft Windows NT Server will use multiple processors with the greatest of ease and split the tasks between the processors.

We've not gotten into any other component yet, and already the cost of the server box has broken $6,000. What you'll gain from this price tag is the ability to simply drop in another processor and relieve the load on the existing system. In the early days of Microsoft Windows NT Server, Microsoft did a test on NT by having over 300 users on one network server. If memory serves me, the processor was a Pentium 90. The overall system performance was dismal, as you may have guessed, but not bad for a 32MB of RAM machine.

The test server had one more Pentium and 32MB of additional memory added, and the performance jumped to within 90 percent of what two Pentiums would do. In essence, 90 percent of a Pentium 90 was effectively used. Keep in mind that adding memory and another processor was all that was done! Subsequent testing added a total of 12 Pentium processors and 256MB of memory in a special Compaq server. Overall system performance went up algebraically, and more users were supported with less server stress and a lot fewer headaches.

This is a very commanding strength of Microsoft Windows NT Server. Can you imagine having 12 of those 200MHz Pentium Pros in one machine? Forget the cost, what about the processing horsepower? What about the heat generated by this system? The case would probably glow in the daylight.

In case you've never played with the likes of a Digital Equipment Corp. VAX/VMS™, a Sun Workstation, or a Silicon Graphics Iris™, these computers are capable of some of the most demanding processing known. One demo that I saw run on the Iris workstation with a 20-inch monitor involved four different full-motion videos of four different sets of two fighter jets practicing their dog-fighting skills. The 20-inch monitor was divided into equal fourths so that one set of jets was in each window pane. Ever see *Top Gun* or *Iron Eagle*? Remember those awesome jet fights and how quickly those jets could turn and maneuver? This Iris workstation (back in 1988) was processing all eight of these jets' similar motions flawlessly and without a single discernible glitch in movement! Now *that's* horsepower. Believe me when I say that such processing is astounding to see.

Well, the point is that now the Intel processors have come full circle with high-powered (and high-priced) workstations. They can handle hundreds of user requests in network environments, such as the Internet, on a single 200MHz processor. Adding a second 200 is like adding a second Iris into the same cabinet. Close enough that you should have the point by now. What's even more amusing about this is that 20 years ago, minicomputers, such as the Wangs and DECs, along with the IBM monsters, handled such matters with ease because they were designed from the ground up as multiuser platforms.

The Intel-based systems were designed initially as a data-entry terminal and were enhanced upward to work as servers. As such, it wasn't until the advent of a Unix variant that ran on PCs, NT Server, or Netware that the Intel-based machines really got a chance to work in these demanding environments. The PC had to mature into the job, while minicomputers were built for the job from the start. This is one reason PCs have had such a hard time filling the role of servers, but now the high-end processors, such as the 200MHz variety, can really do the job with Microsoft Windows NT Server.

There's one last point to be made about processors. Intel recently announced plans for a 233MHz and all the way up to a 300MHz Pentium processor with multiprocessor logic built in. As soon as you get bored with the performance of your machine, just stand still for six months, and a new barnburner will be out. Be sure to plan your server's system board to handle as high of an upgrade as you can possibly imagine. It's sure to come around!

Next, we'll discuss the most recent evolution in memory designs and variety for your server. Keep in mind that the CFO still hasn't recovered from the multiple-processor system board you bought earlier, and the "sticker shock" will persist all the way to the end of this section! Time for the Maalox.

MEMORY

Memory has thus far been the single most expensive component of the server. The memory market went absolutely nuts in the spring of 1994 when an overseas plant that makes crucial chemical components of the memory silicon wafers exploded and destroyed perhaps 40 percent of the world's supply of this component. The law of supply and demand jumped right in and drove up the price of a 4MB 30-pin memory module from an average of $115 to $165 almost overnight. Well, we all know that the supply didn't depreciate that fast, so someone was making a ton of money on a situation that didn't yet exist. Of course, we were all angered at this, but what can a poor systems integrator do?

Memory has stayed in the clouds ever since then, but has started coming down as of early March 1996. Before the pricing came down, a 16MB 72-pin single module averaged $600 for non-parity and nearly $750 for parity SIMMs. In early March 1996, I bought one of these same modules for $375, and two weeks later the same module dropped to $235 in several places. Two days after that, those same places were selling the module for $285. To show the difference, by the time of this book the same module was $125 one week and nearly $200 three days later. Suffice it to say, the memory market is quite volatile. If you look at the stock market and various aspects of it, the memory market is every bit as topsy-turvy as the precious metals market. At one time, gold was cheaper than memory chips!

I went through this spiel to let you know what to expect when designing your primo server. What you spec out today is likely to be obsolete next week in the memory corner. Hard drives, monitors, keyboards, and the like see no such problem. In fact, nearly every aspect of computers is getting somewhat cheaper, except for memory. There is one respite coming along the road that'll help us. New memory types, designs, and capacities are entering the market, so dealers have to clean out the old models before they can bring in the new. That means better prices for the consumer, but the newer models keep overall prices higher.

Some of the newest memory types in the market are the 72-pin designs I've mentioned, and are likely to be the only ones you'll put in your server. The 16MB model is the most commonly used, and its name is usually referred to as a 4Mx32-70. In the 72-pin design, multiply the megabytes rating by 4, and you'll get the capacity—4 multiplied by 4 is 16MB. The *32* in the name refers to 32 data bits, and it designates the non-parity type. The *70* in the name is the speed rating of the module. A 70-nanosecond model is a middle-of-the-road performer and is the most widely sold unit. So, an 8Mx36-54 memory model is a 32MB parity model rated at 54 nanoseconds. This module recently sold for $1,100, but its price is fluctuating just as wildly now as the others are.

One more type of memory that I'd like to mention is the EDO, or Extended Data Out, design. This memory is designed to work in servers to provide faster response and better performance under demanding needs. If you know anything about the system boards, you know that various parts of it can be tuned: the bus speed, CPU responses, cache wait states, and more. Well, the memory subsystem is what is called a *slave device* in the system. Its only job is to perform the task it was given and nothing more. It can't respond back to the processor at all, and it dutifully carries out its tasking. EDO will give you better performance out of memory subsystems, but the modules cost a lot more to use. In heavily used Web servers, you'll find these modules to be a definite advantage, but be prepared to spend the bucks.

Ideally, our optimum Web server would employ the EDO memory and would use a pair of the 8Mx36-40 SIMMs. Do you remember the section earlier where I said that usage of memory was dependent on legal memory configurations? I explained that if you used a pair of 16MB modules and had two memory slots free to give you 32MB of working memory, adding more memory to this server later meant that you had to use the same 16MB modules by adding two more of them. If you needed more than 64MB of memory, then you'd have to remove all 4 of the 16MB modules and buy the 32MB units. In most cases, you can't mix the 16MB and 32MB modules on the same motherboard. Sometimes you can, but usually not. For this reason, I recommend you start with the 32MB modules in this production server.

Let's go back to our basic server. This server was installed at 16MB to test it. The costs were kept to a minimum, and the server proved viable. Fine. Later, we jumped it up to 32MB total using another 16MB module. Two memory slots used, and two free. These slots were capable of supporting the 32MB modules as well, but I opted for the cheaper 16MB units. With 32MB installed, the Web server was brought online and various software components installed. Performance lagged after a while, so memory was bumped up one more module to 48MB. You see the pattern building here. This server has finally made its way up to 96MB of memory by using three of the 32MB modules and removing the four 16MB modules purchased over time. This server now only has one memory slot left, and appears to be headed for a motherboard upgrade soon.

To avoid this problem, start the server with a pair of 32MB modules right off the bat, and then you can jump up to 128MB of server memory later if you have to. The cost is likely to run about $2,000 to start with ECC memory, but it's worth it in the long run.

Disk Systems

Disk drives will be the one area that is likely to please that nervous CFO, especially after that last section. In high-powered Web servers, RAID 5 disk subsystems are the norm. Not only is this for the security of the data but for the increased throughput offered by RAID, which treats all of the physical drives as one logical unit. Because of this scheme, data access is faster due to the RAID controller's usage of the disks that make up the array. Figure 4.7 shows the concept of a RAID system.

This means that if data has to be stored, the controller uses the appropriate disk for the job. If data has to be read, which is perhaps 80 percent of all operations, then the controller determines which disk to use that has the data. It's kinda like rocket science—something that eludes most of us—but the controller and software make the decisions for us by splitting up the data between physical drives in the logical array. All of the adapters for this server should be either EISA- or PCI-based bus adapters. Nothing else will suffice for this demanding environment.

Some vendors of excellent disk RAID controllers include Adaptec's AHA-3940/3940W RAID adapters for PCI. The following are some of the specs on this adapter.

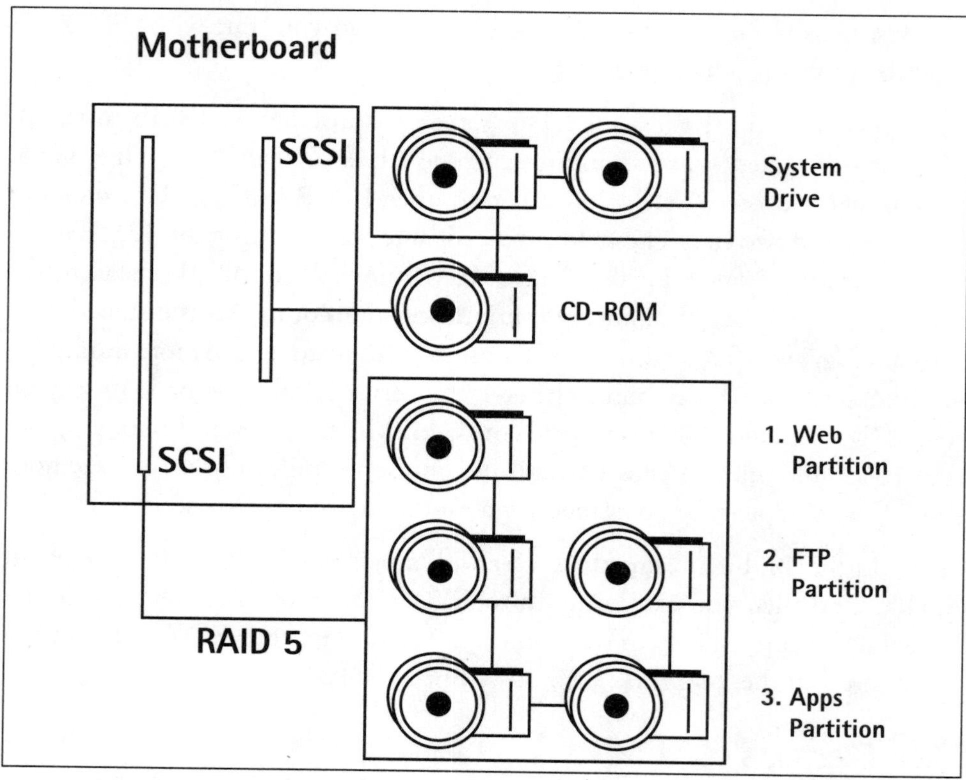

Figure 4.7
Sample RAID disk subsystem.

- *Host PCI bus data transfer rate:* Up to 133MB/sec burst rate
- *SCSI synchronous data rate:* AHA-3940—20MB/sec (10MB/sec per channel)
- *Two-channel Fast SCSI-2:* AHA-3940W—40MB/sec (20MB/sec per channel)
- *Two-channel Fast and Wide SCSI-2*
- *SCSI asynchronous data rate:* AHA-394085—6MB/sec (3MB/sec per channel)
- *Two-channel Fast SCSI-2:* AHA-3940W—12MB/sec (6MB/sec per channel)

- *Three-channel Fast and Wide SCSI-2*
- *RAID levels:* 5, 1, 0, and 0/1

You can find the complete specifications for this adapter at **www.adaptec.com/hiperfio/d_sheets/AHA3940Features_spec.html**. I suggest stopping by if you're interested in seeing all of the things this adapter can do. Another adapter used in the industry is Mylex Corporation's DAC960. I've used this adapter in Banyan VINES, NT Servers, and Novell Netware systems with no problems. It's fast and easy to set up. You can find more information on Mylex's PCI RAID controllers at **www.mylex.com/salemktg.htm**. Dell Computer Corp. also has a disk array for its servers but finding specific information on the disk array was fairly difficult on the company's Web site at **www.dell.com**. From that page, you can get contact information for various countries around the world for your particular application.

This should give you a feeling for the products and their capabilities. Now for some pricing. I'll use the Mylex DAC960 as an example. This controller recently was priced at $850 for no cache memory installed. This price is likely to be different when you buy one, so consult your local vendor for the most current prices. One typical RAID configuration for servers of this magnitude is to run RAID 1 (basic mirroring) on one controller and RAID 5 on a second controller for the data drives. RAID 5 requires three drives minimum, eight maximum, on this controller. RAID 1 requires two drives of the exact same type and geometry, and so does RAID 5. This is where some degree of standardization helps with replacement parts and in purchasing. For example, if you buy Seagate 2 GB SCSI-2 drives, Model ST32430N, then you'll need six of these drives: two for the RAID 1, three for RAID 5, and one spare. Woe be unto the Webmaster who doesn't have a spare drive handy.

This is the only funny part about RAID—it requires drives of the same geometry. This requirement could put you into a precarious position if the style of drive you buy goes out of production this year, and three months later, you need to expand your storage or replace a bad drive. So, many Webmasters purchase several of these drives at once as extras. One option should be noted here. A drive of the next-higher geometry can be used to replace a drive of smaller geometry. An example of this is a RAID 5 system using drives with 2,100 cylinders, 16 heads, and 63 sectors. If one drive goes bad, then you could replace it with a drive of 2,300 cylinders, 16 heads, and 63 sectors. Not all of the disk

Table 4.2

Relative costs of RAID.

Device	Quantity	Price	Total
RAID Controller	2	$850	$1,700
Disk drives	6	$700	$4,200

space on the new drive would be used, but it at least matches the minimum required disk size. Table 4.2 tallies up the damage done so far to the disk subsystem.

Getting pretty expensive, isn't it? The memory we used ran about $2,400 for 32MB; now add $5,900 for the RAID system. That's $8,300 for just the basic core components of the server. Toss in the case, power supply, keyboard, and other odds and ends, and the server can break $15,000 quite easily. And we haven't even added a single piece of software. Take another gulp of Maalox before you tell the CFO that this primo top-end Web server is still not complete.

I/O Devices

This last section on our best-ever Web server involves some peripheral devices not yet discussed as necessary, because they've been considered optional in the other servers. Tape backup is absolutely necessary. Sure, you say, but what kind? Do we just want to save the data or truly backup the server? Next, a CD-ROM drive is a must. Because our high-end server uses SCSI, we'll use a SCSI CD-ROM. No problem. How about uploading the huge quantities of files that you may occasionally put on the server? Why not consider a rewritable optical drive that doubles to handle CD-ROM discs?

When your server gets to be as big as this optimum device, SCSI tape backups greater than 4GB are the only ones that make sense. Not only that, but there's a known problem using IDE tape backups of large capacity—the software won't work under Microsoft Windows NT Server and Workstation. So, SCSI tape drives become mandatory. The drives have come down in price so significantly that it's well worth it. I priced one in March 1996 at $350 with each 4GB tape costing about $28 apiece. The odd part of this is that a truly full-featured backup program to use Microsoft Windows NT Server and the tape drive costs nearly $700. But, once installed, you can back up the server and any workstations on the network, which is useful if this Web server is going to run any workstations.

Optical disks have come a long way, just like tape drives have, and now you can get a 6X speed IDE drive for less than $100 everywhere. One distributor I use offered me a Phillips 6X IDE drive for $95! Granted, that's wholesale, but the picture gets better when I tell you that 5 1/2-inch rewritable drives that can handle CDs are now under $1,000. That's the retail price, too. If you find a friend that resells computer equipment, you're likely to find these drives for as little as $700. Why would you want one of these? Well, if your Web site processes large quantities of data, or you have an exceptionally busy Web site, or the Web server is a standalone machine, you need some way to get this data around. The rewritable drive is the perfect answer. At a rated 1.3GB capacity, it'll solve all but the most demanding needs of your Web site.

One last peripheral device that you may want to explore is the use of a BBS or RAS by way of Microsoft Windows NT Server. This approach provides several solutions to problems you'll undoubtedly encounter in the course of your Web site. One of these is remote management of the Web site. Another is emergency requests for access to your server for files or messages. Still another is access to the server by users that are not on the Internet and who need to get onto the Internet or use the Web resources locally.

Microsoft Windows NT Server's RAS handles up to 256 concurrent users. That would be quite a load for any server, but your primo high-end Web server can handle it. Remember, you built this server to handle large loads, but the standard I/O ports added to computers are limited to four serial ports. Even if you use all four ports for 28.8Kbps modems, you still wouldn't load down this server. By using a multiport I/O card, you can let plenty of remote users onto the server at once. In fact, this is the premise behind many Internet Service Providers.

Microsoft Windows NT Server excels at this by natively supporting intelligent multi-I/O cards, such as the Equinox SST family of cards. I use an SST-4 on my Web server now for remote access for several users who don't have file transfer capability other than something like Procomm communications software. These users dial in using NT Workstation's and Windows 95's remote access software that comes with each system, and they log into my domain natively to copy files. I haven't fully set up the BBS software, yet, but any other users could dial in and get files this way, as well, using Procomm or similar software.

Let's not forget one little piece of ancillary equipment that I almost forgot about, and that's a printer. Did you know that if you can log into a domain, you can do anything remotely that you can do locally? Well, anything given the proper rights, and this includes printing to a network printer. When I'm working on some projects, I need to fax information to customers so they can respond to it. If I email them a word-processing file, they can use it and mark it up as they see fit. If they then log into my network, they can (and have) printed the file directly onto my network printers and saved the fax cost. This is just another way to save money and expedite the operations of a business using Microsoft Windows NT Server.

A Short Summary

This is the end of a relatively long section on the vagaries of Web servers. I'd like to take a minute to do a short summary with you about what we've covered, why we did it, and what you can expect out of each setup toward the goal of building your Web server.

- **Bare-bones server ($1,500)**—Uses existing components around the office; server is comprised of a Pentium 90 with 16MB memory, most any hard disk above 650MB capacity, CD-ROM drive, basic I/O ports. Good for testing theories and running up to 10 users in active usage. Can use a high-speed modem to test the site. If it doesn't work out, return the system to the pool of users wanting a decent 486. Nothing lost but a bit of time and someone's salary to do the work.
- **Mid-range server ($5,000)**—Uses some existing components around the office; server is comprised of a Pentium 133, CD-ROM, 32MB memory, a pair of 1GB drives, or higher storage. Uses basic ISDN lines for low-cost connectivity to support up to 15 concurrently connected users; could support a BBS of up to 5 concurrently connected users at 28.8Kbps. Needs a bit of time spent with it to continue the prototyping and configuring of the Web software, FTP, browsers, users' home stations, and so forth. Expect to take a month of testing and evaluation of the server before you take the server either public or private regardless of the targeted user base. Relatively moderate investment that could be used as an in-house network server for up to 50 users if the Web site doesn't fly.
- **Optimum server ($15,000)**—Pentium 200 class processor with 64MB RAM; RAID 1 and RAID 5 storage for the NOS and data, respectively. Uses all

high-end equipment, such as SCSI disks, tape drive, CD-ROM, and optical storage; uses FT1 or full T1 link to support up to 250 users. Seek this level only if the corporate CFO is sure this is a cost-effective solution to company business goals. This server could double as an enterprise-wide server, so it's not something to take lightly. T1 links cost $15,000 to install and up to $3,500 a month in fees. Enables processing of a full-fledged Web site with all the abilities thereof.

Next, we'll move on to server memory requirements from the application level to see exactly how much memory these applications will use, which will confirm what we've discussed up to this point.

Server Memory Requirements

Now, let's get into the heart of the matter—how much memory this thing is really going to require. I know I just went through a complete server build for three different servers, but I think it bears repeating. Memory can affect your Web server's performance in different ways, so let's look at that now.

Just For NT Server

When you built the Microsoft Windows NT Server, you installed it on a machine without any other software running on it. This means that NT had access to all available memory and had to share none of it. This is important! When you have just NT running and no other applications installed, run the Windows Diagnostics from the Task Manager, and click on the Performance tab to show you how much memory is installed, how much is used, and how much is free, as shown in Figure 4.8.

What you'll notice is the resources and the memory load factor placed on the machine by the operating software and required drivers. Of course, if you add more software and drivers, it takes more memory to run them. By using this tool, you can gauge the impact that various pieces of software have on your server and when you can expect problems caused by them. As a standard rule of thumb, Microsoft Windows NT Server requires 20MB of memory to completely load itself and run before any other drivers or services are loaded. This is for the virgin installation of NT. Now, earlier I did say that you could run Microsoft Windows NT Server on a machine that has 16MB of memory—how is that possible?

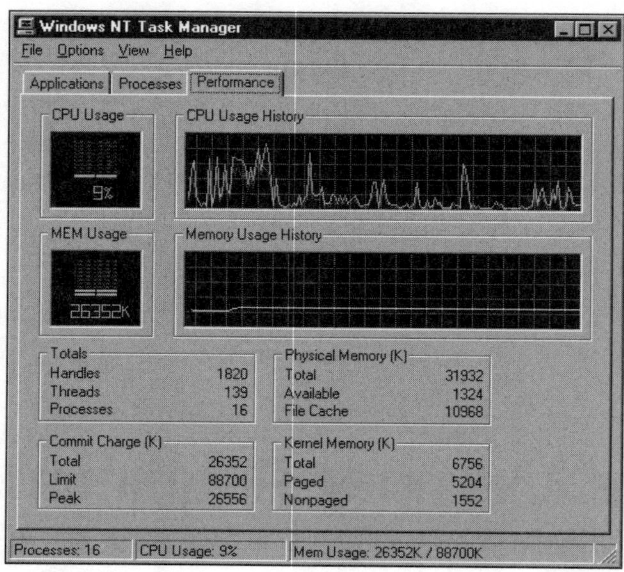

Figure 4.8
NT's Task Manager.

Microsoft Windows NT Server uses a vulture called *virtual memory* to simulate real memory. Virtual memory is nothing more than disk space converted into a single contiguous file called a *swap file*. This swap file is used when physical memory gets low. At that point the unused, or the least recently used, applications and data are moved off to the swap file and out of real memory to make room for the applications and drivers that need to execute. I called it a vulture because swap files are slower than real memory and they tend to gobble up applications, even if they're running in real memory. Even if some applications don't need that much real memory to run, Microsoft Windows NT Server sometimes swaps out applications to the swap file, anyway, but recalls it back to real memory, as necessary.

Because the swap file is fixed, you have to declare a minimum and maximum size for the file. Averages between 25MB and 95MB are common for the lower and upper range in the file. Microsoft Windows NT Server adjusts the size of the file dynamically during operations. I recommend setting NT's requirements to 20MB for a clean setup. You can set the maximum as high as you want.

The Needs Of The Applications

The applications you'll use for your server run the gamut from the actual Web server software up to RAS and the CGI applications you may create over time. Something has to perform the task of the Web pages, and that something includes CGI, HTML, and perhaps the Visual Basic applications you wrote for the CGI part of it. I did some experimenting with my server and came up with the statistics shown in Table 4.3.

This table should give you a hint about what your server may or may not need for application support. The memory requirements may not be as important as the processing demand that these applications place upon the processor. In a few sections, I'll introduce you to the Performance Monitor that comes with Microsoft Windows NT Server and allows you to watch the server's operational characteristics from a different viewpoint. For now, just know that with these few applications' needs, the Web server has jumped from 20MB to 27.5MB of real memory to run its dead-level best without touching the swap file.

Drivers And Your Hardware

Drivers are in a class by themselves when it comes to server memory requirements. This is because if you want to run the device, then you *must* install a driver for it! No questions asked, this is a requirement. Using certain drivers, Microsoft Windows NT Server protects itself from errant applications and utilities. It disallows access, *direct* access that is, to the hardware on the server like Windows 3.x or Windows 95 does. This protection is called the *Hardware Abstraction Layer*, or *HAL* for short. Nothing goes in, out, or through the HAL without NT's control. NT regulates the traffic by using protected mode drivers. One

Table 4.3

Application demands on memory.

Application	Memory	Demand
VB EXEs	250K	High
Perl Interpreter	100K	Low
RAS	800K	Medium
SQL Server	6MB	High

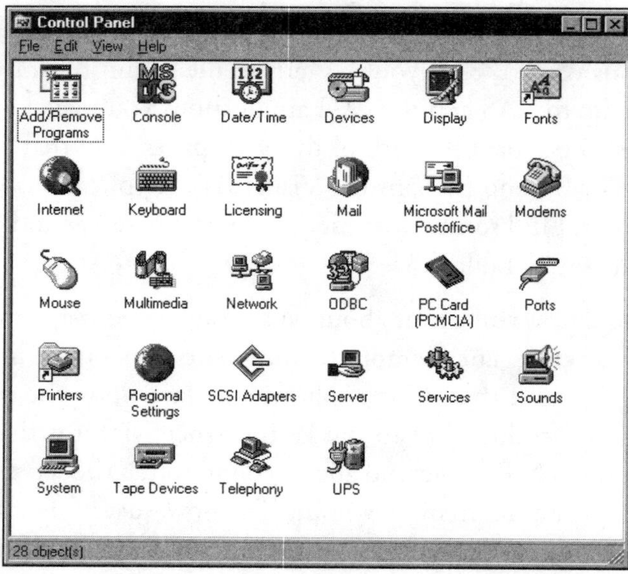

Figure 4.9
Control Panel access to tape drives.

perfect example is the venerable QIC tape drive installed from the Windows NT Setup icon in the Control Panel, as shown in Figure 4.9.

While drivers themselves usually don't take over 250K to run, once loaded, they're running for the duration of the server and can't be removed unless you specifically go to the Control Panel and stop them from running. The main purpose of a driver is as a permanent device in the server, and therefore, it shouldn't be removed anyway! If you need to use the device, then it's generally a system-level device like a tape drive or another disk drive. The memory aside, another performance factor comes into being because NT now has to manage the driver once loaded. Forget the memory, it's something else to manage. Just like crickets crawling on your hand, one or two doesn't matter, but one or two dozen gets to be a pain to manage and takes increasing amounts of your time to take care of. The same is true of NT, as you'll see in a moment.

The Users Of The Server

When you think of users on the server, immediately the mind turns to someone logged in at a workstation. However, Microsoft Windows NT Server has many more users than you may have first thought of, including silent runners. Of course, when you log onto the server, there's the usual user called *Joe User* that makes the connection. However, there's another kind of user in the system called *InterProcess Communications* (*IPC*). To illustrate this, I need to explain a few things about multiple processing systems like Microsoft Windows NT Server.

When a user logs onto the server, it creates a number of functional processing subsystems called *processes.* On a Windows 3.x PC, you might have started your favorite word processor. This program is a process. While you were inside this word processor, perhaps you pressed Alt+Tab to flip over to Program Manager to start another program. When you ran the second program, that too started a process. While running the second program, it may have started some add-in utility to help you do something. This started yet another process. Microsoft Windows NT Server is capable of managing and controlling multiple processes and *spawning* other processes from those processes themselves. This functionality causes more efficient usage of the operating system, but it uses more memory to allow the functionality itself. So, if you install and use applications specifically written for NT, then chances are that it may, at some point, cause you to need more memory.

So, now you have bona fide users logged in, Web server software operating, Perl scripts and CGI running and doing things for the Internet users, and perhaps an incremental tape backup in progress. If you connected your Web server to the in-house network and allowed users to use the Web server as a gateway out to the Internet, the server is being used still more by these logged-in users. All of this translates into memory usage by the server, a truly precious commodity. Next, let's talk about how IPCs can affect server performance and memory usage for the users and remote functions.

InterProcess Communications

InterProcess Communications (IPCs) are the internal functionality between server processes that communicate and carry out tasks where direct users are not involved. This can occur when two servers are communicating with internal tasking or if a remote user connects to the server with incorrect settings. This problem causes the server to generate a *Named Pipe* system service call between the connecting user and the operating system via the IPC, as shown in

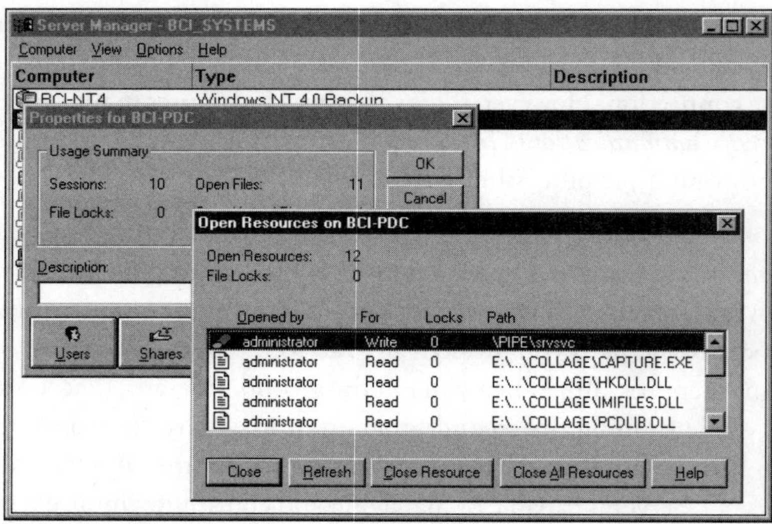

Figure 4.10
Open resources on the server.

Figure 4.10. Without getting into tons of NT nitty-gritty server stuff, this is yet another "user" in the system, which takes another little bit of memory and another little bit of processor time to handle.

You can observe the server performance, as shown in Figure 4.11, by opening the Performance Monitor utility from the Administrative Group and choosing the Processor Time, and then choosing the Percentage Of User Time menu option, or the interrupts per second processing level.

So, now you can see that in even a medium-used Web server, you can count on 32MB of RAM getting eaten up very quickly. While this will degrade server performance somewhat, you can survive, but for how long is indeterminate. Your best bet is to spend the bucks for 48MB of memory to start with. You won't regret it.

In the next section, we'll move forward toward connecting our newly completed Web server to the Internet. We'll want to have the server connected to the Internet and PINGing successfully before we step into Chapter 7 with the Web software.

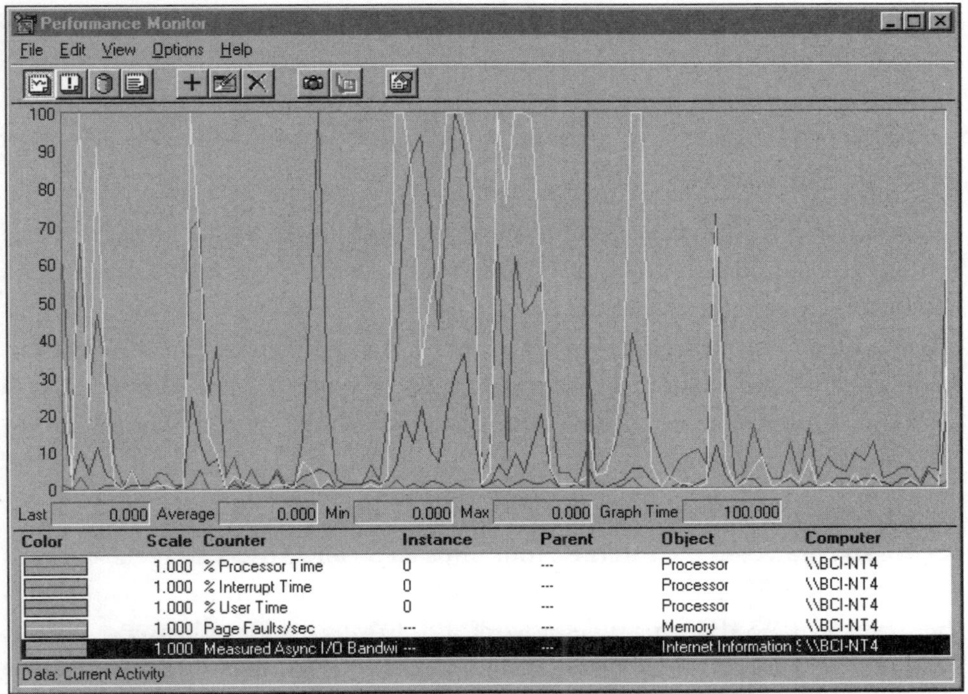

Figure 4.11
Performance monitoring of the server.

Internet Connectivity Devices

In this section, we're going to briefly discuss connecting your server to the Internet by different means. The main goal is to test, develop, and produce a working circuit capable of sustaining data across the link between your Web site and the network users in the business that may be connected to the same Web server. We're assuming that a modem was used to test the Web server's connection to the outside world, establishing that the server's basic communications work fine.

Routers

As I mentioned before, routers perform the task of sending packets of data to the desired destination and preventing undesired packets from getting lost. Users on network A have IP addresses starting with 207.94.233, and users on network B have IP addresses of 207.94.234. Outside users connect to the Web server using IP addresses starting with 207.94.235. Routers say that if data is destined for the user 207.94.233.15 why send it to the Web server on the 235 subnet? Think of the router as a traffic cop in a congested intersection: He sends everyone to their desired location without allowing them to get lost or go down the wrong path.

Routers come in all shapes, designs, purposes, and power levels. There are basic routers that handle Ethernet on thin-net topology for two networks, and that's it. Not much strength to handle beyond 100 users or so, but they don't cost as much, either. Then, there are routers capable of handling enterprise-wide solutions of 1,000 users or more. Count on paying something on the order of $15,000 for such a router, and they can go up to $25,000 for high-end routers. (I can see the CFO sweating now.)

When I got my Web server online for my business, I had eight users that I needed to connect to the Internet: four internal business users, two dial-in users accessing my BBS and gatewaying to the Internet, and two users dialing into the server by RAS. For this style of work, I didn't need a lot of horsepower, but I did need a router to work on my ISDN link. For this job, I chose the Ascend Pipeline Model 50 ISDN router for the job. It's capable of 128Kbps data rates, dial-in demand for the internal users, and multiplexed PPP links so you can get the full 128Kbps capacity. Best yet, it's incredibly simple to set up and use, and it's a router, as well.

When I installed this ISDN router onto my network and configured it, I did a trial run to a favored FTP site where I get lots of goodies. A file transfer of 500K averaged between a 7Kbps and 8Kbps per second rate. If you take into account the 10 percent overhead of the data, I was getting nearly 90Kbps out of the 128Kbps rates of ISDN! Not too shabby, to say the least. A second test with a second network user doing the same thing caused a drop in data rates for the first user, which was expected, but the second user got 4Kbps while the first user sustained 5K. Cumulatively, this means that the ISDN link achieved a sustained rate of 100Kbps of the 128Kbps capacity of multiplexed PPP. This is the reason that smaller sites should take a serious look at ISDN for low-capacity sites. So before we go any farther, let's dive right into ISDN—what it really is, and how it can serve you.

ISDN Equipment

ISDN stands for *Integrated Services Digital Network*, and it's a standard by which fax, phone, and pure data can be transmitted over a single line. All three types of data share the bandwidth of the one line and get separated out by the receiving equipment that you install. These links come in several types relating to style and speed: 32Kbps, 56Kbps, 64Kbps, and 128Kbps. Use 32Kbps for transmitting just voice, fax multiplexed with voice at 56Kbps, or pure data running at any of the four speeds. If you use the 128Kbps rate, then you're actually using a pair of 64Kbps data channels multiplexed together on one virtual circuit. When you connect to the provider, a single 64Kbps data channel is started, and the second 64Kbps channel is started only when the first channel fills.

When you plan on ISDN, you'll need to answer the following questions:

- What do you plan on doing with the link? All data? Mixed data and voice? Fax?
- How many users will be on this link? 64Kbps is recommended for up to 5 users, 128Kbps for up to 12.
- Will you be hooking this up to an ISDN router? A PC? An external modem?
- How long will the link stay connected when you need to get online?

These things are important because the telephone company provider will need to configure its equipment accordingly. For my Web server, pure data was the only requirement. I wanted the highest bandwidth, so I got two data channels multiplexed on one line. This means that I have a pair of phone wires out back coming in from the telco for the ISDN. They look like any other ordinary pair of phone wires, but they're certified as capable of handling higher speeds and a better quality of data delivery.

When you place the initial call for the line, be prepared to wait up to six weeks for the final connection to be made. Most telephone companies will have to do a *loop qualification test* to determine if the currently installed lines are capable of supporting high-quality digital data between your office and the telco's ISDN switch. This takes time for some telephone companies but nothing for others. My telco, Bell South, took four weeks for the test because my site was only the sixth in the entire county to get ISDN. My requests were way beyond their normal operations, whereas Bell Atlantic has well established ISDN presence all over Philadelphia, and you can get ISDN there within a couple of days.

Once the test is done and the go-ahead has been given, the installation will be ready for your site. Because I had never dealt with ISDN before, I elected for Bell South to do the inside wiring at our location, thinking this was some miracle job. Wrong! They used standard phone wire and standard phone jacks with standard jack screws—and I paid $135 for a 10-minute job that wasn't done right to start with. If you know how to wire a phone jack, you can do it yourself. ISDN isn't a miracle, just a mystic. Imagine the same analog modem traffic across a phone wire, now digitize it, and you've got ISDN. It's called Integrated Services because it's capable of supporting fax, voice, and modem at once.

If you want to learn more about ISDN, try Ascend Corporation's Web site, **www.ascend.com/techdocs/isdnuserguide.html**, where they post lots of technical tips and information about ISDN.

Now, let's move on to discuss the ins and outs of the network equipment that you'll need to get your site connected to the Internet.

Network-Specific Equipment

I'm going to break this section out into the three composite parts we discussed earlier: the bare-bones prototype server, the mid-range server, and the optimum Web server. We'll cover how you can connect these server types to the Internet by using a fast modem for the bare-bones server, an ISDN connection for the mid-range server, and dedicated T1 circuits for the optimum server.

The Prototype Server Using A Modem

This isn't too tough to explain, and I won't bore you with too many details. What I will say is that you can use a standard serial port card that most computers come with, but do yourself a favor and get a decent 28.8Kbps modem, such as a US Robotics Sportster. Most of the major vendors work well with NT, but I have a personal affinity for the USRs. Not much more is required to get this prototype server online for testing, except to make sure you have a serial port that uses the 16550AFN UART. This unit buffers high-speed data transfers and is quite useful under poor-quality lines where data has to be retransmitted. You'll need two serial ports, one for the mouse and one for the modem. Beyond that, if you need more than two serial ports, I highly recommend using an intelligent I/O card like the Equinox Super Serial SST-4, which NT uses without you having to worry about all of those interrupt assignments.

The Mid-Range Server On ISDN

This is a little bit more complex to set up, but not much. My site uses the Ascend Pipeline 50 ISDN router, which consists of a 10BaseT twisted pair base, a simple 10BaseT hub, and the wiring to our network server. There are two ways to connect to the Web server, and you'll have to decide on one of them for your needs. If you only have a standalone Web server, then forget the network issues. The two schemes are:

- *Indirectly routed path*—All network traffic has to go through the Web server to get to the ISDN router.
- *Directly routed path*—All network users have a direct path to the ISDN router, bypassing the Web server.

Basically, the connections look something like Figure 4.12.

Because I want my business users on the network to have the fastest route possible to the Internet, I chose the directly connected route, where the ISDN router is connected to the hub. If all of the network traffic has to go through the Web server first, then the Web server has double duty to perform, causing additional load factors on the server. However, if I send all traffic through the Web server in an indirectly connected route, then I can use firewalls and proxy servers to prevent any unauthorized people from coming into my internal networks. You'll have to decide which method is best for you.

I also mentioned the possibility of having dialup users to your Web server using RAS or connecting via your bulletin board, if you have one. These users will connect to the Web server and gateway to the Internet via the Web server, so the Web server will have enough to worry about without additional load factors from these users. This particular Web server was built to handle 20 users connected concurrently, so the additional load of a few dialup users shouldn't affect the server too much.

Another thing to be knowledgeable about is your ISDN adapter. My final bit of advice on this issue is that ISDN requires line termination between the link and your server. The server is digital data, the link is digital data, and the distant end is digital data. So, what's the big deal about? Isn't digital data transferred the same way? Not quite. ISDN uses a different format to move the packets of data, so the digital data coming from your Web server has to be converted to a format

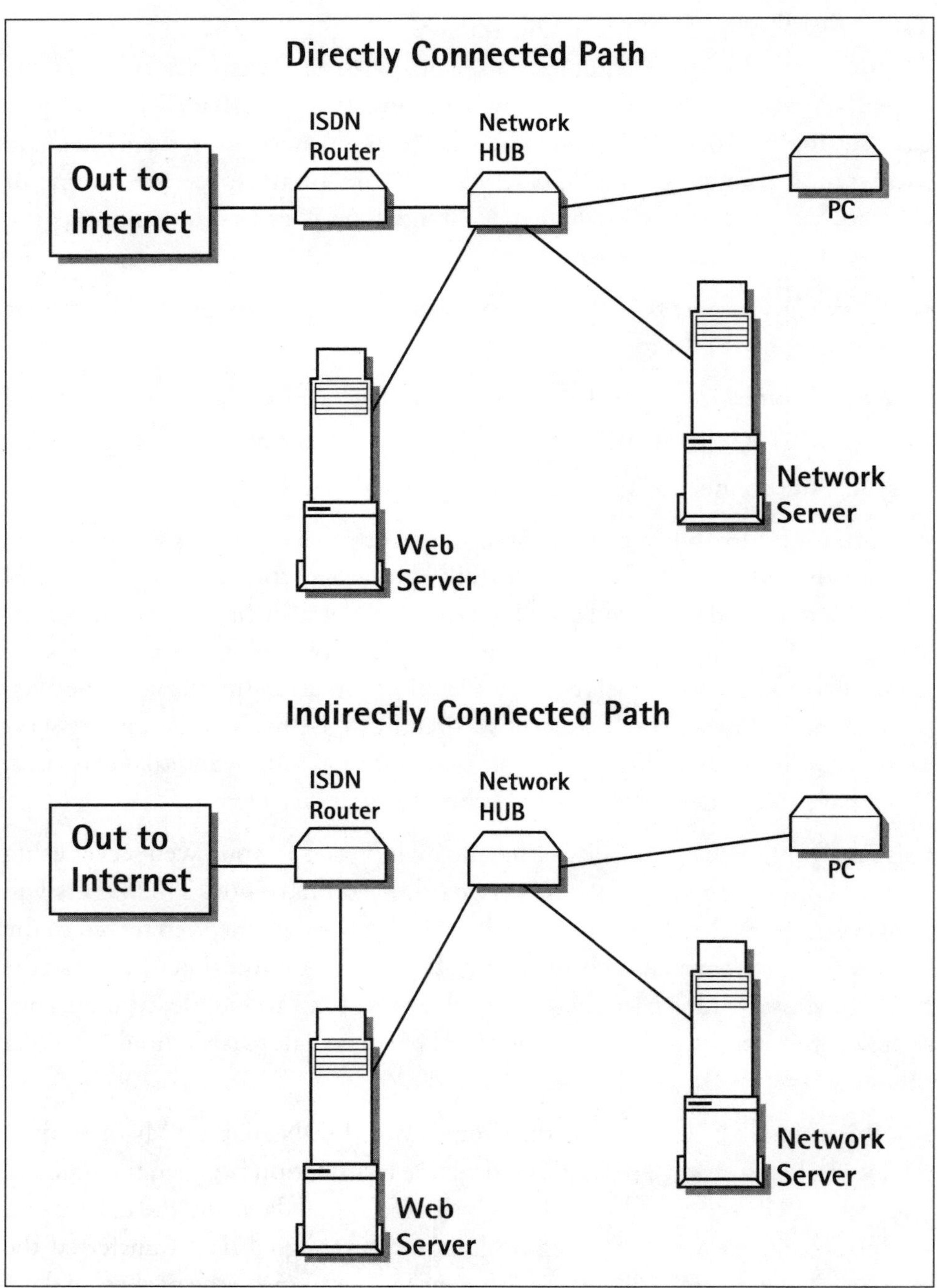

Figure 4.12
Server routing.

suitable for transmission across the link. When the data arrives, the distant end reconverts it back to computerese digital data. This process requires a *line termination* device for the ISDN itself. One way to execute the conversion is to use a *CSU/DSU,* or Channel Service Unit/Digital Service Unit. The CSU adapts and prepares the ISDN line side of the connection to support the DSU, which prepares the Web server side of the connection to connect to the CSU, as shown in Figure 4.13.

Using devices like the Ascend Pipeline does not require a separate CSU/DSU termination because this device, called an *NT-1 Adapter,* does the job in one unit built right into the ISDN router box. Instead of having the Web server connect to the router, which connects to the CSU/DSU, which connects to the ISDN line, we just replace the CSU/DSU and router with a single box—the Pipeline 50.

Our Optimum Web Server On A Dedicated Link

Well, we've connected all of the junior servers, time to spend some bucks for our big server. The server is always operational; now you need to complete the

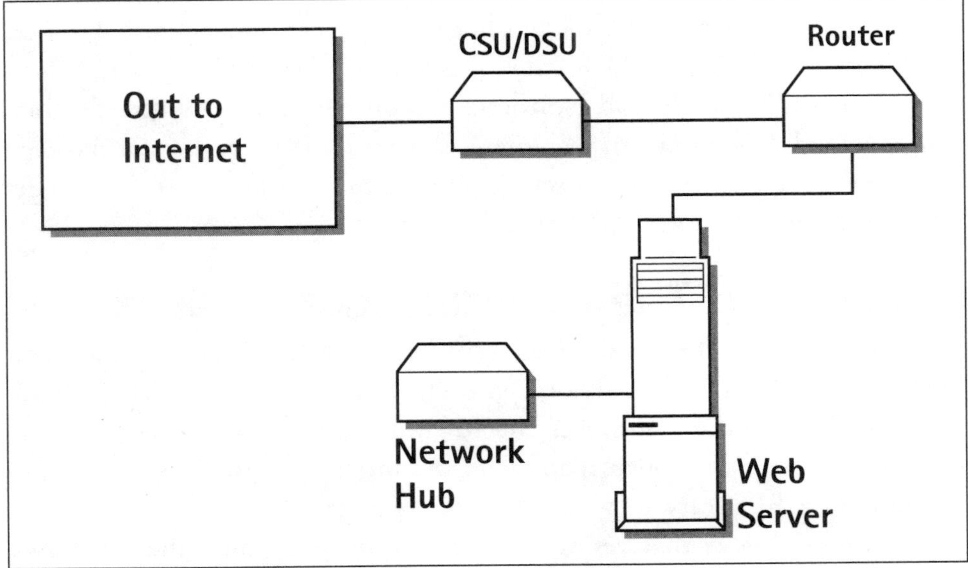

Figure 4.13
Example of a CSU/DSU installation.

task before loading the Web software. Microsoft Windows NT Server comes with all sorts of useful utilities to test the link, including PING, NSLOOKUP, and others.

To get this guy online, we're going to use a full T1 circuit. This is still a copper wire-based circuit, so don't worry about fiber optics as yet. To make this circuit, we can use an external router like the Cisco 2501, which basically does the same job as the Pipeline 50, but for a lot more users and at higher speeds. The Cisco 2501 serial ports provide up to two dedicated serial port interfaces, operating in DCE or DTE mode, compatible with leased lines and packet-switched services at speeds up to 2.048Mbps (megabits per second).

The Cisco 2500 series models 2503 and 2504 also come equipped with a native ISDN Basic Rate S/T Interface (BRI) that replaces an external ISDN terminal adapter (TA). The BRI S/T interface provides one 16Kbps D channel for ISDN signaling information between the router and the ISDN switch, and two 64Kbps B channels for user data access to the ISDN network. The Cisco 2500 series supports the NET3 (Euro ISDN) specification in Europe, as well as VN-2 and VN-3 specifications in France, the 1TR6 specification in Germany, and the SITS 92/48 specification in the United Kingdom. In Japan, the Cisco 2500 series supports the current INS-64 signaling specifications, and in North America, it supports the National ISDN-1 specification, AT&T's 5E6 ISDN specification for its 5ESS switch, and Northern Telecom's DMS ISDN specification. This is a good choice to use if you foresee the need for ISDN users or the need to expand your service between servers at different sites but don't want to get into the expense of another T1 link.

Connecting The Bulletin Board Users

If you want to run a BBS on the Web server, it's important that you understand the background of this connection approach. I want you to understand that if you run a BBS on the Web server, the potential impact can be severe if you're running a dozen users concurrently with the Internet users. These users gateway out of the BBS software via the Web server to get to the Internet, as shown in Figure 4.14. Notice that some of the connections are through the Web server software itself, and more server memory will be used to allow for this functionality.

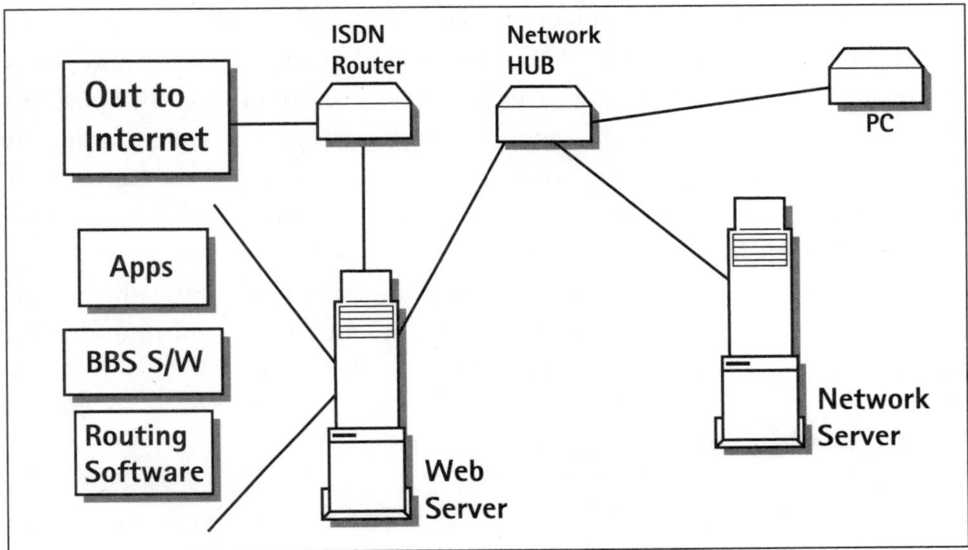

Figure 4.14
Getting BBS users out to the Internet.

Dealing With Your Internet Provider

Your site is spending large amounts of time on this project and lots of the CFO's budget, so something better work right. In fact, when you hit this point, most Internet providers supplying your connections treat you in a completely different light. You've dropped perhaps 10 grand to set up the site and perhaps $3,500 a month in connection fees. As such, you'll probably get fairly good service with your provider. Nonetheless, you need to do your own homework so you understand the system, how it works, and what to expect when it goes wrong. I've seen people duped into buying a new router that cost twice the amount of their existing router to fix a supposed anomaly in the system that only required a firmware upgrade to the original router. Now, I'm not saying that your provider will treat you wrong or try to sell you another router to fix a modem problem, but it's always worthwhile to know what to look for when your site goes down. That way, when you call for support, you and your provider will be on the same wavelength, or close, anyway.

This all comes back to how well the Webmaster is trained to support your site. If you tick off your Internet provider, you'll still get service, but I'll bet that you'll have your share of problems in the shadows. The market is cutthroat right now, but there are plenty of providers around to help you out...and just as many that'll get you into deeper trouble. They're so hungry for your business that some will promise you the moon to get you to sign on. The point here is that the more you know about your site and how to run it, the better your chances are to have a successful site. However, that doesn't mean that you have to take any crap from them. You sign the checks, and that puts you in the driver's seat. Let's face it, if your provider gives you a hard time, a bit of bad advertising on the Net means disaster for them when word gets around. It's a strange world out there, but the providers know that, too.

What's A Backup?

After you've created this Web server and spent hours to configure it exactly to your designs, how would you like for someone to pull the plug on the server and make it crash? What would you think if a rogue user logged into your server and deleted all the files in the FTP directory? These kinds of threats are all too common on new and existing servers. Hardware failure is another ever-present problem. We can never tell when hardware will fail or what will fail. The best defense from these disasters is a good backup philosophy.

Basic Backup Strategies

There are several ways to backup your server, but only a few wise ones. Over the years, I've learned that the backups are only as good as the equipment and tapes that you use. Avoid the generic tapes and instead purchase the higher-quality tapes from known manufacturers, such as Sony, Maxell, and 3M. Buying the preformatted tapes can save hours of formatting time and server operations. I also recommend using tape drives of 4GB and higher capacity to start. If you believe that QIC drives are viable in a serious server situation, you're fooling yourself. While QIC has made definitive gains in capacity and speed, when your server matures over the years, the backups are bound to stream over the 2GB mark and possibly over 4GB within 3 years.

Use top-quality software that is server based yet capable of backing up the work-stations on the network, if you intend to place the Web server onto the internal company network. In this manner, you can use the server-based backup for the critical workstations involved in the server project itself. The backup will also run faster and more efficiently. You'll find centralized control to be a benefit, making security easy to manage. For that reason, SCSI drives in Microsoft Windows NT Server are the only choice above 1GB.

While QIC and SCSI drives can both be used on the server, only SCSI drives are supported in high-end backup programs like Cheyenne Backup for NT. Additionally, the QIC backup tape drive must be located on the server itself. This lends further credence to the SCSI-only disk subsystem on the server.

Better Backups By Design

After acquiring the hardware, it's time to decide how you're going to do the real backup. There are several different forms of backup. Let's review the options:

- *Normal*—Makes a complete copy of the server files, including the registry, and resets the archive bit.
- *Incremental*—Copies only the files that have been added or modified since the last normal backup, and resets the archive bit. Incremental backups use the same tape for each backup if append mode is used.
- *Incremental Copy*—Same as incremental backup, but this option doesn't reset the archive bit.
- *Separate Incremental*—Same as incremental, except you use a different tape each time you backup.
- *Differential*—Copies the files added or changed since the last normal backup, resets the archive bit where applicable, but uses the same tape all the time until it's full or replaced.

You'll have to decide which is best for your server. If not a lot of data changes, say no more than 100MB, then perhaps an incremental is best. You can use the same tape time and time again until it's full or you change the tape. One server I administered used one 4GB tape for two weeks and never used beyond 25 percent of its capacity. The danger here is that if this tape breaks, gets lost, or is otherwise damaged, then all of those backups are lost. The benefit is that you can retrieve files based on dates or different needs, such as locating the third-oldest copy since you started backing up with this tape.

Differential backups are considered by many to be the way to go. The only difference here between differentials and incrementals is that differentials always use a different tape for each backup, regardless of the volume of data backed up. Differentials don't reset the archive bit, so backups are cumulative on each tape. This makes restoration easier when it's needed. This assures that if a tape drive goes bad, then only that set is lost. The downside is the volume of physical tapes required to support this strategy. Small sites won't see much of a storage problem, but at $20 to $35 a copy, this strategy gets expensive in a hurry.

Practical Backup Systems

When you design your server, backup systems should be in the forefront of the design. Integrating backups into the server from the start shows the CFO that not only do you have your act together in planning, but that you're serious about saving data and money. Of the vendors that make backup systems, a relative newcomer gets my aye vote: the Conner TapeStor 3200 SCSI-2 4GB tape backup system. It comes with decent backup software and is easy to install and use. Tapes for this system are around $25 apiece in the retail market, and bundles of 5 can be purchased for just under $100. When I last checked, $700 bought you the whole kit and 5 tapes to get you started. Now, don't get the idea that I'm saying that Conner makes the only good backup, because Hewlett-Packard, DEC, Fuji, and others have really good systems. Seagate's tape divisions are now putting out good products to go with their disk products.

Alternative Backup Systems

One possibility for backups that often is ignored is the use of an optical system. As a standard SCSI device, you can integrate one of these gems onto Microsoft Windows NT Server very easily. While backup software may or may not see the optical drive as a valid backup device, you can copy the critical files over to the optical drive instead of backing them up to tapes. This approach has the added benefit of having the files immediately available to users either by disk sharing or by simply copying the files back to the server's disk drives. These little 230MB drives are made by vendors such as Fujitsu. The drives are around $500, and the cartridges are priced around $22 apiece.

Toasted And Roasted—The Temperature Demon

Perhaps one of the most neglected topics of any server is one of heat and the degradation it causes on server performance, whether it be a Web server or a regular network server. I feel it is important that you know about heat, its effects on a server, and how you can ease the pain.

Why You Should Worry About Heat

Heat is the number one killer of computer components in a server. A study once suggested that for every 15-degree rise in temperature, the operational lifetime of electronics components decreases by 5 percent. This doesn't mean that if your server runs at 130 degrees, your server will only last for one year. What it does mean is that prolonged operation at high temperatures causes adverse reactions to these devices. Motors, bearings, plastics, and many other items inside a computer must work harmoniously and for a long period of time, but all of these components are nothing but man-made devices. It took man to make them, and another man-made device (electricity) to break them down. So you see, your server has a defined beginning, lifetime, and ending. It's the ending that we have no firm grasp on until the users start screaming that it doesn't work anymore. Do you remember the proverb "So hot you could cook an egg on it?" and its implications? Read onward, and see the practical examples.

Preventive Measures

One of the easiest and simplest things that you can do to solve the heat problem is to install a $15 fan strategically located inside the case. In the investigation that I spell out later in this section, placement of the fan is not as crucial to success as just installing the fan. Air stagnation between the circuit cards and disk drives causes the worst problems because the air flow is nearly zero. These fans are ideally 12 volt DC 3 1/2-inch fans rated at between 40 to 85 cubic feet per minute (cfm) of air flow. Fans that run over 100 cfm tend to be rather noisy and run at speeds that closely resemble turbo prop airplanes in takeoff mode. Not only that, but DC fans can be installed using the existing power plugs for a floppy drive or a hard drive.

With fans blowing inside the case, one anomaly can arise that defeats the fans and proper cooling. If two fans are installed inside the case, then the case (if tight fitting) can actually pressurize and cause a negative airflow. Nothing moves in the case because the pressure differential causes additional stagnation. In this case, the cure is worse than the ailment. By and large, two fans rated at 30 cfm each do the job fine.

When measuring the airflow or temperature doesn't lend itself to practical help and the machine is a critical component, then the quickest fix you can do is pull the cover off of the server. This lets the hot air move out of the restricted confines of the case.

A Practical Example

In the course of a computer's lifetime, it, and all components inside of it, experience both physical and thermal shock hundreds of times over. When a hard drive first has power applied to it, an electrical motor is energized to begin spinning the drive's internal component responsible for holding your data. This device, called a *spindle motor*, uses direct current as its powering source and generates heat. This initial surge of power also can be rated as much as 300 percent of the normal running voltage. The same DC current is applied to the various circuit cards installed inside the PC and thus begins the power up cycle we see when you turn on the PC's power supply switch. This seemingly peaceful occurrence is the hardest hit any PC will incur outside of a power surge, and it's the time when many hardware failures occur. Known as the peak inrush current, such a strain on the power supply itself can destroy it. Should you be worried about this fact? No. Modern power supplies are built with internal protection and engineering to withstand a lifetime of on/off cycles. The point is that this is the most stressful time on a PC's components.

In the four computer systems we tested, all were tested from a power off state and were timed for ranges of 4 to 24 hours after startup. Additionally, two were tested for long-range effects of leaving the system powered on throughout the year as seasonal changes occurred. The temperatures measured were compared with the other systems. The following is a list of the systems and their internal configurations:

System #1
Generic clone desktop PC, large case
12MHz 286 with 1MB RAM installed
Standard VGA board
1 serial and parallel port
Floppy controller with two floppy drives
Used as a network workstation
Class B certified

System #2
Same as System #1, but no floppies
Includes network adapter card
Small desktop case
Diskless workstation
Class A certified

System #3
33MHz 386 small case
8MB RAM installed
200MB IDE hard drive, two floppies
Tape drive
Standard AT I/O
SVGA card with 1MB RAM
Additional card
Class B certified

System #4
33MHz 386 Large tower case
12MB RAM installed; 8MB onboard and 4MB on 32-bit RAM board
Tape drive
Standard AT I/O card
Additional AT I/O card
CD-ROM drive and controller
340MB ESDI hard drive and ctrl
additional support card
All 8 slots used
Class A certified

It's important to understand that each system has its own characteristics that set it apart from the others. I didn't include the size of the power supplies because that statistic didn't have any bearing on the outcome of the tests. The sizes ranged from 150 watts to 230 watts, and all had single cooling fans. The item that did seem to matter was that the Class B certified machines all measured temperatures higher than the Class A rated machines. The small desktops also ran at higher temperatures. Changes in seasonal temperature swings simply make the systems run hotter or cooler with respect to the inside temperature of the testing room. Here is a list of the test environment conditions:

- The testing room temperature was set to 68 degrees Fahrenheit.
- Humidity ranged from 35 to 45 percent.
- A temperature probe was placed within two inches of the power supply's air intake screen, inside of the PC, and attached so as to remain in open air.
- Where possible, all systems had one empty slot between circuit cards.

Table 4.4 shows the progression of temperature for each system.

From the statistics shown in the table, you can see a wide range of rates of heating, and in general, the systems stabilized by the two-hour mark. In one system similar to System #3, the system's internal temperature reached 106.3 degrees after the 72-hour mark! So, when you see the moniker of "72 hour burn-in" that many manufacturers state their systems are put through, then you can tell that's quite a test. Now, expand that test to a one-week-long cycle, and you get a system subjected to a rigor virtually guaranteed to find system faults related to heat.

A word of caution, though. When systems are first assembled, brand-new parts tend to withstand this treatment considerably better than one- or two-year-old systems. As part of our reseller program, each system we intend to accept as a trade-in is subjected to a one-week-long continuous diagnostic test procedure. If it fails any part of this test, the system isn't accepted. Due to age, many systems will still run properly in daily usage (one to four hours) but fail when placed in this strenuous test condition.

The solution? After compiling these results, we searched for a suitable cooling fan to be placed in one or two strategic places. The first was to be mounted on the card support cage where all of those seldom-used black card guides are located inside of the system. The second was to be mounted in an unused drive

TABLE 4.4

COMPARISON OF SYSTEM TEMPERATURES.

Time into Test	System #1	System #2	System #3	System #4
15 minutes	68.3	68.8	69.1	68.5
30 minutes	70.5	69.7	70.5	69.8
45 minutes	72.9	71.0	72.3	70.5
1.00 hours	76.4	73.8	75.8	71.0
1.25 hours	78.3	75.1	79.4	72.0
1.50 hours	82.1	76.2	83.3	73.1
1.75 hours	85.5	77.9	85.6	75.2
2.00 hours	87.6	80.2	87.2	77.9
2.25 hours	88.1	81.9	88.2	78.1
2.50 hours	89.9	82.9	89.0	79.3
5.00 hours	92.1	88.7	90.3	82.0
10.0 hours	96.8	94.4	93.6	83.1
18.0 hours	99.4	97.4	95.7	83.3
24.0 hours	103.5	101.9	96.1	84.9

bay immediately above the hard drive, if one was installed, placing a cooling flow of air on the hard drive itself. The first fan placement choice would draw cool air from the outside of the system into the inside of the system. What we found was that to merely move the air inside the card slots resulted in a marked drop of internal temperatures. Because the power supply's fan could only exhaust the hot air within its immediate reach (8 to 12 inches) of the intake screen, the hot spots in between the circuit cards and hard drive would stagnate, resulting in higher temperatures. Sensor probes were placed around the hard drives of all systems under test, and a remarkable finding was made.

Much to our dismay, every system tested, and a few not listed here, were found to have two major hot spots. The first, and most obvious, was the hard drive. Regardless of drive size and type, each ran up temperatures in the range of 115 to 142 degrees Fahrenheit after 24 hours of continuous operation. The exception was the IDE hard drives, new to the PC computer arena. Those units consistently measured 20 degrees cooler than the rest. The second hot spot was the video board. It reported temperatures in the 95 to 105 degree range. For a general reminder, the circuit board slots, the onboard memory, and the CPU chip on many motherboards are all inline with each other in a four-inch-wide path.

In mounting those cooling fans, we thought of the hard drive first, and the sheer amount of heat it generated after 24 hours of operation. In a normal scenario, however, most users operate their system no more than six continuous hours a day, so instead, the video board becomes the major heat generator. Therefore, the first fan was installed on the card guide bracket.

Because heat rises, all of the heat was going to the top of the cabinet but wasn't moving to the power supply's exhaust fan. The card guide fan solved that problem, resulting in a 10- to 15-degree drop in internal temperatures, regardless of the systems detailed back in Table 4.4! System #3, the tightest sealed of the systems, dropped to an average runtime temp of 93 degrees from 103. Furthermore, installing the second fan immediately above the hard drive resulted in an additional eight-degree drop in operating temperature. With the fans installed, the hard drive now averaged 92 degrees, down from 142.

To take this test to further extremes, external cutoff switches were mounted inline with the fans' power so we could control the fan exterior to the system. This way, we could accurately measure the internal temperature without removing the case of the system. What we then found confirmed our earlier observations. Once warmed up beyond the 24-hour mark, stopping the fan above the hard drive resulted in rapid increases in the internal temperatures which the card cage fan could not keep up with. All four systems now averaged internal temperatures 8 to 10 degrees above room temperature, about 85 degrees.

The bottom line is this: Cooling your systems will inevitably result in longer life spans for systems used more than several hours each day. While you won't always be able to install a cooling fan blowing onto each hard drive, perhaps a single fan breaking up the heat around the RAID would be of immense help.

I should note that the fans used were running all the time, so long as the power to the system was on. We then found several fans that could adjust their speed proportionally to the amount of heat sensed. These fans, called *closed loop fans*, are unique. Their primary feature is a temperature sensor mounted within the fan itself, or an external electrical sensor which senses the average air temperature and adjusts the fan's speed accordingly. Although more expensive, these fans reduce the noise characteristically heard inside PCs. You can mount the sensor in the exhaust air, intake air, or anywhere else inside the system for maximum effect.

The best benefit is that as the system's internal temperature stabilizes, the heating/cooling effect in the electronic circuits is greatly reduced. One such effect is called *chip creep*. This condition causes circuit chips (primarily memory chips) to gradually back out of their sockets. Parity errors, unexplainable operation, or other problems may be caused by chip creep. Simply reseating the loose chips usually cures the problems.

Power-Protection Devices

Let's take a few minutes to go over the most important part of the site—proper power protection. Your Web server should have several forms of power protection, not just a single one. Bad weather and bad power have no worse evil twin cousin than dirty power. One lone lightning strike 20 miles away can show up on your doorstep and wreak havoc on your site. Most often, storms within five miles of your site are the prevalent cause of system outages in you area. Let's discuss some of the equipment used in the protection of your server. Also, more and more insurance companies are requiring the use of these devices if you want the hardware covered under a data processing policy.

The Difference Between A UPS, Filter, And Conditioner

Three types of power-protection devices are available to protect your server from power problems, sometimes referred to as *dirty power*. Dirty power refers to unstable power or several other types of power problems. Let's take a look at each and evaluate them in terms of our server's needs.

Most MIS types refer to an *Uninterruptible Power Supply* (UPS) as their way of protecting the network server or servers. A UPS is an alternate power supply, nothing more. If you lose primary AC power in the wall from the commercial source, the UPS kicks in to keep the server running. That's all! The batteries of UPSs average 20 minutes of standby power if primary power fails. This should give you enough time to close all applications and safely shut down the system.

Unfortunately, a UPS is a catchall solution that darkens system administrator's eyes to a larger problem—dirty power.

If you have a power sag or surge, the UPS is useless to you. Your "protected" equipment is likely to reboot or experience erratic behavior.

A filter is a device that senses very sharp and short duration spikes of power, such as lightning strikes, that only last for a few millionths of a second but are in the range of 10,000 volts or more. A filter looks at this voltage and runs it off to ground, much like the lightning rod does for the TV antenna on your house. It does nothing for a sag or surge, as those conditions occur relatively slowly with respect to a power spike. The filter is built to respond to these rapid changes in power situations.

This said, the power conditioner is a device that senses the power changes generated by power anomalies such as an air conditioner, refrigerator, or other high-power equipment turning on. The line voltage momentarily drops below, or rises above, 120 volts AC to something else, depending on the condition. A power conditioner senses these relatively slow changes in power and compensates by adjusting the output power to the device to a constant steady 120 volts AC. No filtering, just maintaining a steady 120 volts. Figure 4.15 shows the various types of power processing.

So, you've been introduced to the three main types of power problems that your site will see. There are others, to be sure, but these are the three that you can buy devices to guard against. Which one do you buy? How will this device help you? First off, changes in the makeup of power-protection devices have drastically improved over the last few years. What was once sold as a pure UPS now incorporates several advanced power-protection features. The UPS I use on the workstation on which I'm writing this manuscript is a 650 volt-ampere UPS that uses power sag and surge features, but no filtering.

Most commonly, you'll see a UPS with power conditioners built into it, which smooth out the input power in most situations and buffers those that are beyond normal conditioning. Those beyond the normal situations are called *brownouts.* In brownouts, power is lost for up to a second, and you'll actually see the lights dim considerably. It's at this time in low-power conditions when servers love to reboot. When the commercial power recovers from the sagging

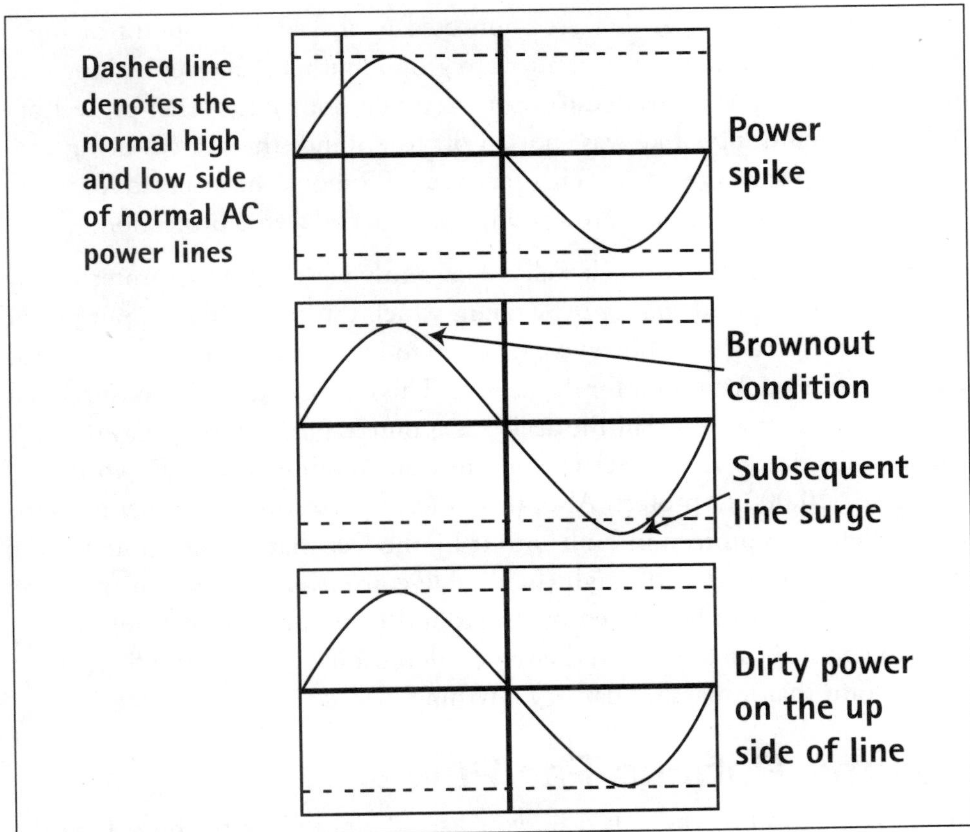

Figure 4.15
Power anomalies encountered by a computer.

power, a power surge usually occurs. Conditioners prevent this sudden surge from hitting your equipment. If the power drop lasts longer than a second or so, you can almost always count on a *blackout*, which is just that—into the dark you go! This is where a UPS will save you every time. I recently had a brownout that lasted a few seconds. Neither of my NT Servers missed a beat—didn't reboot, no harm done, nothing. My own PC has a UPS on it that beeped like a baby missing its bottle, and my fax PC rebooted at the first sign of the brownout.

Lightning Protection

Few devices incorporate power filters into the UPS because of the inherent problems with a UPS handling such large transient voltages. These filters are usually standalone boxes that are connected to the very first point of input power, so any lightning strikes are sent to ground rather than ever making it to the devices. However, this doesn't mean that you don't need other protection. When the lightning strike was shorted off to ground, the devices being protected temporarily lose power. That means a UPS should be installed for them. You're not installing double protection, but rather a layered protection.

There are UPS units that work well concurrently with lightning protectors by using a method called *sine wave power,* in which the commercial input power (which is AC voltage, of course) is converted to DC voltage and then converted back into filtered AC power for the devices. This double protection ensures that the power being consumed by the devices is as pure as possible. You'll pay through the nose for this kind of specialized protection equipment, but it's worth it if you have $20,000 to protect. Also, this kind of protection equipment has inherent lightning protection built into it by the fact that it takes time for the power spike to make it through the double-conversion process. In this time frame, the spike can be filtered off to ground if the protection equipment is built to handle it. In any event, the spike will most likely be drastically reduced to the point that it may not damage anything.

Volume Ratings For Power

When you go to buy these devices, you'll see the rating on the outside of the box. It's nice of the marketing folks to do that, but it's somewhat misleading for your server. That number on the outside is normally the *volt-ampere* (*VA*) rating and not the true wattage rating. Let's look at an example of this. I want to purchase a UPS that protects my workstation, which has a 300-watt power supply. What will be the power rating of the UPS that will serve my needs? Take the wattage and divide it by 0.707, which yields 424. This is the volt-ampere-equivalent rating. Current devices usually include a unit of 450 VA, which should do for most any situation. Most vendors of power-protection devices will advise you to purchase a UPS that is rated at 25 percent higher than the maximum load you expect to put on it. This gives a good working margin for the UPS so it doesn't work too hard. If the UPS runs at 90 percent of its rating all the time, it'll wear out faster. In the vast majority of computers, the power supply in it never runs above 50 percent load, so the 300-watt example could be cut in half and the same computer could possibly use a 250 VA unit safely.

Personally, I advise my own clientele not to use anything under a 600 VA for a safe margin.

But is the computer base unit the only thing you'll put on it? How about the monitor? Modems? Answering machine? All of these take up power. Most monitors run at an average of 2 amperes of current, which equates to 240 watts of power. Add this to an estimated 150 watts of continuous internal power, and now you have about 400 watts of power needs. Divide that by 0.707, and now you have 565 VA of power. So, now? Is the 650 VA enough? You're running this poor 600 VA UPS at 95 percent of its capacity. This isn't a good thing at all. So, you can either get a larger UPS or don't put the monitor on it.

Estimating Your Volume Of Power

To protect yourself adequately, it's important that you're aware of how much power your server uses. To keep it short and direct, let's use Table 4.5 to illustrate the point about estimating power for a Web server.

This should show you that even on an average mid-range Web server, a 1,200 VA UPS is just barely enough to do the job. It's not unreasonable to jump right up to a 2,000 VA UPS and bypass any potential problems with power.

A Word About Extension Cords

Extension cords are one sure-fire way to get your site into trouble with a capital *T*. If you really need additional outlets, that's one thing. But, to use cheap two-wire

Table 4.5

Estimated power requirements for a Web server.

Device	Runtime Wattage	Volt-Amperes
Computer	200	283
Monitor	250	353
External Drives	200	283
Subtotal	650	919
25% Margin	163	230
Total	813	1149

extension cords with multiple outlets is not using proper grounding and can result in shorted-out power supplies.

The usage of poor-quality extension cords can result in fire or possible electrocution. Multiple-outlet devices should consist of only UL-approved cords and outlet devices. Ensure that the total rated power of the devices plugged into the extensions does not exceed the breaker rating of the power source.

There are times when you need more outlets than you have physical wall plugs, and this happens all the time. However, do yourself and the fire marshall a favor, and use proper extensions. One of the best ones to use is the surge-protected, four- and six-plug multi-outlet boxes. Tripp Lite and APC both make fine devices that solve this need well. *No matter what you do, don't exceed the maximum rating of the wall outlet.* No amount of quality extension devices can replace a burnt-down workshop.

Multiple-Outlet Control Centers

One really neat device is the power center or controller that resides under your monitor on the desktop itself. This device is the same thing as one of those rectangular power strips, except that it's a flat pizza box style. The one on my desk is about the size of a small pizza box. It has a switch for the computer box, monitor, printer, modem, and one auxiliary device. It does in fact have a measure of surge protection built into the device, so it makes it nice to have on systems that have no UPS at all. While not a power line filter or UPS, it goes a long way to organizing your power connections, if nothing else, but remember that it's no real replacement for a true UPS or line conditioner.

Backup Generators

The last topic of this section, and the chapter, is one of a power generator. This device actually creates usable power from a motor generator engine. In reality, it's a power-generation station. Perhaps only a few thousand watts of power, but it does the job nicely for small volumes. You've undoubtedly heard of someone using a generator when they lost power because of a tornado, hurricane, or other form of natural disaster to keep AC power to critical equipment. Generators are meant to be short-term solutions to loss of power and not long-term continued usage. These little "personal" generators come in all shapes and designs but, most notably, average 2,000 watts of output power on a continuous basis. If you look at the most essential parts of the network and what it would take to keep the site operational, you'll see that you need 3,500 watts of power for the server, all components of the server, and the router equipment.

One thing that you should keep firmly in your mind is that when you run one of these generators, the output power is not as clean or steady as regular commercial power. To use a generator for a computer, you definitely need a line conditioner and a UPS to keep stable line power going to the server. Also, you may need to turn off the generator at times to let it cool down and refill the gasoline or diesel fuel or whatever is used to power the generator. During this time, of course, the server must come down lest you drain the batteries. Generators have this little thing called a *duty cycle*, which means that the generator is capable of supplying a certain amount of power at 50 percent of the rated speed or capacity of the device. If the duty cycle is exceeded for long periods of time, meaning if you constantly draw 3,000 watts of power from a 3,500 watt capacity generator for hours on end, then the generator will age very rapidly and produce poor power. Not only that, but such a load factor is not advisable on a temporary power source.

Generators are nice, but they have limited outlets. In addition to that, you'll have to run an extension cord from the generator to the devices to be powered. If the distance is beyond 50 feet, then you'll need a power cord of much higher capacity rating than the standard cords you'll see in Kmart or Wal-Mart. Those are fine for normal low-power needs, but this is different. Figure 4.16 illustrates the method my company chose for integrating a generator into the power distribution at my office. By doing it this way, I was able to use standard wiring for heavy usage and standard circuit breakers for power isolation.

Figure 4.16 was approved for our electrical operations. It's meant to provide you with alternative power distribution and redundancy needs. Consult with your electrician to ensure compliance with state, local, and city ordinances before attempting any such power modifications in your office. Failure to do so may render your electrical system unsafe or in violation of your insurance company or local fire regulations.

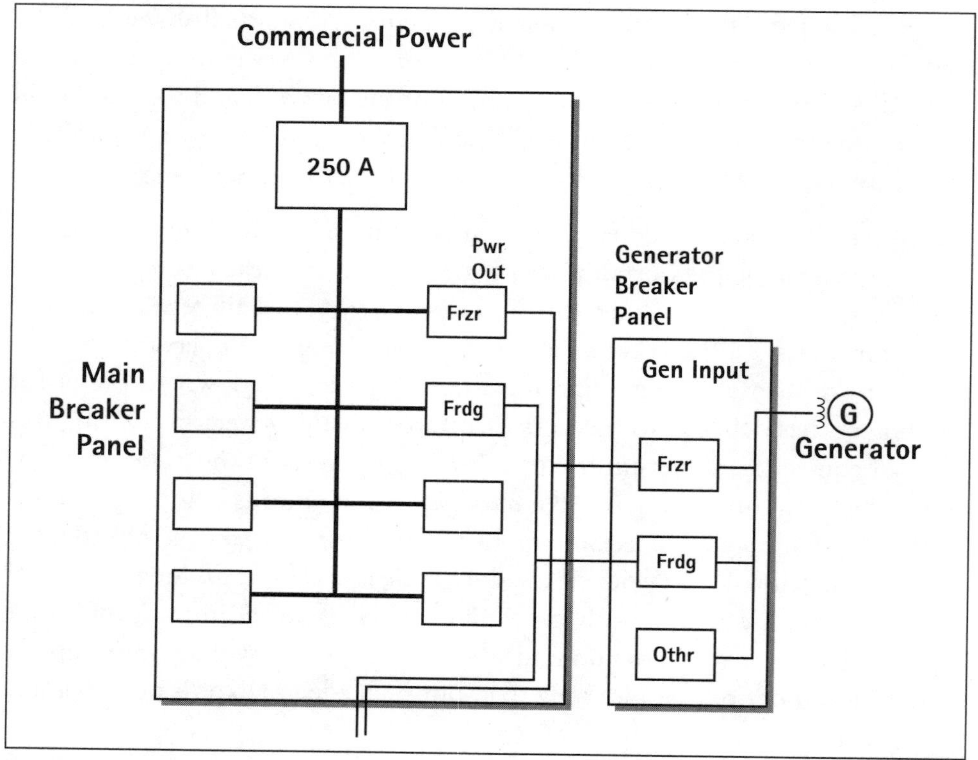

Figure 4.16
Integrating a generator into your power system.

With this scheme, if we lost commercial power, I could turn off the breaker to the commercial source and turn on the breaker to our generator, thereby sending power to the desired in-house equipment by selectively turning on or off the breakers in the main power panel.

The real trick to this is to remember when to turn which breaker on or off. If you forget to turn off the breakers to remove the path to commercial power, then the generator and any associated equipment connected to the generator could be destroyed!

Summary

This has been a really demanding chapter, because every aspect of a Web server has been covered to help enhance your understanding of a Web server and how to build one. Hopefully, you'll take this knowledge forth and build a good server. In reading this chapter, you've learned about:

- Three types of servers and how to apply them
- Various pieces of server hardware to enhance your server's operations and safety
- Connecting your server to the Internet
- How temperature can affect your server
- Some of the dos and don'ts of power protection

In Chapter 5, we'll install the Microsoft Internet Information Server. This server is a native tool of Microsoft Windows NT Server, and it ties directly into the operating system in a native form. We'll discuss the many parts of the Web server, and how it can work for you. So stay tuned for another exciting chapter in the saga of the NT Web Server.

Part 2

Building Your NT Web Server

5 Installing NT Server

Jeff Bankston

This chapter is all about installing NT Server. It covers virtually every part of the basic installation process, and you'll see, beforehand, what the process is all about. NT isn't very difficult to install, but you'll have to make some key decisions along the way to have a successful installation. If there is one chapter worthy of reading before actually doing, this is it! The administrative parts of this installation will be addressed in Chapter 6, so hold on to those thoughts until then.

NT Hardware

There is a small book that comes with your copy of NT Server called the *Hardware Compatibility List (HCL)*. This book lists computer systems and components that are certified by Microsoft to be compatible and reliable for use with the NT NOS. The HCL is usually out of date as soon as it's printed due to the ever-increasing number of certified devices for NT Server. So, if you're planning to purchase newer hardware, you'll need to find a newer, more complete HCL. The most up-to-date and easiest to use HCL is located on the Internet at **www.microsoft.com/ntserver/hcl**. This version of the HCL is created in HTML

(Hypertext Markup Language) so you can view it on the World Wide Web. In addition, a text version of the HCL can be downloaded via FTP (File Transfer Protocol) from the Internet at **ftp.microsoft.com/bussys/winnt/3.51/HCL**. Downloading the document is useful when you want to review the HCL without being connected to the Internet. There is no set timetable for updated releases of the HCL. Microsoft releases an update when enough new information becomes available to warrant a new edition. Therefore, you need to check the online HCL often to ensure that you purchase the right hardware. As you'll see, NT Server is rather picky about some hardware. The next section expounds upon this by examining how NT utilizes hardware.

How NT Server Views The Hardware

By design, hardware can only be accessed in NT through a protective layer. Therefore, if software isn't written to be in this protective environment, it isn't allowed to speak directly with the hardware.

The NT operating system code may run in one of two modes: unprivileged or privileged. The heart of the NT NOS is called the *Executive*. The all-encompassing Executive and its underlying system services operate in kernel, or privilege, mode. All other subsystems and applications operate in user, or non-privilege, mode. Because NT is a client/server operating system, the non-privilege area and above is the client area. All areas below this line operate in kernel mode and belong to the NT Executive (with the exception of the actual hardware). This area is the server area. This defined line of program execution is what gives NT much of its power and flexibility. None of the applications (or non-privilege functions) can reach the hardware without first going through the kernel services. This prevents errant applications from crashing the entire server.

Generally, when instructions come to the Executive, they're executed in *burst mode*. This means a subsystem may make a service call that is handed off to the Executive. The Executive momentarily calls the appropriate manager in kernel mode and then hands the response back to the appropriate subsystem.

Let's next examine how NT's subsystems operate and create the flexibility NT is renowned for.

NT Server Subsystems

Subsystems are mini environments that are specific to an operating system or a CPU. A subsystem interprets a CPU or OS instruction and translates it into understandable NT instructions. When a subsystem is called, it's given its own protected area in which to run. This makes an application feel as if it's running on a machine in its own environment. Let's see what happens when you try to run a program in NT.

When you try to run a program in NT, NT first tries to determine which subsystem an application is written for. If NT figures it out, NT hands the program to the appropriate subsystem, where it is executed. If NT can't figure out which application to run, an error message displays. Simple and elegant. There are a number of NT server subsystems, including Win32, DOS, 16-Bit Windows, OS/2, and Unix Posix. Let's take a look at each subsystem.

The Win32 System

Win32 is responsible for controlling NT's system interface. This is the video, keyboard, and mouse input controller for other subsystems. It's central to NT's functionality. All other subsystems are channeled to the Win32 subsystem, which means that all other subsystems send their translated instructions to Win32 for execution.

The DOS System

Because DOS is not a multitasking OS, this subsystem is treated differently than the others. When NT runs the DOS-protected subsystem, a Virtual DOS Machine (VDM) is created. The VDM is a PC emulator that creates a protected 16MB space for running DOS programs. Unlike other subsystems, each time a DOS program is executed, a new 16MB VDM is allocated. As you can see, it doesn't take long to swallow up resources when running DOS programs.

The 16-Bit Windows System

The 16-Bit Windows subsystem borrows from the DOS VDM. When the first 16-Bit Windows application is executed, a 16MB VDM is created. Unlike the DOS subsystem, only one VDM is created. Then, the WOW (Windows On Win32) Windows emulator runs. This multitasking emulator sets up each new task as a thread within the original VDM and WOW. As with all subsystems, any program trying to directly access the hardware will be terminated and an error message generated.

The OS/2 Subsystem

OS/2 is already a multitasking 32-bit operating system, so no VDM is required. This means that NT has less to do with this subsystem than with the others. However, this subsystem only allows character-based software to run—no GUI software support here! All system calls are mapped to the appropriate NT service. Any illegal hardware calls are trapped by the NT Executive. Keep in mind that NT will not run OS/2 2.X applications—only character-based OS/2 1.X software.

The Posix Subsystem

Here is another character-based subsystem. Unix Posix only accepts character-based software, doesn't require a VDM, and uses the Executive to trap all illegal hardware calls.

Now with a little NT hardware and system background under your belt, let's embark on an installation adventure!

Performing The Installation

Before we get started, you should install, set up, and thoroughly test your hardware, both alone and in conjunction with all other hardware. Now is the time to get out your NT boot disks and CD-ROM. Ensure that you have any special hardware driver disks handy, as well. Assuming you are working with a new hard drive, make sure you have an MS-DOS boot disk handy with Fdisk and Format on it. Boot from this disk, and then use Fdisk to create the partition you want to install NT to and any other work partitions you'll need. Ensure the boot partition is active. Now, let's get going.

Installing NT

To install NT Server, here are the basic steps you should expect to perform during this process:

- Copy initial files
- Automatically create the core NT directories and copy the server files

- Choose the server's devices and configure the network protocols
- Complete final configuration of the server

In this chapter, I'll take you through the steps you need to take for a plain vanilla installation. Insert installation disk #1, and reboot the machine. Ensure the NT 4.0 CD-ROM is in the drive.

You should then see a screen that tells you how to proceed with the installation, providing information about the install and how to perform an installation, repair a damaged installation (which uses the Recovery Disk), or quit the setup.

Most of the other options are self explanatory. We'll cover the Repair option later in this chapter. Pressing F1 here will give you a brief help file on NT installation. If you've forgotten something or arrived here by accident, F3 will allow you to exit gracefully.

The next information screen will inform you about what you can expect to see in the way of mass storage detection. This includes any disk controllers, RAID (Redundant Array of Inexpensive Disks) devices, SCSI CD-ROM drives, and such devices. It is not, however, for the tape drive if you have one.

Next, NT will attempt to detect the major installation components (not all components—just the major installation components).

Detecting Installation Hardware

NT does a pretty good job at detecting installation hardware. NT should detect your SCSI adapter (if you have one) and your CD-ROM. If you plan on using an IDE drive system on a PCI bus machine, this will show up as a PCI/IDE dual device. If NT doesn't detect all your equipment (your Creative Labs Panasonic CD-ROM, for instance), press S, select the equipment NT missed from the list, and continue. If the system hangs on the detect phase, press the reset switch (or CTRL+ALT+DEL), and when you get back to this screen, press S. Then, manually select your equipment from the list, and continue. You will be prompted shortly to insert disk #2, and then onward to disk #3 after the installation proceeds.

At this point, NT displays the mass storage devices found and their native drivers. If no devices were found, and you know that there are indeed SCSI devices, you'll get a chance to load those drivers from the disks or CD-ROM for those units.

You'll be presented with a list of installed devices that NT found. The list of installed devices should be accurate for 95 percent of all your devices. If it's not, move the highlighted bar up and down using the cursor keys. Press Enter to see a list of items, change the item(s) in question, move the highlight bar to The Above List Matches My Computer, and press Enter.

Choose the partition where you want to install NT, or use the tools presented to create the partition. You may also choose to set up partitions in unpartitioned space. If so, highlight the partition, press C, and follow the simple on-screen instructions. When you return to this set of options, highlight the partition you want to install NT (normally C:), and press Enter. If you make a mistake in the unpartitioned area, you can always highlight the partition and press D to delete it. Then, highlight the partition again, create the partition, and press Enter.

Before we continue, a little discussion about partition types is in order.

Partition Types

If you're working with NT Workstation, you can leave the partition in the FAT (File Allocation Table) system. If you're working with NT Server, you should choose NTFS (NT File System). Why? Let's review some of the key features of NTFS.

- NTFS is designed specifically for NT to take advantage of system security. FAT has absolutely no security whatsoever.
- NTFS supports long file names (up to 256 characters), multiple extensions, as well as the old 8+3 convention (eight characters plus a three-character extension). When working with Windows 95 clients, the advantages of long file names are enormous. NTFS saves uppercase and lowercase letters in file names. When searching, NT is case insensitive, however.
- NTFS directly supports RAID levels one and five.
- NTFS keeps tabs on what you're doing in case of a power loss or other type of failure (configuration, for instance). This will allow you to reboot your machine to the last-known good configuration.

The advantages of NTFS far outweigh those of FAT. If your machine will be operating in a multiboot (multiple operating system) environment or as an NT Workstation, leave it as a FAT partition, because operating systems such as

Windows 95 don't recognize NTFS. But then again, if this is a server, you shouldn't be dual booting between a server and a client.

The next thing NT offers to do is to check for corruption on the disk drives. I suggest you allow NT to perform this check in case something is amiss with your drives. Depending on the speed of your equipment, the copying process will probably take 30 to 45 minutes. Be patient, and take another break. When the copying process is completed, you'll need to reboot the server for the changes to take effect.

Initial Installation Restart

When you restart your system, NT checks the hardware, verifies the hard drive (CHKDSK), converts the hard drive to NTFS if you chose that option, sets the default file permissions, and continues the setup process. Next, you'll be presented with the Software License Agreement. Read the agreement, and then click Yes to continue. NT will now prepare you for installation and present you with a request for your server's name and organization.

Enter your name and organization information, then click on Next. Pick the mode of licensing that you've purchased.

I suggest you read the section in your NT manuals about licensing to determine whether you will need *per seat* or *per server* licensing. Most users require per seat licensing. If you are migrating from another NOS, special pricing will be available. Expect migration pricing of around $15 per seat (client) and $30 to $35 for standard purchase. You can purchase licensing along with NT Server as a package deal, also. If I tried to include all the pricing rules in this book, it would take up a considerable amount of space. So, instead, I suggest you contact Microsoft (U.S.) sales at 1-800-426-9400 for more pricing information.

Enter the appropriate number of licenses, then click on Next.

At this point, you should see the Computer Name screen. This is the name of your server as will be seen in the Master Browser.

As discussed earlier in this book, you should pick a machine name that makes sense and is unique on the network. The name must be 15 or fewer characters. If you pick a name that is already in use, you can enter a different machine name later. The next thing you'll decide is the domain controller type, if any.

Enter a machine name, then click on Next.

Deciding On Your Domain

If you're creating a new network and you only have one server on your network, then your server type needs to be a PDC (Primary Domain Controller). If you're working with a new domain and your server will be the primary server for the domain, then choose PDC. Remember, each domain can have only one PDC because a PDC authenticates all logon requests for its domain. Check with your network administrator if you're in doubt. Once you accept a selection on the Server Type wizard screen, it can't be reversed without a complete NT reinstallation. If you're working on an existing network, chances are, a PDC already exists, and your machine should be a BDC (Backup Domain Controller). You may have as many BDCs on your network as you wish. If you want to run your computer as a standalone server, choose option three.

Choose either PDC, BDC, or standalone, and click on Next.

You use this next screen to create the Administrators account and assign the account password. Write down this information, and keep it in a safe place. Don't allow anyone to have access to this information, or they'll have complete access to your network! Choose a password that will be hard for anyone to guess. Combinations of letters and numbers are best. Try to keep the password from 8 through 14 characters long. This makes it harder to break. *Do not* choose birth dates, serial numbers, children's names, and so forth.

Enter your password. Then click on Next.

The Emergency Repair Disk wizard screen appears next.

I highly recommend that you create an emergency repair disk (ERD). An ERD will have all of your system-specific configuration data on it. This information is a must if your NT installation becomes corrupt and you can't boot your system. You'll thank me later for encouraging you to create an ERD. For now, put a disk in your A drive, and click on Next.

The disk will be formatted, and all the hard configuration work you've done thus far will be saved. If you change your configuration, I suggest you update your ERD immediately. This is accomplished by running the file RDISK.EXE located in C:\winnt\system32. In the event you have to repair your installation, you'll be asked for this disk. So label it, date it, and store it in a safe place. If you're paranoid (like me), make two disks in case one disk goes bad. Again, click on Next to continue. Your monitor should now display the Select Components screen.

The default settings work great here. If you're curious, click on one of the boxes, and click on Details to see what is available. If you get confused on what you clicked or didn't click, just click on Reset, and the program will set everything back to the default. When you're finished snooping around, click on Next.

Now, you'll choose the type of connection to your network. Choose whichever action is true for your configuration. Most people installing NT Server will choose Wired To The Network. Choosing this option means that you have a network card (Network adapter or ISDN) in the server and that the server will be your primary connection to the network. New to NT 4.0 is the Remote Access To The Network option, which allows you to become a member of the network through dialup networking. Dialup networking uses a modem in place of a NIC to connect remotely to your network. Once connected, there is no difference between a wired and a remote connection, except speed. Choose the correct method for your installation, and click on Next.

This next screen allows you to install Internet Information Server (IIS), if you so choose. IIS is a Web server developed by Microsoft that allows you to publish and serve HTML documents across the Internet or your intranet. This comes at no additional charge. The IIS also enables you to develop a local intranet, even if you do not want to connect to the Internet. Many corporations are finding that a local intranet is an efficient and effective method to distribute information to employees. Either way, you'll need to install TCP/IP for the IIS to function properly. Keeping this in mind, choose the option you require, and click on Next.

The next thing you'll do is install a network adapter. To have NT Setup search for your network adapter, click on Start Search.

Choosing Your Network Card

For 99 percent of all the NIC cards out there, NT will properly detect them. If NT didn't find the right NIC in your setup, click on Select From List, and see if you can find your NIC manually. If you can't find your NIC, check the disks that came with your NIC to see if an NT 4.0 driver is provided. If not, call your manufacturer or check the World Wide Web. A great place to search on the

Web is at Yahoo!, **www.yahoo.com**. Yahoo! literally has millions of companies and products listed.

Click on Next to see the adapter found. If none was found, you can skip this part now or do a manual install of the adapter.

Click on Next.

The next thing you'll have to do is choose the network protocol used on the server, and this is also what the clients will use to connect to the server.

Choosing The Network Protocol

In an environment of Windows 95 and NT Workstation, NetBEUI can be used where a single segment is present and TCP/IP is not required for Internet access. NWLink is Microsoft's incarnation of SPX/IPX for Netware servers.

If you'll be running a standard Microsoft network with Windows 95, 3.11, or NT clients, install NetBEUI. If you have any NetWare clients on the network, install NWLink. If you'll be connecting your server to the Internet or you'll be setting up an intranet, install TCP/IP.

If you need any of the following protocols, click on Select From List:

- *DLC Protocol*—Used to communicate with IBM mainframe computers and equipment across LANs.
- *Point To Point Tunneling Protocol*—Allows remote users to securely access corporate networks over the Internet.
- *Streams Environment*—Provides a common software wrapper around transport layers.

Otherwise, click on Next.

The next installation screen shows you what services will be installed on your server. You can either confirm the list or go backwards in the process to correct any mistakes. This is a major improvement for NT Server over previous versions. If you noticed a mistake here in earlier versions, you had to start over at the beginning.

Table 5.1 displays additional available network services.

NT will now install the drivers, services, and components necessary to ensure that your network operates properly.

TABLE 5.1

ADDITIONAL NETWORK SERVICES AVAILABLE WITH NT INSTALLATION.

Service	Description
Gateway (And Client) Services For NetWare	Used to access NetWare servers and resources.
Microsoft DHCP Server	Used for dynamic configuration of TCP/IP parameters for network workstations and servers.
Microsoft DNS Server	Used to provide a Domain Name Server (DNS) on Internet networks.
Microsoft TCP/IP Printing	Used to provide print capabilities over the Internet.
Network Monitor Agent	Used to monitor the network data stream.
Network Monitor Tools And Agent	Used to monitor the network data stream.
Remoteboot Service	Used to start MS-DOS and Microsoft Windows workstations over the network.
RIP For Internet Protocol	Routing Information Protocol over IP.
RPC Support For Banyan	Remote Procedure Call (interprocess communication) support for Banyan Vines clients.
RIP For NwLink IPX/SPX Compatible Transport	Routing Information Protocol over IPX.
SAP Agent	Service Advertising Protocol (over IPX) agent.
Services For Macintosh	Macintosh network support.
Simple TCP/IP Services	Basic TCP/IP services.
SNMP Service	Simple Network Management Protocol for network monitoring.
Dynamic Host Control Protocol	Dynamic IP allocation for NT.

Completing The Installation

At different times during the remainder of the installation, dialog boxes will appear asking you for information specific to your server's operation. For example, the first dialog box you'll probably see is the Network Adapter Card Setup dialog box. This dialog box asks for the I/O Port Address (in hex), the assigned Interrupt Number, and the transceiver type (e.g., 10BaseT).

Next, the installation will ask if you have a DHCP server on your network. You'll probably need at least one. Install a DHCP server if your server is the Primary Domain Controller or a Backup Domain Controller.

If you chose remote networking earlier, RAS will be installed and will attempt to detect your modem. If RAS can't determine your modem type, you can choose your modem type manually by clicking Don't Detect My Modem, I Will Select It From A List.

After you set up your modem, you'll be prompted for your area code (mandatory), access numbers for an outside line (if necessary), and tone or pulse dialing. If you selected RAS server, you'll be prompted for the setup information now. If you don't want to allow remote TCP/IP clients to be able to dial in, select Cancel. Otherwise, fill in your network data.

Programs and services will continue to be installed and bound to their respective protocols. If you chose to install DHCP, you'll be asked for the IP address of the DHCP server. Then, you'll get a chance to review and change the bindings for your network.

Click on Next to start the network services that will put the server online to the network.

If you assigned your machine to be a Primary Domain Controller, you'll be presented with a choice to make for the domain name. You'll need to fill in the name of the domain that your machine will be controlling, and, if it isn't filled in for you, the computer name. Don't use spaces in the names, as it causes problems with some client software. If you decide this should be a Backup Domain Controller, then you'll need to enter in the information for the domain name, the domain administrator's account, and password. This causes the BDC to join the domain, have a machine account created, and synchronize the domain accounts between the PDC and the BDC.

When you're done with your selection of the domain controller, click on Next.

Click on Finish.

Final Installation Options

If you chose to install the Microsoft Internet Information Server 2.0 earlier, you'll be presented with a dialog box now for what parts to install. For most applications, the defaults are sufficient.

Click on OK all the way through the dialog boxes. Next comes the Date/Time Properties dialog box. Pick the appropriate time zone, and click on Close.

Now, you'll need to choose video properties compatible with your video adapter. Pick a resolution that will allow you to have a readable-size desktop. Chances are, NT will detect the proper video adapter. If not, choose a compatible one. Make sure you test your picks before you click on OK. If you forget to test, don't worry—NT will remind you and give you a second opportunity.

NT Setup now installs desktop applications, creates shortcuts, sets security on system files, configures your desktop, and saves the configuration. Don't be alarmed if it takes quite a while to save the configuration—this is normal. You will be prompted for a disk to create an Emergency Repair Disk—all pertinent setup data will be backed up on this disk. I recommend you create this second ERD because the first one was for the basic install, and this ERD covers the finished install. Make sure you label it and store it in a safe place.

Congratulations! You have completed a Windows NT 4.0 installation. Press the Restart Computer button, and you are officially finished.

What To Do When The Installation Fails

Installations fail for a multitude of reasons but mostly due to software/hardware incompatibilities. Let's take a look at some of the reasons why an installation may fail, and what you can do about it if it happens to you.

Software/Hardware Incompatibility

If NT starts and tells you that a service failed, open Programs|Administrative Tools (Common)|Event Viewer. Examine the logs to determine which service failed and why. With this information, most times, you can take corrective action.

A System Crash

Many times, if a piece of software fails, you'll get a system crash commonly called a *blue screen*. A blue screen has debugging information that can be used by either a Microsoft tech rep or an experienced programmer to find out the cause of a problem. When the system crashes, the contents of memory (by default) will be written to disk. This gives you several seconds to make observations. If you examine the top of the screen (quickly, before it disappears), you will see the offending program's name. Remove the program, and try to find a replacement from the manufacturer. If the machine has successfully booted at least once, and you have since made changes which caused the machine to fail, reset the machine. Then, on the second boot screen when you see Press Spacebar NOW To Invoke Hardware Profile/Last Known Good Configuration, press your spacebar.

When the next screen displays, press L to boot using the Last Known Good Configuration. If the machine still refuses to boot, you may need to repair your NT installation. To do so, get out the Emergency Repair Disk you made earlier. Put the NT installation disk #1 into drive A, and reset the machine. This will begin the installation process and afford you the opportunity to repair the installation. This process appears to be an installation, but pay careful attention to the screen presented to you.

Choose R to repair an installation.

Your computer will ask you for two more disks, then the Emergency Repair Disk. Critical system files will be copied to your previous installation, in case they have become corrupt.

Pick Overwrite All or you'll be pressing Y at every replacement. When the process is finished, NT will reset and, hopefully, reboot. Keep this repair option in mind, as you'll need to accomplish it whenever your NT installation becomes unusable. If all else fails, install NT from scratch, and overwrite the previous installation.

When you finally have your NT installation running, it's time to try a few connectivity checks.

Testing The New Installation

Now that you have your new NT installation running, you need to try a few connectivity checks. First, open Programs|Administrative Tools (Common)| Server Manager.

You should be able to see your server and any other server within this domain. If not, open the Computer menu, then select Add To Domain. Choose whether this will be an NT Workstation/Server or an NT BDC. Then, enter the computer's name, and click on Add.

Once you view your machine, double-click on it.

You should see a Properties dialog box. If you see the dialog box, then you're communicating with the machine. Windows 95 clients should automatically appear if you have a good network connection. If you're using a Windows 95 client, double-click on Network Neighborhood and the computers registered in the domain should appear. When the dialog box opens, you should see your new server and the rest of the computers on the network, providing they're within the same group/domain.

Now that you've established network connectivity, let's discuss adding users.

Basic User Configuration

For most applications, the default configuration will work fine. But there are times when you might want to add a user to the Administrator's group, restrict the hours in which users can access the server, and so on. Changes to user configurations are accomplished using the User Manager For Domains, located in Programs|Administrative Tools (see Figure 5.1).

You can use the User Manager For Domains to accomplish the following tasks:

- Create new local/global groups
- Add and delete users
- Change user names
- Assign users to specific groups
- Assign user profiles and home directories

Username	Full Name	Description
Administrator		Built-in account for administering the computer/domain
Guest		Built-in account for guest access to the computer/domain
IUSR_SERVER	Internet Guest Account	Internet Server Anonymous Access

Groups	Description
Account Operators	Members can administer domain user and group accounts
Administrators	Members can fully administer the computer/domain
Backup Operators	Members can bypass file security to back up files
Domain Admins	Designated administrators of the domain
Domain Guests	All domain guests
Domain Users	All domain users
Guests	Users granted guest access to the computer/domain
Print Operators	Members can administer domain printers
Replicator	Supports file replication in a domain
Server Operators	Members can administer domain servers
Users	Ordinary users

Figure 5.1
User Manager For Domains.

- Assign specific hours in which users can access the network
- Specify which workstations users may log on to
- Specify account expiration dates
- Grant dialin permissions to users
- Establish policies and trust relationships
- Set user security via NTFS and Share permissions

You probably will not use all of these options, but they're there if you need them. The majority are self-explanatory. Lets look at the most-used options—adding users and assigning user security—in greater detail.

Adding Users

Adding a new user with default settings is very easy. First, start up the User Manager (or the Administrative Wizard). Next, select the User|New User. Figure 5.2 shows the New User dialog box.

Fill in the user's network username. Then, fill in the full name of the user and a brief description about the user (like, which group they are a member of and their contact phone number). I suggest you standardize this information so, as your network grows, finding information will be easy. Next, fill in the user-supplied password. You will have to do this twice for confirmation, and you'll

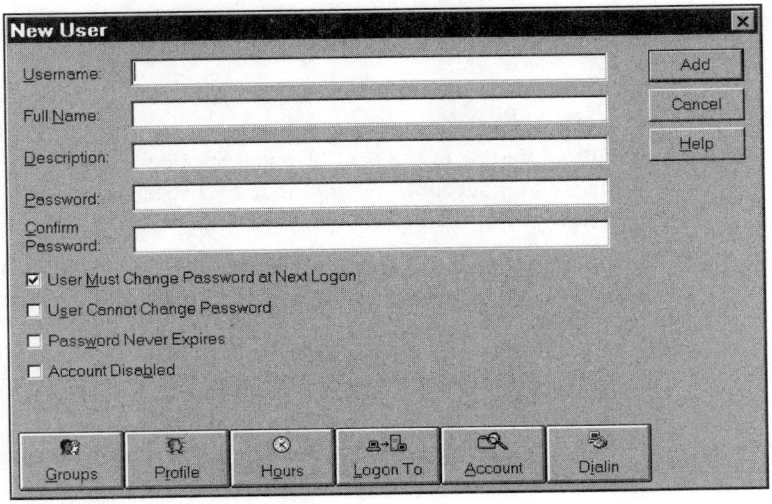

Figure 5.2
User Manager New User dialog box.

not be able to see what you enter. If this information is lost, you'll have to enter a new password. You can't see passwords, as they're masked and encrypted.

Next, if you intend on managing the entire network, I suggest you uncheck the User Must Change Password At Next Logon. Then, check User Cannot Change Password. This will force users to come to you for new passwords. Unless an account is temporary, check Password Never Expires. If you forget, the account will automatically expire in the default 42 days. This default may be changed under the Policies|Account menu option (more on this later in this chapter). Just press the Add button, and your first user will be added. Easy, huh? By default, the user is automatically assigned to the Domain Users group. There are several other available server groups, as shown in Table 5.2.

The groups presented in Table 5.2 can be assigned with the Groups button in the New User dialog box. Or, you can use the Groups button in the User Properties dialog box. If you look at the bottom row of buttons in either the New User or the User Properties dialog box, you can see other functions that you can perform on accounts, including:

- *Profile*—Allows you to assign a profile to a user. This applies to NT Workstations only. Profiles are basically how a machine is set up—colors, screen size, and so forth. The home directory is a protected space in which the user

TABLE 5.2

NT SERVER GROUPS.

Server Group	Description
Account Operators	Allows the use of the User Manager For Domains to create and delete user accounts and information. Account Operators cannot delete any of the default global groups.
Administrators	Grants complete control over the system. This is by far the most powerful group. Administrator rights should be given out very sparingly and only to trusted, knowledgeable users.
Backup Operators	Grants the necessary rights to backup and restore system directories and files.
Domain Admins	Provides full administrative rights to the domain a user is a member of.
Domain Guests	Provides access for occasional users. Domain Guests are given very limited access and abilities. Most are limited to their individual workstation and only on the domain in which their account resides.
Guests	Gives the same access as Domain Guests, except limited rights are extend to the entire network.
Print Operators	Enables operators to create, manage, and delete print shares. Print Operators can also log on to and shut down servers.
Replicator	Assigns privileges to a special group of users whose purpose is to maintain copies of directories between servers.
Server Operators	Enables users to create, manage, and delete print shares and network shares; backup and restore files on servers; format a server's hard drives; change the system time; lock and unlock servers; and log on to and shut down servers.
Users	Grants minimal rights to log on to local NT workstations. Users can also create and manage local groups.

can store files and programs. You may either enter a local path (e.g., C:\users\username) or click on the Connect button, pick a drive letter, and a network path (e.g., \server\users\username). Use the Programs|Administrative Tools (Common)|Administrative Wizards|Managing File And Folder Access (new to NT 4.0) to assign proper permission to the folder, so only the owner and administrators can access it.

- *Hours*—Enables you to assign or restrict the hours in which a person may use the server. To set this option, simply highlight the day and time you want to change, and press Allow or Disallow. When you are satisfied with your work, press OK.
- *Logon To*—Allows you to restrict the workstations a user may log on to. By default, users may log on to all workstations.
- *Account*—Allows you to assign account expiration dates. By default, accounts never expire.
- *Dialin*—Allows a user to use dialup networking to remotely become a member of the network.

The next thing we'll do is look at the user security issues.

Proper User Security

User security starts with understanding the difference between *rights* and *permissions.*

Rights generally apply to users performing tasks—such as allowing a user to back up or restore files. User rights are managed by assigning users to groups using the User Manager For Domains or the Administrative Wizard, Group Management. You should include users in only the necessary groups. Inadvertently adding a user to Domain Admin or Server Operators could create disastrous results.

Permissions apply to specific files and directories. Permissions are managed by using the Administrative Wizard, Managing File And Folder Access. Permissions include the ability to read, write, and delete individual files and directories. As a general rule, rights take precedence over permissions. One suggestion I would like to make is to use the Managing File And Folder Access Administrative Wizard (located in Programs|Administrative Tools (Common)|Administrative Wizards|Managing File and Folder Access) to assign Administrator-only access permission to the server's root directory and any other directory you don't want just anyone accessing.

By default, administrators have read/write/delete access to directories. All other users have read access. Denying read access to users will keep users away from these files. The User Manager For Domains is also useful for managing system audit, account, and user rights policies. You can find the management tools

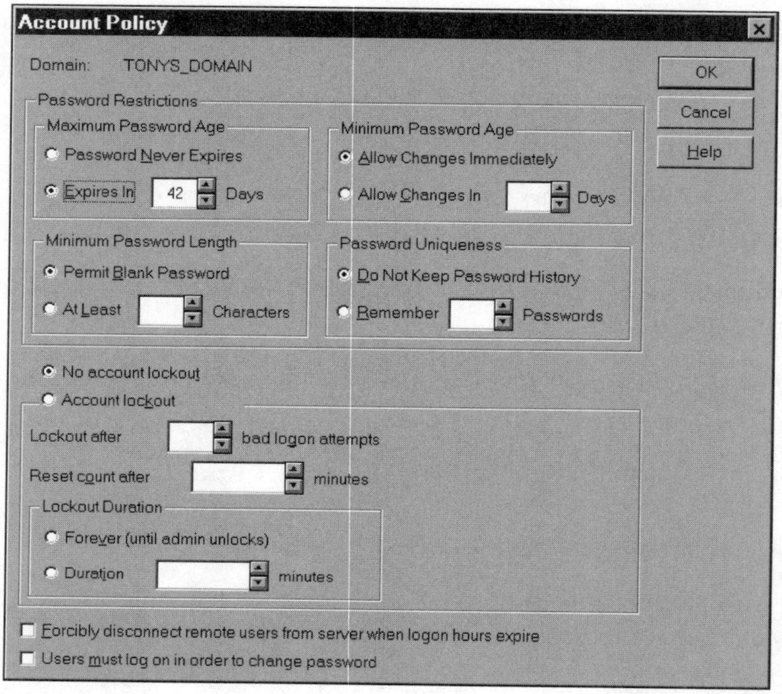

Figure 5.3
User Manager Account Policy dialog box.

under the Policies menu. Figure 5.3 shows the options available on the Account menu. The Account menu options are self-explanatory.

The next menu, User Rights, allows you to assign special specific rights to groups that would not normally have particular rights. The basic rights (or tokens) are as follows:

- Access this computer from network
- Add workstations to domain
- Back up files and directories
- Change the system time
- Force shutdown from a remote system
- Load and unload device drivers
- Log on locally

- Manage auditing and security log
- Restore files and directories
- Shut down the system
- Take ownership of files or other objects

By clicking the Show Advanced User Rights option, the following rights are displayed:

- Act as part of the operating system
- Bypass traverse checking
- Create a page file
- Create a token object
- Create permanent shared objects
- Debug programs
- Generate security audits
- Increase quotas
- Increase scheduling priority
- Lock pages in memory
- Log on as a batch job
- Log on as a service
- Modify firmware environment values
- Profile single process
- Profile system performance
- Replace a process-level token

Discussion on these tokens are beyond the scope of this book. Please refer to detailed reference materials for further information.

Lastly, Audit policies are the way in which you can log server activities into any one of three log files: System, Applications, and Security. The logs may be examined using the Event Viewer under Administrative Tools (Common). To

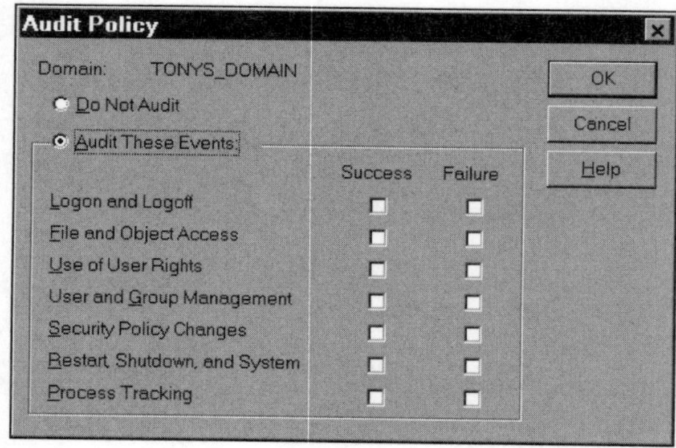

Figure 5.4
User Manager Audit Policy dialog box.

turn individual items on or off, first click the Audit These Events button. Then, log the success or failure of each activity. Figure 5.4 shows each available option.

Summary

This chapter covers many installation issues. Keep in mind that an entire book could easily be written on many of the subjects presented in this chapter—we have only touched on the major points. Chapter 6 goes into deeper issues of administering NT Server. There, we'll configure additional parts of NT and add some very useful services to NT's configuration. Then, in Chapter 7, we'll walk through the rigors of installing and using Internet Information Server v3.0.

6 NT Server 4.0 Administration

Jeff Bankston

Now that you've installed NT Server, you're ready to complete the second half of the battle for control of your users! I laughed when I wrote that sentence, but in reality, that's the essence of a server administrator's role. As a server administrator, you control the users by dictating how they access a server's functions and stored data. This chapter discusses some of the key areas of NT Server administration tasks, including:

- Addressing post-installation security issues
- Creating and maintaining user accounts
- Administering user requirements
- Protecting system security

Without further ado, let's pick up where we left off in Chapter 5.

Post-Installation Security Issues

At the conclusion of Chapter 5, the server was operational and had a basic login for the administrator. That was about it in terms of operational characteristics. Furthermore, we just installed the core components of the NT Server. If there are any other components you require for your installation, just sit tight—many of NT's most commonly used components are addressed later in this chapter. But first, let's take a look at a couple of NT security issues.

The Everyone Group—Danger In The Wind

Ah, yes—a security flaw in NT that Microsoft has yet to address. While this is not a book about NT Security, this is perhaps the very first post-installation issue you should address after installing the NT Server. At this point, not even a service pack fix has been issued for the problem we're going to address here.

Here's the problem: The built-in group Everyone is used for global access to any and all parts of a server and its resources (more about built-in groups in a moment). You can grant permissions based on the needs of a user, but Microsoft has altered the normal course of permissions by allowing the group Everyone *Full Control* permission when any new shared directory is created. Let's step through an example scenario to illustrate the problem.

1. On your newly installed server, start Windows Explorer.
2. Navigate to any directory where you want to create a share for the users.
3. Right-click over the directory, and left-click on Sharing. The Sharing tab is selected by default.
4. Click on the Shared As radio button. Accept the default settings for the share name and Maximum Allowed for the users.
5. Now, click on the Permissions button.

At this point, you'll be presented with the permissions granted by default for *Access Through Share Permissions*, as shown in Figure 6.1.

Look at what came up! The built-in group Everyone was granted Full Control over the share just created (more about built-in groups and shares later in this chapter). This is definitely not what was intended. Sure, you can alter the permissions, but this default behavior is troublesome. I personally know of a few sites caught off guard by this problem. In their haste, the creation of shares was all that was necessary, and they forgot to follow through by checking what permissions were assigned—it's a gotcha to be sure.

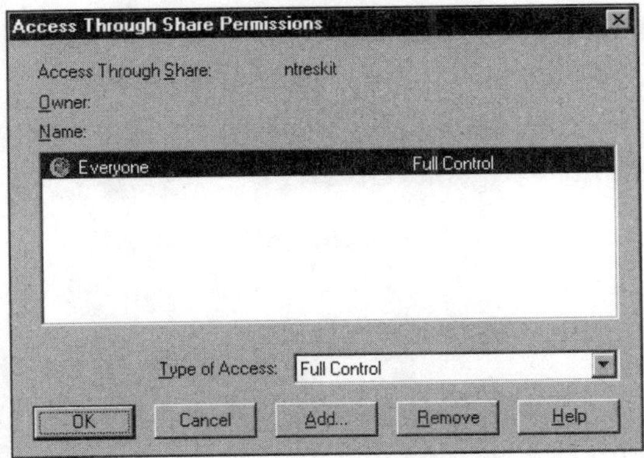

Figure 6.1
Default permissions granted on a share.

Share permissions are used when a more global access is required without the need for a deeper granularity of control. When a more defined security is needed, NT uses NTFS file permissions to completely lock a resource and define tighter access. Return to the share you just created, pull up its properties, and this time, click on the Security tab. Click on Permissions, and look at what comes up! Your default security permissions should look similar to Figure 6.2.

Oops! NT just did the same thing with NTFS permissions! The global built-in Everyone group has Full Control. Can you envision this happening to corporate financial data? Not me, because I double-check permissions regardless. But, believe it or not, it happened to a new site once where critical AutoCAD draw-

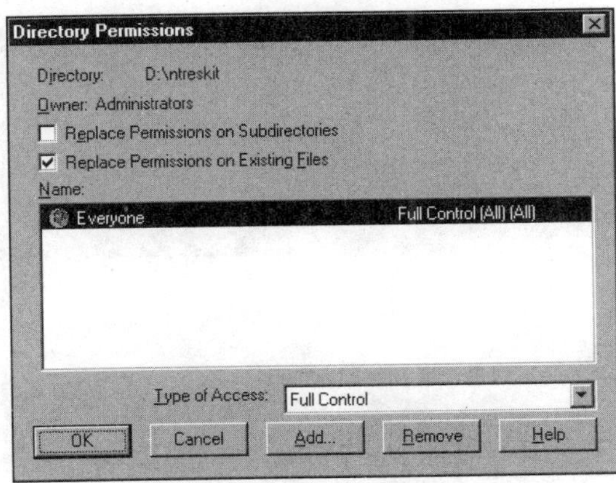

Figure 6.2
NTFS permissions assigned by default.

ings of an engineering facility were kept. An unsuspecting staff member was copying some files to a disk for shipment to a customer and used the Move command to copy some files. Unfortunately, the staff member didn't understand that *Move* meant *Copy And Delete*!

This sort of scenario happens. The point of the matter is that the very first thing an administrator should do after a fresh install is to delete the global built-in group Everyone to ensure tighter security.

Deleting the global built-in group Everyone is the first way NT Server administrators can begin tightening up server security.

Setting Basic Security—Quickly!

There are several directories in which NT sets system-wide security, and it works well. However, hand-in-hand with the previous discussion is the root share in the NT home directory. My server was installed to the C:\WINNT40 location. If I bring up the properties of that share, lo and behold, what do I see? (See Figure 6.3.)

Perfectly disgusting, isn't it? After you delete the global built-in group Everyone, you need to go back and assign share and NTFS security to the shares. How do you know what shares were assigned by the server installation? Go to a command prompt, and type in *NET SHARE* to see what shares are in existence. You should get a display similar to the display shown in Figure 6.4. You'll know were to reapply security now.

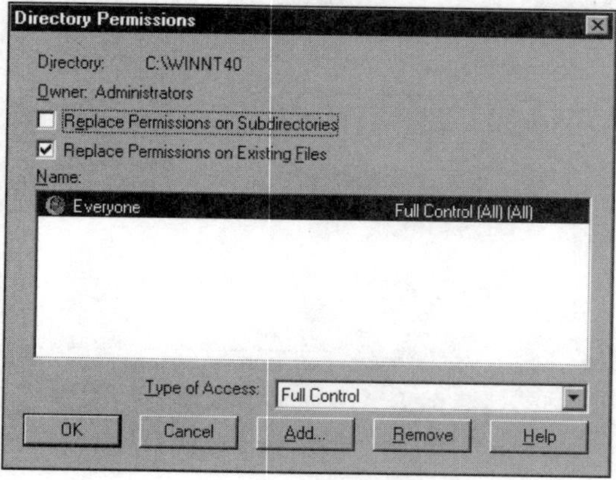

Figure 6.3
NT Server root share permissions.

```
C:\WINNT40\System32\cmd.exe

C:\>net use f: /delete
The network connection could not be found.

More help is available by typing NET HELPMSG 2250.

C:\>net share

Share name   Resource                        Remark

-------------------------------------------------------------------------------
C$           C:\                             Default share
ADMIN$       C:\WINNT40                      Remote Admin
IPC$                                         Remote IPC
print$       C:\WINNT40\system32\spool\drive Printer Drivers
D$           D:\                             Default share
E$           E:\                             Default share
cdrom        F:\
NETLOGON     C:\WINNT40\system32\Repl\Import Logon server share
Deskjet      LPT1:                  Spooled  HP DeskJet 550C
The command completed successfully.

C:\>_
```

Figure 6.4
Default assigned shares.

Use the default shares to reapply and grant appropriate access to the system. Administrators, System, and Creator should be given Full Control of the home NT Server installation. Everyone else's permissions should be based on the needs of the users or desires of the administrator of the server.

Now that our initial security issues are addressed, let's press onward with the basic administration tasks required to get users onto your server.

User Accounts

While this section presents the basics of creating and maintaining user accounts, much more complete chapters are possible (of over 100 pages) dealing with the topic of user accounts. Given the limited space of this text, I'm going to get you going, providing you with enough information so that you can forge ahead and refer to the help files and manuals that came with the server when necessary.

We're going to address three major tasks in this section. Specifically, we'll discuss how to:

- Use built-in groups to centralize control
- Create user accounts
- Create shared data directories

These three tasks can make or break your server. Pay particular attention to the use of the groups—we'll review a very important aspect of groups in the "Creating Shared Data Directories" section.

Using NT's Built-In Groups

NT's built-in groups are created to help centralize control of your server. Built-in groups were defined in Chapter 5, but to remind you, they're groups predefined by NT that are suitable for 75 percent of all of the users and administrators needs. In Chapter 5, Table 5.2 lists the built-in groups created by NT. For the sake of flipping pages, I've listed the table here, again, for ease of reference. (See Table 6.1.) Please pay particular attention to the names of the groups, and you'll notice that there's only one group directly applicable to the users themselves—the User group. My editor may holler at me, but this table is worth repeating. After you review the table, take a look at Figure 6.5.

TABLE 6.1

NT SERVER GROUPS.

Server Group	Description
Account Operators	Allows the use of the User Manager For Domains to create and delete user accounts and information. Account Operators cannot delete any of the default Global groups.
Administrators	Grants complete control over the system. This is by far the most powerful group. Administrator rights should be given out very sparingly and only to trusted, knowledgeable users.
Backup Operators	Grants the necessary rights to back up and restore system directories and files.
Domain Admins	Provides full administrative rights to the domain the user is a member of.
Domain Guests	Provides access for occasional users. Domain Guests are given very limited access and abilities. Most are limited to their individual workstation and only on the domain in which their account resides.
Guests	Gives the same access as Domain Guests, except limited rights are extended to the entire network.
Print Operators	Enables operators to create, manage, and delete print shares. Print Operators can also log on to and shut down servers.

(continued)

Table 6.1 (continued)

NT Server groups.

Server Group	Description
Replicator	Assigns privileges to a special group of users whose purpose is to maintain copies of directories between servers.
Server Operators	Enables users to create, manage, and delete print shares and network shares, back up and restore files on servers, format a server's hard drives, change the system time, lock and unlock servers, and log on to and shut down servers.
Users	Grants minimal rights to log on to local NT workstations. Users can also create and manage Local groups.

The icons in Figure 6.5 are the key. The Global groups are identified by the little green world behind the people. Local groups are identified by the icon of a computer behind the people. Global groups can be added to Local groups, but Local groups cannot be added to Global groups.

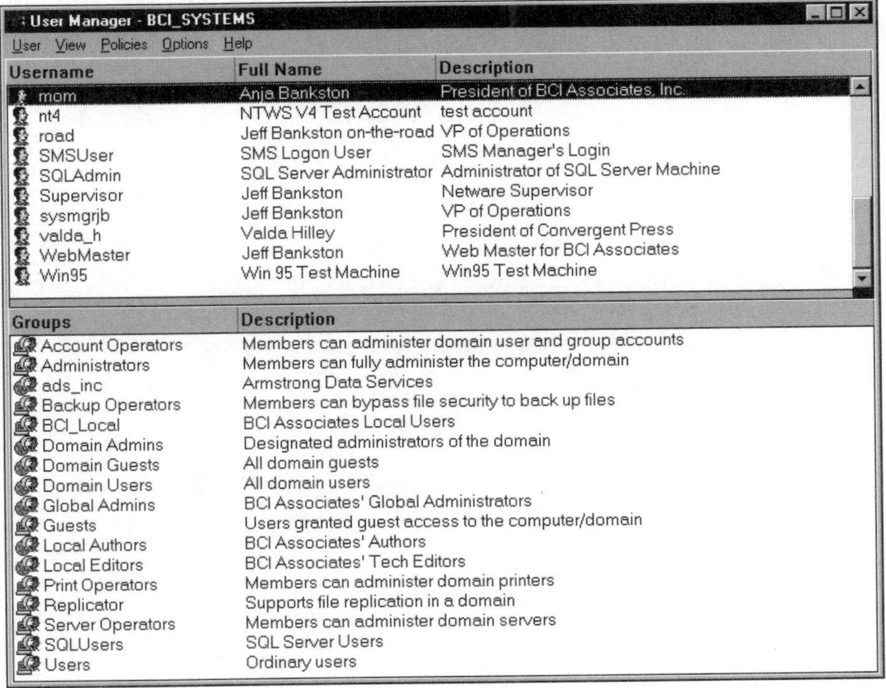

Figure 6.5
NT's groups, and then some!

Why is this so earth-shattering? Misusing groups can make administration of an entire domain a living nightmare. I know, because I've been there, seen it, and nearly done it. So, look again at Figure 6.5 and notice the groups. There are several odd circumstances of interest illustrated in the set of groups that I created for this discussion. First, notice the two groups Local Authors and Local Editors. Both are Global groups! This setting is erroneous because the groups are named as Local groups yet they are designated as global entities. Another oddity is the Global Admins group, which is a Global group, sure, but isn't the built-in group called Domain Admins? In this situation, the Global Admins group is unnecessary because it's a replication of a built-in group.

I've included the odd circumstances in my example because these are two typical problems that most new administrators run into at one time or another. So, use caution when creating groups. Ask yourself, Is there a built-in group that will suffice instead of creating a new group? The key is to look at the purpose of a group—not where the users are located on the server. It's easy to mess up when creating server groups, and unfortunately, the ramifications can be nasty if you have to come back later to fix things up. There are times, however, when none of NT's built-in groups will serve your needs and you'll need to create a new group.

One example of the need for a new Local group can be seen in the SQL Users Local group that I created. With SQL Server installed, I needed to restrict the SQL Users Local group access to users of the SQL Empire (of course, some of the same users are also members of other groups—but we'll get into that later). So, let's look at the contents of the SQL Users Local group, shown in Figure 6.6.

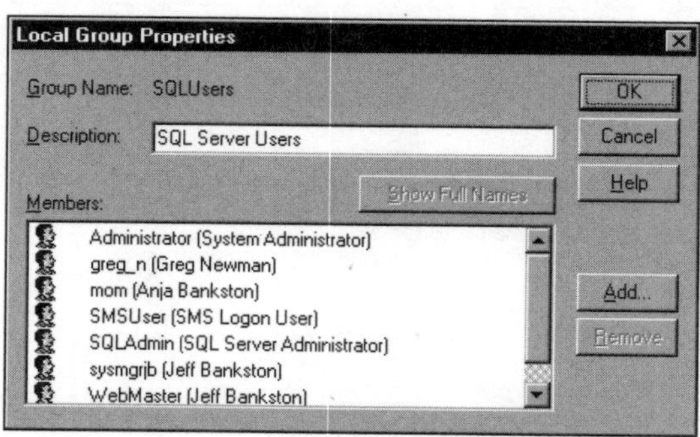

Figure 6.6
Members of the SQL Users Local group.

Guess what? Now, there are two users on the system that are nonstandard users! *Nonstandard* means that these users are not interactively using data files such as spreadsheets or creating documents. One nonstandard user is the SQL Server administrator (which is not the same as the NT administrator), and the other nonstandard user is the SMS User.

One last point of interest. Local groups can only access the local server or servers within a domain. Global groups can access any area within a domain. This is especially apparent with trusted domains where only Global groups in one trusted domain can be added to the trusting domain. You'll never see a Local group of any domain granted access to a different trusted or trusting domain. A *trusted* domain is one that allows other domains to use its resources. A *trusting* domain is one that allows other domains to come to it and use its resources. More in-depth information on trusted domains and the domain model can be found in the NT Server Resource Kit.

Before leaving this section, go ahead and create two Local groups and two Global groups. The Global groups may not be needed if you don't have a second server with a second domain, but create them anyhow for the benefit of our discussion. The names of the groups aren't important. Next, we'll create some user accounts.

Creating User Accounts

Now that you've had a good introduction to the world of groups, let's apply that knowledge and create a new user. Thus far, the basic administrator accounts have been created, but that's all. Now, you'll need to create an account for each user and, perhaps, a few backup accounts for guests and administrative purposes. The accounts I created for myself are examples of creating backup accounts for administrative purposes. On my server, I've created three accounts for myself: one account to use when I'm traveling; another for accessing the network from my office at a customer's site; and yet another for dual login to my NetWare 4.11 server, where I can use dual logon capability and have parallel access to either or both servers on my network.

To show you just how easy NT 4 makes users management, let's create a new user called *NT4*. Open the User Manager For Domains by choosing Programs|Administrative Tools (Common)|User Manager For Domains. You'll be presented with a screen showing the user properties for a new user, as shown in Figure 6.7.

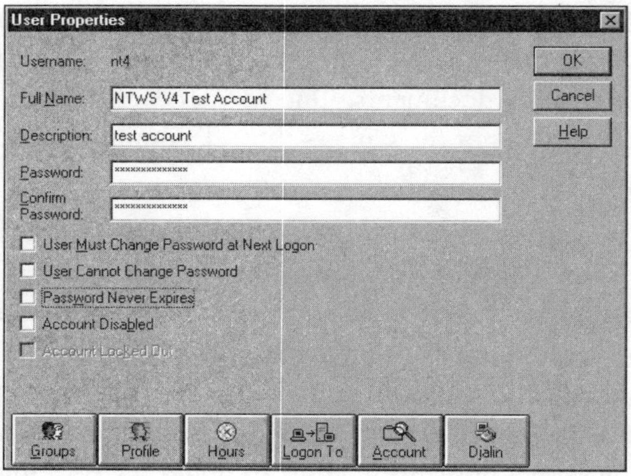

Figure 6.7
Creating a new user.

Figure 6.7 shows the information I added for my new user. Enter whatever information you want. The configuration of the user and the options presented are self-explanatory, so we'll simply look at the group information. Click on the Groups button, and you'll be presented with the Group Memberships screen, shown in Figure 6.8.

Notice the relationship among the groups? NT4 is a member of the Domain Users group, which is global, and a member of the group BCI_Local, which is my core workers group. There's one more important setting to notice—the Primary group. This is a setting devoted to Macintosh or POSIX applications

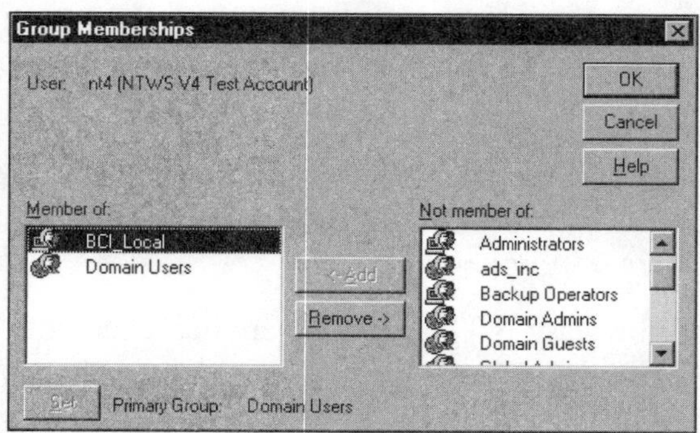

Figure 6.8
Group Memberships screen.

users needing access to the NT domain. Only a Global group can be set as a Primary group. Be careful with your groups!

Guess what—I have a hint for you. Maybe you're thinking that you can't remember all these details. Well, don't sweat it. Before leaving the Group Memberships screen, click on the Help button, and you'll be presented with a help screen that itemizes these topics of these user settings. This level of help is available almost anywhere inside NT4, so don't be afraid to try it out. Sometimes, it actually helps!

Now that you've learned about groups and how to add new users, it's time to put this knowledge to work to create a new share for your users.

Creating Shared Data Directories

Creating shared data directories is one of the most basic tasks you'll do as a network administrator. It's also one of the easiest tasks to accomplish. But first, what is a share? A *share* is a global control mechanism used to provide reasonable access to data and programs. If you want more control over shared data, you can use NT's New Technology File System (NTFS) permissions, which we'll explore shortly. First, let's create a share.

1. Start Windows Explorer, and navigate to the directory on the server that you want to share.
2. Right-click on the directory, and then click on Sharing.

This procedure is much the same as the one we performed earlier in this chapter. The Sharing tab is shown by default.

3. Click on the Shared As radio button, and then add the text for each block of the share.

This is where we diverge from the previous example.

4. Click on the Permissions button, and click on the Remove button to remove the group Everyone from the list.
5. Add the group Administrators with Full Control. On my domain, I've also added the group BCI_LOCAL for my local users.
6. Click on the Type Of Access drop-down box to define the desired permissions.
7. Click on OK twice to complete the share.

You'll see the blue hand go under the directory name signifying the share is in place. Now, everyone that belongs to the groups will have equal access to the data in the share, according to the group membership privileges.

But what if this turns out to be not enough control? How could such an example of this occur? My FTP site, like most other sites, is just such a situation. The share is something like F:\FTP and has a directory structure like this:

F:\FTP

F:\FTP\INCOMING

F:\FTP\PRIVATE

F:\FTP\PUBLIC

The share itself is F:\FTP with the access of the Everyone group having Read permissions, the BCI_LOCAL group having Change permissions, and the Administrators group having Full Control. Keep in mind that this set of permissions cascades down through the entire directory structure. Figure 6.9 shows an FTP site on a different server, but illustrates the point just the same.

This is a fine example of having share-level security, but one problem is masked over when you use shares. Look at the Private directory shown in Figure 6.10.

See what's wrong? The group Everyone has Read access to the private location! Not exactly what the doctor (or boss) ordered. Let's see how applying NTFS permissions can fix this problem.

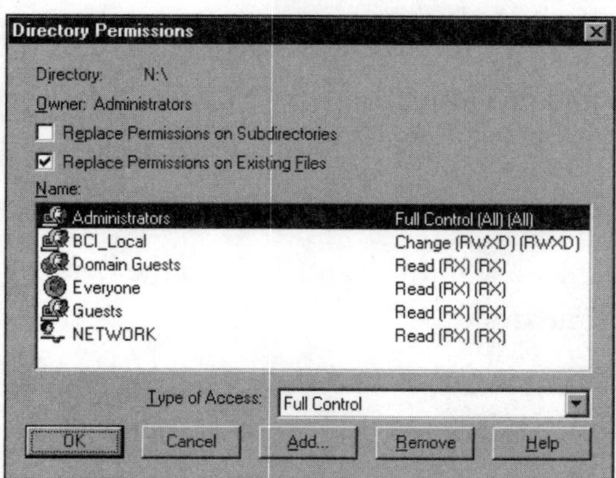

Figure 6.9
FTP site cascaded permissions.

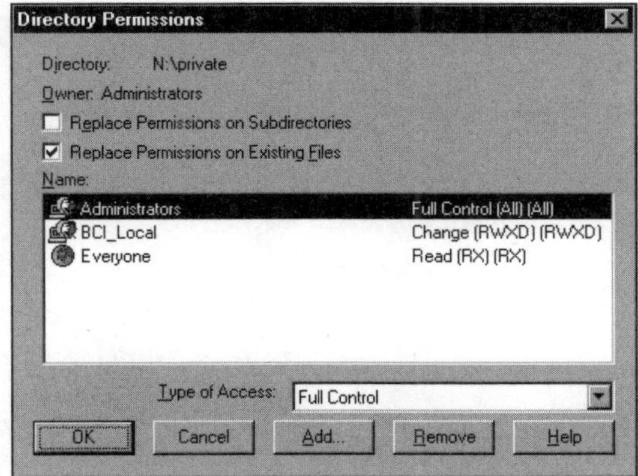

Figure 6.10
FTP site private directory.

Not surprisingly, the fix to the problem shown in Figure 6.10 requires a knowledge of the problem. The group Everyone allows users from untrusted domains to connect to and download files in this location. If you don't want them to gain access to the site, then the best thing to do is override the share-level permissions with NTFS-level permissions. Keep in mind that share-level permissions are at the directory level, whereas NTFS-level permissions allow restrictions down to the file level.

To fix our share permissions problem, perform the following steps.

1. Remove the group Everyone if it still exists, and then click on the Add button.
2. Click on the Show Users button to display the users.
3. Scroll down the list of Names, and you'll see a list of the groups and users.

At this point, you can add individual users to have access to small sections of the server.

4. Click on the Type Of Access button.

You should see the different levels of NTFS permissions possible, as shown in Figure 6.11.

That's all there really is to share and NTFS permissions. Any further discussion would be too complicated for our purposes, so let's move on and look at some other user requirements.

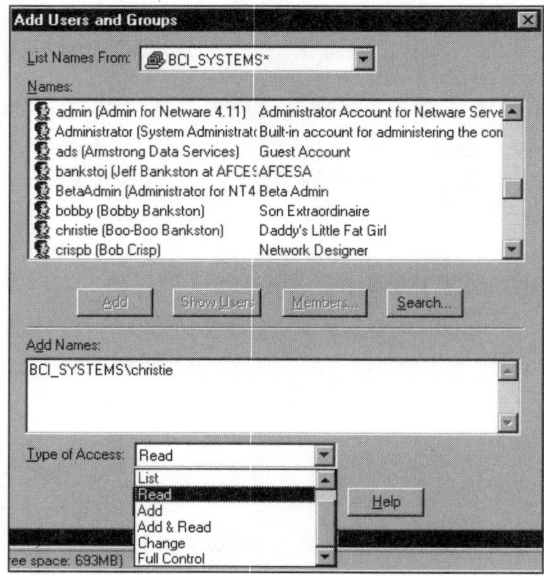

Figure 6.11
NTFS permissions.

User Requirements

Your network users have basically the same requirements as any user of a standalone computer. Network users need access to resources on the network. Among others, these resources can include shared:

- Printers
- CD-ROM drives
- Modems

What you have to do is determine which users, either individually or by group, need which devices. At this point, all permissions should be assigned. So, let's take a look at the two ways to assign user requirements—at the user level and group level. Then, we'll look at the most common user requirement—printers.

User Level

Assigning user resources at the user level means more administrative overhead, but the increased control may be required. As you may recall, Figure 6.11 shows user-level control where NTFS permissions are applied on the FTP site.

Let's look at another application of user-level controls. Let's say there's a shared directory in which the Accounting department stores its files. All network users in the Accounting department need to access the shared directory to change files but not delete them. However, the comptroller has near-final say over the data, and the president of the company has final say. The comptroller is required to purge old files periodically to a saved location, and only the comptroller and president can do this.

In this situation, group-level permissions are applied to the directory, and NTFS user-level permissions are applied for the comptroller. This setting provides the comptroller Full Control of the files while everyone else retains Change permissions.

Other than circumstances similar to this example, user access to data should be applied via a group, as shown in the next section. Microsoft strongly suggests using the group architecture for simplicity of management and migration of data from server to server (in case migration is ever required).

Group Level

Okay, now let's address groups in relation to fulfilling user requirements. As you may recall from earlier in this chapter, Local groups are for accessing untrusted domains—that is, the domain in which a user logged into. This means that a domain called *BCI_SYSTEMS* has users that can't see the resources in a domain called *TEST* unless one domain trusts the other with its data. If TEST trusts BCI_SYSTEMS to access its data, then BCI_SYSTEMS has not trusted out its domain to TEST. Trust relationships are manually created and are in no way automatic. Within each domain, the local users of each domain are restricted to their respective resources. Global groups of each domain can see the other domain's resources provided the trust relationship is created. If a trust relationship fails for any reason, then the Global group users can't get to the other domain's resources—no matter what.

For this reason, the vast majority of the users in any domain are Local. SQL Server, Office applications, and related general-purpose office automation applications never cross the bounds of a domain. While domains frequently separate businesses, domains can indeed be used to separate sensitive corporate divisions. This tactic is not necessarily advised because NTFS and shared permissions can handle this task. But in some cases, Local groups within each domain may be necessary to satisfy business requirements.

Global groups are created by using the User Manager For Domains to add individual users from the domain to create a group. Once the Global group is defined and created, Global groups can be added to Local groups as required. One way to use this feature within untrusted domains is to create a Global group for contractors that may work on a site yet do not need access to the rest of the server resources. More on this topic later in the chapter when we talk about trusted domains. Now, let's look at printer resource requirements.

Printers

Printers are a relatively easy thing to deal with in a domain. They can be connected directly to the server in areas where physical security is not of overriding importance or connected to the network via network cards installed in the printer. An example of this is the Hewlett-Packard JetDirect cards that can be installed into the mid- and high-end printers.

Another way to connect printers is to use print server boxes that plug into the network and then connect to one or more printers. Then, a TCP/IP or a DLC connection is established to the print server where access to the printer is created. A full account of how to create these connections is beyond the scope of this chapter, as it would take an entire chapter to go into all the details. So, for simplicity's sake, let's presume a printer is connected directly to the server. The actual means of connection is not important at this juncture.

Now, let's create one print queue that is directly connected to a server, and then we'll create a connection across a network.

Locally Connected Printers

Assuming that a printer is physically connected and powered on, complete the following steps. When you finish, the screen should look like Figure 6.12.

1. Choose Start|Settings|Printers.
2. Double-click on Add Printer, and you'll get the Add Printer wizard. The default is for a printer connected to My Computer, which in our case is accurate.
3. Click on Next, and choose the port on the server in which the printer is connected.
4. Click on Next.

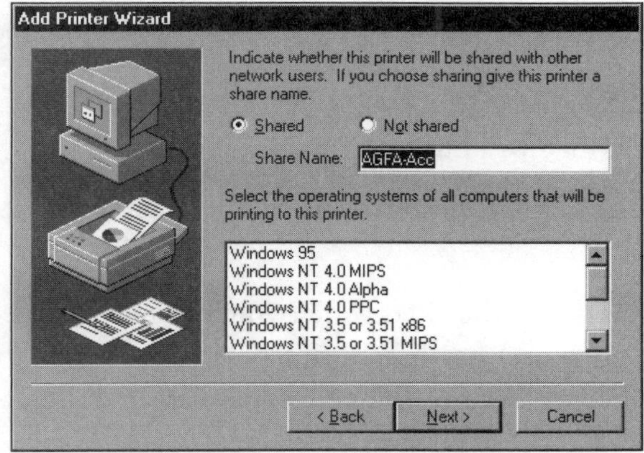

Figure 6.12
Naming a shared printer.

5. Choose the make and model of the printer, and click on Next.
6. Give the printer a descriptive name, and click on Next.
7. Decide if this printer is to be shared, or not. (Of course, why would you connect a printer to a server if it isn't to be shared?)
8. Click on the Shared radio button.

The preceding steps created the printer connection and established the default permissions for the printer. Go back into the Printers menu, and right-click on the newly created print device. Notice that I said print *device* and not *printer*. This is because the users will print to the print device on the server, and in turn, NT Server passes the actual printing job to the physical printer. This is in keeping with NT's architecture of not allowing any user or application direct access to the server hardware.

Network Printers

The only real difference between locally connected and network-connected printers is where the printer is connected to the network. This section pinpoints network printers connected to other devices. After you've connected a printer to the desired print server or another computer, access the Add Printer wizard as we did earlier, but this time, select the Attached To Network option. Otherwise, the process is no different than specifying where the printer is located. Let's take a look at the permissions granted for the newly connected printer.

1. Right-click on the printer icon in the Printers folder.
2. Click on the Security tab.
3. Click on the Permissions button.

You should see the default permissions of the shared printer, as shown in Figure 6.13.

On my new server, notice that Everyone (which has not yet been removed for this illustration's purposes) has basic Print permissions, and the other groups have some form thereof. Mainly, the person who created the document, that is to say printed it, has a special permission called *Manage Documents*. This allows the owner of the document to purge print jobs from the server should one get hung up or fouled up. In many situations, only the network administrators can purge print jobs. Print Operators are usually network administrators with the added ability to manage the print device.

Now that the basics of meeting user requirements have been discussed, let's move on to the final major section of this chapter—system security concerns.

System Security Concerns

Security is an important issue on any server, but it doesn't have to be complicated. I've said this before, but there are entire books written on most of the topics presented in this chapter thus far—this section is no different. So it's no

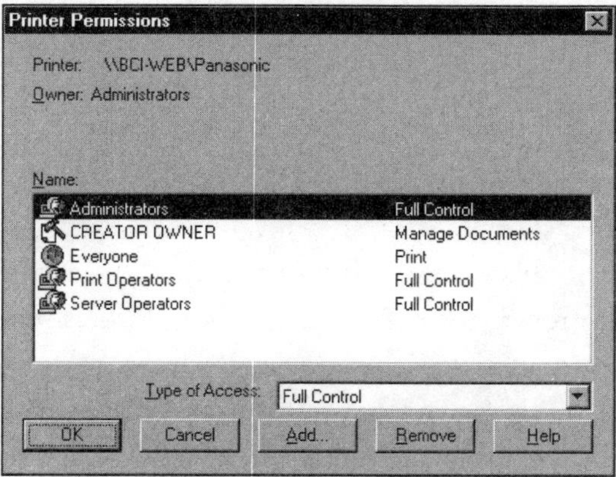

Figure 6.13
Default permissions of the shared printer.

surprise that my goal here is to give you the basics to get you going and leave comprehensive texts on the subject for you to refer to if necessary.

There are two groups key to system security that deserve a bit more attention beyond our previous discussions—Domain Admins and Server Operators. After we take a look at these groups, we'll wrap up this chapter by addressing the issue of domain trust relationships.

Domain Admins Group

The Administrator is the person ultimately responsible for the network. This person has global privileges across the entire domain. In the absence of this person, someone has to administer parts, if not all, of the network. The Domain Admins group serves this need. Domain Admins don't have the power of the Administrator, but close. This group of people is largely considered to be the core administrative people. If a mistake is made by one of the Domain Admins, harm can be done, yet not as fully catastrophic as if the Administrator himself did the deed.

Server Operators Group

The Server Operators group of users is typically more administrators or other trusted people that can make changes to a server's configuration, yet not fully administer the entire server. This group has the ability to create new shares on the server. And while backing up data generally falls into the area of the Backup Operators group, the Server Operators are typically allowed to handle this task, as well. This group is nearly as sensitive as the Domain Admins group, so you'll only want to have people in this group that you can trust completely. Note that Server Operators can't change the configuration of the server at all—just entities, such as the shares.

Domain Trust Relationships

The domain is the central controlling entity of NT Server. Let's take a few minutes to go over domains and what they are. There are four domain models:

- Single Domain Model
- Master Domain Model
- Multiple Master Model
- Complete Trust Model

Let's take a quick look at each model's components.

Single Domain Model

Single domains work best in environments that:

- Have a small network.
- Have the ability to centrally administer the network.
- Have fewer than 15 servers.
- Don't have a Wide Area Network.

Trust relationships are not necessary in the Single Domain Model, and any system administrator can manage the network from one location. Life is very simple. However, this simplicity comes with some problems, which mostly arise when your network grows in size (outgrowing the single domain concept). Some disadvantages of the Single Domain Model are:

- When your network grows, the single PDC has to handle more and more data, jeopardizing performance.
- There is only one PDC. If it fails, the network fails.
- You can't break the network into divisions if some groups want to administer their own servers.
- User lists and, in particular, browse lists may become large and cumbersome to work with.

Master Domain Model

One solution to the problems found in the Single Domain Model is to implement the Master Domain Model. Using the Master Domain Model, you can break a network into separate domains as the network grows. In this model, one domain handles all logon requests and the creation of users and groups. All other domains relay requests of this type to the master domain. The advantages of using the Master Domain Model are:

- Administration is centralized.
- All company divisions can have their own domains.
- Global groups are defined once, in a designated space.

The disadvantages associated with the Master Domain Model are:

- There is only one PDC. If it fails, the network fails.
- User lists and, in particular, browse lists may get large and cumbersome to work with.

Multiple Master Model

With Multiple Master Models, instead of having a single domain to handle all logon requests and account data, several master domains handle these tasks. Each domain has its own PDC and, hopefully, a BDC for redundancy. Each master domain trusts and is trusted by all other master domains. This allows for smooth logons and data sharing. You must preplan a multiple master network to evenly distribute user accounts. For example, I recommend that you set up each master domain to represent a company and subdomains for business units within each company. Two advantages of the Multiple Master Model are:

- Performance issues are minimized because the browse lists are divided among several PDCs.
- Resources can be logically grouped and independently managed.

Among the disadvantages of the Multiple Master Model are:

- Trust relationships must be created and managed.
- Administration is more difficult because user accounts are divided among multiple master PDCs.
- Logical interdepartmental groups have to be created in each domain.

Complete Trust Model

In Complete Trust Models, all domains are both trusting and trusted by all other domains. Use this model when centralized administration is either impractical or unwanted. Each domain in this model has to be separately administered, so you'll need at least one qualified administrator for each domain. A gross number of trust relationships will have to be created at each PDC. This number equates to the **number of domains x (number of domains-1)**. For example, if you have a network with 4 domains you would need 12 trusts [4*(4-1)], 5 domains requires 20 trusts, and so on.

With this explanation of trusts out of the way, let's put theory into practice.

Create A Trusting Domain

I have two domains here at my office: BCI_SYSTEMS and SYSTEMS_TEST. BCI_SYSTEMS is the active domain for our business servers. SYSTEMS_TEST is just that—a test environment. So, I don't want the test machines plundering the production servers, but I might want the business servers to access the test machines. This means that the test domain will have to trust BCI_SYSTEMS. Let's create the trusting relationships.

1. Go to the SYSTEMS_TEST domain controller, and open the User Manager For Domains.
2. Click on Policies, then click on Trust Relationships.

In the Trusted Domains window, there's nothing being trusted at the moment.

3. Click on the Add button, and enter the name of the second domain, *BCI_SYSTEMS* in this case, along with the required password.
4. Repeat the steps in the Trusting Domains section when you want to create a two-way relationship.

This is where you control the model of domain and restrict access based on the mission parameters of your business, as shown in Figure 6.14.

5. Now, go to the trusting domain, and open Windows Explorer.
6. Navigate to any directory, either shared or desired to be shared.
7. Bring up the share properties for the directory, and then share it if it's not already shared.

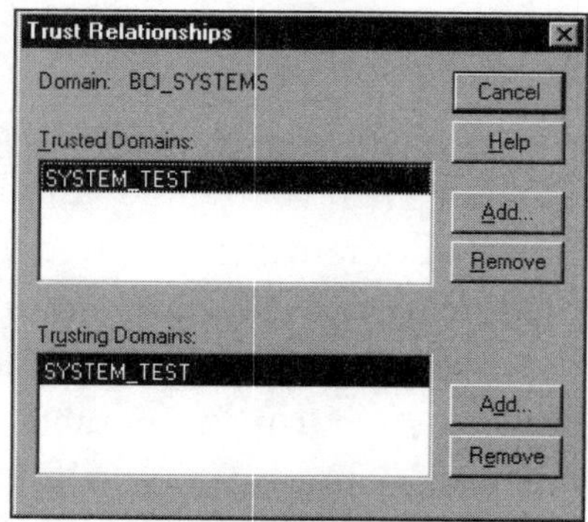

Figure 6.14
Domain trust relationship.

8. Click on the Permissions button, then the Add button.
9. Click on the List Names From drop-down list.

What do you see? Two domains!

10. Click on the trusted domain just created.

There's another nice screen that shows you only Global group users that can be added to the share. The other users' groups of System, Network, and Interactive are built-in groups, not changeable by you in terms of purpose, but you can add users to any of them. I highly recommend that you leave these three groups alone unless you're absolutely confident in what you're doing.

This little exercise illustrates some of the many tasks you'll come across when working with trusted and trusting domains. While the exercise is not all-encompassing in its depiction of trusted domain activities, it's interesting to note how trusted domains can affect your entire domain setup and administration.

Summary

Chapter 6 is an introductory description of the most common administrative tasks faced by administrators when managing NT Server. It's interesting to compare the management tasks against other network systems, such as NetWare. NetWare administrators should recognize many of the tasks presented in this chapter, making migration to NT much easier. In Chapter 7, we'll begin our installation of the Internet Information Server 3.0. Setting up IIS will bring us one step closer to implementing an operational Web site. See you there!

7 Internet Information Server 3.0

Jeff Bankston

With the introduction of NT 4.0, a new era of network systems came into being. There has been plenty of hype and marketing blitz concerning which operating system is the best, which does what better than the other, and the like. However, one thing is clear. When NT 4.0 came onto the scene bundled with IIS, the landscape of the Web changed forever. Unix and Sun Sparcstations were no longer the sole proprietors of the Web.

Nowadays, a lowly souped-up PC with a decent communications circuit can use NT Server and IIS to perform much of the same Web miracles as their high-priced brethren. This chapter is all about the hardware we talked about in earlier chapters coupled with IIS to create a Web site of choice and provide a new presence on the Internet and intranets.

More specifically, this chapter is about:

- Preparing To Install IIS
- Installing IIS
- Upgrading IIS
- Configuring IIS

- Tuning System Memory For IIS
- Using IIS Core Services
- IIS And FrontPage Extensions
- IIS And Active Server Pages

As you'll see—regardless of whether you want to deepen Bill Gates's pockets—the combination of NT 4 and IIS is a sweet deal for those looking for ease of network administration and maintenance. Without further ramblings, let's see why and how this is possible.

Preparing To Install IIS

Before you install IIS, there are several issues you need to consider. Chief among these issues is the nebulous Service Pack 1 that comes with some CD-ROM disks of NT 4. The following considerations are issues you need to think about before installing IIS:

- *Service Pack*—The problem with NT 4 is that it worked fine as the initial release but with a few bugs—that was expected. Service Pack 1 (SP1) came along and struck fear in the hearts and minds of many loyal NT administrators. SP1 was a disaster for many servers and of minuscule help to others, and this isn't even considering the effects of SP1's bugs!

  SP1 began shipping as part of the default installation with new CD-ROMs even as the service pack became available on the Internet. This wasn't immediately apparent to the average administrator because they were getting a brand new CD from Microsoft. This shipment of SP1 snuck in under the net, as the saying goes. When the NT installation is started, pay attention to the install. If SP1 shows up, immediately go to **www.microsoft.com/ntserver**, download Service Pack 2 (which is much more stable than Service Pack 1), and apply SP2 immediately after the installation.

- *Hardware requirements*—IIS only requires about 5MB of disk space and less than 6MB of RAM to run, and then just add the same quantities of RAM and disk space for the extensions and ASP as you'll see later.

- *IUSR_*servername *user account*—One user account comes into play when you install IIS, and that's the one established by IIS at the time of installation.

The account name is IUSR_*servername*, such as IUSR_BCI-WEB. This account is established as the portal for all anonymous Web activity, as you'll see later. The password is defaulted to one established for IIS. Whatever you do, don't mess with this password as it will wipe out the anonymous capability of the Web server.

- *Desired services locations*—This item is of great importance before installing IIS. You need to seriously consider where your services will reside on your network. Your FTP server can grow to enormous proportions and may require you to install more disk storage later on. The Gopher server can be used to provide a browsable view of the Web site. It doesn't require much storage, but it has to have a root area, just like the FTP server. Naturally, the Web server also has to have a root storage location.

  Typical Web sites use no more than 2MB of disk storage, and they use the FTP location with which to FTP files via Web pages. When we get to the "IIS And FrontPage Extensions" section in this chapter, this will be demonstrated along with a few more interesting aspects of Web servers.

Now that we've started to think about the IIS installation process, let's press onward and install IIS.

Installing IIS

IIS comes on the CD that you use to install NT 4 with. So, if you've already installed IIS, bear with me for a moment. Or, uninstall IIS, and follow along here. This installation is based on IIS 2.0, which comes with NT 4. IIS 3.0 was released several months ago, so upgrading to IIS 3.0 requires you to download the IIS 3.0 package from the Microsoft site. Eventually, IIS 3.0 will replace the IIS 2.0 package included on NT 4 CDs. If you're going to follow along, grab your NT 4 CD—it's time to get started.

This installation presumes that NT 4 is already installed, and that the system is configured and working properly.

1. Insert your CD into your CD drive, and navigate to the I386\Inetsrv directory.
2. Double-click on the file named *INETSTP.EXE*.

You'll be provided with plenty of functions to choose from, and you'll be given the opportunity to indicate where to install each function you choose, as shown in Figure 7.1.

Figure 7.1 shows the default choices that work for 99 percent of all IIS installations.

3. Click on OK after making your choices, and then choose the directory structures for the root of the selected services.

At this point, the installation proceeds and then presents you with an important notice about the Guest account on NT. (See Figure 7.2.) Pay attention to the notice, and don't ignore it!

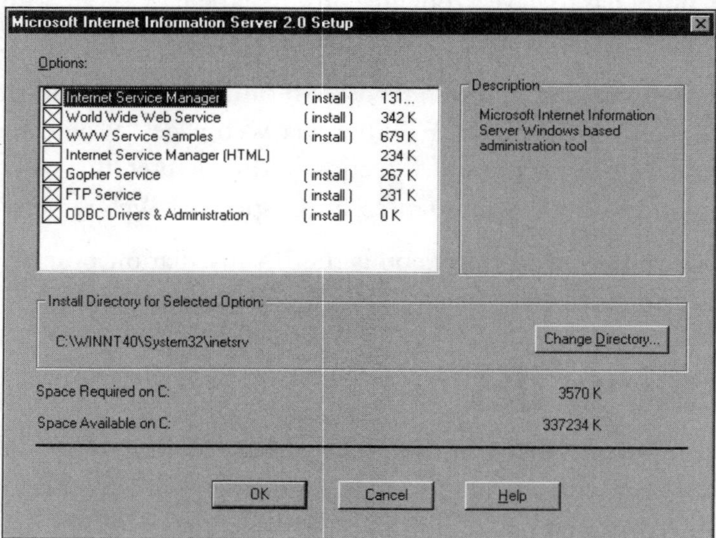

Figure 7.1
IIS opening screen.

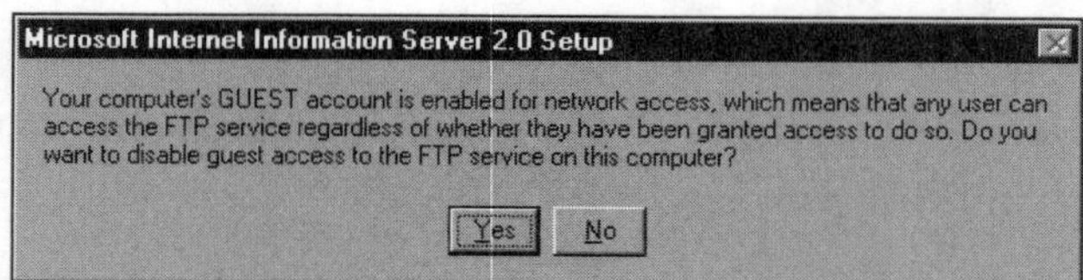

Figure 7.2
Guest account warning.

4. Make your selection as to whether or not you want to use the Guest account, and then choose which database driver(s) you want to install.

By default, only SQL Server is available to be installed. In the Advanced section, there are customized options for the driver manager and translators, but you won't need to change any of these options unless you're running SQL Server in your Web site.

5. Choose OK to move onward.

Onward takes you to the final screen, which lets you know that the installation is complete. That's all there is to it! Next, let's look at upgrading your IIS 2.0 to IIS 3.0.

Upgrading IIS Version 2.0 To Version 3.0

Before you can upgrade IIS 2.0 to IIS 3.0, you'll need to download the 3.0 upgrade from the Microsoft site. Place the upgrade into a working directory on the server. Another source supplying the IIS 3.0 upgrade is the Service Pack 2. The Service Pack 2 can be accessed from a variety of resources, including Microsoft Developers Network CD-ROM and Microsoft's FTP site. At this point, I'll not bore you to tears with the upgrade procedures. It's simple enough.

The IIS 3.0 upgrade for the Web server consists of many add-on components, including the following:

- Active Server Pages (ASP)
- Crystal Reports for IIS
- FrontPage 97 server extensions
- Microsoft Index Server 1.1
- NetShow Live server, client, doc, and SDK
- NetShow On-Demand content creation tools
- NetShow On-Demand Player
- NetShow On-Demand printable SDK and doc (RTF)

- NetShow On-Demand SDK and doc in HTML format
- NetShow On-Demand Server

The add-on components in the preceding list have a cumulative storage of 28MB. So, it'll take some time to download the components by modem. As an alternative, Microsoft offers the upgrade and add-ons via a CD-ROM. All you need to do is complete the online upgrade form found on the Microsoft Web site.

Because I recently installed a new copy of NT Server, I applied Service Pack 2 to achieve the basic upgrade to IIS 3.0. Note that none of the component parts listed in the preceding list are installed as part of Service Pack 2. Microsoft may change this in the future, but as of May 1997, the add-ons weren't included.

With Service Pack 2 installed and IIS 3.0 in place, let's begin the configuration process.

Configuring IIS

IIS is installed with four icons in the menu:

- *Internet Information Server Setup*—Allows you to go back into IIS and update the program with components you may have left out in the beginning. This is basically the same setup program but allows for adding and removing component parts of IIS.
- *Internet Service Manager*—Acts as the core manager for IIS. More on this option will be seen when the Web server portion of IIS is configured.
- *Key Manager*—Allows you to generate security keys to sign your documents on IIS and provide authentication for users. This security feature is being implemented more and more as security continues to grow as a major Internet issue.
- *Product Documentation*—Provides IIS documentation formatted in HTML.

Now that configuration issues have been reviewed, let's look at how to use the components of IIS. A later chapter will look at Key Manager as well.

Tuning System Memory For IIS

Before people start using your Web server, they must have permission to use it. In our particular situation, this book focuses on the use of the Web server as a business tool. Therefore, as a pseudo-private Web site, all connections made are done so as strictly authorized clients. This means that you'll have to go to the NT Server running the Web services and create the user accounts, rights, permissions, and so forth, for each client. Once that's done, we'll address Web administration for IIS.

At any time, you may need assistance. Help is merely a fingertip away because the IIS manual is online in help-file format. To start IIS, click on the Internet Service Manager icon. You'll be presented with a screen similar to Figure 7.3.

Notice that in the lower-right corner of the screen it states *one server* and there are *three services* running! Most interesting. This means that IIS is installed as one Web server but splits out its internal functions as three NT services. Each of the three functions—Web, FTP, and Gopher servers—all operate independently of one another yet as fast as each one can run, depending on the user load.

To demonstrate this concept, I've started the Performance Monitor in NT Server and initialized the Processor Time, User Time, and Interrupts Per Second monitors to see how the physical server is doing while handling a logged in user. Figure 7.4 shows my physical server performance of IIS.

When you look at the statistics of the server, it really isn't that bad. Four users were on the server when Figure 7.4 was captured, and the physical server was running at 40 percent capacity. This server could be doing a whole lot more

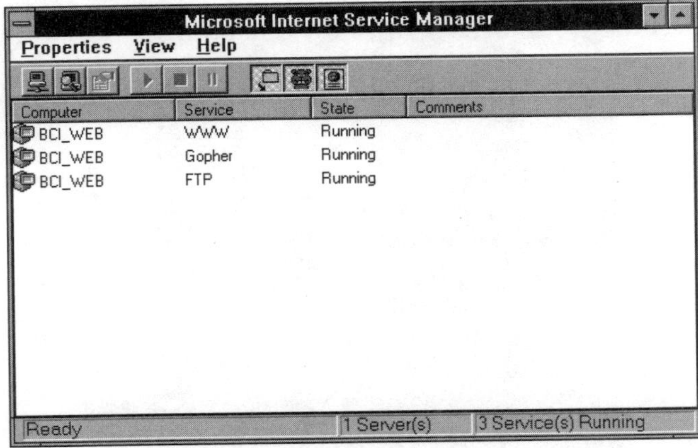

Figure 7.3
IIS Service Manager.

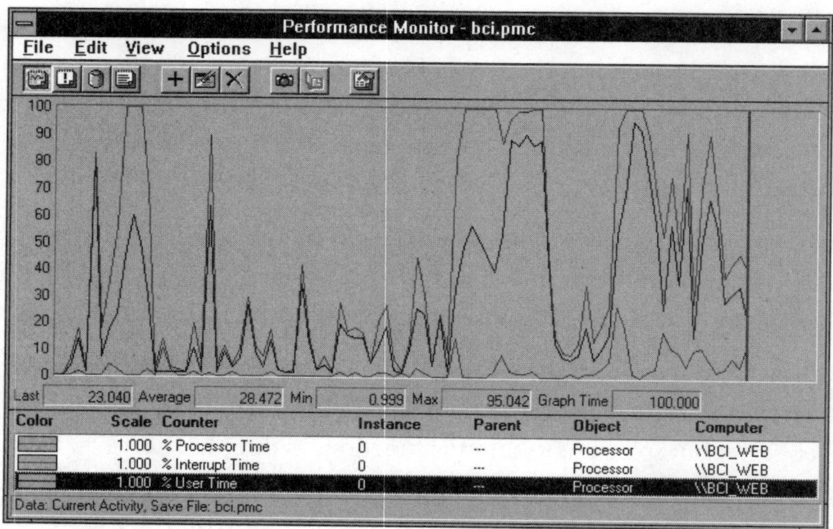

Figure 7.4
Physical server performance of IIS.

work if it needed to, but it isn't right now. While testing this setup, I noticed that the physical server appeared sluggish and otherwise slow to respond to tasks. I made my next discovery by running the Windows NT Diagnostics. Figure 7.5 displays my findings.

Do you see anything wrong here? The tasking bar is red and showing nearly 80 percent workload! This means the Microsoft Windows NT Server proper is closely approaching tasks locking up, slow operations, or even the server itself

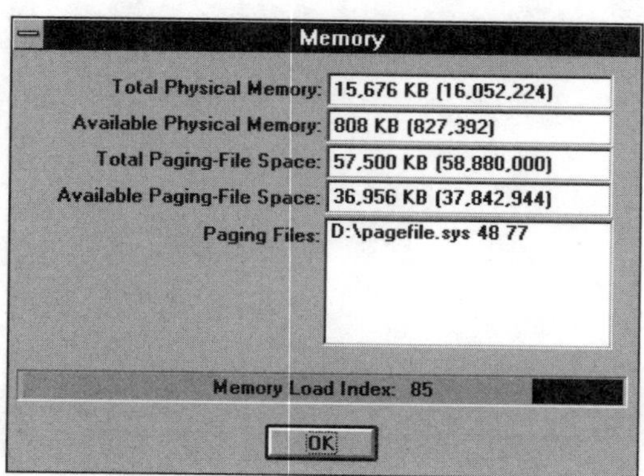

Figure 7.5
Memory tasking diagnostic with 16MB of memory.

locking up. Why? I'm running this Web server on 16MB of memory. That's why! So, in Chapter 6, when I showed you the relative performance between types of servers, this is a key factor in operations of a Web server due to insufficient memory. Figure 7.6 shows the same operations present in Figure 7.5, except, in this instance, the server is running on 32MB of memory.

As you can see, by adding 16MB of memory to create a total of 32MB, the free memory went up to 5.2MB from 1.2MB—a 4MB gain. This means that 12MB of the installed memory went immediately to usage for the operating system, all users, and the drivers. Where the processor was only 40 percent tasked, it now is 30 to 35 percent. Not much of a processor gain, but it shows that beefing up one component of the physical server can assist other facets of the server operations. Installing a faster processor won't help memory loss, but it'll speed up what is using memory. Likewise, adding memory provides more "running room" for applications. Let's take one more look at the memory and server performance at the 48MB level. Figure 7.7 shows the server running with 48MB of memory.

As you can see, the server now has 18MB of free memory after everything is running. When we explored the 32MB installation, we saw that there was roughly 4MB gain of free memory. After adding the 16MB, we should have had slightly over 20MB of memory. But in reality, we're right at 18MB. Why is this? Because Microsoft Windows NT Server dynamically allocates and manages memory and also how you set the tasking in the NT setup via Control Panel in the SYSTEM settings. Thus, Microsoft Windows NT Server used the additional 16MB of memory to load more functions and keeps them loaded in memory.

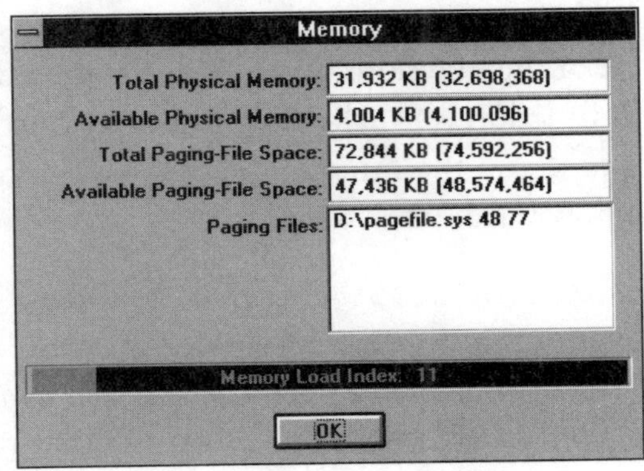

Figure 7.6
Memory tasking diagnostic with 32MB of memory.

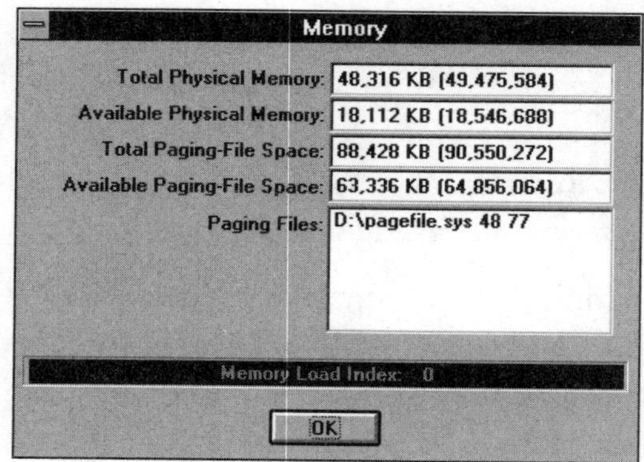

Figure 7.7
Memory tasking diagnostic with 48MB of memory.

This little rendition of server configuration may not have been directly related to the administration of IIS, but I wanted to reinforce the premise that a properly configured server will give you the best performance. Next, let's get right into working with the IIS core services.

Using IIS Core Services

This section is about describing and using each of the three IIS services—Web, Gopher, and FTP servers. Each section will address specific issues behind each server, but one common function is the IIS Service Manager's function, which is nearly identical for all three.

Web Server

When you look at all of the functions that a Web site provides for its constituents, the Web server function is usually the most used. Surfing the Web is the most popular thing to do on the Internet. So, let's take a look at the IIS Web server function and how it can work for us.

> *Note: If you intend to not allow anonymous connections to the Web server, then you must ensure that the proper NT rights and permissions are set for each account you'll provide to the users—just like you do for a normal network setup.*

1. Start IIS Service Manager if you've not already done so.

You'll see the status of all three services (Web server, Gopher server, and FTP server).

2. Make sure all three services have started.

If there are problems, go to the Control Panel, and make sure that each of the services are started. If the services won't start up, then it may be necessary to reinstall IIS.

3. From the Views menu, select the Services view.

The three core services will be displayed.

4. Expand the view of the core services by clicking on the plus sign appearing to the left of the service that you want to see.
5. Double-click on the WWW view, and you'll see a view of the many options by which you can tune and tweak the Web server installation, as shown in Figure 7.8.

I've checked the boxes to allow for anonymous connections and the use of clear text authentication.

6. If you want or need to tighten up security, then check the box for NT Challenge authentication.

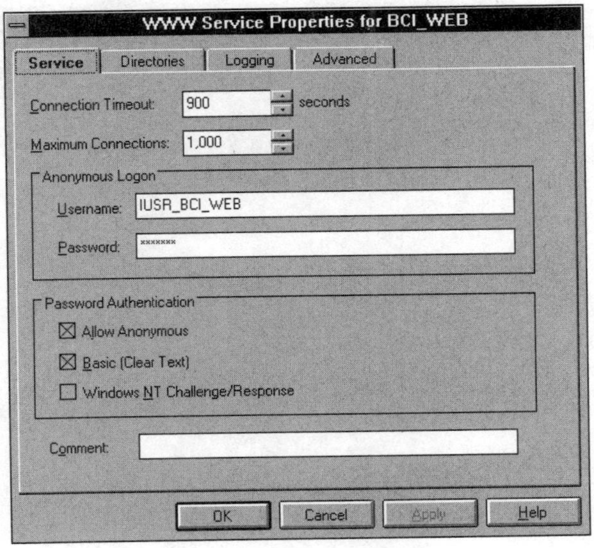

Figure 7.8
Web Server options and preferences.

This type of validation is only usable when clients are using Microsoft Internet Explorer 2.0 or greater, but it ensures added security and lessens the chances of an intruder getting into your site. The NT security is the central point of the server, and you should explore the options here for your Web server.

When you first bring up the Web server properties dialog box, you'll see the Service tab, which presents the basic user issues. These issues include the anonymous account selections, password, and connection limitations.

7. Select the Directories tab.

The Directories tab enables you to select the location of any scripts and HTML pages, including the default home page that users see when they first log on to your site. If you don't modify anything after initial installation, you'll be presented with a default Web page, courtesy of Microsoft. Figure 7.9 displays Microsoft's default home page.

8. Click on the Edit Properties button, and take a peek at some important options for your Web server.

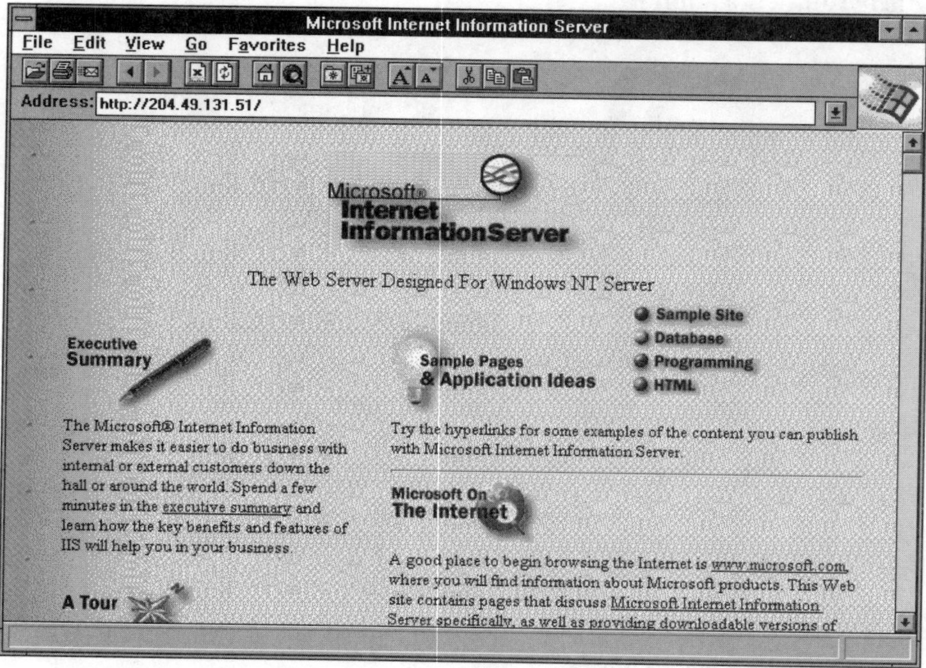

Figure 7.9
Microsoft's IIS default home page.

The first item highlighted on the Edit Properties dialog box is the home directory at the top of the window. This is the default home directory, which is created for you automatically when IIS is installed.

Directly below this selection is a window where you can input an alias directory location which users go to if no other directory is specified. This feature is useful to secure part of one directory tree structure and prevent browsing in others. If you specify a virtual directory using the Universal Naming Convention, such as \\BCI_WEB\APPS\WEBSERVER\IIS, then this option for account information is enabled. Do you remember when we talked about named pipes and network access in Chapter 4? That's exactly what you're doing here when you specify account information in this block. You're creating a named pipe access to another location on the network with account naming and password.

The next consideration in this directory information section is the subject of virtual servers, in which an IP address is assigned to the network card itself (presumably, you've already done this) and assigned to an alias directory. Let's say the real server—the Web server—is at 206.139.150.2. You assign an address of 206.139.150.10 to the virtual server pointing to the \\BCI_WEB\APPS\WEBSERVER directory and give this the alias of *WWW.TEST.COM*. When Internet users enter **www.test.com**, they'll wind up at the UNC specified instead of going to the Web root specified in the IIS setup. We'll talk more about virtual servers later in this chapter.

The next part of this properties section allows you to enable write privileges, in case you want to allow users to alter your Web pages. Read privileges are enabled by default, of course.

The very last item allows you to enable a Secure Sockets Layer (SSL) channel. An SSL channel is a private and public key encryption mechanism that moves data across the server to the clients in a secure format. This may be a crucial feature if your business conducts its affairs with financial or privileged data. If you have SSL installed, this option is enabled, and you can select the box.

Now, let's go on to the other options.

9. Click on the Logging tab.

The options on this card present a really neat way to keep an eye on your Web server. On the left side of the window, you can configure the logging function for the term of log creation and usage, in which the log updates automatically. For instance, if you choose to create weekly reports, then the next report is automatically created on the start of the next week. The old file is retained. If you're using SQL Server, then you can log the file to a database instead of a clear text file. This is really nice if you need to do data analysis in a more automated way. Listing 7.1 is a sample of the text version of the log function.

Listing 7.1 Sample logging file for the Web service.

```
206.139.150.51, -, 6/1/97, 14:59:29, W3SVC, BCI-PDC, 206.139.150.52, 661,
   281, 321, 200, 0, POST, /_vti_bin/shtml.dll, -,
206.139.150.51, -, 6/1/97, 14:59:30, W3SVC, BCI-PDC, 206.139.150.52, 320,
   318, 3482, 200, 0, POST, /_vti_bin/shtml.dll, -,
206.139.150.51, -, 6/1/97, 14:59:32, W3SVC, BCI-PDC, 206.139.150.52, 10,
   408, 147, 401, 5, POST, /ads/_vti_bin/_vti_aut/author.dll, -,
206.139.150.51, sysmgrjb, 6/1/97, 14:59:46, W3SVC, BCI-PDC, 206.139.150.52,
   4656, 451, 36150, 200, 0, POST, /ads/_vti_bin/_vti_aut/author.dll, -,
206.139.150.51, sysmgrjb, 6/1/97, 14:59:47, W3SVC, BCI-PDC, 206.139.150.52,
   491, 437, 3294, 200, 0, POST, /ads/_vti_bin/_vti_aut/author.dll, -,
206.139.150.51, sysmgrjb, 6/1/97, 14:59:56, W3SVC, BCI-PDC, 206.139.150.52,
   650, 415, 5026, 200, 0, POST, /ads/_vti_bin/_vti_aut/author.dll, -,
206.139.150.51, -, 6/1/97, 15:01:00, W3SVC, BCI-PDC, 206.139.150.52, 40,
   166, 1234, 200, 0, GET, /ads/_private/style.htm, -,
206.139.150.51, -, 6/1/97, 15:01:00, W3SVC, BCI-PDC, 206.139.150.52, 60,
   165, 730, 200, 0, GET, /ads/_private/logo.htm, -,
206.139.150.51, -, 6/1/97, 15:01:00, W3SVC, BCI-PDC, 206.139.150.52, 211,
   167, 678, 200, 0, GET, /ads/_private/navbar.htm, -,
206.139.150.51, -, 6/1/97, 15:01:00, W3SVC, BCI-PDC, 206.139.150.52, 40,
   167, 490, 200, 0, GET, /ads/images/undercon.gif, -,
206.139.150.51, -, 6/1/97, 15:01:00, W3SVC, BCI-PDC, 206.139.150.52, 20,
   167, 678, 200, 0, GET, /ads/_private/navbar.htm, -,
206.139.150.51, -, 6/1/97, 15:01:01, W3SVC, BCI-PDC, 206.139.150.52, 370,
   166, 3238, 200, 0, GET, /ads/images/adslogo.gif, -,
206.139.150.51, sysmgrjb, 6/1/97, 15:15:04, W3SVC, BCI-PDC, 206.139.150.52,
   2564, 4714, 1053, 200, 0, POST, /ads/_vti_bin/_vti_aut/author.dll, -,
206.139.150.51, sysmgrjb, 6/1/97, 15:15:31, W3SVC, BCI-PDC, 206.139.150.52,
   581, 416, 3716, 200, 0, POST, /ads/_vti_bin/_vti_aut/author.dll, -,
```

A brief examination of the log file shows the IP address of the visitor, logon name (sysmgrjb), date, time, type of connection, server name (BCI-PDC), IP address of the server, map coordinates of the Web page accessed, type of access which was a GET function (retrieving the Web page), and lastly, the name of the image used to create the map file. What's even more important to be seen here is that the entries are all comma delimited and ready to be imported into just about any database system.

10. Lastly, click on the Advanced tab.

The Advanced tab provides options to set some of the tightest restrictions you can place on Web site visitors. If you know you want to restrict access to your site based on a range of IP addresses, you can restrict an entire class of addresses such as 206.139.000.000 through 206.139.255.255. Or, you can grant access by leaving the exclusions blank. You can also limit the amount of bandwidth usage per user with the setting at the bottom of the page.

Well, I guess you're wondering what's next, right? That's it. Straightforward, simple, fast, and easy access to setting the properties for your Web server.

Next, you need to start developing your Web pages. Figure 7.10 shows a sample directory listing of the Web pages Microsoft includes in the IIS installation. I've simply expanded the directory structure that IIS creates during installation.

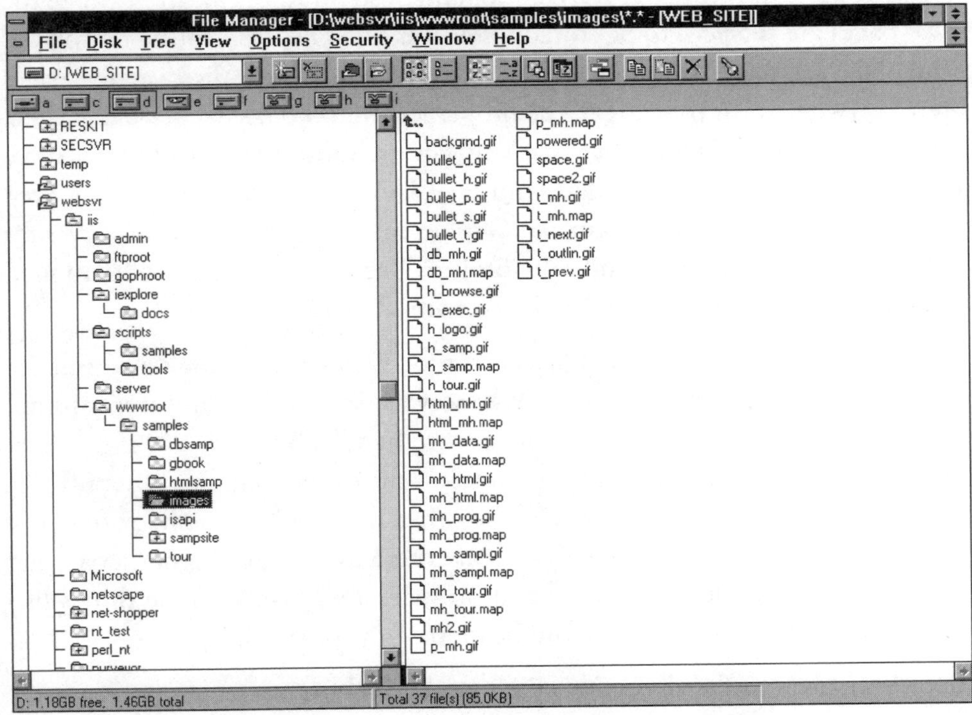

Figure 7.10
IIS directory structure.

Now, we're going to explore the Gopher server and how we can put it to use. You're probably saying to yourself, "What about the HTML programming and designing Web pages?" Don't worry—we'll explore those avenues using Microsoft's FrontPage HTML editor, when we install FrontPage server extensions. Front Page is a full Web page and multimedia authoring program that is worth a look-see. Now, on to Gopher...

The Gopher Server

Let's presume that the Web portion of your server is installed and operational. You've got some really neat Web pages built and posted. Lots of folks are visiting your Web site, and things are hopping for you. Monday when you come back into the office, you find that your Webmaster left you for a new position offering more money. Then, 30 minutes later you get a request to update a Web page with some really hot new material about the latest widget that your business wants to promote.

You start up your favorite HTML editor and head off to the location where the Web pages are *supposed* to be stored. *Supposed* to be because you've not played with the Web pages in quite a while. Unfortunately, you discover the pages aren't anywhere near to being in the proper location. Looks like it's panic time, but fortunately, you remember that you can use most any text file to create a Gopher entry. It's quick, painless, and easy. Is this a replacement for the Web server? No. But it's worth looking at. Gopher can be a quick stand-by server for the Web users while you rebuild the broken Web pages. At least with Gopher, the files and directories of the Web server are accessible.

While Gopher servers aren't a replacement for Web servers, Gopher servers are easier to update and maintain than Web servers. In fact, Gophers were around long before Web servers. Gophers are easy to handle, but they lost their luster because they aren't as flashy as a Web site—they leave out the fun stuff like video and sound presentations. On the other hand, what Gopher offers is a straightforward and direct flow of information to users. The Gopher server that comes with IIS is fully functional and provides a way to advertise things like descriptions of files, directories, publications on your site, and more.

Before we get too far along, let's look at the Gopher server property sheets. With IIS Service Manager started, double-click on the Gopher Server to bring up its properties. You'll notice that the Gopher property sheets are quite similar to the Web server property sheets presented earlier in this chapter. I'm not going into the parameters again, but I recommend that you review the options at your leisure. One thing I'd like to point out is that on the Service card, there's an entry for the system administrator and an area where you can enter an email address for user feedback. You can also provide the username for anonymous logins, if you want to allow that. Aside from this card, the other cards provide the same options as the Web server property cards.

We all know what a Gopher is, right? "Go fer this, go fer that...." And of course, a gopher is a little rodent. In this case, the little rodent scurries around and fetches information stored on Gopher servers. Which brings us to the next question—What's a Gopher server?

What Is A Gopher Server?

A Gopher server is nothing more than a means of using the Internet Gopher protocol to browse a directory and file structure stored on an Internet server. Directories appear as Gopher folders, and the files in the directories appear as Gopher entries inside the folders. That's it! So, if you can create directories and files, know how to use a browser, and can create different file types, then you can build a Gopher server. Plain and simple.

Figure 7.11 shows the Gopher view of my Gopher server.

Now, look at one of the files that Gopher can retrieve for you, as shown in Figure 7.12.

Not much to it, is there? So, let's take a look at how you set up a Gopher server.

Setting Up Gopher

There are a few things to remember when creating a Gopher server. When you create Gopher entries, you follow the same logical steps that you follow when creating an FTP site (creating an FTP site is the subject of a later discussion). For now, suffice it to say that Gopher entries should be arranged in some logical order, like accounting issues in one Gopher directory, logistics data in another, sales flyers in yet another, and so on. The entries that you can create are composed of several types, as identified in Table 7.1.

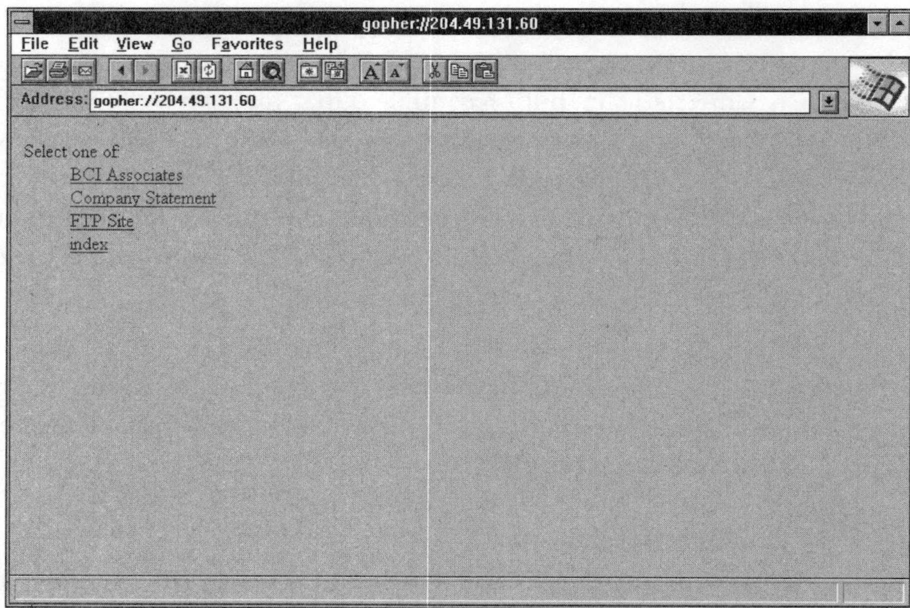

Figure 7.11
IIS Gopher server in basic form for my company.

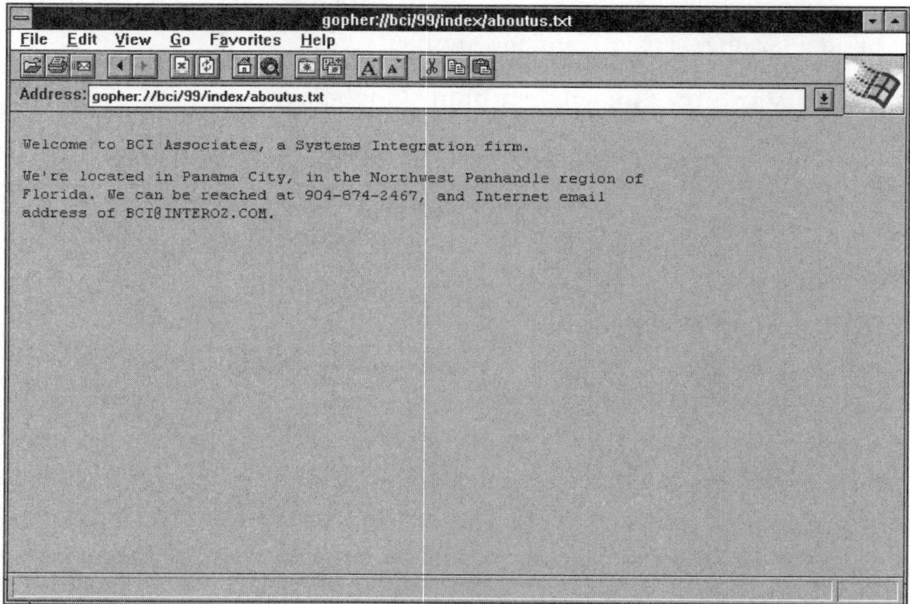

Figure 7.12
File retrieved by Gopher.

Table 7.1

Gopher file types.

Type	Gopher Type	Meaning
TXT	0 (default)	Text File
DOC	1	Text File
ZIP	5	Binary Archive
ARC	5	Binary Archive
UUE	6	UUEncoded
SRC	7	WAIS Index
EXE	9	Binary Executable
DLL	9	Binary Executable
GIF	g	GIF Image
BMP	I	Windows Bitmap
AU	s	Sound Bite
HTM	h	HTML File
HTML	h	HTML File

Table 7.1 shows the standard file types of Gopher servers. One glaring problem with the IIS Gopher server is that these file types can't be changed and additions can't be made to the server. This is a terrible oversight on Microsoft's part, and I hope they fix it in forthcoming versions of IIS. But, don't despair, there's a solution to this if you must alter the file types and you have a Gopher server. First, head to **gopher://gopher.micro.umn.edu**, which is the Gopher server at the University of Minnesota. When you get there, click on the link Information About Gopher, then click on Frequently Asked Questions About Gopher. This takes you to the FAQ sheets for Gopher, in which commonly asked questions are addressed. For example, here's a question and answer I copied from the FAQ:

```
Q1:  Where can I get Gopher software?
A1:  Via anonymous FTP to boombox.micro.umn.edu.  Look in the directory
     /pub/gopher, or use the locator
     <URL:ftp://boombox.micro.umn.edu/pub/gopher;type=d>
     or via gopher itself:
     <URL:gopher://boombox.micro.umn.edu/11/gopher/
```

If you want to see what it means to alter and customize Gopher, download this Gopher server software at the previous URL, and install it on your NT Server. To do so, you must go to the Control Panel|Services, and stop the IIS Gopher server. When you expand the Gopher server from UMN, follow the instructions to install and register Gopher with NT. It's amazingly simple. When you do this, an icon is added to the Control Panel for the UMN gopher. Double-click on this icon, and your screen should look similar to Figure 7.13.

Notice the file options and settings. This is what we wanted to be able to do. Did you ever wonder how you could click on a link in a Web server and have a response come back that includes text like "SQL processing time was 280 ms" or something? In Web servers, the HTML code on a Web page can execute a CGI script that runs a program on the NT Server to handle the task. In a Gopher server, you're providing links to other sites or using the directory structure on your server to disseminate information. Oh, did I say provide links to other sites? You sure can, and that's one of the joys of a Gopher server—easy to configure, maintain, and share information.

As mentioned earlier, Gophers pioneered the Internet for informational flow and sharing of ideas before Web servers took over the show. But Gopher servers aren't totally out of the loop yet. When you need a quick and easy way to get data out to your customers, consider using Gopher as an alternative to using the Web server.

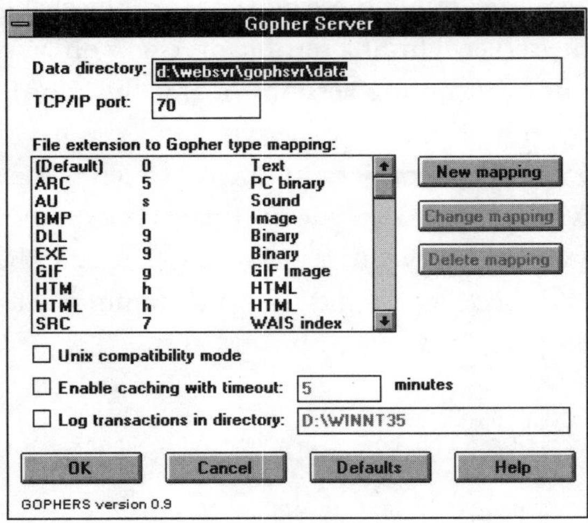

Figure 7.13
Customizable Gopher server.

Of course, as with any computer service, Gopher runs into errors at times. The following section introduces you to error logging your Gopher server.

Error Logging For Gopher

Errors are handled much the same way on Gopher servers as they're handled on Web servers, by logging error instances into the system error log and recording a file as determined by you in the Gopher configuration. Listing 7.2 shows a sample Gopher log listing accesses to our new Gopher. Notice the exact references to the files and directories accessed, and by whom.

Listing 7.2 Gopher log file entries.

```
206.139.150.51, -, 6/12/97, 9:18:57, GopherSvc, BCI-NT4, 206.139.150.51,
   1312, 2, 3, 0, 0, dir, /, -,
206.139.150.51, -, 6/12/97, 9:19:38, GopherSvc, BCI-NT4, 206.139.150.51,
   30, 2, 27, 1, 3, dir, /, -,
206.139.150.51, -, 6/12/97, 9:20:12, GopherSvc, BCI-NT4, 206.139.150.51,
   3755, 2, 12981, 0, 0, dir, /, -,
206.139.150.51, -, 6/12/97, 9:21:32, GopherSvc, BCI-NT4, 206.139.150.51,
   100, 16, 19456, 0, 0, file, /EXCTRLST.DOC, -,
```

Gopher is perhaps the easiest service to set up and maintain, and it's a joy to use. One of the main things that these sites can do is to point users to other sites, such as a related supplier of your super widgets. To create a link, create a text file containing the entries shown in Listing 7.3.

Listing 7.3 Creating a Gopher link.

```
Name=BCI Associates
Host=gopher.bciassoc.com
Port=70
Numb=2
Path=
Type=1
```

Listing 7.3 indicates that the name of the site is *BCI Associates.* The host's location is at alias *gopher.bciassoc.com* using the standard port number 70 for a Gopher and the *Numb* 2 Gopher is the listing on screen. The *Path* to the link file is always relative to the Gopher data location specified in the configuration and *Type* is set to an ASCII text file of *1.* You can easily build Gopher menus by placing multiple Gopher locations in the same link file, as shown in Listing 7.4.

Listing 7.4 Creating multiple Gopher links.

```
Name=BCI Associates
Host=gopher.bciassoc.com
Port=70
Numb=2
Path=
Type=1
#
Name=BCI Associates' Primary Customer
Host=gopher.custone.bciassoc.com
Port=+
Numb=1
Path=0\customers\custone
Type=0
#
Name=Gophers in Europe
Host=sunic.sunet.se
Port=70
Type=1
Path=1/Other Gopher and Information Servers/Europe
```

Listing 7.4 presents an interesting concept of updating and expanding your Gopher server. Look at the listing again, and notice the pound sign (#). The pound sign is the separator between sites. The plus sign (+) used in the second entry indicates that Gopher should use the port number on that particular server. The default is port 70, but sometimes the port number has to be changed, and this is how to allow for that change. In the third entry, the path points to a menu in another Gopher server on another site in Europe. Pretty neat, huh? And so very easy to do. Gopher servers have been around for quite some time, and the mystique behind them has been one of the Internet's hidden secrets. Next, let's take a quick look at WAIS searches, which in some places supplement Gopher.

WAIS Servers By Way Of Gopher

WAIS from Gopher? You bet, and here's a good example. While the full text of building and maintaining a WAIS server is beyond the scope of this chapter, we can take a few minutes to preview the basic steps to using a WAIS server.

Let's say your company has 10 text files that describe various parts of your widgets. As you probably know, a file name sometimes doesn't do justice to what's contained in the file. WAIS is designed to allow for searches in databases for information via Gopher. Here are the basic steps for performing a WAIS operation via Gopher.

1. First, you have to build a WAIS database of the documents that you want to allow to be used.
2. Next, index the database by word and topic.

This lets users search your documents based on a keyword or phrase. When you build the database, you'll need to keep all the source documents in their same directory as when you built the database, or you'll have to frequently index them to refresh the locations of the documents in the directory tree. Once the indexing procedure is done, you'll be ready to implement your new WAIS server for your users by way of Gopher, if that's how you want to use the data.

3. At this point, the only step remaining is to install the WAIS server software itself on the Web server and link in your databases.

I hope this text has shown you just how simple it is to install and maintain a Gopher server. Gopher may not be able to compete with Web servers in popularity, but their sheer simplicity of installation and maintenance certainly deserves consideration and review. Now, let's look at the next IIS service—the FTP server.

The FTP Server

In all of the Internet, perhaps the most frequently used utility among experienced surfers is file transfer. Site support technicians use a vast array of Internet tools, but when it boils down to the nitty-gritty of fixing problems after installations go wrong or system compatibility issues crop up, it's the venerable FTP that comes to the rescue. FTPing files provides an easy way to obtain updated files fast. Let's press onward to see how the IIS FTP server can help us with our file transfer needs. FTP was installed with the rest of the IIS package, so let's bypass the installation procedures and jump right into configuring the system.

Configuration

Before you can start any part of the IIS FTP configurations, you need to make sure that you've defined the FTP area in your system by organizing your directories and files. As you'll soon see, IIS allows you to define many directories and how you access them, but first, the permissions need to be completed on the main server itself. (See Figure 7.14.)

1. Start the IIS Service Manager, if you've not already done so.
2. Double-click on the FTP branch of the tree to bring up the properties of FTP.

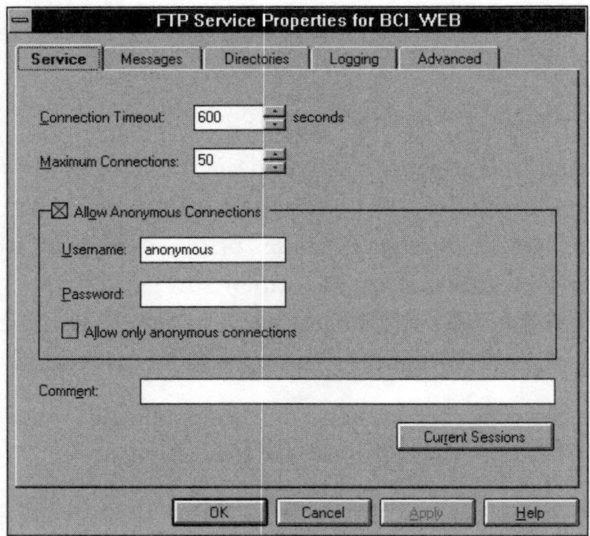

Figure 7.14
IIS main FTP menu screen.

There are five property tabs in the FTP server properties dialog box:

- *Service*—Used to configure connection options.
- *Messages*—Used to customize connection messages users see.
- *Directories*—Used to specify the FTP core locations.
- *Logging*—Used to provide error log information.
- *Advanced*—Used to address advanced issues concerning FTP.

Let's take a minute to explore each of these cards one at a time. I'll not dwell over any options that are the same as we saw on the Gopher and Web server property cards, but I'll at least mention them.

- *Service*—These are the options for the FTP service itself. Options include connection timeout and maximum connections for the server, anonymous FTP settings, and any comments you want to put in for this configuration. The last item here is the Current Sessions button, which shows you who is connected and what their IP address is, along with the amount of time they've been logged on. On a later property card, you'll see how we can define server logging to gather information about finding out who a person is and all

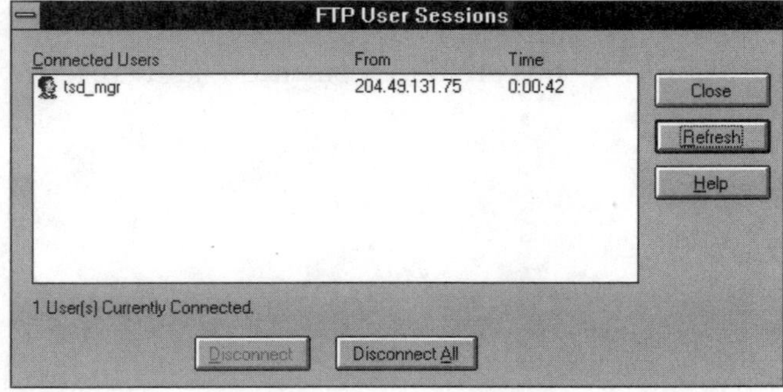

Figure 7.15
FTP user sessions.

sorts of vital information about them. Figure 7.15 shows active user sessions on the FTP server.

- *Messages*—This card enables you to submit customized messages that FTP users see when they connect to and disconnect from the server, and when the server is at its maximum connections as defined in the **Service** property.
- *Directories*—This card provides the one place in the FTP server where you define where the access locations are for the server. My directory structure for the server is four root directories, as follows

```
/incoming
/outgoing
/private
/pub
```

and each directory's usage is self explanatory. The only problem is that you'll need to enter each of these into the **Directories** property card to grant access to them. The only access possible is a global access to any person that can connect to the FTP site. From there, your Microsoft Windows NT Server permissions will regulate who can get to any directory, access any file, or add files. No one can get around to any other parts of the FTP server without being granted permission.

In one glaring difference between the IIS FTP service and the FTP service that comes with Microsoft Windows NT Server, a potential security problem is removed. In Microsoft Windows NT Server's FTP, the directory structure looks like the following on your server. Keep in mind that all directories are on the D partition, which is an NTFS partition, and are at the root level.

```
/WINNT35
/TEMP
/USERS
/APPLICATIONS
/OTHER
/OTHER/FTP
/OTHER/FTP/PUB
/OTHER/FTP/INCOMING
/OTHER/FTP/OUTGOING
/OTHER/FTP/PRIVATE
/CONFIDENTIAL
```

From this listing, let's say that you've installed the Microsoft Windows NT Server FTP server and have configured it. FTP wants to know where the root directory is for the FTP service itself, so you point it to D:/OTHER/FTP as the root for FTP, and you've set Microsoft Windows NT Server's permissions to only allow the FTP users access to this area. When a user logs into the FTP server, they'll be able to traverse the directory tree unless you alter the rights of the users group to deny directory traversing. You also need to hide the directory tree from the users for other locations on the disk.

All of this is possible and is very time consuming to accomplish, but the IIS FTP service takes away the frustrations of having to handle multiple concerns like this. IIS says that so long as the directory and file permissions are set according to your wishes, then IIS takes care of the rest by simply adding in the directory tree. Figure 7.16 shows the alias's setup for the FTP server.

Changing the properties of the FTP locations is a simple affair by clicking on the Edit Properties button. To add a new directory, click on the Add button. It's all self explanatory.

- *Logging*—This card presents the same properties as the Web server and Gopher server services.
- *Advanced*—This card presents options for granting and denying access to the FTP service. The settings are similar to the Advanced options offered for Gopher and Web servers.

The final topic that needs to be addressed concerns the configuration of IIS virtual Web servers.

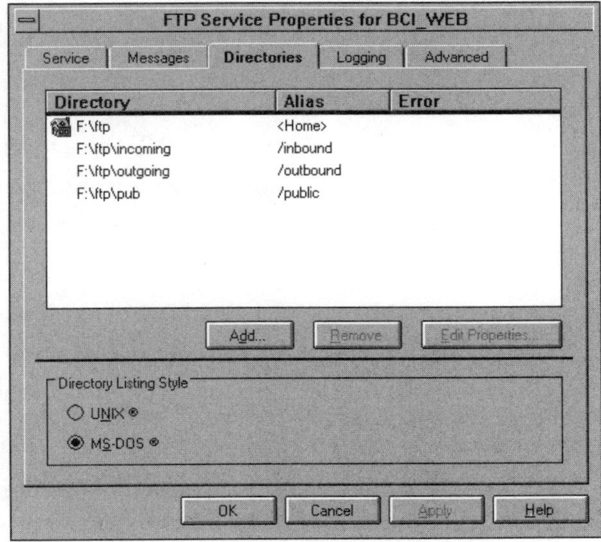

Figure 7.16
Allowing FTP access to specific directories.

Virtual Web Servers

In actuality, a discussion of virtual servers belongs in the Web server section, but I opted to separate it out because not many sites will use this distinct server. Virtual Web servers are hosted on the same physical machine as IIS, but they're separated by a distinct IP address and directory where the Web pages are stored. For further clarification, perform the following steps.

1. Open the IIS Manager and display the properties of the Web server.
2. Click on the Directories tab.
3. Choose a directory that will contain the root Web page for the virtual server, and choose the location for the Web pages.
4. Next, click on the Virtual Directory radio button, and enter the alias for the virtual server.

The alias is used in two situations. First, it's used to access the virtual server by typing in the root IP address or alias plus the virtual server alias. For example, enter the following:

```
http://www.bciassoc.com/~bci
```

To type in the IP address along with the alias, enter

```
http://206.139.150.20/~bci
```

to access the virtual server. Normally, you'd create a DNS entry for this virtual server so that instead of using the alias, it would have its own distinct alias. For instance:

```
http://www.systems.com
```

Figure 7.17 shows that the IP address 206.139.150.26 is assigned to the virtual server. All that's left is to make the DNS entry link this IP address to **www.systems.com** so that the alias of **bci** is no longer needed in the URL address.

If you get an Internet service provider (ISP) that supports virtual servers and FrontPage 97 Web development, this is how they do it. Speaking of FrontPage, the next major section is all about installing FrontPage server extensions and what they can do for you.

IIS And FrontPage Extensions

FrontPage server extensions are drivers, programs, and program extensions of the IIS suite of tools that allow Web pages to be enhanced and modified to

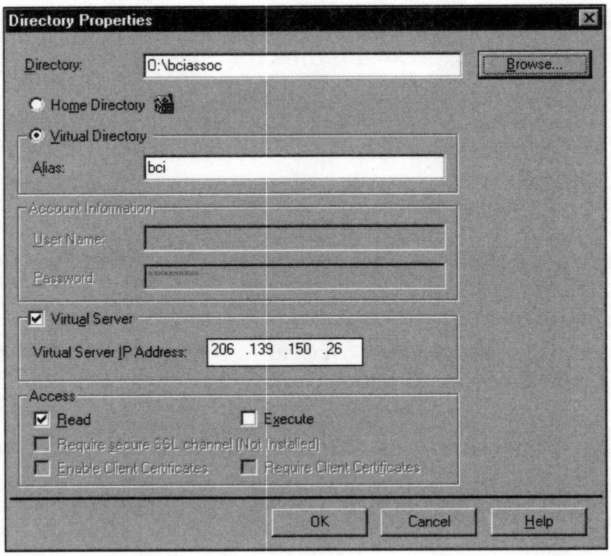

Figure 7.17
Virtual server assignments.

support special functions. These functions are used to present unique Web experiences to viewers with tools like WebBots, MAILTOs, and other options. We'll integrate FrontPage extensions with IIS to present a demonstration of what these extensions can do later in this book. What you need to keep clear in your mind is that these extensions provide a linkage between IIS and Microsoft's FrontPage web editing program so that any web on an IIS machine can be remotely administered via FrontPage Editor.

Extensions are dynamic link libraries, executables, and resource files that take the basic IIS installation to a new plane. By supporting a superset of IIS functionality, they remain backward compatible with FrontPage 1.1. These extensions are part of IIS and should not be tampered with after installation. Speaking of which, let's install the extensions.

1. Start the setup, and click on Next to pass the welcoming screen.
2. Naturally, you'll have to agree with the licensing agreement to continue.
3. Choose the directory for the extensions, and click on Next.

The program will detect the installed servers and offer the ones needed before you install the FrontPage extensions.

4. Click on Next to proceed with the selections made, which will be displayed on your screen for review, as shown in Figure 7.18.

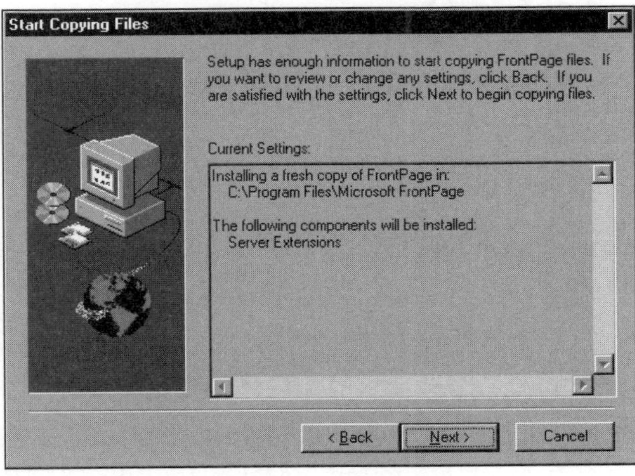

Figure 7.18
Confirmation of FP97 server extension installation.

You can back up to correct any of your setup choices. After you accept your choices, your newly extended IIS server will be fit and robust enough to support the new functions of FrontPage and IIS. You'll then have to pick the NT Server account that will administer the webs created by the FrontPage program itself. The default is the account you used to log on to the NT Server.

5. Click on OK, and the FP97 extensions will be bound to port 80 of the Web server.

One step remains—to restart the Web server so the changes will take effect.

6. Click on Yes to restart the Web server.

One last note. Basic Authentication must be enabled to allow earlier versions of FrontPage to edit Webs. If someone is using version 1.1 of FrontPage, enable this feature. If not, disable it.

Setup of the IIS FP extensions is now complete. Nothing more needs to be done except to use and enjoy the new functionality of IIS. While the extensions are only one part of extending IIS, it is perhaps the most important in terms of easing administration and support for your Webmaster. Next, let's install Active Server Pages to the same IIS server to further IIS capabilities even more.

IIS And Active Server Pages (ASP)

This section deals exclusively with ASP. We'll discuss how to:

- Understand ASPs
- Install ASPs
- Use the documentation for ASPs

Let's get started.

What Are Active Server Pages?

ASP is one more way to present Web surfers with an enhanced view of the Web, by integrating the Microsoft programming language called *ISAPI*, which ties in Internet protocols with back-end processing of databases and Web pages. That's the easy explanation; more details will be presented in Chapter 11.

Installing ASP

Installing ASP is nearly as simple as installing FrontPage extensions. The ASP archive is nearly 9MB and expands to approximately 25MB of files during the install process. Here's the installation process.

1. Double-click on the archive executable, and wait for the ASP setup program to complete the extraction.
2. Accept the licensing agreement to continue the install.

You'll be next presented with a generalized welcome message.

3. Click on Next to continue.

If there are any running services from IIS, you'll be prompted to shut them down before proceeding. Do so. Figure 7.19 displays the IIS reminder that services must be stopped to effect some of the required changes.

4. Next, choose the type of database services you want to install.

ASP core functions require at least 2.5MB of disk space. The ODBC drivers take another 5MB with online docs, and yet another requires 5MB. I highly suggest using the online docs.

5. Now, choose a destination for the ASP files.

I left my files to default to the location where IIS was initially installed. The files are now copied and configured internally with IIS. You're next presented with a screen like Figure 7.20, which shows you what is installed where.

6. Click on OK, and then click on Yes to restart your IIS components stopped for the ASP install.
7. Once Step 6 is completed, choose Start|Programs|Microsoft Internet Server (Common), and you'll see the installed components.

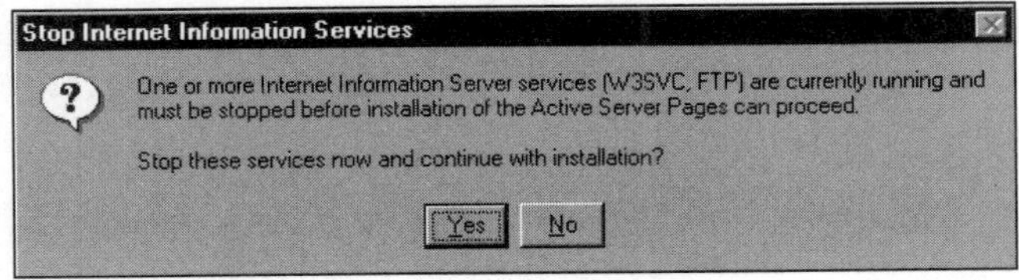

Figure 7.19
IIS services warning.

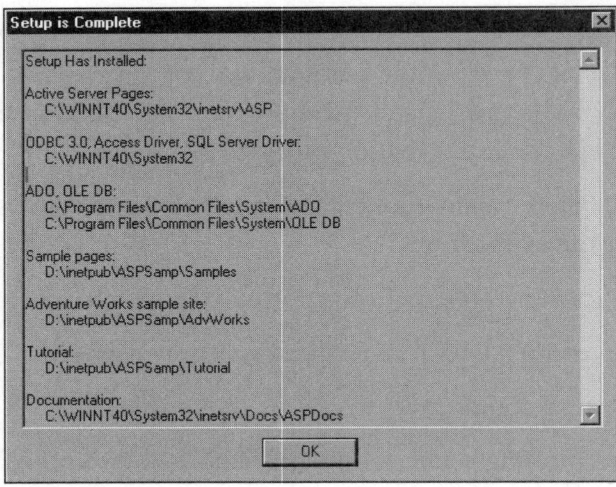

Figure 7.20
Final installed components.

The ASP Documentation

If you click on the Active Server Pages Roadmap, you'll be presented with a view of ASP and how the many functions work. The map provides a pathway to learning how to implement ASP, and it's an excellent learning tool. Figure 7.21 shows the main documentation screen.

This is another major move toward having the HTML format used for documentation, as Microsoft and other vendors have been doing for the past year or so. Using HTML enables any Web browser to read a document. Like any HTML page, you can search it, save it, or bookmark it with a URL. Kind of neat, to be sure. All you do is click on one of the plus signs located to the left of a topic header to expand the topic header, and then drill down into the documentation to find what you want. Searching is quicker, but when searching won't find what you want, this is the next-best method. Besides, sometimes, it's more fun to plunder the docs instead of approaching them in a more organized manner! Figure 7.22 shows the code in the example and the documentation itself.

As you can see in Figure 7.22, the expanded topics look much like the HLP file formats of the old Windows. So the feeling here should be similar to that format.

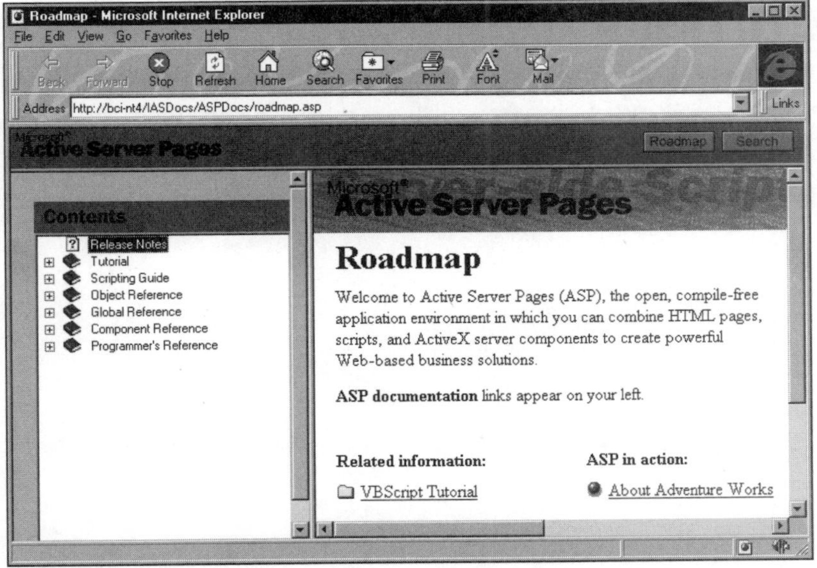

Figure 7.21
The ASP documentation in HTML format.

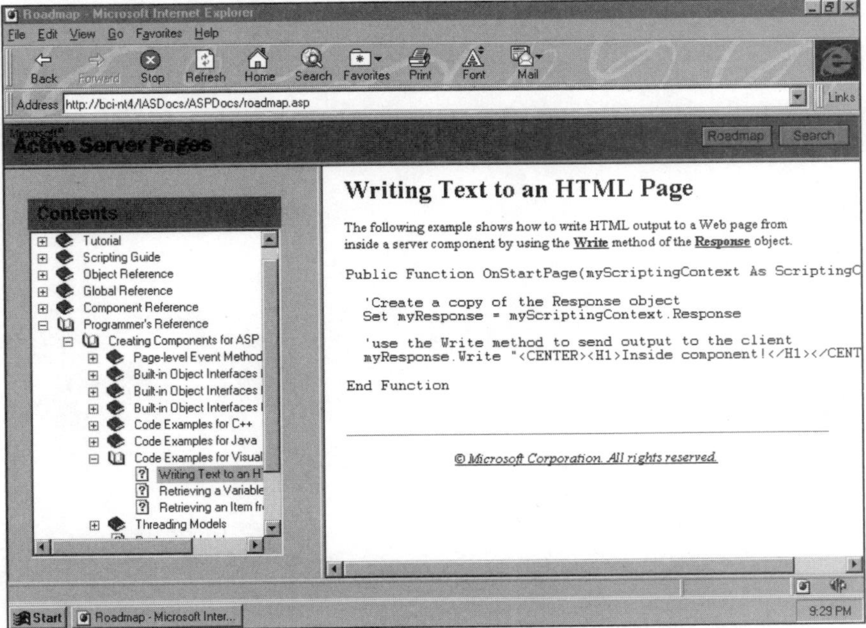

Figure 7.22
Expanded topics.

Summary

This chapter is about installing, configuring, and adding IIS functionality to your NT 4 setup. We looked in fairly good depth at IIS configuration and services. Forthcoming chapters will manipulate ASP and the FrontPage extensions to show you how IIS provides a superior Web serving platform.

Part 3

Extending Your Web Site

8 Implementing Microsoft Proxy Server

Robert Ellis

If your goal on the Internet is to provide a means for Internet clients to view Web pages, download (or upload) files, or search an index, then the Internet Information Server is all you really need. On the other hand, perhaps you want to do more than publish files on the Internet. Perhaps, you are more concerned about security and want to use the Internet Information Server as the backbone of a proxy server to limit access to your Internet/intranet. This chapter describes the Microsoft Proxy Server, which can turn your IIS installation into a full-featured proxy server.

The Microsoft Proxy Server

To protect your network from potential hackers or restrict your network clients from accessing specific Internet resources, you need a little more than the basic software included with the Internet Information Server. The Microsoft Proxy Server might be just what the doctor ordered in this situation. You can order the Proxy Server directly from Microsoft, or you can download a 60-day trial version from the Web at **www.microsoft.com/proxy**. This proxy server can actually protect your network much better than the mini-firewall option, because the granularity is so much finer. You can limit access by user or group to any Internet protocol or TCP/IP port. This means, you can specify which users on your internal network can browse the Web, chat online, download files, and so forth. The Microsoft Proxy Server provides several benefits that can add a significant performance boost to networks using a slow Internet connection. For example, the Microsoft Proxy Server can:

- Cache frequently accessed Web pages.
- Automatically connect to the Internet using Dial-Up Networking when an Internet request is detected so users do not need a persistent Internet connection.
- Mask internal IP addresses while providing Internet access for private (commonly called *non-routable*) IP addresses.

When using the Microsoft Proxy Server, the key to benefiting from the system and easing some of the administrative burden is that you must assign users to groups (using User Manager For Domains) and then use the groups when assigning permissions to specific Internet protocols. This works in exactly the same manner as assigning permission to directories or files to restrict access.

The Microsoft Proxy Server actually includes two separate proxy services. The first is called the *Web Proxy* and is used to support Web browser clients that support the CERN proxy protocol. This includes Internet Explorer, Netscape Navigator, and most other Web browsers. The second is called the *WinSock Proxy* and is used to support WinSock 1.1 compliant applications.

With the addition of third-party software, you can enhance the Microsoft Proxy Server to restrict access to specific Web sites, add virus protection, create dynamic Web pages for individual users, and perform other operations. For more information about third-party enhancements, check out the Web page at **www.microsoft.com/proxy/partners.htm**.

Installing The Microsoft Proxy Server

Let's walk-through the actual installation and configuration process for the Microsoft Proxy Server.

1. Execute the self-extracting file, which you downloaded from the Microsoft Proxy Server Web site, or run the setup program if you obtained the Microsoft Proxy Server on CD-ROM.

The Microsoft Proxy Server Setup dialog box should appear, as shown in Figure 8.1.

2. Click on the Continue button.

The Proxy Server install program prompts you to enter a key to install the software. This key can be found on the back of your CD-ROM jewel case. For the downloadable version, the key is 375-1749043, although you should take note of this key when you download the evaluation version, as it may change from time to time.

3. Enter your key, then click on the OK button to continue.

The product ID dialog box should appear.

4. You should write the product ID number down in case you need to call Microsoft for technical support. If you do not, you can still obtain the ID by

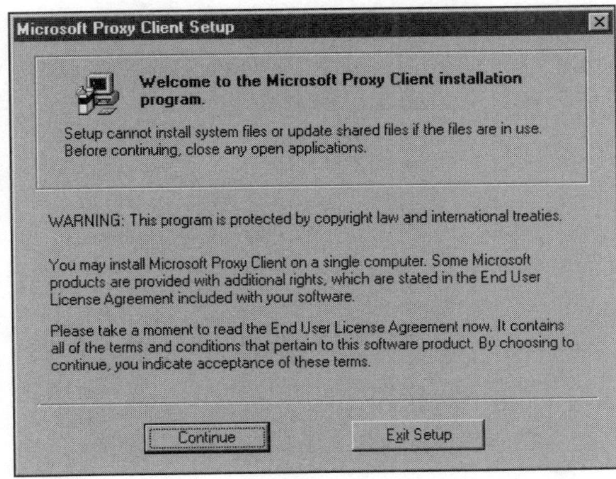

Figure 8.1
Installing the Microsoft Proxy Server.

viewing the Service tab for the proxy service in the Internet Service Manager. When you have finished writing down your product ID, click on the OK button to continue.

The Microsoft Proxy Server Setup dialog should appear, as shown in Figure 8.2.

5. Click on the Browse button to specify an alternate location for the Microsoft Proxy Server files if the default of C:\MSP is not acceptable.
6. To specify which components should be installed, click on the Installation Options button, and the Microsoft Proxy Server—Installation Options dialog box shown in Figure 8.3 should display.

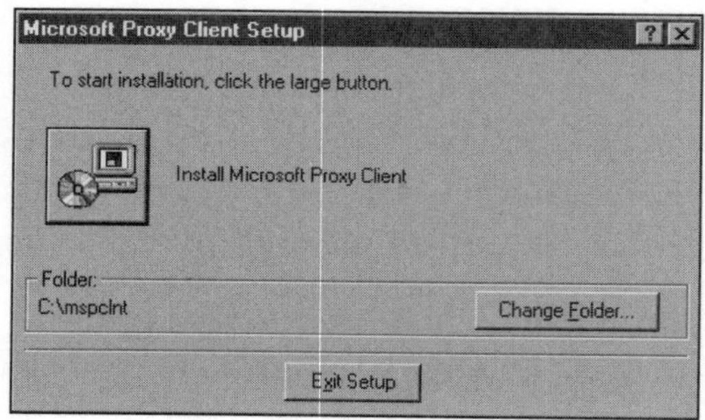

Figure 8.2
Specifying the Microsoft Proxy Server installation options.

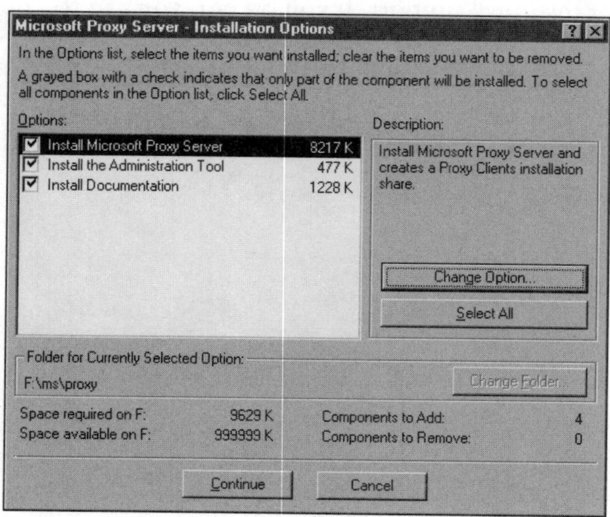

Figure 8.3
Specifying the Microsoft Proxy Server components to install.

7. To specify the types of clients to support, highlight the Install Microsoft Proxy Server option, then click on the Change Options button.

The Microsoft Proxy Server—Install Microsoft Proxy Server dialog box shown in Figure 8.4 should appear. While you can install all of these components, it is best to install only the software for the clients you plan to support on your network. For example, if you plan to support only Intel platforms for Windows NT and Windows 95, then you should uncheck the Install NT Alpha Client Share, the Install NT PPC Client Share, and the Install Win 3.x Client Share.

8. Make your installation selections, then click on the OK button to return to the Microsoft Proxy Server—Installation Options dialog box.
9. When you have completed your selections, click on the Continue button to proceed with the installation.

The Microsoft Proxy Server Cache Drives dialog box should appear. For each drive detected on your computer, you may specify the number of MB to be used by the Proxy Service for cached HTML pages. This option can be used to increase the performance for your clients for frequently accessed pages. It performs the same basic functions as the local cache used by Internet Explorer except the caching occurs as a global system cache for the entire network.

10. Make your drive specifications, then click on the OK button to continue.

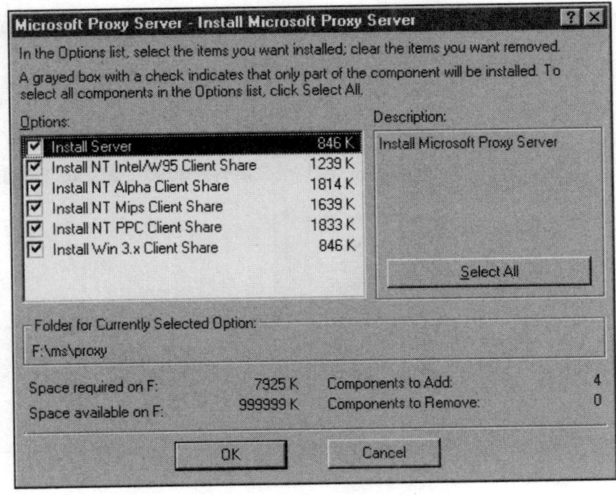

Figure 8.4
Specifying the clients to be supported by the Microsoft Proxy Server.

The Local Address Table Configuration dialog box shown in Figure 8.5 should display. This dialog box is used to specify the internal IP addresses used on your network. You can set this option in two ways:

- Specify a starting and ending range of IP addresses in the From and To fields in the Edit group, and click on the Add button. If you are using DHCP to assign IP addresses, you can enter the DHCP scopes in these fields. Don't forget to include the DHCP server IP addresses, however.
- Click on the Construct Table button, and have the setup program attempt to locate the internal IP addresses for you. While this option sounds attractive, it can actually require more work because it might detect IP addresses in use outside of your internal network. Should this occur, you will have to remove the addresses manually.

11. Enter your internal IP addresses using either procedure described, then click on the OK button to continue.

The Client Installation/Configuration dialog box should appear, as shown in Figure 8.6.

This dialog box is used to configure the proxy client configuration. The defaults should suffice for almost every installation; however, it never hurts to know a little more about the configuration options.

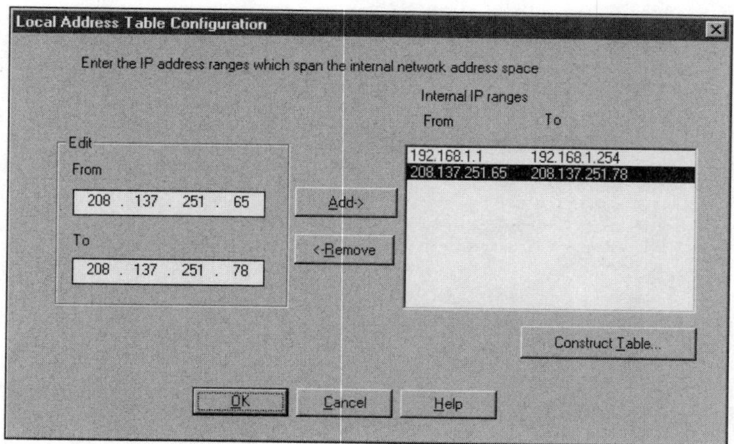

Figure 8.5
Specifying the IP addresses in use on your area network.

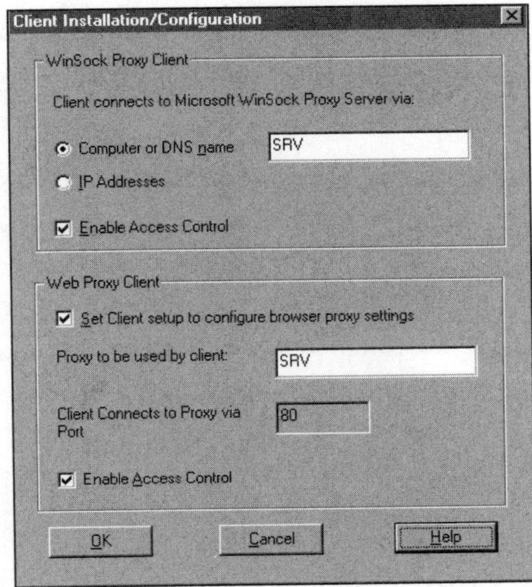

Figure 8.6
Configuring Client IP information.

These options include:

WinSock Proxy Client group

- *Computer Or DNS Name*—Specifies the NetBIOS name, which the proxy clients use to access the proxy server.
- *IP Address*—Specifies an IP address, which the proxy clients use to access the proxy server.
- *Enable Access Control*—Specifies that only authorized users can access the proxy server and gain access to Internet and intranet resources using a Windows Socket application.

Web Proxy Client group

- *Set Client Setup To Configure Browser Settings*—Specifies that the client setup program attempts to automatically configure the Web browser client.
- *Proxy To Be Used By Client*—Specifies the name of the proxy server to be used by the client during an automatic configuration attempt.
- *Client Connects To Proxy Via Port*—Specifies the TCP/IP port to be used by the client for access to Web services.

- *Enable Access Control*—Specifies that only authorized users can access the proxy server and gain access to Internet resources using the FTP, Gopher, WWW, or SSL protocols.

The Enable Access Control is a powerful option. With a single switch, you can either limit access to all Internet resources (when enabled in the WinSock Proxy group), limit access to all Web browser functions (when enabled in the Web Proxy group), or throw the door wide open and allow complete access. While you can disabled this option to make your administrative duties a little easier, I do not recommend it because this defeats the "limit access to those who really need it" feature of the proxy server and raises the potential for Internet abuse.

12. Make your proxy client configuration selections, then click on OK to continue the installation and copy the proxy server files to your computer.

The Microsoft Proxy Server Setup dialog box appears informing you that the setup completed normally.

13. Click on OK to exit the setup program.

Configuring The Microsoft Proxy Server

After you have installed the Microsoft Proxy Server, you must configure it for optimum operation. First, you have to configure the Web Proxy and WinSock Proxy Services. Then, if you are using Dial-up Networking as your Internet pipeline, you need to configure the auto-dial options. Finally, you need to configure your client Web browsers to use the Proxy Server for all Internet access.

The most important part of the Proxy Server configuration process is to assign permissions (or access rights, if you prefer) to restrict access to various Internet protocols/services. The mechanics to assign permissions are actually quite easy and are performed in the Web Proxy and WinSock Proxy Services' Permissions property sheets, which you'll step through later in this section. More importantly, it is the application and methodology of applying permissions that requires real consideration.

You can, for example, assign permissions based on individual user accounts. However, this can cause a significant administrative burden. The better methodology is to assign permissions based on groups. Managing groups is easier for an administrator than managing users. Why? Simply because when applying permissions to an object—a directory, file, named pipe, service, and so forth—it is easier to specify it at the highest level. If you use groups properly, you can specify permissions to multiple objects. This makes it much easier for the administrator to grant or reject user access to an object.

> ***Note:*** *For more information on group management and basic network administration, you might want to look at another book of mine called* Microsoft BackOffice 2 Administrator's Survival Guide, *by Sams Publishing. This book covers the basics of network administration along with various tips and tricks to aid you in your administrative pursuits.*

The basic method to assign permissions using groups breaks down into the following basic actions.

1. Create your local groups. These local groups can be created using User Manager (if IIS is installed on a server) or User Manager For Domains (if IIS is installed on a domain controller).
2. Assign your users to the local groups. You can do this by directly placing your user accounts directly into the local groups. This works, but it is also more work for your network administrator. The preferred method is to place a global group that contains your domain user accounts into a local group. This way, when you create a new user account, you can assign it to the appropriate global group, and the system can apply the correct Internet permissions automatically.
3. Utilize the groups to assign permissions to the various protocols specified in the Web Proxy and WinSock Proxy Services.

To review the process, let's assume you want to limit your network clients ability to use their Web browser to access the Internet. You have three basic types of personnel at your company. These include your administrators that require full access to the Internet, technical personnel that require limited access to the Internet, and the rest of the company that just requires Web access. You could create three local groups called FullInternetAccess, LimitedInternetAccess, and

WebAccessOnly. Next, assign the global groups containing your domain administrators (Domain Admins) and perhaps a global group containing your upper-level management to the FullInternetAccess local group. Follow this by assigning your global group containing your technicians to the LimitedInternetAccess local group and your regular domain users (Domain Users) global group to the WebAccessOnly local group. Finally, you can use the local groups you've created to actually implement your security restrictions for the Web Proxy, as described later in this chapter, in the section entitled *Assigning Web Proxy User Permissions.*

To grant Web-only access to your domain users, for example, you could grant the WebOnlyAccess group permission to the WWW protocol in the Web Proxy Service Permissions property sheet. This would allow your regular domain users to view Web pages on the Internet but not access any secure Web sites using the SSL protocol (perhaps in order to purchase a product), download or upload any files using the FTP protocol, or search a Gopher database. For your technicians, you could grant the LimitedInternetAccess group permission to the WWW, FTP, and Gopher protocols so that they could do anything but access a secure site. Finally, for your administrators, you could grant the FullInternetAccess group permissions to the WWW, FTP, Gopher, and Secure protocols so that they could perform any action required.

To restrict access to the Internet even further, you can specify permissions in the WinSock Proxy Service, as described later in the section entitled *Assigning WinSock Proxy User Permissions*, on a per protocol basis. If an Internet protocol is not specified, you can actually add it. This opens up a great deal of flexibility in granting or restricting Internet access to your network clients and in preventing Internet hackers from gaining access to your internal network.

Don't let this ability to specify permissions on the proxy server go to your head; however, because it is possible for your network clients to bypass your proxy server by reconfiguring their software (assuming they know how to do so). In order to prevent this possibility from occurring, the proxy server must be a "chokepoint." By this, I mean that the proxy server must be physically between your network clients and your Internet connection (router or dialup server). Furthermore, the server that is executing the Microsoft Proxy Server must not forward (or route) IP packets. Otherwise, your network clients could specify your server's IP address or your router's IP address as their default gateway and bypass your proxy server altogether.

Configuring The Web Proxy Service

The Web Proxy Service configuration options can be divided into five specific areas. You may set the basic service properties; specify permissions for the WWW, FTP, Gopher, and Secure protocols used by Web browsers; specify the URL caching options; configure the service logging options; and specify a security filter based on IP address or Internet domain name. Each of these options are accessible from the Internet Service Manager as a property sheet in the Web Proxy Service Properties dialog box. To display this dialog box, just highlight the computer name (such as SRV) associated with the Web Proxy Service, and choose Service Properties from the Properties menu. As an alternate method, highlight the service associated with the Web Proxy Service, then right-click on the highlighted service, and select Service Properties from the popup menu.

The fastest method to display the Web Proxy Service Properties dialog box is to double-click on the computer (such as SRV) associated with the Web Proxy Service.

Once the Web Proxy Service Properties dialog box is displayed, as shown in Figure 8.7, you can configure the service as described in the following sections.

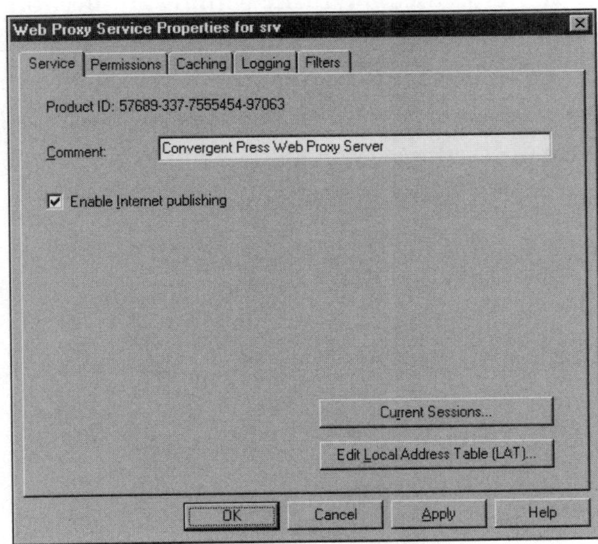

Figure 8.7
Configuring the Web Proxy Service.

Configuring The Basic Web Proxy Service Properties

The General property sheet is the default property sheet displayed in the Web Proxy Service Properties dialog box shown in Figure 8.7. This dialog box looks quite simple in appearance. The functionality is easily accessed; however, the power behind these simple checkboxes and buttons is very impressive. Within this dialog box, you can perform the following configuration options:

- Specify a comment to be displayed in the Internet Service Manager in the Comment field.
- Limit the published data to your intranet only or open up your ability to publish data on the Internet and your intranet. This is accomplished by checking or unchecking the Enable Internet Publishing checkbox. If this box is left unchecked (the default), then external clients can not access your Internet Information Server services.
- View the currently connected users by clicking on the Current Sessions button. This displays the Web Proxy Service User Sessions dialog box. This dialog box displays the user name, IP address, and total time for all of the currently connected users.
- Specify the IP addresses used internally within your network by clicking on the Edit Local Address Table (LAT) button. This displays the Local Address Configuration Table dialog box (see Figure 8.5, presented earlier in this chapter) where you may enter your IP address ranges. To manually specify an IP address or range of IP addresses, execute the following steps:

    1. Enter the starting IP address in the From field.
    2. Enter the ending IP address in the To field.
    3. Click on the Add button, and the IP address (or range of IP addresses) appear in the Internal IP ranges field.

If you are using DHCP to assign IP addresses, you can enter the DHCP scopes (or IP address range) in the From and To fields. However, don't forget to include the DHCP server IP addresses.

4. Repeat Steps 1 through 3 for each IP address range used within your internal network.

Note: *If you'd like to try and automatically build this list of internal IP addresses, click on the Construct Table button. Depending on whether all of your network clients are currently active, whether you are currently connected to the Internet, and whether any Internet clients are currently connected to your site, the list may be generated properly. If any external IP addresses have been detected, you have to manually remove them. Because it is difficult to control all of these variables, I prefer to manually create the LAT list and suggest you do so, as well.*

Assigning Web Proxy User Permissions

Assigning permissions, or access rights, is really where the power of the Web Proxy Service comes into play. Within this property sheet, you get the opportunity to specify which users can access the Internet using the World Wide Web (HTTP and S-HTTP), File Transfer Protocol (FTP), Gopher, and Secure Sockets Layer (SSL) Internet protocols from their Web browsers. Assigning permissions is quite simple to accomplish and can be performed with the following steps.

1. Select the Permissions tab to display the Permissions property sheet, as shown in Figure 8.8.

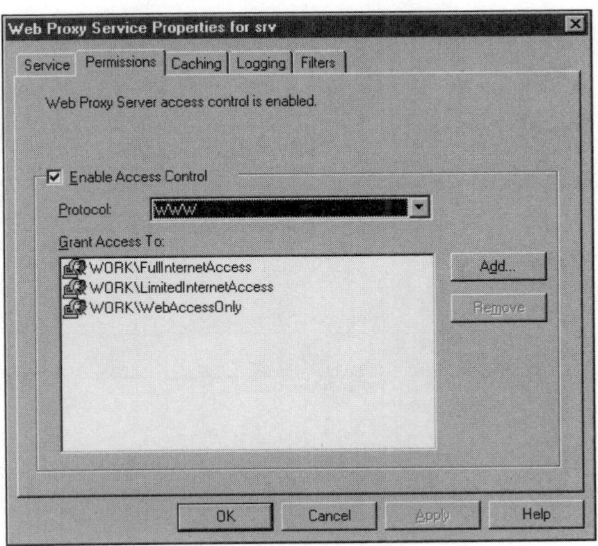

Figure 8.8
Specifying Web Proxy Service access rights.

2. Check the Enable Access Control checkbox. This enables the rest of the dialog box options.

If you encounter problems or need to temporarily disable access control, uncheck the Enable Access Control checkbox. The changes take effect as soon as you click on the Apply button or exit the dialog box by clicking on the OK button.

3. Select the protocol to limit access by choosing WWW (full World Wide Web access), FTP Read (File Transfer Protocol download capability), Gopher (full Gopher access), or Secure (Secure Socket Layer capability) in the Protocol drop-down list box.
4. Click on the Add button to display the Add Users And Groups dialog box, as shown in Figure 8.9.
5. Select a group name in the Names field, and click on the Add button. To select an individual user account, click on the Show Users button first. This updates the Names field to include all user accounts. Then, select the user account, and click on the Add button. As you add each group or user, they will be copied to the Add Names field. When you have completed your selection, click on the OK button.

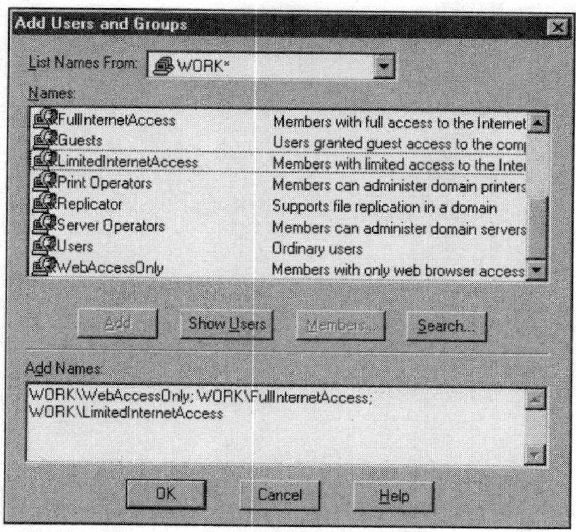

Figure 8.9
Specifying the Web Proxy Service users and groups access rights.

At this point, the users and groups appear in the Grant Access To field (see Figure 8.8). These are the users or groups with permission to use the selected Internet protocol. Any user or group not listed can not use the selected protocol.

If you have established a trust relationship with other Windows NT domains, you can enter global groups from these domains by selecting the domain name in the List Names From drop-down list box. This updates the Names field with entries from the trusted domain.

6. Repeat Steps 3 through 5 for each additional Internet protocol. When you have completed your selections, click on the OK button to close the Web Proxy Service Properties dialog box and return to the Internet Service Manager.

Specifying The Caching Options

One of the greatest performance benefits to a network with a slow Internet connection is the proxy server's ability to cache frequently accessed Web objects. This can provide the following benefits:

- *Improved Client Performance*—If an object is in the cache when a network client requests it, then it is returned at the speed of your network connection (up to 100MB per second) rather than limited to the speed of your Internet connection. If the object is not in the cache, the proxy server retrieves it and places it in the cache for the next user.
- *Improved Storage Management*—By using the proxy server as a centralized Web object cache, you can save disk space on your network clients. How? By disabling the local caching options of Internet Explorer or Netscape Navigator.
- *Added Ability To Actively Or Passively Cache Objects*—An active caching methodology is proactive. The proxy server automatically retrieves a frequently accessed page when its TTL (Time To Live) period has expired. This process usually occurs during off-peak hours. A passive caching methodology, on the other hand, only caches objects as they are requested.

These benefits may prove to be more valuable to you than security restrictions, if you only access the Internet via a dialup connection, because it can significantly lower your phone bill. To obtain the maximum benefit, you should experiment with the size of the cache and when to update the cached objects. This can be accomplished by performing the following steps.

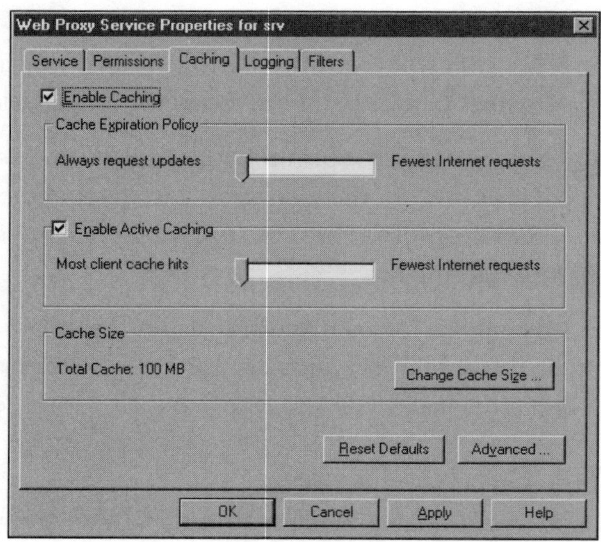

Figure 8.10
Specifying Web Proxy Service caching options.

1. Select the Caching tab to display the Caching property sheet, as shown in Figure 8.10.

2. Check the Enable Caching checkbox. This enables the rest of the dialog options, including the Cache Expiration Policy slider. This slider setting determines how long objects remain in the cache (the TTL) before being refreshed. Move the slider toward the Always Request Updates to lower the chance of displaying stale data but increase the amount of Internet bandwidth used. Move the slider toward the Fewest Internet Requests to lower the amount of Internet bandwidth used but increase the chance of displaying stale data.

3. Check the Enable Active Caching box. This enables active caching of Web objects, which can improve performance. As with the Cache Expiration Slider, the Active Caching Policy slider (though the slider name is not displayed in the dialog box) has a tradeoff between Internet traffic and cache performance. Move the slider toward the Most Client Cache Hits to update the cache more frequently but increase the amount of Internet bandwidth used. Move the slider toward the Fewest Internet Requests to update the cache less often but decrease the amount of Internet bandwidth used. To disable active caching and perform passive caching, clear the Enable Active Caching checkbox.

4. To specify a different cache size, click on the Change Cache Size button to display the Microsoft Proxy Server Cache Drives dialog box. This is the same dialog box displayed during the setup process and is used to specify which drives to use for caching objects and how much space to use on the drive.
5. To specify which Web sites to cache or to not cache, click on the Advanced button. This displays the Advanced Cache Policy dialog box, as shown in Figure 8.11.
6. To specify the maximum size of an object to cache, click on the Limit Size Of Cached Objects To checkbox, and enter the maximum size (in K).
7. To specify that a cached object be returned to the user (which might be a stale object) when the actual site is not available, click on the Return Expired Object When Site Is Not Available checkbox.
8. To specify which Web sites the proxy server should cache or not cache, click on the Add button. This displays the Cache Filter Properties dialog box, as shown in Figure 8.12.
9. Enter a relative URL in the URL field.

A relative URL is a site name (**www.microsoft.com**) or a site name plus a path name (**www.microsoft.com/inetdev**). The asterisk (*) can be used as a wildcard

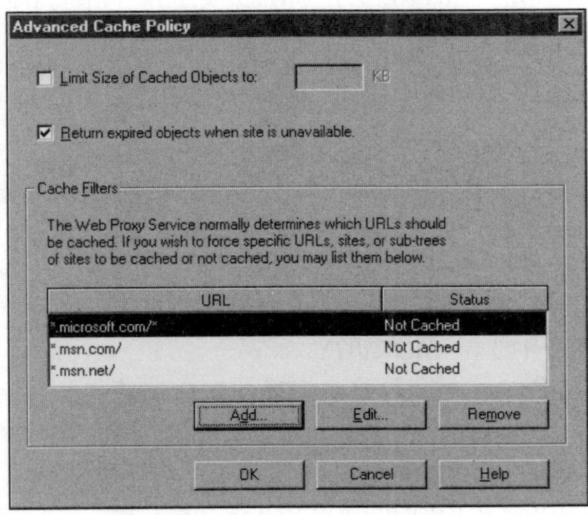

Figure 8.11
Specifying the Web Proxy Service advanced caching options.

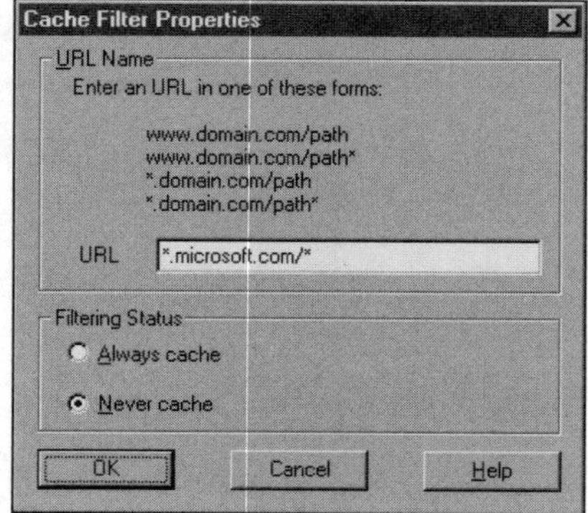

Figure 8.12
Specifying the Web sites to cache.

character. For example, **www.microsoft.com/*** caches all Web objects within the Microsoft Web site (if you do this, make sure you have a lot of space on your Web server). Then, choose a Filtering Status option:

- *Always Cache*—Specifies that the proxy server always caches Web objects within this relative path.
- *Never Cache*—Specifies that by the proxy server never caches Web objects within this relative path.

10. Click on OK. This adds the URL to the Cache Filters list.
11. Repeat Steps 8 through 10 for each URL to cache or not cache. When you have specified all of the URLs, click on the OK button to return to the Web Proxy Service Properties dialog box.
12. Once all of your caching settings have been specified, click on OK to close the Web Proxy Service Properties dialog box and return to the Internet Service Manager.

Logging Web Proxy Activity

Logging your Web Proxy activity is one way you can determine how active your site is, as well as determine if anyone is accessing data they should not have access to. There are two methods you can use to log your Web Proxy site's activity: You can store the information in a standard text file, or you can store it in an ODBC database. If you use an ODBC database, you must create the database and then set up an ODBC data source name (DSN) using the ODBC Control Panel applet. To enable logging, perform the following steps.

1. Click on the Logging tab in the Web Proxy Service Properties dialog box to display the Logging properties sheet, shown in Figure 8.13.
2. Click on the Enable Logging radio button. This enables the rest of the dialog box.
3. Next, specify the amount of activity to log. You can choose to log only a subset by enabling the Regular Logging radio button, or you can log all activity by enabling the Verbose Logging radio button. I recommend that you start with Verbose Logging, then after a month or two, change to Regular Logging. This gives you a chance to verify that everything is working as expected.
4. To log your Web Proxy site's activity to a text file, click on the Log To File radio button. This enables the following options:
   - *Automatically Open New Log*—This option specifies that a new log will be created based on one of the following criteria:
     a. *Daily*—Every day.
     b. *Weekly*—Once a week.

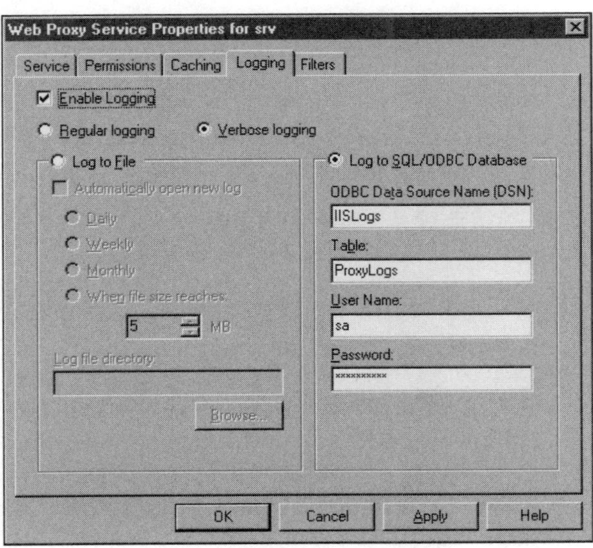

Figure 8.13
Configuring the Web Proxy Service to log activity.

c. *Monthly*—Once a month.

d. *When Log File Size Reaches*—Whenever a log file exceeds the size specified in the MB field.

- *Log File Directory*—This option specifies the location where the log file resides.

5. To log your Web Proxy site's activity to an ODBC database, click on the Log To SQL/ODBC Database radio button. This enables the following options:

   - *ODBC Data Source Name (DSN)*—Specifies the name of the data source to use to access the ODBC database.
   - *Table*—Specifies the table within the ODBC database to use for logging.
   - *User Name*—Specifies a user name to use to access the table within the ODBC database.
   - *Password*—Specifies a password for the associated user account.

6. Click on OK to close the Web Proxy Site Properties dialog box and return to the Internet Service Manager.

Controlling Access To Internet Sites And Your Network

Almost everyone is concerned about the security of their network. Some companies are also concerned with limiting the sites their network clients can access to make sure that their employees are working rather than checking the sport scores on the ESPN Web site. You can use the proxy server's filtering option to specify the Internet sites your network clients can access. You can use this filtering option to block access to a single computer, a group of computers, or an entire Internet domain by following the steps presented in this section.

1. Click on the Filters tab in the Web Proxy Service Properties dialog box to display the Filters properties sheet (see Figure 8.14).

2. To limit access to a specific set of clients, click on the Denied Access radio button. Then, click on the Add button to display the Grant Access On dialog box.

   To specify a single computer to give access to your Web site, click on the Single Computer radio button, and enter the IP address of the computer in the IP Address field.

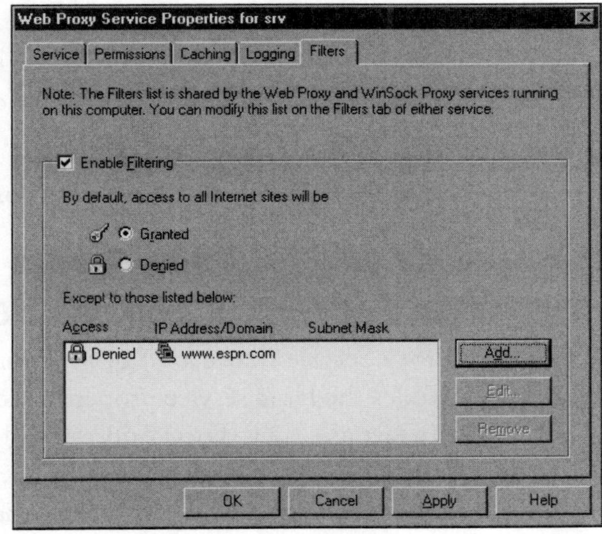

Figure 8.14
Preventing access to specific Web sites.

To specify multiple computers to give access to your Web site, click on the Multiple Computers radio button, and specify an IP address and subnet mask in the IP Address and Subnet Mask fields.

To specify an entire Internet domain, click on the Domain radio button, and enter the domain name in the Domain field. Then, click on the OK button.

3. To grant access to all but a specific set of clients, click on the Granted Access radio button. Then, click on the Add button to display the Denied Access On dialog box.

   To specify a single computer to deny access to your Web site, click on the Single Computer radio button, and enter the IP address of the computer in the IP Address field.

   To specify multiple computers to deny access to your Web site, click on the Multiple Computers radio button, and specify an IP address and subnet mask in the IP Address and Subnet Mask fields.

   To specify an entire Internet domain, click on the Domain radio button, and enter the domain name in the Domain field. Then, click on the OK button.

4. The domain name or set of IP addresses and subnet masks you specified in Step 2 or Step 3 is displayed in the Except To Those Listed Below list box. Repeat Step 2 or Step 3 for each additional domain or set of computers you want to deny or grant access for your network clients to visit.
5. Click on OK to close the Web Proxy Site Properties dialog box and return to the Internet Service Manager.

Configuring The WinSock Proxy Service

Configuring the WinSock Proxy Service shares a bit of functionality with the Web Proxy Service. This includes the basic service properties, logging properties, and filtering properties. In fact, the LAT (Local Address Table) and filtering options you apply to one of these services is automatically applied to the other. Rather than repeat this information, you should just look at the previous section for configuring these options. This way, we can concentrate on the options that are different from the Web Proxy Service.

Unlike the Web Proxy Service, which is limited to the WWW, FTP, Gopher, and Secure Internet protocols, the WinSock Proxy Service supports any Internet protocol or Internet port. If one is not listed, you may add it. This gives you the ability to grant or deny access to any Internet protocol or port. Not only can this be used to prevent network clients from using one of these protocols or ports to access the Internet, it can also be used to prevent external threats (Internet hackers for example) from gaining access to your corporate network.

The following sections show how to specify the Internet protocols and ports to monitor, and how to grant permission to use these protocols and ports. Each of these options is accessible from the Internet Service Manager as a property sheet in the WinSock Proxy Service Properties dialog box. To display this dialog box, just highlight the computer name (such as SRV) associated with the WinSock Proxy Service, and choose Service Properties from the Properties menu, or highlight the service associated with the WinSock Proxy Service, right-click on the highlighted service, and select Service Properties from the popup menu.

The fastest method to display the WinSock Proxy Service Properties dialog box is to just double-click on the computer (such as SRV) associated with the Web Proxy Service.

Specifying The Internet Protocols To Monitor

Before you can grant or reject permission to use an Internet protocol or monitor its usage, you must first define it. An Internet protocol definition, such as HTTP (for WWW access) is really just a subset of the TCP (Transmission Control Protocol) or UDP (User Datagram Protocol) protocols. Most of these Internet protocols use one or more port(s). The HTTP protocol, for example, is a subset of TCP and uses port 80. There are many predefined protocols for the WinSock Proxy Service; however, at times, you may need to add or modify a definition. You may need to expose the TCP port used to access an SQL Server installation, expose the America Online TCP port, or The Microsoft Network TCP port, for example. To add a new protocol, follow the steps presented in this section.

1. Select the Protocols tab to display the Protocols property sheet, as shown in Figure 8.15.
2. Click on the Add button to display the Protocol Definition dialog box. (See Figure 8.16.)
3. Specify a unique name in the Protocol field, such as HTTP for the Hypertext Transfer Protocol.

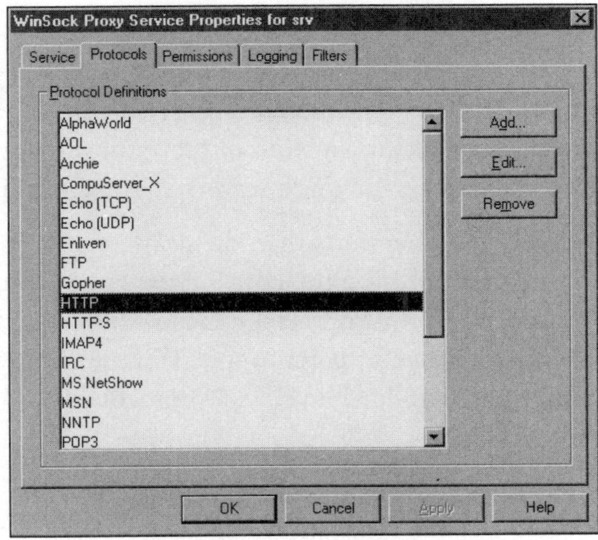

Figure 8.15
Specifying the Internet protocols and ports to monitor.

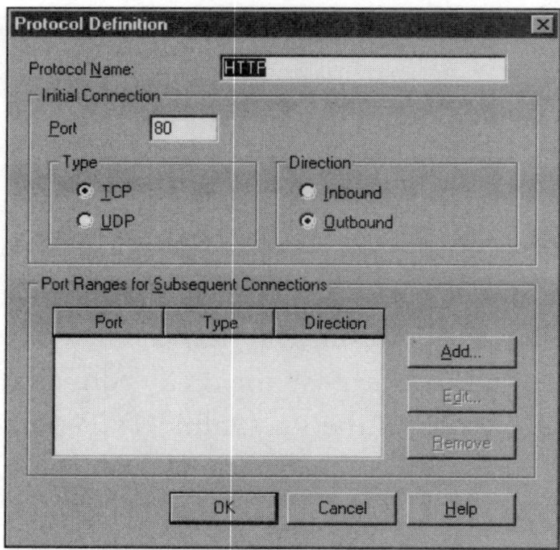

Figure 8.16
Adding a new Internet protocol and ports to monitor.

4. Specify an initial port value in the Port field. By default, the HTTP protocol uses port 80. If you have configured the Web server to use another port, you should change this value to match.

5. Specify the type of protocol (either TCP or UDP) in the Type field. The HTTP protocol uses TCP.

6. Specify the direction for the protocol (either inbound or outbound) in the Direction field. We are interested in monitoring or restricting access to the HTTP protocol to our network clients (instead of preventing access from Internet clients who we want to access our Web server), so the direction is outbound.

7. If this protocol will use other ports than the primary port listed in the Port field, click on the Add button in the Port Ranges For Subsequent Connections group. This displays the Port Range Definition dialog box where you may specify a port (or range of ports), type (TCP or UDP), and direction (inbound or outbound) to add. The HTTP protocol does not use any other ports, so leave this blank.

8. When you have completed the protocol definition, click on OK to return to the WinSock Proxy Service Properties dialog box.

9. Repeat Steps 2 through 8 for each additional protocol to add to the list to monitor or restrict access.

10. When you have completed all of the protocol additions, click on OK to close the WinSock Proxy Service Properties dialog box and return to the Internet Service Manager.

Editing an existing protocol or port definition follows similar steps as those described in this section. The only difference is that instead of clicking on the Add button, as described in Step 2, you should select an existing protocol definition then click on the Edit button. The rest of the steps remain the same. Should you decide that you no longer need a protocol definition, you can delete it by selecting it then clicking on the Remove button.

Assigning WinSock Proxy User Permissions

Once you have added the protocols you want to monitor or restrict access to, as described in the previous section, you can apply user access rights to the protocols. This can be accomplished by following the steps presented here.

1. Select the Permissions tab to display the permissions property sheet, as shown in Figure 8.17.
2. Check the Enable Access Control checkbox. This enables the WinSock Proxy Service's ability to control access to specified Internet protocols. It will also enable the rest of the dialog options.

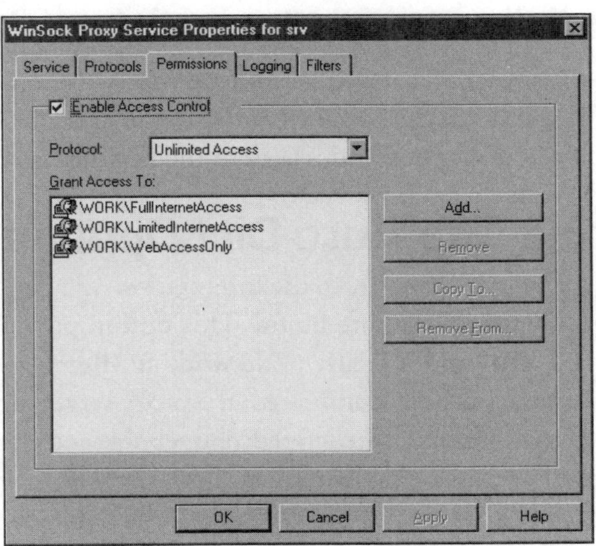

Figure 8.17
Limiting access to an Internet protocol.

3. Select a protocol to grant access to in the Protocol field.

The Unlimited Access protocol includes all protocols and all ports on the server. Use this protocol with care because it essentially bypasses the proxy server restrictions.

4. Click on the Add button to display the Add Users And Groups dialog box. (See Figure 8.9.)
5. Select a group name in the Names field, and click on the Add button. To select an individual user account, click on the Show Users button first. This will update the Names field to include all user accounts. Then, select the user account, and click on the Add button. As you add each group or user, they will be copied to the Add Names field. When you have made the selection, click on the OK button.

At this point, the users and groups appear in the Grant Access To field (see Figure 8.17). These are the users or groups with permission to use the selected Internet protocol. Any user or group not listed can not use the selected protocol.

If you have established a trust relationship with other Windows NT domains, you can enter global groups from these domains by selecting the domain name in the List Names From drop-down list box. This updates the Names field with entries from the trusted domain.

6. Repeat Steps 3 through 5 for each additional Internet protocol. When you have made the selections, click on the OK button to close the WinSock Proxy Service Properties dialog box and return to the Internet Service Manager.

Configuring The Auto-Dial Options

If you are using a server as a gateway to the Internet, you may find the Microsoft Proxy Server auto-dial option quite useful. This option provides an interface between network clients and a Dial-Up Networking (Remote Access Session, or RAS) session. When properly configured, the proxy server can automatically connect to the Internet using a predefined phonebook entry whenever a network client requests access to the Internet. If the network client is using the Web Proxy Service (via their Web browser), then the connection will only be attempted if the Web object is not in the proxy server's cache or if the cached object TTL has expired. The auto-dial connection can also be used directly by the proxy server to update its internally cached Web objects. This can be particularly useful because it can update these pages during off-peak hours, thereby possibly lowering phone bills. To configure the auto-dial options, just follow the basic steps presented in this section.

1. Select the Auto Dial Configuration applet in the Microsoft Proxy Server program group. This should display the dialog box shown in Figure 8.18.
2. Check the Enable Dial On Demand checkbox to allow the proxy server to connect to the Internet as needed.
3. Specify the times the proxy server may connect to the Internet. This is accomplished by clicking each box on the displayed chart. In the example shown in Figure 8.18, the proxy server can only dial up the Internet between the hours of 5:00 A.M. and 6:00 P.M., Monday through Friday.

To quickly select all days and any hours, click on the gray box in the upper-left corner. To select all hours within a day, click on the day button. To select an hour for all days, click on the gray button in the appropriate hour column. You can also use the mouse to outline a selection, if desired.

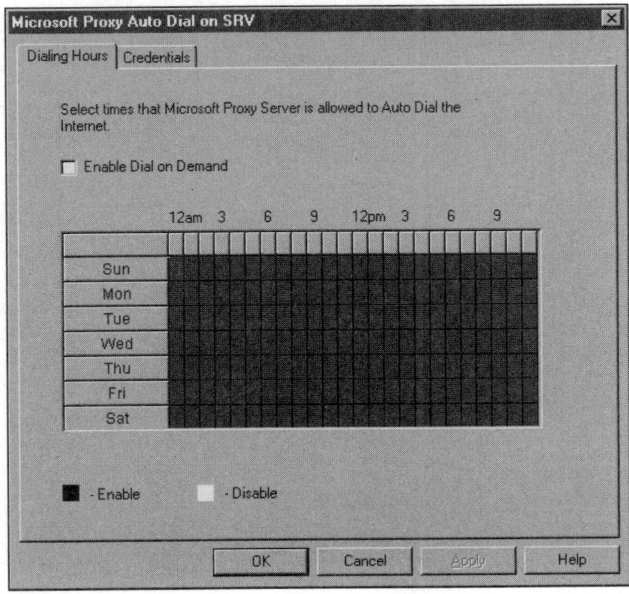

Figure 8.18
Configuring the auto-dial connection times.

4. Once you have specified the time that the proxy server may connect to the Internet, click on the Credentials tab to display the Credentials property sheet. (See Figure 8.19.)
5. Choose a phonebook entry from the Entry Name field. If there are no entries, you must create a new phonebook entry using the Dial-Up Networking client.
6. Enter the user account name for your Internet connection in the User Name field.
7. Enter the associated password for the user account in the Password field.
8. If this account requires an Internet domain name, enter this value in the Domain Name field. Otherwise, leave this field blank.
9. When you have finished, click on the OK button to close the Microsoft Proxy Auto Dial dialog box. The Microsoft Proxy Server uses these settings immediately.

Configuring The Client Software

Okay, so you've installed the Microsoft Proxy Server between your Internet connection and your network. All of your Windows 95 and Windows NT clients

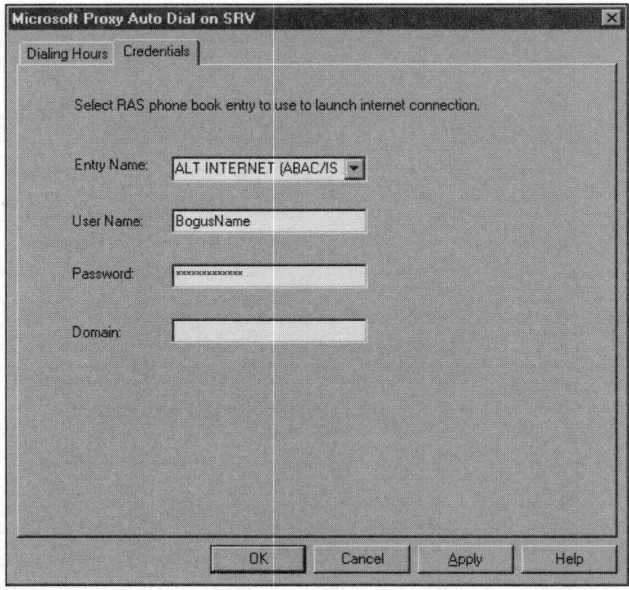

Figure 8.19
Specifying the phonebook entry parameters to use for the dialup connection.

are using the Microsoft Internet Explorer or Netscape Navigator, and you want to configure them to use the proxy server to connect to the Internet. So, how do you do it, you ask? Well, there is the easy way, and then there is the hard way. The easy way is to connect to the MSPCLNT share on the server where you installed the Microsoft Proxy Server. For the server named *SRV*, this would be \\SRV\MSPCLNT, for example. Once you have connected to the share, just run the setup program located in the root directory. This installs the client software and automatically configures the client Web browser to use the proxy server.

If your Web browser isn't the Microsoft Internet Explorer or Netscape Navigator, or you have a Web browser on a non-Windows platform (such as Unix or Macintosh), then you have to do it the hard way. But don't distress, it's not really *that* bad. While the methodology may differ a bit on where to enter the information, almost all Web browsers include a configuration dialog box where you can specify the information for a connection via a proxy server. To manually enter this information for Internet Explorer 3.x for Windows NT, for example, just follow the steps presented here.

1. Choose Options from the View menu. The Options dialog box should display, as shown in Figure 8.20.

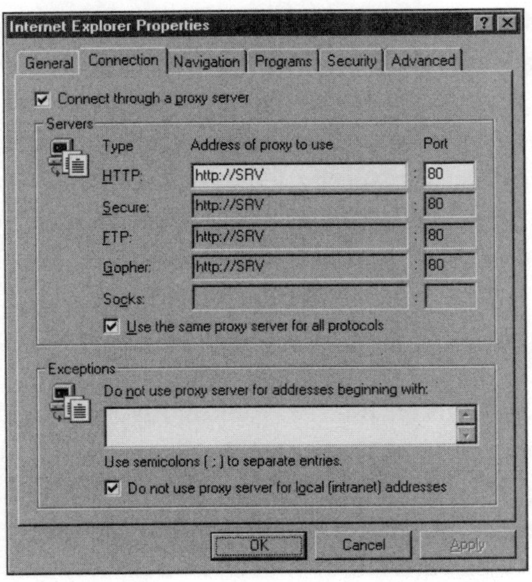

Figure 8.20
Specifying the Internet Explorer connection properties.

2. Check the Connect Through A Proxy Server checkbox to enable the rest of the dialog box options.
3. Enter the IP address of the computer running the Microsoft Proxy Server in the HTTP address field. Enter the port number of the HTTP server in the HTTP port field.
4. Check the Use The Same Proxy Server For All Protocols checkbox.
5. Check the Do Not Use Proxy Server For Local (Intranet) Addresses checkbox.
6. Click on OK to close the Options dialog box and return to Internet Explorer.

Now, that wasn't so hard was it? There are a few additional things you should know, though, before you try this on non-Microsoft Web browsers. First, if it is at all possible, use an IP address rather than a DNS name. A DNS name is usually bound to the same IP address as the network card connected to the Internet. This could cause the name to not be accepted by the proxy server as a valid intranet name, which would cause an unresolvable name or not found error. It is possible to use a NetBIOS name for TCP/IP and IPX/SPX clients. For example, you could specify the HTTP address field as **http://SRV** instead of the IP address **206.170.127.65**.

Do not install the Proxy Server client software on a computer running Exchange Server. This installs the WinSock proxy client software and may cause Exchange Server to fail to operate. This, in turn, would prevent Exchange Server from receiving or delivering any email. If you need to specify a proxy server in such a situation, follow the previous steps, and manually specify the connection properties for your Web browser.

Summary

Microsoft's Proxy Server is an Internet tool tightly integrated into IIS. It provides basic and medium level protection for your users, and for the network resources. It's fairly easy to set up and configure given its intended purpose. While it does a decent job, if you need an industrial strength proxy, you can either wait for Proxy Server v2.0 or find a third party solution. For first time administrators of a proxy, Microsoft's Proxy Server is an excellent learning tool.

9

Introducing Microsoft Index Server And Active Server Pages

Jeff Bankston

This chapter presents an introductory-level discussion about two applications that extend IIS's functionality—Microsoft's Index Server and Microsoft's Active Server Pages. Talking about these tools in combination seems natural because both tools integrate very tightly into IIS and extend IIS capabilities beyond the services provided by most other servers. IIS's additional features make the NT Server and IIS combination stand out.

The first half of this chapter is about Microsoft's Index Server, a tool used to create an index of the documents on an IIS platform. This index is used to quickly and concisely find any document—Web page, text document, and so forth—anywhere on your Web server where proper permissions are granted. Keep in mind, this searching function only applies to your Web server, and not to any other servers in your network.

The second half of this chapter discusses Microsoft's Active Server Pages. ASP enables you to use programming tools to incorporate dynamic HTML, provide database access, and include additional information in your Web pages, without having to manually enter a lot of HTML source coding. Granted, some manual HTML work is usually required at some point during Web page creation, but ASP greatly reduces your workload. Reducing your workload probably sounds good right about now, and we'll get to ASP's features soon enough. But first, let's look at the benefits of using Microsoft's Index Server.

Microsoft's Index Server

As mentioned, Microsoft's Index Server is a tool used to create searchable indices of documents on an IIS platform. It does this by using the directories specified in the WWW properties. In this section, you'll specifically learn how to:

- Install Index Server
- View Index Server components
- Build initial indexes
- Analyze a sample search
- Use Index Server
- Troubleshoot Index Server problems
- Recover data

Figure 9.1 shows a sample of what Index Server can do for you. Go to the Microsoft Web site to find an example of what Index Server is capable of. It'll turn up a listing of all documents found on the site by the text you told it to find.

> ***Note:** Before you install Index Server, you need to have Microsoft Internet Explorer installed on your system. MSIE 3.xx is sufficient, and version 3.02 for Windows 95 and Windows NT Workstation 4 is the most recent. MSIE 4 is due to be released soon, but as of this writing, it is a beta product, so it will not be used here.*

Now, let's install Index Server. Before actually creating indexes or working with Index Server, ensure that you have Web documents on the IIS Web root location to give it something to find and index.

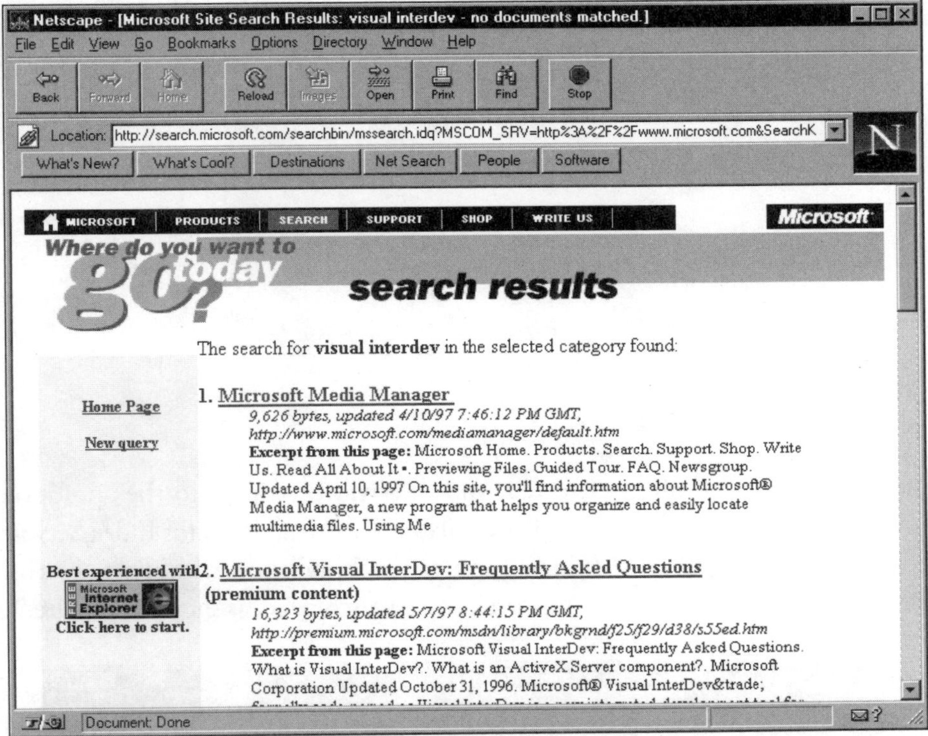

Figure 9.1
A sample Index Server search result.

Installing Index Server

You can download the Index Server archive from the Microsoft Web site, just like we did for the other IIS upgrade components in Chapter 7. If you don't have the Index Server, take a moment now to go get it. It's only 1.8MB and shouldn't take much time to download. Then, install it over the existing IIS server that we've been building thus far by executing the following steps.

1. Copy the archive (which is a self-extracting installation tool) to somewhere on your IIS server.
2. Double-click on the archive, and click on Yes to accept the licensing agreement.

Index Server will be extracted, and you'll be prompted to confirm that you want to install it.

3. Click on Continue to confirm the installation, as shown in Figure 9.2.

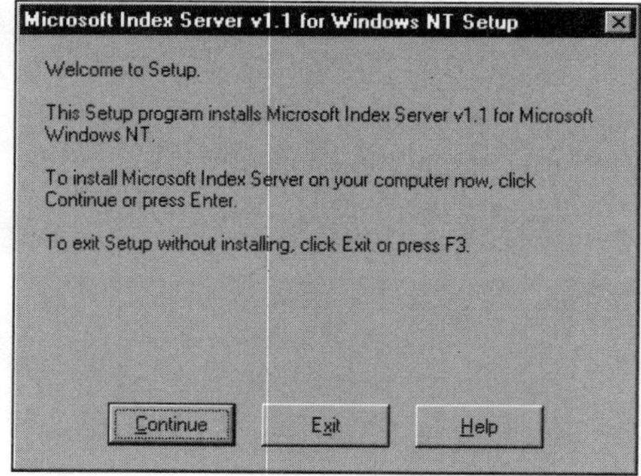

Figure 9.2
Confirm installation of Index Server.

The IIS installation will be detected, and files will be copied to the appropriate locations for the InetSrv directory. IIS services will be shut down for Index Server to be initially configured with IIS. As soon as the installation completes, you'll be presented with the opportunity to see a sample search page, as shown in Figure 9.3.

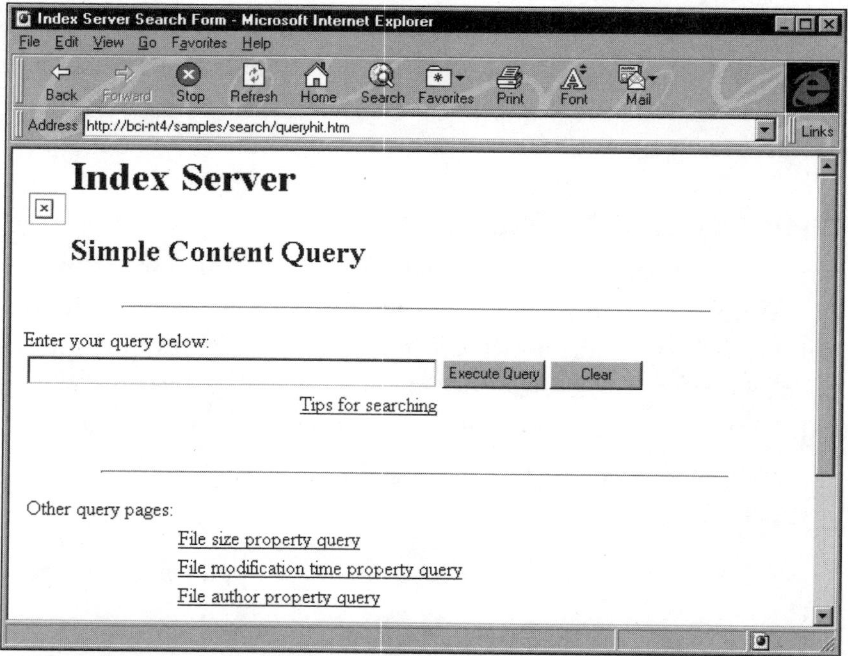

Figure 9.3
Sample search page.

Now that the initial install has been accomplished, let's review the Index Server components and build the initial indexes.

Viewing Index Server Components

You can view Index Server's components by clicking on Start|Programs|Microsoft Index Server (Common). The Index Server consists of the following four components:

- Index Server Administration
- Index Server Online Documentation
- Index Server Release Notes
- Index Server Sample Query Form

The component names do just what they imply, so I won't bore you to tears with simplistic explanations. However, the administration program is what we're after at the moment, because we need to build some initial indexes.

Building Initial Indexes

To build your initial indexes, you need to use the administration program.

1. To start the program, select Start, Programs, Index Server, Index Server Administration, and you'll see a screen much like the one displayed in Figure 9.4.
2. To build the initial indexes, click on the View/Update Indexing Of Virtual Roots button.
3. Click on the Directories tab on the properties page, and you'll see the aliases that were established during your IIS and add-in installations, as shown in Figure 9.5.

The first time you run the administration subroutine, you'll have to force the scan of the virtual roots, which is the last option and what you'll need to do in Steps 5 and 6.

4. Click on the Start button, and you'll be presented with Figure 9.6, which shows the search results of your query. (Of course, in our case, it's not really a query because we're performing the initial setup of Index Server.)

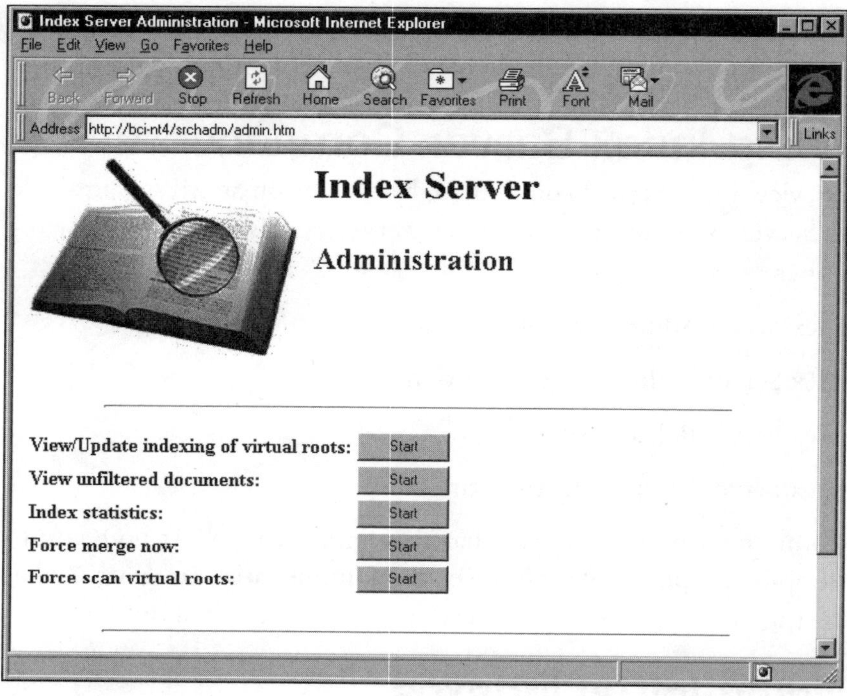

Figure 9.4
The main menu of the Index Server Administration program.

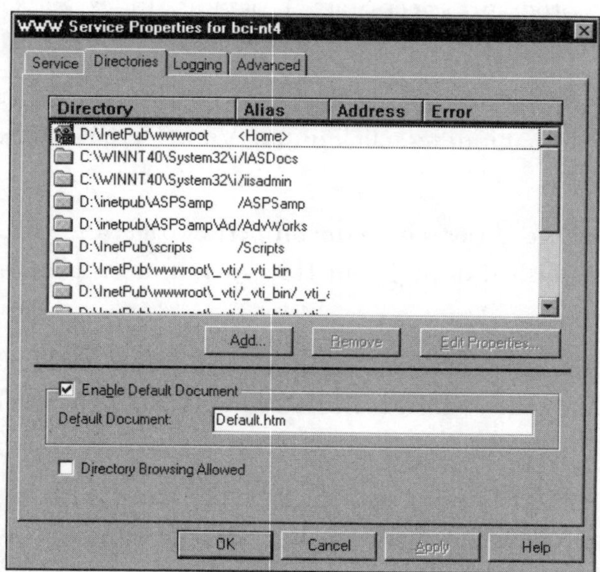

Figure 9.5
Properties of IIS Web Server.

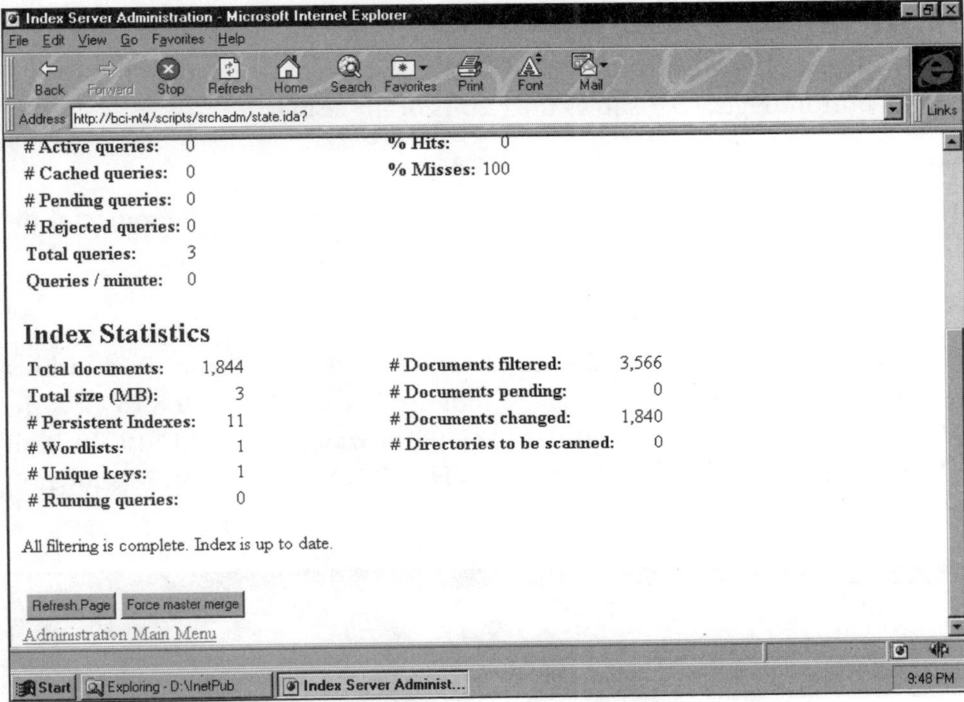

Figure 9.6
Indexing process progress.

5. In the Type Of Scan section, click on the Full radio button for all virtual roots, and then click on Submit Changes to create the initial indexes.

   Note: *This initial indexing procedure may take quite some time depending on the volume of Web pages on IIS.*

6. When the changes have been made, submit the forced build of the indexes.
7. When this completes, scroll down the screen, and look at the statistics in the lower half of the page.

You can now perform searches on your Web server. The sample query form now becomes a powerful search tool. As an example, I'll conduct a search on a Web site that I'm developing so you can see the power of the Index Server.

Analyzing A Sample Search

Using the sample search form, I entered *itd* as the search string, then pressed the Search button. Figure 9.7 shows the results of my search.

How does Index Server work? Let's take a look.

1. With the query form on screen, use your browser to view the source of the HTML form.
2. Once open, scroll two-thirds of the way down.

You should see the point where you enter text for a query. All you see is nothing less than programmatic access via the indexes. Look at Figure 9.8 to view the HTML code for the QUERYHIT.HTML file provided on the CD-ROM. This file performs a search using the QUERYHIT.IDQ search form, as shown in Figure 9.9.

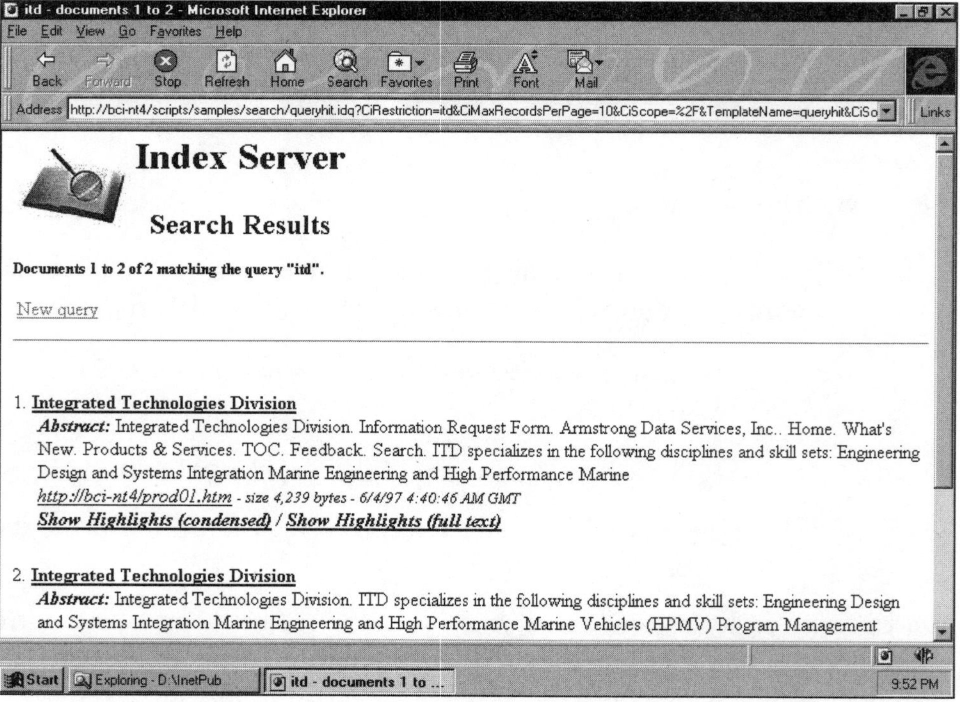

Figure 9.7
Search results for the string *itd*.

Queryhit.htm - Notepad

File Edit Search Help

```
<p>

<FORM ACTION="/scripts/samples/search/queryhit.idq" METHOD="GET">
    Enter your query below:
    <TABLE>
        <TR>
            <TD><INPUT TYPE="TEXT" NAME="CiRestriction" SIZE="60" MAXLENGTH="100'
            <TD><INPUT TYPE="SUBMIT" VALUE="Execute Query"></TD>
            <TD><INPUT TYPE="RESET" VALUE="Clear"></TD>
        </TR>

        <TR>
            <TD ALIGN=right><A HREF="/samples/search/tipshelp.htm">Tips for sear
        </TR>

        <INPUT TYPE="HIDDEN" NAME="CiMaxRecordsPerPage" VALUE="10">
        <INPUT TYPE="HIDDEN" NAME="CiScope" VALUE="/">
        <INPUT TYPE="HIDDEN" NAME="TemplateName" VALUE="queryhit">
        <INPUT TYPE="HIDDEN" NAME="CiSort" VALUE="rank[d]">
        <INPUT TYPE="HIDDEN" NAME="HTMLQueryForm" VALUE="/samples/search/queryhi
    </TABLE>
</FORM>

<BR>
```

Figure 9.8
QUERYHIT.HTML form processed.

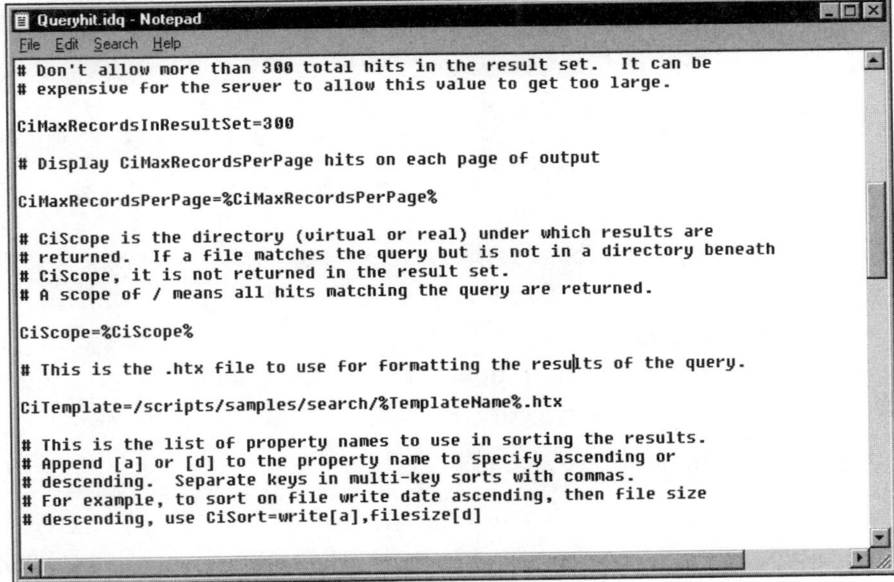

Queryhit.idq - Notepad

File Edit Search Help

```
# Don't allow more than 300 total hits in the result set.  It can be
# expensive for the server to allow this value to get too large.

CiMaxRecordsInResultSet=300

# Display CiMaxRecordsPerPage hits on each page of output

CiMaxRecordsPerPage=%CiMaxRecordsPerPage%

# CiScope is the directory (virtual or real) under which results are
# returned.  If a file matches the query but is not in a directory beneath
# CiScope, it is not returned in the result set.
# A scope of / means all hits matching the query are returned.

CiScope=%CiScope%

# This is the .htx file to use for formatting the results of the query.

CiTemplate=/scripts/samples/search/%TemplateName%.htx

# This is the list of property names to use in sorting the results.
# Append [a] or [d] to the property name to specify ascending or
# descending.  Separate keys in multi-key sorts with commas.
# For example, to sort on file write date ascending, then file size
# descending, use CiSort=write[a],filesize[d]
```

Figure 9.9
QUERYHIT index search code.

Both of these forms, the HTML form and the IDQ programmatical searching code, are editable and can be customized for your own likes, dislikes, and specific uses.

At this point, we've completed our installation, viewed Index Server's components, built our initial indexes, and analyzed a sample search. Now, finally we get to the good stuff—using Index Server.

Using Index Server

Index Server is a constantly updating tool that relieves the Webmaster of many tasks usually associated with Web site administration. Index Server is not like SQL Server, where administrators are required to constantly work with users for data access and tune the databases for specific needs. Index Server needs none of this.

Basic query functions include the use of boolean features such as AND, OR, and NOT, and the properties tools such as =, <, >, and <>. These functions add power and versatility to the HTML forms created by the administrator.

Let's look at the following sample set of free form text to illustrate how Index Server works and how indexes are created:

```
President Clinton said today that he supports the principles of free speech
on the Internet, but he vowed to sign legislation regulating what can be
posted on Web pages.
```

Politics aside, Index Server looks at this sentence and creates an index based on keywords, such as President, Clinton, principles, free, speech, and Internet. These words are then used as the basis for text retrieval and hit counts for any sentence. Whenever a Web page is updated or replaced, Index Server automatically updates the indexes to reflect the change.

Other features of Index Server include:

- Supports "fuzzy" queries that use the asterisk (*) wildcard character. For example, searching for *run*** would return values such as *runtime* and *runt.*
- Provides full language support for multiple languages plus context switching from English to Spanish and back to English. This is a very useful feature when accommodating an international Web server.

As you may know, with every tool comes the potential for errors. The next section addresses how to troubleshoot potential Index Server problems.

Troubleshooting Problems

Errors in Index Server fall into several categories:

- Query syntax
- Form syntax errors
- Index corruption
- Other related system errors (such as ACL permissions)

These errors can be reported back to the user via HTML output or placed into the Windows NT Server Application Error log.

Some errors in the query error structure are those such as forgetting the "(" or the "]" characters used to terminate a query field. The usage of reserved tokens such as the comma placed in locations where such was not expected is an example of a programming syntax error.

All of these forms of errors are described in the Index Server documentation, which should have been installed when you performed the Index Server installation. Feel free to peruse the error codes in the online documentation, as all of them are there. Figure 9.10 presents an example of an error in the search string.

Figure 9.10 leaves quite a bit to be desired, but it does offer to take you to Query Syntax Help. However, going there will probably prove quite useless because there's no clue as to what went wrong. As an alternative, you could peruse the code in the IDQ search file. Opening the IDQ search file for the example error shown in Figure 9.10 might be more helpful than accessing the Query Syntax Help. Listing 9.1 shows the messed-up code found in Figure 9.10's IDQ search file.

Listing 9.1 IDQ SEARCH FILE.

```
# These are the columns that are referenced in the HTX files
# when formatting output for each hit.
CiColumns=filenamesize,rank,characterization,vpath,DocTitle,write
# Do a recursive search (i.e., all directories under CiScope).
# The opposite is SHALLOW
CiFlags=DEEP
```

```
# The CiRestriction is the query. Here, it's just passed in from the
# form in the HTML file.
```

Notice on line 3 that there's no comma between **filename** and **size**. That's a syntax error! These are the kinds of problems that will drive you up the wall. Simple syntax errors are killers (especially when the pressure is on) because you're usually looking for logic errors in the code, not syntax errors. One thing I learned long ago is that "anything after midnight is fair game." It doesn't matter if it's programming, debugging, writing, or whatever—after midnight, I'm convinced that the human body is designed to shut down. Especially the brain! So once the clock strikes midnight, give it up until the morning.

Recovering Data

Every once in a while, Index Server may be subjected to lost files if hardware problems strike. Among these issues are lost indexes. Index Server assists in recovering

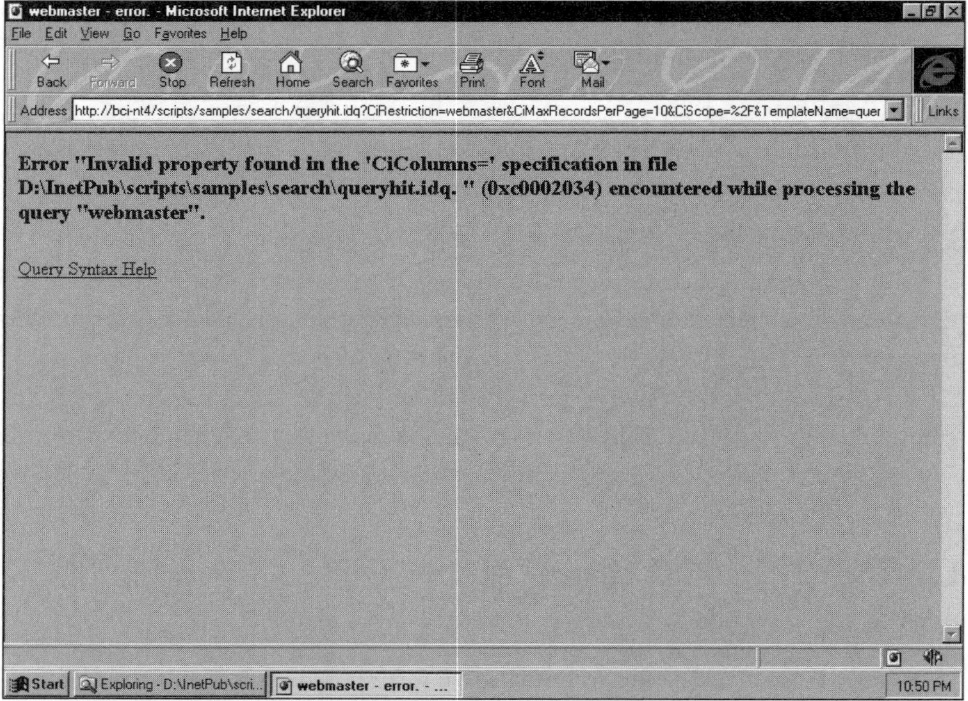

Figure 9.10
What happens when the search string is formatted badly?

lost data in a number of ways. If only one or two files are lost and Index Server determines that these files are not crucial, the files will be rebuilt upon the next incremental rebuild. No user intervention is necessary. If these files are major databases, restoration from backups may be required. If you lose connection to a virtual path across a network, then Index Server automatically scans the network to reestablish the lost connection and restores service. Even though it's a condition that should never occur in an adequately monitored server, a disk full condition is monitored and reported via NT's own event log and via Index Server.

Finally, if a catastrophic event occurs, such as a power outage or massive corruption of the indexes or databases, Index Server detects this and attempts to initiate an automatic re-indexing process. If an automatic re-indexing can't be performed, then an administrator will need to restart Index Server, which performs automated data recovery and reindexing of the master indices.

Index Server is an outstanding tool to create fast and customizable searches for the people visiting your site. It's a significant advance in Web server administration and functionality for IIS. Now if only Microsoft would make a generic indexer for other popular Web servers.

The second half of this chapter takes an introductory look into another tool which is tightly integrated into IIS, called Active Server Pages.

Microsoft's Active Server Pages

In this half of the chapter, we'll install Microsoft's Active Server Pages and discuss how to use ASP. Specifically, we will:

- Install Active Server Pages
- Use the ASP documentation
- Review the ASP model
- View HTML pages
- Compare CGI and ASP
- Write ASP scripts

Active Server Pages was a huge jump in progress for Web servers for Microsoft. ASP integrates with IIS to form what is called *server side processing.* Server side processing means a Web browser can send a request to a Web server, and then the Web server will process the query and return pertinent information to the browser. ASP offers other advantages, as well, but first we need to discuss how to install Microsoft's Active Server Pages.

Installing Active Server Pages

Installing ASP is as simple as installing Index Server. Before you install ASP, you need to have IIS version 2 installed with its basic components. That's it for the prerequisites. If you happen to have the FrontPage Server Extensions already installed, don't worry—ASP won't hurt your FrontPage settings one bit.

After you verify that IIS version 2 is installed on your system, go get Service Pack 2 for NT Server 4. Next, download the ASP archive from Microsoft's site. Applying Service Pack 2 is, in effect, installing IIS 3, as mentioned earlier in this text. Now that the preparation is complete, let's walk through the ASP installation and configuration.

1. Start the ASP installation by double-clicking on the archive, which is a self-installing program.

The setup will extract the necessary files and present you the dialog box shown in Figure 9.11 after you accept the licensing agreement.

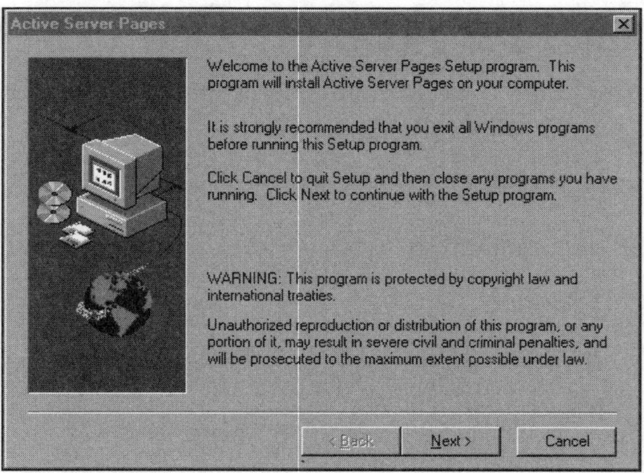

Figure 9.11
Starting the ASP installation.

2. Click on Next.

Most likely, you'll see a screen that warns you that one (or more) of IIS's services is running, and that ASP needs the services to be stopped before continuing the installation.

3. Click on Yes to stop the services, as shown in Figure 9.12.

Next, you'll be presented with a screen similar to the one shown in Figure 9.13. This screen gives you the chance to choose what parts of ASP you want to install. Of course, ASP core components must be installed. To aid in your decision-making process, the size of each component is listed.

4. Next, choose the directory where you want the ASP files to be installed.

5. Click on Next.

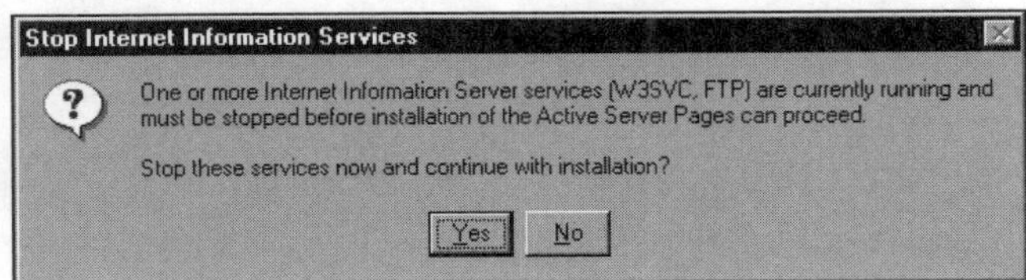

Figure 9.12
Stopping running services on IIS.

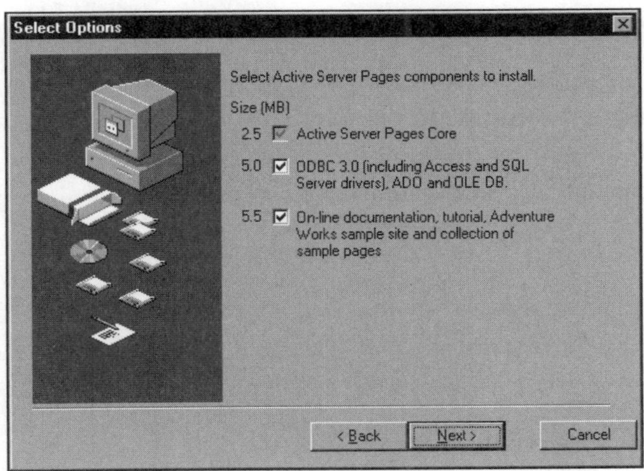

Figure 9.13
Choosing which ASP components to install.

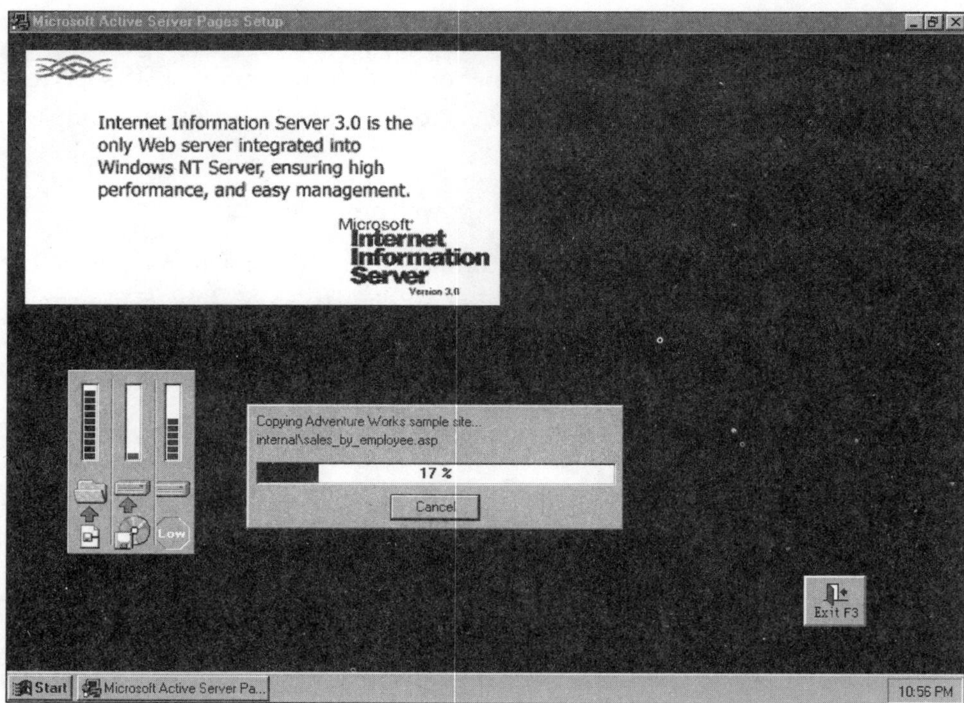

Figure 9.14
Installing components.

Notice, ASP defaults to the directory where IIS is installed. The program files will now be installed and server configuration performed, as shown in Figure 9.14.

After the installation is complete, permissions will be set, and the basic configuration will be completed for you automatically. The last item you'll see is a screen similar to Figure 9.15, acknowledging what was installed and where it was installed.

6. Restart the IIS services for your changes to take effect.

If you want one more measure of verifying a good installation, reboot the server, and ensure that no errors come up as a result of your ASP installation. After you verify that your installation was a success, you might want to review the ASP documentation to get acquainted with some of ASP's features.

Using The ASP Documentation

One part of the ASP installation places the ASP documentation onto your server. Before you can use this documentation, you need to have Internet Explorer

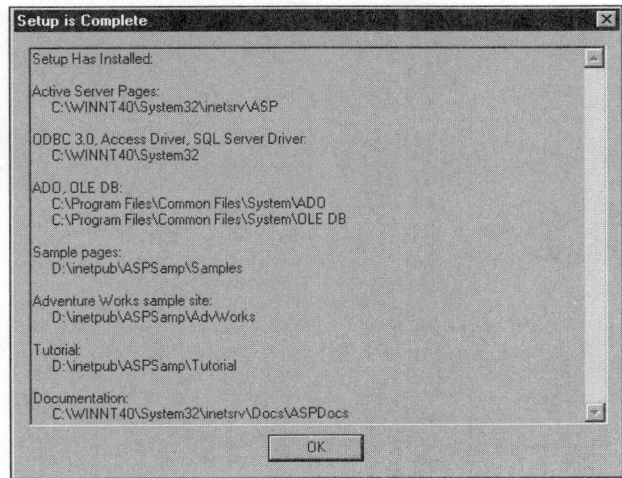

Figure 9.15
Completed installation notice.

3.xx installed and operational. To view the documentation, click on Start|Programs|Microsoft Internet Server (Common)|ASP Roadmap. This brings up the home page of the ASP documentation (which uses frames), as shown in Figure 9.16.

The ASP documentation is pretty good, but it lacks a few things, such as a search function. To use the documentation, just click on a plus sign to expand a topic. (See Figure 9.16.) For example, let's say we want to learn what capabilities the person's browser has by using ASP functions. The baseline capabilities are listed in the file named *BROWSCAP.INI*. Here are the steps we would follow.

1. Expand the Component Reference topic, then expand the Browser Capabilities Component subtopic.
2. Click once on the BROWSCAP.INI file listing in the left pane to bring up the subject contents in the right pane.
3. Scroll down the list to see what ASP properties are supported in this feature.

This is just one example of how the documentation can help you learn how to use ASP. Let's continue our exploration.

4. Collapse the Component Reference topic all the way back up.

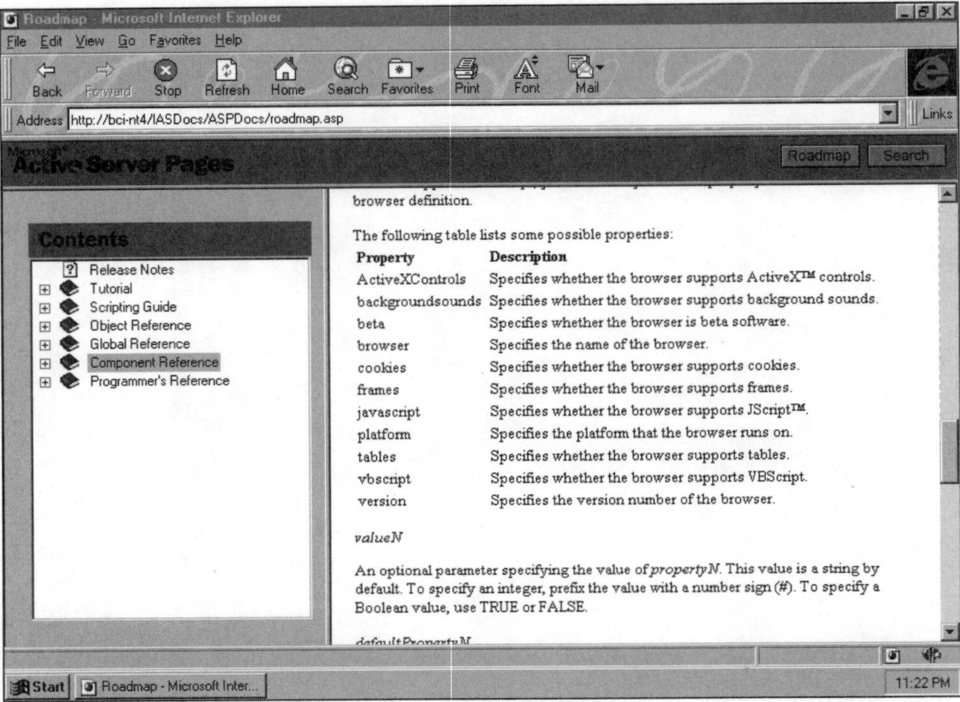

Figure 9.16
ASP roadmap documentation.

5. Expand the Programmer's Reference.
6. Then, expand the Creating Components For ASP topic, as shown in Figure 9.17.

Now, spend some time browsing through the documentation on your own. When you're finished exploring, we'll move on and take a look at the ASP model.

Reviewing The ASP Model

ASP is constructed of several types of tools that form the ASP Model, including objects, components, and languages. In the following sections, we'll take a look at each area of the ASP model, starting with a discussion about ASP objects.

Objects

It helps to have a good understanding of the underpinnings of ASP's objects, so you need to know what the objects are. ASP consists of five objects, including:

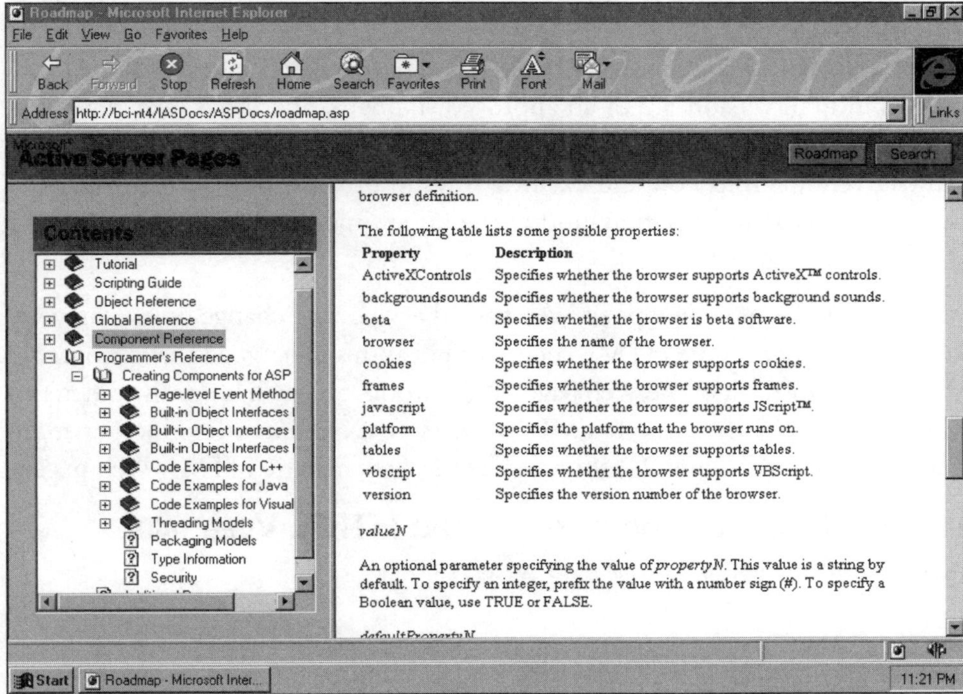

Figure 9.17
Programmer's reference.

- *Request Object*—Retrieves information from a user
- *Response Object*—Sends information to a user
- *Server Object*—Performs control operations on an ASP operation
- *Session Object*—Retains information about a Web session with the user
- *Application Object*—Shares information between certain users of a shared application

Each of these objects has properties and programming methods used to access ASP and HTTP information in processing the user's request. This kind of programming is beyond the scope of this book. Rather than go into examples of each object, let's concentrate on how ASP can be used to provide users with valuable information and ease the Web surfer's job by next looking at the HTML pages.

Viewing HTML Pages

Hypertext Markup Language, or HTML, has been around for quite some time. It's currently in version 3.2 of an approved standard, and it has been extended countless times by Web browser vendors such as Netscape and Microsoft. These browser vendors find new and exciting ways to provide Web surfers with cool pages and lots of information, and at the same time, they bring new, exciting gizmos to the party.

Static Web pages are one type of Web page that does not change unless someone intentionally changes the HTML code. As rigid as this is, it's good that changes are not possible for most of the Web pages in the world. So you'll know the difference when you see the dynamic HTML in the ActiveX chapter, let's look at some static Web pages. Listing 9.2 shows an example of a static HTML Web page.

Listing 9.2 Example of a static HTML Web page.

```
<!DOCTYPE HTML PUBLIC "-//W30/DTD HTML//EN">
<HTML>
<HEAD>
<TITLE>BCI What's New Page</TITLE>
<META NAME="FORMATTER" CONTENT="Microsoft FrontPage 1.1">
</HEAD>
<BODY>
<P> <IMG SRC="images/logo.gif" ALT="[Company Logo Image]"
BORDER="0" WIDTH="120" HEIGHT="24">  </P>
<H1> What's New</H1>
<P> [ <A HREF="index.htm">Home</A> | <A HREF="news.htm">What's
New</A> | <A HREF="products.htm">Products &amp; Services</A> | <A
HREF="toc.htm">TOC</A> | <A HREF="feedback.htm">Feedback</A> | <A
HREF="search.htm">Search</A> ]</P>
<P> <IMG SRC="images/undercon.gif" ALT="[Under Construction]"
BORDER="0" WIDTH="40" HEIGHT="38"></P>
<H2>Web Changes</H2>
<P> This is where we'll announce the most recent additions to our
Web site. If you've visited us before and want to know what's
changed, take a look here first. </P>
<P>  </P>
<DL>
   =<DT> <IMG SRC="images/smallnew.gif" ALT="[New!]" BORDER="0"
      WIDTH="35" HEIGHT="22"> <STRONG>BCI Associates, Inc.
      Establishes Internet Presence</STRONG></DT>
   <DD>See the <A HREF="pr01.htm">press release</A> for more
      details. </DD>
   <DT><STRONG>Sample Product Announcement</STRONG> </DT>
```

```
   <DD>See the <A HREF="prod01.htm">product data sheet</A> for
      more details. </DD>
</DL>
<HR>
```

As you can see from this Web page, there's nothing in it that could be substituted via programming methods to provide updates or have any indication of new material, such as automatic variables in Visual Basic programming or in Active Server Pages code, which you'll see next.

Comparing CGI And ASP

A long time ago, way back when the Web was getting organized, the National Center for Supercomputing Applications developed a set of standards that collectively formed a Common Gateway Interface (CGI). Basically, CGI is a set methodology of communicating between a server and the client (a competitor to ASP itself). Let's take a look at how the two compare to one another.

Common Gateway Interface

CGI scripts are text documents that are executed on the server when a Web document calls the script. Each time this script is called, it is compiled by the Web server and executed on the computer. When this occurs, an operating system process is initiated that handles the script and returns the data to the user. Each time a CGI script is executed, this mini application is executed. Can you imagine a thousand of these miniature applications running concurrently on the server? Well, that is exactly what CGI does each time a Web server is accessed. This places quite a load on a server and heavy demands on the hardware.

As server demands increased, there had to be some reprieve. Microsoft rose to the challenge by releasing ASP for IIS. Now, with ASP, CGI scripts are unnecessary because the HTML request is passed on to IIS's Web server internal processing.

Active Server Pages

To start, let's look at an example of Active Server Pages on the Internet at Microsoft's Web site, shown in Figure 9.18 (**www.microsoft.com**).

Take a close look at the URL in the Location section of Netscape. Do you see the file name in the URL? It says it is *DEFAULT.ASP*, which is an Active Server

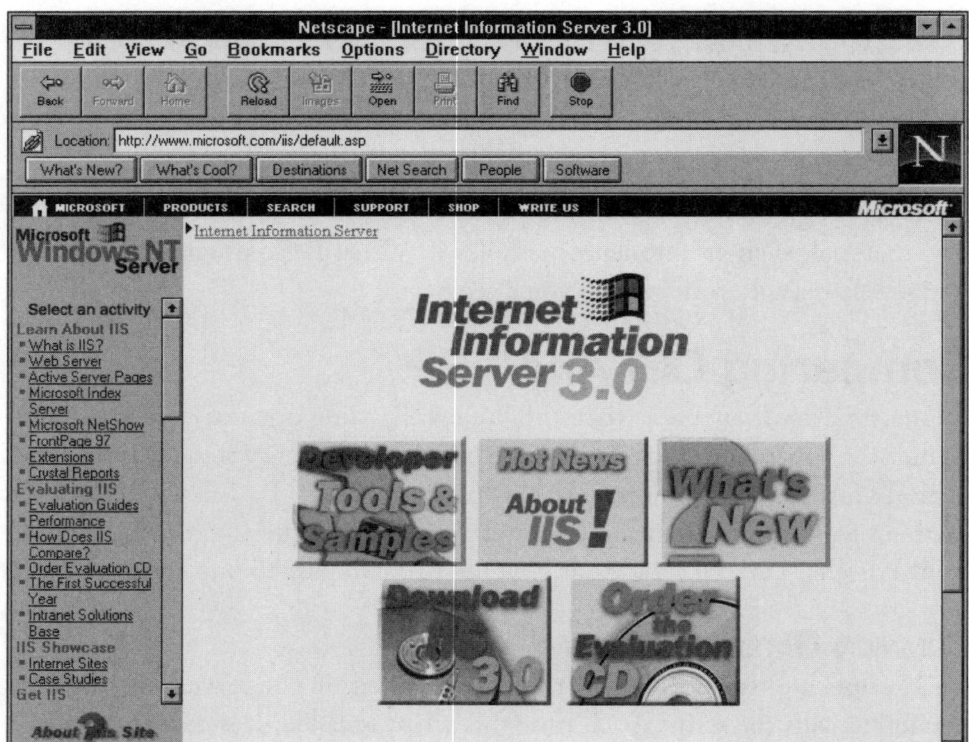

Figure 9.18
Active Server pages in action at Microsoft Corp.

Pages script. Do you see all of the items at the left side of this Web page? These are ASP script properties used to embellish the Web page for ease of understanding the information that Microsoft is presenting to the visitor. Click on View|Document Source, and you'll see the contents of the HTML page for this Web page, as shown in Figure 9.19.

Notice the second line item inside of the **<FRAMESET>** created for this document. On the right side of the figure, near the middle, you'll see that **MENU.ASP** is used to create part of the menu structure for the Web page, in addition to standard HTML code. This is the basic premise behind ASP and HTML—ASP removes the necessity of CGI and PERL scripts and, instead, uses a tighter server processing scheme to serve up Web pages to your users.

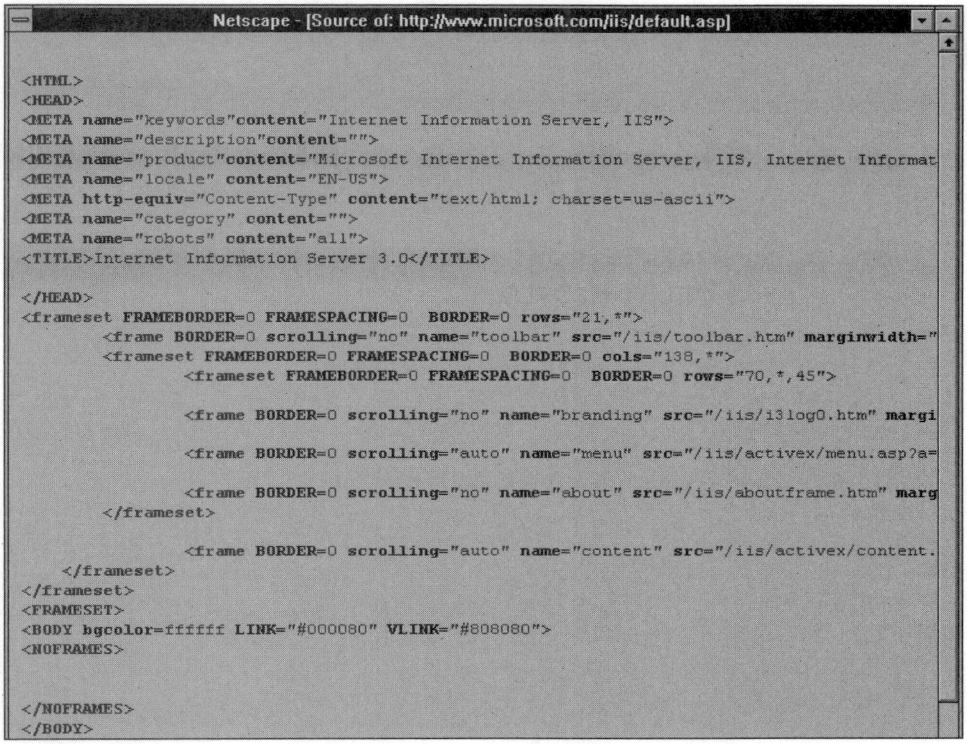

```
Netscape - [Source of: http://www.microsoft.com/iis/default.asp]

<HTML>
<HEAD>
<META name="keywords"content="Internet Information Server, IIS">
<META name="description"content="">
<META name="product"content="Microsoft Internet Information Server, IIS, Internet Informat
<META name="locale" content="EN-US">
<META http-equiv="Content-Type" content="text/html; charset=us-ascii">
<META name="category" content="">
<META name="robots" content="all">
<TITLE>Internet Information Server 3.0</TITLE>

</HEAD>
<frameset FRAMEBORDER=0 FRAMESPACING=0  BORDER=0 rows="21,*">
        <frame BORDER=0 scrolling="no" name="toolbar" src="/iis/toolbar.htm" marginwidth="
        <frameset FRAMEBORDER=0 FRAMESPACING=0  BORDER=0 cols="138,*">
                <frameset FRAMEBORDER=0 FRAMESPACING=0  BORDER=0 rows="70,*,45">

                <frame BORDER=0 scrolling="no" name="branding" src="/iis/i3log0.htm" margi

                <frame BORDER=0 scrolling="auto" name="menu" src="/iis/activex/menu.asp?a=

                <frame BORDER=0 scrolling="no" name="about" src="/iis/aboutframe.htm" marg
        </frameset>

                <frame BORDER=0 scrolling="auto" name="content" src="/iis/activex/content.
    </frameset>
</frameset>
<FRAMESET>
<BODY bgcolor=ffffff LINK="#000080" VLINK="#808080">
<NOFRAMES>


</NOFRAMES>
</BODY>
```

Figure 9.19
The document source for the page shown in Figure 9.18.

Writing ASP Scripts

Before you can write ASP scripts, you need to learn the language itself. The scripts are based on three core languages: Java, C++, and Visual Basic 4 or higher. Each of these three programming languages requires its own level of expertise, and each also has its own level of extensibility.

Java requires some knowledge of C. There's tons of information on the Web to help you learn Java. Both VB and C++ require a lot more investment in software and time before you can write ASP scripts. So, to make things simple, let's look at a Java example of how to write text to an HTML Web page.

1. Return to the ASP documentation, and open the Programmer's Reference.
2. Expand the Code Examples For Java folder.
3. Left-click once on the Writing Text To An HTML Page topic.

The code's source shows up in the right pane. Most of the code consists of HTML command tags commonly used in Web pages. The other text consists of Java commands that are used to form the script, as shown in Figure 9.20.

Listing 9.3 presents another sample of ASP code. The code in this listing displays *Hello World,* with each letter increasing in size incrementally.

Listing 9.3 Sample ASP script that increments Hello World.

```
<HTML>
<HEAD><TITLE>Creating Hello World with Incremental
Text Size Increase</TITLE></HEAD>
<BODY BGCOLOR=#FFFFFF>
<% for i = 3 to 7 %>
   <FONT SIZE=<% = i %>>Hello World</FONT><BR>
<% next %>
<BR>
<BR>
<!--#include virtual="/ASPSamp/Samples/srcform.inc"-->
</BODY>
</HTML>
```

This sample ASP script shows that not only can you use ASP scripts to do Java-like things, but that ASP uses programmatic methods, like include files, to enhance a Web page with programming tools. Look at the include file contents in Listing 9.4, and you'll see what I mean. Other ASP files are being used to form the entire tool suite.

Listing 9.4 Contents of the include file.

```
<AHREF="/ASPSamp/Samples/code.asp?source=
    <%=Request.ServerVariables("PATH_INFO")%>">
<IMG SRC="/ASPSamp/Samples/Vsource.GIF" WIDTH=85 HEIGHT=45
  ALT="View Active Server Page Source" ALIGN=CENTER BORDER=0></A>
```

These two code examples from the ASP installation show that even basic HTML can be used to extend a Web site with simple coding.

This all seems too easy to be that powerful. Well, the fact of the matter is that we've barely scratched the surface of ASP capabilities—and it only gets better. After all, we've only discussed ASP's installation and looked at a couple lightweight examples. Take a walk through the other code samples provided with

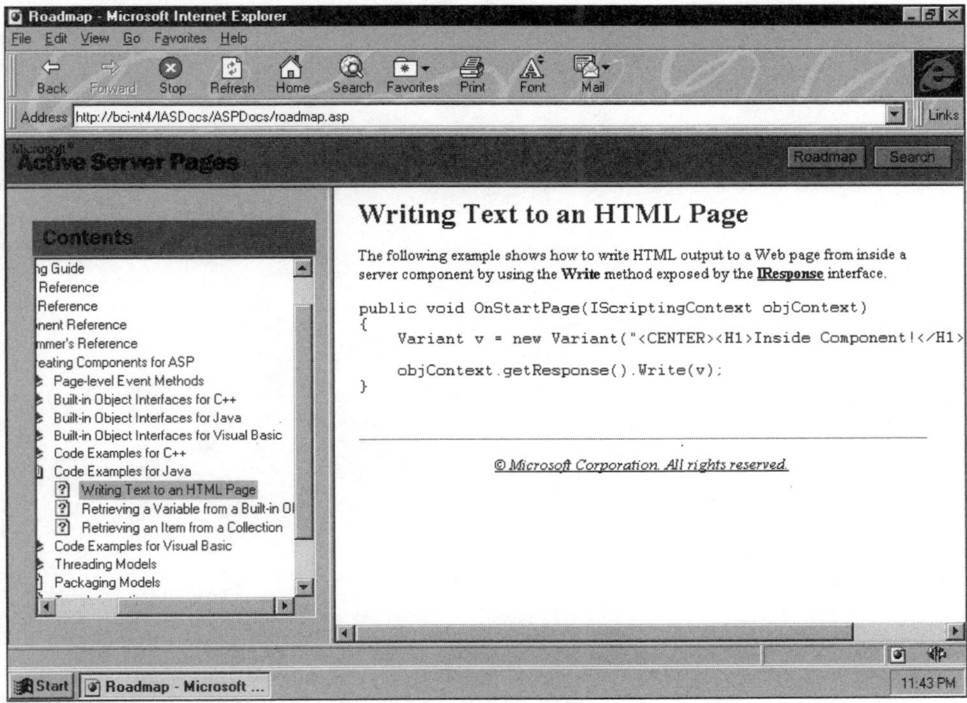

Figure 9.20
Sample Java code.

the ASP installation, and you'll get more of a feel for what is possible with ASP. You'll be pleasantly surprised at what you see.

Summary

This chapter introduces you to Microsoft's powerful add-ins for IIS: the Index Server and Active Server Pages. Index Server is a powerful search and retrieval tool with astoundingly easy-to-use functions and extendible features. ASP assists in adding advanced features to your Web pages. We'll talk about ASP again in Chapter 12. In that chapter, we'll look at how ASP and ActiveX technologies can be used to modify various parts of IIS to support some very neat Web pages.

10 Serving Up Active Server Pages

Robert Ellis

Cruise the Net and you will encounter two types of documents: *static* documents, which are standalone documents that never change, and *dynamic* documents, which can change their content and/or appearance and even interact with the user. This chapter focuses on dynamic documents and explores their creation with Microsoft's Active Server technology.

Characterizing An Active Server Page

An Active Server Page (ASP file) is a unique type of HTML document in which processing actually occurs on the Web server rather than on the Web browser (the client). The Web server passes a series of HTML codes to the Web browser. Then, the Web browser displays the document based on the HTML codes. The document is dynamic in the sense that the Web server determines what HTML codes to send to the browser at the time the user interacts with the Web server.

One of the interesting characteristics of an Active Server Page is that it can support three scripting languages: VBScript, JavaScript, and Microsoft's JScript. Microsoft licensed technology from Sun to create JScript, which is Microsoft's version of JavaScript. JScript has been optimized for the Microsoft platforms and includes functionality not available from JavaScript.

If you plan on using any server-side components of the JScript language, you need to download and install Microsoft VM for Java on your Web server. You can download these files for the Intel platform at **www.microsoft.com/java/jvmi386.cab**, for the Alpha platform at **www.microsoft.com/java/jvmalpha.cab**, and the PowerPC platform at **www.microsoft.com/java/jvmppc.cab**.

Writing Your First Active Server Page

The first step in writing an Active Server Page is to choose a language. While you can write the code using VBScript, the examples shown here use JScript. But before turning to the code, take a look at the actual output of the code, as displayed on a Web browser (see Figure 10.1).

What you are looking at in Figure 10.1 is the phrase Welcome to Paradise, shown in a series of font sizes—ranging from size one through size seven and then back again to size one. If you select View|Source, you'll see the corresponding HTML source code, as shown in Listing 10.1.

> *Note: The numbers displayed to the left of the code samples throughout this chapter are shown for clarity only. They are not actually part of the source code.*

Listing 10.1 The HTML code used to display the document in Figure 10.1.

```
<HTML>
<HEAD>
<META NAME="Author" CONTENT="Robert H. Ellis">
<META NAME="Description" CONTENT="Welcome to Paradise">
<META NAME="Subject" CONTENT="Active Server Page - JScript Sample">
<TITLE>Visual Developer Active Server Page Sample</TITLE>
</HEAD>
<BODY BACKGROUND="blulight.gif" BGCOLOR="#C0C0C0">
<FONT SIZE=1>Welcome to Paradise</FONT><BR>
<FONT SIZE=2>Welcome to Paradise</FONT><BR><FONT SIZE=3>Welcome to
Paradise</FONT><BR><FONT SIZE=4>Welcome to Paradise</FONT><BR><FONT
```

```
SIZE=5>Welcome to Paradise</FONT><BR><FONT SIZE=6>Welcome toParadise
</FONT><BR><FONT SIZE=7>Welcome to Paradise</FONT><BR><FONT
SIZE=6>Welcome to Paradise</FONT><BR><FONT SIZE=5>Welcome to Paradise
</FONT><BR><FONT SIZE=4>Welcome to Paradise</FONT><BR><FONT
SIZE=3>Welcome to Paradise</FONT><BR><FONT SIZE=2>Welcome to Paradise
</FONT><BR><FONT SIZE=1>Welcome to Paradise</FONT><BR>
</SCRIPT>
<HR>
<A HREF="Source.HTM">View Active Server Page Source</A>
<P>
<TABLE BORDER="0" WIDTH="100%">
   <TR>
      <TD VALIGN="top" WIDTH="50%"><FONT SIZE="2"><EM>Copyright
      © 1997 Robert H. Ellis. All rights reserved</EM></FONT><FONT
      SIZE="2"><EM><BR>
      </EM></FONT>For comments or suggestion send e-mail to:<BR>
      <A HREF="MAILTO:beach@paradise.com"> beach@paradise.com </A></TD>
      <TD ALIGN="right" VALIGN="top" WIDTH="50%">This page was
      last modified on:<BR>
      <!--webbot bot="Timestamp" startspan s-type="EDITED"
      s-format="%A, %B %d, %Y" -->Monday, June 30, 1997<!--webbot
      bot="Timestamp"
      i-checksum="60550" endspan --></td>
   </TR>
</TABLE>
</BODY>
</HTML>
```

Listing 10.2 is an example of using the Response method to introduce users to the Web site with a standard text string. The commands illustrate how easy ASP is to implement.

Listing 10.2 ASPSample.ASP—An Active Server Page sample.

```
<%@ Script RunAt=Server Language=JScript %>
<HTML>
<HEAD>
<META NAME="Author" CONTENT="Robert H. Ellis">
<META NAME="Description" CONTENT="Welcome to Paradise Active Server
Page Sample">
<META NAME="Subject" CONTENT="Active Server Page - JScript Sample">
<TITLE>Paradise Active Server Page Sample</TITLE>
</HEAD>
<BODY BACKGROUND="blulight.gif" BGCOLOR="#C0C0C0">
<%
```

```
11. var WelcomeString;
12. WelcomeString = "Welcome to Paradise";
13. for (i=1; i <= 7; i++)
14.     {
15.     Response.Write("<FONT SIZE=");
16.     Response.Write(i);
17.     Response.Write(">");
18.     Response.Write(WelcomeString);
19.     Response.Write("</FONT>");
20.     Response.Write("<BR>");
21.     }
22. for (i=6; i > 0 ; i--)
23.     {
24.     Response.Write("<FONT SIZE=");
25.     Response.Write(i);
26.     Response.Write(">");
27.     Response.Write(WelcomeString);
28.     Response.Write("</FONT>");
29.     Response.Write("<BR>");
30.     }
31. %>
32. </SCRIPT>
33. <HR>
34. <!--#include file ="CopyRight.INC"-->
35. </BODY>
36. </HTML>
```

Obviously, the code in Listing 10.2 is quite different from the HTML output shown in Listing 10.1. In fact, only a few lines in Listing 10.2 (Lines 9, 33, 35, and 36) can be matched to lines in Listing 10.1. Listing 10.2 might appear to be a bit confusing, even if you know C++ or JavaScript because some of the functions may not be familiar. You can examine the code a bit more closely while I explain how it works.

The first thing to notice in Listing 10.2 is Line 1. Line 1 includes the command **<%@ Script RunAt=Server Language=JScript %>**, which tells the compiler that the scripting commands contained within the document are JScript commands and that they should be executed on the server. If you choose to use VBScript instead, you can skip the language element because VBScript is the default and will be assumed by the compiler. Like most HTML tags, **<SCRIPT>** has a corresponding end tag shown in Line 32 (**</SCRIPT>**), although in this example, the end tag really isn't required. I've used it only for clarity's sake. Using the **<SCRIPT>…</SCRIPT>** tag set enables you to mix and match

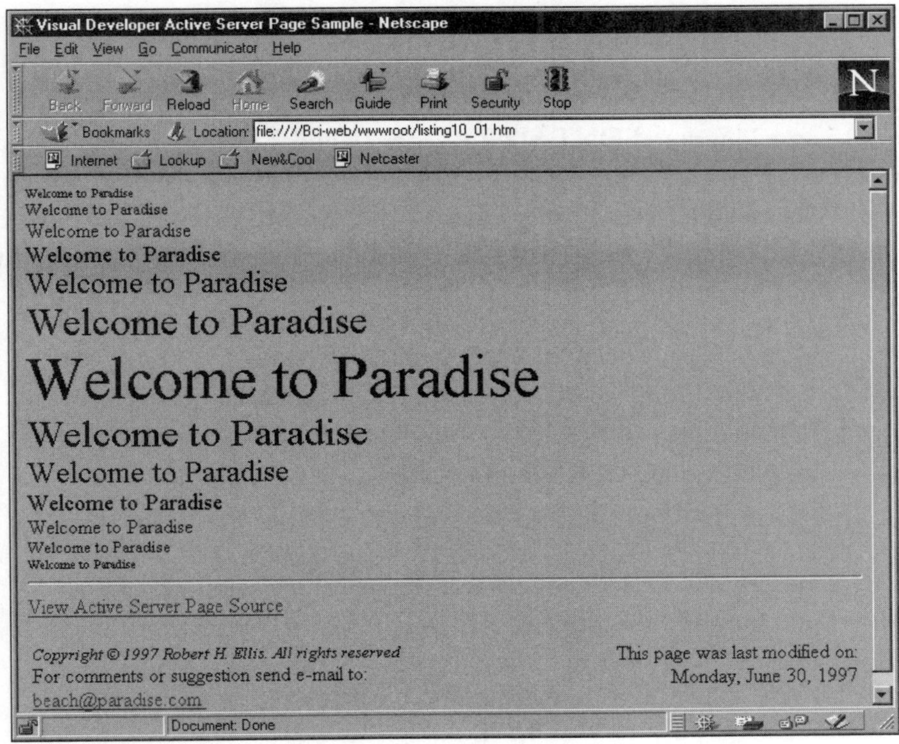

Figure 10.1
The sample Active Server Page displayed on Internet Explorer.

VBScript and JScript in the same document. This feature allows you to reuse an existing code base or perhaps use a third-party code base within your documents.

The next item to notice in Listing 10.2 is the text contained within Lines 10 through 31. This is where the heart of the script comes into play. Lines 10 and 31 delimit the starting and ending points of the script. Everything within these delimiters must be JScript code; otherwise, a compile time error occurs. Line 11 creates a string variable called **WelcomeString**, which is assigned the value **Welcome to Paradise** in Line 12. Line 13 begins a loop that counts from 1 through 7 and is delimited by the braces in Lines 14 and 21. Line 22 begins a loop that counts down from 6 through 1 and is delimited by the braces in Lines 23 and 30.

Lines 15 through 20 and 24 through 29 perform the same task. The task is repeated each time the loop condition is **true**. The important feature about these lines of code is the **Response.Write** portion of the statement. This portion of code actually writes the HTML output you saw in Listing 10.1. What you are seeing here is the use of the **Write** method for the **Response** object. Each statement writes a portion of the HTML code into the HTTP data stream. Lines 15 and 24 write **<FONT SIZE=**. Lines 16 and 25 write the loop counter. And Lines 17 and 26 write > (the end of the tag). Lines 18 and 27 write the actual **Welcome to Paradise** string. Lines 19 and 28 write the end tag **</FONT>**, while Lines 20 and 29 write a **
** tag into the output stream. The final result is Line 9 of Listing 10.1.

Make sure you remember the **Response** object, as it can be difficult to find in the Microsoft documentation. If you have the Index Information Server installed on the same site, then you can use the Search option (within the Active Server Page Roadmap) and perform a search on the phrase *Response object*. This search should get you to the page where the **Response** object methods are documented and explain how to use the object to write information into the HTTP data stream.

If you have never encountered a *server-side include* (SSI) before, then Line 34 in Listing 10.2 should prove interesting. Line 34 inserts a complete file into the HTTP data stream. The inserted file is called CopyRight.INC. The source code of the included file is shown in Listing 10.3.

Listing 10.3 CopyRight.INC—The included.

```
<A HREF="Source.HTM">View Active Server Page Source</A>
<P>
<TABLE BORDER="0" WIDTH="100%">
  <TR>
    <TD VALIGN="top" WIDTH="50%"><FONT SIZE="2"><EM>Copyright
    © 1996 Robert H. Ellis. All rights reserved</EM></FONT>
      <FONT SIZE="2"><EM><BR>
    </EM></FONT>For comments or suggestion send e-mail to:<BR>
    <A HREF="MAILTO:beach@paradise.com">beach@paradise.com</A></TD>
    <TD ALIGN="right" VALIGN="top" WIDTH="50%">This page was last
      modified on:<BR>
    <!--webbot bot="Timestamp" startspan s-type="EDITED"
    s-format="%A, %B %d, %Y" -->Monday, June 30, 1997<!--webbot
      bot="Timestamp"
    i-checksum="60550" endspan --></TD>
  </TR>
</TABLE>
```

Notice that the HTML code in Listing 10.3 is exactly the same as the HTML code generated in Listing 10.1. Server-side includes can be very useful for your development efforts because they can reduce the amount of code you need to generate and improve usability.

Now that you know that you can include files within your HTML documents, you probably want to know more about how to accomplish the task.

Including Files In An Active Server Page

Before you start to insert files, I'd like you to consider that you can also include other objects. For example, you can insert the file size into the HTML output stream. Or perhaps, you'd like to execute a CGI application and send its output into the HTML output stream. All of this, and more, is possible.

The basic format of the HTML insert statement is

```
<!--InsertTagHere PathType=PathName-->
```

where InsertTagHere is a directive that determines the type of information to be inserted into the HTML output stream and PathType specifies the type of path to use (either **VIRTUAL** or **FILE**). PathName is the actual path to the object. These directives are summarized in Table 10.1.

> *Note: A FILE path is assumed to be relative to the directory of the parent document (the document with the* ***#include*** *directive), whereas a VIRTUAL path is assumed to be relative to the IIS WWWRoot directory.*

One of the really neat features of server-side includes (STM files) is the ability to include Active Server Pages within the HTML document. You can't just use the **#include** directive to insert an ASP file, however. If you do, the file contents will be embedded into the document, but they will not be executed on the server. Instead, to include an ASP file, use the **#exec** directive. You could, for example, use

```
<!--#exec cgi="/PageInfo.ASP"-->
```

which would insert the HTML output generated by the PageInfo.ASP file into the HTML data stream.

TABLE 10.1

INCLUDE DIRECTIVES TO INSERT FILE AND APPLICATION INFORMATION INTO THE HTML OUTPUT STREAM.

Directive	Description	Example
#include	Inserts a file into the HTML output stream.	<!–#include file="CopyRight.INC"-> <!–#include virtual="/Books/Samples/CopyRight.INC"–>
#flastmod	Inserts the file's last modification date into the HTML output stream.	<!–#flastmod virtual="/Books/Samples/CopyRight.INC"–>
#fsize	Inserts the file's size into the HTML output stream.	<!–#fsize virtual="/Books/Samples/CopyRight.INC"–>
#echo	Inserts the output of a CGI variable into the HTML output stream.	<!–#echo var=CONTENT_TYPE–>
#config	Specifies how error messages, the date time format, and the file size format will be issued to the client.	<!–#config errmsg="An error has occurred attempting to include a file. Please email the administrator"–>
#exec	Executes a given CGI application, command shell, or ISAPI application, and outputs the result into the HTML output stream.	<!–#exec cmd="DIR"–>

You can use your Web browser to find more information on how to use server-side includes. Just use the URL **yourserver.yourdomain/iasdocs/aspdocs/ssi/isiall.htm** where YourServer is the name of the IIS server and YourDomain is your Internet domain name.

Before ending this chapter, I need to discuss some of the more basic administration issues faced when using Active Server Pages. Otherwise, you might find that although you can write JScript code, use server-side includes, and generate tons of ASP files, you can't actually execute any of them.

Additional Considerations For Active Server Pages

The first thing to consider is that an Active Server Page is not a normal HTML document, nor is it a regular script file. The client only reads a normal HTML document. The client only executes a normal script file. The standard permissions applied to a home directory or virtual directory with the Internet Server Manager is read only for HTML directories and executes only for scripts.

These permissions work fine for HTML documents and script files. If you place ASP files into either of these directories when they are loaded into the client's Web browser, however, you are not going to like the results. Instead of being interpreted by the Web server and converted into a standard HTML output stream, the documents load as is into the Web browser if the directory is marked as read-only. Consequently, the client will see any HTML code you might have, ignores all the scripting commands, and just displays the script commands as regular text. In most cases, the client displays an empty page! If the directory is marked as execute, but not read, then the client gets an access violation when attempting to load the file. To avoid these problems, just make sure that any directory you use for ASP files has both read and execute permissions—which leads to the second item to consider—security.

How can you prevent users from loading all your ASP pages? You may, for example, have created various private Active Server applications for use within your intranet. If these pages access sensitive data, you obviously do not want to allow just anyone to run them. One way to prevent unauthorized access is to use permissions to limit access to the files. However, this method requires that the documents be physically stored on an NTFS partition and that you use File Manager or Windows Explorer to assign permissions to limit access to the files.

Summary

This chapter demonstrates some of the basic functionality provided by Active Server Pages. The most important concept you should remember is that Active Server Pages are executed on the server, rather than on the client. As a script is processed, it is converted to HTML, which, in turn, is sent to the client. This technique is very different from processing scripts locally on the client. It also opens up new ways for developers to take advantage of the server's horsepower.

11

Enhancing Your Web Site With Microsoft NetShow And Crystal Reports

Robert Ellis

This chapter is a combination of two applications associated with Web servers and NT: NetShow and Crystal Reports. In this chapter, we'll discuss using streaming audio and video with Microsoft's NetShow multimedia product, as well as look at Crystal Reports, a utility used to generate reports based on data obtained from a Web server. All in all, these two topics are relatively short in nature and easy to understand. While there are many ways to use NetShow, each use is an off-shoot of the principles presented in this chapter. With that stated, let's get started. First, we'll first review NetShow, then we'll discuss Crystal Reports.

Streaming Audio And Video With NetShow

The introduction of Microsoft's Internet Information Server 3 places streaming multimedia capability within financial reach of almost anyone. Streamed multimedia differs from regular multimedia in that a streamed multimedia file is sent over the wire in packets. Each packet is then played on the client's computer as it is received. This process is quite different from the usual method of playing an AVI or WAV file, in which you must first download the complete file. Then, only after a complete download can you play the file using Media Player or other application. In contrast, a streamed multimedia file plays as it downloads. Microsoft's version of this new streaming technology is called *NetShow*.

What Is Microsoft NetShow?

Microsoft's NetShow is a client/server tool consisting of several components. The core component of NetShow is the Microsoft Internet Information Server (IIS). You need to use IIS version 2 or higher before you can install NetShow. You must also be running Windows NT Server 4 or higher because you cannot install the NetShow components on a Windows NT workstation. NetShow consists of the following five components:

- *NetShow On-Demand Server*—This component executes as a Windows NT 4 Server service. It can supply multiple-bit-rate audio, video, or interleaved audio/video multimedia streams to Windows NT and Windows 95 clients.
- *NetShow On-Demand Server Administration Utilities*—This component consists of the Internet Service Manager Add-In, the Trace Facility, and the Log Facility.
- *NetShow On-Demand Player*—This component consists of the two client-side tools required to view a streamed multimedia file: a standalone player and an ActiveX control that can be embedded in an HTML document. You can also use the ActiveX control within Visual Basic or Visual C++ applications.
- *ActiveX Streaming Format (ASF) Editor*—You can use this editor to assemble audio, video, or audio/video files into a data file. It is a crude tool designed to assemble files into an ASF file. However, I expect third-party manufacturers to hop on the bandwagon and create better tools.

- *Various Conversion Tools*—These tools include VIDTOASF.EXE, which converts AVI and MOV files to the ASF file format, and WAVTOASF.EXE, which converts WAV files to the ASF file format. All I can say is that the tools work (which means that they can at least get you started in developing ASF files).

You might have noticed a few disparaging remarks in the preceding descriptions. I'm not faulting Microsoft or its developers in any way. I've been a developer for many years, and I understand that new technologies introduce new requirements into the industry. If we, as developers, had to wait until all of a product's tools were written before the product was introduced, then we would never get anything done. Third-party manufacturers need a little time before they can get their tools out on the market, and this rule applies to Microsoft, as well. First, the underlying product is developed. Then, and only then, can development teams (from Microsoft and third parties) get involved.

What this sequence of events means is that, if you want to implement streaming technology, you will need to use additional tools available in the market, including tools to record and edit audio files. You'll also need a tool capable of capturing, editing, and assembling audio/video files. Luckily many of these types of tools are readily available. The bad news is that none of the current tools can work with the native ASF file format. Therefore, you have to edit your files, convert the files, assemble the files, and then use the ASF Editor to build the ASF file. If you are unhappy with the result, you must repeat the entire cycle. With this caveat out of the way, let's talk about streams, what they are, and how NetShow uses them.

What's A Stream?

If you have ever listened to a RealAudio presentation on the Internet, then you might already have used streamed audio. But, perhaps you want to know a bit more about how a stream works. Essentially, a stream is an assemblage of audio only, video only, or audio and video files synchronized to a common timeline. These files are interleaved in the data stream so that when the image is rendered or an audio file plays, it is assembled from the various bits and displayed or played at the correct time.

With NetShow you can stream audio, video, or a mixture of the two, to the target audience on an intranet or on the World Wide Web via the Internet. Keep in mind, every network has limited bandwidth. The network can handle only so many bits before the network chokes and dies. Nothing chews up bandwidth like multimedia files. High-quality audio/video files can consume bandwidth faster than you would believe. However, NetShow employs very good *codecs* (a piece of software used to compress/decompress audio and video files) that you can use to compress audio and video files. Without the ability to compress data streams, even 100MB/sec. networks would suffer from the large demands of streaming technology. Even with compressed data, you should limit the number of simultaneous connections and users on the network to avoid potential problems.

> ***Note:*** *If you choose to provide a more open connection standard, then you need to use less video and more audio. Audio consumes far less bandwidth than video.*

Now that we've defined streaming technology, let's look at the stream types offered by NetShow.

NetShow Stream Types

There are three types of streamed data you can assemble with the ASF Editor and then play back using an ASF player (like the NetShow player). The pros and cons of each type of data are summarized in Table 11.1. You should evaluate each format to determine whether it is suitable for the intended application. Consider the bandwidth requirements, noting that you can support only a limited number of clients based on your available network bandwidth. For example, a high-quality audio/video file limits the number of simultaneous clients able to access the file in comparison to the number of clients that would be able to access an audio-only file. The moral is that if you need to support many simultaneous clients, you should consider using a less-bandwidth-intensive format.

Next, let's use this information to build a streaming audio/video file.

Building A Streaming Audio/Video File

This is where the fun starts! First, choose your tool. You can use the ASF Editor, the video-to-ASF converter, or the WAV-to-ASF converter. Because the ASF converters are simpler, you should start with one of them. ASF converters are command-line tools that have the command-line arguments shown in Tables 11.2 and 11.3.

> ***Note:*** *Some of the options listed for the command-line arguments in Tables 11.2 and 11.3 are not displayed when you use the /? argument on the application, but they are supported.*

Table 11.1

SUPPORTED STREAMED FILE TYPES.

File Type	Descriptions	Comment
Audio Only	High quality audio-only data.	You can use any supported WAV file format as your input file format. These formats include Mono render or Stereo from 11.025 to 44.1KHz. The higher the frequency, the better the quality. The higher frequencies also require an increased network bandwidth to play properly. You should use the higher frequencies (44.1KHz) only for sound sources that require it. For example, CD-quality music uses 44.1KHz.
Illustrated Audio	A mixture of static images and interleaved audio.	This format is an excellent choice for narratives, such as PowerPoint slide shows. Although it uses more bandwidth than an audio-only format, it can provide more information.
Interleaved Audio/Video	A high-quality audio and video interleaved file that can display full-motion video (24 through 30 frames per second).	Using fewer frames (15fps) can significantly lower the bandwidth requirements and still provide acceptable animation. Requires an extreme amount of network bandwidth for full audio processing. It can basically provide the same quality as broadcast television right on your network.

The command-line arguments for VIDTOASF.EXE are shown in Table 11.2. The command-line arguments for WAVTOASF.EXE are shown in Table 11.3.

TABLE 11.2

COMMAND-LINE ARGUMENTS FOR VIDTOASF.EXE.

Command	Argument	Description
IN	FileName.EXT	Specifies the file name and extension of the input file you want to convert. This file can be an AVI file or a QuickTime movie, although not all QuickTime movie file formats are currently supported.
OUT	FileName.ASF	Specifies the output file name.

Continued

Table 11.2 (continued)

Command-line arguments for VIDTOASF.EXE.

Command	Argument	Description
WAVESPAN	MSSpan	Specifies the wave span in milliseconds. The wave span is the time frame in which an audio file can smear in the file. It is used to compensate for lost data packets. If you have a highly reliable network, you can disable spanning by setting this value to 0.
LEADTIME	MSTime	Specifies the time to wait to play an input file after buffering it. The default is 1,000 milliseconds.
VIDEO	StreamToUse	Specifies which data stream in the file to convert. This argument is applicable only for source files with multiple audio or video data streams.
AUDIO	StreamToUse	Specifies which data stream in the file to convert. This argument is applicable only for source files with multiple audio or video data streams.
ECCSPAN	ECCValue	Enables (ON) or disables (OFF) error correction.
SCRIPT	ScriptName	Specifies the script file used to insert URLs and markers into an output file.
SEEKABLE	SeekValue	Specifies that the file includes seekable frames (ON), even when there are not enough key frames. The default is OFF.
AUDIOFILE	AudioFileName	Specifies the name of an audio file to be used instead of the audio file in the original audio/video source file.
BITRATE	BitRate	Specifies the bit rate to convert the file to use. The default is to allow the application to determine the bit rate.
BUFFERTIME	BufferTime	Specifies the maximum time to use for buffering the input file when played on the client.
OPTIMIZE	OptimizeValue	Specifies a percentage (the default is 5 percent) for the application to maintain when calculating the maximum bit rate.
PACKETSIZE	PacketSize	Specifies the network packet size to use.

Using the ASF Editor, as shown in Figure 11.1, is easier than using the command-line conversion programs because it is a Windows application. Figure 11.1 shows the sample ASF file included with the NetShow Creation tools. It

Table 11.3

Command-line arguments for WAVTOASF.EXE.

Command	Argument	Description
IN	FileName.WAV	Specifies the file name of the input file to convert. This file must be a WAV file.
OUT	FileName.ASF	Specifies the output file name.
LEADTIME	MSTime	Time required to set up conversion.
ECCSPAN	ECCValue	Enables (ON) or disables (OFF) error correction.
SCRIPT	ScriptName	Specifies a script file used to insert URLs and markers into the output file.

displays images in green and yellow (on the top of the timeline) and the associated sound file in blue (on the bottom of the timeline). Adding images and sounds is as simple as dragging them from the bottom window (the source window) of the application and dropping them into the timeline. You can drag files from Windows Explorer into the source window, or you can use the Add Files command from the File menu.

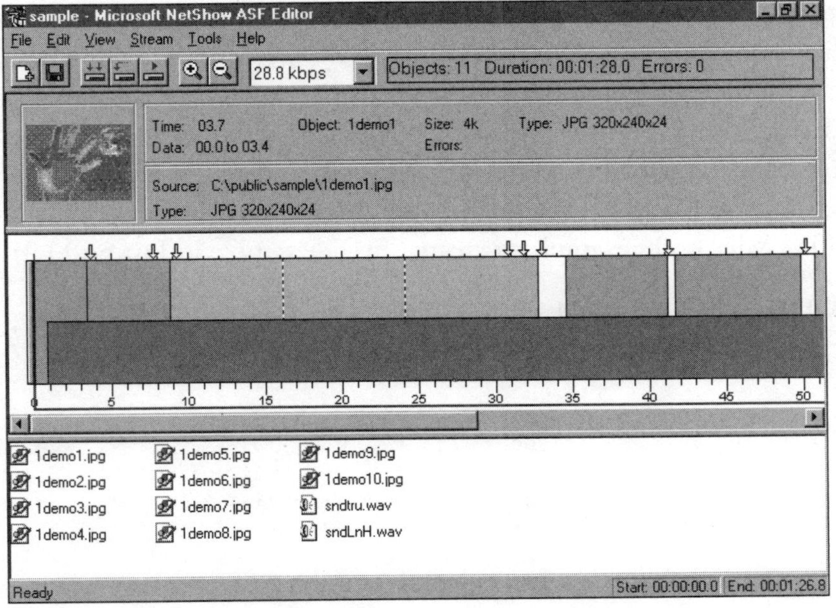

Figure 11.1
The ASF Editor in action.

The important feature to note about this program (which is really very basic in its capabilities) is that it can convert various graphic formats into a presentable form for streamed media. I've found that the most compressible option is the VDONet/VDOWave format. It converted the sample file from 1.5MB to 140K—more than a 10 to 1 ratio! You can also select a targeted bit rate for streamed media—14,400Kbps, 28,800Kbps, or 112,500Kbps—right from the toolbar. Just remember, pick the bit rate before you start working with the ASF Editor to import media because this setting affects the timeline significantly.

The timeline specifies how long it takes an image to be downloaded and rendered on the client computer. Audio files generally render quickly, whereas video files take noticeably longer. Therefore, if you decide to mix audio and video in the same file, you should make sure the audio stream is long enough to cover the time it takes to download and render the video images. The Stream Test menu option can help you with this calculation.

Once you have created an ASF file, you need to find a way to display it on your client's computer. To do this, you need to pull the technology together in some way.

Putting It All Together

You can display your ASF file on client computers in two ways. First, you can let clients download the ASF file and play it on their computer, much like any other multimedia file. However, this defeats the purpose of streaming the file. The second method is to provide an HTML page with the Microsoft NetShow On-Demand Control embedded in it. This task is really easier than you might expect because Microsoft provides a very nice sample. In fact, I have slightly modified Microsoft's example to create the code sample in Listing 11.1.

Listing 11.1 An example of NetShow in action.

```
<!DOCTYPE HTML PUBLIC "-//IETF//DTD HTML//EN">
<HTML>
<HEAD>
<META HTTP-EQUIV="Content-Type"
CONTENT="text/html; CHARSET=iso-8859-1">
<META NAME="GENERATOR" CONTENET="Microsoft FrontPage 2.0">
<TITLE>NetShow Sample Page</TITLE>
</HEAD>
<BODY BACKGROUND="blulight.gif">
<H1 ALIGN="center">A leopard on the move!</H1>
```

```
<HR>
<DIV ALIGN="center"><CENTER>
<TABLE BORDER="3">
   <TR>
      <TD><OBJECT ID="NSOPlay"
      CLASSID="clsid:2179C5D3-EBFF-11CF-B6FD-00AA00B4E220"
      codebase="http://www.microsoft.com/netshow/
               download/nsoplay.exe#version=1,0,0,475"
      ALIGN="baseline" BORDER="0" WIDTH="260" HEIGHT="62"><PARAM
      NAME="_ExtentX" VALUE="18574"><PARAM NAME="_ExtentY"
      VALUE="22410"><PARAM NAME="AutoRewind" VALUE="-1"><PARAM
      NAME="AutoStart" VALUE="-1"><PARAM NAME="ControlType"
      VALUE="2"></OBJECT></TD>
   </TR>
</TABLE>
</CENTER></DIV>
<HR>
<TABLE BORDER="0" WIDTH="100%">
   <TR>
      <TD VALIGN="top" WIDTH="45%"><ADDRESS>
         <FONT SIZE="2"><EM>Copyright © 1997 Ellis
         Consulting. All rights reserved<BR>
         </EM></FONT>For comments or suggestion send email
         to:<BR>
         <A HREF="MAILTO:beach@paradise.com">beach@paradise.com</A>
      </ADDRESS>
      </TD>
      <TD ALIGN="right" VALIGN="top" WIDTH="40%"><ADDRESS>
         This page was last modified on:<BR>
         <!--webbot bot="Timestamp" startspan s-type="EDITED"
         s-format="%A, %B %d, %Y" -->Monday, June 30, 1997<!--webbot
         bot="Timestamp" i-checksum="999" endspan -->
      </ADDRESS>
      </TD>
   </TR>
</TABLE>
<ADDRESS>
   <SCRIPT LANGUAGE="VBScript"><!--
Sub window_OnLoad()
   dim servername 'create a variable
   servername=Location.Hostname
   SetNetShowFileName( "leopard.asf" )
end sub
sub SetNetShowFileName( szNSOFile)
   Dim dwTruncPoint, GetCurrentPath
   dwTruncPoint = 1
```

```
   while( InStr( dwTruncPoint, window.location, "/" ) )
      dwTruncPoint =  InStr( dwTruncPoint, window.location, "/" ) + 1
   wend
   while( InStr( dwTruncPoint, window.location, "\" ) )
      dwTruncPoint =  InStr( dwTruncPoint, window.location, "\" ) + 1
   wend
   GetCurrentPath = Left( window.location, dwTruncPoint - 1 )
   dwTruncPoint = instr( GetCurrentPath, "///" )
   if( Not( IsNull( dwTruncPoint ) ) ) And ( 1 < dwTruncPoint )  then
      GetCurrentPath = Left( GetCurrentPath, dwTruncPoint ) &
         Right(GetCurrentPath, Len( GetCurrentPath) - dwTruncPoint - 1 )
end if
   On Error Resume Next
   NSOPlay.FileName = GetCurrentPath & szNSOFile
   if( 2 < Len( Err.Description ) ) then
      Res = Msgbox( Err.Description, 16, "NetShow On-Demand Player" )
      exit sub
   end if
   Err.Clear
end sub
--></SCRIPT>
</ADDRESS>
</BODY>
</HTML>
```

When the code in Listing 11.1 is executed, the HTML page shown in Figure 11.2 displays the streamed file with the control. Users have full control over how the object plays on their computers. At this point, a user simply specifies an action, either by clicking one of the buttons or right-clicking the control to specify various properties.

The document includes an ActiveX embedded object (within the **<OBJECT>... </OBJECT>** tag set) and associated Visual Basic script. You could do without the Visual Basic script entirely if you were to set the **FileName** property for the object to the full URL of the ASF file.

> ***Note:*** *Any HTML document with an ActiveX control used to enhance NetShow can only be viewed using Internet Explorer 3 or later, or Netscape 3 with an ActiveX plug-in.*

This completes our discussion of Microsoft's NetShow. The remainder of this chapter discusses how to use Crystal Reports with your Web server.

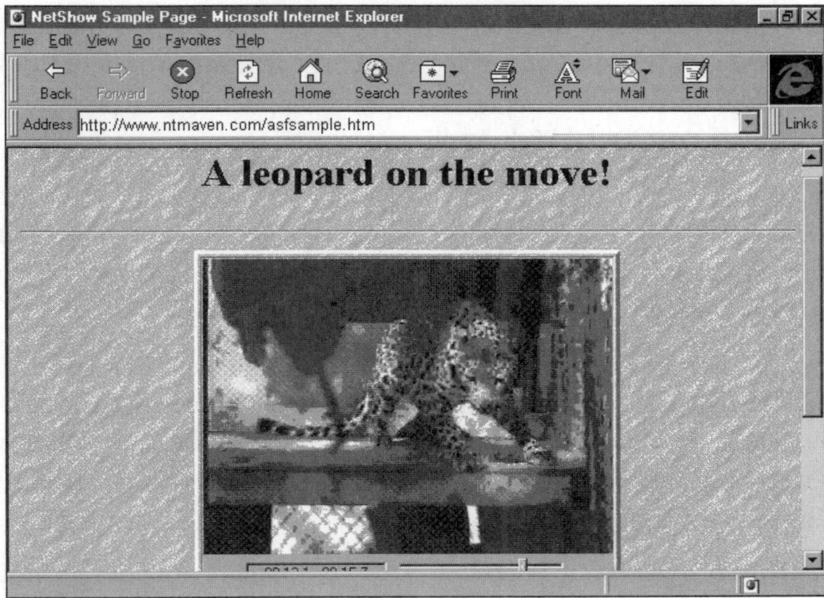

Figure 11.2
A streamed audio/video file using NetShow.

Crystal Reports

When you install the Internet Information Server, you have the opportunity to install Seagate Software's Crystal Reports For The Internet Information Server. This is a special version of Crystal Reports specifically designed to generate reports using IIS log files. Crystal Reports can be used to view IIS formatted log files, NCSA formatted log files, and IIS logs stored on an ODBC compliant database. Crystal Reports also includes the ability to generate live reports using Active Server Pages. In the upcoming sections, we'll explore some of Crystal Reports' capabilities.

What Is Crystal Reports For The Internet Information Server?

Crystal Reports For The Internet Information Server consists of several components. Not all of these components are accessible directly by the user, however, as you will see once you start working with the product. The product components include the following.

- *Crystal Web Publishing Interface*—This component is a Windows application that utilizes a WYSIWYG interface to aid in generating presentation-quality reports. You can print these reports on a printer or publish the reports directly to the Web via the Crystal Web Application Interface.
- *Crystal Web Activity DLL*—This component provides an interface between the Crystal Report Engine and the Web server log. It treats all log files as a common database with standard fields. These fields can then be used to create in-depth reports.
- *Crystal Reports Engine*—This component retrieves selected data from a database. The data is sorted, summarized, and grouped as specified by the report. The data is then presented in a presentation-quality format. A Web developer can use the Crystal Reports Engine to add reporting capabilities to Web pages with minimal coding.
- *Crystal Web Application Interface*—This component provides an interface between Web pages and the Crystal Reports Engine. It provides a mechanism to allow parameters to be passed to the Crystal Reports Engine to specify report information.

Next, let's see how to create a report using Crystal Reports.

Creating A Report

If you use Crystal Reports on log files rather than ODBC-compliant databases, then the samples provided with the product should get you up and running in no time. The first thing you need to do for each report is to specify the location of the IIS log files using the Crystal Reports application.

To change the log file location, follow the steps presented in this section.

1. Choose Set Location from the Database menu. The Set Location dialog box should appear.
2. Make sure the **in960628** entry in the Databases field is selected. Then, click on the Set Location button.

At this point, you will have to wait for a few minutes. Why? Because the default location for the log files is on a shared directory called *LogFiles* on a remote server called *VADER*. It will take a bit for the request to connect to this server or

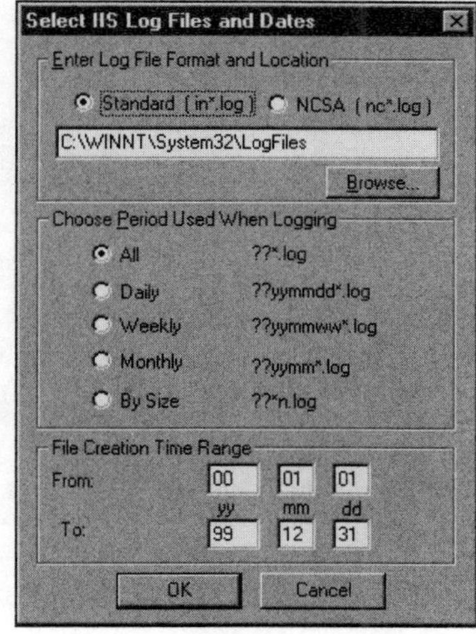

Figure 11.3
Specifying the location of the IIS Log files.

for it to fail. Eventually, the Select IIS Log Files And Dates dialog should appear, as shown in Figure 11.3.

3. Enable the Standard (in*.log) radio button.
4. Specify the correct location for the log files. The default log file location for an IIS installation should be %SystemRoot%\InetSrv\LogFiles.
5. Choose a file format type by enabling an option in the Choose Period Used When Logging section. These types directly relate to the naming convention used when you enabled logging using the Internet Service Manager.
6. Specify a file creation date to help eliminate files by specifying a start and end date in the From and To fields.
7. Click on OK. The Choose SQL Table dialog box should display. Do not be concerned by the name of this dialog box. It is configured to use the database files that you specified rather than an SQL Server table. (See Figure 11.4.)
8. Click on OK to continue.

> ***Note:*** *If you are using ODBC databases instead of IIS log files, then you have another step or two to complete. When you get to Step 8 in the previous process, click on the Log On Server button to display the Log On Server*

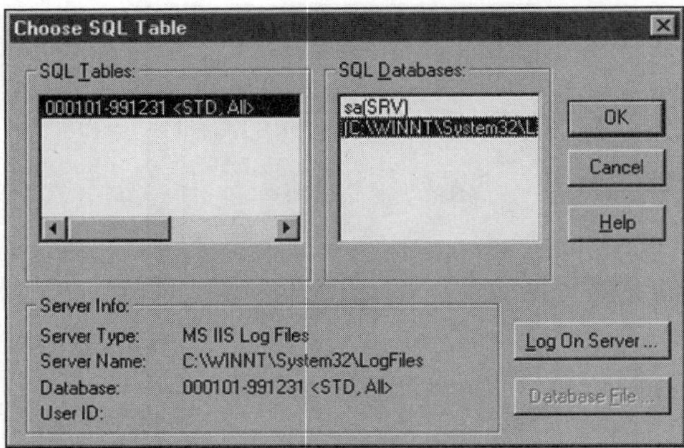

Figure 11.4
Specifying the IIS log files to be used by Crystal Reports.

dialog box. In the Server Type list, select the Microsoft SQL Server entry or the ODBC DSN that you are using to connect to the IIS log database. Then, click on OK. The Select Data Source dialog box should appear. Select the DSN you use to connect your database, and click on OK. If a logon dialog box appears, enter the user identification and password, and continue. Then, select the appropriate table and database to use in the Choose SQL Table dialog box, and click on OK.

You will return to the Set Location dialog box. The location information displayed on the bottom of the dialog box should now reflect the correct location of your IIS log files.

9. Click the Done button to close the Set Location dialog box and return to the Crystal Report Editor.

You might find that your reports have a few errors relating to data types when they are executed. If this occurs, you should use the modified reports included on the CD. Only they have been modified to log on to an ODBC database, and the type-related errors that occurred have been removed. In addition, you will need to modify several bits and pieces of the sample HTML documents in order to make them work with an ODBC database.

Now that you have an understanding of what Crystal Reports are, let's go through a real life reporting session.

Using Crystal Reports

It is possible to use the same reports you created from HTML pages on your Web server. If you used an ODBC or Microsoft SQL Server data source, then a logon screen can be generated automatically. The samples included with the Crystal Reports package are designed for use with the IIS log files. I've taken the samples and modified them (with appropriate comments) to work with an ODBC database. Here's how the process works.

1. The sample requires Active Server Pages (ASP), so make sure you have installed the Microsoft Active Server Pages software before trying to run the sample applications.
2. Using the Internet Service Manager, create a new virtual directory for your ASP files. This directory must have both read and execute permissions.
3. Using the steps presented in the previous section entitled *Creating A Report* as a guide, change the database location to point to your IIS log files—either local files or tables on an ODBC database.
4. Open your Web browser, and load the file INDEX.HTM. You must supply a URL in the form of **http://YourServerName.YourDomainName/YourVirtualDirectory/Index.HTM** in order for this process to work correctly.
5. The Web page shown in Figure 11.5 should appear.
6. Select the report type to view in the Select The Report To Generate field.
7. Enter a start and end date to use as the base data for the report in the Start Date and End Date fields, respectively.

   Note: *You might notice that my page automatically sets the start date to be one month less than the end date (the current date). I modified the source code to do this automatically so you can obtain a status report for the preceding month.*

8. Click on the Generate Crystal Report button. A page will be displayed informing you to wait while the report is generated. Immediately after that, a logon dialog box will be displayed, as shown in Figure 11.6.
9. Enter a valid user name with access to the database, and click on OK. For my live reports, I created a user account with only select (i.e., read) permissions. It only has access to the IISLogs database. The user name is *Guest*, and

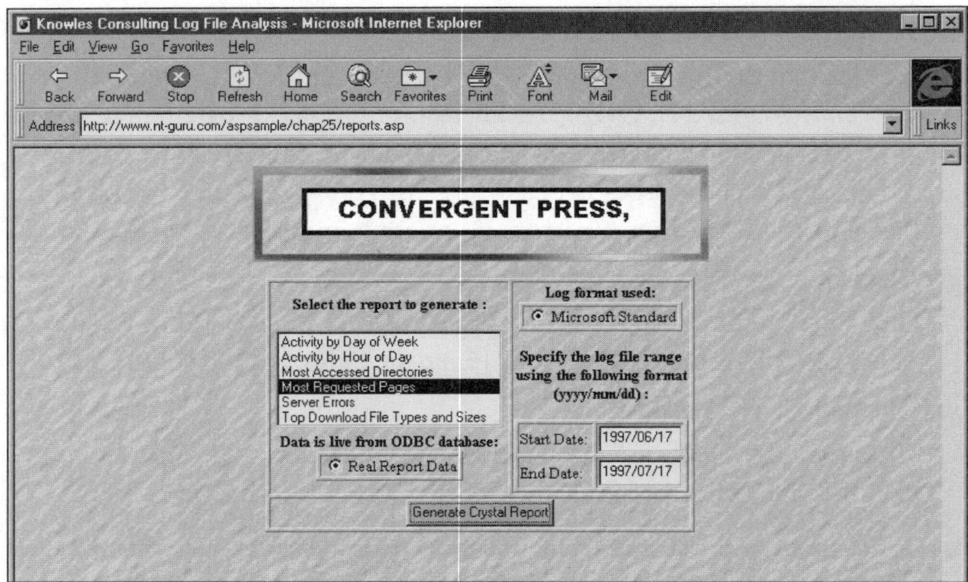

Figure 11.5
Generating a report on the Web using Crystal Reports.

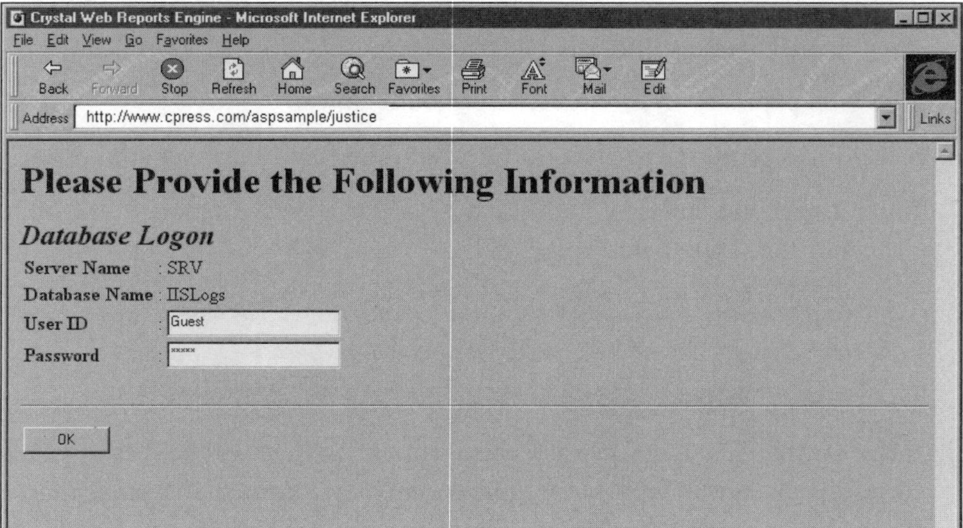

Figure 11.6
Logging on to the database.

the password is *guest*. Feel free to try out the reporting capabilities. Unfortunately, I can't promise how long this feature will remain on my site.

After you click on OK in Step 9, it will take a while for the query to execute and the report page to be created. The longer the time period (specified by the start and end dates), the longer it will take for the query to process. Once the process completes, however, you will see a report similar to the report shown in Figure 11.7. Don't bother to click one of the URLs within the reports. From what I can tell, the reporting module has a bug in the HTML code. As of this writing, the URLs do not work properly. Hopefully, this problem will be fixed in version 5.

Summary

The opening portion of this chapter explores some of the basic features of Microsoft NetShow and shows you a bit about streaming multimedia and the

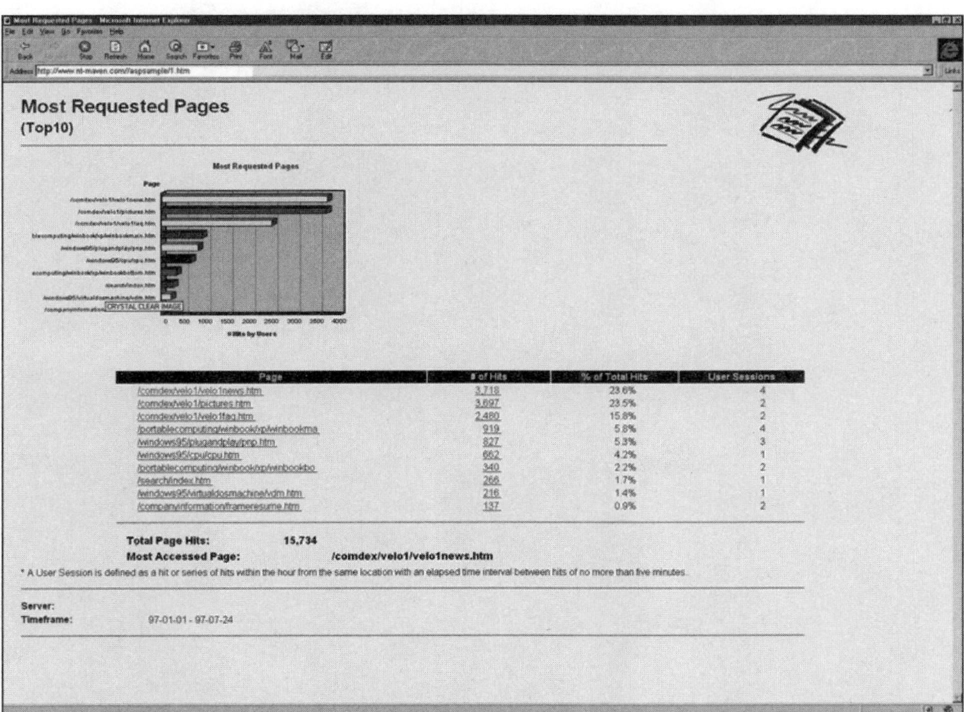

Figure 11.7
A live report on the Web server.

various formats that NetShow supports. The section also briefly examines the ASF Editor and associated conversion tools.

The remainder of the chapter explores some of the possibilities of Crystal Reports For The Internet Information Server. The product is extremely useful for generating high-quality reports. You should examine the source code carefully to see how ASP files are used to call the Crystal Report Engines.

12 Working With ActiveX Technology

Robert Thayer

ActiveX is one of the hottest buzzwords in the computer industry today. Microsoft claims that this "new technology" will revolutionize the way we use the Internet and, on a grander scale, how we'll use computers in general. But just exactly what is this "exciting new technology" we've been hearing so much about?

Surprisingly, ActiveX is little more than a new name for a group of components that have existed for quite some time: Hypertext Markup Language (HTML), COM, 32-bit OCX controls, VBScript, Java, and the list goes on and on. ActiveX simply acts as the "glue" that binds everything together. And while that may not seem like cutting-edge technology, it is when you add the secret ingredient—the Internet.

What the concept of Object Linking and Embedding (OLE) did for desktop computing, ActiveX promises to do for the Internet. Web pages can now be transformed from primarily one-way communications into rich multimedia applications that are truly interactive, much like a CD-ROM program. Indeed, it is rumored that the next generation of Microsoft's Windows operating system will attempt to meld elements of the desktop and the Internet.

The goal is to create a seamless computing environment that is no longer limited to the applications contained on a single computer.

Microsoft has been extremely aggressive in its bid to dominate the Internet market. In order to wrest control away from Netscape (Microsoft's main competitor in the Internet market), Microsoft has begun offering a wide variety of free tools and applications. Among the free offerings is the Internet Explorer (MSIE) Web browser, which is quickly gaining in popularity over Netscape's Navigator. Many tools for Webmasters have also been released, with almost every facet of Web development covered. To add icing to the cake, Microsoft did something that was completely unprecedented. It gave away a beta version of its most popular programming environment, Visual Basic 5.

Why would Microsoft do this? The answer is simple: To promote its new ActiveX technology. This new version of Visual Basic does something previous versions did not. It allows the creation of 32-bit OCX controls (now called *ActiveX* controls). Prior to the release of VB5, ActiveX controls could only be created using languages like Visual C++. Now, millions of Visual Basic programmers—even beginners—have the ability to make their own ActiveX components. They can then use these components to enhance their applications or Web pages.

In the next section, we'll take a look at ActiveX controls and how to integrate them with the Internet.

ActiveX And The Internet

To the programmer, the most important part of ActiveX is the ActiveX control. Controls are the building blocks that are used to create applications. Several ActiveX controls are included with VB5: **PictureBox**, **CommandButton**, **Slider**, **Spin**, and so forth. These controls make up the toolbox that every VB programmer knows so well.

Many more ActiveX controls are available for free on the Internet or can be purchased from third-party vendors. In fact, there are over 2,000 of them—and that number is no doubt going to grow quickly now that VB5 provides an easier way to create these controls!

> ***Note:*** *VB5 cannot use any 16-bit controls (VBXs). Only 32-bit ActiveX controls (OCXs) can be used. This means that if your applications utilize*

any VBXs that you purchased from third-party vendors, you'll need to obtain new ActiveX versions of those controls in order to recompile the same applications in VB5.

In the same way that controls (or *objects*) can be placed on a form to create an application, they can also be placed on a Web page to give it additional functionality. And just as properties can be set to change the size, location, or effect of an object used in an application, they can also be set for an object used on a Web page.

But how is this accomplished? Web pages, which use HTML, are not like Visual Basic. You cannot simply select an object from the toolbox and create an instance of the control on a form like you can in VB. And how does an OCX control get from a Web page to the user's computer so it can be executed? Well, that's where ActiveX comes in.

To begin with, an ActiveX control is placed on a Web page using the **<OBJECT>** HTML tag. An **<OBJECT>** tag can, in turn, enclose several **<PARAM>** tags which are used to set the object's properties. For example, the background color of a control on a Web page can be controlled directly through HTML by setting the object's **BackColor** property with a **<PARAM>** tag.

Many controls used on Web pages—especially those provided by Microsoft—may already exist on a user's system. But if a new control (or a new version of a control) is used, there must be some way to transfer that control to the user. This process is all handled transparently by an ActiveX-enabled Web browser such as Microsoft's Internet Explorer 3.x. The overhead of having to transfer one or more controls does take some time during the user's initial access of an ActiveX Web page (just how much time depends primarily on the file size of each control). However, subsequent accesses are much quicker because the controls would already exist on the user's system.

Note: *Netscape Navigator can also be used to view Web pages with ActiveX controls. However, a special plug-in from NCompass Labs is required to give Navigator ActiveX support. The plug-in is available for free via the Internet.*

In addition to properties, Internet ActiveX controls can also have methods and events. They work the same way as they do in regular VB applications.

Methods And Events

Methods are functions that can be called using code or a scripting language (such as VBScript). These functions cause the control to do something. For example, let's say you designed a control that uses a digitized voice to tell the current time, and you named it SayTime. You'd probably want to include a method that could be called to have the time announced. If the name of this method was Announce, it could be called from VBScript using the following line of code:

```
SayTime.Announce
```

Events are things that happen while the control is running that can be used to make it take some kind of action. Going back to our previous example of the **SayTime** control, you may decide you want the time announced whenever the user clicks on it. The code to do this (by calling **SayTime**'s **Announce** method) would be contained in the control's **Click** event. When the user clicks on the control, the **Click** event is triggered, and the time is announced. The best part is that you've enhanced the functionality of your control with only a single line of code!

Enhancing Web Pages With ActiveX

Now that you have a basic idea of what ActiveX is, you're probably already thinking of ways you can use it to enhance your Web pages. If you are, that's great! But if you're having trouble visualizing how you can use ActiveX, try thinking of your Web page as a simple application. Right now, all it probably does is present information in the form of text and graphics. But if it was a Visual Basic program, you would no doubt have some kind of interaction with your users. Try to think of ways in which you can add that same interaction to your Web page, and, before you know it, you'll have many great ideas for ActiveX controls!

To illustrate the process of enhancing a normal Web page with ActiveX, let's start with a sample page and see what we can do with it. Figure 12.1 shows a regular Web page that uses only text and a few graphics to present information about some former Presidents of the United States.

Not bad as Web pages go but still pretty static and dull. Plus, there's not much interaction with the user. But let's see what we can do by adding a few ActiveX controls. Figure 12.2 displays a new version of the sample Web page using ActiveX.

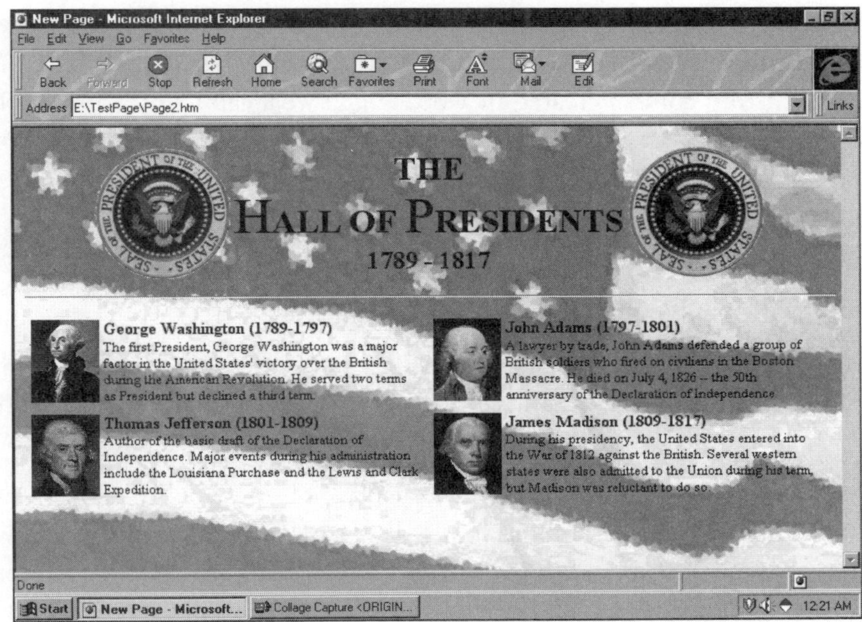

Figure 12.1
A sample Web page that uses only standard HTML.

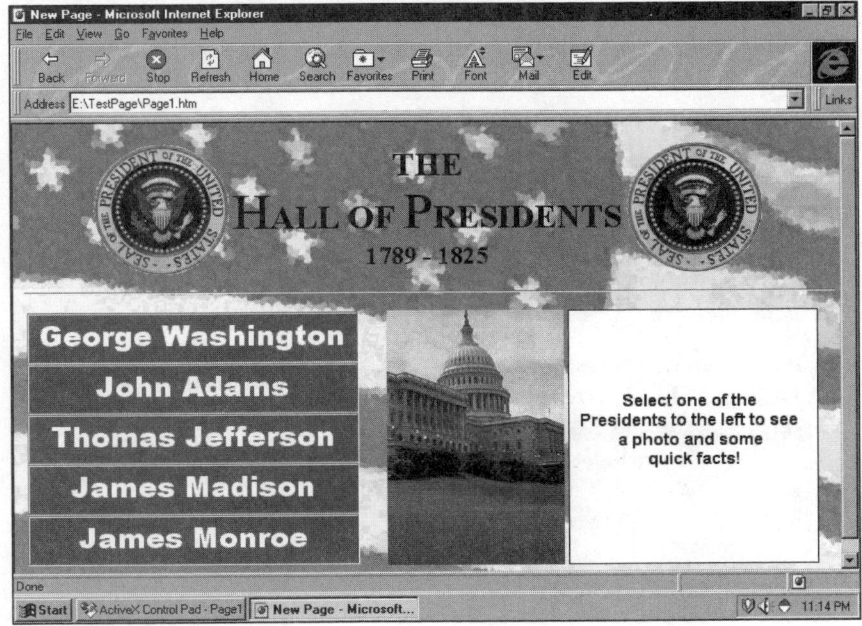

Figure 12.2
The new version of the sample Web page, greatly improved using ActiveX.

As you can see in Figure 12.2, three ActiveX controls have been added—two of which (**PictureBox** and **Text**) are standard tools from VB's toolbox. The other control, a custom control created in VB5, which we'll call ChoiceBox, appears on the page several times. Note that the control only needs to be loaded once even though there are multiple instances of the control on the page.

The Web page looks a lot nicer now, but where's all the extra interaction? Well, let's click on one of the President's names (the **ChoiceBox** controls) and see what happens (see Figure 12.3).

When the cursor is clicked on a President's name, the name becomes highlighted, a picture is displayed, and some brief data about the President is shown beside the picture. When another name is selected, different information is displayed to reflect the new choice.

Granted, this is a pretty simple example. But with only a handful of ActiveX controls, we've jazzed up an otherwise dull Web page and made it truly interactive. Perhaps this example will provide you with some inspiration in thinking up your own ideas for ActiveX controls.

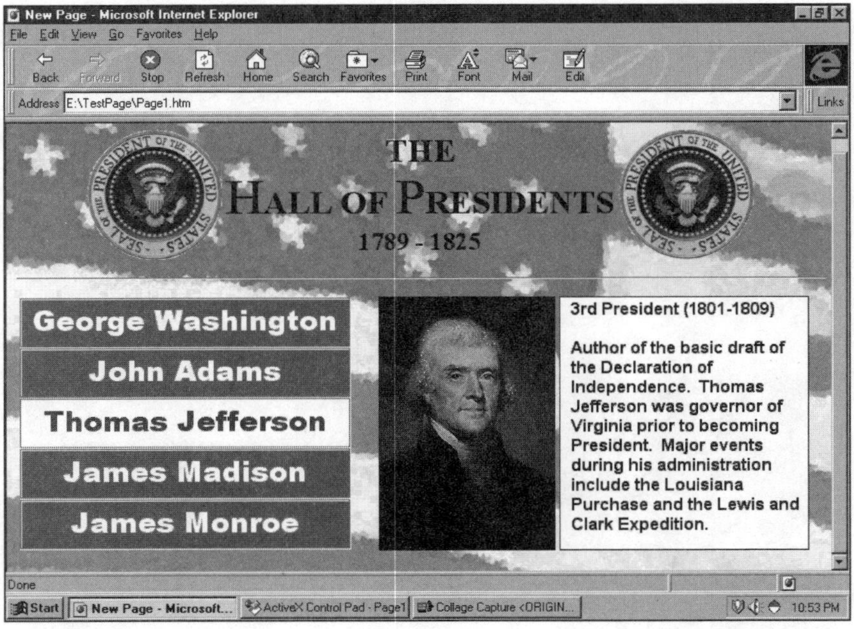

Figure 12.3
The sample Web page becomes interactive by using a few ActiveX controls.

Armed with the knowledge presented thus far, you could probably create many great ActiveX controls using VB5. But, if you add a general knowledge of COM (Component Object Model) and DCOM (Distributed Component Object Model) to your repertoire, you will be able to design much more robust ActiveX controls. It will also give you a greater insight into the underlying concepts of ActiveX.

COM And DCOM

This section provides a quick overview of COM and DCOM. It does not discuss some of the many details involved in a complex object model like COM. If you'd like to find out more about the Component Object Model and how it works, there are several excellent documents available from Microsoft that can be freely downloaded from the Internet. Their URLs are listed in Appendix B.

The Old Way Of Programming

Not too many years ago, most PC-based programs ran under DOS. They consisted mainly of a single EXE file, with all of the program code contained within. The concept of object-oriented programming or the ability to reuse objects was very new, and no means for doing so was yet available. About the best a programmer could hope for was to reuse functions and subroutines by cutting and pasting them into the code.

But it wasn't very long before object-oriented principles of programming began to take root. Code libraries, in the form of DLLs, or dynamic link libraries, were soon being used (and are still being used today). A programmer could create (or purchase) a DLL that contained several useful functions or routines. Code that called those routines would be included in a program, and the DLL could be linked to the compiled program's object module to create an EXE. This was one of the first instances of reusing code, and it worked pretty well—but it definitely had its limitations.

To begin with, DLLs could not be modified or expanded upon unless the programmer had the DLL's source code. And even if the DLL was changed for the better and had increased functionality, other applications that utilized it might not work because of the new changes. Version 2 of a DLL might not work with applications that are expecting to use Version 1.

Another problem occurred when several applications were using the same DLL simultaneously. While this wasn't much of a problem when running a program in DOS, it was a problem in multitasking environments like Windows. Even though the same DLL could be in use by multiple applications, a separate copy of the library module had to be loaded into memory for each DLL. If the DLL was 200K in size and was being used by five different applications, it would take up 1MB of memory space—this at a time when 4MB of memory was considered a lot!

Microsoft's attempt to solve these problems resulted in the development of COM, the Component Object Model. Although COM is mainly a specification of how objects are expected to interact with one another, there is some operating system-level code that is included with any OS that utilizes the COM method. This is referred to as the *COM library*, a collection of API functions and other services for facilitating its use. The first version of COM shipped with Microsoft's Windows 3.1, but it has since been implemented in Windows 95, Windows NT, and Apple Macintosh.

What Is COM?

COM is the underlying method upon which higher technologies like OLE and ActiveX are based. It provides the fundamental ability for multiple applications or software components to cooperate with one another. It doesn't matter what language the components are written in or who programmed them. It doesn't even matter if the components are running on different computers or different operating systems. COM provides an elegant way for everything to work together.

COM also promotes the concepts of object-oriented programming. Under the COM method, objects (software components) can be reused and expanded upon while still providing backward compatibility with applications that have been programmed to use previous versions.

To explain how COM works, let's take a look at a sample application (PICVIEW.EXE). The purpose of the PICVIEW program is to allow the user to view images that are in GIF87a format. To save on coding, PICVIEW's programmer utilized an object (SEEGIF.OCX) that provides the ability to decode and view GIF files. Figure 12.4 shows how COM is used to facilitate the interaction between PICVIEW.EXE and SEEGIF.OCX.

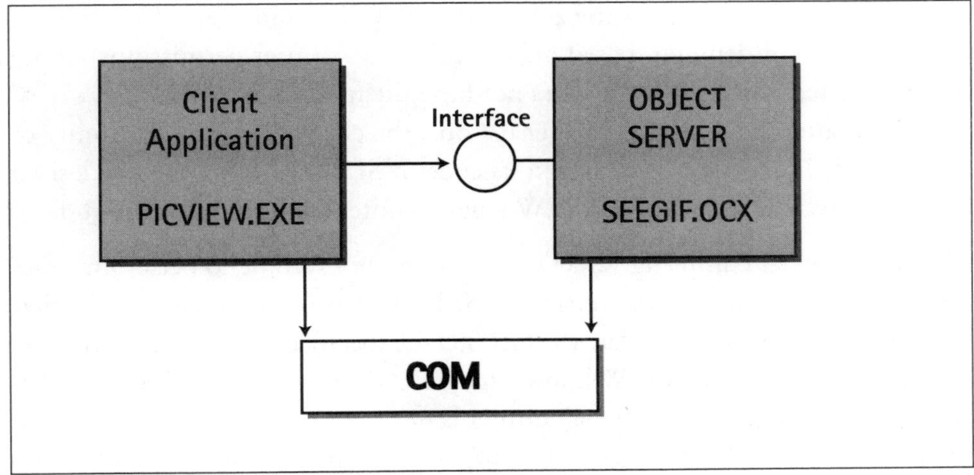

Figure 12.4
COM establishes an interface between the client application and the object server.

PICVIEW (in this case, a *client* object) does not initially interact directly with SEEGIF (an object *server*). It goes through COM first, and COM gives PICVIEW an *interface pointer* by which it can communicate with SEEGIF. Once the connection between PICVIEW and SEEGIF has been established, COM is no longer used as a middleman for communication.

All interaction between clients and object servers is done via interface pointers, and a client never has direct access to an object in its entirety. An interface is a clearly-defined contract between a client and a server that specifies how the two objects will work together.

> *Note: Although this example uses an OCX file, object servers can be several different file types, including DLLs and EXEs.*

When PICVIEW attempts to gain access to SEEGIF through COM, it is given an interface pointer to SEEGIF's IUnknown interface. All server objects have an IUnknown interface. IUnknown allows a client to do two things and two things only: partially control the lifetime of the object (using *reference counting,* which we'll go over later) and invoke the object's **QueryInterface** function.

The **QueryInterface** function allows a client to ask an object if it supports the functionality that it desires. In our example, PICVIEW would use **QueryInterface** to ask SEEGIF if it supports the ability to view GIF87a images. SEEGIF then has the option of denying (based on security issues or user permissions) or accepting the request. If SEEGIF does not have the functionality that PICVIEW needs or denies the request for other reasons, the client has the opportunity of accommodating for that situation in its code. If SEEGIF does have the desired functionality, it returns to PICVIEW a new pointer to the requested interface.

This is somewhat confusing, so let's expand on our example to better illustrate this concept. Say that a new version of SEEGIF has been released, and it has been enhanced to accommodate the GIF89a file specification as well as GIF87a. The programmer of PICVIEW knows that SEEGIF now supports both GIF87a and GIF89a images, but the programmer is not sure which version of SEEGIF the user of PICVIEW will have. The programmer would like to accommodate both versions of SEEGIF so the program will work with any version of the SEEGIF.OCX.

The PICVIEW client begins by using COM to obtain the initial interface pointer to SEEGIF, as we saw in our earlier example. It then uses SEEGIF's **QueryInterface** to see if an interface for GIF89a (SEEGIF version 2) is available. If it is, then PICVIEW knows that it can provide support for viewing GIF89a images. If an interface is not available, then PICVIEW can compensate for that in its code and support only GIF87a image formats. In effect, **QueryInterface** allows a client to be written to take advantage of as much of an object's functionality as it would ideally like to use instead of being limited to the lowest common denominator.

What happens if the user of PICVIEW obtains the new version of SEEGIF? The PICVIEW application is immediately able to provide support for GIF89a images even though the application has not been replaced or updated. And if a third version of SEEGIF comes out and the PICVIEW user obtains that also, then what happens? PICVIEW continues to work as it always has, but it does not take advantage of any of SEEGIF's new functionality—that is, at least, not until an upgrade is made to the PICVIEW program.

This brings us to the topic of *versioning*. Under COM, multiple versions of an object are contained in a single object module. Instead of changing the object's interface to accommodate newer versions, additional interfaces are added to the object. That way, a single object module can provide backward compatibility and can support multiple versions, even though one version may be drastically different from previous versions. In our example, SEEGIF.OCX contains two versions in one object module.

You may be wondering how a client knows how to identify the particular interface that it is looking for. After all, an OCX that provides the same functionality that SEEGIF does will not necessarily be called SEEGIF, and its interfaces may go by different names than those used in the SEEGIF object. So, how does a client know what is available on the current system?

Interfaces are not identified by COM using names—names are simply a programming convenience. COM uses *GUIDs* (pronounced *gwids)* exclusively to reference interfaces. A client specifies the class of an object that it requires. Locator services, which are a part of the COM library, use class identifiers to determine which server object implements the class and where on the system the object can be located. A catalog of all available GUIDs on a system can be found in the system registry in Windows 95 and Windows NT.

GUIDs are long, 128-bit integers that are used to identify every interface and every object class. Because of their size, each GUID is virtually guaranteed to be unique, even on systems or networks that contain thousands or millions of objects. If human-readable names were used rather than GUIDs, a conflict would be imminent. When the **<OBJECT>** tag is used in an HTML document, the GUID of the desired object is included in the tag.

Keeping Track Of Objects

Earlier in this chapter, we had briefly mentioned the process of reference counting. Reference counting is a way for a server object to keep track of how many clients are currently using them.

Unlike operating systems of the past, new operating systems can only load an object into memory once, no matter how many applications are using it. This solves the problem of a single object being loaded into memory multiple times and hogging valuable system resources. But, it raises another problem: How does an object know when its clients are done with it?

This is accomplished by reference counting. An object is itself responsible for keeping track of the clients that use it. It doesn't care *which* clients are using it, only how many. When a client is finished using an object, the object is notified. Once it gets to the point of no longer being used by any clients, it removes itself from memory. Problem solved! Of course, an object is reloaded whenever another client requests it, and the process starts all over again.

We've talked a lot about COM, but not much has been mentioned about DCOM (Distributed Component Object Model). What's the difference between COM and DCOM?

DCOM, Location Transparency, And ActiveX

DCOM is simply a version of COM that facilitates COM's functionality over a network. In fact, DCOM was previously referred to as *Network OLE*.

One of COM/DCOM's more interesting features is its provision for *location transparency*. *Location transparency* refers to COM/DCOM's ability to use an object in the exact same way whether it is local or not. In other words, an object server can exist on the same system that also houses its client, or it can exist on a completely separate system that is connected via a network.

With location transparency, objects may also be running in-process (in the same address space as its client) or out-of-process. No matter where an object exists—locally (either in-process or out-of-process) or on another system—COM/DCOM serves it to the client in the same way. No special coding is required by the client for using out-of-process objects.

However, there are times when an object needs to make special considerations when it is being used over a network. Usually, they are based on performance concerns. An object designer can choose to support a process called *custom marshaling* within objects. Custom marshaling lets an object take special action if it is being accessed via a network. Of course, this is all done transparently to the client, and objects do not need to support this process.

Just as OLE builds on COM to create a more sophisticated model of interaction between objects, ActiveX builds on DCOM. ActiveX uses DCOM to facilitate communication between applications (or applets) and object servers. The most important thing to remember is that ActiveX (and DCOM) allow a client to communicate with an object, no matter what programming language is used to create the object. This is ActiveX's main strength, and it's what makes ActiveX an extremely viable technology for the future of Internet- and network-based applications.

You may be wondering how ActiveX actually uses COM/DCOM to allow controls to be embedded into Web pages. How do ActiveX controls work from within a Web browser like Internet Explorer? Well—read on!

How ActiveX Works

When Internet Explorer (MSIE) loads a Web page that contains the **<OBJECT>** tag (indicating an embedded ActiveX control), it looks for the object's GUID in the system registry. Remember, it was stated earlier that the GUID of each object is included within its **<OBJECT>** tag. If MSIE finds the GUID of the object class that it's looking for, MSIE creates an instance of the object on the Web page. If the object class is not found, MSIE transfers a copy of the object to the local system. The location of the object on the Internet can be specified using a special **CodeBase** property.

It's important to note that Web pages are not like forms. They have no memory and cannot remember even simple items like property settings. Whenever a Web page is reloaded, new instances of any ActiveX controls that it contains are created.

If a Web page has no memory, then how can there be interaction between different controls? It's true that ActiveX controls wouldn't be of much use if they couldn't interact with one another in some way. This interaction is usually accomplished by using a scripting language such as VBScript or JavaScript. Internet Explorer supports both scripting languages, but Netscape Navigator currently supports only JavaScript. It is beyond the scope of this book to give detailed information about how to use VBScript with ActiveX controls.

Microsoft's Role In ActiveX

ActiveX was initially designed to have an open and cross-platform framework. It is the concept of openness that prompted Microsoft to pass along control of ActiveX to an impartial committee.

Microsoft is so committed to promoting ActiveX that it decided not to be the main body governing its further development. Instead, Microsoft has passed control to a group consisting of its customers, ISVs, and platform vendors. Microsoft is still involved as a part of the new decision-making committee, but it is no longer the sole developer of the new technology. In this way, Microsoft has greatly helped to ensure ActiveX's success. Any new decisions regarding ActiveX will be based not on Microsoft's best interests but on the best interests of the computer industry in general.

Summary

Microsoft's ActiveX technology is vying for the hearts and wallets of developers and Internet users alike with its enhanced functionality for Web pages, and back end server extensions. ActiveX brings this extended feature set at the expense of a more complex environment that is in direct competition to Sun Microsystems' Java and JavaBeans. While each have their respective developer followings, it remains to be seen just how important the users judge such feature sets. However, Microsoft is betting the farm that you'll appreciate and demand ActiveX on your Web server plate for the future.

13 The Power of Scripting

Marshall Copeland

It's time to dig in and create your own Web pages, and I'll take you through all the steps that are required to make your Web site both useful and easy to use. I'm assuming that you know the basics of Hypertext Markup Language, or HTML, which is the basic language for all Web pages. In this chapter I'll explain how to create forms, using CGI and VB4 scripting, so that you can interact with the people who are reading your pages. Forms can provide a vital link between you and your customers.

A myriad of tools are waiting on the Internet to assist you in building your Web pages and to get your Web site up and running quickly. With all these tools it's possible for you to build Web pages and forms without ever laying an eye on the HTML code in raw form. And there are even tools that help you create the forms themselves, like Form-Gen or WebSite's HotDog, all without your having to learn scripting. But you guys are past that, right? You can't wait to get your hands dirty.

And that's just what we're going to do. We're going to be covering HTML, forms, and CGI to create complete applications without the aid of helper tools. Don't get me wrong; these tools are important and can be used to speed up your Web site production, but they may also limit your page design capabilities.

Always be on the lookout for new ideas; and the best place to find them is right in your own backyard. Let's face it, we can get a lot of good ideas for our Web site by surfing the Internet and noting how other sites are constructed. You can take new information and incorporate it into your own applications and improve on an existing design. (Unfortunately, not all of the new techniques we see on the Internet can be used on a Web site.) Keep in mind how your Web site appears and is used by your staff, as well as your customers. Your Web site should be designed with an audience in mind—Internet or intranet—and how they connect should be of consideration. Modem connections from the sales staff in another state or the casual connection from a home user will have a much slower response time than a high-speed business, government, or university connection.

So without any further delay, roll up your sleeves and let's do a little catching up with our not-so-distant past and present technology.

Getting Your Bearings

The Internet has been defined and described in a vast number of ways. You can call it the Net, Internet, Web, WWW, W3, World Wide Web, the Net of networks, or whatever else you want. When it comes right down to it, the Internet is most simply and best defined as, "The world's largest and most up-to-date multimedia encyclopedia." And you never have to buy the new version like you did with the old World Books. The Internet is a complete wealth of information on subjects ranging from technology to movies and everything in between. The real challenge of today's technology is finding or generating the information and providing better management solutions. How are we able to see, not to mention *use*, so many different information pages, business applications, and useful Web sites?

The Internet is built upon different existing protocols, as well as future technologies. It may help to remember that a protocol is simply a set of standard instructions; it is not machine, nor is it platform specific. Let's get a few specifics on the table. The HTML pages are transported using the HTTP (Hypertext Transfer Protocol) of the Web site. The CGI (Common Gateway Interface) is a method used by the HTTP to transfer information to and from a Web site and to make extensive use of the resources available at that site. The end user (customer, client, or staff) uses their Web browser to see your Web pages and request specific information. Your Web server receives the request through the HTTP that then passes it to/through the CGI to process the information through the necessary applications. That's a lot of information moving about, but it really isn't as confusing as it sounds. Take a look at Figure 13.1 and you'll see what I mean.

Don't confuse the protocol transfer method, HTTP, with the page layout language of HTML. HTML coding is possible because it is an application of SGML (Standard Generalized Markup Language).

SGML is an international standard used for definitions of devices, systems, and electronic text applications. It was designed to help define a form of language

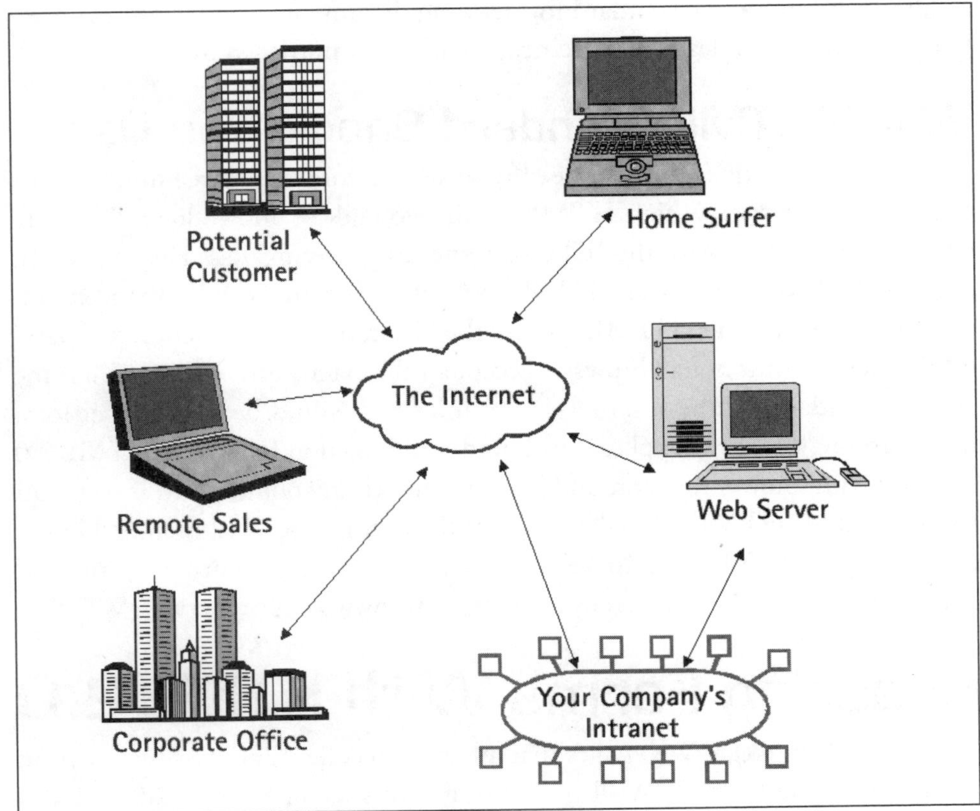

Figure 13.1
A pictorial representation of an Internet/intranet process.

description or a description of each document part. The interpretation of the descriptors and the appearance of the document is handled by the browser. Today, markup is sometimes referred to as *encoding*, which is a way of presenting a body of text in a specific format. SGML was originally designed to allow someone else to read your SGML application and vice-versa. SGML even has an ISO (International Standards Organization) designation: ISO-8879-1. Because of this standardization, many institutions—sectors of U.S. government and industries—have adopted SGML as a standard in their document construction. To find out more about SGML take a look at the SoftQuad sponsored page at **http://www.sil.org/sgml/sgml.html**.

A descriptive markup language uses codes, or *tags*, to describe the document elements to a browser. The description allows the browser to display documents differently without changing the original content. Because SGML has become an almost international standard for defining documents, it was used to create HTML, which was designed specifically with the Internet in mind.

Which HTML Standard Should You Use?

There's one more question you need to answer before you start building your company's Web site: Which HTML should you adopt and follow? There are currently three standards: the IETF (Internet Engineering Task Force) HTML 2.0, the WWW Consortium HTML 3.0, and Netscape's 3.0 enhancement. The not-yet-established HTML 3.0 and the Netscape enhancements offer powerful functions, but not all browsers accept all the extensions. HTML 2.0 is the current standard for the Internet community and would be the safe bet for a new Web site. All of the applications found in this section follow the HTML 2.0 standard with some of the more advanced features clearly pointed out. If you want to get a feel for HTML 2.0, take a look at the example tutorial included in the accompanying CD-ROM. To keep yourself abreast of the current status and features of HTML 3.0, surf on over to **http://www.w3.org/hypertext/WWW/**.

Creating Forms With HTML 2.0

In a nutshell, *forms* are Web pages that are used to collect and pass information to and from the browser. We'll be creating forms using HTML 2.0 and also using Visual Basic 4.0 (but we'll hold off on that portion until a bit later in the chapter). By now, you are probably familiar with most of the basic elements (or tags) of HTML 2.0. However, before we proceed, take a look at Listing 13.1, which shows the basic structure of an HTML 2.0 document. To be able to use the Internet and your Web site you will need to be able to read and write HTML.

Listing 13.1 Required components of the standard HTML document.

```
<HTML>
<HEAD> Title on the WWW Browser </HEAD>
<BODY>
The Information
and
Really Cool Stuff
</BODY>
</HTML>
```

There are only three necessary sections to an HTML document: the declaration (**<HTML> ... </HTML>**), head (**<HEAD> ... </HEAD>**), and body (**<BODY> ... </BODY>**). Notice that two tags are required for each section, an opening **<TAG>** and closing **</TAG>**.

Understanding How Forms Work

Web pages can do more than simply provide a one-way flow of information. As I mentioned earlier, Web pages can be designed to collect and pass information to and from the browser using forms. Forms pass information to a Web site using an *action statement* that specifies the name of the program that will process the form's information. Forms also include a *method attribute* to specify how the data requested in the form is sent back to the program. The two methods are **GET** and **POST**. The **GET** method is the default value for the method attribute. The syntax is:

```
<FORM METHOD=how_to_send ACTION=where_to_send>
```

Unfortunately, the **GET** method will choke if too much data is submitted at one time (more than a few hundred bytes). This situation happens because the server is passing the data to the form-processing program via a shell command line, which has a fixed length. This problem does not exist with the **POST** method. We'll explore this in detail later on.

Designing A Form

Let's begin by designing a useful form that is simple to construct and understand. We will be able to view the form with our browser, as shown in Figure 13.2, to see if our formatting is correct. Later in the chapter we'll change the form to collect information for our Web site database using Visual Basic 4.0.

This is what we would like our customers to see when they take a look at our home page on the Internet. Keep in mind that this is just the first example of a form and it does not have all the bells and whistles of hidden images and background images, *yet*! We will take an in-depth look at form construction in Chapter 14, but for now, this explanation should suffice. Listing 13.2 shows the HTML code used to generate the form from Figure 13.2.

Listing 13.2 HTML script for our Guest Book example.

```
<!--  GUEST BOOK Example --!>
<HTML>
<HEAD>
<TITLE>Create / Maintain an NT Server </TITLE></HEAD>
<BODY BGCOLOR = FFFFAA>
<H1> Company Guest Book </H1>
<P> If you would like to be on our mailing list, fill out all fields, then
CLICK Register:</P>
<HR>
<FORM METHOD=POST ACTION="http://WEBSERVER/cgi-win/guestbk.exe">
<PRE>
   First Name:          <INPUT  FNAME="fname">
   Last Name:           <INPUT SIZE=25 LNAME="lname">
   E-mail Address:     <INPUT SIZE=35 ENAME="email">
   Address Line 1:     <INPUT SIZE=35 ADDR1="addr1">
   Address Line 2:     <INPUT SIZE=35 ADDR2="addr2">
   City, State & Zip: <INPUT SIZE=15 CITY="city"><INPUT SIZE=2
                        STATE="state"><INPUT SIZE=5 ZIP="zip">
</PRE>
Comments ?<P>
<TEXTAREA ROWS=5 COLS=65 NAME="comments">
</TEXTAREA><BR>
<P><INPUT TYPE="submit" VALUE="Register"><BR>
<INPUT TYPE "reset" VALUE="Clear this Form"></P>
</FORM><HR>
</BODY></HTML>
```

Forms are not automatically set apart from the rest of a document. Try using the <HR> (horizontal rule) tag before and after a form to cleanly differentiate it from surrounding text and/or other forms.

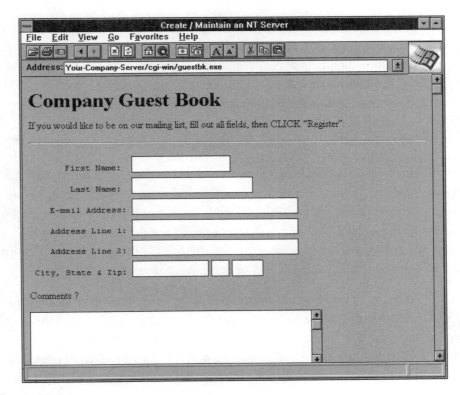

Figure 13.2
Our Guest Book example viewed through Netscape.

Let's take a close look at the HTML script for our Guest Book example. We'll begin with the standard header information, which is followed by the line:

```
<FORM METHOD=POST ACTION="http://WEBSERVER/cgi-win/guestbk.exe">
```

The **<FORM>** tag is an action tag that uses the **POST** method to send the information to the URL **http://WEBSERVER/cgi-win/guestbk.exe**. Because we are writing programs in Visual Basic 4.0 (32 bit) to run in a Windows environment, the program that processes the information the **FORM POST** statement sends is stored in the CGI-WIN subdirectory. The program that will process all of the information from our guest book HTML form is titled guestbk.exe.

Because these programs were written for WebSite v1.1, which creates and sets up the CGI-WIN subdirectory, we can't just create this subdirectory with the File Manager and expect it to work. This is true with all of the server software that can be used for your Web site—specific directories are created for specific CGI programs. We are writing programs in Windows (32 bit) environment, so all of our programs will be saved into the CGI-WIN subdirectory. If you have questions please refer to the help files inside the 60 Day Test Drive of WebSite ver. 1.1(which you can download for free from **http://website.ora.com**) or the manual if you purchased the product.

The **<PRE>** tag is used because we want the text and input boxes to line up in a specific format. The next line uses an **<INPUT>** tag to place the user's information into the field "fname", which will be used to hold the value of the First Name. On the **<INPUT>** tag for fname we used the default box character size, but in the following lines of code we set the **SIZE** option. This is because a person's last name and address tend to need more input space.

Your first priority in designing a Web page is to make it easy for the casual surfer to use. Long gone are the days when we designed the program and made the user learn our software. Just remember, if your Web site is difficult to use, no one will use it! And word *does* get around.

The next line sets **SIZE** to 25 to give our input box a longer look than the previous line. The browser takes care of the characters that the user enters; if they exceed the length of the input box the browser scrolls to accommodate the additional text. The same is true for the **<TEXTAREA>** tag; we set the input size for columns and rows to make it easier for the user. The **<TEXTAREA>** tag is used to record any comments the user wants to make at the bottom of the form. Each **<INPUT>** tag takes the user's information and places it into the corresponding field, such as "fname" for their first name, "ename" for their email address, etc. The information is then sent to the Web site with the following lines:

```
<P><INPUT TYPE="submit" VALUE="Register"><BR>

<INPUT TYPE "reset" VALUE="Clear this Form"></P>
```

We use the first **<INPUT>** tag above to allow the user to send the information in our form back to the Web browser specified in the **<FORM POST>** statement. A Register button is provided on the HTML page to start the **POST** process and pass all of the information the user has input into each option. Yes, we could instead use an image for the user to click on, but we won't get to that until Chapter 14. The next line is used to clear or reset all of the inputs the user has entered on the HTML page.

This type of form is a standalone HTML document and could be linked from the Web site home page using the hyperlink anchor like this:

```
<A HREF="http://WEBSERVER/home_docs_dir/guestbk.htm"> Enter our
  Guest Book </A>
```

The form shown back in Figure 13.2 would be sent to the browser making the request, and the information would then be routed to the Visual Basic program we wrote to process the data. We could generate the form "on-the-fly" by adding the same script into our Visual Basic 4.0 program.

Understanding Form Tags

To create quality forms that work, you need to have a solid understanding of the HTML code you'll need to use. Inside a form you can have anything except another form. Once you've created a form using the <FORM> tag, you can then specify elements of the form using the <INPUT>, <SELECT>, and <TEXTAREA> tags.

The <FORM> Tag

Let's begin with an example of a <FORM> statement:

```
<FORM ACTION="URL" METHOD=POST>
```

The <FORM> tag specifies a fill-out form within an HTML document. More than one fill-out form can be in a single document, but forms cannot be nested. Let's take a look at the attributes of <FORM>:

- **ACTION** is the URL of the query server to which the form contents will be submitted; if this attribute is absent, then the current document URL will be used.
- **METHOD** is the method (either **GET** or **POST**) used to submit the fill-out form to a query server. Which method you use depends on your server, but I strongly recommend using POST.

- **GET** is the default method and causes the fill-out form contents to be appended to the URL as if they were a normal query. When the user presses the submit button on a form when the **GET** method is used, the contents of the form will be assembled into a query URL that looks like this:

  ```
  action?name=value&name=value&name=value
  ```

- **POST** causes the fill-out form contents to be sent to the server in a data body rather than as part of the URL. The contents of the form are encoded exactly as with the **GET** method, but rather than appending them to the URL specified by the form's **ACTION** attribute as a query, the contents are sent in a data block as part of the **POST** operation. The **ACTION** attribute (if any) is the URL to which the data block is **POST**ed.

The <INPUT> Tag

Inside the **<FORM> ... </FORM>** tags, any number of **<INPUT>** tags are allowed, mixed with other HTML elements (including **<SELECT>** and **<TEXTAREA>**) and text. The **<INPUT>** tag is used to specify a simple input element inside a form. It is a standalone tag; it does not surround anything and there is no terminating tag. **<INPUT>** tags have many attributes, most of which we referenced in Listing 13.2. Let's take a closer look at the attributes for this tag. All of the attributes in the **<INPUT>** tag are shown in the following line:

```
<INPUT TYPE="text|password|checkbox|radio|submit|reset" NAME="symbolic
  name" VALUE="on|off or name on button" CHECKED(use only if box should be
  checked) SIZE="number" MAXLENGTH="maximum number of characters accepted">
```

- **TYPE** indicates the type of input you are requesting on the form. **TYPE** can be any of the following:
  - text—Text entry field; this is the default.
  - password—Text entry field; entered characters are represented as asterisks.
  - checkbox—A single toggle button; on or off.
  - radio—A single toggle button; on or off.
  - submit—A button that causes the current form to be packaged up into a query URL and sent to a server.

  - reset—A button that causes the various input elements in the form to be reset to the default values (more on this in Chapter 14).

- **NAME** is the symbolic name (not the name displayed on the screen—**VALUE** or standard HTML within the program is used for that) for this input field. This must be present for all types except "submit" and "reset," because it is used in the query string that is sent to the remote server when the form is submitted.
- **VALUE** is used in a text or password entry field to specify the default value of the field. For a checkbox or a radio button, **VALUE** specifies the value of the button when it is checked (unchecked checkboxes are disregarded when submitting queries); the default value for a checkbox or radio button is on. For types submit and reset, **VALUE** can be used to specify the caption for the button.
- **CHECKED** (no value needed) specifies that this checkbox or radio button is checked by default.
- **SIZE** is the physical size of the input field in characters in text and password entry fields. If this attribute is not present, the default is 20. In our first example (Guest Book), we used both default and custom values. You can specify multiline text entry fields as **SIZE**=width, height.

The **SIZE** attribute should not be used to specify multiline text entry fields now that the **<TEXTAREA>** tag is widely used in current browser programs.

- **MAXLENGTH** is the maximum number of characters that are accepted as input in single-line text entry fields and password entry fields. If this attribute is not present, the default will be unlimited. The text entry field is assumed to scroll appropriately if **MAXLENGTH** is greater than **SIZE**.

The <SELECT> Tag

Inside <FORM> ... </FORM>, any number of <SELECT> tags are allowed. <SELECT> creates a pulldown menu of choices for the user. Unlike <INPUT>, <SELECT> has both opening and closing tags. Inside <SELECT>, only a sequence of <OPTION> tags, each followed by an arbitrary amount of plain text (no HTML), are allowed. Listing 13.7 shows how to use the <SELECT> tag properly.

Listing 13.7 Using the <SELECT> tag.

```
<SELECT NAME="my select menu">
<OPTION> First option.
<OPTION> Second option.
</SELECT>
```

Let's take a closer look at the <SELECT> tag's attributes:

- NAME is the symbolic name for this element, and must be present because it is used in the query string for the submitted form.
- SIZE if SIZE is 1, or if the SIZE attribute is missing, SELECT will be represented as an option menu. If SIZE is 2 or more, then <SELECT> will be represented as a scrolled list with the value of SIZE determining how many items will be visible.
- MULTIPLE specifies that the <SELECT>tag should allow multiple selections. The presence of MULTIPLE forces the pulldown menu to be represented as a scrolled list, regardless of the value of SIZE.

The <OPTION> Tag

The attribute for <OPTION> is SELECTED, which specifies that this option is selected by default. In some instances, multiple options can be specified as being selected.

The <TEXTAREA> Tag

The <TEXTAREA> tag is used to place a multiline text entry field with optional default contents in a fill-out form. The <TEXTAREA> element requires both an opening and a closing tag. A <TEXTAREA> tag with no default contents looks like this:

```
<TEXTAREA NAME="Text Here" ROWS=4 COLS=40></TEXTAREA>
```

A <TEXTAREA> tag with default contents looks like this:

```
<TEXTAREA NAME="Text Here" ROWS=4 COLS=40>
Default contents go here.
</TEXTAREA>
```

Let's take a closer look at the attributes for <TEXTAREA>:

- **NAME** is the symbolic name of the text entry field.
- **ROWS** is the number of rows (vertical height in characters) of the text entry field.
- **COLS** is the number of columns (horizontal width in characters) of the text entry field.

<TEXTAREA> fields automatically have scrollbars; any amount of text can be entered in them.

Using Visual Basic 4.0 To Generate A Form And Process The Information

You should have already installed Visual Basic 4.0 (VB4) using the 32-bit option, so let's start it now. Open the File menu and use the Remove File option to remove FORM1 from our program, temporarily. Because we are writing this VB4 program for a server using WebSite v1.1, we have to add the CGI framework to our program. WebSite comes with a set of routines called the *framework model* that takes care of most of the interface work. This module handles communication between the browser and server software for us. Open the File menu, select Add File, and select cgi32.bas from the WebSite\cgi-src subdirectory.

This framework module defines the main routine for your CGI program and defines the variables to use. It also defines a number of functions with error handling and establishes a global exception handler to catch runtime errors and produce browser error messages that can be used to debug your program. I suggest you take some time to look at the routines in the framework module so you can get a better understanding of some of the CGI variables and utility routines. Table 13.1 shows some of the more common variables.

Most of the variables have intuitive names. And, as I'm sure you can tell, these variables can come in pretty handy. If the browser sends us information back in a form, we may want to gather some demographic information to use for our Web site design. Remember, a system administrator's work is never done! For example, it might be useful to file away the number of times a browser from a

TABLE 13.1

SOME COMMON VARIABLES IN WEBSITE'S CGI FRAMEWORK.

Variable Name	Description
CGI_ServerSoftware	Version of the server HTTP.
CGI_ServerName	Server's network host name.
CGI_ServerAdmin	Email of the server's administrator.
CGI_Version	Version of CGI spoken.
CGI_RequestMethod	Method is POST or GET.
CGI_RequestKeepAlive	Client connection reused (yes/no).
CGI_Referrer	URL of the referring document.
CGI_From	Email of the browser (if set).
CGI_UserAgent	Browses software of the "surfer".
CGI_RemoteHost	Browser's network host name.
CGI_RemoteAddr	Browser's network address.
CGI_AuthUser	User's name.
CGI_AuthPass	User's password.

sub-Net address comes into our Web site. We can get information from that browser and the user to help better construct our server.

The cgi32.bas module also has a large array of utility functions that we can use in building our Internet/intranet Web site. Table 13.2 lists the more common functions.

The utility functions all use the syntax name = value, where the value is passed into the name provided in the form and in the VB4 program. In our first form example, we get the email address sent to our program from the <INPUT> tag that saved the value in the variable email. In VB4, the code to accomplish this task looks like this:

```
sEmail = GetSmallField("email")
```

It is good programming practice to use names that have meaning and also adhere to the standard naming convention recommended for VB4 functions and routines (refer to your Visual Basic users manual).

Table 13.2

Some common utility functions in WebSite's CGI framework.

Function Name	Description
GetSmallField()	Retrieves the contents of a named <FORM> field.
FieldPresent()	Tests for a preset value (used in checkboxes).
Send()	Sends the "string" to be spooled (back to the browser).

There are a few things we need to do before we can turn our HTML code into VB "script" that can be inserted into VB4 code. Open the Insert menu and select Module, which will allow us to write some routines. We'll begin with the CGI_Main routine, shown in Listing 13.3, which is called by the CGI framework to check if the CGI request is passing information to be processed or requesting that an HTML form page be generated.

Listing 13.3 CGI_Main.

```
Sub CGI_Main()

 If CGI_RequestMethod = "POST" Then
        Enter_Data
    Else
        Send_Form
    End If

End Sub
```

The first line of code does a check to see if the request method was from a <FORM ACTION=POST> tag. If it was, then we have data that we need to process and we call a routine called Enter_Data (more on this routine in a bit). If the request method is null or empty, then the program was called from inside an HTML document and we need to generate a form and send it to the requester via Send_Form. The coding for Send_Form is shown in Listing 13.4.

Listing 13.4 The Send_Form routine that uses coded script to produce the HTML form.

```
Sub Send_Form

Send ("Content-Type : text/html")

Send ("")
```

```
Send ("<HTML><HEAD><TITLE>Create / Maintain an NT Server </TITLE></HEAD>")

Send ("<BODY><H1> Company Guest Book </H1>")

Send ("<P> If you would like to be on our mailing list, fill out all _
      fields, then CLICK "Register":</P>")

Send ("<HR><FORM METHOD=POST ACTION=""http://WEBSERVER/cgi-win/ _
      guestbk.exe""><PRE>")

Send ("        First Name:  <INPUT  FNAME=""fname"">")

Send ("         Last Name:  <INPUT SIZE=25 LNAME=""lname"">")

Send ("     E-mail Address: <INPUT SIZE=35 NAME=""email"">")

Send ("     Address Line 1: <INPUT SIZE=35 ADDR1=""addr1"">")

Send ("     Address Line 2: <INPUT SIZE=35 ADDR2=""addr2"">")

Send (" City, State & Zip: <INPUT SIZE=15 CITY=""city""> _
      <INPUT SIZE=2 STATE=""state""><INPUT SIZE=5   ZIP=""zip"">")

Send ("</PRE>")

Send ("Comments ?<P>")

Send ("<TEXTAREA ROWS=5 COLS=65 NAME=""comments""></TEXTAREA><BR>")

Send ("<P><INPUT TYPE=""submit"" VALUE=""Register""><BR>")

Send ("<INPUT TYPE=""reset"" VALUE=""Clear this Form""></P>")

Send ("</FORM><HR>")

Send ("</BODY></HTML>")

End Sub
```

This code is almost as simple as HTML code! Refer to the HTML form example and you'll see that the only changes we have to make include the spacing on each **<INPUT>** line so the VB coded script produces the same format for our **<INPUT>** boxes. You may also notice that I've included a space followed by an underscore on lines that continue. It looks like this: " _" (without the quotation marks, of course). This technique makes code easier to follow and read.

One other routine we need to write is Inter_Main, shown in Listing 13.5. If the CGI executable is started from the File Manager on the Web server, this routine is used to display a message indicating that the program cannot be executed in that manner.

Listing 13.5 Inter_Main.

```
Sub Inter_Main

msg = "CGI Program for Create / Maintain an NT Server"

MsgBox  msg

End Sub
```

This code will produce a simple message box that informs the user what this program is and will then exit. If this program is executed from the File Manager, the user will see the screen shown in Figure 13.3.

Figure 13.4 shows the entire guestbk.mak project. You can type the code yourself or load the program from the CD included with this book.

> *Note: For the remainder of this section, I will refer to HTML text that is sent from inside a VB4 program as coded script.*

If CGI_Main's check for the **POST** method resulted in a true value, then we need a routine to save the data into our database and route a simple "Thank You" document back to the requester. There are several different methods to use to communicate with a database. One of the simplest is to create a new form in VB4 (using Insert|Form) and then add the DataBound control to link our program with an existing database. In our example, we'll only be placing information into the database, so we won't need any other controls. Figure 13.5 shows the DataBound control on the VB4 form.

Figure 13.3
guestbk.exe executed from the File Manager on the NT Server.

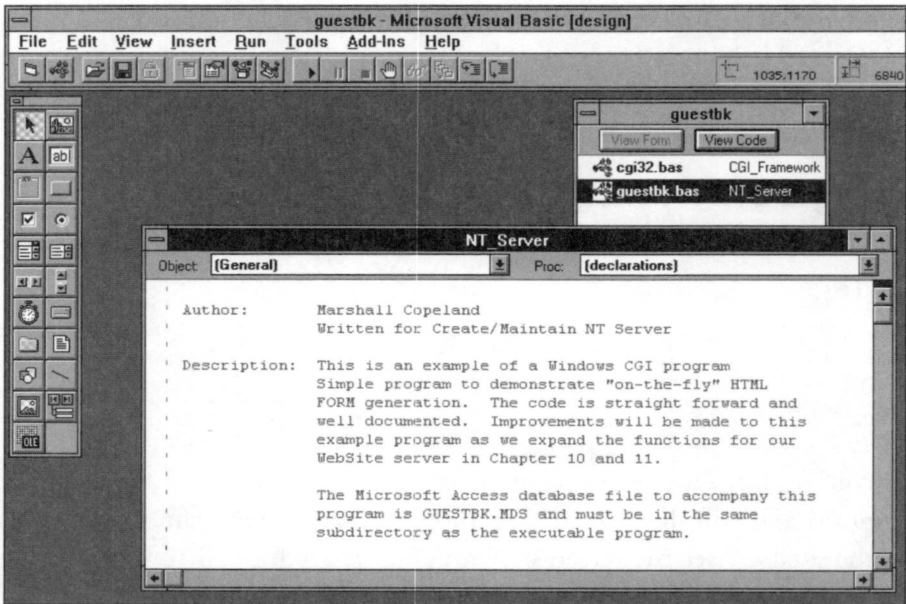

Figure 13.4
The guestbk.mak project as it appears in VB4.

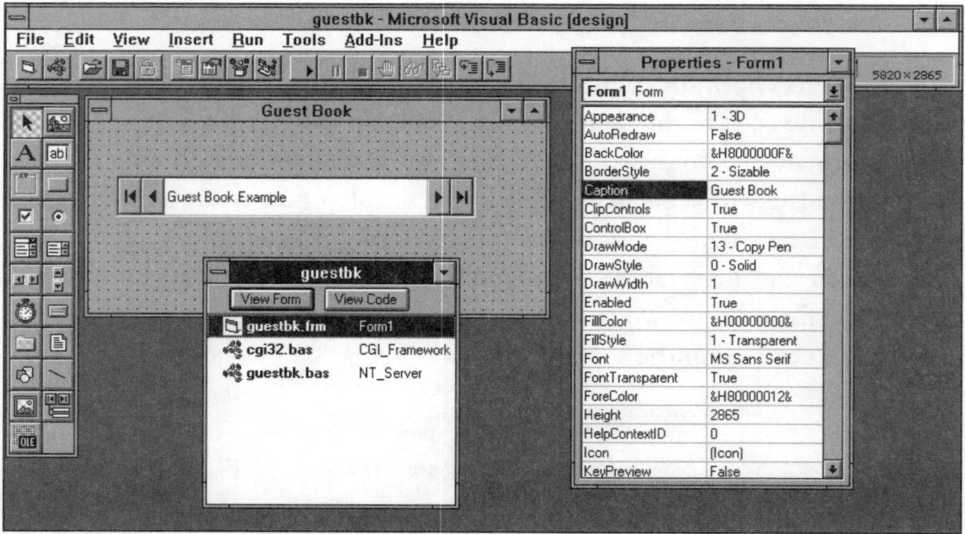

Figure 13.5
Guest Book example using a DataBound control in a VB4 form.

Using a VB4 form may not be the best solution for our task because of the length of time it takes to execute a routine or an entire program. Numerous other ways exist to add, delete, or query information in a database through VB4, but they all have their limitations, as well. Let's look at another, more elegant way that we can use a VB4 form to enter information into our database using SQL commands.

The routine Enter_Data, shown in Listing 13.6, allows us to enter information into the database without using a DataBound control, by setting up the necessary dimensions so we can read the values from the browser and prepare them for storage in our database.

Listing 13.6 Enter_Data receives data from the browsers for our database.

```
Sub Enter_Data()

'This routine stores the values passed by the
'browser software

    Dim sFname As String
    Dim sLname As String
    Dim sEmail As String
    Dim sAddr1 As String
    Dim sAddr2 As String
    Dim sCity As String
    Dim sState As String
    Dim sZip As Integer
    Dim sComments As String
    Dim sDate As String
    Dim sBrowser As String
    Dim fn As Integer

    'Since the POST command was used we can read the data
    'that is passed from the browser

    sFname = GetSmallField("fname")
    sLname = GetSmallField("lname")
    sEmail = GetSmallField("email")
    sAddr1 = GetSmallField("addr1")
    sAddr2 = GetSmallField("addr2")
    sCity = GetSmallField("city")
    sState = GetSmallField("state")
    sZip = GetSmallField("zip")
    sComments = GetSmallField("comments")

End Sub
```

This procedure collects the information passed from the browser, and stores the data into the variables that we set up for our database. We will stay with Microsoft's VB4 naming conventions by using s=String on all of the values used to store information. Keep the naming conventions understandable and logical so that you won't get confused when you use the same variables in both the VB4 coded script and the VB4 code. Our next step is to write a routine to open the database, write the record, update the database, and close the file.

Summary

This chapter has given you the necessary background to create basic interactive Web pages using HTML 2.0 and VB4. We learned that generating HTML documents inside VB4 increases the flexible services that we can offer our customers and staff from our Web server. Understanding the process of passing information to and from an Internet/intranet browser program provides you with the essentials for building powerful "back-end" programs and routines that could cross platform boundaries to accelerate your company's growth.

The next chapter continues with our discussion of forms and the use of HTML and Visual Basic. I'll provide multiple examples to demonstrate methods for receiving and interpreting users' responses, dealing with multiple forms to produce the information the client requests, and designing better user interfaces. Server programs are used to demonstrate connectivity methods with other office software, such as email, spreadsheets, and databases, and I'll explain how these methods can continue to enhance solutions for your company's Web server. You'll soon realize that the more you do to make your Web server easier for your customers/clients to use, the more your company will excel.

14 FORMS OF THE WEB

Marshall Copeland

Now that you have the basics of HTML snugly in your pocket, we can expand our discussion to in clude some of the more interesting elements currently proposed for inclusion in the HTML 3.0. Of course, you must keep in mind that the goal of your site is to serve your customers, which requires staying on top of the latest market trends. For example, Netscape has earned over $400 million in the first quarter of 1996. From this information, you can see that the Netscape browser enjoys a large market share of total Internet browser sales. Developing HTML pages, then, without considering the use of Netscape extensions could be potentially damaging to your Web site.

In this chapter, we'll take an advanced look at creating forms using HTML 3.0—including the addition of text entry and password security

Creating Forms

In this section, we'll build on your knowledge of HTML Level 2.0 to incorporate the advanced features of HTML Level 3.0 into your forms—both standalone documents and those you generate inside VB4.

As you know, we use the **<FORM>** tag inside the HTML document to submit a set of responses to a Visual Basic program or to generate the form itself. Inside the form we can have any other HTML tag—except another **<FORM>** tag—which allows us to produce a more in-depth selection of user inputs to retrieve information. We can use this information in our database to help with marketing, to help the user specifically select the query information, or both. Of course, our first priority is to understand the intricate uses of the various HTML tags so that we can design our pages to be user friendly—not intimidating or frustrating to the users. We can even design our form to request a password before access is granted to a specific section of our Web site.

Using the <SELECT> Tag

We briefly reviewed the <SELECT> tag in Chapter 13, but there are a few more uses for this tag that I'd like to cover here. We're going to build on the Guest Book form from the previous chapter; if you need to refresh your memory, refer back to Chapter 13. We're going to implement some changes to provide the user with some options. We'll begin by asking a few "marketing" questions in the form to collect information about our users.

We can provide a list of options from which the user can select one or more items. Using the **<SELECT>** tag requires the use of the **<OPTION>** "attribute" tag for each item in the list. I call it an "attribute" tag because it is used only with the **<SELECT>** tag and does *not* require a closing **</OPTION>**. As with other HTML tags, you can use the name and size arguments to define the field variable. The general syntax for creating our list of options is

```
<SELECT attributes> </SELECT>
```

where *attributes* can be:

- NAME="*VariableName*" where V*ariableName* is the name of an input field.
- SIZE=*n* where *n* is the number of options.
- MULTIPLE, which allows multiple selections using the **<OPTION>** tag.

The **<OPTION>** tag itself has several possibilities:

- <OPTION> VariableName1.
- <OPTION> VariableName2.
- <OPTION SELECTED> VariableName3; this selection is the default.

The <SELECT> tag's attributes help us not only in designing the form, but also when we pass information to the server. Because the server receives this information as raw data, we need to choose logical name variables to aid the "flow" of information. Listing 14.1 shows the <SELECT> tag added to an HTML document.

Listing 14.1 Using the <SELECT> and <OPTION> tags.

```
How did you see/hear about our Web site? <BR>
<FORM method="POST" action="http://webserver/cgi-win/PROGRAM.EXE">
<SELECT name="RequestArea">
<OPTION SELECTED>Internet
<OPTION>Magazine
<OPTION>Radio
<OPTION>Television
<OPTION>Other
</SELECT>
</FORM>
```

We provide a prompt for the user followed by a break (the **
** tag), and select the default value with the line **<OPTION SELECTED>** Internet. We could have selected any item in the list as the default, it does not have to be the first item. When viewed through a Web browser, the user will see the label, the word "Internet" in a text box, and a down arrow used to indicate more options. Figure 14.1 shows the listing as it appears in a browser.

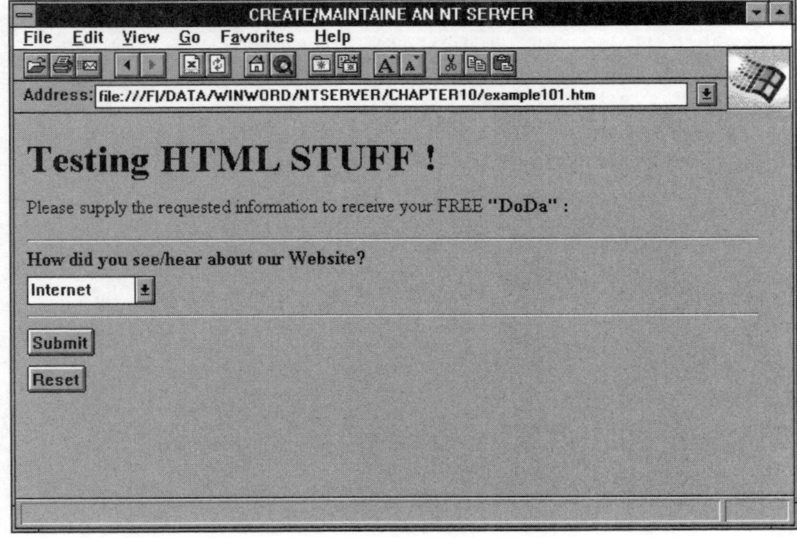

Figure 14.1
Providing multiple choices for your users by using the <SELECT> tag.

As you can see, this is a fairly straightforward form. There are a number of different variations that you can use to change the design of the form page. Let's look at one more example. We'll use the same variable names but change the "look" by using more attributes. The **MULTIPLE** attribute defaults to a text box that displays four variables at one time; the remaining variables can be viewed using the scroll bars. To change our form just a bit more we use the **SIZE** attribute to reduce the display of attributes to three. These modifications are shown in Listing 14.2.

Listing 14.2 Using <SELECT> with the MULTIPLE and SIZE attributes.

```
How did you see/hear about our Web site? <BR>
<FORM method="POST" action="http://webserver/cgi-win/PROGRAM.EXE">
<SELECT name="RequestArea" MULTIPLE SIZE=3>
<OPTION>Internet
<OPTION>Magazine
<OPTION>Television
<OPTION>Radio
<OPTION>Other
</SELECT>
</FORM>
```

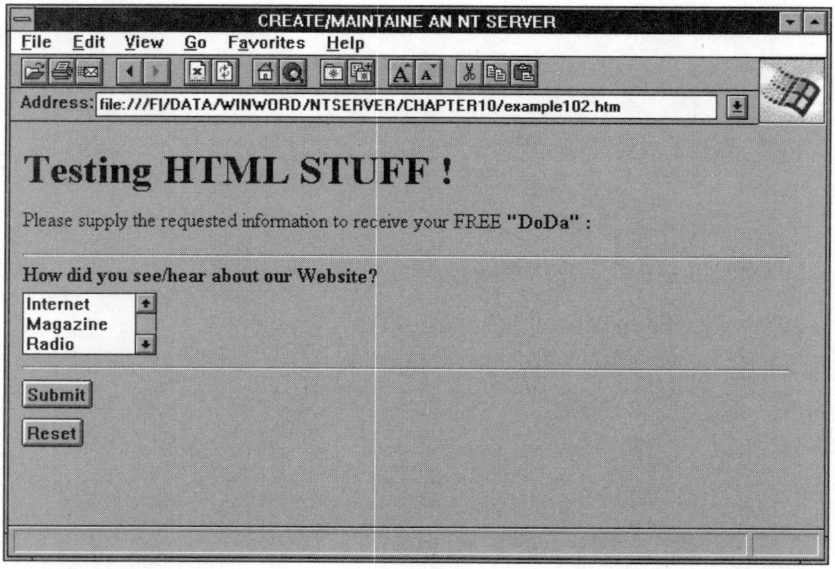

Figure 14.2
Displaying multiple options for the user.

Something to keep in mind is that when you use the **MULTIPLE** attribute you can no longer select the default variable with the **<OPTION SELECTED>** tag. This may change in the future. Figure 14.2 shows the modified form.

Adding Text-Entry Capabilities

The <TEXTAREA> tag provides you with another way to get helpful information from your users. This approach allows users to enter specific information into the form—personal information about them, or feedback about your site. The general syntax for creating a text entry option is

```
<TEXTAREA attributes> </TEXTAREA>
```

where the *attributes* can be:

- NAME="*VariableName*" where V*ariableName* is the name of an input field.
- ROWS=*n* COLS=*n* where *n* is the number of rows across and columns down; ROWS = 4 and COLS = 30 are the default values.

Listing 14.3 shows how to incorporate the <TEXTAREA> tag into your form, and Figure 14.3 shows the form with the added text-entry capability.

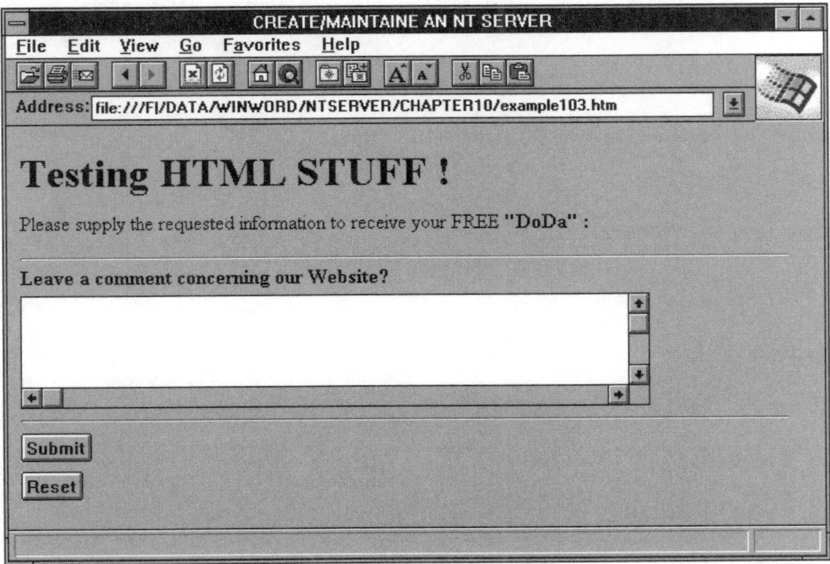

Figure 14.3
Requesting more information from users.

Listing 14.3 The <TEXTAREA> tag.

```
Leave a comment about our Web site? <BR>
<FORM method="POST" action="http://webserver/cgi-win/PROGRAM.EXE">
<TEXTAREA NAME="comment" ROW=5 COLS=70>
</TEXTAREA>
</FORM>
```

One thing you need to consider is the amount of text users will enter in this section of your form. Currently, the amount of text that can be received in the <TEXTAREA> tag is unlimited. To make sure you collect everything the user enters, be sure to define a memo field in your database to store this information with the rest of the record. Of course, our example shows only one way to use the <TEXTAREA> tag. You can use it anytime you want users to enter text.

Modifying Your Forms With <INPUT>

If you remember from our brief discussion in Chapter 13, one of the most important tags we use in our HTML form is the <INPUT> tag. It has attributes that provide us with options for text entry, security, quick response to our questions, and submitting or resetting the form. As you'll see, the <INPUT> tag is very versatile and can be used in several different sections of our form by mixing and matching the attributes. The general syntax for the <INPUT> tag is

```
<INPUT attributes>
```

where the *attributes* can be the following input types:

- TYPE=TEXT
- TYPE=CHECKBOX
- TYPE=RADIO
- TYPE=IMAGE
- TYPE=SUBMIT
- TYPE=RESET
- TYPE=PASSWORD
- TYPE=HIDDEN

The input types can be further defined by using the following attributes:

- NAME="*value*" to supply the name of the field.
- CHECKED to set defaults via checkboxes or radio buttons.
- SIZE=*n* to set the box size in characters for the TEXT attribute.
- MAXLENGTH=*n* to limit the user input TEXT attribute size.
- VALUE=default value of the field if no other is specified.

The <INPUT> tag uses variables that have a specific variable *name,* which uses a defined input field *value.* This field value must be of a specific data type that corresponds with the possible values of the field. For instance, if you used a numeric field, you wouldn't want text characters in it. One example of the <INPUT> tag can be found near the end of Listing 14.4, where the input types of mail vendors are listed.

Creating Text Fields

Single-line text fields <INPUT TYPE=TEXT> are used for entering short text strings, such as names, numbers, and dates. The visible width of the field in characters can be set with the **SIZE** attribute. The **MAXLENGTH** attribute can be used to specify the maximum number of characters permitted for the input string. If the **TYPE** attribute is missing, the <INPUT> tag is assumed to be a single-line text field. The **NAME** attribute is used to identify the field when the form's contents are converted to the NAME=*value* list.

Checkboxes And Radio Buttons

Checkboxes and radio buttons provide an alternative to using the <SELECT> tag, and provide benefits for both the end user and the server administrator. End users can select the options quickly, which is helpful to entice them to provide information to subscribe. And administrators receive far more detailed information for the profile database. The **CHECKBOX** and **RADIO** types are toggle fields; that is, they either are selected or are not selected.

The Windows environment has existing conventions for input on a form. For example, Tab and Shift+Tab are used to navigate among fields, and Enter is used to submit the form. These conventions stem from the days before the mouse became popular, and are still implemented for those users who are "rodent impaired."

Each field normally is given a distinct name. However, several **<INPUT>** tags with the **TYPE=RADIO** attribute can share the same name to specify that they belong to the same group. If you use this naming technique, understand that only one button in the group can be selected, or *active*, at one time. Unselected checkboxes and radio buttons don't appear in the submitted data, but we can initialize **CHECKBOX** to a preselected state by using the **CHECKED** attribute. Only the selected radio button in the group generates a **NAME=***value* pair in the submitted data, and both **NAME** and **VALUE** are required for radio buttons.

Listing 14.4 shows a typical form that uses menus and radio buttons to obtain data from users, and Figure 14.4 shows the form as it appears in a browser.

Listing 14.4 Using <SELECT> and <INPUT TYPE=RADIO> tags.

```
<HTML>
<!--This is a comment Field -->
<HEAD>
<TITLE>CREATE/MAINTAIN AN NT SERVER</TITLE>
</HEAD>
<BODY BGCOLOR=FFFFA0>
<H1>Testing HTML STUFF !</H1>

<FORM method="POST" action="http://WEBSERVER/cgi-win/PROGRAM.EXE">

<CENTER>
<STRONG>Choose an AREA and a DATE to "Calculate" a delivery charge for Your
  Purchase!</STRONG><BR>
</CENTER><HR NOSHADE>

<CENTER><PRE><B>AREA     MONTH     DAY</B></PRE></CENTER>

<CENTER>
<SELECT name="RequestArea">
<OPTION> Canada
<OPTION> South America
<OPTION SELECTED> North America
<OPTION> Europe
<OPTION> Asia
<OPTION> Africa
<OPTION> Japan
<OPTION> China
<OPTION> England
</SELECT>
```

```
<SELECT name="Month">
<OPTION>January
<OPTION>February
<OPTION>March
<OPTION>April
<OPTION>May
<OPTION>June
<OPTION>July
<OPTION>August
<OPTION SELECTED>September
<OPTION>October
<OPTION>November
<OPTION>December
</SELECT>

<SELECT name="Day">
<OPTION>1
<OPTION>5
<OPTION>10
<OPTION SELECTED>15
<OPTION>20
<OPTION>25
<OPTION>29
<OPTION>30
<OPTION>31
</SELECT>
</CENTER>

<HR>
<CENTER><STRONG>What Vendor would you prefer?</STRONG><BR>
<INPUT TYPE=RADIO name="MailVendor" Value=UPS>UPS
<INPUT TYPE=RADIO name="MailVendor" Value=FedEx CHECKED>FedEx
<INPUT TYPE=RADIO name="MailVendor" Value=Courier>Courier
<INPUT TYPE=RADIO name="MailVendor" Value=US Mail>U.S. Mail <BR>

<HR>
<STRONG>How would you like it Sent? </STRONG><BR>
<INPUT TYPE=RADIO name="MailSpeed" Value=Gnd>Ground
<INPUT TYPE=RADIO name="MailSpeed" Value=ON>Overnight
<INPUT TYPE=RADIO name="MailSpeed" Value=Second CHECKED>2nd Day Air

</CENTER>

<HR NOSHADE>
<INPUT TYPE=SUBMIT Value="Request Estimate">
Send your choices for an "Estimate"<BR>
<INPUT TYPE=RESET Value="Clear FORM">
```

```
Clear your "options" and try again
</P>
</BODY>
</HTML>
```

As I mentioned earlier, time is of the essence when it comes to getting users to fill in forms (and simplicity doesn't hurt either!). The **<INPUT TYPE=RADIO>** tag provides a method for making quick choices and avoids the "clutter" of drop menus used in the **<SELECT>** tag. Another way to get readers to sit up and take notice of your form is to add a little flash. This is exactly what we did with the line **<BODY BGCOLOR=FFFFA0>** at the beginning of the document. This tag statement changes the background color, which we hope will catch the users' attention. Very simple, but very effective.

Polishing Your Form Design

When it comes to attracting users, a good form relies as much on its ease of use and functionality as it does on general appearance. A professional-looking form is a form that gets responses! The Internet provides the ability for any business or

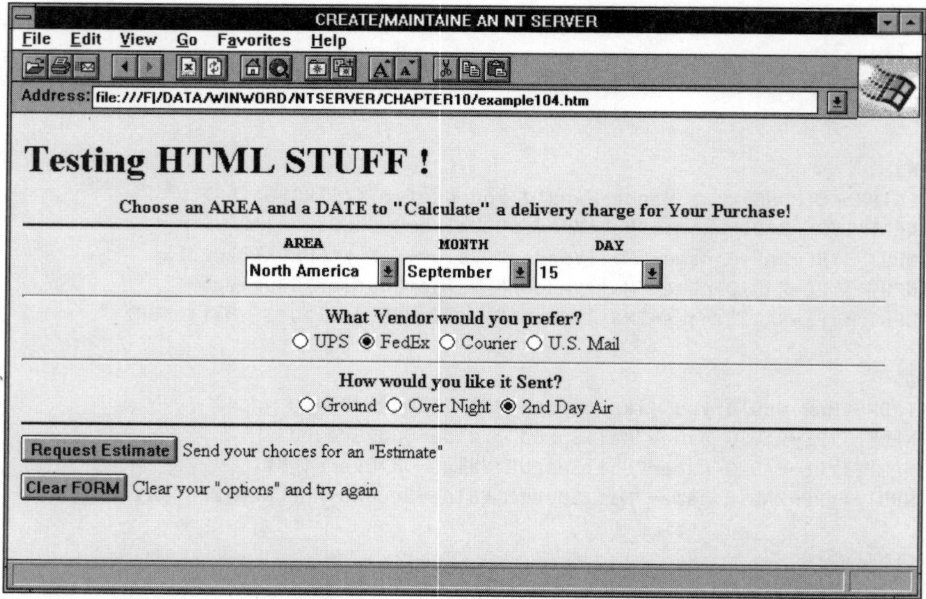

Figure 14.4
Creating a form with menus and radio buttons.

company—no matter how small—to give the appearance of a large well-established business. Your forms and other HTML documents will speak for themselves.

We're going to make a few changes to the form shown in Listing 14.4 to help in your understanding of the **<INPUT>** tag attributes and to add an artistic flair. We'll begin by adding an eye-catching image instead of the Request Estimate button to get users' attention. We'll also change the background by choosing a GIF for the **<BODY BACKGROUND="URL">** tag. These changes, shown in Listing 14.5, are simple but add a polished look to the document, as shown in Figure 14.5.

Listing 14.5 Polishing the form design.

```
<HTML>
<HEAD>
<TITLE>CREATE/MAINTAINE AN NT SERVER</TITLE>
</HEAD>
<BODY BACKGROUND=bkgnd.gif>

. . .

<HR><IMG SRC="new.gif">
<STRONG>How would you like it Sent? </STRONG><BR>

. . .

</CENTER><HR NOSHADE>
<INPUT TYPE=IMAGE  SRC="rfinger.GIF"><IMG SRC="space.gif">
Send your choices for an "Estimate"<BR>
```

Here we used a simple image for the background of the form to produce a different overall feel. The image background was made transparent so the edges would not be so apparent and also to provide a more seamless method of combining text and images in the same HTML document. We also used various small images to add color and text to the document. For example, we added the word "new" to an option by inserting the NEW.GIF image, and we replaced the Request Estimate button with an image. When the user moves the mouse pointer on top of the image, it displays the familiar hypertext link pointer to indicate an action for the image.

There are many dazzling features that you can add to your HTML documents, but many require lengthy downloads. Many sites have an option, for the users who prefer to get information quickly, that

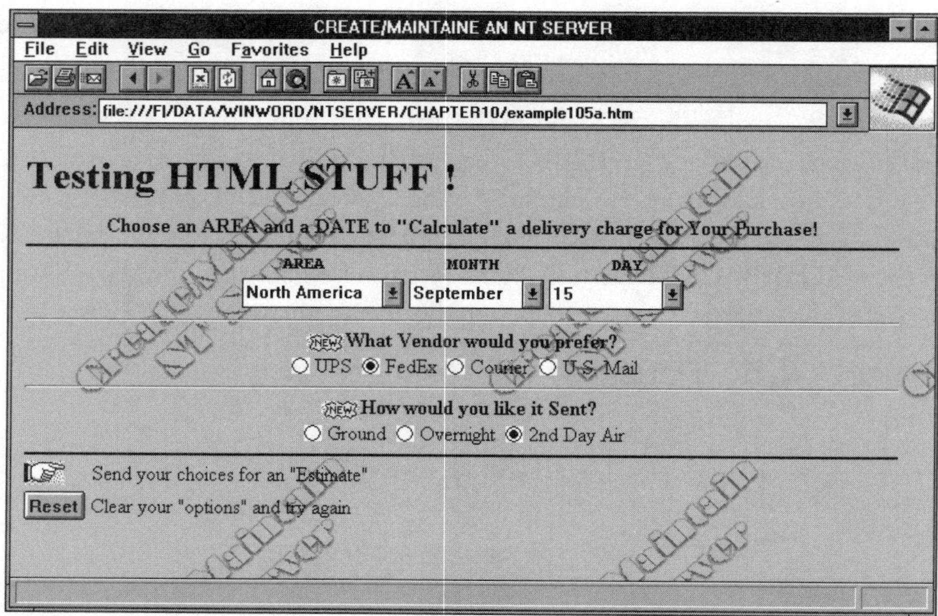

Figure 14.5
Using GIFs to create a more eye-catching form.

allows them to view text only. This option displays a duplicate set of HTML documents without all of the extras. Of course, this means you have to create two sets of HTML documents.

There are only two possible command button functions for forms: Submit and Reset (<TYPE=SUBMIT> and <TYPE=RESET>). Submit, of course, submits the contents of the form to the WebServer\cgi-win\VBprogram.exe. Reset causes the contents of the form to be reset to the default values. Each command button can use a label or a graphic to describe its function.

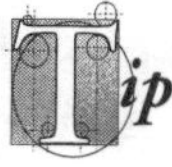

Use a small, transparent GIF image to add space in you HTML documents, or place the GIFs into an HTML table without a border. Either of these options will provide necessary spacing to produce a polished look.

Adding Security To Your Forms

Sometimes it might be necessary for a user to view sensitive information at your Web site, but you don't want everyone to have access. For example, you might want a large distributor, and not an individual buyer, to see your wholesale price list. HTML has responded to this need with the **<TYPE=PASSWORD>** attribute. This attribute restricts users from "classified" information by requiring a password to view it. Listing 14.6 and Figure 14.6 show password protection in action.

Do not let this lead you to believe that HTML security will fully handle your Web server's security issues. Any serious hacker will breach right through HTML-generated password files, so you should refer to the NT Server security manual or your Web server's manual.

Listing 14.6 Adding security to your forms.

```
<INPUT TYPE=PASSWORD name="RegistedUser" MAXLENGTH=11> <BR>
<INPUT TYPE=SUBMIT Value="Send Password">
Send your password to the server!<BR>
<INPUT TYPE=RESET Value="Clear Password">
I messed up, CLEAR and try again !
```

Here we used the **<TYPE=PASSWORD>** and **MAXLENGTH** attributes to require a password from the user. As the user enters the password, an asterisk character (*) is displayed in the text area for each character typed. The user can see how many characters have been typed but not *what* was typed.

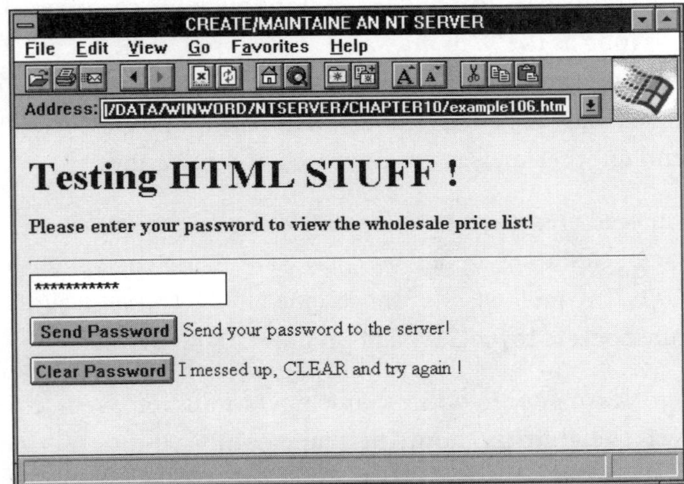

Figure 14.6
Using a password to help restrict site access.

Even though the data being entered to the password field is hidden from the user on the screen, there are no security features to protect the information when it is transferred over the Net. Therefore, the password field alone is insufficient to protect the confidentiality of private information passed over the Internet.

MAXLENGTH is set to 11 because of the old "eight-dot-three" (eight characters plus a three-letter extension) DOS filename limitation, but you can change the setting.

Controlling Access To Your Server With HTML

You can restrict access to specific documents or subdirectories on your server with an HTML form that requests a username and a password before access is granted. Your server software will dictate the type of security you can use, but most restrict through either IP connections, filters, or URLs.

WebSite 1.1 restricts users by URL (or control point). When a browser tries to access a document that is below a particular control point, the server sends a form to the Web client requesting a username and a password. If the username and password are authenticated, the information is returned to the Web browser. The username and password are needed only once for each control point. In other words, as long as the Web browser is not closed, then the access is granted once the proper username and password have been provided. Once the client software is closed and reopened or a different control point is encountered, the server will send another message requesting authentication.

If you need greater security for your Web server for functions such as credit card transactions, you may want to use encryption-based security. Two methods that are designed for high-level security are: Secure Sockets Layer (SSL) and Secure HTTP (S-HTTP).

If you want to learn more about secure operations for Web servers, try the Netscape's Web site at **http://home.netscape.com**.

Summary

Chapter 14 has supplied you with a brief overview of forms on the Web and how they can work for you. It included key topics of interest in creating forms using HTML. While the examples here may seem simplistic, they're meant to show you how much information you can generate by placing forms on your site. Whether you want simple demographic information or online ordering—simply decide what information you need from your site's users, and there's a way to receive it, using forms and HTML.

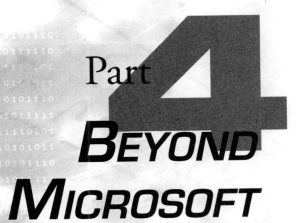

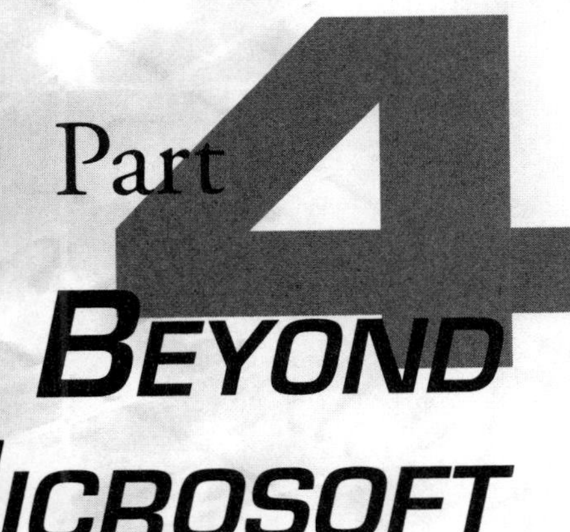
Part
4
Beyond
Microsoft

Oracle WebServer

Jeff Bankston

In Internet circles, the dominant Web servers for NT are largely regarded as Microsoft's Internet Information Server and Netscape's FastTrack. Netscape's Enterprise Web Server is a significant Web server for NT, but it's tiered for the large and complex Web sites that need the advanced features that Enterprise offers. There are many other Web servers, such as O'Reilly's WebSite and Process Corp's Purveyor Web servers, but these options are not nearly as popular as IIS or FastTrack.

To that end, Oracle Corporation has come out with, and has greatly improved upon, its own Web server in Oracle WebServer version 2.1, the current release. Web Server version 2.1 is a fully Internet-ready Web platform used to create and maintain a full Web presence. It smoothly integrates into the Oracle version 7.3 database platform that has long been the namesake of Oracle.

This chapter is about Oracle's WebServer, and how to install and run it on NT Server. Unfortunately, there isn't time nor space to show how to integrate the Web server into the database platform, but you'll find that it integrates quite well. To kick off this discussion, the upcoming section talks about procuring the Oracle WebServer. Then, as dictated by logical progression, the installation of Oracle WebServer is presented in detail.

Procuring The Oracle WebServer

You can procure the Web server from Oracle or one of its many distribution points. However, I downloaded the trial product directly from the Oracle site at **www.oracle.com/products/trial/html/trial.html**, as shown in Figure 15.1.

When you get to the Web page shown in Figure 15.1, scroll to the section on the Oracle Web Application Server (WAS) version 3. WAS version 3 is for Unix, but you'll see version 2.1 for NT Server as the last option in this section. You'll want to download version 2.1 but, at 29MB, be prepared for a lengthy wait while it downloads. You'll also be required to fill out a registration form for Oracle. The registration form serves two purposes: It gathers information for Oracle's marketing team and provides export controls for the security.

> ***Note:*** *You'll need 29MB of disk space for the archive itself and another 60MB for the extraction process, for a total of 89MB (minimum) of free disk space.*

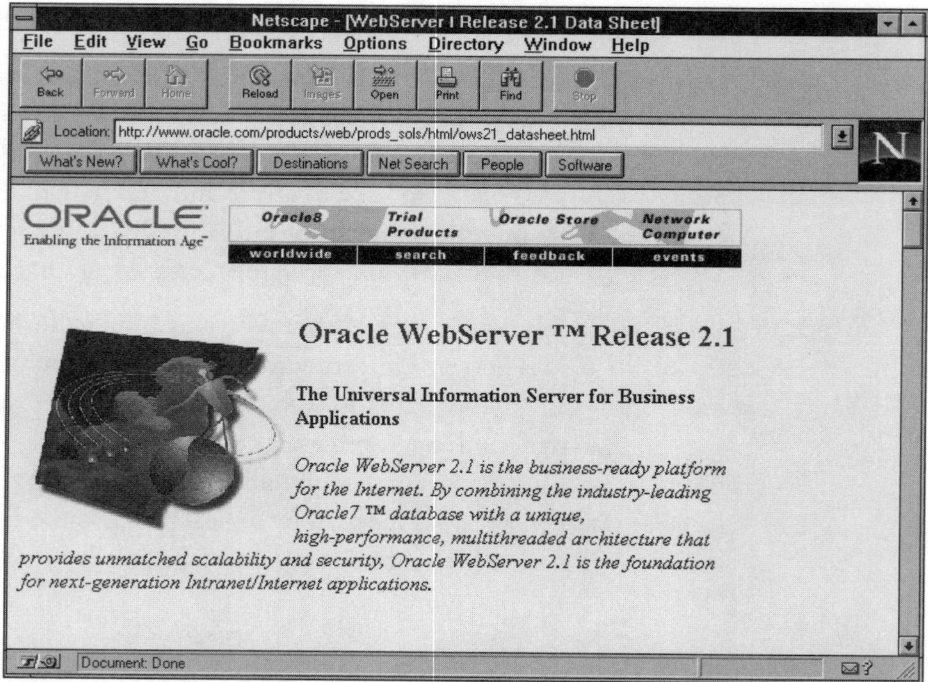

Figure 15.1
Downloading the trial version of Oracle WebServer.

Once downloaded, copy the archive to a temporary working location. From the DOS prompt, enter the name of the self-extracting file, and be sure to use the **-d** option to preserve the directory structure.

Installing Oracle's WebServer

Once the extraction process is complete, you're ready to install the software. To install the software, follow the steps presented in this section.

1. Double-click on the setup program to begin.
2. You'll have to agree to the 60-day license to continue, so click on OK.
3. Enter your company name and the destination location where you want the Web server to be installed, as shown in Figure 15.2.

If you're currently running Oracle database server, this installation will search for, and upgrade, the component parts of the Oracle database system to support the Web server. Installing the Web server will not harm an existing Oracle system, but you should ensure that all installed Listeners are turned off before proceeding. To do this, go to NT's Control panel, Services section, and stop any Oracle Listeners.

4. Choose your installation type.

Typical is used for a basic installation. The Custom setting allows you to pick and choose which parts of the Web server you want to install. I chose to perform a Custom installation. Figure 15.3 shows the optional components of the Web server that can be installed.

5. Select the components you want to install by deselecting any component(s) that you don't want installed.

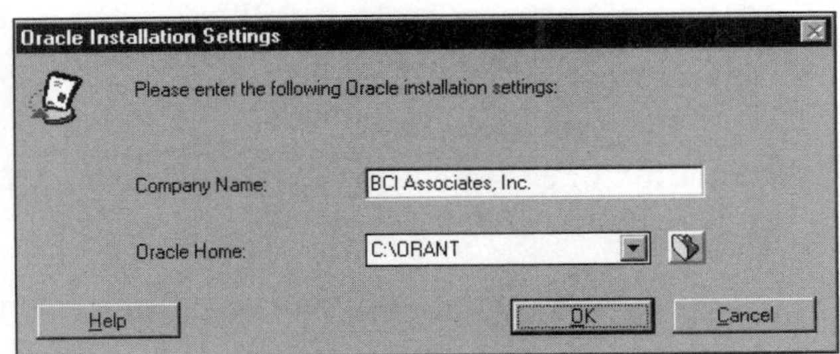

Figure 15.2
Choosing the company name and server location.

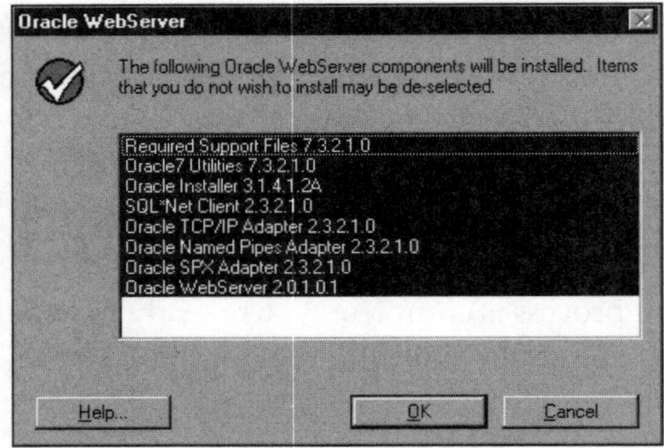

Figure 15.3
Choosing the components to install.

6. Click on OK to continue.

You might receive a version warning if you're using a current version of Oracle database system products. This warning tells you that the files being installed as part of the Web server are out of date compared to what exists in your database system. You'll see this message for all out-of-date Web server parts to be installed. Do not allow the outdated files to be written to your system. You should use your existing database system files if your files are more current than the files you downloaded. If you're not using Oracle database system files, you'll never see this message.

7. Click on OK.

Administrator's Information

You'll next be presented with a screen asking for the information for the Web server administrator.

1. Enter the Host Name, Web Listener Name, and Port Number, as shown in Figure 15.4.

Following is an explanation of each item to be entered on the screen shown in Figure 15.4:

- *Host Name*—The given name of the computer as recognized on the Internet. The host name consists of the computer's name plus the domain name, using dot notation.

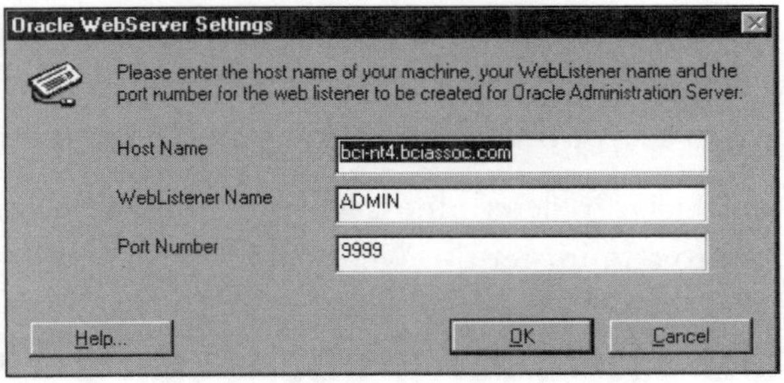

Oracle WebServer Settings

Please enter the host name of your machine, your WebListener name and the port number for the web listener to be created for Oracle Administration Server:

Host Name bci-nt4.bciassoc.com

WebListener Name ADMIN

Port Number 9999

Help... OK Cancel

Figure 15.4
Choosing the company name and server location.

- *Web Listener Name*—The Web server account name used by another application to communicate with the Web server or by a user administering the Web server.
- *Port Number*—The operating system's way to connect to, and communicate with, the Web server. Internet standards dictate certain numbers for standard ports, such as **21** for FTP or **80** for WWW. **9999** is recognized as the administrative port. You can use any port so long as it does not conflict with currently used ports, as defined in the NT Services section of Control Panel.

2. Click on OK.
3. Enter a name for the Web server administrator, complete with password.
4. Click on OK.

At this point, the installation should begin, as shown in Figure 15.5.

5. After the files have installed, click on the Accept button to agree with the terms of the licensing.

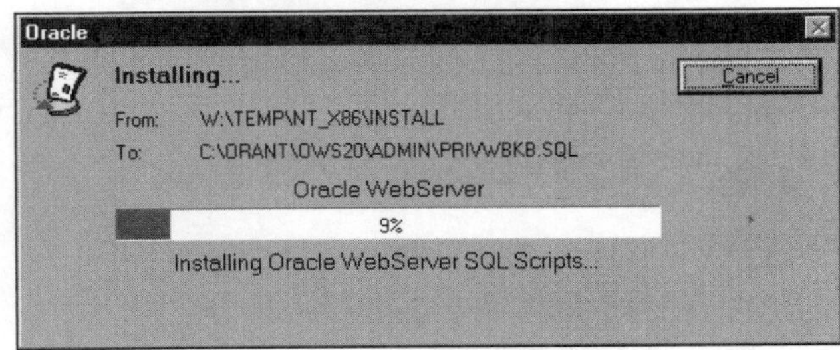

Figure 15.5
Installing the program files.

I found it rather odd to be accepting the license at this point, especially because the files are now copied to the server's disk. But regardless of when the process occurs, you'll have to accept the license if you want to use the software.

The next thing you'll have to determine is whether to use Oracle's PowerBrowser Web browsing tool to administer the Web server.

Setting Up The Administrator's Browser

In this section, we'll use the PowerBrowser Web browsing tool to administer the Web server, as shown in Figure 15.6. The generic setup is just that, and not much more. The other two setups presume your physical server has a connection to the Internet where setup information will be obtained for your new site.

1. Choose the New User Information link for the Web server, and click on OK to proceed.

Basically, this action creates a user on the Web server that you'll use for testing.

2. Enter the required information, and click on OK.

The PowerBrowser setup performs the basic configuration steps required, and then presents you with Figure 15.7, after you've entered the administrator's username and password.

This completes the basic installation. The next item on our agenda is to configure the Web server itself.

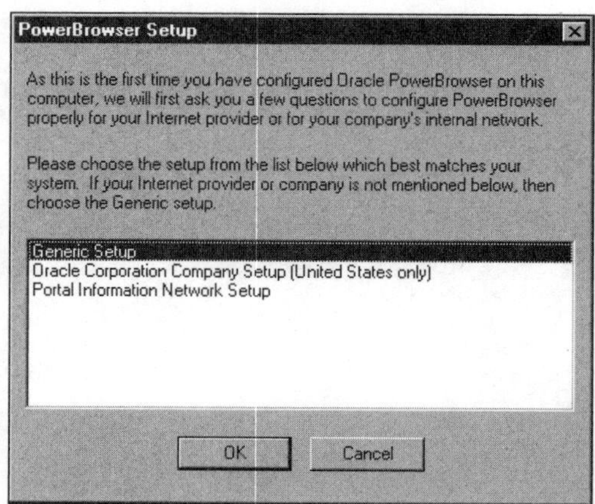

Figure 15.6
Choosing the PowerBrowser setup.

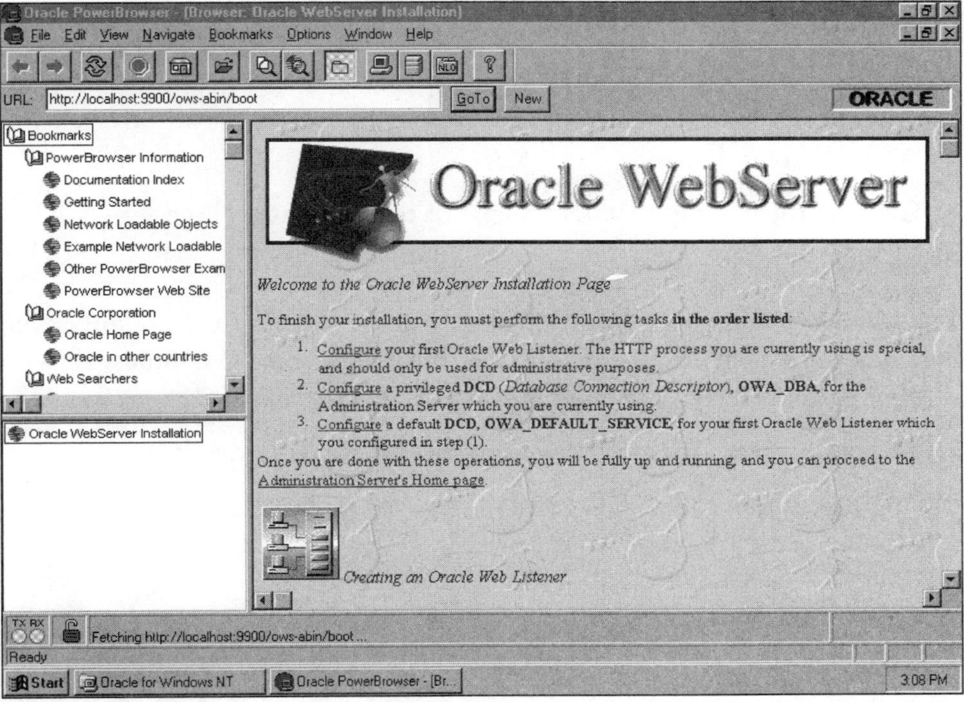

Figure 15.7
Completed PowerBrowser setup.

Configuration

Configuration consists of the three processes shown in Figure 15.7. Those processes are:

- *Configure the Web Listener for administrative use.* You'll use a Web browser to administer, change, and troubleshoot the Web server.
- *Configure a Database Administrative connection.* Even the Web Server version 2.1 (when you're not using an Oracle database system) uses a Database Administrative connection to store user information in local tables.
- *Configure a default service for the Web Listener.* This is the listener you created in the first step.

Let's complete the configuration of each of these services, one at a time.

Configuring A Web Listener For Administrative Use

You should still have the PowerBrowser open. If not, start PowerBrowser, and log in as the administrator.

1. Click on the Configure link in Step 1 of the Installation Page.
2. Enter the Listener's name.

The Listener's name must be six characters or less. In Figure 15.8, notice my host name and port are already filled in, but the port name conflicts with an existing IIS Web server. I entered *8080* to overcome this conflict.

3. Click on Create Listener after you've entered the desired text.

When this has been completed, you'll be returned to the Installation Page. Now, let's configure the Database Connection.

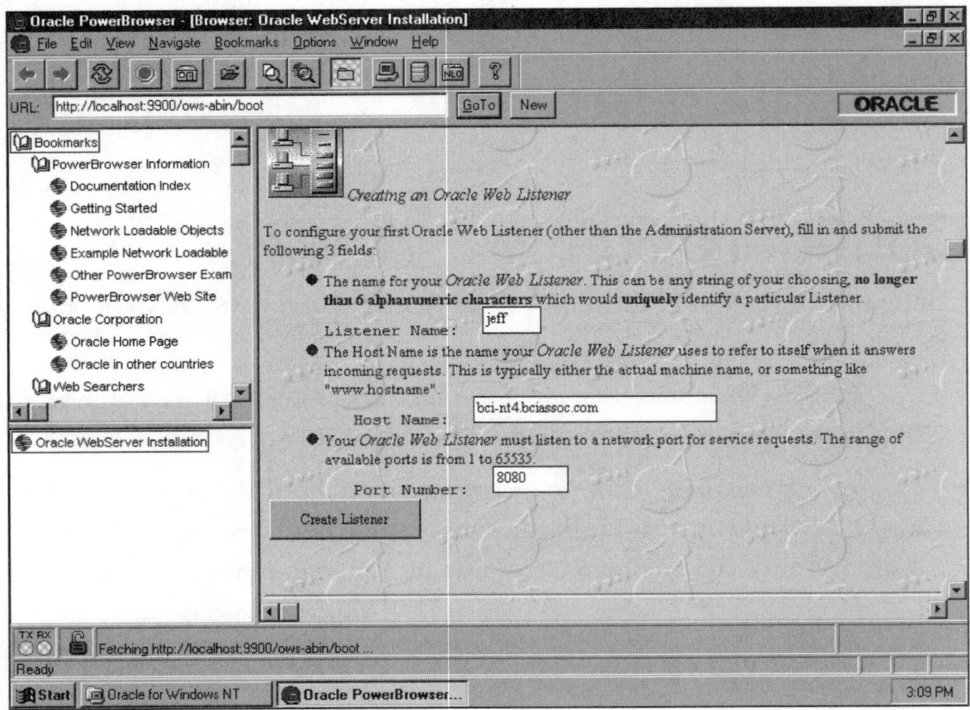

Figure 15.8
Creating the Web Listener.

Configuring The Database Administrative Connection

Follow these steps to configure the database administrative connection:

1. Click on the Configure link in Step 2 of the Installation Page.
2. Click on the OWA_DBA radio button to identify that the Database Administrative connection is being created.
3. Scroll down, and identify the Web user used for the DBA.

Notice that user WWW_DBA has been already selected as the default.

4. Enter the password you'll use for the WWW_DBA.

The home directory for Oracle is already filled in for you, but you can change it to wherever you installed the software.

5. The TCP port number will be detected for the DBA, so leave this setting alone for now.
6. For remote databases to be used with this Web server, enter the appropriate information.
7. Click on Create Listener after the information has been entered, as shown in Figure 15.9.

When the DBA connector is created, you'll be taken back to the main Installation Web page, where you'll see the word *Done* just under the step that was completed. There's one final step, and that's to create the standard default service for the Web Listener. Let's do that now.

Configuring A Default Service For The Web Listener

Follow these steps to configure a default service:

1. Click on the Configure link in Step 3 of the Installation Page.
2. You'll be taken through the same process as the DBA connection process, only this time, choose the OWA_DEFAULT_SERVICE.

Notice that the default username is WWW_USER. You can change this, if you'd like, but there's no harm done if you don't change it.

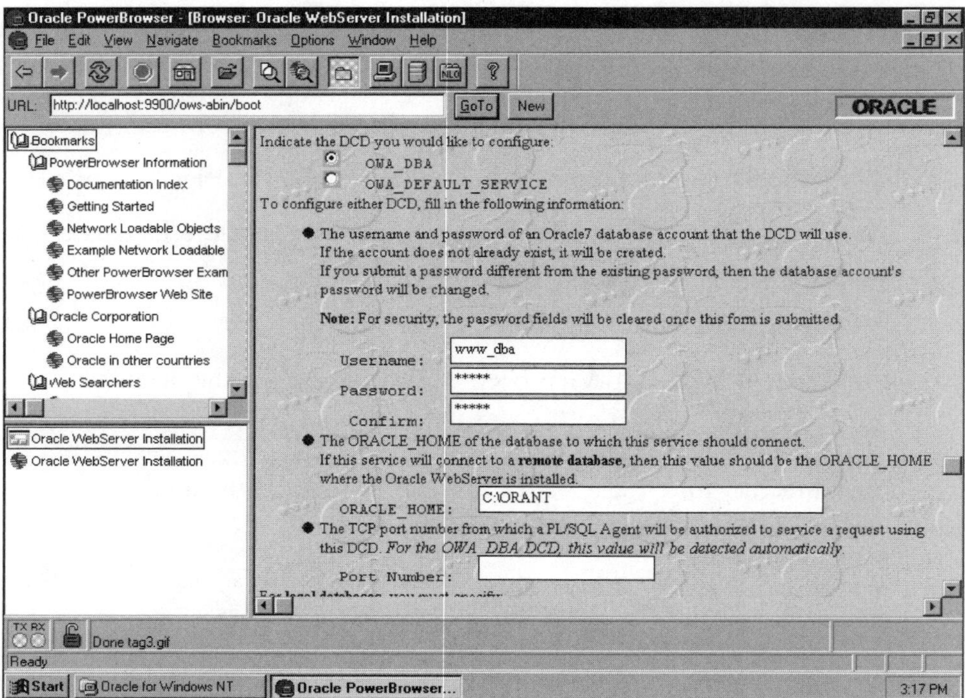

Figure 15.9
Creating the DBA Web Listener.

3. Name your default user account, and enter a password, as shown in Figure 15.10.

Notice in Figure 15.10, the port number is *8080*, which is what I indicated in my settings earlier, because I already have another Web server running on the same server. It's crucial that you remember to set the port number. If you forget to set the port number for a user, then the user will never be able to find the Web server. In addition, it's very important that you remember which port is assigned to which device.

4. If the user will access remote databases, then scroll down, and fill in the appropriate user information as per your database administrator's directions.
5. Now, click on the Create Service button at the end of the Web page to create this new service.

The service will be created, and then the new Oracle WebServer version 2.1 installation and configuration will be complete, as shown in Figure 15.11.

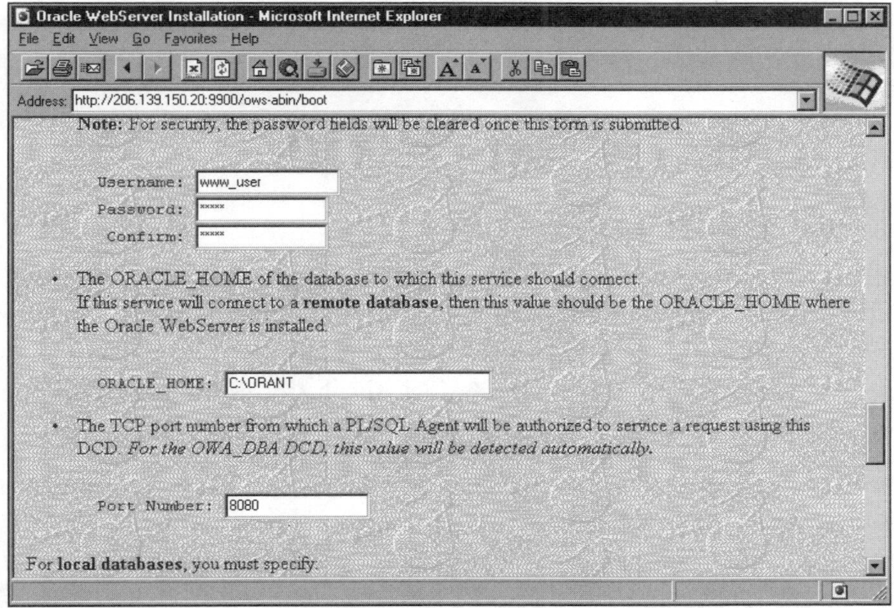

Figure 15.10
Creating the default Web user account.

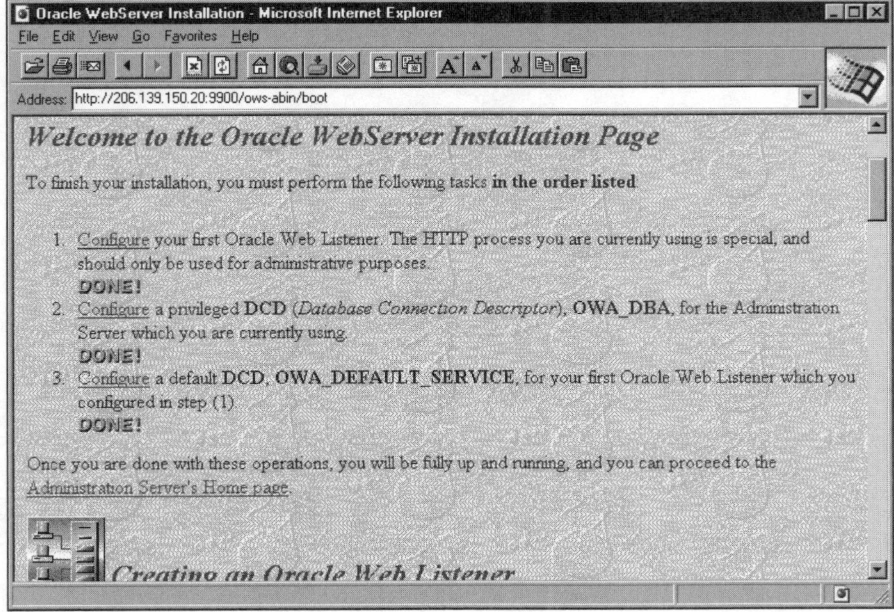

Figure 15.11
The completed configuration.

The next section involves administering the Web server and using online documentation.

Administration Of The Web Server

While our initial setup of the Web server used PowerBrowser, I'm going to administer the Web server using Microsoft's Internet Explorer. You can administer your server with nearly any browser, but at some point, support of HTML tables will become essential. The use of MSIE illustrates the independence of Web servers and browsers.

Once the configuration is completed, click on the link at the bottom of the page that takes you to the Administrative page, as shown in Figure 15.12.

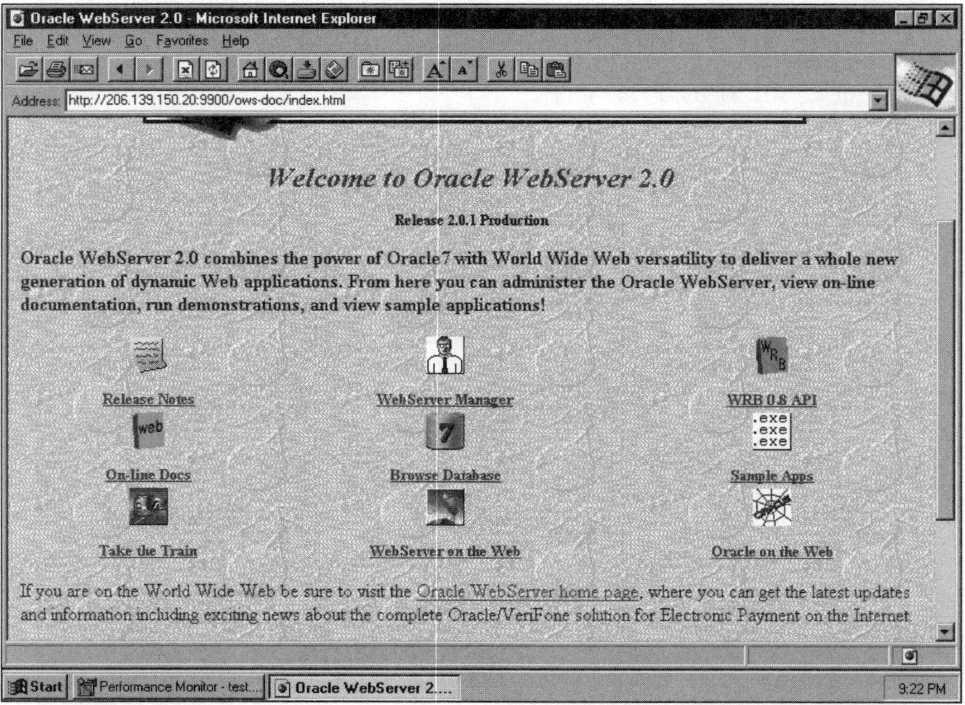

Figure 15.12
The Administrative Web page.

The Oracle WebServer functions can be addressed using the Administrative page. The bottom three options are all marketing items and concern finding more Oracle stuff on the Web, so I'll let you peruse those links at your leisure. For now, let's breeze through a brief description of the nine Administrative options:

- *Release Notes*—Provides last-minute updates to the documentation.
- *Web Server Manager*—Allows for administration of all Web server functions.
- *Web Request Broker (WRB)*—Provides programmatical access to Oracle database systems in which a full-scale intranet/Internet application can be developed independent of HTTP servers. This is a direct comparison to Microsoft's IIS and MS SQL Server usage in BackOffice.
- *Online Documentation*—Provides Oracle WebServer documentation at your fingertips.
- *Browse Database*—Manages Oracle database system users if you have the Oracle SQL Server installed and operational. Administrative access is required to use this function, and the use of a browser that supports tables is essential.
- *Sample Apps*—Provides a combination of C, Java, and SQL code for performing nearly any HTTP connection request to a Web server. Many of these HTTP functions are explored in Chapter 12 when we discuss ActiveX technologies.
- *Take The Train*—Provides a series of demos of the Oracle WebServer's features and versatility.
- *Web Server On The Web*—Takes you to Oracle's Web site for more information on its Web servers and related tools.
- *Oracle On The Web*—Displays Oracle's home Web site.

Of these nine functions, only two will be of major use to us during this phase of using the Web server: Online documentation and Web Server Manager. At times, we may take a peek at browsing the database and see what's there, so Browse Database will be used also.

Online Documentation

To view the online documentation, go to the index, then click on the link to the documentation. This is an HTML-based representation of the written documentation, which includes the use of Adobe's Acrobat viewer for other related documents. The four primary functions of the documentation are presented. The four functions serve the following purposes:

- Identifying the online documentation's structure.
- Instructing how to use Acrobat viewer with the documentation.
- Providing a more in-depth structure of the documentation.
- Providing the actual table of contents for the documentation.

You can peruse the first three items at your leisure to learn about those topics. The fourth topic—the table of contents—is what we're interested in. Scroll down the Web page TOC, and review the many topics you can learn about.

If you're a first-time Web administrator of an Oracle product, I highly recommend that you take a ride on the Roadmap To The Oracle WebServer. The Roadmap is a well-written, clear description of Web servers, protocols, and Oracle's integration features. After you've reviewed the Roadmap, let's move on to our primary area of interest—the Oracle WebServer Management pages. This section of the documentation tells all about managing the Web server, creating a secure Web channel with an Oracle WebServer, and much more, including Java and PL/SQL programmatical issues.

Continue scrolling down the page, and you'll come across the PL/SQL Web Toolkit Reference manual. Knowing PL/SQL is one of the keys for successfully integrating HTML and SQL to create interactive Web pages. Further down on the same page, you'll find a complete listing of the Oracle WebServer messages that PL/SQL might generate during the course of an application's development.

Overall, it's really nice to see some good documentation on a product. Oracle has done a good job with its Oracle WebServer documentation. Now, let's make a few things happen by using the WebServer Manager to perform a few common tasks.

WebServer Manager

From the main administrative login Web page, click on the WebServer Manager link. This action should take you to the central administrative tools of the Web server, as shown in Figure 15.13.

Figure 15.13
The main administrative tools.

The following encapsulates the purpose of each main administrative tool:

- *Oracle7 Server*—This tool allows the administrator to make changes to any existing databases used by the Oracle WebServer. New databases can't be created, nor can existing databases be deleted, although existing databases can be stopped or restarted should some problem occur within the database.
- *Oracle Web Listener*—This tool is the primary tool used to alter or change the Web server, and we'll review the Oracle Web Listener tool later in this chapter.
- *PL/SQL Agent*—This tool is used to create new database connections and modify existing database connections. We'll look at this option a bit more later in this chapter.
- *Web Request Broker*—This tool is the programmatical side of the Web server that we don't have time to go into, but we'll touch on it briefly, so you can

become familiar with the sections of the Web Request Broker that can be modified.

Each tool is discussed in further detail in the upcoming sections.

Oracle7 Server

The Oracle7 Server is a tool used to stop, start, or abort an action of Oracle databases in existence on the Web server. In Figure 15.14, the only database is the ORCL main database used for the users of this Web server. Not too much to it, as you can see.

Oracle Web Listener

The Web Listener is the primary tool used to configure the Web server. You use the Web Listener to define where a Web page is stored, who uses the Web, what access restrictions exist, and where to create virtual Web servers. There are three principal functions of the Web Listener.

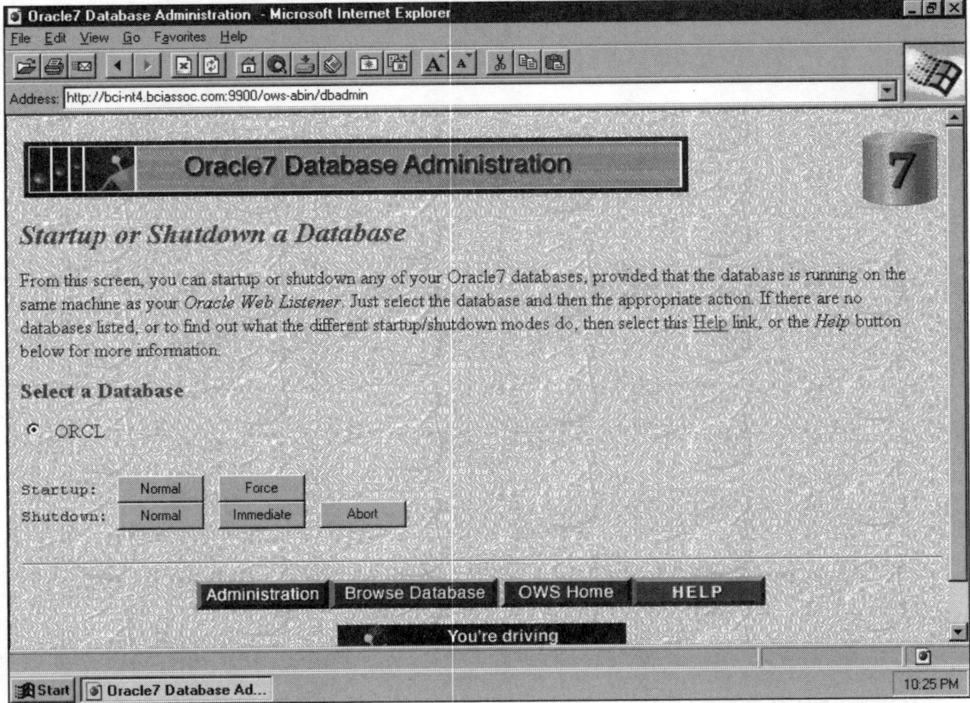

Figure 15.14
Starting or stopping an Oracle database.

- *Create*—Creates a new listening function for the server, such as for virtual servers.
- *Modify*—Allows for changing an existing Listener.
- *Start, Stop, Or Delete*—Does just what its name implies (starts, stops, and deletes the Web Listener).

In looking at the Web Listener, here's a list of the settings you can change in this function:

- *Web Address*—Indicates the host name and port address of the Web server itself, such as **bci-nt4.bciassoc.com:8080**. The number **8080** is the port number previously mentioned.
- *Maximum Connections*—Specifies the highest count of users concurrently allowed on the server.
- *DNS Resolution*—Allows for definition of when to resolve the DNS name of requests. Options are Always, Never, Lazy, and Lazy With CGI. *Lazy* means to resolve only when the actual demand has been placed upon the Web server. *Lazy With CGI* is the same as Lazy, but only when a CGI request has been sent from the Web server.
- *Redirection Server*—Defines where excess requests should be sent when the Web server is maxed out with the number of connections.
- *Log File*—Defines where the error log file is located.
- *Log Time Style*—Defines the time format in which all events are stored. Options are Local or GMT.
- *Configuration Directory*—Defines where the administrative control files for the Web server are located.
- *Initial File*—Defines the name of the baseline file used in a Web. The default is INDEX.HTML.
- *Default MIME Type*—Specifies the default format to use if a URL does not support any of the known MIME standards of the requests. *application/octet-stream* is filled in the form.
- *Default Character Set*—Defines the character set that is used by default. *ISO 8859-1 English* is entered for you.

- *Preferred Language*—Specifies the language to use. By default, this option is set to *en*, which stands for English.
- *Image Map Extension*—Defines the file type for image maps. This is preset to *map*, such as in a file named *bciassoc.map* for our company map.
- *Directory Indexing*—Determines whether the Web server allows for directory indexing.
- *Service Timeout*—Defines the time in seconds that the service waits for completion of the start or stop action requested. This option is used only on NT Server or Windows 95.
- *CGI Timeout*—Defines the number of seconds that the CGI scripting engine waits for completion of a script before terminating the script. Setting this option to a value less than two helps keep the Web server running smoothly during periods of heavy scripting.
- *Keep Alive Timeout*—Specifies the value used to define how long to wait before inactivity terminates the connection. The default setting is 10 seconds.

As an example of modifying the Listener, let's first modify an existing Listener currently running on our new Web server. As an added exercise, we'll create a new Listener for a virtual server. On installation, my Listener was named *jeff*, and it's the only Listener. I want to define where the Web pages are stored, so I'll be changing the current configuration of the Listener, shown in Figure 15.15.

1. Click on the Configure link, which takes you to a rather lengthy Web page describing the possible ways to change the current Listener configuration.
2. Scroll down about one fourth of the way, and you'll come to a section titled *Oracle Web Listener Configuration Parameters.*

The *Oracle Web Listener Configuration Parameters* is the most important section of the entire Web server. Oracle puts everything in HTML format and, in my humble opinion, is significantly easier to manage and navigate than Microsoft's IIS Manager.

As I mentioned earlier, the directory where Web pages are stored is my target for this first change.

3. Click on the Directory Mappings link, and a screen similar to Figure 15.16 should display.

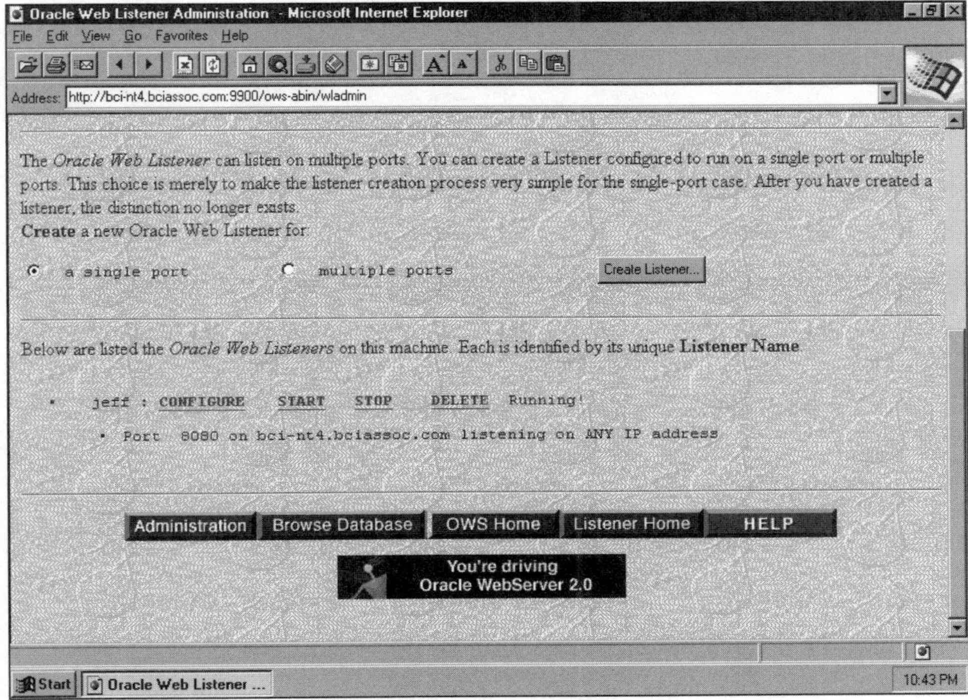

Figure 15.15
Installed Web Listeners.

This section allows you to create up to nine virtual paths for this one Listener. If you need more virtual paths, you should create more Listeners. To create virtual paths:

1. You first need to create the actual directories themselves. Use the root-level alias as shown in Figure 15.16's first mapping. Any additional mappings should be a subdirectory below this one. This is the only caveat to the procedure.
2. As shown in Figure 15.16, type the directory name in the longest field.
3. Immediately below this directory, type the alias to the directory.
4. Set the flags for the mapped directory—C for contains CGI scripts, R for subdirectories should be mapped recursively, and N if subdirectories should not be mapped recursively.
5. Click on Modify Listener for the changes to be applied.

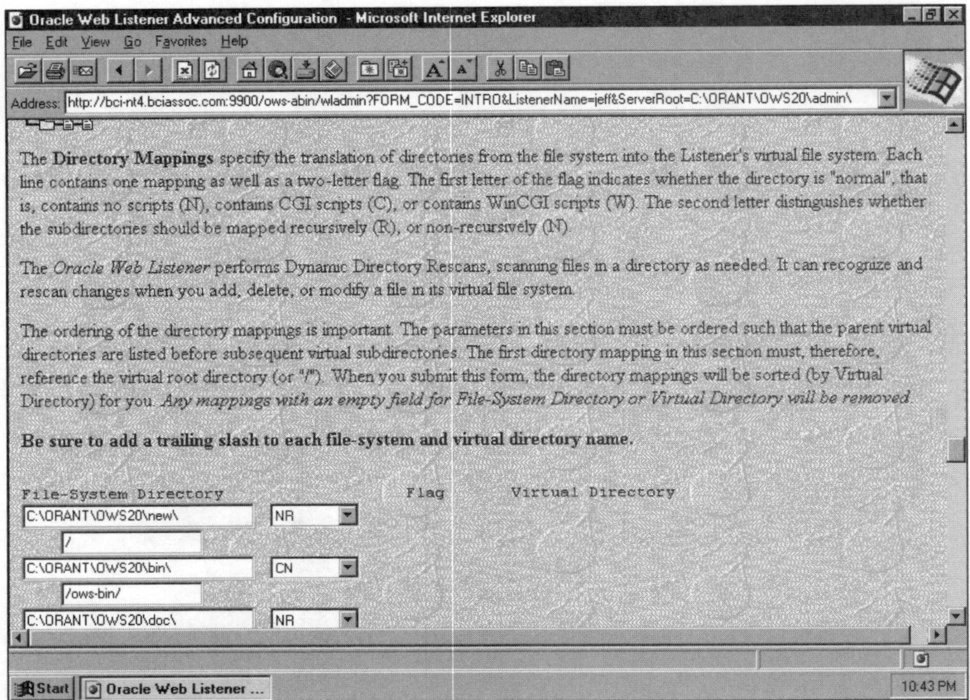

Figure 15.16
The Directory Mappings tool.

(In future versions, I'd like to see a browse function to aid in inserting the names of the directory for those really long names.) Be sure to stop and restart the Listener to ensure your changes take effect.

Now, as promised, we'll create a new Listener.

6. Display the Main Administrative page, and click on the Create Listener button, located on the right side of the page.
7. Enter the name of the new Listener.
8. Enter a new port number that does not conflict with an existing port.

Rest assured, if you use a conflicting port number, Oracle will let you know. I used *8085* as my new number.

9. Scroll down, and you'll notice that many settings are filled in for you.

For a new Listener, I prefer creating a new admin directory just to keep things separate. Also, create a new document directory for the Web pages.

10. Click on the Advanced button.

You'll be taken to the ever-lengthy Web page that shows the settings for the network, directories, special configurations, and much more.

11. When you've completed your configuration settings, click on Create Listener, and you'll come back to the Main Administrative page, now showing two Listeners running on the server, as shown in Figure 15.17.

Not too bad! Now, if only the rest of the Web servers in the world were as easy to run. Let's take a glance at the two remaining functions of the admin Web page before we wrap up this chapter.

PL/SQL Agent

As mentioned earlier, PL/SQL Agent is the tool used by the database system to configure the database requestor service. This requestor is how the Web server's Oracle databases are accessed by things such as intranet applications or database

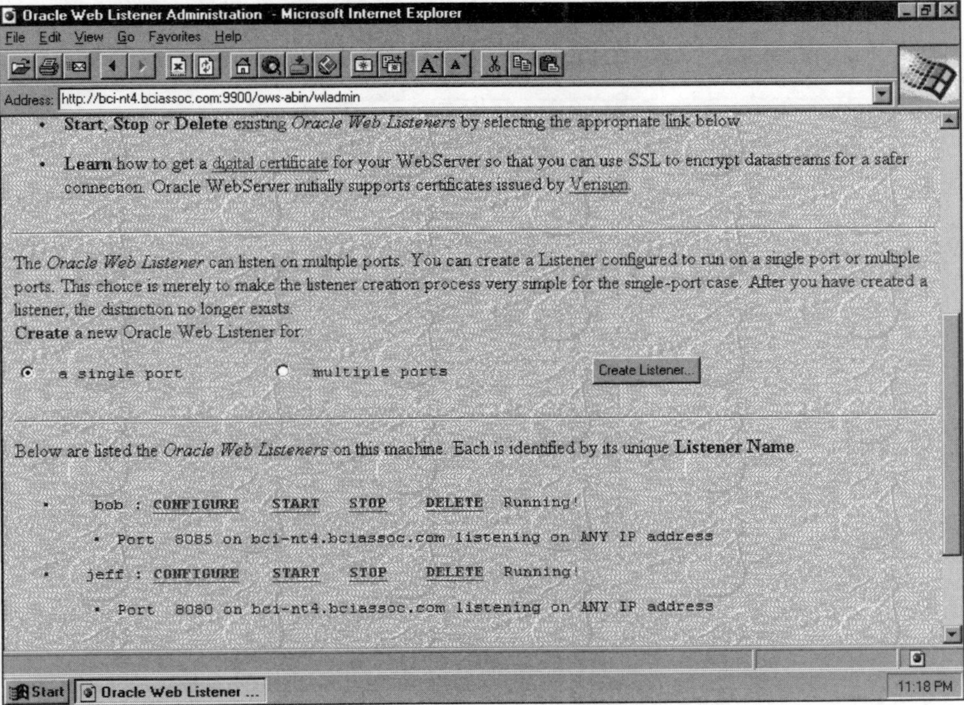

Figure 15.17
The new running Web Listener.

administrative tools, and the PL/SQL Agent is the connection between the application and the database.

1. Click on the PL/SQL link, and you'll see the DBA and Default Service that are running.
2. As an exercise, click on the Default Service's link.
3. Scroll down a little, and you'll be presented with a screen similar to Figure 15.18, showing the settings for the Default Service.

For any service created, this is where you'll modify or repair settings for your database connections. Again, Oracle makes it a dream to use.

Web Request Broker

The Web Request Broker, or WRB, is a key component of the overall Oracle WebServer system. The WRB is a set of Application Programming Interfaces

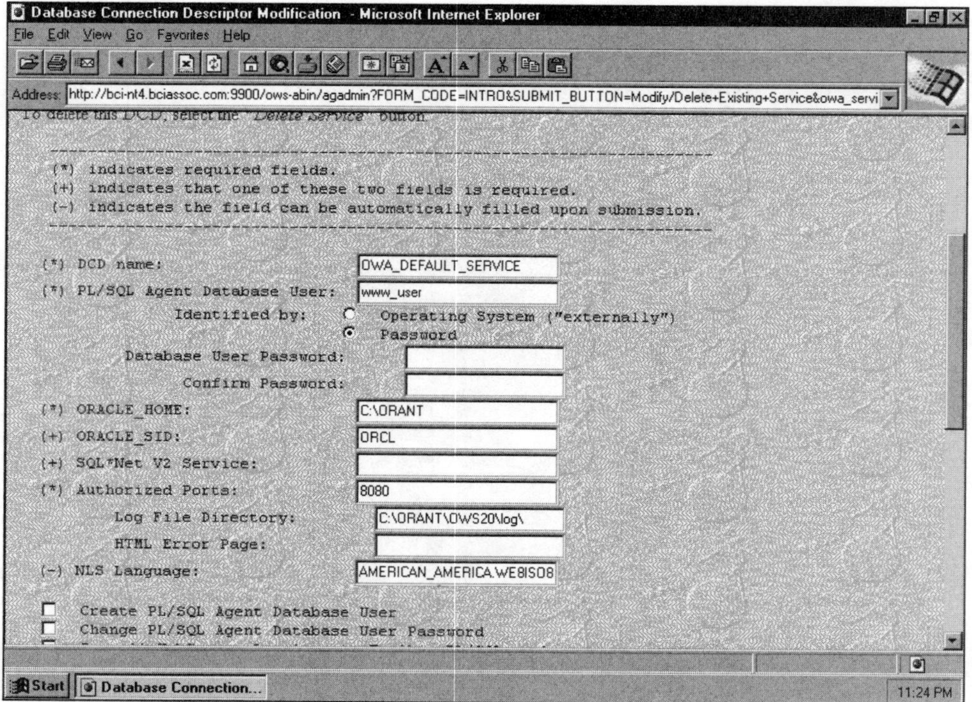

Figure 15.18
The Default Service settings.

used to access Oracle databases by way of browsers. Let's run through an example application to see how this works.

Our company has an assortment of name listings for our customers and contacts. This information is updated by the order entry system and contacts made during the normal course of business. By logical design, there are dozens of tables within each database for the entire business. Spanning several servers, these tables contain information that needs to be accessed by our designers and customers alike.

While many of the users travel out to customer locations, this information needs to be accessed frequently and must be the most up-to-date information possible. To make this possible, WRB is used to allow access to the Web server while this person is at the customer's site. Browsing the Web pages of the server, WRB is actually making the connection via the PL/SQL Agent extracting the required information.

As far as the customer knows, this data is coming from a Web page back on one of our servers. They believe the data is the same as what they see while they're at home, except that the connection back to the home office Web server is via modem or some other form of connectivity. Roughly speaking, this functionality is equivalent to Active Server Pages.

Summary

Oracle's WebServer is a really nice and efficient tool for distribution of your business information. While not within the scope of this book, Oracle makes excellent products for extending this Web server. Among them is their premier development tool, Developer 2000. Developer 2000 is a front end application, roughly corresponding to PowerBuilder, except it's tightly integrated into Oracle database systems.

16

Netscape's FastTrack Server

Robert Ellis

In today's computing environment, the value of a network is measured more and more by how well it exploits the global Internet. As you probably know, a good interface to the Internet has become a major factor in the survival of operating systems in the next century. However, in order to provide a good interface to the Internet, it is essential to have a good product to administer and manage the Internet. Netscape FastTrack Server delivers the power of a Netscape Internet Server in an easy-to-use package. In this chapter, we'll take a look at Netscape FastTrack Server.

What Is Netscape FastTrack Server?

Netscape FastTrack Server enables users to install a server in minutes and create Web content simply and easily, using Netscape Navigator Gold 2. FastTrack provides this functionality without forcing users to make sacrifices in performance, security, or platform selection. Netscape FastTrack Server also provides leading edge development tools using Java and JavaScript.

Who Should Use Netscape FastTrack Server?

Netscape designed FastTrack for companies, individuals, and workgroups who need a very easy entry point for creating and publishing documents on the Internet or a corporate intranet, but who also require security, scaleable performance, and a migration path to the full-featured Netscape Enterprise Server. Businesses can use Netscape FastTrack Server to quickly establish a presence on the Internet. On an intranet, departments and individuals can use Netscape FastTrack Server to publish information for a workgroup or across an entire organization. For example, a human resources department could publish company procedures and policies; marketing managers could publish product plans, collateral, and presentations; and R&D teams could publish technical specifications and product schedules.

Now that you know the who and what—let's look at the *how*. The remainder of this chapter deals with installing, configuring, and administering FastTrack Server.

FastTrack Server Windows NT Installation

Netscape FastTrack Server is tightly integrated with Windows NT. It runs as an NT service and is integrated with the NT registry. FastTrack supports SMP through extensive NT thread usage, supports performance monitoring using NT PerfMon, and writes error logs to the NT Event Viewer. Once installed, you can manage FastTrack Server like any other server program integrated into Windows NT.

In this section, we'll walk through the FastTrack Server installation under Windows NT. But before you install FastTrack, make sure you first fulfill the following preinstallation requirements:

- You'll need a minimum of 30MB of hard disk space and, depending on some systems disk cluster sizes, you might need 50MB of disk space for installation.
- Make sure you have installed the latest service pack for Windows NT Server, which is available at Microsoft's Web site (**www.microsoft.com**).
- Make sure you have installed Netscape Navigator version 2 (or higher) or Netscape Navigator Gold. Also, make sure that JavaScript is enabled so that

you can administer FastTrack Server using Server Manager forms, as described later in this chapter.

To install the server, perform the steps presented here:

1. Insert the CD-ROM into your CD drive, and then choose File|Run from the Program Manager.
2. If you have a 486 or Pentium-based system, enter *D\:FastTrak\NT_i386\setup.exe* in the dialog box. If you have a Digital Alpha-based system, enter *D:\FastTrak\NT_Alpha\setup.exe*, where *D:* is the drive letter for your CD-ROM drive.
3. Press Enter. The Welcome screen appears. After reading the Welcome screen, click on Next.
4. The Software License Agreement appears. Click on Yes to accept the license.
5. The Choose Destination Location screen appears. The default location for the server files is C:\Netscape\Server. Click on Next. The installation program copies the server files to the directory you specified.
6. The Configure Netscape FastTrack Server 2 screen appears. Click on Next.
7. Enter the full name of your server, and then click on Next.
8. Enter the user name for administration server access. The default is *admin.*
9. Enter the administration server access password, which can be up to eight characters. Enter it again for verification. Click on Next.
10. Enter the path for your primary document directory, which is where your server's content files will be stored. The default document directory is C:\Netscape\Server\docs. Click on Browse to navigate your file system. (You can use the Server Manager to change the primary document directory after installation.)

    Note: *If you enter an existing document root, the sample HTML files won't be copied to the existing document root.*

11. The Finish screen appears. Click on Finish. Your new server's home page appears after installation is complete.

The next thing we need to do is add the users for the Web server.

Create A User Account For The Server

You should create a user account for your server and set it up so that the server has restricted access to system resources and runs under a nonprivileged system user account (one that has a limited set of system permissions to your system). If you don't know how to create a new user on your system, consult your server documentation.

When the server starts and runs, it runs under its user account. (During installation, the server uses the LocalSystem account, which has a limited set of privileges.) Any threads the server creates are created with this user account as the owner.

You can change the user account for a server after the installation process. You can then configure the user account to have permissions to get files on another machine, which lets your server serve files that are mounted from another machine. The next section explains how to change the user account.

Changing The User Account

After installing the administration and Web servers, you might want to change the user account that the administration server uses. By default, the user account is LocalSystem. To change the user account after installation, follow the steps presented in this section:

1. Open the Server Selector. Figure 16.1 displays Netscape's Server Selector.
2. Click on Configure Administration.
3. Click on Daemon Configuration.
4. Enter the server user account you want to use.
5. Scroll down the form, and click on OK.
6. Go to the Control Panel, and double-click on the Services icon.
7. Select Netscape Admin Server.
8. Click on Start Up.
9. In the Logon As section, enter the account name you want to use.
10. Enter the password for that account, then enter it again for confirmation.

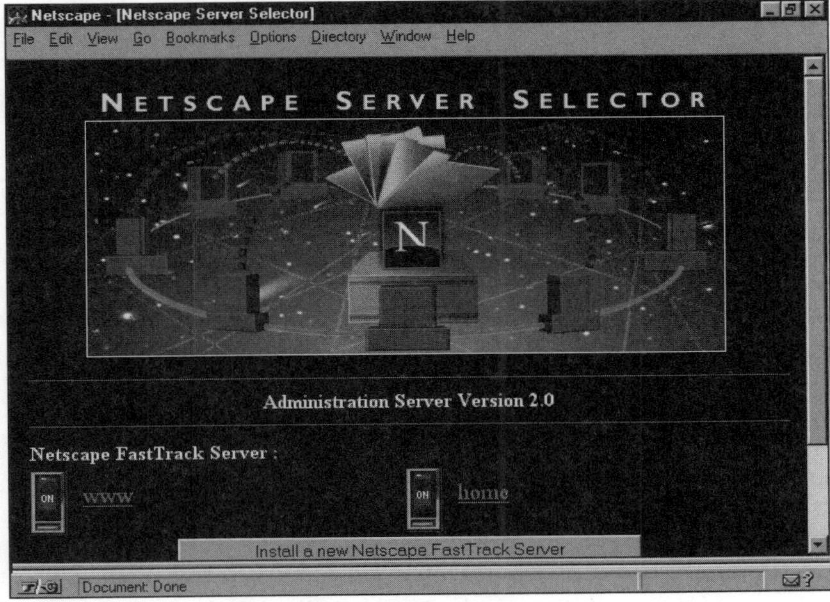

Figure 16.1
Netscape's Server Selector.

11. Click on OK.
12. Restart the server using the Services program or the Server Selector.

The next thing to be aware of is how to upgrade the Web server.

Upgrading An Existing Server

If you're running a 1.1 server, the installation program takes configuration information from your 1.1 server and puts it into a new version 2 server in a new server root directory (you specify this directory). You should stop running the 1.1 server before upgrading. Make sure you have Netscape Navigator 2 or later installed on your computer before upgrading.

To upgrade your server, follow the steps presented in this section:

1. Insert the CD-ROM in your CD drive, and then choose File|Run from the Program Manager.
2. If you have a 486 or Pentium-based system, enter *D:\FastTrak\NT_i386\setup.exe* in the dialog box. If you have a Digital Alpha-based system, enter

D:\FastTrak\NT_Alpha\setup.exe, where *D:* is the drive letter for your CD-ROM drive.

3. Press Enter. The Welcome screen appears. After reading the Welcome screen, click on Next.
4. The Software License Agreement appears. Click on Yes to accept the license.
5. The Configure Netscape FastTrack Server 2 screen appears. Click on Next.
6. An upgrade dialog box appears. To upgrade your existing server, click on the upgrade checkbox. If you choose not to upgrade and install a new server, you'll be prompted for a server port number and server name. Click on Next.
7. The Finish screen appears. Click on Finish. Your server's home page appears when installation is complete.

To ensure that your 1.1 server's configuration information is completely converted, you should run a program called *Upgrade 1.1x* that is in your server's program group. If your 1.1 server had SSL enabled or had access control enabled and configured, you need to run Upgrade 1.1x in order for your version 2 server to be secure and retain the access control configuration information from your version 1.1 server. Any NameTrans information is also properly updated after running the program.

To run the upgrade program, double-click on the Upgrade 1.1x icon that is in your server's program group. When the program has completed, restart the server in order for the changes to take place.

Copy any necessary documents from your version 1.1 document to your new version 2 document directory.

Occasionally, you may need to create multiple Web servers if you are an ISP hosting many customers.

Installing Multiple Web Servers

You can use FastTrack Server's Server Select menu button called Install A New Netscape FastTrack Server to install another Web server on your machine without going through the installation program. The new server can share its configuration with the current Web server on the system or use its separate configuration files.

The FastTrack Server license allows you to have as many Web server instances as you desire on one system. Each Web server you install can run only on a TCP/IP port on your system. You cannot run two Web servers on the same port at the same time. However, if your system is configured to listen to more than one IP address, two or more Web servers can share the same port as long as they use different IP addresses. If your system is not listening to multiple IP addresses, you do not need to enter an IP address for each server.

To install another Web server with its own configuration files, follow the steps presented in this section:

1. Click on Install A New Netscape FastTrack Server from the Server Selector. You will get to the screen shown in Figure 16.2. And as you scroll down, you will see Figure 16.3.
2. Enter the following information in the specified fields:
    - *Server Name*—Enter the fully qualified domain name for your server. If your are installing a second server for a custom domain, enter the domain name here.

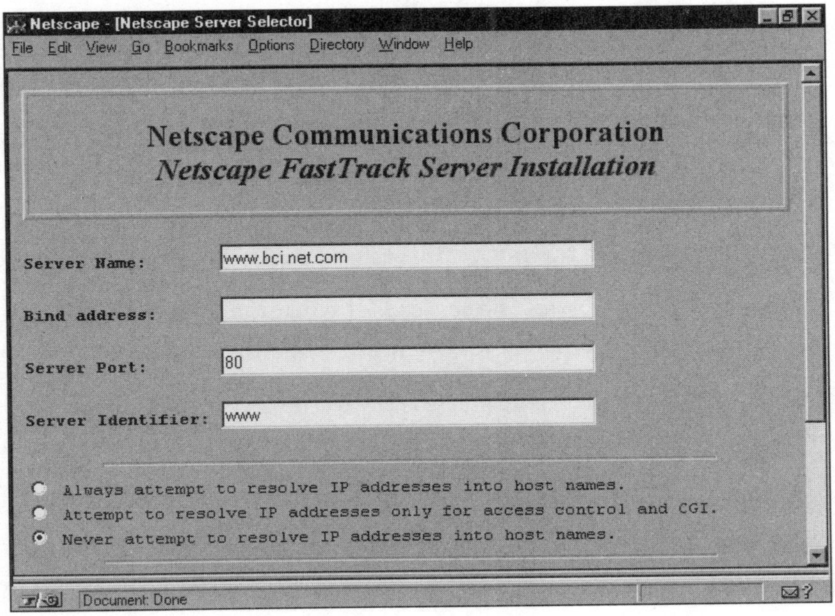

Figure 16.2
FastTrack Server—new Web server installation options.

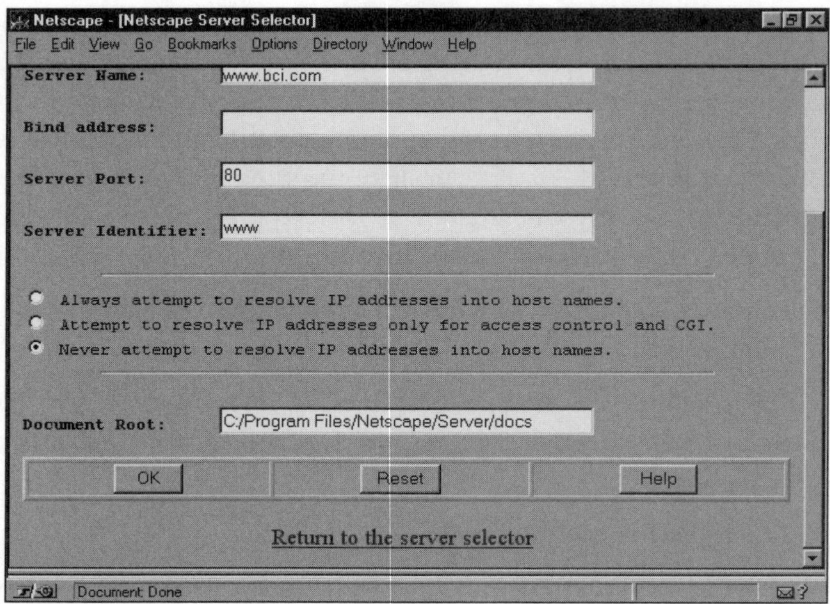

Figure 16.3
FastTrack Server—new Web server installation options (continued).

- *Bind Address*—Leave this field blank if you are not going to use multiple IP addresses. If you are installing another server in order to have your machine answer to multiple IP addresses, enter the IP address that the server should listen to. Your system should already be configured to listen to multiple IP addresses.
- *Server Port*—Enter the port number you want the server to listen to.
- *Server Identifier*—Enter the server identification that the administration server will use for your server, such as *Marketing_Server*.
- *Enable DNS*—Select whether to always resolve host names, to resolve host names for access control and CGI, or to never resolve host names.
- *Document Root*—Enter the server's document root, which is the directory that will contain most of your server documents.

3. Click on OK.

Now, let's see how you can remove a Web server if that action is ever needed.

Removing A Web Server

As shown in Figure 16.4, the second button in the Server Selector screen is Remove A Server From This Machine. Ensure that you do not need a server before you remove it.

To remove a server from your machine, follow the steps presented in this section:

1. Shut down the server before removing it by clicking on the On/Off icon to the left of the server name in the Server Selector.
2. Click on Remove A Server From This Machine from the Server Selector.
3. Select the server you want to remove, as shown in Figure 16.4.
4. Select whether you want to remove the administration binaries, as shown in Figure 16.5. The administration binaries include the server's configuration files and the server's binaries.

Note: Make sure you do not remove administration binaries if there is more than one server installed.

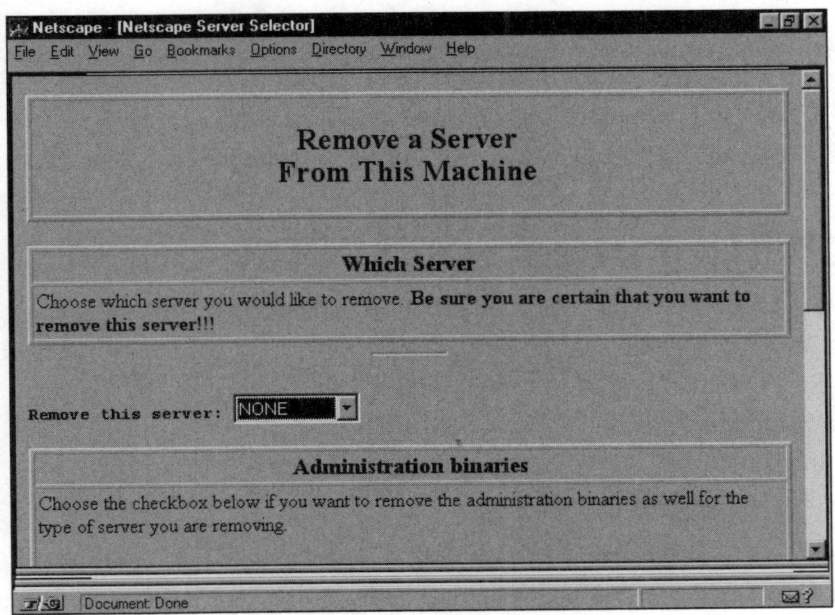

Figure 16.4
Selecting the server you want to remove.

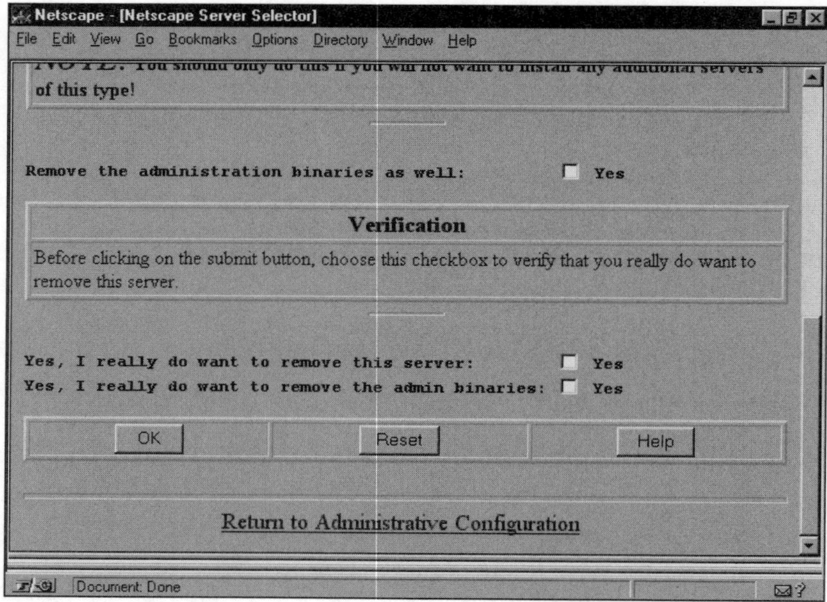

Figure 16.5
Server administration binaries removal option.

5. Verify that you want to remove the server and the administration binaries.
6. Click on OK.

Now that FastTrack Server is installed, let's configure it.

Configuring FastTrack Server

As mentioned earlier, FastTrack Server has two components: the administration server and the Web server. The administration server, which is installed on a different port than the Web server, allows you to manage the Netscape Web server or multiple servers from the Server Selector (shown earlier in the chapter, in Figure 16.1).

You can access the Server Manager through the Server Selector. The *Server Manager* is a collection of forms used to change the settings and options of the server. The administration server must be up and running before you can use the Server Manager.

Let us start our configuration discussion by configuring your administration server after the initial installation is complete.

Configuring Your Administration Server

This button is used to configure the following items of the administration server:

- Daemon Configuration
- Access Control
- Options

Let's look at each item one by one, moving down the list, as shown in Figure 16.6. As you scroll down, your screen should appear similar to the screen displayed in Figure 16.7.

Daemon Configuration

If you click on Daemon Configuration, your screen should look similar to the screen displayed in Figure 16.8.

Let's look at the individual options:

- *Admin Server Port*—This is the port number used for server administration. It should be different from the port you used for the HTTP server.

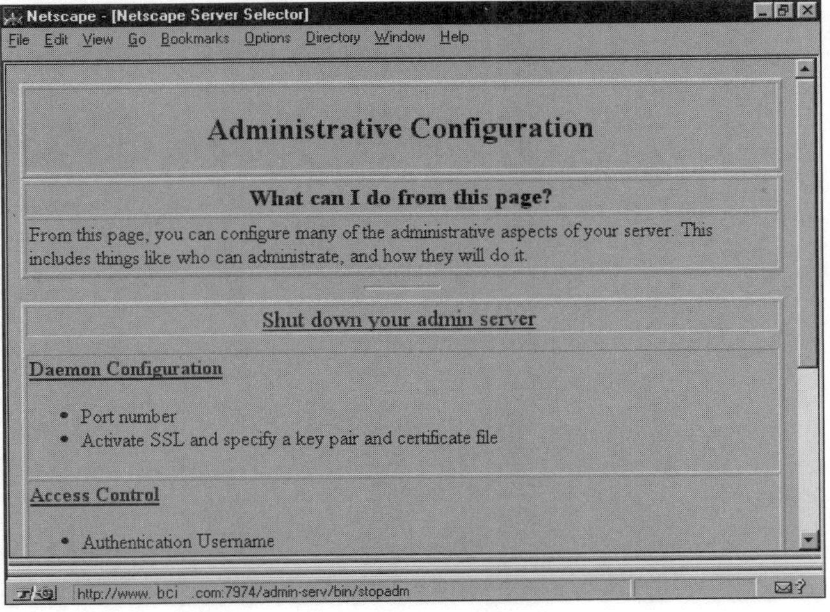

Figure 16.6
Administration Server options.

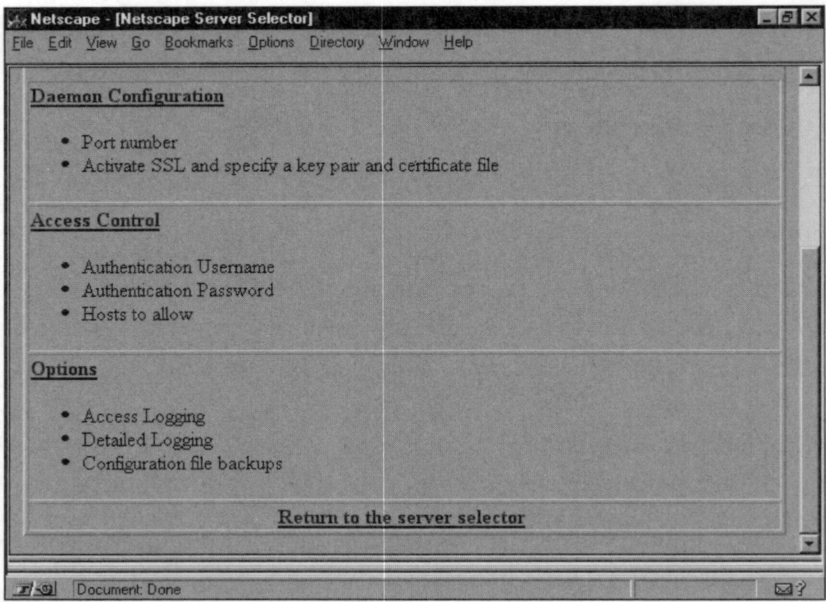

Figure 16.7
Administration Server options (continued).

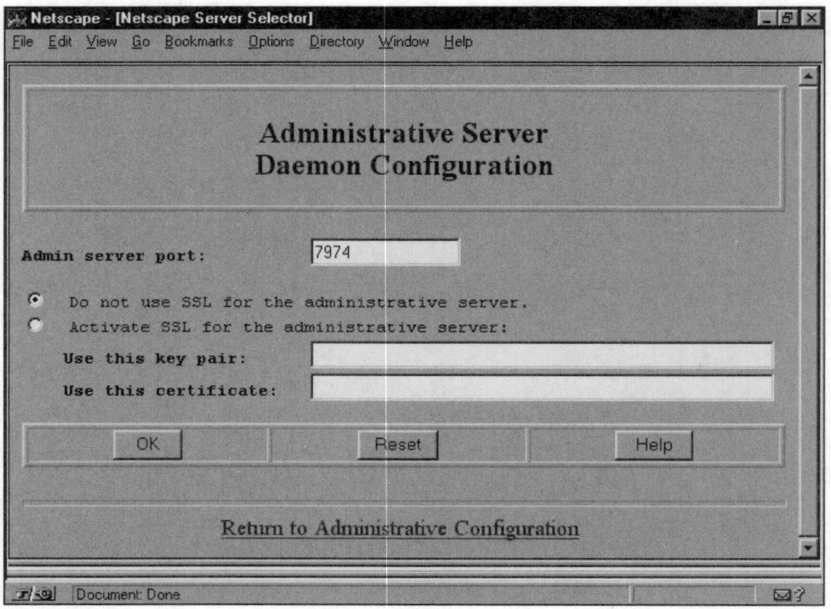

Figure 16.8
Administration Server Daemon Configuration.

- *Activate SSL And Specify A Key Pair And Certificate File*—You can configure the administration server to run in secure mode by activating SSL. But before activation, you need a certificate file and a key pair file for the administration server.
- *Admin Server User (Windows NT Only)*—This user name is the user name that can run the administration server. This user account should have both Administrative and Log On As A Service rights, and a password. For NT installations, the rights can be changed using the NT User Manager program. If you leave the password field blank, it will leave the admin server user unchanged.
- *Authentication password*—This password is used to authenticate the administration server user. Remember to enter the password in the Password (Again) field for verification.

> ***Note:*** *Make sure that you enter the path correctly when activating SSL for the administration server. If you make a mistake, the administration server will not start. However, if you do make a mistake, you can correct it by changing Security to Off in [server_root]\admserv\ns-admin.conf.file or editing the key pair file or certificate lines.*

Access Control

Click on the Access Control button, shown in Figure 16.9. You should see a screen similar to the screen displayed in Figure 16.9.

Administrative options include the following:

- *Authentication User Name*—The name that is entered to verify the server administrator can be changed. This is the name you entered during installation. This is an HTTP user name and can be used within the server only. The server will create the user specified in this field.
- *Authentication Password*—The password for the user name you specified can also be changed. If you leave the password field blank, it will not remove the password but stay the same. In other words, it will remain unchanged. The password can be up to eight characters.
- *Hosts To Allow*—You can change what hosts are allowed to administer the server. The access can be restricted by host name or IP address. It is more

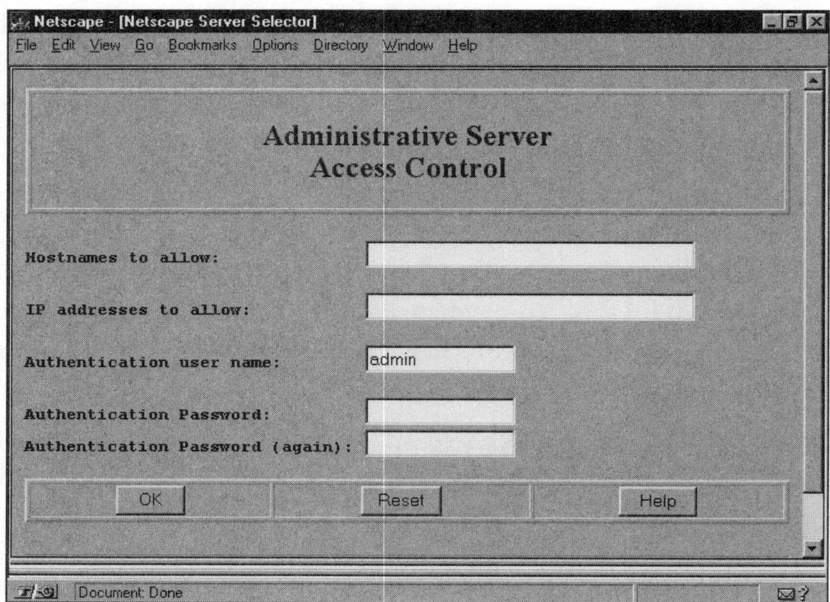

Figure 16.9
Administration Server Access Control.

flexible to specify the host name. If a system's IP address changes, you do not need to update the server. However, using IP addresses is more reliable. If a DNS look up fails for the connected client, host name restriction cannot be used.

Options

In the Administration Configuration screen, click on Options. You should see the screen displayed in Figure 6.10.

The server options are:

- *Access Logging*—The administration server can keep access logs using the common log file format, which is the format HTTP servers normally use. If you leave this field blank, it will deactivate access logging. If you want to activate logging, enter a relative path from your administration server root or a full path to where you want to keep the access logs.
- *Detailed Logging*—Administration server also allows you to keep a log of the configuration changes you make to the server. It works the same as the Access Logging feature. If you leave the field blank, it will deactivate detailed

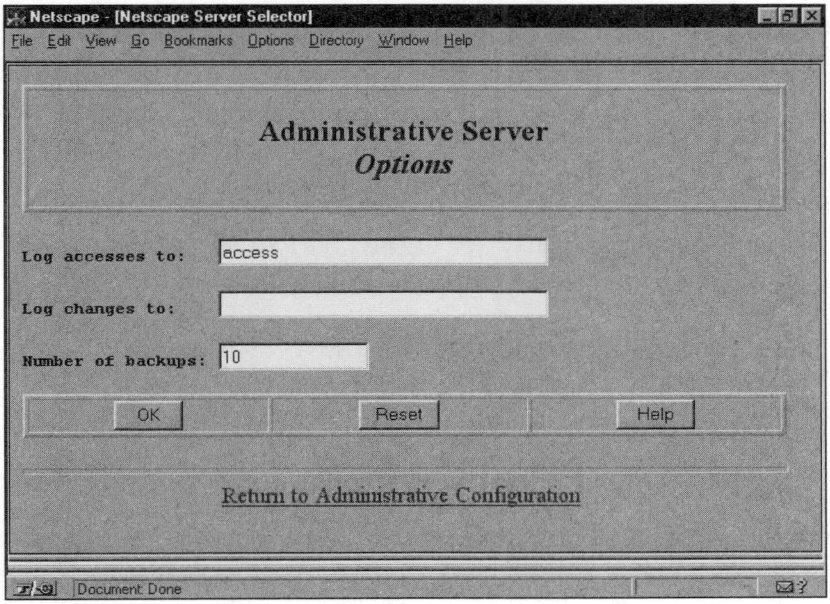

Figure 16.10
Administration Server Options.

logging. You can enter a path name from your administration server root or a full path name to where you want to keep the logs.

- *Configuration File Backups*—The administration server can also keep backups of a Web server's configuration files. Backups are made every time the server configuration changes. Backups are stored in the following directory in the admserv\http-[server_name] server root.

Another function that you can perform from the Server Selector is starting and stopping a Web Server.

Starting And Stopping A Web Server

You can start and stop any server listed on the Server Selector by clicking on the On/Off icon located to the left of the server's name. If the server is on, there is a green light under the icon. Click on the icon to turn the server off, and simply click on the icon again to turn it back on. The green light shows you that it is on.

Well, you have just learned all the major function that can be performed using the Server Selector. Up until now, we've discussed accessing the Server Selector functions locally on the server. Server Selector can also be accessed remotely.

Remotely Accessing Server Selector

As long as you have access to the client software like Netscape Navigator, you can access the Server Selector from anywhere to configure the Web server. To remotely access the Server Selector, follow the steps presented in this section.

1. Ensure that you are using a browser that supports frames and JavaScript (for example, the Netscape Navigator or Internet Explorer), and enter the URL for the administration server, in the following format:

```
Http://[servername].[your_domain].[domain]:[port_number]/
```

For example:

```
http://www.cciinet.com:7974/
```

The port number that you select is the port number of the administration server and not the Web server. (See Figure 16.11.) You will be prompted to enter the user name and password.

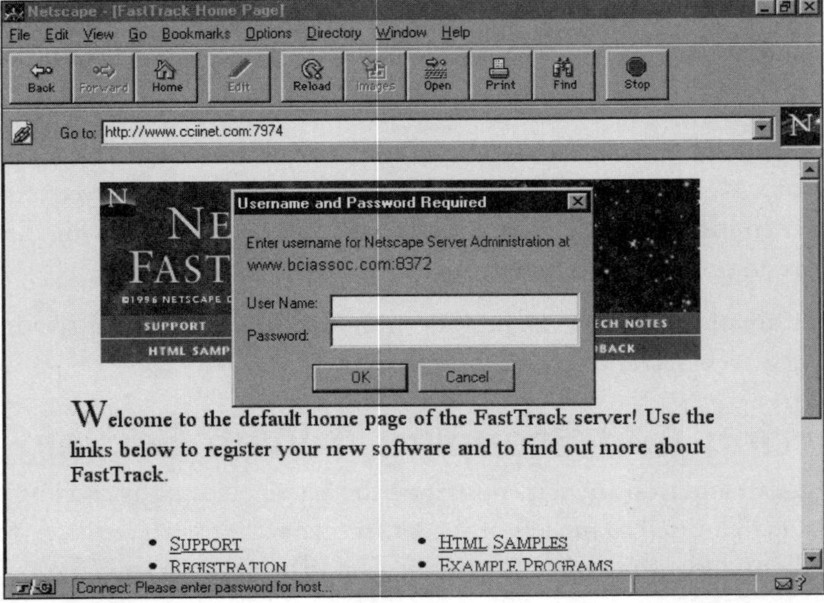

Figure 16.11
URL and port number, user name, and password pop-up window.

2. Enter the administration server user name and password that you specified during installation.

The Server Selector should appear. It lists all the servers installed on the system.

3. Click on the server you want to configure.
4. Configure your server.
5. After you finish configuring, you should shut down the administration server to avoid break-ins or any other security violations.

Now that the setup and configuration is completed, let's go into some administrative tasks for FastTrack.

Administering FastTrack

Administering FastTrack is a breeze to do. The HTML driven interface is common among Web servers just like the Oracle WebServer, and is comparable to the IIS method.

Go to Options in the Netscape menu bar, and click on Network Preferences. In the Network Preferences screen, you will see the Preferences tab. Click on the Preferences tab, and your display should appear.

Within this set of options, you can:

1. Create an alias for the server.
2. Choose a unique port for the administration and the Web servers. The standard Web server port name is 80. The standard SSL-enabled server port number is 443.
3. If you are going to use host names during the FastTrack Server installation, you have to make sure the DNS is properly configured and your server has an entry in the DNS server. If DNS is not running on your system, you have to make sure that you use IP addresses instead of host names during installation. You also need IP addresses when accessing the Server Selector pages of the administrator server.

Once all of this set of configurations and core administrative work is completed, you'll next need to stop the administration server.

Shutting Down The Administration Server

There are two different ways to shut down the administration server. Let's look at these two methods and how to accomplish them.

Using The Server Selector

To shut down from the Server Selector follow the procedure described in this section:

1. From the Server Selector, click on Configure Administration, and click on Shut down your administrative server. Then, click on Shut down the administrative server, as shown in Figure 16.12.

Using Windows 95

If you want to shut down the administration server from Windows 95, follow the steps listed in this section:

1. From the Windows 95 task bar, choose Start|Settings|Control Panel.

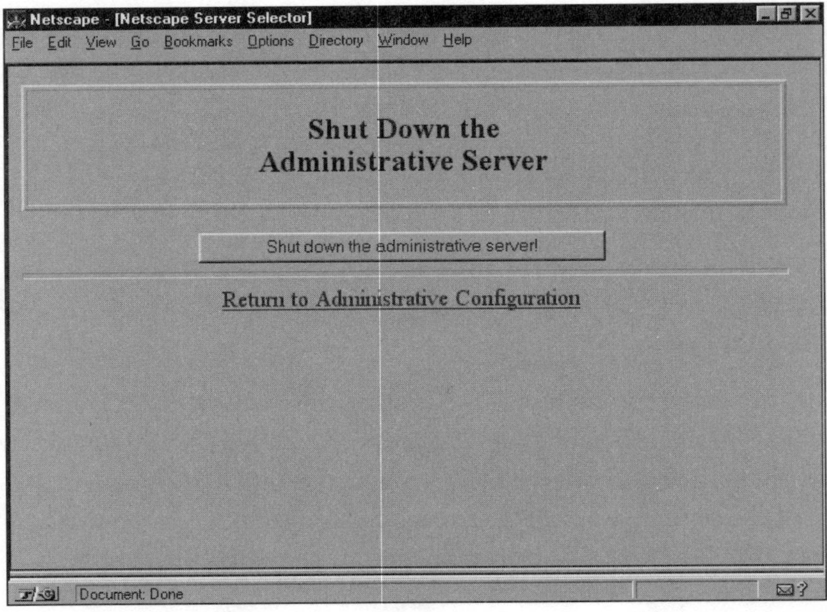

Figure 16.12
Shut Down the Administrative Server.

2. Double-click on the Netscape servers icon. The Netscape Server Management dialog box should appear.
3. Click on Admin Server.
4. Click on Stop.

Summary

In this chapter, you learned about high-level features and unique functionality of the FastTrack Server. If you compare Netscape FastTrack Server to Internet Information Server, you'll find that it has comparable features. However, you may want to give FastTrack Server serious consideration if you plan to deploy your Web servers on more than just the Windows NT platform.

17

Web Server Administration

Jeff Bankston

Although previous chapters have focused on specific products or applications of ideas, we haven't yet completely dissected the ins and outs of Web server administration. It has been apparent for some time that administration takes up where the installation leaves off, but to what degree? What are your options for managing the Web server? How can you or your business benefit from the different types of administration? These are some important questions, deserving some detailed answers.

This chapter presents answers to these questions and discusses several other ideas, including:

- Remote Access Server considerations
- Management tools
- Daily Web server administration
- Emergency actions when the server goes haywire

When Web servers run fine, they're great to have around. When they have problems, it can be a terrible nightmare. Problems happen; it's part of a normal course of server life. Arming yourself to combat those problems can make a huge difference in lessening the nightmare. As you read onward, understand that the solutions we'll discuss are not all encompassing, but rather present some of the easiest and most proactive methods of Web server administration.

NT's Remote Access Server

Microsoft Windows NT Server includes one of the most welcomed communications packages around in the form of a standard PPP (Point-to-Point Protocol) connection. This protocol is used by most Internet servers to allow dialup connections from Joe User who wants to surf the Internet. The other protocol, called SLIP (Serial Line Interface Protocol), is the most commonly used protocol for Internet clients; however, PPP improves on SLIP by offering more security, better error correction, and better streamlining of data movement by reducing overhead slightly. All in all, PPP is the way to go if such a connection is available.

You've already seen how running the Web server software affects performance of the physical server itself. Allowing anyone to connect to the Microsoft Windows NT Server by way of dialup modems puts pressure on server resources in an incremental manner. Although RAS doesn't reduce the strain on a server's ability to serve the users, configuring your physical server with RAS in mind is key to a successful site.

Server Considerations

Each user accessing your server takes up approximately 600K of server memory in normal operations. When high-speed modems are being used, the server must be able to handle the increased data throughput of the users. At one site where I consulted and assisted in the planning of the site, a Pentium 133MHz system running 64MB of memory was sufficient to handle 48 concurrently connected users at speeds of 28.8Kbps. The processor was "clocked" at approximately 75 percent utilization with memory utilization around 65 percent.

Obviously, this server could accommodate a few more users, but one thing remains to be said: Even if 48 users were connected to the server at the same time, it's doubtful that every user would be getting full 28.8Kbps bandwidth out of the connection—the phone lines could be terrible, the modems themselves may not match up the speeds completely, and the list goes on of possible irritants to the server. In a real-world setting, these and other uncontrollable factors can affect the operations of the user dialup lines. Your best bet is to use error-correcting modems on the RAS connection and employ the use of the PPP options, which we'll discuss later in this section.

Installing RAS

Installing RAS couldn't be easier, but we need to discuss a few decisions that you'll need to make first. In the Microsoft Windows NT Server world of networking and connectivity, the NetBEUI protocol has long been the Microsoft standard. Over time, however, Microsoft began to use the IPX (InterPacket eXchange) protocol more often for networking connectivity. And the world standard for network connectivity is TCP/IP, which Microsoft Windows NT Server can use, as well.

You'll have to decide which protocols you want to allow the users to request for the connection:

- *NetBEUI*—The network protocol specific to Microsoft operating systems such as Windows for Workgroups and NT Workstation.
- *IPX*—The network protocol that accommodates NetWare clients and Microsoft clients using IPX identifiers.
- *TCP/IP*—The Internet standard.

Go to the server where you'll install RAS. You'll need the NT Server CD-ROM for this operation. The remainder of this section assumes that your Microsoft Windows NT Server is already operational with TCP/IP installed for the normal network operations, and that you're adding RAS as a side element of operations.

1. On the desktop, right-click on Network Neighborhood, and click on Properties. Click on the Services tab next.
2. Click on the Add button to bring up a list of available applications that can be installed on your server.
3. Scroll down and find the option for Remote Access Service, as shown in Figure 17.1.
4. Select the service, and click on OK to proceed.
5. Tell NT where the files are that must be installed.

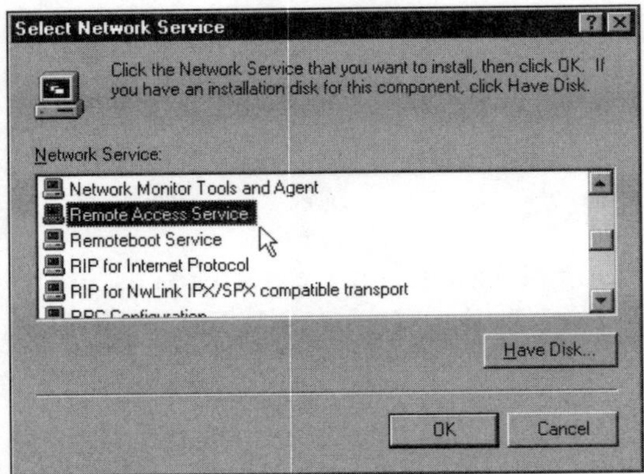

Figure 17.1
Remote Access Service.

The process will copy the files, perform some automatic configuration, and then prompt you to invoke the modem installer to find a compatible modem.

6. Click on Yes to allow the program to start the Modem wizard.

The Modem wizard will prompt you to allow it to search for a modem, and I suggest you allow it to do so, as shown in Figure 17.2.

7. When the wizard finds your modem, select the proper one given in the choice or click on the Change button to make the selection yourself. This may be required for some modems that are of a rather obscure nature.

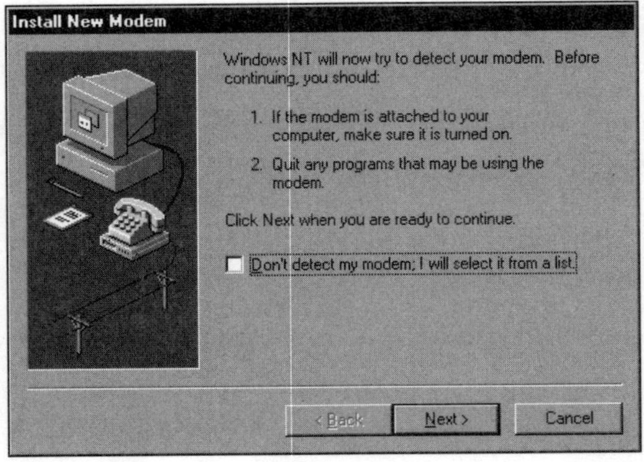

Figure 17.2
Modem wizard invoked.

8. Click on Next.
9. Enter the area code and other dialing information when prompted.
10. Click on Next, and then click on Finish to complete the task.

You're now presented with a dialog box used to add a RAS device.

11. Choose the modem you just installed, and click on OK.

The next dialog you'll see is now the semi-completed RAS setup, as shown in Figure 17.3.

12. Click on Configure.

You'll be asked to confirm the mode of operations for the modem, either dial out only or dial out and dial in.

13. Click on the proper mode of operation radio button, and click on OK to proceed.
14. Click on Network, and you'll be presented with the dialog box shown in Figure 17.4.
15. For any device used thus far, pick the protocol desired.

For the most part, TCP/IP is required for access to the Internet. If you're using Windows 95 or NT Workstation on a laptop, and you want to access the corporate LAN while traveling, then you'll need to choose NetBEUI and/or IPX protocols. Notice that there are two sections of choices: one for dial in and one for dial out, as shown in Figure 17.5.

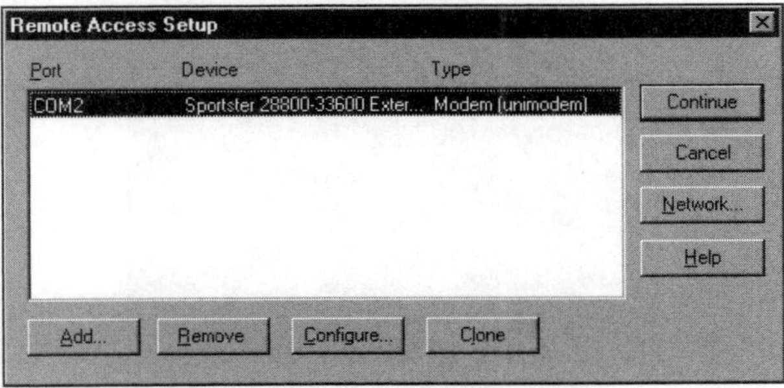

Figure 17.3
RAS setup almost completed.

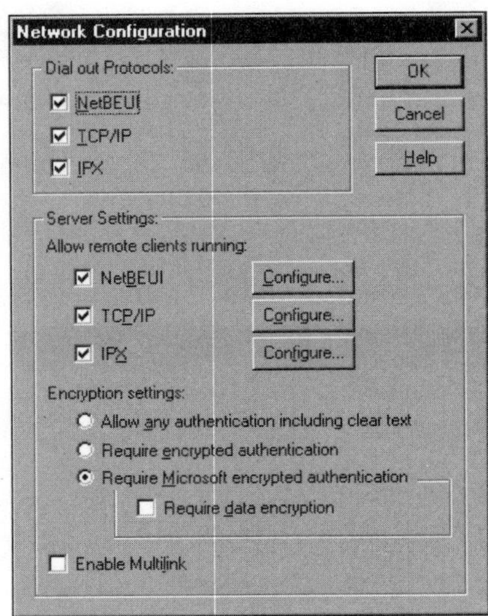

Figure 17.4
Choosing the network options for the RAS device.

Choosing NetBEUI and IPX/SPX merely lets you decide if you want to allow access to the whole network or just to the RAS computer itself. However, TCP/IP allows for a whole new set of options with which to control and determine how the RAS user is recognized on the network.

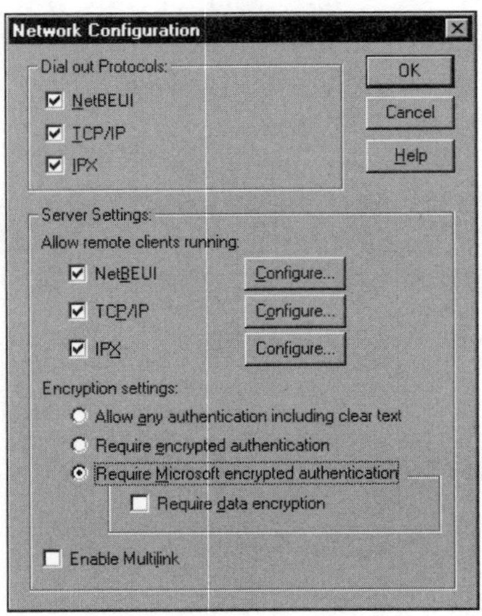

Figure 17.5
Choosing the protocol for the RAS device.

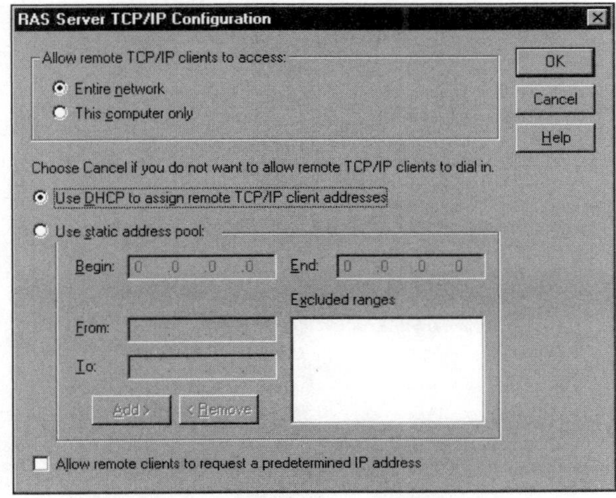

Figure 17.6
Choosing the TCP/IP protocol options for the RAS device.

16. Click on the TCP/IP button, and you'll see a dialog box like the one shown in Figure 17.6.

Note that there's a section to determine if the user can access the network or just this server, a section to determine if DHCP assigns an address, and one more section to assign a static IP pool of addresses in case a DHCP server is not running. One last radio button is provided to allow the user to request a predetermined IP address. ISPs rarely allow this to be used, and there are few reasons to ever allow it.

17. Click on OK when you're done with the TCP/IP selections.
18. Click on OK again to close the Network Configuration dialog box.
19. Click on Continue to have the RAS selections bound to the operating system.

You'll be presented with one more dialog box letting you know the installation is complete and enabling you to use Remote Access Admin to grant access to your users. Granting user access is next on our list of things to do, right after the final binding has been performed with the operating system, as shown in Figure 17.7.

Now that the installation is complete, let's do some configuration for the users.

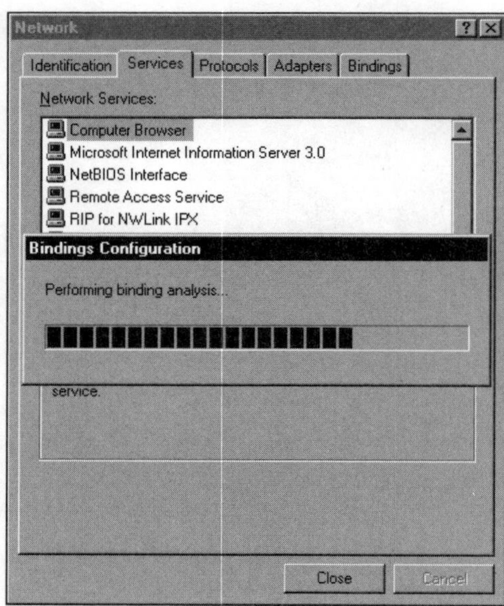

Figure 17.7
Binding the RAS devices to the operating system.

Configuring RAS

RAS has a few simple configuration options. We'll begin with the options that weren't covered in the installation of RAS.

1. Click on Start|Programs|Administrative Tools (Common)|Remote Access Admin.
2. From the menu bar, select Users|Permissions to display the user permissions options shown in Figure 17.8.

In the list of users section on the left, note the Grant Dialin Permission To User checkbox. If this option is not turned on (and is not checked by default), then the user will never be able to connect to the server. Period! The other options below this checkbox deal with the ability to dial into or out of the server by calling back to validate the call. *Call Back functions* are commonly used in a secure environment to prevent unauthorized access.

3. Ensure that these last two options are set, and then exit the administrative part of RAS.

Now that we've set permissions for the user, we need to configure RAS so users can connect properly. Let's take a few minutes and go over the process in which a RAS-enabled client will be connecting to the Web server.

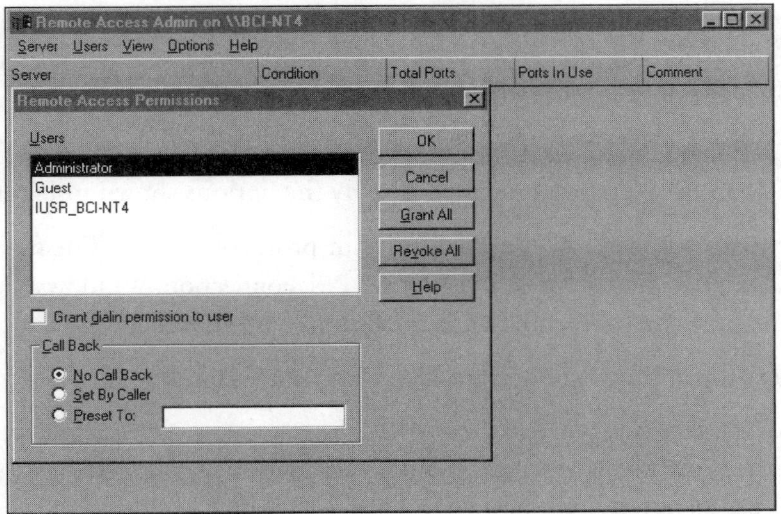

Figure 17.8
Granting dialin permissions.

4. Start RAS by clicking on the RAS button in the RAS program group.

Because you've just installed this component, no entries exist in the phone book, so we'll add one in just a moment. Also, the RAS monitor will start up automatically. The monitor is a graphical representation of what is happening to the modem line, showing received and transmitted data, errors in transmission, and carrier detection. Each option has a corresponding light. All the lights are green except for the error light, which is red, as you might expect.

5. To add a phone book entry, click on the Add button, and fill in the blanks for the Entry, Description, and Phone Number.
6. Clear the Authentication checkbox, because we're not using the NT registry of users to validate the user.
7. Click on the Advanced button to show the network settings that must be configured.
8. Click on the Modem button, set the required parameters for your modem, then click on OK.

Some modems will not work properly on a dirty phone line if the Compression option is checked. If you experience problems connecting or maintaining connections, clear this option.

The next two buttons, X.25 and ISDN, pertain only to those settings requiring these items—for example, when you've got an ISDN adapter connected to the server. While ISDN is taking off in a big way, you don't need to worry about it in this context. Skip these options.

9. Click on the Network button to display the options shown in Figure 17.9.

It's here that you need to begin making your protocol choices. The first choice you'll make is deciding between a SLIP and a PPP connection. Windows clients can use either, but when presented with the option, you should always choose PPP.

10. Select the appropriate options for your connection types.

NT binds the protocols you select to the RAS Server; the more functions you choose to offer, the more physical server resources are used. For most settings, TCP/IP is the only protocol required. Notice in Figure 17.9 that I selected the NetBEUI protocol as well as TCP/IP. I did this to allow WFWG computers to connect to the server when the user has no knowledge of how to configure TCP/IP.

If you're using RAS to connect to an ISP, then the ISP will generally assign you an IP address. In this case, the Server Assigned IP Address checkbox should be selected. Likewise, the Server Assigned Name Server Addresses checkbox should also be selected, which allows the ISP to define the DNS server. The user-defined options in both sections are therefore grayed out. In the case of my network, I defined all the parameters for each workstation on the network. For my traveling laptop users, I also have them follow the preceding two settings so they don't have to worry about assigning IP addresses to their computer.

Figure 17.9
Configuring the RAS client.

11. Accept the default Security settings.

Normally, the ISP handles the security authentications. In a purely Windows environment like this, you can tighten up security by selecting Microsoft encryption as the most secure form of connections.

12. Close this section.

Now, it's time to test accessing the server!

Using RAS For The Web Server

Now that we have RAS fully configured, we can test access to the server.

1. Open the RAS program group from the computer you configured to connect, and click on the Dial button to connect to the server.

Despite the settings that you entered earlier, RAS insists that you enter the username, password, and domain.

2. Type in your username and password, clear the domain entry, and then click on OK to connect.

When RAS connects for the first time, a dialog box appears asking if you want the program minimized upon connection, displays the type of protocol that successfully connected with the server, and also asks if you want such messages suppressed in the future.

3. Select all options, double-click on the minimized icon, and bring the RAS dialer back up on screen.

4. Click on the Status button to display connection information, as shown in Figure 17.10.

This screen shows the IP address you were assigned by the server, the connection settings of the modems, and more. You are now considered a full user of the server to which you've connected! If you have the privileges set on the remote server, you can map to directories, send or receive email, move files, and do anything else that you could do if you logged into the server locally. The same goes for your customers. Once connected, they'll have access to all the regular network services, including printing.

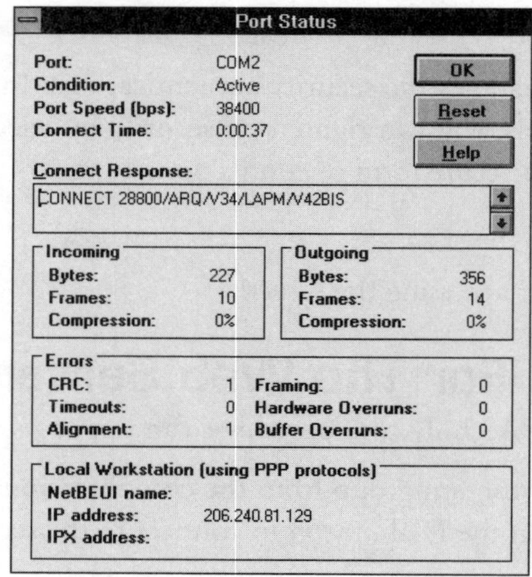

Figure 17.10
Showing the completed connection.

The next topic that will be explored is the addition of more serial ports so that the server can function as a scaled down ISP, or to provide for additional modem support for remote users.

Adding Additional RAS Serial Ports

When I was checking the marketplace for the solution to this issue, I came across the *SuperSerial Technology* (*SST*) intelligent processor made by a little-known company called *Equinox*. This card is a souped-up version of a PC's serial port built onto one card, with several ports on the card operating as highly enhanced serial ports. This card comes in several models that run in Unix, NetWare, NT Server, DOS, and Windows 3.x or 95. Bus structures included are ISA, EISA, PCI, and Micro Channel. If you have the slots, you can add 8 ports at a time until you run out of slots, or hit the limit of 256 ports.

Not feasible, you say? How about running a 20-slot passive backplane server with a single board computer. That leaves 19 slots free, so 16 of these cards could be added. Equinox has cards running 2, 4, 8, 64, and 128 ports. If I had one bad thing to say about the SST line, it would be that I would like to see a 16- and a 32-port model to minimize the number of cards to be installed. The

16-port model is a common installed item with BBS systems. In fact, the Digiboard, which is a competitor to Equinox, has a 16-port model, but a comparable SST out-performed the Digiboard by as much as 25 percent in our testing. If you want more information on the SST card, call Equinox at 954-746-9000 or fax the company at 954-746-9101. Its email address is **info@equinox.com**. The next couple of sections discuss how to install and configure the SST.

Installing The SST

The first thing you have to do is know what hardware is currently installed in the server. The ISA card requires a unique I/O port address, and you'll have to select one. PCI, EISA, and Micro Channel cards have no such requirement. You'll need to shut down the Microsoft Windows NT Server itself, and power it off. Install the SST card into a spare slot, and restart the server.

Failure to observe proper safety precautions can cause loss of life. Ensure that all power is turned off before installing the SST card. The technician performing the installation of the card should be using the proper electrostatic protection devices to prevent destruction of the circuit cards.

Configuring The SST

After restarting the server, NT knows nothing about the card until you install the driver for the respective device. In the *Software Installation And Reference Manual*, locate the NT section. The installation instructions for the driver are incredibly simple. When you're done, reboot the server to initialize the card. Now, we'll configure the SST.

1. Go into Control Panel, and bring up the Network Properties dialog box.
2. Click on the Equinox card, and then select the Configure button to see the settings for the card.

The SST has two settings: First COMPort and ISA Memory Block.

3. Click on the First COMPort drop-down menu, and you'll see that the first port that the SST can use is highlighted by default.

On my server, I already have two serial ports, so COM 3 is selected as the starting port for the SST card. If you scroll down to the end, you'll see that 256 ports are possible, which is the maximum that one RAS server can use.

4. Click on the ISA Memory Block drop-down menu, and you'll see the various memory ranges possible for the card. If you only use one ISA card, I suggest you leave it set to Auto and let NT handle the matter.

That's about it as far as the Equinox settings go. Now, you can use the additional ports for any function that NT supports, including RAS. In fact, you can mix and match RAS users on half the ports and BBS users on the other half. NT takes care of the intricacies of port management.

5. Before leaving the Network Properties, click on Remote Access Service, and click on Configure.

This brings up the Remote Access Setup.

6. Click on Add.

This brings up the available ports.

7. Click on the drop-down list box, and you'll see the added serial ports—instant expansion, as shown in Figure 17.11.

You now have four additional serial ports which can be used for any serial port service—possibly additional modems for Internet access? Yes, this is how Internet Service Providers (well, the smaller ones anyhow) establish a new ISP. High-end providers use other types of equipment, but the premise is the same.

Next, let's look at one of the more popular Web analysis tools to see how well your Web server is performing.

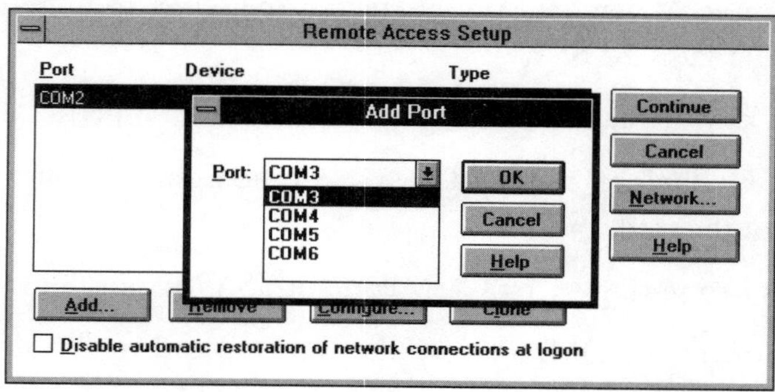

Figure 17.11
Adding more serial ports to RAS.

WebTrends—An NT Server Management Tool

In any Web server, it's always nice to know how the Web server is doing and who is accessing it. The WebTrends system analyzer can perform these very essential operations. WebTrends uses the log files generated by the various Internet servers running on your machine, and it produces clear reports in HTML and GIF file format. WebTrends is compatible with nearly every Web server on the market. You can reach the makers of WebTrends on the Internet at **www.Webtrends.com** or by phone at 503-294-7025.

Installing WebTrends

Installing WebTrends is quite simple. The program is stored on a single 3 1/2-inch high-density disk. When you execute the Setup program, it looks for any previous installations of WebTrends and offers to install the software anywhere you want, as indicated in Figure 17.12. As a matter of habit, I installed my copy in a common directory beneath my other Web server software.

After you've installed the program, install the additional WebTrends software that handles the interpretation of the known Web sites in the world. This portion of WebTrends comes on two 3 1/2-inch high-density disks, which expand

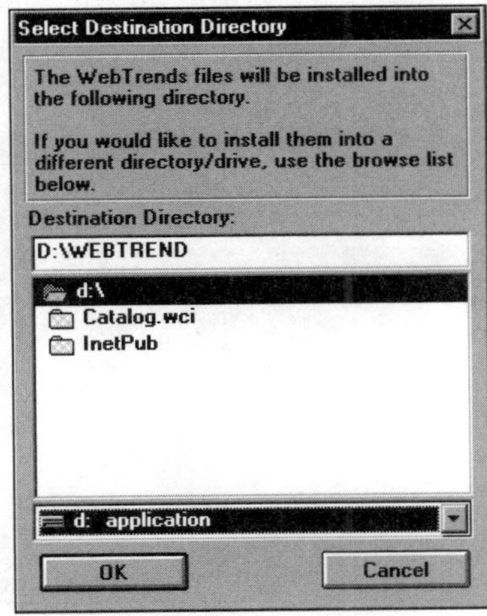

Figure 17.12
Choosing the directory for WebTrends.

out to one monster file of nearly 5MB. After installing WebTrends, you'll need to configure the software.

Configuring WebTrends

WebTrends allows you to choose a path to a browser for the output files, and define or edit the templates used for the various reports. You can choose from corporate, business, quick summary, and technical outputs, as shown in Figure 17.13. You'll find these templates a tremendous help when it comes to troubleshooting a flaky Web server. In the next section, I'll run one of these reports so you can see how helpful they are.

I added a template for my business's Web server to cover the accesses to the site by cataloging the log file produced and recorded to the Microsoft Windows NT Server log file. WebTrends uses the NT Server system log files to perform the analysis. By default, WebTrends looks into the SYSTEM32 directory, so you'll need to let WebTrends know where these files are if you've stored them elsewhere. You'll perform this configuration change in WebTrends in the next section.

Using WebTrends

After you've configured WebTrends, it's only a matter of starting the trend analysis against the log file.

1. Ensure that you've specified a Web browser for WebTrends to use to view a report by using the Configure button.

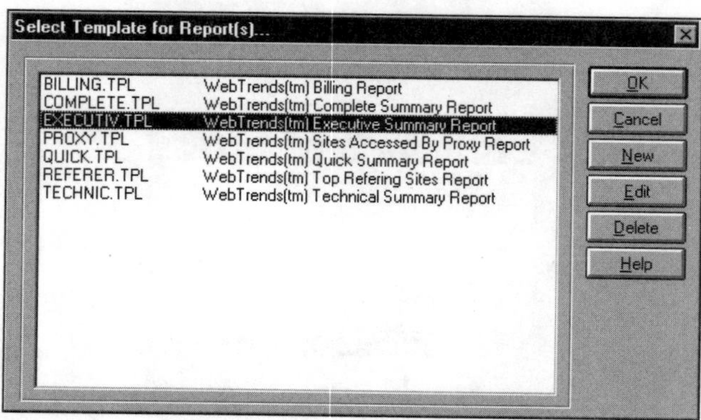

Figure 17.13
Stock templates provided with WebTrends.

2. Start WebTrends, and then click on the Report button.
3. Select the log file to run the report against.

> ***Note:*** *The analysis process takes several minutes for each file process, and can easily take 10 minutes to process on a Pentium 100 if your site is very active. Be patient during the process.*

After the process completes, WebTrends automatically starts the chosen Web browser and presents you with a colorful report and analysis in HTML and GIF file format, as shown in Figure 17.14. The reports are saved, and they're regenerated between each session in case the log file changes.

The report is chock-full of useful data showing you which HTML files were accessed, how many times, who accessed each file, and much, much more. Page down to see the rest of the report that the browser is holding for view. Only one

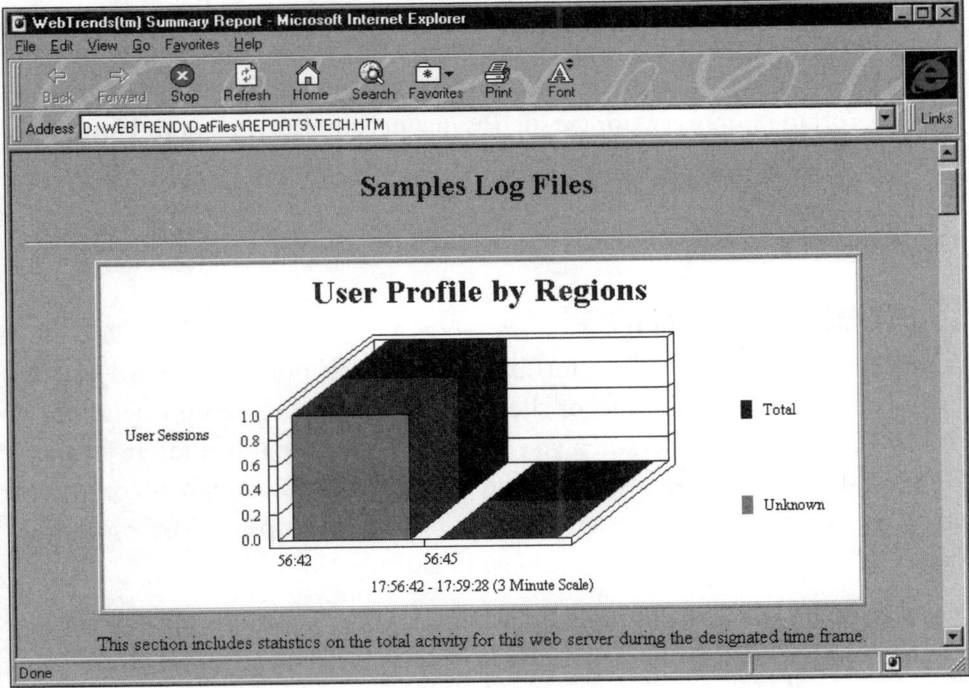

Figure 17.14
Report generated from last week's Web access.

section of the report can be seen at a time. This sure beats the heck out of looking over the log files and manually picking out the information you need.

In the next major section, we'll explore many of the daily administration tasks for your new Web server.

Daily Web Server Administration

At this point, we should address some of the daily Web server administration issues. For instance, you need to monitor your FTP server, perform daily backups, and prepare for an emergency restoration (better safe than sorry!). Let's take a quick look at these daily tasks.

FTP Server Disk Management

One matter of interest to you in your daily Web server tasks is to ensure that the FTP server disk space doesn't fill up. There are several new NT utilities coming to market that watch an FTP disk for usage, allocate and manage space, and handle the hierarchical storage management tasks—moving the least recently used files off to temporary storage such as magneto-optical drives and journalled tape backup. Some servers also use backup mirrored servers to move old files off to conserve disk space. Whatever utility you use, you should make sure that you are monitoring your FTP disk space on a regular basis.

System Backups

Another task that you'll be performing is a daily (if not more often) backup. Here's an exception to the rule of cheap and effective Web server operations. If this is your first Web server, then you're likely making the transition from an all-IDE disk-based disk storage system to one that's mixed IDE and SCSI, or perhaps all SCSI. If this is the case, then your options for backups on Microsoft Windows NT Server systems have just been drastically reduced.

You can no longer turn to the standard tape backup solutions for NT because the built-in backup for NT uses QIC drives. QIC drives are nearly impossible to use due to their limited capacity, and thus require a move to SCSI solutions. I've tested several tape backup solutions for my servers and came up with using Conner TapeStor 4000 drives as one method. As I'm writing this, I'm using the

Arcada Backup Exec for NT Workstation v6.1, which is working fairly well. It has its quirks, but otherwise seems to work the best for our configuration.

Emergency Restoration

The last thing any Webmaster wants to hear is the whining of a crashed disk drive or the ringing of the phone (for the umpteenth time) with a user asking why files or Web pages are inaccessible. Even if you're confident it's only a security problem, the whining of the disk still sends shivers from your nose to your toes. A horrid thought, but one that you may be faced with eventually. Don't say it can't happen to you, because it can. In fact, I was faced with such a situation while writing this book, and it cost me a day to rebuild the server. I had been tinkering around with the software and had only just reinstalled the server. I had more software to install, so I had not created an emergency disk, saved the partition configuration, nor done a backup. The worst possible time for a disk failure....

One policy we adopted some time ago was to create two separate backups of the Web server—one for NT and one for the data files of the Web server. Not the applications, just the data files, such as the HTML source, Visual Basic source, and the like. The applications have to be registered with NT when installed, but the data files can reside anywhere and thus can be restored from tape to anywhere. If the server crashes, you'll have to reinstall the applications anyhow, so what's the use in backing up your applications every time? Not much point in that, really, for a Web server. But lose the source files, such as HTML and CGI PL files, and watch what happens to your job security! Those took hours upon hours to create, and even more to rebuild and test.

Microsoft Windows NT Server installs and remembers what hardware it's running on and, therefore, needs to have that same hardware in the backup system.

One last word of advice for you. If your site becomes critical, meaning that you can't afford to be down for more than several hours, you should have a completely installed and mirrored Web server. This is rather expensive as a backup mechanism, so if your company needs the emergency support, but can't afford it, you have an alternative: Use another server to install the software onto another hard drive, so at least the operating system is ready to accept the Web server. In fact, some administrators install the Web server software as well as applications.

If you take this approach for emergency services, be sure to observe software licensing.

Summary

In this chapter, we covered the hazards and fun you can have taking care of a Web server. Because you already know how to manage Microsoft Windows NT Server, I opted to show you how to use alternative communication functions to access and manage the server by adding additional serial ports that could be used as a makeshift ISP. In addition, we talked about how WebTrends can help you find and remove any rocks in the Web server road without scraping yourself to shreds. In the next chapter, we'll delve into Web server and NT security issues as they apply to your site.

18 Web And NT Server Security Models

Jeff Bankston

Security is a very important part of any computing environment. The fun and exploratory nature of the Web brings with it a new set of problems, including virus attacks and intrusions. This chapter is designed to present the problems and the solutions to the problems of security and your Web server. This overview is different than the security we looked at pertaining to the Web server itself, and concentrates on an enterprise-wide view of the issues.

More specifically, the issues presented here cover:

- The Department Of Defense (DOD) security standards
- Standard NT Server security types and applications
- Implementing NT's C2 security level
- Firewall security models
- The reverse DNS lookup model as a security measure

This order of approach should give you an introductory-level overview of security measures from a layman's perspective. While each of these topics has a much deeper explanation, this chapter presents the core technology of each so you'll understand the whys and wherefores of Internet security.

Established DOD Security Levels

By design, the Internet is a wide open frontier given to the vices and virtues of the people inhabiting cyberspace. As such, it has been raided and pillaged on numerous occasions. Any site supervisor worth his or her salt will tell you horror stories of what either has happened or almost happened with an intrusion or unauthorized usage of a system. Intrusions aren't something administrators want to talk about for embarrassment or security reasons. Whatever the cause, any network used for outside connectivity has once upon a time been subjected to this ill will.

DOD security is arranged into four progressively tighter security realms—D, C, B, and A, from least to most secure. Within each region of security, some sub-levels exist and all will be touched upon in this chapter. Also, with each increase in security comes a corresponding increase in cost to implement that level. The following sections take a look at each level, from least to most secure.

Level D

This is level D1, the least secure of any computing environment. In fact, there's no security at all. The whole system or network is wide open for anyone to see and use. Typically, this is a regular MS-DOS PC or a Windows-based computer. On a network, the users have open access to the server's applications, and not even password security is invoked. But this is a rare situation. The most predominant thought here is that anyone at the keyboard cannot be discerned from the next person using the same computer.

Level C

This level has two sub-levels of coverage: C1 and C2. C1 is the next level up the security chain from D1 because username and password pairs of authentication are used for validation. The system administrator uses the NOS tools to assign file and directory access attributes for each user. The administrator may use group profiles for mass rights and permissions settings, remote system access, and printer rights. However, the system administrator has global access throughout the entire system, and there's no tracking mechanism to say what was changed or otherwise altered by the administrator. This level has another hole in it because any user with the administrative password can access the system globally, undifferentiated from another administrator.

Level C2 addresses these C1 issues, and C2 is what Microsoft Windows NT Server implements. C2 restricts users to accessing areas of the network that they have rights to as well as have permissions to reach the files and only the files explicitly open to them. OK. To explain the double-speak, this means that a user may have the right to go to a certain directory and view the files, but this user may not have the permissions granted to use the files. If the user has the permissions and begins using the files, the user leaves an audit trail that NT Server puts into the log file as a record of access, as shown in Listing 19.1.

Listing 19.1 NT authentication audit trail.

```
5/6/96     10:21:40 AM     Print     Information     None     10
   sysmgrjb     BCI_PDC     Document 15, Microsoft Word--PERMISS.DOC owned
   by sysmgrjb was printed on Domain Laser via port LPT1:.  Size in bytes:
   82114; pages printed: 2
5/6/96     8:52:44 AM     Print     Information     None     10
   sysmgrjb     BCI_PDC     Document 14, Microsoft Word--chap13.doc owned
   by sysmgrjb was printed on Domain Laser via port LPT1:.  Size in bytes:
   70742; pages printed: 2
5/5/96     8:34:59 PM     NETLOGON     Information     None     5711
   N/A     BCI_PDC     The partial synchronization request from the server
   BCI_WEB completed successfully. 1 changes(s) has(have) been returned to
   the caller.
5/5/96     12:17:57 PM     Print     Information     None     10
   sysmgrjb     BCI_PDC     Document 8, Microsoft Word--chap14.doc owned by
   sysmgrjb was printed on Domain Laser via port LPT1:.  Size in bytes:
   347417; pages printed: 6
5/5/96     10:54:57 AM     Print     Information     None     10
   sysmgrjb     BCI_PDC     Document 7, Microsoft Word--chap14.doc owned by
   sysmgrjb was printed on Domain Laser via port LPT1:.  Size in bytes:
   179875; pages printed: 4
5/5/96     12:52:09 AM     NETLOGON     Information     None     5711
   N/A     BCI_PDC     The partial synchronization request from the server
   BCI_WEB completed successfully. 1 changes(s) has(have) been returned to
   the caller.
```

```
5/4/96     9:48:47 PM     Print     Information     None     10
   sysmgrjb     BCI_PDC     Document 6, Microsoft Word--chap12.doc owned by
   sysmgrjb was printed on Domain Laser via port LPT1:.  Size in bytes:
   1210740; pages printed: 20
5/4/96     8:35:26 PM     Print     Information     None     10
   Webmaster     BCI_PDC     Document 5, Collage Complete owned by
   Webmaster was printed on Domain Laser via port LPT1:.  Size in bytes:
   251369; pages printed: 1
5/4/96     8:13:26 PM     NETLOGON     Information     None     5711
   N/A     BCI_PDC     The partial synchronization request from the server
   BCI_WEB completed successfully. 1 changes(s) has(have) been returned to
   the caller.
5/4/96     8:00:02 PM     NETLOGON     Error     None     5722     N/A
   BCI_PDC     The session setup from the computer HOME_SVR failed to
   authenticate. The name of the account referenced in the security
   database is HOME_SYSTEMS$.  The following error occurred: Access is
   denied.
```

Notice that the date and time are inserted along with the reason for the entry. On the second line is the username (**sysmgrjb** in the first few entries) and then the domain controller that was recording the event (**BCI_PDC**). The rest of the entries are self-explanatory. This kind of information tracks who did what and when. Even the system administrator gets logged into this system and is unalterable. However, there are alterable events that affect all users that the system administrator can define, as shown in Figure 18.1. This figure clearly shows where events are chosen for the security monitoring process.

> ***Note:*** *If you try to track the entire world's events, then the size of the event file will match it! It's not unreasonable for a one week System log to reach 2MB in size for a 10-user network.*

To define the auditing specifications, go to the Administrative program group, then open the User Manager For Domains program. When you do this, click on the Policies top menu, then Audit submenu. This brings up Figure 18.1.

Later in this chapter, I'll show you how to implement C2 level security on NT Server, but let's get through the rest of the security model first. And before progressing onward, let's address the rather large file that can be created during the auditing process. This can be controlled by going to the Administrative Tools group, starting Event Viewer, and then clicking on the Log Menu. When this menu comes up, click on the Log Settings submenu, and make the necessary

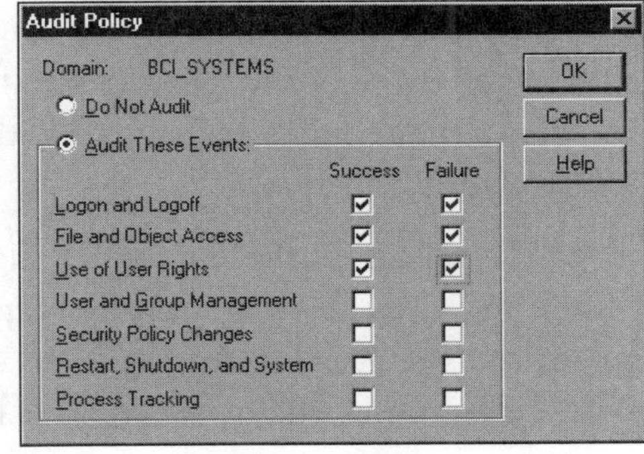

Figure 18.1
Setting the audit options.

changes to the sizes and control of the log files. The drop-down menu shows you all three possible logs that can be controlled, as shown in Figure 18.2.

Level B

This level has three subsections to it, addressing increasing orders of security. The levels are, appropriately enough, named *B1*, *B2*, and *B3*.

B1 Security

Above C2, B1 is the next tightest security level, which means that an object that is under mandatory control by the system will not allow the owner to change any of the permissions of the object (usually an *object* is a file or directory, but it also can be a piece of equipment, such as a tape drive). For instance, if one of the computer operators at your site is classified as the owner of a tape, and the

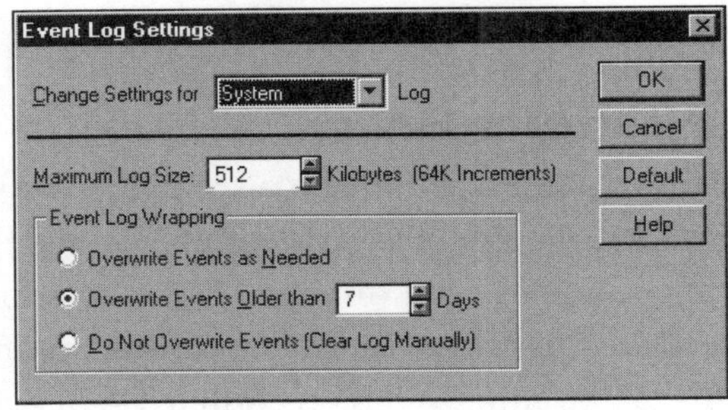

Figure 18.2
Log file size settings.

tape drive has read and write permissions so backups can be done, then the operator can't change the permissions of the tape drive so that a different tape itself could be used to overwrite the operating system with different rights. I think an example might explain this better.

Let's say Susie created a tape called *Accounting* (which classifies Susie as the Owner of that reel of tape), and Chuckie creates a reel of tape called *Master OS*, because Chuckie is one of the system administrators. Access to tape drives is under strict control of the MIS group, usually. When Susie logs into the system to access the tape drive, she only has permissions to use tapes that she created under B1 security, and she can't change the permissions of the tape or contents thereof. Because Chuckie's tape has privileged information on it, Susie might have physical access to the tape but can't do a thing with it because she can't change the rights of the tape to restore the operating system. Such a job might change the rights and permissions of the entire system, opening it up to intrusion!

Oh, and in case you're wondering where the good ol' U.S. Military security falls into the scheme of things, it's right here in B1 level. I could tell you how and why, but then I'd have to shoot you...and burn the book.

B2 Security

B2 says that every object in the domain must have a label affixed to it. For instance, the disk drive that contains the operating system might be called *BOOT DISK*, and the accounting department could be named *THE MONEY PIT*. This further decreases the likelihood of mismanaged security rights because a user's rights and permissions would be indelibly tied to the object. Additionally, object-to-object security can now be formed, placing some objects in a hierarchical tree of control.

B3 Control—Hardware Style

This is where it really gets expensive to run a secured environment. When secure systems are tightened up to this level, you can be assured that most everyone has a security clearance and has been through an extensive background check. In the B3 level, specialized hardware is used to enforce security accesses to the system. One way this can be employed is on clustered systems where disk drives are shared among servers. A circuit card is installed that is programmed to allow access from specific domains in general, although some cards can get down to

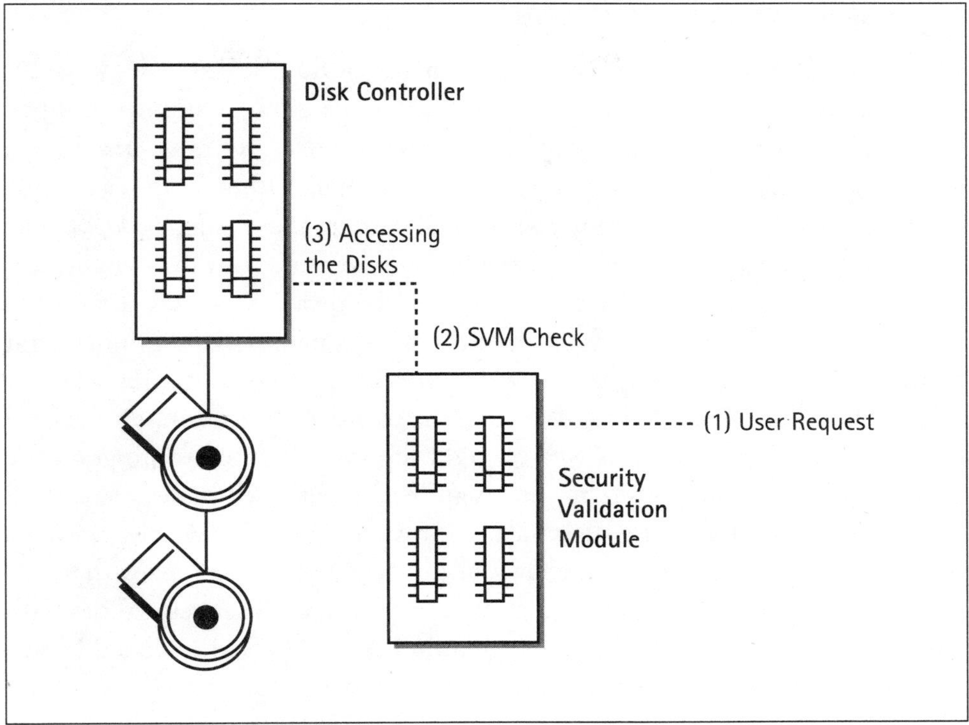

Figure 18.3
Hardware-controlled security access.

the user level, as shown in Figure 18.3. That specificity is not normal, but it's possible, and definitely expensive!

The procedure is usually classified or deeply confidential, but the procedure usually goes something like this.

1. The user makes a disk request, like storing a file. Then, the request from the application goes to the security validation module (SVM).
2. The SVM card performs a lookup of the requester's identification and compares it to the list of authorized users.
3. A match allows the requested operation to be completed. An unauthorized request results in activation of a security alert or a log entry, or perhaps their ejection seat sends them through the roof!

That's the basics of how hardware security works.

Level A

This is the most stringent level of security in the DOD Book of Rules for security. This level is where the SVM card used in the preceding example is shipped from the vendor under tightly controlled and well-known routes of travel, such as the U.S. Postal Service's registered or certified mail. Other methods include special courier services, but not commercial carriers like FedEx or UPS. The intent is that the package is tracked over every step of the way during virtually every minute of its transportational life. The hardware that uses the card is closely monitored during transit. The card itself is manufactured under tight controls, including monitoring who did it, how it was done, and a host of other issues. The firmware circuits used to store the user database are closely guarded under lock and key. As if this isn't enough, the software used to program the card is written by programmers with high-level security clearances, and paid about a skijillion dollars a year in salary. Only the most trustworthy get these programming slots, and they're usually well compensated. The company that performs this work is usually a DOD contractor that has close security ties with our government. Several that come to mind are General Electric, Martin-Marietta, Loral Federal Systems, and Ford Aerospace.

Now that you understand the government security features and functions associated with computers, it's time to see how this applies to Microsoft Windows NT Server's security.

Normal NT Security Issues

If you already know the details of NT's security, you might want to skip this section and go directly to the C2 implementation. In this section, we'll address user, group, and NT share security levels.

User-Level Security

Any user connecting to NT has to pass some sort of security parameters within the server, whether it be login rights or file attributes. It's easy enough to define and control users by way of the User Manager For Groups function. I won't go into each and every right or permission for NT because that's in the *Administrator's Guide* publication. You can also refer to the Microsoft Windows NT Server Resource Kit for a deeper explanation of the rights and permissions.

For the time being, go to your server and start the User Manager. Select any one of the users on your system, and then click on User|Properties to see this person's attributes. There are five buttons with which to select the changes for access, and notice the five checkboxes on the left side. The very bottom one you can't check, but is automatically checked if the account gets locked. If that occurs, you'll have to uncheck it to allow the user back into the network. Choosing any of the many options causes some sort of restriction to be placed on the user, whether it be for the time and day that the user can log in, or group permissions, or to simply restrict what PCs the user can log into on the network.

Group Security

Plan your groups carefully, or you might wind up in trouble giving out full system admin access to guest users!

I usually don't start a section with a tip or a caution, but in this case, it's well worth it. Most administrators don't really think about the overall security issues and how the issues apply to users or collective groups until they start adding users to the NT domain. It's not unreasonable for the integrator of a system to use the old-fashioned paper-and-pencil way to plan out the network, and I wholeheartedly approve. The basic reasoning is that to mess up security means that your system is no longer C2-compliant, if that's how the system was designed, and your Web server is no longer secure, if that's what you wanted in the first place.

In my work with The Microsoft Network as a Category Manager, I had rights to perform certain tasks closely related to the system administration of a server, but not quite as much as an administrator. Some of the other managers on the service had similar rights, but only for other areas specific to their job. As a result, their rights were a subset of mine. At certain times of changes in the service, I noticed that these other managers somehow had rights into my functional area for no apparent reason. Investigating the problem proved that a mistake in group rights had been granted by someone administering the server. Things had gotten so complex that there was no real way to discern what was wrong without spending oodles of time tracking it down. This is exactly what the administrators did to fix it, but this scenario underscores the importance of proper tracking of user and group rights, as demonstrated in Figure 18.4.

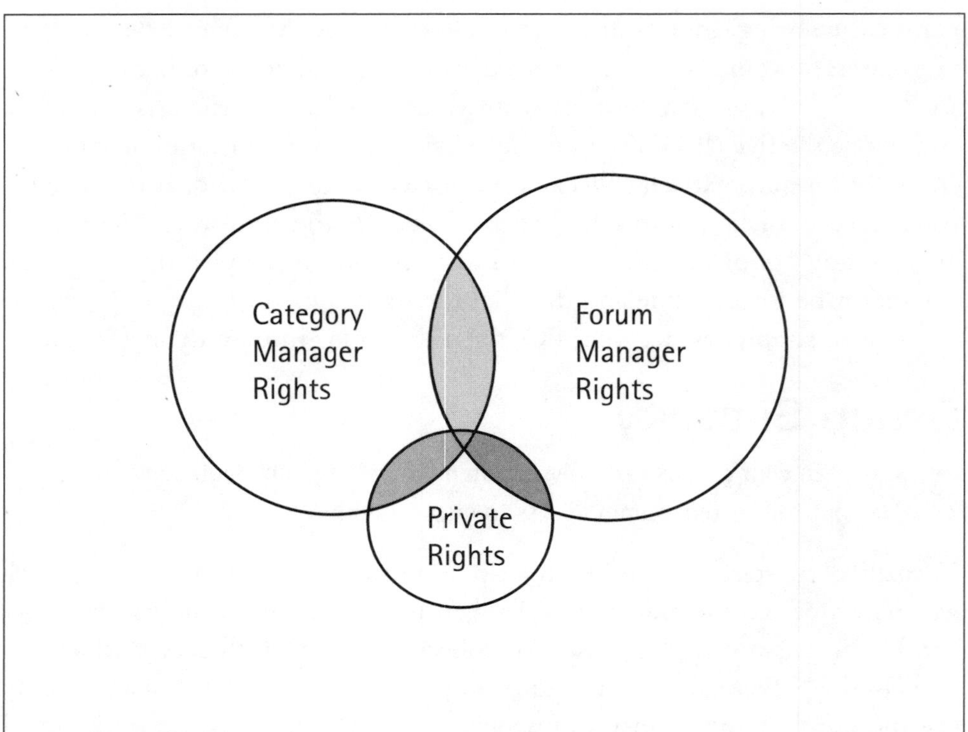

Figure 18.4
Various group rights overlapping.

The zigzag lines in Figure 18.4 denote where the accidental rights were granted to a forum manager where none should've existed! The private rights shown with the little boxes were category manager rights normally granted in an overlapping fashion, but they were cut up by the improper group rights selection. This was not done on purpose, but with some 700 users on the server, something like this was bound to happen. There's no telling how long this condition existed, but it was easy to spot when it occurred. The point is that you should be very careful and have your server's rights and user rights assignments clearly documented.

NT Share Security

Shares is a method that NT uses (as do other operating systems) to make server resources available to the users in a controlled manner. A share can be a printer, or it can be an entire server's disk space, including the NT operating system data areas. The share tells NT which users are authorized to access the resource, and how they're allowed to access it, such as only reading it, writing to it, or the ability to add or delete directories.

As long as a share is in force, any user connecting to the server will be able to see the share, even if the user doesn't have the proper permissions set to access the data within that share. This has been known to open a server to intrusive users.

The key issue here is to only grant access to and share a resource with the bare minimum number of users that use the data or applications. Figure 18.5 shows a share that forms an aggregation of the applications used for my Web server. In one fell swoop, I've limited the users to one controlled area of the server.

The drawback in a situation like this is that the security model is less flexible because so many applications are managed by the share. All I have to do is change the permissions for the individual applications within the share to deny access to anyone I don't want accessing the applications. The plus side is that when I map a drive letter to this server share, only one letter is used. My PC uses drive letters C through K for hard drive partitions and optical drives, so I'm automatically using lots of drive letters. I'm the system administrator for four networks, so I have drive letters mapped to three of these servers resulting in the use of seven more drive letters. Anytime someone uses this many resources, either the user needs lots of disk space (that's me!) or they have no firm concept on disk management. Look at Figure 18.6 for one example of having plenty of shared resources. This shows only a few, but large organizations can have dozens!

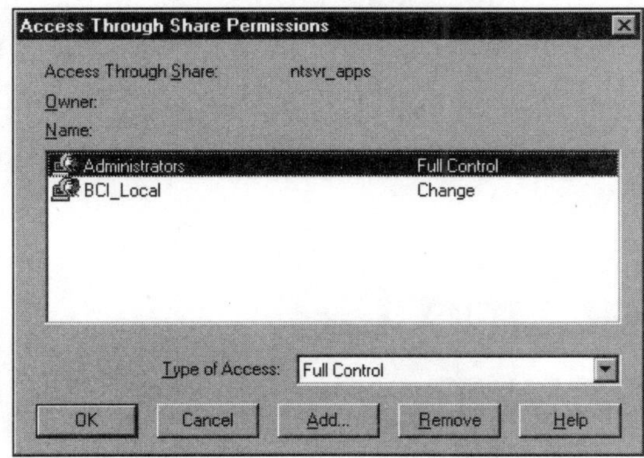

Figure 18.5
Limiting access with a shared location.

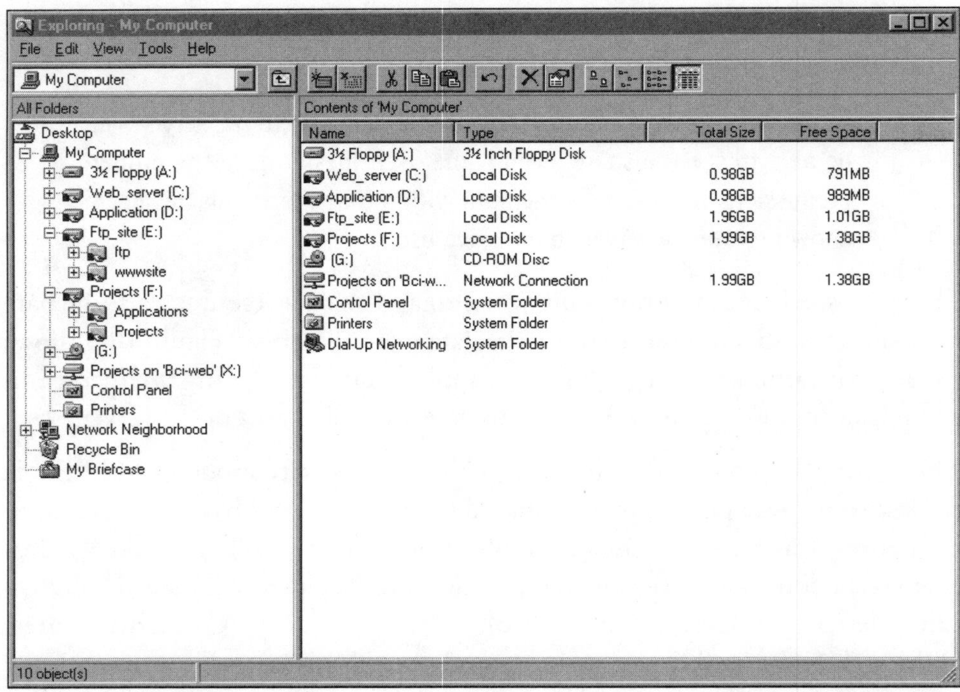

Figure 18.6
Multiple server shared resources.

The key issue here is that the more group shares you make, the more demands you place on the server, and the more chances you have of a security problem cropping up as a result of the users getting mapped to multiple shares. When this happens, some user is likely to have a nonworking application directory, and an administrator might goof granting the wrong (or too many) permissions.

This brings us to the conclusion of the security presentation. Next, we'll focus on the task of implementing the C2 security level that Microsoft has boasted about in Microsoft Windows NT Server.

Implementing C2 Level Security

Microsoft steadfastly insists that NT is capable of C2 level security. There are a few issues involved that will be discussed in the next sections. Just in case you don't know this, you can also implement C2 security in an NT workstation provided the partitions are running NTFS. In this section, we'll take a look at what C2 security is, and what it isn't.

What C2 Is...

C2 is a comparable balance between resources that a user owns if their PC runs NT and the requirements to secure an operating environment to the level that intruders can be effectively denied access. It's a straightforward methodology for a network administrator that understands security, networks, access controls, and systematical approaches to user controls. If you follow the C2 guidelines to the letter, then you'll most likely have a server secure enough for the most demanding and intrusive users or computer fiends. In order to implement C2, your server must meet the requirements shown in Figure 18.7.

Look at each of the functions listed in the figure, and you'll see a lock figure to the left of it. If the lock is in the unlocked position, then the NT function will not allow C2 to be implemented. When locked, the icon is red, and the lock mantle is in the down position, indicating that the function meets C2 requirements. In this configuration, nothing about this NT workstation meets the C2 security level. As a comparison, I implemented partial C2 on my domain server to show you the difference, as shown in Figure 18.8.

Thus, to fully secure a server to the C2 level means that the server can't be running any software that opens a hole to intruders, such as a DOS partition where a user could access it by booting the server from a DOS floppy and

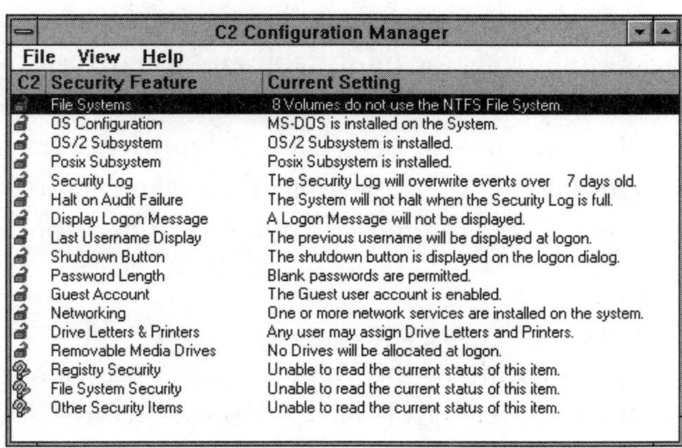

Figure 18.7
C2 security implementation details.

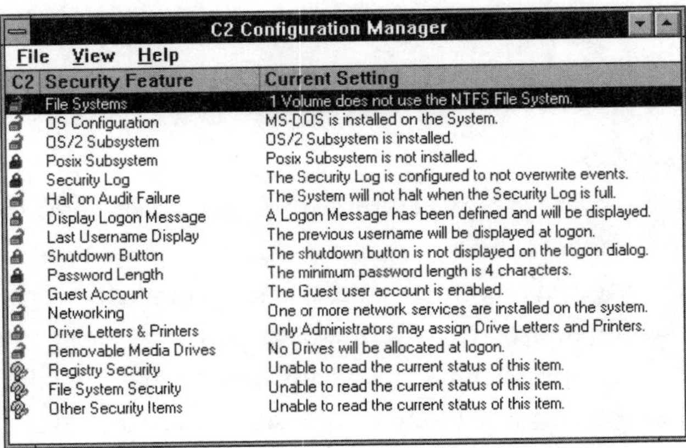

Figure 18.8
Partial C2 security employed.

seeing the partition. If you look at each of these requirements and wonder how you can understand them to their fullest, you'll find an explanation of them in the Microsoft Windows NT Server Resource Kit 4, available from Microsoft Corporation or your local computer dealer. To go in each of these functions would easily take up a complete chapter in itself, so I'll refer you to the Resource Kit.

And What C2 Isn't...

Looking at the C2 functions and understanding what they do might give you an idea that a fully C2-compliant server is the cat's meow for denying intrusion. What you should *not* do is drop your guard if you implement C2 to its fullest extent! C2 is meant to provide the most stable and secure server possible given the type of computers we use today. What it can't possibly do is anticipate every possible new development in viruses or hackers' knowledge learned by prying into computers. I'm not saying that Microsoft's implementation of C2 doesn't work—it truly deters all but the most adamant intruder from breaking into the server.

The Web by its own design is an open atmosphere and subject to break-ins due to the programmatical nature of the Web. CGI and programming tools like C++ are so powerful that, in capable hands, a program written to break passwords and login security is possible given enough time and computational power. You need to maintain your vigil, keeping an eye on user passwords and physical access to the server. Don't fully count on the programmatical implementation of C2 to keep your computing world safe.

The last topic I'd like to share with you in the security department is the use of firewalls to help secure an entire network.

Firewall Security

A firewall can be thought of as a guard shack at an international border crossing. When you cross from one country into another, you have to present a passport to the guards. If you have the proper credentials, you're let through, otherwise, you're refused passage. Firewalls do the same, only with a TCP/IP address of the source and destination computers.

A Simple Firewall

One of the simplest firewalls you can implement is the usage of multiple network interface cards in the same computer. This forms a method of internal routing that is sometimes used in place of purchasing an expensive external router to guide and direct network traffic between network segments. However, within NT, you can use software to perform network routing between the networks, as shown in Figure 18.9, as well as the proxy installed in Chapter 8.

This is a common trick that is sometimes referred to as a *Poor Man's Router*, but it can be used for segmenting networks. This reduces the load on a server by keeping network traffic for one segment to that segment only, and only routing traffic to other segments when it's required. The same technique can be employed to segment external Internet traffic from the internal business network, as shown in Figure 18.10.

The other part of the equation is the use of hosting software running on the firewall computer, which serves to further secure the networks. As of the time I wrote this chapter, I was unable to locate host software for firewall agents to perform this function as a solely dedicated function. All of the solutions I found were Unix-based, and there were plenty of them.

Enhanced Firewalls

If you really need to secure your internal network and retain connectivity to the Internet, then there's a way to form a double gauntlet of protection, sometimes

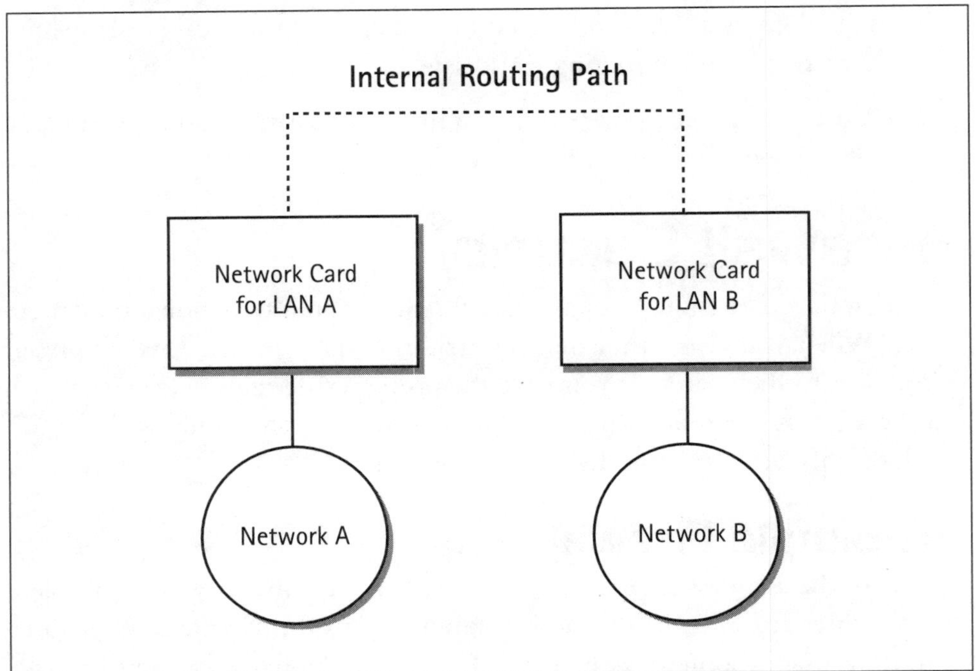

Figure 18.9
Using multiple network cards in a server.

referred to as a *bastion host.* When run in conjunction with a router that screens or remaps the TCP/IP addresses, it filters those that reside on the internal network and prevents entry onto your network of unwanted guests. MAC layer means *Media Access Control,* and it's the second lowest layer in a network card's interface, next to the physical connection of the cabling. The basic theory is to use the technique employed in Figure 18.10, and add a router between the firewall computer and the external connection. This router serves to filter the incoming traffic first, and then forward the traffic that passed the filter on to the firewall computer. This strategy forms a very secure two-way barrier to external intrusion.

If all of this is not enough for you, and you absolutely must have a completely secure environment and tie your internal networks to the Internet, there's one more technique you can employ.

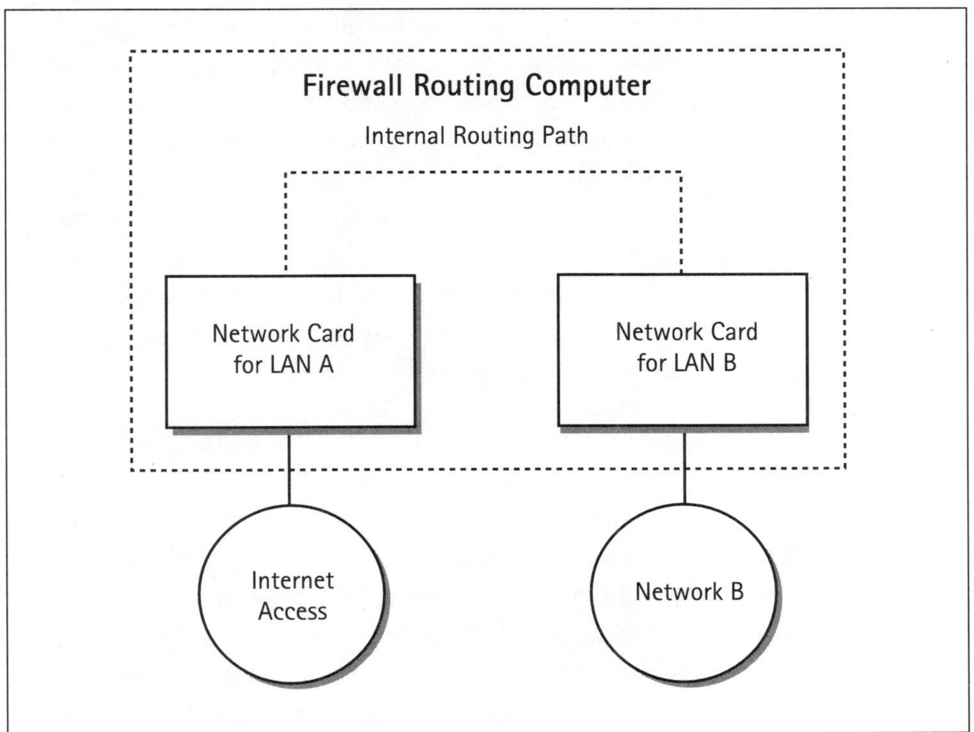

Figure 18.10
Separating external and internal networks.

Double Firewalls, Proxy Servers, And Sacrificial Hosts

This firewall technique, called a *sacrificial host*, is a very expensive solution. This system is used to store and forward incoming packets after having been filtered by the first-line router and the outside firewall host. If the outside router says that the incoming data passes the filtering test, then the packets are sent to the outside firewall, which is after the outside router. Once this far, the packets can be interpreted by the outside host computer, such as an external Web server, where, if anything goes wrong, there's no great loss. Sure, the Web server comes down, but the internal networks are saved.

If the packets make it this far, then the inside firewall serves as a proxy server to interpret and pass only the packets that pass the filtering test to make the trip to the internal network. This method provides a double layer of protection by creating two avenues of opportunity for the administrator to stop intrusions. This setup is normally all that an organization could expect to create for the ultimate in C2 security. Beyond this, the B level of security demands the use of fiber optics and cryptological devices to scramble the packets using the DES (Data Encryption Standard) created by the U.S. Government. DES encryption is commonly used in functions where the very best in protection is required, and it's so good that it can't be exported outside of the U.S. In fact, several excellent utilities, such as PCTools for Windows, employ encryption algorithms that cause the application to be distributable only in the U.S.

Summary

The end has been reached on another part of our journey to create and maintain Web servers, but we've taken a slight detour from normal Web functions to look at server security from a different perspective. I've introduced you to the different levels of security that may be necessary to implement a protective scheme for your Web server and internal networks. I wish I had time and space to go on, because security is so vitally important that I could write an entire book on Internet security alone. However, we must move on. Here's to a secure Web site and its productive future.

19

When It All Goes To Pot!

Jeff Bankston

Any electronic or electrical device is subject to failing at any time—and without warning. Computers are no exception. There are many reasons why computers fail, and few reasons or methods available to prevent failures. Truly effect preventive methods are few and far between. This chapter shows you how to respond to system disasters either just before or just after they occur. We'll discuss what you can do to recover from:

- Subjective power failures
- Temperature-induced disasters
- Theft of equipment
- Vandalism and sabotage
- Virus attacks

Subjective Power Outages

Subjective, huh? It never fails. There is usually someone in the crowd who purchases a UPS unit for a server to ensure all bases are covered, but then forgets to connect the serial cable between the UPS and the physical server, or fails to install the proper software to control the shutdown of the server when the UPS senses a power loss. Let me elaborate.

True story: An experienced network administrator installed a new UPS unit on a network server that was to begin doing double duty as the company's Web server. All of the standard precautions were followed during the installation. The UPS software was installed, and the administrator even went to the Control Panel and made the proper settings via the UPS program. NT knew the UPS was there, and all looked fine. A week later, the administrator came into the computer room smelling smoke—the acrid smell of fear is what it really was. Frantically chasing down the source of the burning, the administrator discovered that the UPS itself had fried and the server had shut down. The administrator breathed a sigh of relief, thinking the UPS did its job and shut down the server. Moments later, the administrator discovered that not only did the UPS fry, but so did various parts of the server!

Rightly so, the administrator thought the CFO was going have his head for breakfast. Lots of money was going to be spent now, for sure. Fortunately, the administrator remembered that the UPS warranty covered any attached equipment up to $25,000 in replacement value. Whew! That was a close call. So, the administrator called the UPS vendor, reported the claim, and the vendor dispatched a locally available technician to write up a report. Promising swift turnaround of the paperwork, the vendor set about with the investigation, and the network administrator set about getting the spare server operational.

Both finished about the same time. Then, the vendor's technician handed the administrator the bad news—the warranty was null and void! The UPS was connected into a power source that was not properly grounded, had a 15-volt difference of potential between the neutral leg and ground, and had an intermediate power extension running off of it that was not NEMA rated. Any one of the three problems just mentioned was enough to void the warranty, and the UPS destruction was all but assured. It also answered the nagging questions of erratic server problems, which had prompted the company to buy the UPS in the first place.

This real-life disaster shows that there are plenty of gremlins hiding in every part of your computer installation. One gremlin that is frequently overlooked is that the power infrastructure of your site (which can run a typewriter and coffee pot just fine) may not be adequate for your computer system (which is much more sensitive than most electrical appliances). Having your grounding system checked and validated once a year is a very good idea. If your equipment is in an office complex, it may be a wise idea to ask the building manager to survey the power structure for problems.

Temperature-Induced Disasters

Another silent bombshell waiting for the opportune (or inopportune) moment to strike is searing temperatures within the computer case and distributed throughout the server. Every component generates heat to different levels of intensity, and it's all cumulative. The end result is a gradual degradation of performance in every component. To what degree this temperature affects performance is somewhat of a mystery. However, the following sections discuss methods of reducing heat and applying cooling components.

Direct Equipment Cooling

Direct cooling refers to the use of heat sinks and cooling fans to reduce or eliminate heat. You probably recognize that heat sink and cooling fan combinations exist for processors, but do you know fans are available for I/O cards? Cooling fans for I/O cards are nothing more than full-length cards mounted with two 3-inch fans. The fans break up the hotspots between the cards and move the hot air to the top of the case faster.

The same is true for hard drives. Vendors are recognizing the need for additional cooling where many drives are installed one on top of another, creating one massive heat generator. Such a situation is common in RAID drive installations, where three or more drives are installed in a vertical stack. One cooling solution is to use 1 1/2-inch fans that blow air onto the drive stack. Not meant to explicitly cool the drives, the fans merely circulate air from the case and into the drive stack, resulting in a disruption of the heat buildup. In most server-sized cases, there's ample room to mount air-circulation fans, as depicted in Figure 19.1.

Indirect Cooling

In the majority of tower cases, the power supply is located in the top rear of the case with its own cooling fan. What a lot of folks don't realize is that the heat

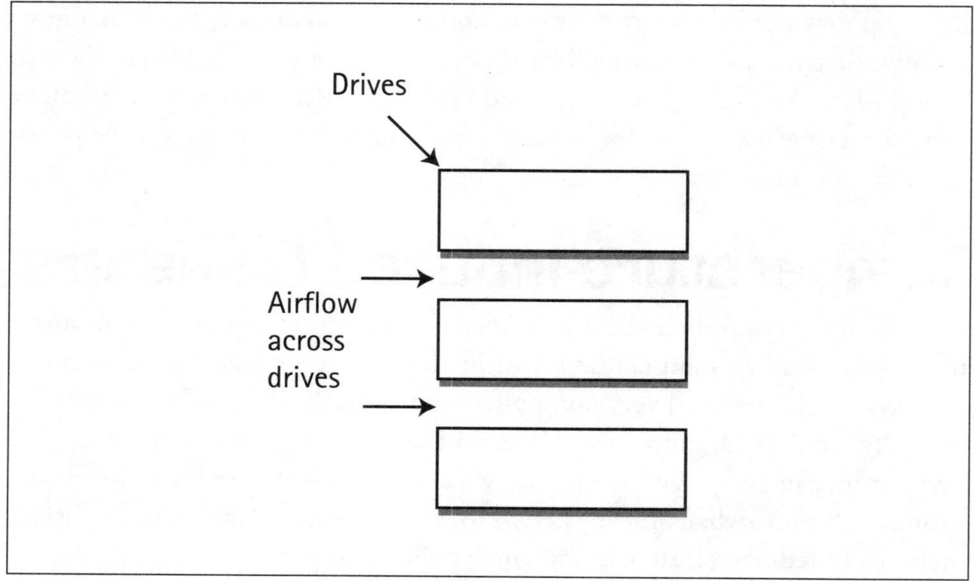

Figure 19.1
Direct cooling methods.

that rises to the top of the case is being exhausted by being drawn into the power supply and blown out the back. The power supply is therefore being heated further by the internal heat generated by components. Not that the power supply runs cool on its own, but the additional heat isn't helping the power supply at all. In fact, the extra heat causes the power supply to run less efficiently.

As such, there needs to be a way to reduce the heat everywhere before something melts down Chernobyl-style. There are several ways this can be accomplished, inexpensively and otherwise. Full-size tower cases built today routinely have a prebuilt place in the top of the case for a second fan to be added to draw out the heat in the case without heating up the power supply.

Yet another way to keep your system cool is to use thermoelectric cooling plates that transfer heat from one surface to another. These plates are meant to be installed directly onto a device, but they can also be installed onto the case in a location that causes cool air to be generated. You wouldn't want to install one of these directly onto a hard drive, but indirect case cooling works great.

Rack-Mounted Systems

This last section looks at the most expensive proposition presented thus far, but this setup offers the greatest benefits. When your computer facilities grow to several servers, then perhaps you'd be better served (pardon the pun) by installing your computers into floor-mounted stand-up racks. These devices are industry standard 19-inch wide racks where you mount the computer into a special chassis drawer that slides in and out on rails. The entire computer components, including drives, are mounted inside this case. The case has vents and two or more cooling fans in the rear of the case that exhaust the air out the back and cause fresh air to be drawn into the front of the case.

When rack-mounted case and cabinets like these are used, you can then use air conditioners to blow cool air through the facility's subfloor computer room. Never seen one of those? Imagine the room where your computers are sitting now on the floor. The air they get now is regular room ambient air. A raised-floor computer room is one in which the computers sit on a false floor that is raised about one foot above the concrete floor, by way of special floor mounts, as shown in Figure 19.2.

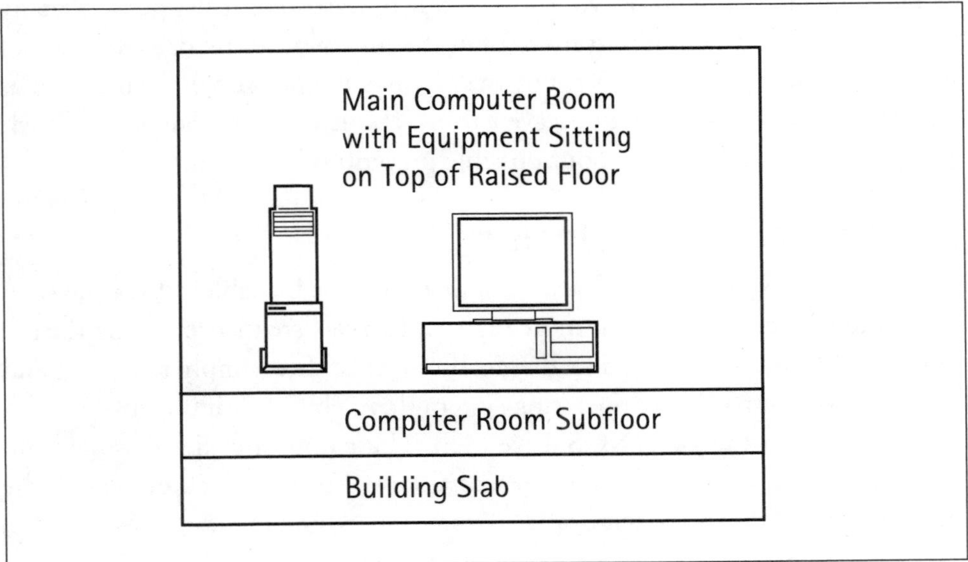

Figure 19.2
Computer room raised floor.

When you have a situation like this, the rack-mounted equipment is mounted directly over an opening in the raised floor, so cool air flows into the bottom of the cabinet and circulating fans can blow cool air into the racked equipment. Sensors arranged all around the equipment are set to monitor both airflow and temperature. If either gets out of whack, you could be notified automatically by beeper or have the equipment shut down, to prevent possible damage.

Don't have the money for a complete raised-floor computer room? Well, not to fret, because there are solutions for that, too! If you want to use rack-mounted servers, then you might want to explore floor-mounted miniature air conditioners. These little gems are rated in many capacities from 300 to 5,000 BTUs of cooling capacity, which is more than enough for a single rack. Operating on 120VAC power, they produce enough cold air to satisfy a full rack of equipment.

The Sticky Finger Syndrome

It never fails. Every computer operation is subject to the less pleasurable moments in computing life, such as theft. These kinds of disasters leave you holding the bag with no possible way out—period. Pilferage in a computer room may or may not be a problem in your office, but rest assured, it happens in many locations. It could be nothing more than the loss of a floppy drive or a set of mounting rails for a hard drive, but the obvious major problems are there, as well. Many sites managers don't even think about the consequences of theft and, therefore, rarely think about possible prevention methods.

Lockable Hard Drives

If a hard drive is installed into a server, how can it be lockable? Open the case, and there's the drive. True, but more high-end servers are incorporating the use of removable and hot swappable drives. If one fails, then simply remove it and replace it with a spare. The operating system then rebuilds it if possible, assuming that it wasn't the main NOS drive itself. These units are all accessible from the front of the server and use a hexagonal key of sorts to lock or unlock the drive, or spin it down for removal.

Lockable Computers

When lockable drives aren't possible or you have special needs requiring you to secure the server, lockable cabinets and server cases becomes a fundamental problem. This is because very few server vendors make a truly secure case. Sure, it has a key lock on the front of the case, but it's more like a steel latch hooking on a plastic case block. This isn't my version of a lockable case. It should be a steel lock slide onto a portion of the steel case itself. Additional security should prevent unauthorized access to the floppy drives and tape drive. This would prevent someone from rebooting the server with a floppy and gaining access to the server software.

Lockable Computer Rooms

The last physical security issue is of the entire computer room. In the office where I used to work, over $1 million in server and networking equipment existed to serve our local 200 plus users as well as users across our wide area network. In this situation, the computer room was secured by magnetic striped cards tying into the locked room with a computer that controls each door in the entire facility. A user must swipe the card through the entry point device, much like you would at an ATM, and then punch in a password. A valid card and a valid password gets you into the facility. This is the ultimate in protection and the ultimate in expense to match. Fully implemented, this tactic also lets you sleep well at night if your computer room is that valuable.

Insuring The Investment

This is an obvious protection mechanism, but it's usually an afterthought at best. If you have to seek reimbursement for covered equipment, then the damage has been done. In the case of insurance, you should be aware of several concerns:

- Very few companies insure beyond several thousand dollars in personally used computers.
- Insurance underwriters for major data processing equipment have a variety of requirements that you'll have to fulfill before you can get the proper amount of coverage.
- Policy premiums can easily hit a mark of $10 per thousand in coverage. For the average network or Web server, this is a premium of $250 a year for just one server.

- Insurability is sometimes judged by an independent survey from another computer firm. No matter how competent you and your people are, an underwriter may require you to pay for a survey from an outside source.

In arranging the coverage for my equipment, I was required to have the computers and any networked devices centrally located in one facility that was bricked up on the outside, and all of the servers had to be running on UPS units certified by the underwriter as acceptable. One such UPS is the American Power Conversion (APC) UPS, which comes with a $25,000 protection policy for any equipment plugged into it. For my policy to be in force, I had to strictly adhere to the instructions that came with the APC unit.

When Sticky Fingers Aren't Enough—Theft Vs. Vandalism

Theft is an outright loss of property used to complete your mission. However, theft isn't the only outside hazard capable of deteriorating your site's operation. Computer vandalism comes in several forms, ranging from someone cutting a cable between drives, smashing fiber optic cables, and otherwise finding ways to disrupt normal operations. Both theft and vandalism cost businesses money to repair and replace parts, and businesses must absorb the loss of revenue if the damaged equipment keeps the business from functioning. However you size it up, it boils down to securing as much of your equipment as possible, within reason. Obviously, there's nothing you can do about the external cable plant operations between buildings or running along the telephone poles.

You can protect your business's internal investment with the physical security implementations mentioned earlier, but be aware that petty theft can prove to be a mere shadow compared to treacherous vandalism. One type of vandalism that has villainous effects is when a programmer creates a back door into your system or creates a time bomb in a server. When you hire your programmers, check their references, and verify their trustworthiness. Even though programmers are essential to many network operations, you should understand that they have access to every single part of the network, regardless of what server-level security you implement. All someone would have to do is understand enough of the operating system to create a little utility that works at the NOS level, and boom! You could be left wide open to a heck of a surprise. On the other hand, if you implement sufficient security, you'll prevent this from ever occurring.

The Impact On Your Web Site

The overall impact of vandalism is crystal clear—loss of productivity and money. In addition, you may have certain contractual issues to deal with if you can't provide the necessary support to your customers. Such an impact tends to be felt for some time to come as you recover the site. On some occasions, the destruction itself masks the marauders' entrance and exit, so you'll never know what hit, or when. The best preventive measures here are to have frequent and separate backups of your data files away from the operating system and use password protection that the trusted employees (and only the essential ones) know.

Preventive Measures

Perhaps the best defense against vandalism is to work with your people and ensure that everyone involved understands the operations, what they can and can't do, and what will happen if the system is vandalized. Normal security measures can only go so far—a peaceful working relationship goes a lot further and is cheaper in the long run. A quarterly audit of equipment and software is another useful process, if not for insurance purposes, then to let employees know that the equipment is valued and accounted for at various times. You can also implement tight server-level security to prevent files from being copied or used after certain times of the day or days of the week.

Unfortunately, no matter how well you institute physical protection for your server, there's always the presence of a sly and devious creature called the *computer virus*. We've all been exposed to some degree to virus attacks in one form or another. The repercussions of a virus attack are the same as those experienced when theft or vandalism occurs—loss of server time and added monetary costs to restore the system. Yet, for all the potential damage a virus can do, users often ignore preventive measures. The next section discusses viruses.

A Silent Marauder—Viruses

What was once a mysterious and seldom fatal attraction has rapidly become the scourge of computing. Viruses are oftentimes thought of as a prank or sick joke played on an unsuspecting public, but they've gotten more dangerous as time goes on. This section is intended to wake you up to the stark realization of what virus attacks can do, how to prevent them (or reduce the threat), and illustrate a real-life occurrence of what one virus did to a major network.

NT's Built-In Protection

Built-in protection is often a misnomer, but NT really does have a form of virus protection available, provided the NTFS file system has been implemented. NT's increased performance and operating characteristics comes from the various parts of NT itself. One particular function of NT is called the *Hardware Abstraction Layer*, or the HAL, which performs the actual accessing of the physical hardware installed in the server. HAL serves to create a shield and a level of independence for applications and programmatical functions. As such, ordinary applications that run fine under Windows 3.x or Windows 95 and directly access the hardware, will not work under NT. The same is true for a virus because a virus is an application, as well. Even TSR driver viruses can't install in NT once NT is operational because of this shield.

While NT provides a shield against viruses, you're not completely protected against virus attacks. You need to do everything you can to protect yourself from viruses. Do not forget about the possibility of a virus attack on a Microsoft Windows NT Server based system.

Software Protection

For added virus protection, you should check out one of the many fine antivirus software kits available. Among the leaders in the market is Symantec's Anti-Virus for NT. Other popular vendors offering NT-based solutions include McAfee and Cheyenne Software. As always, diligence in maintaining a schedule of scanning and protection must be adhered to, or all is for naught. Also, you should invest in protection for every desktop PC that brings in data to the system. If you don't, then one possible pitfall might be created while backing up data to tape storage—you could actually store a virus on your backup tapes! Of course, you'll never know you stored the virus until you restore your files—and the virus—from the backup. The last thing you need when restoring files (which is a bad sign in itself) is to be hit with a virus.

When A Virus Attacks

What I'm about to tell you is another one of my true stories of computer disasters. In a company I used to work with some time ago, most of the MIS types didn't care much about virus protection, and those that did care didn't have a clue about how to protect their systems correctly. The circumstances surrounding the entry of the virus into the network were never fully pinned down, but the damages were clearly documented.

The entire computing community consisted of 14 networks spread across a campus-wide intranet of some 13,000 users. A multiple FDDI ring was in place to connect all of the buildings and servers together. Several of the servers were of the Sun Workstation variety in which five of them formed a cluster of operating software that worked together, forming an apparently single unit. If you're not familiar with clustered systems, two or more computers connected together can pool their resources to build a considerably more efficient computing environment. A server working at only 10 percent capacity can do some of the work of another server running at 95 percent capacity. This balances the workload and smooths out the overall performance of the entire system.

Sometimes in clustered systems, operating software on one server must be running to enable another physical server to work. When systems tie in tightly like this, disruption of one server frequently wreaks havoc on the others. This was the case when the virus hit the campus network. It was thought that the virus entered the network via a DOS-based machine, proliferated into one of the neighboring networks, and then migrated into another building where it infected several desktop PCs on its way to the building's network server.

The virus was discovered when a user in the fourth network called the MIS group asking what MIS had done with his data files on another PC. Checking into the problem, MIS found out that the PC's hard disk was absolutely clean. Clean as in not even a partition existed! This was a key sign that something was definitely wrong, but the MIS person missed the wake-up call. The PC was repartitioned and the software was reloaded. The MIS person thought a corruption wiped out the disk. The user then restored the data files from a recent backup, and away he went. Actually, he went off to lunch and returned to find his other PC wiped out as well. By this time, the network server for the entire building had been infected and wiped out.

At that point, the MIS group realized that a virus was on the loose and destroying data, but they mistakenly thought that it was a DOS-only problem and that the Unix machines were not affected. Wrong! This was the second big mistake the MIS group made, and eventually, it proved to be the worst. With this network physically disconnected from the WAN, they cleaned up the infection, not thinking to disconnect the desktop PCs from the network while repairs were underway. They also failed to notify anyone else.

Well, by this time the virus had replicated and morphed into another strain of virus and proceeded to infect the clustered machines, wiping them out as well. MIS wasn't sure how this happened, and still aren't to this day. All they know is the system was shut down for four days while the virus was eradicated. It should tell you that even if you're a small fry, you should take viruses very seriously or be prepared to pay the price.

Summary

Chapter 19 brings us to the conclusion of the book. Disaster situations previewed here actually occurred and, unfortunately, are continuing to recur in many businesses. Hopefully, armed with the information provided here, you'll be able to implement precautions that will help your system maintain optimal performance throughout the years. I've really enjoyed sharing this information with you, and I'd like to leave you with one final thought: If we plan ahead, computers will serve us, not us them!

EPILOGUE

Jeff Bankston

Installing and maintaining NT Web Servers is merely one more fact of life in the chain of network operating systems. In fact, NT is just another vendor's way of bringing the Internet to the once peaceful (albeit more simple) network infrastructure. Internet services, regardless of which operating system hosts the Web server itself, are going to be the number one challenge for businesses at the crossing of the millennia. It will be a challenge because the Internet is growing at a 200 percent rate each year with servers and clients running things like shopping malls, chat rooms, the ever-present smut rings, and many other topics and services of interest that can be stored on a server.

What makes this scenario scary is the use of the PC hardware to perform these tasks. You really have to keep in mind that, initially, the PC was intended to serve a single user, way back when IBM and Microsoft first started this adventure 15 years ago. What is now happening is that mission-essential operations, access to the Internet, and other critical components of business computing are being conducted on this entity called a PC. So, you should always remain keenly aware that when things go terribly wrong and you're ready to seek revenge on the salesman who sold you the system, it's all based on a PC—perhaps a massively powerful one but, nonetheless, a PC.

Is this a condemnation of the PC and NT Server? Not at all, but it's a realization that not everything in the networking world is for everyone. If you love a challenge and look forward to each day's adventures on your network, then this book should help you with all of the little problems involved in starting up your own NT Web Server. It's my sincerest hope that the important issues have been addressed by this book within the topics I've selected. My own experiences, both painful and pleasing, have been shared here in the reverent hope that it will benefit you like it has me, but without the bumps for you that I experienced along the way.

Appendix A

Jeff Bankston

Active Server Pages—The Microsoft initiative that extends Internet Information Server by providing a linkage between server extensions and IIS.

ActiveX—The Microsoft technology that extends functionality of any OLE component or application, such as Internet Information Server.

ARPA—A form of reverse DNS resolution allowing Web servers to check the alias used backwards against the calling server. This allows for a more secure server, but only if reverse resolution is enabled.

ARPANET (Advanced Research Projects Agency Network)—The first network infrastructure, which evolved into what is now called the Internet.

Bandwidth—The property of an electronic data circuit that specifies how much data can be safely carried on the circuit at one time. ISDN circuits have a maximum bandwidth of 144,000 bits per second, although most of the time only half of that is in actual use.

Bottleneck—A restriction preventing any device from performing at maximum capability. In a disk drive system, slower physical drives can be a bottleneck, even though the disk controller is capable of faster performance.

C2 Security—The mid-level security that Microsoft Windows NT Server implements to form a secure computing environment. C2 was created by the U.S. Department Of Defense.

DNS (Domain Naming Service)—The mechanism by which an alpha name (such as **www.bci.com**) is converted to the numerical IP address equivalent (**206.139.150.35**).

Filter—A function that checks an IP address or alias and allows the data to pass on to the destination or to be rejected.

Firewall—A device, usually software, that prevents or allows users who are outside of your internal network to see your Web site. Normally, firewalls are created to prevent unauthorized users from entering your site, but they can be used to prevent intranet users from getting to the Internet, as well.

FrontPage—Microsoft Corporation's HTML editor (originally owned by Vermeer Software). Allows the user to create full-featured and integrated Web pages.

Gopher—The Internet protocol that creates menus from disk drive directories and files. This was an early forerunner of the Web.

Hop Count—The number of routers or processing devices that handle each data packet from the source to the destination.

HTML (Hypertext Markup Language)—The basic programming source code of the Internet Web page.

HTTP (Hypertext Transfer Protocol)—The language used to communicate between Web servers and Web clients, or browsers.

IIS (Internet Information Server)—Microsoft's premier Web server integrating HTTP, FTP, and Gopher protocols into one environment.

Index Server—Any operation that creates a quick listing to a larger database of listings. Speeds up access to large databases.

Internet Domain—The function that creates and defines a Web site. Each domain is a "territory" covered by an Internet provider, with blocks of 256 IP addresses and services for customers of dialup modems. However, some domains are private sites that do not resell connectivity.

IPX/SPX—The protocol standard used primarily by NetWare operating systems to enable communication among servers and clients. NT Server also uses IPX/SPX for certain functions such as Remote Access Server.

ISDN (Integrated Services Digital Network)—A 144Kbps link in which a pair of 64K channels is used to transfer digitized data between source and destination. (Standard modems are analog in nature.) A separate 16K signaling channel is also employed for setup and breakdown of the link. ISDN is much better at processing data and is less susceptible to line noises than traditional analog lines.

Java—The language pioneered by Sun Microsystems used to create C programming language applets that can manipulate Web page components and information.

Linux—The Unix derivative operating system used by many first-time Unix users to learn Unix.

NNTP (Network News Transfer Protocol)—Creates and distributes news server information.

NT Server Domain—The NT Server principle of a collective computing environment. An NT Domain is usually an entire business having several different departments, such as accounting, engineering, and logistics.

POP (Post Office Protocol)—One of the languages that email servers use to communicate and transmit email.

PPP (Point-to-Point Protocol)—One of two common protocols used to connect clients to Internet servers using modems. PPP uses a much-improved error-correction mechanism to ensure better data processing as opposed to using SLIP.

Proxy Server—Software, used sometimes in conjunction with a firewall, to build an impenetrable barrier to intruders. A proxy gives users the illusion that they're accessing a Web site, when in reality, the proxy sends the user to another Web site based on administrator-provided parameters.

RAID (Redundant Array Of Inexpensive Disks)—A system that uses two or more disk drives to form a logical disk drive, using a highly reliable scheme of data storage based on various levels of protection (referred to as RAID 1, RAID 2, and so on).

RAS (Remote Access Server)—Microsoft's suite of communications tools used to provide remote connectivity for NT Server clients.

Reverse DNS—Used to validate user access rights to a Web server. When you connect to a site, the site checks with the server you use to make your Internet connection, and then validates who you are.

Router—The network device used to send data packets to the desired destination. The router helps prevent the data from going to the wrong location.

Server Extensions—Enables the Web server to perform more functions than it is normally capable of, by integrating additional drivers and software.

SLIP (Serial Line Internet Protocol)—The first Internet access method used by analog modems to connect to the Internet.

SMTP (Simple Mail Transport Protocol)—The Internet mail standard used to send email to outbound servers. SMTP is capable of attaching files to the email messages using various formats such as BINHEX and UUencoding.

Storage Channel—A high throughput disk drive subsystem in which data is moved at rates of 100MB or higher. This is the next generation of data storage for RAID systems, and it uses fiber optics as the medium instead of cables.

TCP/IP (Transmission Control Protocol/Internet Protocol)—The communication standard used to transfer data across the Internet.

UPS (Uninterruptible Power Supply)—Used to prevent power loss to a device when primary power is lost or when the primary power is in an unstable condition.

Virtual Circuit—A communications path used by computers in which the path is not over the same physical server at any one point in time. This allows for a more flexible movement of data across links that could fail unexpectedly.

Virtual Server—The function within IIS that allows IIS to emulate another Web server by assigning a TCP/IP address to an individual directory under the control of IIS.

Web Server—The core operating software used to provide HTTP services from the server to the client.

Appendix B

Jeff Bankston

Computers are great tools when they work for us, but they can be a nightmare when things go wrong—and, as you know, things usually go wrong at the most inopportune times. Often, you'll be able to solve a problem by yourself, using your wit, wisdom, or just plain blind luck. However, the one time in your computing life when absolutely everything must run smoothly, everything in the world will go wrong. For instance, the cat chews through the power cord, you spill Coke in the keyboard and the motherboard objects, or you remember that you forgot to plug in the UPS just about the time you see the first flash of a lightning bolt.

For whatever reason, disasters will test your merit and inner strength. When your strength gets a bit frazzled (often around 3 a.m.), you'll be reaching for a helping hand. Your list of resources will vary from site to site, so I've compiled a list of helpful resources that will aid you in troubleshooting Web server problems.

Microsoft Developer's Network

Wait—a programming reference? Isn't this appendix in a book about *Web servers*? Sure, it is. But plenty of programming is involved with CGI code, Visual Basic, and the Internet protocols themselves when you're managing a Web server. Microsoft

Developer's Network, referred to as *MSDN*, is a collection of documentation, bug fixes, technical facts, and programming interface specifications for nearly all of Microsoft's stable of software. Not just for C++ or Visual Basic programmers, MSDN also contains information about the Microsoft Office Developer's Kit, Windows 32-bit Developer's platforms, and more. MSDN has three subscription levels:

- *Level 1*—Contains libraries of files and documents, and costs $195 a year for quarterly updates.
- *Level 2*—Offers the same benefits as Level 1, with additional documentation, SDKs, and developer's tools. Level 2 costs $495 a year to receive quarterly updates, with interim updates of special CDs, such as beta products.
- *Level 3*—Contains a complete set of all Microsoft software documentation plus Level 2 tools and drivers, including a 5-user license of BackOffice for roughly $1,495.

So, how does this help you with your Web server? Let's say you're creating a very specialized front end to an SQL database using CGI and Visual Basic. The task requires you to send an email message back to the system administrator when a certain user accesses the database, and this username check is performed every hour. In order to perform this check, you need to spawn another process on the Web server (actually on NT Server), but how do you do this in CGI?

The following steps presume you already have MSDN installed, and for those of you who don't subscribe to MSDN, this process will underscore MSDN's usefulness.

1. Start MSDN while thinking of a keyword that will fit your topic.

Just like any other search utility, you'll have to search a massive database with very distinct and accurate keywords, unless you want to receive 10,000 topics selected as possible solutions.

The left side of the screen shows the major subjects supported on the CD. Many are non-supported, antiquated systems, but Microsoft is listing the information to assist in the transformation from older systems into modern-day technology.

Anyhow, back to the CGI issue.

2. Click on the large pair of binoculars in the top center of the menu bar.
3. Click on the Query tab to type in the keyword that you're searching MSDN for.

At this point, you can also specify a subset of information to search.

4. In the search field, enter *CGI*, and click on the Query button.

This search should uncover several prospective answers to your CGI problem. Scroll down the list of topics found to examine the list of prospective fixes, and you're likely to see one close to your problem. This list of found topics is kept available until you restart the search and clear out these results, so you can view one prospective fix and come back to the results of the search to see more fixes. This is the essence of MSDN, and how it can solve some of your programming needs for NT-based Web servers.

Microsoft TechNet

TechNet is another Microsoft tool that helps solve Web server problems. It comes in monthly updates at a cost of $195 a year. This set of two CDs differs from MSDN in that it contains technical facts about Internet protocols, Intranet configuration problems, and useful tips for Microsoft products. TechNet looks and runs like MSDN in every step of operation but is geared more closely towards technical problems. MSDN is more closely aligned as a programmer's tool. If you know how to operate one, then you'll know how to operate the other. Figure B.1 shows TechNet's opening screen.

CompuServe Information Service (CIS)

Since the beginning of the computer revolution, online services have dominated the world of vendor support. These services can help you set up your Web server in a number of ways, including providing updated drivers, testing facilities for software, and establishing places where users can gather to talk about their experiences. CompuServe is one such service that started years ago when the online services industry was in its infancy, and it has held a firm footing with a longstanding customer base.

CompuServe Information Service (CIS) is made up of forums and electronic bulletin boards where users post questions and (hopefully) get answers to their problems. Vendors, such as Intuit Software, have a support forum on

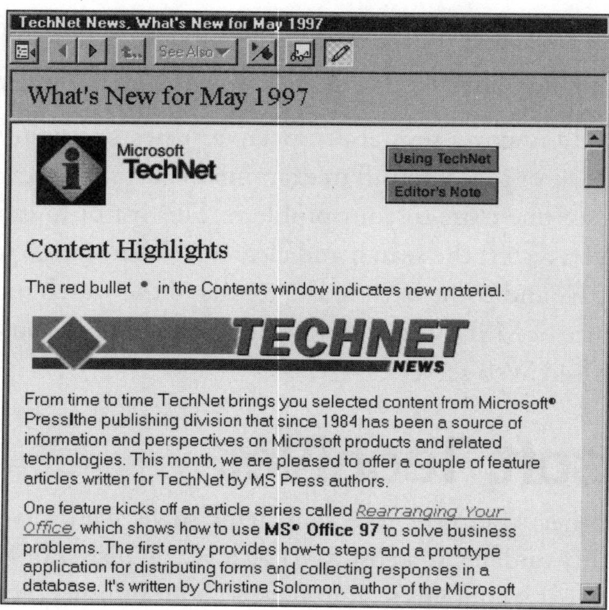

Figure B.1
TechNet's opening screen.

CompuServe where they provide updates and bug fixes to their users. All told, there are over a thousand such forums of support across CIS.

Microsoft Network (MSN)

This is Microsoft's answer to CompuServe for information services and technical information. It's a private network owned by Microsoft, and membership is required. It has technical forums, chat rooms, bulletin boards, and file download areas. MSN uses a backbone connected to the Internet and is hosted by dozens of NT Servers, IIS systems, and FTP servers supporting well over a million users.

IBM Network (IBMNET)

IBMNET is a subset of forums on CIS that supports IBM products and services. IBMNET is broken down into forums such as IBMAPP (applications), IBMSYS (systems level support), and IBMHW (hardware support), to name just a few. Because it's named *IBMNET*, you might think that it's purely an

IBM area, but that's not true. You can get some of the most complete answers to problems here, from a very knowledgeable group of programmers. To get to the IBM Network, use the keyword *GO CIS:IBMNET*.

NT Resource Kit

The NT Resource Kit is a five-volume set of manuals on managing NT Server and NT networks. The kit includes a CD-ROM that is chock-full of useful utilities, updated drivers for NT, and tips on general maintenance of your NT Server. Two of my favorite resources are the domain planner (which is used to define a network, as we discussed in Chapter 2) and the NetWatcher utility (which allows you to see who is connected to which NT resource on the server, regardless of the application). The NT Resource Kit is available from Microsoft and your local computer dealer for $395.

Usenet Groups

Don't overlook the Usenet newsgroups and circles available on the Internet. These are frequently staffed or moderated by experienced users who, at one time or another, have been where you are now. One of the biggest advantages of Usenet newsgroups is that users are online 24 hours a day around the world, and you're bound to find someone that can help solve your problem.

Online Learning Institutions

One such learning institution is ZDNet University (**www.zdu.com**), which is run by Ziff-Davis, Inc., the publisher of *PC Magazine*. Ziff-Davis has a long history of providing technical expertise via CompuServe forums, and now the company has moved that expertise onto the Web. In addition to ZDU, Ziff-Davis runs ZDNet (**www.zdnet.com**), the most popular site for news and information about computing and the Internet. Both ZDU and ZDNet provide a cool online experience.

List Servers

List servers are nothing more than large mailing lists of users that closely approximate forum participation in an online service like CIS. You get an email, answer it, and repost it on the list server. Someone else sees your message, answers it, and sends the response back to you. One thing different here is that in a list server, everyone on the list gets the messages, not just the two carrying on the conversation. This can result in rather large message traffic across the Internet.

Summary

This appendix barely scratches the surface of available Web server resources, but the overriding purpose here is to convey that there are numerous resources available to help you with your Web server (and other computing) problems. Really—there's no need to get hysterical in the middle of the night because of your NT server. Remember, when you think all is lost, there are plenty of people who have been there and are willing to help you.

INDEX

A

B

C

P

Q

R

S

T

X

Y

Z

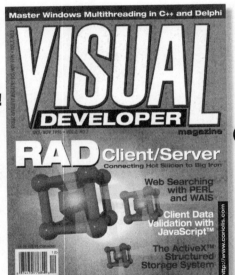